CHARACTER EDUCATION

Grades K–6
Year 2

by John Heidel and
Marion Lyman-Mersereau

Incentive Publications, Inc.
Nashville, Tennessee

Acknowledgments

We would like to acknowledge the many people who supported us in this project. We are indebted to these people who have given of their time and energy to help bring this project to completion.

First, we would like to name the Character Education Committee of Punahou School which conceived of the idea for this project. They set us on the right path with suggestions for what they need, as teachers, to better help in the intentional character education of our students. Special thanks to the Review Committee who offered encouragement and thoughtfully critiqued our work.

In addition, we would like to thank the many other people who provided their time and expertise in developing this complete Character Education program.

Illustrated by Marta Drayton
Cover by Bill Latta
Edited by Jennifer E. Janke

Library of Congress Catalog Card Number: 98-75493
ISBN 0-86530-428-9

PRINTED IN THE UNITED STATES OF AMERICA

TABLE OF CONTENTS

INTRODUCTION

Twenty-five hundred years ago, Socrates defined education as helping students gain both knowledge and virtue, to become both smart and good. In recent decades, schools sometimes consciously and sometimes unconsciously have lost their focus on this historic mission. Now, however, educators are being called back to help children gain the virtues, the embedded habits, which constitute good character. Often those calling for character education are parents. Increasingly, they are politicians articulating the will of worried citizens. A few scholars have recognized the current lack in our schools and have become champions for character education. While these voices have been articulate in pointing out the problems of a value-neutral school or a school that rejects responsibility for character formation, these voices are limited. They lack the knowledge of and experience with the instructional issues surrounding this topic. They do not speak to the real world of schools. The authors of this book possess that knowledge and experience.

John Heidel and Marion Lyman-Mersereau have written a book that takes character education to a new level, a level that enables teachers and administrators to go beyond the abstract into that real world of their classrooms and their schools. *Character Education* is based on the authors' action research project at one of the truly lighthouse schools of our nation, the Punahou School in Hawaii.

The book reflects a complete plan for engaging a school community in the mission of character development. Central to their work and to the organization of the book is a school-wide, monthly focus on a particular virtue, such as respect or courage. In this, they are addressing one of the core problems with school's efforts to respond to the call for character education. Americans, and particularly American educators, have frequently replaced the language of moral values and virtue with the language of psychology. Cheating is referred to as "inappropriate behavior" rather than "wrong." The goal has been "student development" and "adjustment," but development *into what* and adjustment *to what* has been left vague or unstated. This book and the program it offers educators, while on the one hand being new and fresh, returns us to an older, richer language system, one based on views of human excellence.

Over a two-year cycle, students are introduced to a deeper meaning of common words, such as loyalty, commitment and wisdom. It is here that the authors' gifts as educators become apparent. Students are not simply told the meaning of these virtue words. They are immersed in them. During the months that a particular word is being studied, each day there is a new activity which will give them greater experience and thus deeper understanding of the concept behind the word. Activities range from journal writing to a structured conversation with parents, from creating a poster about the virtue to listing ways students can practice the virtue in their everyday lives.

One of the most plaguing problems of American education is the continuing search for "the one right way": the one right way to teach reading, the one right way to evaluate student performance, the one right way to discipline students. As character education is again becoming a concern of educators, this same one-right-way mentality is becoming evident. The authors of *Character Education* take a very different approach, one that recognizes that children have very different ways of learning and that the best way to master something is to acquire it in several different learning modes. Therefore, the book offers students and teachers a rich reservoir of stories, sayings, and biographical sketches, which together bring out the depth of these concepts and show how they exist in a human life.

Character formation has been described as what we do to help students *know the good, love the good,* and *do the good.* This book addresses all dimensions of that description. The great power and benefit of *Character Education* is its appeal to the student's head, heart, and hands.

Kevin Ryan
Director of the Center for the Advancement of Ethics and Character,
Boston University

PURPOSE

Since one of the primary concerns of this program specifically relates to the total development of students, it is important to remember what a complete student is. A complete student is one who succeeds academically, but also portrays a strong moral character, with a clear sense of right and wrong.

It is probably a good exercise to reflect on how educators are doing. Most people would agree that schools across the country are doing well with academic goals and not so well with character goals. We have many students who don't know how to properly love themselves or each other, or who cheat on their schoolwork. There is teasing, gossiping, inappropriate language, and stealing. There are problems with litter and a general lack of common courtesy and good manners. We have a lot of work to do before we can fulfill the dream of a nation filled with complete students.

Thomas Lickona, developmental psychologist and author of *Educating for Character*, asserts that " . . . character must be broadly conceived to encompass the cognitive, affective, and behavioral aspects of morality. Good character consists of knowing the good, loving the good, and doing the good. Schools must help children understand the core values, adopt or commit to them, and then act upon them in their own lives."

While it might be difficult to teach values, the educational process at least can make known to students certain universal values. Students can be motivated and inspired to incorporate these values into their lives. The final step of acting out these values can be taken by giving students opportunity for community service and showing them how these values can be acted out in the community, on the playground, in the cafeteria, and in the classroom.

The purpose of this program is to design a structure whereby teachers can be more focused and intentional in their efforts to provide character education. Teachers should keep in touch with each other about activities that work, and design ways to involve parents and the wider community so the values will be reinforced. Teachers need to be conscious of who they are as role models and what values are reflected by their actions.

In all ways, our purpose is to assist teachers in their efforts to create a classroom environment where students can grow socially and spiritually, as well as intellectually. If these ideas prove useful we will be very gratified. We acknowledge the right of teachers to make this choice and to decide on their level of involvement. We know teachers enjoy autonomy, so there is room for flexibility and the development of personal style.

Much has been written about the present moral environment from which our children and youth choose their values. We know about the decline of the family, the lack of good adult models, the pervasive influence of the media, the problems of public schools, and the troubling trends in youth character. Another reason for this changing scene of morality can be traced through the gradual shift in the operative values that have characterized American life. Since the arrival of the Puritans and their lifestyle of honesty, faith, and hard work, there has been a big change. Sociologist Max Lerner made a study of American values in the mid-1950s and published his findings in *America As A Civilization* in 1957. He maintains that the idealistic values of early America became contaminated by money, materialism, competition, and success. "By the turn of the twentieth century a new pattern of life purposes emerged. Its components were success, prestige, money, power, and security." This "five-goal system" seemed to characterize the basic drives and behavioral patterns of most Americans. These five questionable values are alive and well today.

We are hopeful this program will offer other choices and have a positive impact on the daily life within each classroom and with relationships outside the classroom. This is the primary step that educators can take in reordering the moral environment of America with universal values that affirm life and enhance everyone's health and happiness. We can play an important role in the process of restoring a sense of what is right and good for our common life as Americans.

VALUE OF THE MONTH

The framework around which this project is designed is the idea of emphasizing a specific value each month. We chose eighteen values to be the featured values over a two-year cycle and thirty-six others as supportive values. We decided on eighteen because that would give us a two-year cycle of nine values a year. This way we won't be repeating the same values each year and, with a different focus in each grade level, the values should stay fresh.

There is a specific reason for beginning with respect, following with responsibility, and leading toward compassion, faith, and commitment. It will be explained how one leads to the next and how each remains connected to all of the previous values. Some relate to seasonal themes and others become part of a total picture. However, this format is completely flexible and educators may develop their own schedule if students or current events warrant it.

VALUE OF THE MONTH BY TWO-YEAR CYCLE

In the first year, students studied:

September	**Respect**	*Acceptance*	*Kindness*
October	**Responsibility**	*Self-discipline*	*Reliability*
November	**Compassion**	*Service*	*Generosity*
December	**Faith**	*Hope*	*Trust*
January	**Commitment**	*Loyalty*	*Effort*
February	**Love**	*Friendship*	*Sincerity*
March	**Wisdom**	*Knowledge*	*Understanding*
April	**Health**	*Holistic Living*	*Serenity*
May	**Humor**	*Joy*	*Enthusiasm*

In this second year, students expand their character development by learning about:

September	**Honesty**	*Integrity*	*Truth*
October	**Cooperation**	*Family*	*Unity*
November	**Humility**	*Gratitude*	*Appreciation*
December	**Peace**	*Harmony*	*Forgiveness*
January	**Patience**	*Perseverance*	*Confidence*
February	**Courage**	*Tenacity*	*Conviction*
March	**Creativity**	*Wonder*	*Resourcefulness*
April	**Environmental Awareness**	*Beauty*	*Sacrifice*
May	**Freedom**	*Social Justice*	*Equality*

LEVELS OF FACULTY INVOLVEMENT

Basic

Aware of how busy teachers are and how much is already asked, the basic involvement is quite simple. Yet, if we accept this project as important, there is great value in everyone's involvement. A clear message of the school's intention will be sent to the students and to the wider community. Hopefully, there will be a general feeling of cohesion as teachers share stories about what works and as students talk about each value from their own experience.

Therefore, basic involvement would mean supporting and following the value-of-the-month idea. Specifically, it would mean posting a sign bearing the current month's value, making the students aware of it, finding a connection with your curriculum once a week, and citing an example of someone acting out that value once a week; preferably "catching a student," but also examples from the community and the world. You can take this as far as your time and interest allow, from a short announcement to a discussion.

A Little Extra

You may want to do a little extra for any of the following reasons: the value of the month goes well with your subject area or curriculum, it relates to a current event or issue within the school or worldwide, it reflects one of your concerns, or you just want to explore the possibilities a little more.

In that case, use the extensive information provided on each value in this handbook. There will be suggested activities and, where appropriate, material that will deal with specific issues such as inappropriate language, cheating, or stealing. These activities will include stories, quotations, material from world religions, biographies of heroes and heroines, values in other languages, discussion questions, and community service ideas. Another suggestion is to follow up a school assembly presentation with a discussion or writing assignment. This level of involvement would mean utilizing these resources two or three times a month.

Beyond the Call

Some people may become so excited about the possibilities of this program that they will use many or all of the suggested calendar activities. In that case, go for it!

Calendar

At the beginning of each month there is a calendar of suggested activities outlining a lesson plan for that month. No matter the level of involvement chosen, this calendar should help educators fit *Character Education* into their monthly routine. These calendars show daily activities which focus on the value of that month. The calendar can be used to help educators develop creative ways to teach *Character Education*. The schedule need not be followed exactly—this is only one example of how a *Character Education* lesson plan might look.

COMMENTS FROM TEACHERS

- The character education program has given us a focus each month, and points of reference to remember during the entire school year. When problems arise in class, we often discuss the various values . . .

- In the past we have incorporated character-building and values education in our daily teaching; the curriculum project . . . certainly helped us to include these topics with our classroom activities in a more organized way . . .

- The Values of the Month that were put together . . . were a tremendous asset to the school.

- I would like to extend my appreciation . . . for the Character Education program which has set the tone to this year . . .

- I am so pleased that Punahou has included values as an integral part of our curriculum. As an educator, there is no way I would downplay knowledge; yet as a parent and concerned adult I believe that to be truly enlightened, a person must possess clear and honorable values and a moral character.

- I can't help but feel that our focus on values has brought about a positive change in our day-to-day goings-on. Good mornings and pleases and thank-yous abounded . . .

- The Character Education Handbook filled with guidelines and ideas for the incorporation of given values into the daily curriculum is one of the most significant steps that has taken place at Punahou . . . It resets a standard that speaks to the community at large about Punahou's stand regarding the necessity of spiritual values in daily living.

- I felt the character education program was a great success. Having the quotes in the daily bulletin and the signs in the classroom, cafeteria—everywhere—was very effective; it kept those values in the forefront of our day . . . [it] made us realize that these values were not just something to "teach" our kids, but they were ideals to be sought after by every adult on campus. In a sense they unified us . . . the signs/values provided me and my students with a common language for our discussions of themes in our literature.

- The addition and recognition of character education as an integral part of the total curriculum of the school has been long awaited and fully embraced by all students, parents, faculty, staff and administrators alike.

- Start at the kindergarten level and continue through academy years, if not already doing so. There cannot be too much character development!

* These comments were unsolicited and were written after the first year of the program as piloted at Punahou School.

PARENTAL AND COMMUNITY INVOLVEMENT

The statement "It takes a whole village to raise a child" refers to the community of support necessary for the upbringing of students. We acknowledge that this is not a task that educators do alone. Much of a school's success is a result of parental involvement. Parental support in reinforcing a school's educational goals for their children is imperative. We, therefore, feel it is important for parents to be aware of this particular program so that they may more actively participate in reinforcing these goals of *Character Education.*

Through announcements, newsletters, and various other methods of communication, educators can keep parents informed of the value of the month, related activities, and opportunities to attend workshops or selected speaker engagements.

Our dreams for *Character Education* go beyond the triangle of parents, teachers, and students to include the community outside of school. As Thomas Lickona writes, the long term success of any values education depends on " . . . the extent to which families and communities join schools in a common effort to meet the needs of children and foster their healthy development."

Here are some excerpts from letters of support our project has received from parents and the community around our school:

> *I am writing to applaud and commend you for attacking what I think is at the very heart of a world wide epidemic . . . During the next 1½ years, I will encourage physicians to focus on the importance of personal responsibility and other attributes of character building. I will encourage physicians to assist in spreading this message via the media and to address the community with appropriate speeches.*
> — Carl W. Lehman, M. D.
> President, Hawaii Medical Association

> *While I do teach at a Buddhist-affiliated school, the general philosophy and the values on which the Character Education program is based are universal. I will be sharing the program with all Middle School teachers and the Reverends who instruct the students in religious education.*
> — Lynette Araki
> Hongwanji Mission School

> *The Character Education program . . . is a breath of fresh air, and I encourage you . . . to vigorously continue this initiative for the sake of our children, our community, and our country.*
> — M. G. MacLaren

> *Your "village" concept has led me to conclude that we probably have more villages than we realize . . . , and, more importantly, that those villages don't communicate with each other very well. That is probably our ultimate challenge before we can really solve some of the underlying issues.*
> — Ed Case
> Representative, 23rd District, Hawaii

SUGGESTED LETTER TO PARENTS

Dear K–6 Parents,

As we begin the second year of our *Character Education*, we continue to encourage parental and community involvement in the hope that we can make an integrated effort to influence our students' positive character development from as many directions as possible. We will continue our work inside and outside the classroom to develop the character of our students.

Mark Twain's quip, "To be good is noble, to teach others to be good is nobler—and less trouble," speaks to our work in *Character Education* and is reminiscent of G. B. Shaw's often-heard droll remark, "Those who can, do . . . " Kurt Hahn, the father of Outward Bound, wilderness schools of experiential education, offers the following suggestion for teachers, which is more helpful than Twain and Shaw, when we think about *Character Education*:

> *There are three ways of trying to win the young. There is persuasion, there is compulsion, and there is attraction. You can preach at them, that is a hook without a worm; you can say, "You must volunteer," that is [compulsion]; and you can tell them, "You are needed," that appeal hardly ever fails.*

Once again, the program will emphasize a value of the month with two partner values. This year's values for each month are:

September	**Honesty**, Integrity, Truth
October	**Cooperation**, Family, Unity
November	**Humility**, Gratitude, Appreciation
December	**Peace**, Harmony, Forgiveness
January	**Patience**, Perseverance, Confidence
February	**Courage**, Tenacity, Conviction
March	**Creativity**, Wonder, Resourcefulness
April	**Environmental Awareness**, Beauty, Sacrifice
May	**Freedom**, Social Justice, Equality

We look forward to continuing to work with you on this joint effort of providing a complete education for your children.

Sincerely,

September

Honesty

SUPPORTIVE VALUES

Integrity • Truth

DEFINITIONS

Telling the truth; straightforward conduct.

The definition for **honesty** goes beyond being truthful in speech, it also assumes a way of conducting oneself. Shakespeare's classic and timeless piece of advice in *Hamlet* from Polonius to his son probably best describes the partnership of honesty and behavior toward others: "To thine own self be true, And it must follow, as the night the day, Thou canst not then be false to any man."

Integrity is the firm adherence to a moral code. Integrity is the state of being complete or undivided. Synonyms for integrity are incorruptibility and completeness and the antonym which furthers our understanding of the word is duplicity.

Truth is sincerity in action, character, and speech. When we examine the word further we see it is often capitalized and refers to a spiritual reality. In some spiritual traditions, Truth is synonymous with God.

PURPOSE

In a school faculty survey, honesty came up third in number of votes after respect and responsibility as the most important value for students to learn. It is obvious that teachers are concerned about the prevalence of cheating on schoolwork and tests and the "but everybody else does it" attitude which accompanies this behavior. The win-at-all-costs, dog-eat-dog ethic appears to be entrenched among many students. The value of honesty clearly has been undermined by the importance placed on achievement and the rewards and recognition which accompany the accomplishment. We somehow need to express our indignation at dishonest conduct, and communicate how much we esteem honest actions. Honor codes in the classrooms and sportsmanship in athletics, demonstrated by calling fouls on oneself, would affirm expectations we have for appreciating and valuing honesty.

Honesty

Day One:
Discuss the meaning of honesty using the definitions on page 17.

Day Two:
If you discover someone has lied to you—how does that make you feel? Make a list of words which describe your feelings. Does it matter what that person lied about? Why or why not?

Day Three:
In a total class setting, review and pronounce (as best you can!) the list of words meaning the same as honesty in other languages on page 19.

Day Four:
As a class, create a list of categories of people that you expect to be honest. (A few to get you started are: family, government officials, law enforcement officers, and teachers.)

Day Five:
Why is it sometimes difficult to be honest? Why should you be honest even when it may get you in trouble? Select a bookmark from page 28 to keep in your desk to remind you to be honest even when it might be uncomfortable to do so.

Day Six:
Discuss cheating. Why is cheating being dishonest? How would it feel if someone cheated on you? What would you say to that person to explain how you feel?

Day Seven:
Read a story about honesty from pages 21–27. Discuss the message the story carries about honesty.

Day Eight:
Read about the lives of the heroes and heroines of honesty on pages 29–30. What can we learn about how to be honest from the actions of these people?

Day Nine:
To be an honest person takes commitment. Write yourself a letter of encouragement to be honest.

Day Ten:
Why are good relationships dependent on honesty? How would you feel about a person who was always lying to you?

Day Eleven:
Create a bumper sticker to remind people to behave honestly in daily life.

Day Twelve:
Write a journal entry about a time in your life when you were tempted to behave in a dishonest manner.

Day Thirteen:
Discuss the importance of family members being honest with each other and ways a sense of family trust is built.

Day Fourteen:
In a total class setting, read the story of the life of Abraham Lincoln. Create a class mural to show scenes from his life to demonstrate why he was called "Honest Abe."

Day Fifteen:
Why is honesty an important value to embrace throughout your life? Brainstorm a list of the benefits of a lifetime of honesty.

Day Sixteen:
Review the letter you wrote to yourself about honesty. Have you remembered to be honest?

Day Seventeen:
Design a certificate of appreciation for someone you feel you can trust to behave honestly with you at all times.

Day Eighteen:
Make a list of words that mean the opposite of honesty and discuss the effect they have on relationships. (Lying, cheating and stealing are some to get you started.)

Day Nineteen:
Discuss ways students in your school are encouraged to be honest with themselves and with other students. Are there some school rules that are especially helpful in this regard? Is there evidence to show that honesty is considered an important school value?

Day Twenty:
Reflect on the lessons about honesty that you have learned this month. Can you commit to a lifetime of embracing honesty?

HONESTY IN OTHER LANGUAGES

Chinese   *cheng*   sincere; true; honest; to make sincere
                shi   solid; substantial; hard; real; true

French   *l'honnêteté*   characteristic of a person or of
                                    behavior which shows conformity to
                                    rules of morality, probity or loyalty

German   *ehrlichkeit*   honesty, honorable dealing, fairness

Hawaiian   *kupono*   upright, honest (ku means "to stand"
                                    and pono means "goodness,
                                    uprightness, morality")

Japanese   *makoto*   to make what you say happen or to do
                                    what you say

Korean   *jin shil*   right and straight; integrity

Latin   *probitas*   from Latin "honestus" (honorable);
                                    from "honos" (honor) (something that
                                    is held in honor)

Spanish   *honradez*   honesty, integrity, uprightness

Tagalog   *katapatan*   being fair, upright, and just in all
                                    aspects of personal behavior

DISCUSSION QUESTIONS

- How have you or a parent been honest lately?

- Why is it important to "do your own work," especially your schoolwork?

- Why is it wrong to lie in order to get something you want?

- Why is it sometimes hard to tell the truth? Give an example.

- Do you like yourself when you say or do something dishonest? Do you think others will like you if you are dishonest? Why?

- Why is it easy to like someone who is honest?

- What does the Golden Rule ("Do unto others . . . ") say about being honest? Give an example.

- Why is it important to be honest when you express your feelings?

- How can we express an honest opinion without hurting someone's feelings? How could you say it?

- What are some situations where it is difficult to be honest?

- Why is it difficult to maintain a friendship with someone who doesn't tell the truth?

- What is a "white lie"? Why is it potentially harmful?

- Why is it wrong to cheat on your homework or on a test?

- Why do people cheat? Does it lead to other kinds of dishonesty?

- Would you be brave enough to express your disagreement with someone who is dishonest? Give an example.

- Why is it important to be honest with oneself?

STORIES AND THOUGHTS FROM SPIRITUAL TRADITIONS

Hinduism

Truth and non-violence are the two wheels of the chariot of God.
— *Mahatma Gandhi*

A lie once told is like leprosy, that affects all who come into contact with it.
— *Tradition*

The damage caused by a false accusation can never be undone, and it causes the speaker to be reborn as a ghost.
— *Tradition*

Buddhism

Honesty is simple truthfulness in every action of body, speech, and mind. Dishonesty means deceiving others, with our speech or through gestures. Whether motivated by desire, hatred or ignorance, dishonesty creates confusion and entangles us in a web of deceit. Dishonest actions give rise to similar results: we are constantly deceived and cheated. Moral integrity is essential to spiritual progress.

In Tibet, there was a great yogi named Milarepa, the "cotton clad." After his father died when he was a young boy, his aunt and uncle seized his family home and property through treachery. Under the influence of an evil teacher, Milarepa unleashed a hailstorm in revenge, killing a large number of horses and people. Later regretting his action, he began to study the true path under the great teacher Marpa. Years went by, but Marpa only put him to work and never gave him spiritual instruction. Frustrated, Milarepa forged a letter from his teacher and went to seek meditation instruction from another. He meditated with all his might according to these instructions, but was never able to achieve even the slightest realization. After months and months of seeing Milarepa's fruitless practice, the instructor said, "This is very strange! Are you sure you have your teacher's permission?" Confronted like this, Milarepa confessed that he had forged the letter from Marpa. Because his spiritual practice was based on a lie, his efforts were all in vain. Without a foundation of moral integrity, even if he were to practice for 100 years, he would never be able to achieve realization. Realizing his error, he returned to Marpa and confessed all he had done. In time, after Milarepa had purified his negative deeds through years of strenuous effort, Marpa bestowed the highest empowerments and sent Milarepa to the snowy mountain peaks to practice. Dressed only in a thin cotton cloth in the frozen climate of Tibet, Milarepa meditated with sheer determination. Inspired by genuine compassion and unmoved by worldly fame or gain, he practiced persistently until he reached the highest state of enlightenment.

Ethical conduct is the foundation of every success, both mundane and spiritual. To refrain from killing, stealing, and sexual misconduct are the three virtues of body. To refrain from lying, abusive speech, divisive speech, and idle gossip are the four virtues of speech. To refrain from malice, covetousness, and perverted views are the three virtues of mind. A life guided by these ten virtues will be uncomplicated, wholesome, and happy.

Zen Buddhism

It is often said that truth is something that is universally valid. To put it simply, it is something which can be applied anytime, anywhere, and to anyone. For instance, fire is hot no matter what time it is. Fire was hot thousands of years ago, as surely as fire will be hot hundreds of years from now. Of course, fire is hot today. Furthermore, fire is hot in America, and it is hot in Russia as well as in Japan. Fire is hot no matter where.

Christianity

"Lead me in your truth and teach me."   *– Bible, Psalm 25:5*

"The one who walks in integrity walks securely, but the one who perverts their way will be found out."

– Bible, Proverbs 10:9

The Two Sons

"What do you think about this? A man with two sons told the older boy, 'Son, go out and work on the farm today.' 'I won't,' he answered, but later he changed his mind and went. Then the father told his youngest, 'You go!' and he said, 'Yes, sir, I will.' But he didn't. Which of the two sons was obeying his father?"
They replied, "The first, of course!"

– Bible, Matthew 21:28-31

Islam

Verily, truth is goodness, and goodness leads to paradise; and verily lying is wickedness, and wickedness leads to the fire (of hell).
— Selections from Mishkat-ul-masabi [928] p. 208
Ibni Mas'ud, MU

Cheats Are Not True Muslims

Passing through the marketplace, the Prophet noticed a man selling from a heap of grain. The Prophet ran his fingers through the grain whereupon his fingers became wet. "How is it that your grain is wet?" he asked the owner, who said that it was because of the rain. "Then why not put the wet portion on top, so that people can see it," said the Prophet, adding: "Those who deceive others do not belong with us."
— God-oriented Life p. 147 (Al-Bukhari, Muslim)

Chinese

"I do not see what use a man can be put to, whose word cannot be trusted. How can a wagon be made to go if it has no yoke-bar or a carriage if it has no collar-bar?
— Confucius

"In the old days a man kept a hold on his words, fearing the disgrace that would ensue should he himself fail to keep pace with them."
— Confucius

The Empty Pot

Long, long ago in China, there was a boy named Ping. More than anything else in the world, Ping loved flowers and had the gift of being able to make anything grow. He could plant any seed and up would grow beautiful blossoms and rich green leaves. Ping's family and friends would marvel at the wonderful things he was able to grow.

Now, the Emperor in those days was also a great lover of flowers and loved to spend time in his garden, which was filled with beautiful shrubs and fine fruit trees. Each day he would tend to all the lovely things growing there.

But unfortunately, the good Emperor was growing old and was becoming more and more worried about finding someone who would rule fairly after he was gone. How should he choose someone, he wondered daily. Finally, he decided that because he loved flowers so much, he would let the flowers do the choosing.

The very next day, the Emperor issued a proclamation throughout the land.

All the children in the realm were to come to the palace. Each child would be given special flower seeds to plant. "Whoever returns with the best in a year's time will inherit my throne!" were the Emperor's words.

Everyone was so excited by the possibilities and the next day all the children of the land gathered in a long line to await their seeds from the Emperor.

Ping, so anxious to have something to grow for the Emperor, traveled the long distance from his home to the palace. He waited patiently in the long line until, at last, he gladly received his seed from the Emperor. Ping was overjoyed. He was certain that he would grow the most exquisite flower with such a seed.

When he arrived home, he chose a sturdy pot and filled it with good soil. Each day he watered it lovingly and made sure it got the sunshine it needed. He could not wait to see it sprout and grow into a beautiful flower!

Days passed, and Ping waited patiently, but nothing happened. He became worried and put the seed in a larger pot with more good soil. He watered it carefully and made certain it received sunlight, and still nothing happened. Finally, he put the seed into an even better pot and made sure it had the richest soil. He continued to care for it, and watched over it for months, yet no sprout came. Month after month Ping tried and waited until finally the year was up.

The day had arrived for all the children to return to the palace with the flowers they had grown. They flooded toward the palace gates, eager to to be chosen as the next emperor. Ping watched as children with azaleas, peonies, and chrysanthemums streamed by. He saw roses and lilies and orchids like he had never seen before. He was so ashamed of his empty pot. He could not believe that for once he had not been able to make a flower grow.

Just then his friend passed by, holding a beautiful white lily. "Ping!" he cried. "What are you doing with that empty pot? Couldn't you grow anything at all? I'm on my way to the palace with this great big flower now. Where's yours?" The boy did not wait for Ping to answer. He sped off to see if he would be chosen by the Emperor.

A tear trickled slowly down Ping's cheek. "I've grown many flowers before," he said to himself. "I don't know why this seed would not grow."

Ping's father heard Ping's sad words. He placed his hand on Ping's shoulder and said, "Son, you did your very best, and that is good enough for the Emperor. If the best you could do is in that empty pot, then that is what you must show him."

Nodding, Ping picked up the empty pot and headed directly for the palace.

When he arrived there, the Emperor was already examining the hundreds of flowers brought by the eager children. He stopped at each one, but said nothing.

Finally, he came to Ping and his empty pot. Ping hung his head, hoping that the Emperor would not be angry with him.

The Emperor spoke to Ping. "Why did you bring me an empty pot?"

Tears trickled once again down Ping's cheeks. With his head bowed, he replied, "I planted the seed you gave me. I gave it a nice pot with good soil. I watered it each day, but it did not sprout. I put it in a better pot with rich, dark soil. I cared for it lovingly for a year and still it did not grow. So all I have to show you is an empty pot. It is the best I can do."

A smile swept across the Emperor's face and, holding Ping's hand high in the air, he exclaimed, "I have found him! I have found the next emperor! It is this boy and this boy alone who is worthy!" Then he spoke sternly to all the other children who had gathered with their flowers. "I do not know where the seeds for all of your beautiful flowers came from, for the seeds I gave you had all been cooked, making it impossible for them to grow." Placing his hand upon Ping's shoulder, the Emperor said proudly, "Ping is the only one who returned to me with the truth in his empty pot. It is for his courage and honesty that I reward him with my kingdom and my throne!"

Hawaii

The Lost Kapa Beater

Kalei had lost her favorite kapa beater. In ancient Hawaii, a kapa beater was a very important implement for the women, since women were the ones who were responsible for the hard work of pounding the water-soaked strips of bark from mulberry shrubs, which became clothing for their families.

Kalei looked everywhere for her kapa beater, which looked like a small club with intricate designs carved into it. It had a unique sound, which only she could recognize, and as she walked from one end of the island of Oahu to the other, listening to the women in their villages pounding kapa, she listened for the sound of her kapa beater. She had traveled all day and all night and was tired, so she finally stopped to rest under a tree.

The exhausted woman soon slept, and in her sleep a soft breeze carried a faint sound of the pounding of a kapa beater. She quickly awakened and realized the sound was carried by a gentle breeze, which was coming from the mountains to the valley where she had stopped to rest.

The sound was familiar to Kalei and she began to walk in the direction from which it came. As she walked, the sound became louder and louder. It was a sound that was so dear to her she began to cry, knowing that she would soon see her beloved kapa beater again. For awhile she had to walk beside a stream, which eventually led her to a cave where a woman was pounding her kapa with Kalei's kapa beater. Kalei spoke to the woman, "That sounds like my kapa beater. How did you get it?" The woman reluctantly gave the club back to Kalei, replying, "I found it floating in the stream which flows from the mountain."

The woman followed Kalei back to her home on the other side of the island, far from the mountain cave, to see if Kalei was being honest. When she reached Kalei's village, she tied a bundle of large leaves together and tossed it into the stream near Kalei's home, then returned to her mountain cave.

After a few days, the woman saw the bundle of leaves floating in the stream near her home and was satisfied that Kalei was indeed the owner of the kapa beater she had found.

India

The Banyan Tree

Sagardas of Pallipur was known to be an extremely good man. One day, while he was returning from a distant village, he was greeted by Sushil, a man from a neighboring village. "It seems you are coming from far," observed Sushil. "Yes, a merchant owed me some money. I went to realize the amount," replied Sagardas.

"Sir, it must be a good amount! Otherwise you could have sent your servant to realize it," observed Sushil once again.

"Well, it is five hundred rupees," said Sagardas. Then, as courtesy demanded it, he asked Sushil, "Where are you going?"

Sushil drew a heavy face. Wiping his eyes, he said, "Sir, must I narrate my misfortune to you? The monsoon is about to set in. I have not been able to repair my thatch. I don't know how my children would live under the leaking roof. I am looking for a loan of two hundred rupees. I will pay back the loan as soon as I have raised the new crop. I have already been to three moneylenders, but in vain!"

Sagardas had declared that he had money with him. How could he pass by a man who was in such dire need of a part of it? "Sushil," he said, "you may take the amount you need from me. I hope you will return it in a year's time!"

"Sir! Why should I let a year pass? I will pay it back in six months!" exclaimed Sushil. Sagardas gave him the amount and Sushil bowed to him and thanked him profusely.

But two years passed and Sushil did not pay Sagardas his due. Several times Sagardas saw Sushil in the weekly market, but Sushil avoided him.

However, one day they came face to face, "Sushil, what about my money?" asked Sagardas.

"Your money? What do you expect me to say about your money?" asked Sushil in turn. Sagardas immediately understood that Sushil planned to play treachery with him. He stared at him. "Don't show your red eyes to me!" shouted Sushil. Some people who knew both Sagardas and Sushil well and who were passing by were surprised. Sagardas told them what had happened between Sushil and himself. They led the two to the landlord of the locality who was famous for his wit and wisdom.

The landlord heard the case and asked Sagardas, "Who was the witness to your giving money to Sushil?"

"None. We met under a banyan tree. There was nobody nearby," said Sagardas with a sigh.

"How do you say so? The banyan tree itself is the witness!" said the landlord. "Go and ask the banyan tree to come here," he added.

Sagardas looked at the landlord in utter disbelief. But the landlord told him, once again, to go and call the banyan tree.

Sagardas went away. All those present there wondered if the landlord had gone mad. Sushil looked perplexed. Did the landlord know any magic by which he might bring the banyan tree there? He kept standing with anxiety.

Half an hour passed. The landlord looked at Sushil and asked in a very casual tone, "Why is he so late? How far is the banyan tree?"

"Sir, the banyan tree is a mile away. He cannot be back here so soon!" replied Sushil.

"Which banyan tree?" asked the landlord meaningfully. But then it was too late for Sushil to come out with an explanation. "You liar, you ungrateful creature! Bring Sagardas's money at once or you will be severely punished," roared the landlord.

All praised the landlord's wisdom. Sushil had to return Sagardas's money. The people of the locality lost their faith in Sushil forever.

PROVERBS AND MAXIMS

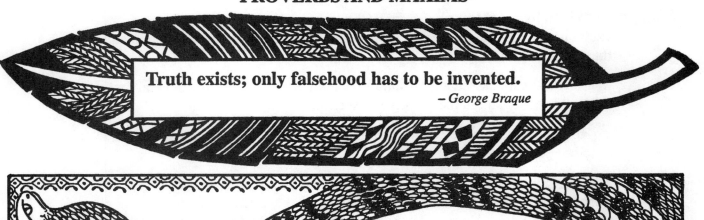

Truth exists; only falsehood has to be invented.
— *George Braque*

The truth is more important than the facts.
— *Frank Lloyd Wright*

In the mountains of truth, you never climb in vain.
— *Friedrich Nietzsche*

If you tell the truth, you have infinite power supporting you; but if not, you have infinite power against you.
— *Charles Gordon*

We must love them both—those whose opinions we share, and those whose opinions we reject. For both have labored in the search for Truth and both have helped us in the finding of it.
— *St. Thomas Aquinas*

HEROES AND HEROINES

DIETRICH BONHOEFFER (1906–1945)

Born in Breslau, Germany, he moved with his family to Berlin when he was six. He received his doctorate in Theology from Berlin University when he was only twenty-one. After one year as pastor of a church and one year at Union Theological Seminary in New York City, he returned to Berlin University, where he became a lecturer in Theology. His writing had a major influence on post-World War II Protestant Theology. He could easily be an example of the values of commitment, courage, faith, freedom, or peace, but he is mentioned under honesty because he spoke the truth during a time when it would have been safer to lie. He was one of the first German Protestants to see the evil of Nazism and speak out publicly against Hitler. He called for Christian involvement and was executed by the Nazis for his actions.

CONFUCIUS (551 B.C.E.–478 B.C.E.)

Born as Kung Fu-Tze (Confucius is a translation into Latin) in what is now the province of Shantung, China, he probably wasn't religious in the traditional sense, yet many scholars consider him a holy man. Confucius considered himself a teacher of four basic subjects: literature, human conduct, being one's true self, and honesty in social relationships. The heart of his teachings was what he called "shu": "Do not do unto others what you would not have others do unto you." Confucius strongly believed that a person's first duty was to be virtuous; this would create a strong community of harmony and peace. Though more philosopher than theologian, his ideas about morality became the state religion of China—Confucianism.

COCHISE (1815–1874)

Born in the mountains of southern Arizona, this Native American followed in a long line of Chiricahua Apache chiefs. He was both feared and respected as a leader, and was chief of the Chiricahuas during the time white settlers were trying to take their homeland. Cochise was raised in the ancient tradition of leadership that encompassed both war and peace. Until the white settlers broke their trust, Cochise maintained a relationship of peace and was known for his honor and for keeping his word. Before he died he affirmed the importance of truth and honesty even to those who were untrustworthy. He urged his sons to maintain the peace and always be honest; this would be an example of the honorable way to live.

BARBARA JORDAN (1936–1996)

Born in Houston, Texas into a very poor home, she and her sister were reared in a strict family. Her father was a Baptist minister and her mother was trained as an orator in the church. As a child, she showed a talent for public speaking and became the star of her high school debating team. While she had interests in pharmacy, she changed her mind upon hearing a black woman attorney speak at her school's career day. She graduated with honors in political science and history from Texas Southern University and entered Boston Law School in 1956. She was the first black woman to be elected to the Texas Senate and credited her success to a personal interest in the people and a dedication to speaking the truth. She was elected to the U.S. House of Representatives in 1972. She is remembered as a champion for the poor, a hero to the oppressed, and a model for anyone who aspires to be an honest politician.

MARTIN LUTHER (1483–1546)

Born in Eisleben, Germany, he was the son of peasant parents who worked hard to give him a good education. Two career fields were open to educated people: the law and the church. Hans Luther, Martin's father, was anti-church, and pushed Martin toward law; by 1505 he was well on his way. However, Martin experienced a religious crisis and, out of fear, decided to become a priest. In 1512, he received his doctorate in theology, and was destined to teach theology all his life. His basic honesty did not allow him to turn his back on the dishonesty of the Church and his disagreements with Church theology. In 1521, he was brought to trial and had to choose between his personal views and the will of the Church. His decision forced his removal from the priesthood and he became instrumental in the Protestant Reformation. He is perhaps the greatest figure of the Reformation and is still a symbol of honesty and moral courage.

PUT HONESTY INTO ACTION

- Thank someone in your family for being honest.

- Tell your parents about a mistake you've made.

- Tell the truth when you've done something wrong.

- Learn as much as possible by doing your own work.

- Express your real feelings without anger, without blaming others, without exaggerating, and without hurting the feelings of someone else.

- When someone wants to copy your work, politely explain that it isn't right and that it's best to do your own work.

- Compliment a friend or family member for being honest.

- Turn in something that is lost and encourage others to do the same.

- Admit a mistake you've made and apologize to anyone it might have affected.

- Do all your schoolwork honestly and as best as you can.

- Be truthful with your friends and thank them for being truthful with you.

- When you ask someone to be honest with you don't get angry with them if their honesty isn't what you wanted to hear.

COMMUNITY SERVICE IDEAS

- Write a letter of thanks to a politician or community leader who has taken a stand on a controversial issue.

- Visit a senior citizens center to play board games with the residents. Make very honest moves as you play.

- Share the meaning of honesty, as you understand it, with your family. Ask them to share their ideas with you. As a family, develop your own definition of honesty.

- Remind members of your community to be honest. Decorate public areas with signs telling about the value of honesty.

- Create a classroom honor code. Write it down and hang it up in the classroom, so that everyone can see it all year long.

- Plan a class field trip to a daycare center to tell stories with themes of honesty to young children. The Chinese tale *The Empty Pot* (page 23) would be a good one to begin with.

EMBRACING ———————————————————————— *Honesty*

BOOKS ON HONESTY

Anansi and the Moss Covered Rock. Janet Stevens. New York: Holiday House, 1988.
Strega Nona. Tomie De Paola. Englewood Cliffs: Prentice Hall, 1975.
True Francine. Marc T. Brown. Boston: Little, Brown, 1981.
True Story of the 3 Little Pigs! Lane Smith and Jon Scieszka. New York: Viking Kestrel, 1989.

The Book of Virtues. William J. Bennett, ed. New York: Simon and Schuster, 1993.
   "The Boy Who Cried Wolf" – p. 602
   "The Boy Who Went to the Sky" – p. 634
   "The Frog Prince" – p. 623
   "George Washington and the Cherry Tree" – p. 605
   "The Good Bishop" – p. 644
   "The Honest Woodman" – p. 602
   "The Indian Cinderella" – p. 612
   "The Pied Piper of Hamelin" – p. 627
   "Pinocchio" – p. 609
   "Someone Sees You" – p. 604
   "Truth and Falsehood" – p. 636

Cooperation

SUPPORTIVE VALUES

Family • Unity

DEFINITIONS

Common effort of a group for their mutual benefit.

"There is no 'I' in team." "United we stand, divided we fall." "No man is an island." If all of these statements speak to the importance of cooperation, to the idea that we live interdependently, it is then necessary that we do so as effectively as possible. **Cooperation** is as much a cornerstone of this country as is independence, and both values, as paradoxical as it seems, are highly honored in our society.

Family is commonly defined as a group of people who share common ancestors. In a broader sense, family can also include all people everywhere, by virtue of our common link as human beings. Montaigne said, "Every man beareth the stamp of the whole human condition." The nuclear family, extended family, and the family of humanity are the focus of the partner value, family.

Unity connotes oneness. Unity is what is required for cooperation and for a well-functioning family.

PURPOSE

As our world becomes smaller, as a result of mass communication and our networking technology, we are becoming more aware of how necessary it is, for our own survival, to work with other people cooperatively. Competition has long been the driving force of our democratic society; yet if we look at the history of this country we see that it was cooperative effort which created and continues to sustain America.

"The whole is greater than the sum of its parts," speaks to the importance and the strength derived from unity. We also know that in creating a team, or a unified effort of any kind, it is wiser to stay together than stand as individuals.

The importance of understanding that we are interconnected with our environment, as well as interdependent with humanity, is an understanding without which we cannot survive as a species. The demand for cooperation in the world is obvious and has already affected the way most educators conduct classes. The rewards of cooperation are numerous; as students move out of their sometimes self-centered molds and work with others, they reinforce many of the preceding values, which are inherent in the cooperative process. The Sioux state these ideas simply: "With all beings and all things we shall be as relatives."

Cooperation

Day One:
In a total class setting, discuss the meaning of cooperation based on the definitions on page 35 as compared to your own definition of cooperation.

Day Two:
What does "many hands make for light work" mean to you? Draw a picture to share and compare with your classmates.

Day Three:
With a group of classmates, create a list of things that people do which take cooperation. (Here's a few to get you started: build a house, play baseball, have a party.)

Day Four:
Conduct a three legged race. The pair that cooperates the best nearly always wins!

Day Five:
Create a "Pear of the Week" award to present to two students whose cooperation serves as an example for others. Make a pear tree to hang the "Pear" award on each week. Add pears to the tree all month.

Day Six:
Read and discuss one of the stories about cooperation on pages 39–46.

Day Seven:
Use what you have learned so far about cooperation to answer the discussion questions on page 38.

Day Eight:
Write a short story about a village where no one cooperates with each other. What limits are placed on the lives of these people?

Day Nine:
Some animals know the value of cooperation. Research one of these animals and prepare a short presentation or drawing to share with your class about how this animal cooperates. Some cooperative animals are: Canadian geese (flying), humpback whales (feeding), fish (swimming), wolves (hunting).

Day Ten:
Embrace the spirit of cooperation by completing a homework assignment with a partner. How much time would you estimate was saved through your cooperative efforts? How did you use this extra time?

Day Eleven:
Determine to embrace cooperation today! Think of one way you can cooperate with another person either at school or at home and then do it!

Day Twelve:
Draw a picture or write about your experience yesterday with cooperation. Display and marvel at all the different ways your classmates cooperated with others!

Day Thirteen:
Read about the heroes and heroines of cooperation on pages 48–49. What would our world be like today if these people had not embraced the value of cooperation?

Day Fourteen:
Choose, color, and cut out a bookmark on page 47. Choose a book to keep it in to remind you of the value of cooperation.

Day Fifteen:
Work in cooperative learning groups of four or five students to plan a special celebration for your class.

Day Sixteen:
Present the celebration plans made by each group and vote on the one to actually be carried out.

Day Seventeen:
Working in the same small groups, assign tasks to each group for carrying out the celebration and provide time for the preparations.

Day Eighteen:
Enjoy the celebration!

Day Nineteen:
Review the celebration with an evaluation of how work groups cooperated to make it happen.

Day Twenty:
Reflect on the lessons you have learned this month about cooperation and decide to embrace it as a lifelong value!

COOPERATION IN OTHER LANGUAGES

Chinese	*xie*	united in; agreement; mutual help; to aid; to help
	li	power; strength
French	*la cooperation*	collaboration with others; to act jointly with someone
German	*zusammenarbeit*	to work together
Hawaiian	*laulima*	cooperation, joint action (lau means "very many, numerous" and lima means "arm, hand")
Japanese	*kyooryoku*	to put everyone's ability and energy into one kyoo—to put power and energy into one ryoku—power, energy, ability
Korean	*hyup dong*	together and same
Latin	*adiumentum*	from Latin "cum" (together with) + "opus" (work) (working together)
Spanish	*cooperación*	cooperation
Tagalog	*pakikiisa*	united effort or labor; working together to accomplish what can't be done alone

DISCUSSION QUESTIONS

- How do you cooperate with your family?

- What can you do to have more fun at recess with your friends?

- Why do we talk about the school community as a family?

- What do you enjoy the most, a group that works together or a group where each person does whatever he wants? Why?

- What do you like best about competition? About cooperation?

- Can competition be harmonious?

- How would you describe a happy family?

- As competition in sports provides motivation to do the best we can, can cooperation provide similar motivation for the good of the community?

- How big is your family? Is it possible to create a human family of all the people of the world?

- How is the future of our planet connected with the way in which we live in harmony with all creation?

STORIES AND THOUGHTS FROM SPIRITUAL TRADITIONS

Hinduism

The joys of liberation are for then, the joys of a loving family are for now.
— Tradition

Never may brother hate brother or sister hurt sister. United in heart and in purpose, commune sweetly together.
— Atharva Veda

Buddhism

Cooperation comes through realizing the interdependence of all living beings.

Once there were four friends: an elephant, a rabbit, a monkey, and a bird. Each of them looked enviously at the ripe mango fruits high on the treetops. They each in turn tried with all their might to get to the fruits hanging on the branches, but the fruits were too high to reach. Finally, they hit upon a plan. With a little cooperation, they could all eat their fill. First, the elephant stood sturdily at the base of the tree. Then the monkey helped the rabbit climb up on the elephant's back. Then the monkey leaped up and stood on the rabbit's back. And finally the bird perched on the monkey's back. Collaborating like this, the four friends were able to pluck one ripe mango after the other and pass them along until everyone got to eat as many mangoes as they liked!

Zen Buddhism

Water is known as H_2O. It consists of the mixture of hydrogen and oxygen at the ratio of two to one. However, it is impossible for us to drink only the oxygen or the hydrogen part of water. They say that the bird named hamsa-raja is capable of separating water from milk and drinking on the concentrated milk. We human beings, however, cannot perform such a feat. The analysis of human beings in terms of individuals, classes, or races certainly serves to deepen our view of human beings. However, the one-sided emphasis on any particular one of the above groups with the exclusion of others is undesirable. There is no other way to reward such men of inflexible thought than by commanding them to drink the hydrogen component of water alone, if indeed they can.

*C*ooperation———————————— UNDERSTANDING

Christianity

"How good and pleasant it is when brothers and sisters live together in unity."
– Bible, Psalm 133:1

"If one member suffers, all suffer together; if one member is honored, all rejoice together."
– Bible, I Corinthians 12:26

"Working together we encourage you to accept the Grace of God."
– Bible, II Corinthians 6:1

Joshua and Jericho

The Gates of Jericho were kept tightly shut because the people were afraid of the Israelis; no one was allowed to go in or out.

But the Lord said to Joshua, "Jericho and its king and all its mighty warriors are already defeated, for I have given them to you! Your entire army is to walk around the city once a day for six days, followed by seven priests walking ahead of the Ark, each carrying a trumpet made from a ram's horn. On the seventh day, you are to walk around the city seven times, with the priests blowing their trumpets. Then, when they give one long, loud blast, all the people are to give a mighty shout and the walls of the city will fall down; then move in upon the city from every direction."

So Joshua summoned the priests and gave them their instructions: the armed men would lead the procession followed by seven priests blowing continually on their trumpets. Behind them would come the priests carrying the Ark, followed by a rear guard.

"Let there be complete silence except for the trumpets," Joshua commanded. "Not a single word from any of you until I tell you to shout; then shout!"

The Ark was carried around the city once that day, after which everyone returned to the camp again and spent the night there.

At dawn the next morning they went around again, and returned again to the camp. They followed this pattern for six days. At dawn of the seventh day they started out again, but this time they went around the city not once, but seven times. The seventh time, as the priests blew a long, loud trumpet blast, Joshua yelled to the people, "Shout! The Lord has given us the city!"

So when the people heard the trumpet blast, they shouted as loud as they could. And suddenly the walls of Jericho crumbled and fell before them, and the people of Israel poured into the city from every side and captured it!

– Bible, Joshua 6:1-16, 20-21

Islam

The master next told a story about Shaykh Najib ad-din Mutawakkil: "Many times he wanted to set to writing a compilation of Sufi anecdotes, but his income was so tight that he could not manage to purchase the instrument for writing and also to pay wages for a scribe; if a scribe did become available, he could not afford to pay him, or if he somehow found the means to pay him, he could not obtain additional funds to buy paper and the other provisions necessary for writing. Then one day a scribe named Hamid came to him. Shaykh Najib ad-din told him: 'For a long time now I have wanted to commit to writing a compilation of Sufi anecdotes, but I have not found the means to accomplish that objective.' 'What are your present resources?' asked Hamid. 'I have one diram [a silver coin equivalent to about 4 cents],' replied Shaykh Najib ad-din. Hamid took that one diram and bought paper with it. Now everyone knows how little paper one diram can buy, and Hamid had not finished writing on that paper before Shaykh Najib ad-din received another charitable donation, with which he purchased more paper and the other necessities for writing. Money for the scribe's salary also came to hand. More and more charitable donations continued to arrive, and as a result the book was quickly and satisfactorily completed. The point is: Even a work begun with difficulty will be completed, as long as one persists; and without cooperation, the book could not have been completed."

— Nizam Ad-Din Awliya: Morals of the Heart p. 110
I. Assembly 26
Saturday, the 23rd of Ramadan, A.H. 708 (15 March 1309)

Our treatment of our fellow human beings must always be in accord with our common humanity. This surah of this verse was delivered nine years after the migration to Madinah, at a time when the Muslim community was growing rapidly, drawing on the peoples of many different tribes. It was known as the Year of Deputations for by now representatives of diverse tribal and political interests were visiting the Prophet in official recognition of Islam. It was at this time of Islam's increasing power that Allah enjoined us to remember that we are brothers and sisters, descended from the first man and woman He created. The importance of this injunction has continued to grow as Islam's role in the world has grown.

— The Essential Teachings of Islam p. 207
320: The Inner Apartments (Hujurat) 49:13

The Prophet of Allah said: "If a man has three daughters and brings them up well, educates them and clothes them from what Allah has given, and gives them in marriage to decent people, they will become a shield to protect him from hell-fire."
Then (his companions) said: "What if he has only two daughters?"
He said: "Yes, even two daughters will protect him."
They said: "What about one?"

He said: "Yes, even one."

Men are the protectors of their daughters in this life, but as in all relationships in Islam, there is reciprocity. A well-cared-for daughter will be to the benefit of her father in the Hereafter. The Laws of Allah are just.

– The Essential Teachings of Islam p. 189
296: Hadith
Ibn.-I-Majah: Book of Virtue, Good Manners
and the Joining of Ties of Relationship 3669

Chinese

"He who sets to work upon a different strand destroys the whole fabric."
– Confucius

"Moral force never dwells in solitude; it will always bring neighbors."
– Confucius

"Simplicity in the doing of the will of every person would put an end to vain ambitions and desires."
– Lao Tzu

Chi Kiang-tzu asked whether there were any forms of encouragement by which he could induce the common people to be respectful and loyal. The Master said, "Approach them with dignity, and they will respect you. Show piety towards your parents and kindness toward your children, and they will be loyal to you. Promote those who are worthy, train those who are incompetent; that is the best form of encouragement."
– The Analects, Book II

The Master said, "The case is like that of someone raising a mound. If he stops working, the fact that it perhaps needed only one more basketful makes no difference; I stay where I am. Whereas even if he has not got beyond leveling the ground, but is still at work, the fact that he has only tilted one basketful of earth makes no difference. I go to help him."
– The Analects, Book IX

India
The Little Squirrel Becomes a Savior

On the branches of an old banyan tree in the forest lived a squirrel couple. A bonny child was born to them. It was as handsome as it was frolicsome.

"He ought to grow up into a remarkable creature—remain a squirrel like us forever," his mother told his father.

"Yes, he has every sign of becoming great—like one of those deer here," agreed the little one's father. He did not wish his son to become anything else because they had not known any other animal. And because the deer had hair and stripes like those of the squirrels, the squirrel couple thought that they were just bigger squirrels though known as deer!

"But how can he grow up to become a deer?" asked the mother squirrel.

"Well, how do other kids grow into deer? There must be some method," observed the father squirrel. He was always logical like this, and the mother squirrel could not contest his wisdom. "We'd better ask them," she said.

At night a herd of deer slept around the banyan tree, amidst bushes. The place was surrounded by rocks or tall anthills, with very few openings. So, they considered the cozy place quite safe.

It was a moonlit night. The deer gathered there as usual. The squirrel couple addressed them from a branch of the banyan tree and told them all about their ambition regarding their son, drawing their attention to the little one.

The first to speak was a hefty deer. "I too was a little squirrel when I was born. But through sheer willpower I grew to what I am."

"And look at me," rejoined a heftier deer, "I grew up to this stature through regular exercise, discipline and wrestling with some stout boars."

"And if all the tigers of the forest are scared of me today, it is because I have gathered more muscle-power than them," said a third deer who was no less hefty.

The squirrels, of course, did not know what was meant by 'tigers.' Nevertheless, they were impressed.

"That is fine, but how can our little baby become like you? What should he do, to begin with?" asked the mother squirrel.

"To begin with? Hm!" said the hefty deer.

"Well, to begin with, um, um . . . ," the heftier deer stopped there.

"It is late enough tonight. We will pass on the secret to you another time," said the no-less-hefty deer, and he added in a commanding voice, "Now, all to sleep!"

And all fell asleep—but not the little squirrel. He kept on gazing at the deer. He wondered how they could become so big. Yes, they too had stripes and they too had hair like his parents, though their hair differed slightly in color.

His parents were asleep. He hopped down to a bush and then leaped on to a rock to have a closer look at the deer. But what did he see? Two human beings were stealthily doing something. He knew the human beings to be very clever animals who lived outside the forest. He observed that these two human beings had closed all the openings with their nets. They were now putting a finishing touch to closing the last opening.

Why were they doing this? Surely not to catch the squirrels! They must be planning to catch the deer. They worked so cautiously and quietly that no deer was aware of the terrible fate awaiting them.

As one of the humans was tying the last knot, the little squirrel jumped onto his nose. The man gave out an involuntary shriek. The net fell from his hand. The deer woke up. They found all the openings shut, but got away through the solitary opening which had not been shut. The little squirrel's parents too had awakened. They became anxious when they found that their son was missing. But soon the little one was back with them, and told them what he had done.

An old owl, who lived in the hollow of a neem tree nearby, told the deerfolk when they were back, "You loudmouths! What happened to your muscle-flexing and frightening the tigers? Today all of you would have been captured by the human beings. You would have been killed for flesh or imprisoned in a zoo. The little squirrel saved you. Bow to him and confess your lies to him. Nature has made him a squirrel as Nature has made you deer and made me an owl. Our ideal should be to be good and brave, not to become someone else. Just as a squirrel can be a noble squirrel, a deer can be an ignoble deer or vice versa."

The deer stood ashamed. They apologized to the squirrels.

Judaism

When Two Sing Together

The Rabbi Pinahas said that when one person who is singing but cannot lift his voice is joined by another who can lift her voice, then the first one will be able to lift his voice also. This is the secret bond between spirit and spirit.

The Strength of Community

The Baal Shem was very troubled because the clouds had hidden the moon and it was time for him to say the Blessing of the Moon after the Day of Atonement. He struggled with all of his power to bring the moon from behind the cover of clouds. His followers knew nothing of their master's struggle and joyfully danced just as they did every year at this time. They danced into his room, where they ignored his gloomy state and pleaded with him to join in the dance. All of a sudden someone called from outside. The moon had finally emerged from beneath her blanket and showered the night in her luminous glow. The strength of the community was more powerful than the master's solitary efforts.

Russian

The Turnip

Once upon a time there lived a very old man called Dedoushka. He had lots of land and he loved to farm it. One day as he was walking through his fields he came upon a single turnip seed. "Ah!" he declared joyfully, "What a wonderful little gift! I shall find the perfect place to plant it so that it can grow very large indeed."

He hobbled up to the top of a little hill where he knew it would get just the right amount of sun and rain. He dug a little hole in the earth, placed the turnip seed in it, and covered it ever so carefully again with soil. Each day Dedoushka would gaze out upon the little hill, knowing that the sun was shining on the turnip, and the rain was watering the turnip, and soon it would be very large indeed.

Finally, after many days of waiting, Dedoushka set out for the top of the hill. There he found that his turnip had grown very, very large indeed!

"Ah!" he cried, "What an enormous turnip!" He reached down to pull the gigantic turnip from the earth. He pulled and he pulled, and finally he sighed, "Oh, this turnip is too large. I must call my dear wife Baboushka. Baboushka! Baboushka!" Dedoushka called loudly.

"Yes, my darling," answered Baboushka.

"You must come and help me with this turnip. It is very, very large!" cried Dedoushka.

"Of course, my darling," replied Baboushka and she started up the hill. When she got to the top, she exclaimed, "Ah! What an enormous turnip!"

So Baboushka pulled Dedoushka, and Dedoushka pulled the turnip. They pulled and they pulled, but the turnip would not budge. "Oh, this turnip is too large. We must call our granddaughter, Mashenka. Mashenka! Mashenka!" Baboushka called loudly.

"Yes, dear grandmother," answered Mashenka.

"You must come and help us with this turnip. It is very, very large!" cried Baboushka.

"Of course, dear grandmother," replied Mashenka, and she started up the hill. When she got to the top, she exclaimed, "What an enormous turnip!"

So Mashenka pulled Baboushka, and Baboushka pulled Dedoushka, and Dedoushka pulled the turnip. They pulled and they pulled, but the turnip would not budge. "Oh, this turnip is too large. We must call our little dog Geoutchka. Geoutchka! Geoutchka!" Mashenka called loudly.

"Yes, mistress," answered the little dog, Geoutchka.

"You must come and help us with this turnip. It is very, very large!" cried Mashenka.

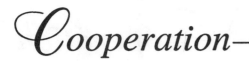

"Of course, mistress," replied Geoutchka. He ran up to the top of the hill and when he saw the turnip he exclaimed, "Oh mistress, what an enormous turnip!"

So Geoutchka pulled Mashenka, Mashenka pulled Baboushka, Baboushka pulled Dedoushka, and Dedoushka pulled the turnip. They pulled and they pulled, but the turnip would not budge.

"Oh, this turnip is too large. We must call our little friend, Keska, the cat. Keska, oh Keska!" cried Geoutchka loudly.

"Oh, what is it now?" yawned Keska, the cat. "Why must you wake me from my nap?"

"You must come and help us with this turnip. It is very, very large!" cried Geoutchka from the top of the hill.

"Oh, I suppose I can help, now that I am awake," said Keska, as she wound her way leisurely to the top of the hill. When she saw the turnip she exclaimed, "What an enormous turnip! And what delicious soup it will make!"

So Keska pulled Geoutchka, Geoutchka pulled Mashenka, Mashenka pulled Baboushka, Baboushka pulled Dedoushka, and Dedoushka pulled the turnip. They pulled and they pulled, but the turnip would not budge.

"Oh, how ridiculous! This turnip will never come out," cried Keska in dismay.

"Yes, it will," insisted Dedoushka. "We must call the little field mouse to help."

"The little field mouse?" the others chorused in surprise. "Why should we bother calling the little field mouse for help?"

"Because we need just a little more help, of course," replied Dedoushka. "Little field mouse! Oh, little field mouse!" Dedoushka called loudly.

"Yes. What can I do for you?" squeaked the little field mouse.

"You must come and help us with this turnip. It is very, very large. If we all try together I am sure we can pull it out and then we will have the most delicious turnip soup for supper," declared Dedoushka.

"Of course, I will help," said the little field mouse as he scampered to the top of the hill. "Oh my, what an enormous turnip!" said the little field mouse as he reached the others. "Let's pull!"

So the little field mouse pulled Keska, Keska pulled Geoutchka, Geoutchka pulled Mashenka, Mashenka pulled Baboushka, Baboushka pulled Dedoushka, and Dedoushka pulled the turnip. They pulled and they pulled—and out popped the turnip!

"You see," cried Dedoushka, "I told you we could do it together! Now together we will eat the most delicious turnip soup!"

PROVERBS AND MAXIMS

We may have all come on different ships, but we're in the same boat now.
— *Martin Luther King*

The hidden harmony is stronger than the visible.
— *Heraclitus*

"Nemo solus satis sapit."
(No one is that wise on their own.)
— *Plautus*

There is no more sure tie between friends than when they are united in their objects and wishes.
— *Cicero*

The more cooperative the group, the greater is the fitness for survival which extends to all of its members.
— *Ashley Montague*

HEROES AND HEROINES

DAG HAMMARSKJÖLD (1905–1961)

Born in Jönköping, Sweden into one of Sweden's oldest families, Dag grew up in Uppsala, Sweden, where his father was a provincial governor. He earned a law degree from Uppsala University and a doctorate in political science from the University of Stockholm. He became the vice-chairman of Sweden's delegation to the United Nations in 1952. A year later he was elected Secretary General of the United Nations, a position he held until his death in a plane crash in Zambia while on a peacekeeping mission. He practiced "quiet diplomacy" to reduce conflict. A publication of his journal, *Markings*, revealed him as an intensely religious person who was concerned with the contrast between the ideal of world peace and the reality of human frailty. He was awarded the Nobel Peace Prize after his death.

JOHN ROBERT WOODEN (1910–)

Born in Martinsville, Indiana, John Wooden seems to have been destined for a life of basketball. He attended high school there, winning all-prep honors three years in a row and leading his team to the Indiana State title in 1927 and as runner-up in 1926 and 1928. He had a similar career at Purdue University, where he led the Boilermakers to two Big Ten Conference titles and the 1932 NCAA Championship. He began his coaching at Dayton High School in Kentucky, but returned to Indiana, where he coached at South Bend Central High School. After World War II, he went to Indiana Teachers College (now Indiana State University), where he served for two seasons as Athletic Director and basketball and baseball coach. In 1948, he went to the University of California at Los Angeles (UCLA), where he compiled a record that is unsurpassed by any coach in the history of sports. In 40 years of coaching he had an 885–203 win-loss record that is unequaled. His coaching philosophy was built upon a "pyramid of success" that had values like cooperation and friendship at the base, self-control, team spirit, and confidence in the center, and honesty, sincerity, patience, and faith as supportive values along the side. His honors recognize him not only as a great figure in sports but also as a great humanitarian (1995—Lexington Theological Seminary Service to Mankind Award; 1985—Bellarmine Medal of Excellence; 1995—AYA Humanitarian Award.)

MARGARET MEAD (1901–1978)

Born in Philadelphia, Pennsylvania, she grew up in a liberal and highly intellectual home. Her father was a college professor of finance and commerce and her mother was a sociologist and an early advocate of women's rights. Margaret became one of the world's foremost anthropologists and developed research methods that helped turn social anthropology into a major science. She worked with the American Museum of Natural History from 1926 until her death, and taught at Fordham and Columbia. She made expeditions to Samoa, New Guinea, Bali and other parts of the South Pacific, which led to many books and articles that introduced the concept of culture into education, medicine, and character development. She was active in environmental concerns, women's rights, and racial harmony.

EMBRACING ———————————————————— *Cooperation*

RABINDRANATH TAGORE (1861–1941)

Born in Calcutta, India, the youngest of 14 children, he was the son of the "Great Sage," Maharishi Debendranath Tagore. He was educated at home and started writing at an early age. Part of his home schooling was the influence of his father, who worked to purify Hinduism, stressing ethics and service as leading to a direct experience with God. Rabindranath Tagore was known as a gifted and creative artist of abundant gifts; he wrote poetry, short stories, novels, essays, and plays, painted in an unorthodox style, and is considered one of India's best songwriters. His first collection of poems and stories, published in 1890, included his first social and political poems. The influence of his writing and lecturing earned him a reputation in India as an educational, social, and religious reformer on a par with Ghandi. He had a deep concern for social justice and an appreciation for different cultures. He embraced Western Civilization, giving India ways to assimilate the West without becoming a mockery of it. His writing emphasized cooperation between nations, businesses, and religions. He was a myriad-minded man that saw the expressions of beauty within different cultures as a means for stimulating thought, conversation, and action. He dedicated his work to the concept of harmony between people and nations.

WRIGHT BROTHERS (ORVILLE 1871–1948, WILBUR 1867–1912)

Wilbur was born near Millville, Indiana, and Orville was born in Dayton, Ohio. They were the sons of a United Brethren Church Bishop, and very early demonstrated abilities in designing and building machines. They opened a bicycle shop and soon became interested in aviation. They started experimenting with gliders, building their first one in 1899. Their first airplane was powered by a twelve-horsepower gasoline engine and was first successfully flown on December 17, 1903 at Kittyhawk, North Carolina. But that was only the beginning, and it took years of patient experimenting before their airplane was perfected. Their third design, built in 1905, could turn in circles and stay in the air a half-hour. In 1909, they founded an aircraft company and began producing two planes each month, gaining the respect of the entire world. Though Wilbur died of typhoid fever at age 45, Orville enjoyed many years of research. The Wright Brothers gave the world a perfect example of how much people can accomplish when they cooperate and work together.

RALPH BUNCHE (1904–1971)

Born in Detroit, Michigan, the grandson of a slave and the son of a barber, he moved to Los Angeles when he was thirteen, after both of his parents died. He worked his way through the University of California at Los Angeles as a janitor and carpet-layer. He earned a masters and doctorate at Harvard University and taught political science at Howard University from 1928–1942. Because of his knowledge of colonialism and government, he moved to the State Department and then to the United Nations, where he became a trouble-shooter in Palestine, working on the Jewish and Arab disagreements. His efforts led to an armistice in the first Arab-Israeli War, and he became the first African-American to receive the Nobel Peace Prize.

Cooperation———————————————EMBRACING

PUT COOPERATION INTO ACTION

- Happily do what your parents ask you to do.

- Play the game your friends want to play even when you would rather do something else.

- Help someone by opening a door or helping to carry something.

- Help find a compromise when a group is in disagreement.

- Always play fair when playing games. Be a good loser.

- Invite someone who is alone or "left out" to join your group.

- Help family members realize the importance of family cooperation by demonstrating a spirit of cooperation in your daily activities.

- Become involved in a community service project.

- Ask your friends to help you do something to preserve the environment.

- Practice good sportsmanship.

COMMUNITY SERVICE IDEAS

- Contribute clothes to a community service organization serving families in unfortunate circumstances.

- Adopt a beach or park and keep it clean.

- Volunteer to help with a project to promote community safety.

- Learn about how you can become prepared to help with disaster relief.

- Make and display posters to help the Heart Association with their campaign for healthy hearts.

- Plan a "share a book day" to contribute books to a children's hospital or after-school program.

BOOKS ON COOPERATION

Anansi the Spider. Gerald McDermott. New York: Holt, 1972.

Sam Johnson and the Blue Ribbon Quilt. Lisa C. Ernst. New York: Lothrop, Lee & Shepard Books, 1983.

Stone Soup. Marcia Brown. New York: Atheneum, 1947.

Wilfred Gordon McDonald Partridge. Mem Fox. Brooklyn: Kane/Miller Book Publishers, 1989.

Zinnia and Dot. Lisa C. Ernst. New York: Viking, 1992.

The Book of Virtues. William J. Bennett, ed. New York: Simon and Schuster, 1993.

    "The Devoted Friend" – p. 674

    "Why Frog and Snake Never Play Together" – p. 284

Chicken Soup for the Teenage Soul. Jack Canfield, "etal." Deerfield Beach: Health Communications, Inc., 1997.

    "The Gravediggers of Parkview Junior High" – p. 298

    "Helen Keller and Anne Sullivan" – p. 294

A 3rd Serving of Chicken Soup for the Soul. Jack Canfield and Mark Victor Hansen. Deerfield Beach: Health Communications, Inc., 1996.

    "Make A Wish" l – p. 217

    "You Very Good; Your Very Fast" – p. 215

A 4th Course of Chicken Soup for the Soul. Jack Canfield, "etal." Deerfield Beach: Health Communications, Inc., 1997.

    "Angel in our Backyard" – p. 214

Humility

SUPPORTIVE VALUES

Gratitude • Appreciation

DEFINITIONS

Having no arrogance, being modest.

Humility, the quality of being humble, without arrogance or pretense, is our focus this month. Modesty is a synonym often used to explain the word humility.

Being pleased, when comfort is given or discomfort alleviated, is certainly a good reason for **gratitude**. It is not the only reason, however. Counting our blessings helps us maintain a positive perspective in life, but being grateful for the opportunities which disguise themselves as problems or tragedies elevates gratitude to another level.

Appreciation is a sense of feeling admiration, approval, or gratitude. Expressing our thanks and being sensitive and aware of ourselves and others is appreciation at its best.

PURPOSE

Humility is a difficult value to define, but you know it when you see it. With the media highlighting arrogant professional athletes and rock stars, it becomes a challenge to support the value of humility. In helping our students realize the talents they are born with, we can encourage them to develop those talents with humility and gratitude and the knowledge that their talents are gifts. In this same way, we can encourage them to be mindful of the many privileges and opportunities they have which they can then learn to humbly appreciate. A little humility would deter the "Life-owes-me-a-living" attitude which is so prevalent in our society.

Too often we take for granted the abundance we have. We are so caught up in our own lives of "busyness" that we don't take the time to truly appreciate our blessings and those events in our lives which present themselves as problems, but are really challenges and opportunities for our own personal growth.

Giving with the knowledge of our abundance becomes an expression of humility, gratitude, and appreciation.

Humility

Day One:
Use the definitions on page 53 as a springboard for discussing the meaning of humility.

Day Two:
Use the discussion questions on page 56 to further your understanding of humility.

Day Three:
Name some words that are the opposite of being humble? Why is being humble a desirable value while arrogance is not?

Day Four:
Read and discuss the stories about humility on pages 57–70.

Day Five:
Choose one of the stories from yesterday to illustrate.

Day Six:
Choose two bookmarks from page 71 to cut out and decorate. Save them for later.

Day Seven:
Can you be proud of your accomplishments with a spirit of humility? Discuss with your classmates.

Day Eight:
Think of a person whose humble spirit you appreciate. Write to that person and tell him or her of your appreciation. Include with the letter one of the bookmarks you decorated.

Day Nine:
One way we show humility is through expressing gratitude to another person. Think of a person for whom you have deep gratitude. Write a short note telling this person why you feel gratitude for him or her. Include the other bookmark which you created earlier.

Day Ten:
Read and pronounce as best you can the foreign words meaning humility on page 55.

Day Eleven:
Work in small groups to create stories comparable to the ones you read on day four. Make sure the characters in each story demonstrate humility in their actions.

Day Twelve:
Share the stories written yesterday and hold a class election to determine which story best reflects a humble spirit.

Day Thirteen:
Do you know the Thanksgiving story? It was a celebration of appreciation and gratitude! Plan to re-create the original thanksgiving feast, either with real food or with drawings of the feast.

Day Fourteen:
Native Americans showed great humility when they shared their knowledge of agriculture with the Puritans and the Puritans exhibited gratitude by sharing their feast. Do you know this story? Draw a picture of the indians helping the new settlers.

Day Fifteen:
Remembering the relationship between the Puritans and Native Americans, list examples of other friendships based on sharing and caring.

Day Sixteen:
Plan a service project for the specific purpose of sharing the talents and abilities of class members to spread Thanksgiving joy in a grateful and humble manner.

Day Seventeen:
Carry out your service project as you planned yesterday.

Day Eighteen:
What does humility mean to you? Write a few sentences or draw a picture representing how you will embrace humility as an important value.

Day Nineteen:
Based on what you have learned this month about humility, as a class, create your own definition of humility. Create a poster to display, which will remind you of the value of humility.

Day Twenty:
Reflect on what you have learned about humility and endeavor to embrace it as a lifelong value.

HUMILITY IN OTHER LANGUAGES

Chinese   *qian*   retiring, humble, modest;
                 xu   hollow, empty, vacant;
                                           pure, unprejudiced, humble

French   *l'humilité*   state of mind or attitude of a person
                                           who looks honestly at himself or
                                           herself without denying his or her
                                           faults, and who tends to downplay his
                                           or her own merits or worthiness

German   *bescheidenheit*   modesty, diffidence, discretion,
                                           demureness, moderation

Hawaiian   *ha'aha'a*   low, lowly, humble

Japanese   *kenkyo*   to respect with pure mind and not say
                                           words
                                           ken—to be humble
                                           kyo—empty, do not have malicious
                                           intention

Korean   *kyum son*   self-effacement, modesty

Latin   *humilitas*   from Latin "humilis" (lowly); from
                                           "humus" (ground) (having eyes to the
                                           ground)

Spanish   *humildad*   humility, humbleness

Tagalog   *kababaang-loob*   a lack of pride; meekness

DISCUSSION QUESTIONS

- Can you think of an example of someone showing humility?

- What is the opposite of humility? Why isn't it a virtue?

- What are the things in life for which you are most thankful?

- How often and how do you express your thankfulness?

- What are the little things in life you appreciate? How do you express your appreciation?

- Why is it important to share what we have with others?

- How does a humble person act toward others?

- How would the world be better if more people practiced humility?

- What are the aspects of your life that make you happy?

- Do you always express appreciation to those who take care of you, help you and do nice things for you?

- Is appreciation always expressed in words? What are some other ways?

- What are the lessons of gratitude that can be learned from the problems of life?

- What are people saying about themselves when they try to be the center of attention?

- Can a person be proud and humble at the same time?

- Make a list of things for which you are thankful. How many relate to your physical comfort? How many are about relationships? How many are spiritual? Is there a good balance?

- How do you express your appreciation of these blessings?

- How much do you share with others?

- How can you turn challenges and difficulties into positive opportunities?

STORIES AND THOUGHTS FROM SPIRITUAL TRADITIONS

Hinduism

Therefore I tell you:
Be humble, be harmless,
Have no pretension,
Be upright, forbearing,
Serve your teacher
In true obedience,
Keeping the mind
And the body in cleanness,
Tranquil, steadfast,
Master of ego,
Standing apart
From the things of the senses,
Free from self;
Aware of the weakness
In mortal nature,
Its bondage to birth,
Age, suffering, dying;
To nothing be slave,
Nor desire possession
Of man-child or wife,
Of home or of household;
Calmly encounter
The painful, the pleasant;
Adore me only
With heart undistracted;
Turn all your thought
Toward solitude, spurning
The noise of the crowd,
Its fruitless commotion;
Strive without ceasing
To know the Atman,
Seek this knowledge
And comprehend clearly
Why you should seek it:
Such, it is said,
Are the roots of true wisdom:
Ignorance, merely,
Is all that denies them.

– Bhagavad Gita

In reality, there is no hero or coward, no great or lowly. All beings are but wooden puppets controlled by the hands of God.

— *Ramcritmanas*

Buddhism

Pride is the last obstacle on the way to spiritual attainment and humility is its antidote.

Humility is appreciating that I am one whereas other are many. Where did we ever get the idea that we are more important than others? This grand delusion is the root of all conflicts and problems. My own benefit is the benefit of just one person, while the benefit of others is infinite.

The Tibetans have a saying: we see the faults of others even when they are as small as a flea, but don't see our own faults even when they are as big as an elephant!

Nangsa Obum

Once upon a time in Tibet, in an ordinary family, an extraordinary child was born. The mother, after doing extensive spiritual practice with a pure heart, had an auspicious dream. In the dream, a female Buddha named Tara told her, "Be happy! You will give birth to a daughter who will be better than any son!" Overjoyed, the parents gave donations to many beggars, and offerings to monasteries, requesting prayers. As soon as the baby was born, the mother said, "Homage to Tara! I have taken birth to benefit all sentient beings."

The baby, Nangsa Obum, was as beautiful as a goddess, and her heart was full of wisdom and compassion. As she grew older, all the young men of the land wished to marry her, but she was interested only in spiritual practice.

Finally one day the king caught sight of her at a festival and asked her to marry his son. Because the king was such an important person, her parents could not refuse his request. So Nangsa was sent off in a grand procession on horseback, and the wedding celebration went on for many days, with much singing, dancing, and merriment. Nangsa was loved and respected by everyone in the kingdom and her husband was completely devoted to her. After seven years, she gave birth to a beautiful baby boy.

About this time, out of jealousy, Nangsa's sister-in-law began treating her badly. This reminded Nangsa of the futility of worldly life and turned her mind strongly to religion. One day when some wandering yogis came for alms, she longed to give up household life and go meditate in the mountains. When her sister-in-law saw her give alms to the yogis, she beat her badly and tore out her hair. Then she went to her brother with the hair in her hand and said, "See what Nangsa has done to me? And she was flirting with the yogis!"

When Nangsa's husband accused her of beating his sister, she kept quiet rather than create a rift between brother and sister. So her husband, assuming she was guilty, beat her until she was bleeding and had three broken ribs. When the servants heard her screams, they pleaded with the prince, "Please stop! How can you beat our lovely Nangsa?"

That evening, as she sat with her young son, Nangsa heard the voice of a wandering beggar outside her window. Distraught by the day's events and convinced of the meaninglessness of worldly life, she asked him for the name of a good spiritual teacher. The beggar said, "Fair goddess! Tibet is a religious country and there are many excellent teachers, but the most famous is Milarepa, living not far from here. You can go there." At the sound of Milarepa's name, Nangsa's hair stood on end and she knew she must go to meet him. She took several turquoises and corals from her necklace and gave them to the beggar.

Just then, the king approached and heard a man's voice in Nangsa's room. When he looked in, he saw Nangsa handing jewels to the beggar. 'This is too much,' he thought. 'She really is a bad woman.' So he began beating Nangsa himself and took her son away from her. The little boy was so sad that he cried and cried and cried.

That night one of the servants sneaked the boy in to see his mother, but when she entered the room, they found Nangsa cold and dead. Nobody could believe she was really dead. They prepared a huge funeral, trying to create good karma to offset the bad. When they asked for a divination, they were told that she would revive after seven days.

During those seven days, Nangsa visited all six realms of rebirth and received teachings on karma from the Lord of Death. After seven days, she came back to life. She sang a lovely song of renunciation and resolved to practice meditation in the mountains. The king and her husband were both filled with remorse. Her small son wept, her husband apologized, and everyone begged her to stay. Nangsa knew that if she returned to the palace, there would be many obstacles. But thinking she could help them by explaining the Buddha's teachings, she relented and returned.

Very eloquently, she explained about karma, the law of cause and effect, but nobody seemed to listen. So she felt very sad and finally asked permission to go visit her parents. Along the way, everyone was delighted to meet the beautiful queen, for they had all heard about her dying and coming back to life. When they asked her to sing, she sang about wishing to trade her silks and jewels for the robes of a nun. She won their hearts and they all promised to give up unwholesome deeds.

When she arrived home, her parents greeted her with great joy. She humbly helped her mother with the weaving, and whoever heard her songs was inspired to spiritual practice. Eventually, though, her mother urged Nangsa to return to her husband and the palace. She even threw ashes in her face and beat her. Reflecting that, 'Death can come at any time, and I have already died once,' Nangsa escaped from the house one night when everyone was asleep and went off to the mountains to practice meditation. When she arrived at the guru's cave, she sang a lovely song of renunciation. After testing her determination, he gave her a small hut for meditation.

When the king finally discovered where she had gone, he was furious and set off with his army to capture her. Arriving with their soldiers, the king and his son trampled many meditators with their horses, and seized the guru from his cave. They were shocked to see Nangsa in the plain garb of a nun, and berated her. As they approached the guru with their swords to slay him, Nangsa sang a moving song about the law of karma and flew into the air, using her shawl as wings. Amazed, the soldiers dropped their weapons and prostrated on the ground. The king and his son regretted their evil deeds and vowed never to repeat them.

From that time on, Nangsa stayed in the mountains and practiced meditation. Not only did she fly, she also left her footprints in stone in many places. All the people of the land, including her sister-in-law, turned to the path of virtue, practicing wisdom and compassion for the rest of their lives.

Zen Buddhism

When ordinariness and holiness exist no more, how is that? An octagonal grindstone is turning in empty space; a diamond pestle grinds to dust the iron mountain.

Christianity

"Do justice, love kindness and walk humbly with your God."
— Bible, Micah 6:8

"When pride comes, then comes disgrace; but with the humble is wisdom."
— Bible, Proverbs 11:2

"Pride goes before destruction, and a haughty spirit before a fall."
— Bible, Proverbs 16:18

The Pharisee and the Publican

Jesus told this story to some who boasted of their virtue and scorned everyone else:

"Two men went to the Temple to pray. One was a proud, self-righteous Pharisee, and the other a cheating tax collector. The proud Pharisee 'prayed' this prayer: 'Thank God, I am not a sinner like everyone else, especially like that tax collector over there! For I never cheat, I don't commit adultery, I go without food twice a week, and I give to God a tenth of everything I earn.'

"But the corrupt tax collector stood at a distance and dared not even lift his eyes to heaven as he prayed, but beat upon his chest in sorrow, exclaiming, 'God, be merciful to me, a sinner.' I tell you, said Jesus, this sinner, not the Pharisee, returned home forgiven! For the proud shall be humbled, but the humble shall be honored."

– Bible, Luke 18:9-14

Islam

Aishah recounts how a poor woman who came to see her one day wanted to give her some gift, but how, out of pity for her circumstances, she preferred not to accept it. The Prophet later told Aishah that she should have accepted it, and then given her something in return. "I think you were looking down on her. Be humble, Aishah, for God likes those who are humble, and has the greatest aversion for those who are proud." *– God-oriented Life p. 84 (Hilyat al-Auliya')*

Tafsir ibn Kathir records the Prophet as saying: "Whosoever humbles himself before the Lord will be raised by Him on high; he may think little of himself, but he will be great in the eyes of men." *– God-oriented Life p. 86*

The servants of God must live in humility.

Chinese

"The good man does not grieve that other people do not recognize his merits. His only anxiety is lest he should fail to recognize theirs."

– Confucius

"He does not preach what he practices till he has practiced what he preaches."

– Confucius

"To reward merit is to stir up emulation; to display desirable things is to excite the disorder of covetousness."

– Lao Tzu

"Gold and jade endanger the house of their possessor. Wealth and honors lead to arrogance and envy, and bring ruin."

— Lao Tzu

The Master said, He does not mind not being in office; all he minds about is whether he has qualities that entitle him to office. He does not mind failing to get recognition; he is too busy doing the things that entitle him to recognition.

— The Analects, Book IV

Someone said, "Jan Yung is Good, but he is a poor talker." The Master said, "What need has he to be a good talker? Those who down others with clap-trap are seldom popular. Whether he is Good, I do not know. But I see no need for him to be a good talker."

— The Analects, Book V

The Arrogant Azalea and the Humble Pine

Each spring for thousands of years, the Queen of Flowers held a festival to which she invited one hundred of the prettiest flowers. She and all of her guests celebrated the beauty and wonder of spring in the forest.

Once, many years ago, Azalea had been invited, due to her brilliant color and great beauty. She began primping and preparing for the great event, quite certain that she would be the loveliest there. She knew that only the most beautiful flowers would be invited, and even next to them she would be spectacular. Oh, how excited she was! It was all she could think about.

Imagine Azalea's surprise when one day the scraggly little Pine Tree approached and said, "Azalea, dear friend, shall we go together to the Queen's celebration? It would be so much more fun to go with a friend."

Azalea burst into laughter at Pine Tree's suggestion. "Surely you haven't been invited to the festival! You are not even a flower and you are hardly beautiful! In fact, you are small, crooked, and quite homely. There must be some mistake."

Tears ran from Pine Tree's eyes as she tried to sweep them away with one of her branches. "It is true I am not very tall or straight, but I do so love the company of my friends. I am so grateful for the loveliness of spring and for the beauty of all the flowers of the forest. I may not be beautiful, but since the Queen invited me, I will go." Then Pine Tree turned sadly and left Azalea.

"What a bother," said Azalea, ruffling her crimson petals. "It's time now for my beauty sleep." Then Azalea rested her head on her glossy leaves and fell fast asleep.

Meanwhile, Pine Tree made her way slowly to the Queen's festival. Upon her arrival at the gates she was greeted warmly by the Queen of Flowers. A camellia smiled her way and an orchid waved. They were all happy to see the gentle pine tree. She was so happy to be among friends. After all had enjoyed the party for quite some time, the Queen beckoned to Pine Tree. "My dear Pine, I would like to present you with the award for Greatest Beauty."

Quite startled, Pine Tree said, "But I am not a beautiful flower at all."

"Ah, my little friend, you always see the best in others, you find gifts where others find faults, you see the bright side of life. You possess great inner beauty," said the Queen, stroking Pine Tree's young branches.

Just then Azalea arrived, quite indignant at all the attention Pine Tree was receiving. She scowled at Pine Tree, unable to enjoy the celebration and the happiness which surrounded Pine Tree. She gazed on Pine Tree with a hollow, bitter heart. Ever since that moment, Azalea's stems have been hollow as well. Even today, while azaleas continue to be lush and beautiful flowers, they live short lives.

The Pine Tree, however, heartened by friendship and strengthened by love, grew to be very tall and strong, and lived a long and happy life.

India

Yayati

Emperor Yayati was one of the ancestors of the Pandavas. He had never known defeat. He followed the dictates of the sastras, adored the gods, and venerated his ancestors with intense devotion. He became famous as a ruler devoted to the welfare of his subjects.

He became prematurely old by the curse of Sukracharya for having wronged his Devayani. In the words of the poet of the Mahabharata: "Yayati attained that old age which destroys beauty and brings on miseries." It is needless to describe the misery of vigorous youth suddenly blighted into age, where the horrors of loss are accentuated by pangs of recollection.

Yayati, who found himself suddenly an old man, was still haunted by the desire for sensual enjoyment. He had five beautiful sons, all virtuous and accomplished. Yayati called them and appealed piteously to their affection: "The curse of your grandfather Sukracharya has made me unexpectedly and prematurely old. I have not had my fill of the joys of life; for not knowing what was in store for me I lived a life of restraint, denying myself even lawful pleasures. One of you ought to bear the burden of my old age and give his youth in return. He who agrees to this and bestows his youth on me will be the ruler of my kingdom. I desire to enjoy life in the full vigor of youth."

He first asked his eldest son to do his bidding. That son replied: "O great king, women and servants would mock at me if I were to take upon myself your old age. I cannot do so. Ask of my younger brothers, who are dearer to you than myself."

When the second son was asked, he gently refused with the words: "Father, you ask me to take up old age, which destroys not only strength and beauty but also—as I see—wisdom. I am not strong enough to do so."

The third son replied: "An old man cannot ride a horse or an elephant. His speech will falter. What can I do in such a helpless plight? I cannot agree."

The emperor grew angry when he saw that his three sons had declined to do as he wished. He hoped for better from his fourth son, to whom he said: "You should take up my old age. If you exchange your youth with me, I shall give it back to you after some time and take back the old age with which I have been cursed."

The fourth son begged to be forgiven, as this was a thing he could by no means consent to. An old man had to seek the help of others even to keep his body clean, a most pitiful plight. No, much as he loved his father, he could not do it.

Yayati was struck with sorrow at the refusal of the four sons. He paused for some time and then supplicated his last son, who had never yet opposed his wishes: "You must save me. I have got this old age with its wrinkles, debility and grey hairs as a result of the curse of Sukracharya. I cannot bear it. If you will take upon yourself these infirmities, I shall enjoy life for just a while more and then give you back your youth and resume my old age and all its sorrows. Pray, do not refuse as your elder brothers have done." Puru, the youngest son, moved by filial love, said: "Father, I gladly give you my youth and relieve you of the sorrows of old age and the cares of State. Be happy." Hearing these words, Yayati embraced him.

As soon as he touched his son, Yayati became a youth. Puru, who accepted the old age of his father, ruled the kingdom and acquired great renown.

Yayati enjoyed life for a long time and, not satisfied, went later to the garden of Kubera and spent many years with an apsara maiden. After long years spent in vain efforts to quench desire by indulgence, the truth dawned on him.

Returning to Puru, he said: "Dear son, sensual desire is never quenched by indulgence. I had heard and read this, but till now I had not realized it. No object of desire—corn, gold, cattle, and women—nothing can ever satisfy the desires of man. We can reach peace only by a mental poise beyond likes and dislikes. Such is the state of Brahman. Take back your youth and rule the kingdom wisely and well."

With these words, Yayati took back his old age. Puru, who regained his youth, was made king by Yayati, who retired to the forest. He spent his time there in austerities, and in due course attained heaven.

Germany

The Modified Horse

Once upon a time, in a small kingdom, there lived a sculptor. His beautiful works in stone were appreciated by one and all. Soon his fame spread far and wide. A day came when the king of the land ordered a statue of himself to be done in marble. The humble artist was overjoyed at this royal assignment. He worked hard all day long and well into the midnight hours.

Days passed into weeks and weeks into months. At last, the great work was completed and installed in the public square. The artist had taken great pains to carve the figure of his beloved ruler. On an appointed day, the king rode from his castle, flanked by his favorite courtiers. The statue was unveiled amidst much pomp and show. All stood spellbound! His statue seemed so real that the king was unable to believe that it was made of marble.

"Marvelous! Beautiful! Perfect!" he exclaimed, and, turning to the sculptor, shook his hands warmly like a good old friend. "You are indeed a great artist! I feel honored that you are one of my subjects. Here, take this sackful of gold as your reward."

But some of the courtiers seethed with jealousy and anger. "We're the king's favorites and his constant companions. But never have we met with such warm affection from him," they thought to themselves. But they dared not pick any flaws in the statue of their lord, for the king himself had already declared it perfect! What should they do to humiliate their rival?

"Indeed, Your Majesty," began the first one, taking courage, "your marble figure is perfect and we hail the great artist for his skill! But the steed you're mounted upon is not as handsome."

"Yes," joined another, "the figure of the horse is surely out of proportion. Its tail is too long and its head too large."

"The statue of the horse is absolutely a failure. The fall of its manes and the turn of its neck are rather awkward," added the third.

"If only the fold of the horse's left hind leg could be changed, it would stand much smarter," said the fourth.

Thus, one after another all the jealous courtiers found some fault in the animal's figure. The king nodded to their comments, for they were his counselors. So many of them could not go wrong!

The humble sculptor listened quietly. He then said with a faint smile, "Your Majesty, these honorable men are not very happy with my sculpture of the horse. Allow me seven more days, I shall try to change it to their taste."

The king agreed to his request. The artist ordered temporary curtains to be put over the statue to enable him to work undisturbed. Day in and day out was heard the clang of hammer and chisel. The honorable courtiers did often pass by the enclosure. They were delighted by the sound and chuckled, looking at one another meaningfully.

Soon the seven long days passed, and the people who lived nearby gave a sigh of relief. For the loud noise of hammer and chisel had at last stopped. All gathered in the central square. The king arrived, flanked by his favorite courtiers. The screens were drawn and the statue was unveiled once again.

The ruler exclaimed at its beauty and beamed a smile at its creator. The sculptor looked at his first critic and said, "Revered sir, your comment was so much to the point that I devoted two full days to modify the figure accordingly. How do you find it now?"

The artist then turned to one after another of all his critics and praised them for their high aesthetic sense, asking them if they were satisfied with the modified horse. Indeed, they were thoroughly satisfied!

"Perfect!" said the eldest of the courtiers. "The steed is the most handsome that I have ever set my eyes upon."

"Yes, the work is now finely proportioned, with the animal's elegant head, and its tail not too long," said the second earnestly.

"How graceful are the fall of its manes and the turn of its neck!" exclaimed the other.

"Much smarter is the position of the horse's rear left leg. Indeed, it enhances the beauty of the work now!" said the fourth, pretending to be one with the fine aesthetic taste in the court.

"O sculptor," said the king at last, "all my courtiers are happy with your creation. They think that it is now perfect, after you have improved upon it according to their suggestions."

But the modest man smiled and replied in a measured tone, "Your Majesty, I'm indeed fortunate to have such great and educated critics of art. But alas, the fact is, I have changed nothing. The work is as it was when you first saw it."

All stood amazed, once staring at the great statue and then at its creator.

"What do you mean? Didn't we hear the sound of your tools?" asked the king, rather surprised.

"O Lord, indeed you heard the sound of chisel and the hammer. I was only hammering at the virtuous quality of your loyal courtiers, who found faults in my work simply because they were jealous," explained the sculptor with a low bow.

The king turned towards his men. They stood, heads hung.

"Bravo, my dear good man! Bravo!" exclaimed the king, affectionately patting the sculptor on the back. "You've not only created a marvelous piece of art but also hammered my courtiers' pride and reputation to pieces!"

African

The Tug of War

One hot day, Rabbit was hopping at the edge of the river when he tripped and landed hard into Hippo's nose. "Watch where you're going, you clumsy little beast! Don't you know any better than to be stumbling around my home? Why, I am the greatest animal in these parts and too important to be bothered by the likes of you!" scolded Hippo.

"I'm sorry, sir. I didn't mean to bother you. I just tripped over that root," apologized Rabbit.

"I don't care if you fell from the sky! You should be careful when you are around someone as powerful and important as I am, you foolish creature," said Hippo angrily.

"Oh, I know how important you are, sir," said Rabbit, with a twinkle in his eye. "I didn't realize that you were powerful, as well."

"Why, I am the strongest and most cunning animal in these parts. There is no one who can beat me at anything!" exclaimed Hippo.

"Not anything?" asked Rabbit, wide-eyed.

"Not a single thing," declared Hippo proudly.

"Hmmmmm," thought Rabbit, "not even at Tug of War?"

"Why, of course not!" laughed Hippo. "I can beat anyone at Tug of War, especially someone the likes of you."

"Would you like to try? Tomorrow?" inquired Rabbit. "I'll meet you here at the river bank with the rope at noon."

Hippo could not contain his laughter. "All right then, you scrawny little fool.

I'll see you here at noon. You won't last two seconds against me. I am the greatest!"

So off hopped Rabbit into the forest to collect vines with which to braid a rope. As he was jumping here and there he leapt right onto Elephant's trunk. "Hey, you little runt! Watch where you're going! Don't you know you should be more careful in my forest? You should be bowing before me instead of colliding into me. After all, I am the greatest animal in these parts!" scolded Elephant.

"I'm sorry, sir. I didn't mean to intrude. I was just wandering through the forest," apologized Rabbit.

"I don't care if you were swinging through the trees! You should watch yourself when you are around someone as powerful and important as I am, you clumsy oaf," said Elephant angrily.

"Excuse my clumsiness and my ignorance as well. I knew that you were important, but I didn't realize that you were powerful," said Rabbit, most politely.

"Why, there is no one stronger or more cunning than I," declared Elephant. "I can beat anyone at anything!"

"Really! Anything! Even, hmmm . . . Tug of War?" asked Rabbit.

"Don't be ridiculous! I can beat anyone at Tug of War!" boasted Elephant.

"Well, how about a game tomorrow with me?" inquired Rabbit. "I'll meet you here in the forest with the rope at, let's say, noon?"

"How amusing!" guffawed Elephant. "It will be over before you can blink your beady little eyes. But if you insist on being so foolish, I'll see you here at noon."

As Elephant turned haughtily and left, Rabbit continued to gather vines and finally braided a strong rope for the next day's challenge.

At noon the next day, Rabbit greeted Hippo at the river bank. "Here's your end of the rope. I will pick up the other end in the forest and when I say 'Go!' begin to pull."

"I know the rules, you little pipsqueak," snorted Hippo. "I'll make quick work of you!"

Then Rabbit raced into the forest and greeted Elephant with the other end of the rope. "Here's your end of the rope," smiled Rabbit. "The other end is at the river bank. When I get there I'll yell 'Go!' and we'll start to pull."

"I know exactly what to do. It's you who ought to be worried about this game, Rabbit!" bellowed Elephant.

Rabbit scampered off to find the middle of his rope at a point halfway between the forest and the river bank. Once he arrived there he hollered "Go!" All at once, Hippo began pulling on his end of the rope from the river bank and Elephant began pulling on his end from the forest. They pulled and pulled, harder and harder.

"My," said Hippo from the river bank, "that little Rabbit is stronger than I thought he was!"

And from the forest Elephant exclaimed, "Goodness! That little Rabbit is much stronger than he looks!"

They continued to pull and tug with all of their strength, unable to gain any ground. "Why, I've never known a Rabbit with such strength," said Hippo, straining.

"This Rabbit is certainly determined to win!" said Elephant, perspiring.

Just then Rabbit began nibbling at the center of the rope with his strong, sharp teeth. He nibbled and nibbled until there was just one strand left. All of a sudden he heard a great splash as Hippo flew into the river when the rope snapped. At the very same moment he heard an enormous crash as Elephant flew into the trees with his half of the rope.

"Oh my," said Hippo from the river, "that Rabbit was much better than I thought!"

"Oh dear," said Elephant from the forest, "I shall not underestimate that little Rabbit again!"

Japanese

The Stonecutter

Once, long ago, there was a humble stonecutter named Tasaku. Each morning he rose early to go to work at the base of a mountain where he chipped away the stone with his hammer and chisel. Every day, he was content to carve the great blocks of stone from which beautiful palaces and temples would be built. He was very happy with his task and asked for nothing more. Tasaku's good and simple outlook made the Spirit of the Mountain very happy, and the Spirit was pleased by Tasaku's kind nature.

But one day, as Tasaku was busy with his hammer and chisel, a great and beautiful procession passed by. First, there came a large army of proud soldiers. Then Tasaku saw a fine prince who was dressed in splendor and carried aloft by many servants. There were lovely dancers and musicians parading behind. Tasaku watched the magnificent stream of people with awe until they moved out of sight.

After witnessing such splendor and the prince in all his finery, Tasaku could not bring himself to return to his humble work. He no longer wanted to spend his life at the base of the mountain cutting stone. He envied the prince. His heart longed for a life of wealth and power. The Spirit of the Mountain heard the desires of his heart and, that very night, transformed the lowly stonecutter into a fine prince.

Tasaku awoke the next morning in a beautiful palace surrounded by servants ready to do his bidding. He wore magnificent robes of the finest silk, and dancers moved before him while musicians played for his enjoyment. He was overjoyed with his new life.

Each day he would stroll in his garden, enjoying the lovely blossoms and fruit trees. One day, he sought shelter from the heat of the sun beneath the branches of a tree and he noticed that the sun's searing rays had withered some of his precious blooms. He thought about the great power of the sun and became discontent. The sun's power was far greater than that of a prince. Tasaku longed to be as powerful as the sun!

Once again, the Spirit of the Mountain heard Tasaku's desires and transformed him instantly into the sun. The feeling of such power thrilled Tasaku. He shone so brightly and proudly in the sky that it was not long before he scorched fields and burned crops. His strong rays began to dry the lands and the people became desperate for water.

At long last, a large group of clouds came over Tasaku and covered his rays completely. Tasaku then realized that the clouds were even more powerful than the sun. Once more, he became discontent and longed to become a great cloud. The Spirit of the Mountain heard his wishes and transformed him into an enormous cloud.

Haughtily, Tasaku puffed himself up and began to rain powerfully over the land. Proud of his new strength, he sent huge storms over the fields. He flooded fields and homes in his excitement, and finally even temples and palaces were washed away. All was gone, destroyed by his power. All but the mountain.

Tasaku was enraged by the immovable mountain. Angry that the mountain was more powerful than the cloud, he cried out, "Turn me into the mountain!" Without hesitating, the Spirit did so and departed, knowing that there was nothing more that he could do to please Tasaku.

So all at once, Tasaku became the mountain. At last, he thought, he was more magnificent than the prince, more powerful than the sun, and far stronger than the cloud. He stood there so proudly. Finally, he was greater than everything around him.

Suddenly, he felt a sharp pain at his feet. It was the sting of a chisel! There, far below, was a lowly stonecutter, hammering slowly but surely at his base.

While bits of stone cracked and crumbled from him, so did Tasaku's heart.

PROVERBS AND MAXIMS

I believe the first test of a truly great man is his humility.

— *J. Ruskin*

Gratitude is the heart's memory.

— *French Proverb*

If the only prayer you say in your whole life is "thank you," that would suffice.

— *M. Eckhart*

If you compare yourself to others, you may become vain and bitter; for always there will be greater and lesser persons than yourself.

— *Desiderata*

Great character has no facades. It shines with honesty, respect, true humility, and an inner faith that knows we are but the recipients of a great gift.

— *T. Pagna*

HEROES AND HEROINES

SACAGAWEA (1786–?)

Born in territory which is now part of Idaho, she was of the Shoshone tribe of Native Americans, but was captured by an enemy tribe and sold to the Missouri River Mandans. She married a French Canadian fur trader who lived in the Mandan village. When Meriwether Lewis and William Clark appeared on the river in 1804 on their way west, her husband was hired as an interpreter for the expedition and Sacagawea was allowed to accompany him. Her abilities as a guide, interpreter, and diplomatic liaison with other tribes proved invaluable to Lewis and Clark. Nothing is known of her life after the expedition ended in 1812, but she is remembered for her courage, her love of adventure, and her loyalty to family and friends.

MARY MCLEOD BETHUNE (1875–1955)

Born in Mayesville, South Carolina, she was the daughter of former slaves, who had seventeen children; Mary was the fifteenth. She was raised on a farm and educated in a Presbyterian mission school. While she had a serious mind, she still enjoyed music and dance and was an acknowledged leader of her classmates. She graduated from the Moody Bible Institute and, unable to pursue her desire to become a missionary in Africa, became a teacher. She opened a school for African-American girls in Daytona Beach, Florida in 1904. The school survived, merged with a boys' school, and eventually became Bethune-Cookman College. In 1936, President Franklin Roosevelt appointed her director of African-American affairs in the National Youth Administration. She is recognized as one of America's great educators, an advisor to several American presidents, and a powerful champion of racial equality.

JIMMY CARTER (1924–)

Born in Plains, Georgia, as James Earl Carter, he was the 39th president of the United States from 1977–1981. Of humble birth, he was the son of a farmer and a nurse; he listed his occupation as a peanut farmer and warehouseman. He was the first president to use his nickname at his inauguration and the first one to walk from the Capitol to the White House afterward. His administration was characterized by a human rights policy that he considered an integral factor in the relationship between the United States and other countries. Following his term as president, he remained active in a local Baptist church as a Sunday school teacher, worked as a volunteer for Habitat for Humanity, and represented the United States as a peacemaker in several trouble spots around the world.

MOHANDAS GANDHI (1869–1948)

Born in Porbandar, India, into a wealthy family of the Vaisya, or merchant caste, he was a small, quiet boy who disliked sports and was only an average student. He wanted to study medicine but was prevailed upon by his father to study law. His belief in non-violence was fostered by racial discrimination and violence in South Africa, by a reading of Thoreau's essay on *Civil Disobedience*, by correspondence with Leo Tolstoy, and by reading John Rushin's *Unto this Last*. He became a vegetarian, took voluntary vows of poverty and chastity, and created a cooperative commonwealth for civil resistors called the Tolstoy Farm. He devoted his life to Indian independence from England, equal justice for all of the people of India, and unity between Hindus and Moslems. While attending prayers, he was shot and killed by a Hindu extremist.

PUT HUMILITY INTO ACTION

- Do something nice for someone without their knowing who did it.

- Always be polite.

- Make a list of all the things for which you are thankful.

- Find a way to thank every person who has contributed to something on your list.

- Share something every day with someone (time, an idea, lunch).

- Help someone without expecting a favor in return.

- Thank someone for doing an unexpected, unselfish act.

- Make a list of everything that contributes to your happiness.

- Express your appreciation to every person who contributed to something on your list.

- Contribute to someone else's happiness.

- Be part of the group, not the star of the show. Share the credit.

- Be strong in character and gentle in criticism.

- Find ways to express your thankfulness to the people who have contributed to your happiness.

- Contribute to someone else's happiness.

- Get involved in a community service project.

COMMUNITY SERVICE IDEAS

- Volunteer to collect food for disadvantaged people.

- Make placemats or tray favors for the annual Thanksgiving dinner for the hungry of your community.

- Write a letter thanking the people who clean your classroom; have everyone in the class sign it.

- Visit an elderly shut-in to help with chores or just to share a smile.

BOOKS ON HUMILITY

A Chair for My Mother. Vera Williams. New York: Greenwillow Books, 1982.

Raven. Gerald McDermott. San Diego: Harcourt Brace, Jovanovich, 1993.

Sylvester and the Magic Pebble. William Steig. Simon, 1969.

A Call to Character. Colin Greer and Herbert Kohl, eds. New York:
Harper Collins Publisher, 1995.
"The Frog and the Ox" – p. 360
"A Childhood Story to Treasure" – p. 361
"Simple Gifts" – p. 69
"The Head Man" – p. 72

Chicken Soup for the Teenage Soul. Jack Canfield, "etal." Deerfield Beach: Health
Communications, Inc., 1997.
"The Oyster" – p. 259

A 3rd Serving of Chicken Soup for the Soul. Jack Canfield and Mark Victor Hansen.
Deerfield Beach: Health Communications, Inc., 1996.
"The Cookie Thief" – p. 199

The Moral Compass. William J. Bennett, ed. New York: Simon and Schuster, 1995.
"The Mandarin and the Tailor" – p. 767
"The Melon and the Professor" – p. 745
"Robert of Sicily" – p. 725
"The Golden Tripod" – p. 729

Peace

SUPPORTIVE VALUES

Harmony • Forgiveness

DEFINITIONS

A state of tranquility, harmony in relationships.

There is an outer **peace** and an inner peace. There is the peace which refers to communities where there is no violence and everyone is able to live a fulfilled life. There is a peace which refers to self, where security and self-worth enable a person to feel at peace with oneself. These are the two kinds of peace which we are referring to in this month's value.

Harmony is a word we usually couple with peace. We also think in terms of musical harmony where many voices or instruments play different melodies, creating more depth and beauty in the composition.

Forgiveness is ceasing the feeling of resentment towards someone who has offended or hurt you in any way.

PURPOSE

We are aware of the state of unrest in our world; there are wars in many countries as well as increased violence in our own cities. We look outward and forget that if we truly desire peace on earth, it needs to begin with each one of us. Our actions toward ourselves and those around us speak clearly about the degree to which we are at peace with ourselves. Inner peace is a good place to start.

As students strive for inner peace and to become more attuned to themselves and to each other, they can create a more peaceful world.

We always hope for forgiveness, but often have difficulty giving it when we feel we've been wronged. When we learn to forgive ourselves, we are more forgiving of others. An inability to forgive, bearing a grudge for some past hurt, is an obstacle on the path to inner peace. Teachers need to strive to be forgiving of our students if we expect them to be forgiving of each other and of us.

Peace

Day One:
Use the definitions on page 77 as a springboard to discuss the meaning of peace.

Day Two:
Answer the discussion questions on page 80.

Day Three:
What symbols can you think of which represent peace? List as many as you can.

Day Four:
Create a banner to promote peace to hang up outside your classroom. Be sure to decorate it with several symbols of peace from yesterday's list.

Day Five:
Practice saying the words for peace in other languages on page 79.

Day Six:
Make a bookmark from a proverb on page 84. Keep it in your history book as a reminder of peace.

Day Seven:
Do you know what the Nobel Peace Prize is? If not, find out. Research and learn about the life of one Nobel prize winner.

Day Eight:
Based on what you learned about the Nobel Peace Prize, name the person in your class you would nominate for a class peace prize winner. Tell why you selected the person for the class prize.

Day Nine:
Design an award for someone you know who encourages others to act in a peaceful manner. It could be a blue ribbon for a school helper, a star for a classmate, an apple for a teacher, a note or picture for a neighbor, etc. Present the award and tell the person why they received it.

Day Ten:
Consider what you would do if someone who did not value peace tried to fight with you or treated you badly. Share your ideas in a small group and together decide on the best resolution to the problem. Each individual group should then share their idea with the class as a whole.

Day Eleven:
Read and discuss one of the stories about peace on pages 81–83.

Day Twelve:
How can you promote peace in your own life? Make a list of peaceful acts which you can do today. Choose one act and follow through to promote peace.

Day Thirteen:
Create a petition for students and their families to sign—pledging their support for peace and committing to promote peace in their own environment and around the world. Be sure to give everyone in your school an opportunity to sign the pledge.

Day Fourteen:
How would we be different if there were world peace? Write a short story about life in a peaceful world or draw a picture of what this world would look like.

Day Fifteen:
Name some things family members can do to create a peaceful home environment. Tell how each of these actions can influence peace in the home:
1) quarreling;
2) complaining;
3) showing lack of respect for family rules.

Day Sixteen:
Why is it important for family members to work together to make the home a place where family members can expect to find peace at all times. Write or draw about something you can do to make your home environment more peaceful.

Day Seventeen:
Discuss ways people of your age can promote peace in your community, in your country, and in the world. How are the three lists alike and different?

Day Eighteen:
Do you think television influences people's respect for peace? Do you think it causes less or more violence? Explain your answers.

Day Nineteen:
Work in small groups to make lists of questions about the causes of war. Share the questions in a total group setting and name specific things that might be done to change the causes.

Day Twenty:
Review what you have learned about peace this month and reflect on how you can begin now to endeavor to embrace peace on a daily basis.

Character Education Year 2 Grades K–6

LEARNING ABOUT ——————————————————— *Peace*

PEACE IN OTHER LANGUAGES

Language	Word	Meaning
Chinese	*ping*	level; even; just; equal; average; ordinary; common
	an	quiet; still; peace; tranquility
French	*la paix*	state of concord, agreement among members of a group or nations. tranquility; lack of noise, agitation, disorder; serenity of mind
German	*friede*	peace, tranquility
Hawaiian	*maluhia*	peace, quiet, tranquility, serenity
Japanese	*heiwa*	quiet harmony hei—flat wa—harmony
Korean	*pyung hwa*	evenly harmonized; reconciliation
Latin	*pax*	from Latin "pax" (peace)
Spanish	*paz*	peace
Tagalog	*kapayapaan*	freedom from war or strife; a public quiet, order and security

*P*eace ————————————————————— LEARNING ABOUT

DISCUSSION QUESTIONS

- Why do kind words and actions make you feel peaceful?

- What is a peaceful response to someone who says or does something unkind? Is that forgiveness?

- Describe something peaceful.

- Why is harmony so important in good friendships?

- When you have a disagreement with someone, what is the peaceful thing to do? Why is this difficult?

- Have you ever apologized to someone and asked for forgiveness? How did it change your relationship? Could nations do this?

- Do you think all people should be seen as equal no matter what kind of job they have or how much money they have? Why?

- What makes you feel peaceful?

- How does being unfair to someone take away from that person's freedom?

- In a song we sing are the words, "Let there be peace on earth, and let it begin with me." How is this possible?

- Is there a situation where you have forgiven someone? Did it establish a kind of peace?

- Describe a time when you are at complete peace.

- When people are striving for harmony during a disagreement, are they suggesting people change their minds or that they try to understand the other's position?

STORIES AND THOUGHTS FROM SPIRITUAL TRADITIONS

Hinduism

Peace can be reached by concentrating on that which is dearest to the heart.

– Sivananda

When one goes beyond the duality of the external world, then one finds true peace, for it exists alone within.

– Upanishads

Christianity

"Glory to God in the highest, and on earth, peace and goodwill among all people."

– Bible, Luke 2:14

"Live in harmony with one another. Repay no one evil for evil. Live peaceably with all."

– Bible, Romans 12:16-18.

Love your Enemies (A Portion from The Sermon on the Mount)

"The law of Moses says, 'If a man gouges out another's eye, he must pay with his own eye. If a tooth gets knocked out, knock out the tooth of the one who did it.' But I say: Don't resist violence! If you are slapped on one cheek, turn the other too. If you are ordered to go to court, and your shirt is taken from you, give your coat too. If the military demand that you carry their gear for a mile, carry it two. Give to those who ask, and don't turn away from those who want to borrow.

There is a saying, 'Love your friends and hate your enemies.' But I say: Love your enemies! Pray for those who persecute you! In that way you will be acting as true sons of your Father in heaven. For he gives his sunlight to both the evil and the good, and sends rain on the just and on the unjust too. If you love only those who love you, what good is that? Even scoundrels do that much. If you are friendly only to your friends, how are you different from anyone else? Even the heathen do that. But you are to be perfect, even as your Father in heaven is perfect."

– Bible, Matthew 5:38-48

Islam

I found this inscribed on the hilt of the Prophet's sword: 'Forgive him who wrongs thee; join him who cuts thee off; do good to him who does evil to thee, and speak the truth although it be against thyself.'
— *Selections from Mishkat-ul-masabi [243] p. 56*
'Aliy, RA

But if the enemy inclines towards peace, then you should also incline towards peace, and trust in Allah, for He is the One that hears and knows all.

The root of the word Islam means, amongst other things, Peace. To incline towards peace is to incline towards Allah. War is at times an unavoidable step to peace. It is the price we pay for free will, for it is the ultimate expression of conflicting wills. But whenever there is a possibility of peace with our enemies we should take it, rather than continue fighting out of fear or suspicion. If, indeed, it is a trick by our enemies, then Allah and the solidarity He has given us amongst ourselves will come to our aid.
— *Selections from Mishkat-ul-masabi [253] p. 164*
Spoils of War (Anfal) 8:61

Chinese

"If out of the three hundred songs I had to take one phrase to cover all my teaching, I would say, Let there be no evil in your thoughts."   — *Confucius*

"Never do to others what you would not like them to do to you."
— *Confucius*

"Let us make our sharpness blunt; let us loosen our complexes; let us tone down our brightness to the general obscurity."   — *Lao Tzu*

"Who can clear muddy water? Stillness will accomplish this. Who can obtain rest? Let motion continue equably, and it will itself be peace."
— *Lao Tzu*

India
Character Certificate

Kumar was the son of a farmer. He approached Ramanath, a rich trader, who was looking for an assistant. Ramanath told Kumar he would give him a job provided Kumar gave a security deposit of a thousand rupees. "Alternatively, you may ask four prominent persons to stand surety for you. I'm wary of employing strangers," he told Kumar pointblank.

"All right," agreed Kumar. "If you'll go with me in the evening after you close your shop, I shall get you a thousand rupees or four sureties."

Late in the evening, Kumar took Ramanath to moneylender Vairabh. He told the moneylender the purpose of his visit. "Kumar, you're honest and good," said Vairabh in the presence of Ramanath. "You're not given to telling lies. All this I know well, and I know for certain, too. But, I can't give you a loan. How'll you return the amount? I know your financial status. So, please don't press me for a loan."

Kumar then took Ramanath to Muthuswami, who was a prominent figure of that town. He listened to the youngster's pleas. "I know you even from your childhood; you're also the son of my best friend. You don't quarrel with others for anything and everything; you're also honest. But all that will not prompt me to give you a thousand rupees—as a loan or a gift. I hope you won't insist or bother me again and again."

Kumar's next visit was to the village chief Manikyam. "Look here! I know everybody in your family, Kumar. I also know you well—that you're clever, competent, honest, and won't cheat. But all that will not be sufficient for me to stand surety for you, my boy!"

Kumar was disappointed. He came out and told Ramanath, "See how difficult it is to get a loan. It's all my misfortune!"

"Don't worry, Kumar," Ramanath consoled him. "The certificates of surety I wanted you to get me, I've already received. I don't need them in writing any longer. I've heard all of them describing you and your honesty. That's more than sufficient. You may join my company tomorrow."

Kumar was happy. Though no one was willing to give him a loan of a thousand rupees, it was not a reflection on his character. They did not want to help him with money. At the same time, they all spoke highly of his character. That was enough for Ramanath to assess Kumar. More than a surety certificate, what he wanted was a character certificate.

PROVERBS AND MAXIMS

This is the way of peace: Overcome evil with good, falsehood with truth, and hatred with love.

– Peace Pilgrim

To err is human,
to forgive, divine.

– Pope

It is right for him who asks forgiveness
for his offenses to grant it to others.

– Horace

Peace is not an absence of war, it is a virtue, a state of mind,
a disposition for benevolence, confidence, justice.

– Spinoza

Go placidly amid the noise and haste, and remember what peace there may be in silence . . . be at peace with God, whatever you conceive Him to be, and whatever your labors and aspirations, in the noisy confusion of life keep peace with your soul.

– Desiderata

HEROES AND HEROINES

MADELINE KORBEL ALBRIGHT (1937–)

Born in Prague, Czechoslovakia, she moved to London when she was two years old and to America in 1948. She attended Wellesley College, graduating with honors and a degree in political science in 1959. She married Joseph Albright, a newspaper reporter, a few days after graduation. She enrolled in graduate school at Columbia University, eventually earning a masters and Ph.D. At the same time, she was working for Senator Edmund Muskie, and in 1978 joined the staff of the National Security Council under Zbigniew Brezejinski, who was President Jimmy Carter's national security advisor. She has served as the United States permanent representative to the United Nations since 1993. She has acted not only as a spokesperson for the executive arm of the government but as a significant behind-the-scenes strategist and policy-maker. She has earned a reputation as an expert in foreign policy and has already made significant contributions as an advocate for peace.

RIGOBERTA MENCHU (1959–)

Born in the village of Chimel in northwestern Guatemala, she is a member of the Quiche, one of twenty-two groups of Mayan Indians. By age eight she was toiling on the coffee plantations under conditions that approximated slavery. Her family's efforts to improve conditions and to resist the Guatemalan soldiers from taking their land resulted in the torture and killing of her father, mother and younger brother during 1979 and 1980. In 1981 she escaped to Mexico, where she has lived in exile ever since. She continues to speak out for justice and a peaceful resolution in Guatemala. She yearns for a normal life of family and peace, but repeated death threats keep her "homeless" and in isolation. She was awarded the Nobel Peace Prize in 1992.

YITZHAK RABIN (1922–1995)

Born in Jerusalem of Russian parents who moved to Palestine during World War I, he received his education in Tel Aviv and in a kibbutz. He planned to become a pioneer farmer, but World War II interrupted his studies in Berkeley and he joined the Pulmach, the highly trained commando force of the Haganah. By 1964 he had achieved the rank of Major General in the Israeli army. Upon retirement from the military he became ambassador to the United States and entered Israeli politics. A military hero who evolved into a peacemaker, he became Prime Minister of Israel and negotiated several peace accords with Yasir Arafat of the PLO. He shared the Nobel Peace Prize with Arafat and Israeli defense minister Shimon Peres. While leaving a Tel Aviv "Peace Now" rally at which he had just spoken, he was shot to death by a right-wing Israeli Jew.

ANWAR SADAT (1918–1981)

Born in a Nile delta village in Egypt, he was one of thirteen children of a devoutly Moslem family. He studied the Koran in a local religious school, and in 1925 his family moved to Cairo, where he went to high school. He developed a passion for ending the British influence in Egypt and became a military officer and a close friend of Gamal Abdel Nasser. He continued his work for the freedom of Egypt and became President of the United Arab Republic in 1970. When the conflict between Egypt and Israel worsened, he worked with Israeli Prime Minister Menachem Begin to restore peace. In 1978 he and Begin were awarded the Nobel Peace Prize.

DESMOND TUTU (1931–)

Born in the gold-mining town of Klerkadorp, South Africa, he moved with his family to Johannesburg, where he attended high school and college. He taught in a high school from 1954–1957 but decided to enter the ministry of the Anglican Church when the government instituted an inferior system for blacks. This change coincided with political developments in South Africa and the beginning of the anti-apartheid movement. He became a leader of the South African Council of Churches and a voice of moderation in the struggle against apartheid. His work resulted in his being awarded the Nobel Peace Prize in 1984. He continues to express his belief that "there is no peace because there is no justice. We are struggling not to oppress somebody else but in order to free everybody."

ELIE WIESEL (1928–)

Born in Sighet, Rumania, he was raised within the Hasidic Jewish tradition by his parents, who fostered in him the importance of the Hasidic spirit, studying and living a life that was devoted to God. When the Nazis occupied Rumania in 1944 his family was sent to the Birkenau concentration camp, where his father died of starvation and his mother and younger sister perished in the gas chambers. In 1945 he was transferred to Buchenwald, where he was liberated in April of that year. He studied philosophy in an effort to understand the horrors he had experienced, and became a journalist, traveling widely while trying to learn and write about human suffering. It was ten years before he could write about his encounter with the evil of the concentration camps. His subsequent writing, teaching, and lecturing on behalf of the victims of violence everywhere led to his being awarded the Nobel Peace Prize in 1986.

EMBRACING———————————————————————*Peace*

PUT PEACE INTO ACTION

- Practice random acts of kindness until it's a habit.

- Respond with kind words when someone says something unkind.

- Be honest, nice, and patient with everyone, no matter what their age.

- Sit quietly and have peaceful thoughts.

- When you disagree with someone, disagree politely and end the conversation as friends.

- Apologize to someone you have wronged.

- Sit quietly, every day, and have a peaceful thought.

- Follow the rules and question those who are unfair to others.

- Make peace with someone you have disagreed with.

- When someone apologizes, accept it gratefully and sincerely.

- Find a time, every day, when you can have a few minutes of peace.

EMBRACING

COMMUNITY SERVICE IDEAS

- Volunteer to be trained as a peer-mediator through a neighborhood justice center.

- Volunteer with an Education Program.

- Organize Christmas caroling for a hospital.

- Volunteer with an organization that works to prevent child abuse

- Collect toiletries, toys, clothes for a shelter for abused spouses.

- Write to your representatives in Congress and the Senate. Ask these people to pursue a policy of peace in all their dealings with foreign nations.

- Spread the message of peace to your community by hanging up signs and passing out copies of the bookmarks on page 84.

- Discuss the meaning of peace with your family. Decide how your home can always be a place of peace.

BOOKS ON PEACE

Billy the Great. Rosa Gui. New York: Doubleday Books for Young Readers, 1992.

Butter Battle Book. Dr. Seuss. New York: Random House, 1984.

Island of the Skog. Steven Kellogg. New York: Dial Press, 1973.

Smoky Night. Eve Bunting. San Diego: Harcourt Brace, 1994.

Teammates. Peter Golenboch. San Diego: Harcourt Brace, Jovanovich, 1990.

The Book of Virtues. William J. Bennett, ed. New York: Simon and Schuster, 1993.

    "The Arrow and the Song" – p. 341

    "Bausis and Philemon" – p. 303

    "Helen Keller and Ann Sullivan" – p. 312

    "Rocking Horse Land" – p. 286

    "Ruth and Naomi" – p. 296

    "A Wayfaring Song" – p. 312

    "Why Frog and Snake Never Play Together" – p. 284

January

Patience

SUPPORTIVE VALUES

Perseverance • Confidence

DEFINITIONS

Being able to bear difficulties calmly and without complaint.

One definition of **patient** is "steadfast despite opposition, difficulty, or adversity." The capacity for calmly waiting; for ideas, for growth, for achievement, regardless of obstacles in our path, is patience. *Ahonui,* the Hawaiian word for patience, literally means "large breath," something we need to do (inhale deeply) when we're struggling with our patience. *Ho'omanawanui* is another Hawaiian word for patience which literally means "to make time large," an interesting perspective for looking at the concept of time in regard to patience.

Another word for **perseverance** is persistence. The idea of continuing or persisting in a certain action or on a specific course in spite of any deterrent describes the value of perseverance.

Confidence stresses faith in oneself and one's talents without any suggestion of conceit or arrogance.

PURPOSE

In an age where instant gratification is the norm, it is understandable that our students expect immediate results. In lives that are so goal-oriented and schedule-oriented, patience is a virtue which sometimes seems beyond our grasp. Impatience is often accepted as a natural characteristic of youth. However, as we mature and experience life, we realize that the greatest human achievements in our world all required patience, perseverance, and confidence.

When we are patient with ourselves and others we are able to persevere in any situation. When we are confident about our abilities we are aware that it is just a matter of patience and perseverance before we will succeed in our goals.

As educators teach and interact with students, let us strive to demonstrate that being patient, although not easy, is necessary, not only in regard to achievement but especially in regard to relationships and building character.

Patience — January

Day One:
Use the definitions on page 91 as a springboard to discuss the meaning of patience.

Day Two:
Why is it sometimes difficult to be patient? With your class, think of ways to help an impatient person become more patient.

Day Three:
Select one of the bookmarks on page 100. Use it to help remind you to be patient with yourself and others every day.

Day Four:
Read a story about patience from pages 95–99. Discuss what was lost or could have happened because of impatience.

Day Five:
Remember a time when you had to be patient for something. Write a short story or draw a picture about your experience. Was being patient worth the reward in the end?

Day Six:
Patience requires a good amount of self-control. Practice your ability to be patient by trying as a class to be quiet for five entire minutes. Afterwards, discuss whether students had an easy or difficult time being patient.

Day Seven:
Remembering your exercise in patience yesterday—work as a total group to recommend tips on being patient to help those who had a tough time exercising patience.

Day Eight:
Integrate your list of suggestions from yesterday into a chart to display in your classroom, so that students may refer to it whenever they find a lack of patience. Students might then make their own copy to take home to display.

Day Nine:
Read about the heroes and heroines of patience on pages 101–103. Do you think you could have exercised the same patience that they did? What can you learn from these people about the rewards of patience?

Day Ten:
Make a plan to help a classmate with a math or spelling lesson. Remember to use patience!

Day Eleven:
Have you ever had a difficult time learning something? Do you remember the teacher or parent who patiently took the time to help you? Draw a picture showing the event.

Day Twelve:
Why is it important for teachers to be patient with their students? Discuss ways teachers and students show patience for each other during the school day.

Day Thirteen:
Patience is like a muscle. To be patient more easily, you must practice using your "patient muscle." Where do you think a patient muscle would be in your body? What do you think it would look like? Draw a picture and share your idea with the class.

Day Fourteen:
Why is it as important to be patient with yourself as it is to be patient with others. Frustration is a feeling you can get when you are impatient with yourself. Plan what you will say to yourself when you feel yourself becoming frustrated. Write it down and don't forget your own good advice!

Day Fifteen:
Discuss the meaning of the word impatience. Can you think of examples of impatience that led to complaining, a temper tantrum, tears, or quarreling?

Day Sixteen:
Select one of the behaviors discussed yesterday to use as the basis of a creative story or drawing to show the consequences of impatience.

Day Seventeen:
Think about a time in your own life when impatience caused you to behave poorly. Ponder on what you could have done differently.

Day Eighteen:
Work in small groups to create posters or banners to encourage students to be patient with each other.

Day Nineteen:
Share and discuss the banners created yesterday and display them in the hallway or school cafeteria to encourage a school-wide spirit of patience.

Day Twenty:
Reflect on what you have learned about patience this month. Discuss reasons why patience is a value worth embracing?

PATIENCE IN OTHER LANGUAGES

Chinese	*ren*	to endure; to bear; to repress; to forbear
French	*la patience*	aptitude for enduring with constancy or resignation the problems or unpleasant aspects of existence; characteristic of someone who can wait or persevere without irritation or fatigue
Hawaiian	*ahonui*	patient, enduring (aho means "breath, to breathe" and nui means "big, large, great")
Japanese	*nin*	blade on your heart
Korean	*in rae*	patiently persevere, tolerance
Latin	*patientia*	from Latin "pati" (to suffer, endure) (enduring suffering)
Spanish	*paciencia*	patience, forbearance
Tagalog	*tiyaga*	steady effort and perseverance to accomplish a task or responsibility

Patience ——————————————————— LEARNING ABOUT

DISCUSSION QUESTIONS

- What does it mean to be patient? Are you patient? Would you like to be patient?

- Do you agree with the quotation, "If at first you don't succeed, try, try again"? Why is this wise?

- What is an example of something about which people are confident?

- Who in your life is a good example of someone who is patient? How are they patient?

- Are patient people admired and well-liked? Why?

- Do you admire people who don't give up when working on a project? Why?

- Why are people with a lot of confidence sometimes hard to get along with?

- What or who makes you lose your patience? How could you develop more patience?

- Why are patient people easy to get along with?

- When or how are you confident?

STORIES AND THOUGHTS FROM SPIRITUAL TRADITIONS

Hinduism

Who has no patience, has no strength. Who has no strength, has no contentment. Who has no contentment, has no peace.

— Tradition

Buddhism

Anger is the greatest downfall, and patience, its antidote, is the greatest virtue.

Two Brothers

Once upon a time in India, there was a great king named Brahmadatta who had two sons. Despite all the luxuries of palace life, the older son wished to renounce all worldly attachments and live the spiritual life of a wandering monk. Seeing the steadfast resolve of his beloved son, with great sadness and many tears, the king finally gave his permission. The prince left the comforts of the palace and went to live in solitude in the forest. There he meditated on loving kindness for all beings, befriending and pacifying the wild elephants and lions. Subdued and serene, he became known as Kshativadin, the Patient One.

One day his younger brother, now King Kalabhu, went with his many wives to frolic in the forest. Eventually, he dozed off on a sleepy meadow, and as the women wandered off to pick flowers they came upon the ascetic Kshativadin, meditating peacefully. Attracted by his serene countenance, they bowed before him. When King Kalabhu awoke, he was furious to find his women admiring the sage. Not recognizing his own brother, he drew his sword to attack him. With one blow, he severed both the monk's arms, screaming, "How patient are you now?" When Kshativadin showed no anger, he was further infuriated and cut off both the monk's legs, snarling, "How patient are you now?" Still, Kshativadin remained calm and tranquil, saying, "Although I suffer tremendously, I feel no anger. Instead of cutting off my limbs, you should cut through your own anger and impatience."

As a result of Kalabhu's wicked actions, famine and epidemics raged in the land, creating untold miseries. When the astrologers told Kalabhu that he was to blame, the king went to the forest and bowed before the monk Kshativadin, saying, "I sincerely regret my evil deeds and all the suffering they have caused." To this Kshativadin replied, "Just as a seed produces fruit, so each action we create produces its result. I bear you no grudge, nor do I feel despondent. If this is true, let my body become whole."

With this, his severed limbs became reattached. The king was astonished and, bowing at his feet once more, begged for his mercy and compassion. The sage Kshativadin pledged to free his brother from delusion once he became enlightened, and when he became a Buddha, he did.

Catching the Ox

> If he tries to detain it,
> He does not feel good.
> That accounts for the truth
> Of their relationship.
> To what avail will it be
> To get hold of the raging ox?
> The harder he pulls on the rein,
> The bolder the ox becomes.

Christianity

"Love is patient and kind."

— Bible, I Corinthians 13:4

Islam

The Prophet was passing by a woman who was weeping near a grave, and he said, "Fear God, and be patient." She said, "Away from me! My calamity has not befallen thee, and thou dost not know it." The woman was afterwards told that it was the Prophet; whereupon she came to the door of the Prophet where she found no door-keeper. She said to the Prophet, "I did not know thee, O Prophet of God!" The Prophet said, "Patience is only (becoming) at the first (stroke) of grief."

— Selections from Mishkat-ul-masabi [554] p. 123
Anas, BU: MU

Chinese

The Master said, Even when walking in a party of no more than three I can always be certain of learning from those I am with. There will be good qualities that I can select for imitation and bad ones that will teach me what requires correction in myself.

— The Analects, Book VII

India

Narada and the Two Yogis

The great saint Narada was passing, one day, through a forest. There, in the middle of the forest, he saw a large ant-hill. When ants are digging into the earth to make an underground nest, the soil they carry away is put in a heap nearby. It makes quite a big mound. Narada looked at this ant-hill and was surprised to see that at the top of the ant-hill was a yogi's head.

"What is this?" he thought. "How can there be a yogi's head at the top of an ant-hill?"

He went closer and saw that the yogi's eyes were shut.

"What are you doing here in the middle of an ant-hill?" Narada said in a loud voice.

The yogi opened his eyes and looked at Narada.

"Oh, Narada, it is you!" he said. "How fortunate I am that you have come this way. I came to the forest to meditate, and I have been sitting here meditating for so long that these ants have built their ant-hill round me. Where are you going, Narada?"

"I am on my way to heaven," Narada replied. "I am going to see God."

"Oh, will you see God?" the yogi said. "When you see Him, would you ask Him a question for me?"

"Certainly," Narada replied. "What question do you want me to ask Him?"

"What I want to know is," the yogi answered, "how much longer must I sit here meditating? When shall I see God and realize Him so that I do not have to be born again and again? Would you please ask Him that for me?"

"Yes, certainly," Narada assured him, "I will ask God your question." Narada then went on his way through the forest. After some time he began to hear someone singing in a loud voice. Narada walked on, and then he saw the owner of the loud voice. A yogi was jumping about, singing and dancing. As soon as the yogi saw Narada, he ran to him and said, "Narada, Narada, I am so glad to see you. Where are you going?"

"I am going to heaven," Narada replied.

"Oh, are you going to heaven?" cried the yogi. "Then will you do something for me?"

"Yes, certainly," Narada said. "What can I do for you in heaven?"

"Narada," the yogi replied, "I know that I shall have to be born again and again until my heart becomes so pure that I can see God, but what I want to know is, How many times must I be reborn? Please ask God that for me, will you?"

"Yes, certainly," Narada assured him. "I will ask God your question."

Narada walked on and on through the forest, and at last he reached heaven. Narada stayed in heaven for some time, and then went back to earth. He traveled about the earth, visiting many different places, and one day he happened to walk through that same forest, and there he met the yogi who was meditating in the middle of an ant-hill.

"Oh, Narada," said the yogi, "did you ask God about me?"

"Yes," Narada replied, "I did."

"You did? What did He say?" asked the yogi eagerly.

"God told me," Narada said, "that you must go on meditating through four more lives. Then you will be free."

"What? Four more lives?" exclaimed the yogi in despair. "Oh, that is terrible! I have meditated and meditated. I have meditated so long that the ants have built their ant-hill round me! Now you say even that is not enough. I have four more lives! Oh, I am so sad!" And the yogi began to weep.

"You have only four more lives," Narada said quietly. Then he went on his way.

Soon he met the other yogi, who was singing and dancing.

"Oh, Narada," said the singing yogi, "did you ask God about me?"

"Yes," replied Narada, "I did."

"You did? What did He say?" asked the singing yogi eagerly.

"Well, now," Narada replied, "you see this tamarind tree? How many leaves has it? Count them. As many leaves as there are on this tamarind tree, so many times you will be born again, and then your heart will become pure and you will see God."

"Oh, how wonderful!" cried the singing yogi. "Narada, your news has made me very happy. I did not think that I would see God so soon. As many leaves as there are on this tamarind tree, that number of times I shall be reborn! Oh, Narada, that is but a short time—and then I shall be free!" Then the yogi began to dance and sing in great joy.

At that moment there was a flash of light, and a voice came from heaven.

"My child," said the voice to the singing yogi, "you are free at this moment. God is pleased with you because you have great patience and strength of mind. The tamarind tree has a great many leaves and yet you are willing to be born again and again as many times as there are leaves on that tree. That shows that you are steadfast and firm in your decision to see God and win your freedom. Therefore God has made you free here and now. You will not be born again, but you will live with God."

Judaism

The Bird Nest

Once the Baal Shem was in the House of Prayer with his disciples. He was praying for a long time, although his disciples had long since finished. They waited for long while, then they got tired of waiting and went home. He explained to them later that it was a painful separation for him when they left him alone to pray. He told them this parable.

There are birds who fly to warm countries in the autumn. One year the people in one of those warm countries saw a beautiful bird of all colors in the midst of a flock, which was flying on their annual journey. No one had ever seen such a beautiful bird. It perched itself on one of the tallest trees and sat comfortably in its leaves. When the king of this country heard about this bird he commanded some men to make a human ladder which could reach the bird, and get the bird for him. The men stood on each other's shoulders until their formation was high enough to reach the nest. Just before the last man could reach it, the men closest to the ground lost patience and the human ladder collapsed.

So Be It

A rabbi was invited to a circumcision ceremony in a neighboring village. For this ritual, as in many Jewish rituals, it is important to have ten men present. There were only nine men present when he arrived. The rabbi was very upset about having to wait for the tenth man, especially since it was raining, making it difficult to get someone who happened to be passing by. After awhile the group was able to ask a beggar who was passing by to attend the ceremony, to which he replied, "So be it." After the circumcision the beggar was invited to the meal and he replied, "So be it." When he was offered warm tea, his reply was the same. Finally someone asked him why he always said the same thing to which he responded, "It is written: Happy is the person for whom it is so!" He then vanished before everyone's eyes.

That night the rabbi couldn't get to sleep. The phrase of the beggar's, "So be it," kept repeating itself in his mind. He suddenly realized that it must have been Elijah, the prophet who attends circumcision ceremonies, and Seder, who was scolding him for being so impatient and reminding him that, "Happy is the person for whom it is so."

PROVERBS AND MAXIMS

Only those who have the patience to do simple things perfectly will acquire the skill to do difficult things easily.

— Anonymous

A handful of patience is worth more than a bushel of brains. *— Dutch Proverb*

All things come round to him who will but wait. *— Longfellow*

How poor are they that have not patience! What wound did ever heal but by degrees? *— Shakespeare*

Failure is the path of least persistence. *— Anonymous*

HEROES AND HEROINES

SUSAN B. ANTHONY (1820–1906)

She was born in Adams, Massachusetts, one of seven children; her American ancestry goes back to her family's settlement in Rhode Island in 1634. She attended Quaker schools and began teaching when she was 18. Her family moved to Rochester, New York in 1845, where she was influenced by her father's work with slavery abolitionists like Frederick Douglas. She took up the cause of women's rights in 1851 and began campaigning door to door and with speakers for the rights of women and the abolition of slavery. She organized the National Women's Suffrage Association, was arrested for voting in the 1872 presidential election, and spent the rest of her life working for an amendment to the constitution that would give women the right to vote. She was active until the day she died at age 86. At her death only four states had granted women the right to vote, but the 29th Amendment, enacting this legislation, was passed fourteen years later.

SHIRLEY ANITA ST. HILL CHISHOLM (1924–)

Born in the Bedford-Stuyvesant section of Brooklyn, New York, she was the daughter of emigrant unskilled laborers; her father was from Guyana and her mother was from Barbados. To save money, Shirley was sent to Barbados when she was three years old to live with her grandmother. She recalls being lectured about the virtues of pride, courage, and faith. She returned to Brooklyn at age eleven, graduated from a girl's high school, and entered Brooklyn College to study sociology. She also earned an M.A. degree in elementary education from Columbia University. She became a recognized authority on early education and child welfare, serving as an educational consultant for New York City's bureau of child welfare. At the same time, she became involved with the Democratic Women's Workshop, the League of Women Voters, and other local political groups. She entered politics in 1964, becoming the first black woman from Brooklyn to serve in the State Assembly. In 1969, she became the first black woman elected to Congress. Though she seems small and frail in physical stature, her voice on behalf of millions of disinherited Americans has been strong and vital.

MARIE CURIE (1867–1934)

Born in Warsaw, Poland, she was a brilliant student, but because Poland did not allow women to attend college, her sister helped her gain entrance to the Sorbonne in Paris in September 1891. In 1894, she began her work with Pierre Curie at the University of Paris. Their friendship resulted in their marriage in 1895 and an extraordinary partnership in scientific work. While searching for sources of radioactivity they discovered polonium (named after Poland) and radium. Together they published 32 scientific papers, including the announcement that, when exposed to radium, diseased tumor-forming cells were destroyed faster than healthy cells. They jointly received the Nobel Prize in Physics in 1903.

AMELIA MARY EARHART (1897–1937)

Born in Kansas City, Missouri, she lived with her wealthy maternal grandparents in Atheson, Kansas, but spent her summers in Kansas City. Because of her father's struggle with alcoholism, she attended schools in several states and finally ended up in Chicago where the Hyde Park yearbook described her as "A.E.—the girl in brown (her favorite color) who walks alone." After a year at Columbia University, she moved to Los Angeles, where she saw her first air show and took her first airplane ride. She learned to fly, but couldn't afford such an expensive hobby, so she moved back to Boston and became a social worker. In 1928 she joined a crew that was flying across the Atlantic and met her future husband, George Palmer Putnam. He chose her as his "Lady Lindy" (after Charles Lindbergh) and became her manager in arranging flying engagements. She became world famous as the first woman to fly solo across the Atlantic. She became an advocate of aviation and women's rights. On July 2, 1937, she disappeared over the Pacific while trying to circumnavigate the earth.

VIKTOR EMIL FRANKL (1905–1997)

Born in Vienna, Austria and educated at the University of Vienna, he was one of Europe's leading psychiatrists. After three horrible years at Auschwitz and other Nazi prisons, he gained freedom only to learn that almost his entire family had been wiped out. However, during his ordeal and because of his experience in the death camps, he developed his theory of Logotherapy. The suffering and degradations of those harrowing years taught him much about the human spirit, what it takes to become a whole person, and humanity's quest for a higher meaning in life. He became professor of psychiatry and neurology at the University of Vienna and President of the Austrian Medical Society for Psychotherapy. He was a visiting professor at Harvard University and a frequent lecturer around the United States. His experiences in the concentration camp and his theories are found in his book *Man's Search for Meaning*. His survival and his wisdom are examples of the strength of the human spirit and the power of a belief in God.

BABE DIDRIKSON ZAHARIAS (1914–1956)

Born in Port Arthur, Texas, as Mildred Ella Didrikson, she was one of the greatest American athletes of the first half of the 20th century. She was a record breaker in high school and participated in basketball, baseball, golf, swimming, tennis and volleyball (she wasn't allowed to play football). In college, she was an All-American basketball player. She also won eight events and tied for a ninth in the women's national track and field meet. In the 1932 Olympic games, she earned two gold medals, one for the javelin throw and another for the 80m hurdle event. In 1935 she turned to golf and became the leading U.S. woman golfer, winning 17 straight titles in 1947. She married George Zaharias, a wrestler, in 1938. She developed cancer in 1953 and survived an operation to win two more golf titles in 1954. She is noteworthy not just because she was a gifted athlete, but because of her dedication to excellence, her courageous spirit and her inspiration of women athletes.

BENJAMIN FRANKLIN (1706–1790)

Born in Boston, Massachusetts, into a family that was religious, frugal and self-reliant, he was very bright and had a deep desire to learn. Because of economic reasons, he had only two years of formal education, but designed a lifelong career of self-education. He became an apprentice in his brother's printing shops and read everything that passed by. At age fifteen he began writing social commentaries but, because his brother was tyrannical, often beating him, he ran away to Philadelphia at seventeen. He opened his own print shop and, even though life was difficult, his persistence, patience, and hard work began to pay off. He and a group of friends met every Friday night to discuss current issues and philosophy. Together they founded the first subscription library (1731), a fire company (1736), a public academy for needy boys that eventually became the University of Pennsylvania (1749), and America's first medical center (1751). He became a leading scientist, inventor, publisher, and politician. He was the only founding father to sign all four documents related to America's independence; The Declaration of Independence, The Treaty with England, The Treaty with France, and The Constitution.

MADELEINE L'ENGLE (1918–)

Born in New York City, New York, she was the only child of Charles Wadsworth Camp and Madeline Hall Barnet Camp. Her father was a writer and journalist and her mother was a talented pianist. As a child, Madeleine kept herself busy reading and writing; she wrote her first book at age five. Because of her father's work she grew up in New York, France, Switzerland and England. She graduated from Smith College in 1941 and pursued graduate studies at the New School for Social Research. She married actor Hugh Franklin in 1946 but continued using the name "Madeline L'Engle" for her writing. She has written poetry, prayers, fantasy, fiction, and novels for adults and young adults; as such, she could easily be thought of as a heroine for creativity, but is included as a model for patience because one of her best known works, *A Wrinkle in Time,* was rejected by more than twenty publishers. She lives in New York with her granddaughter and continues to write.

PUT PATIENCE INTO ACTION

- When something starts to bother you, wait as long as you can before you express your frustration. Wait even longer the next time.

- When something doesn't work out right, try again and again.

- Be patient with your parents when you need something, especially when they are busy.

- Don't lose your temper when something upsets you.

- Keep working at something that is difficult until you complete it.

- Try to understand someone who has a strong opinion.

- Always finish what you start.

- Focus on someone or something that ordinarily makes you lose your patience and try to understand it (and don't "lose it").

- Don't give up on difficult jobs or situations.

- When you disagree with someone's strong conviction, keep talking calmly with them, trying to understand them.

COMMUNITY SERVICE IDEAS

- Help with the paper recycling project at your school.

- Organize a campaign to promote good study habits in your school.

- Volunteer with a local food bank.

- Volunteer to work in the library, at a nature center, or in an animal shelter doing tasks that require a great deal of patience.

BOOKS ON PATIENCE

Bringing the Rain to Kapiti Plain. Verna Aardema. New York: Dial Press, 1981.

Grandma Gets Grumpy. Anna G. Hines. New York: Clarion Books/Ticknor & Fields, 1988.

Oxcart Man. Donald Hall. New York: Viking Press, 1979.

Very Busy Spider. Eric Carle. New York: Philomel Books, 1984.

Very Quiet Cricket. Eric Carle. New York: Philomel Books, 1990.

The Book of Virtues. William J. Bennett, ed. New York: Simon and Schuster, 1993.

    "The Crow and the Pitcher" – p. 532

    "The Little Hero of Holland" – p. 53

    "The Little Steam Engine" – p. 530

    "Perseverance" – p. 565

    "Persevere" – p. 529

    "The Stars in the Sky" – p. 542

    "The Tortoise and the Hare" – p. 529

    "Try, Try Again" – p. 532

    "You Mustn't Quit" – p. 536

February

Courage

SUPPORTIVE VALUES

Tenacity • Conviction

DEFINITIONS

Firmness of mind and will in danger or difficulty.

Just the sound of the word **courage** makes one think of mental and moral strength. It's a word which challenges us to face and overcome our fears. We sometimes believe that a person of great courage is one who has no fear when in fact they are the ones who have acknowledged and conquered their fear. Cervantes reminds us, "He who loses wealth loses much; he who loses a friend loses more; but he who loses his courage loses all."

Tenacity comes from the Latin root *tenax,* which means "tending to hold fast." It is one thing to have courage to think in a moral way but it is quite another to actually follow through on thoughts with actions and to keep following through. It is uncommon to have the tenacity to cling to an idea which may be difficult or dangerous.

Conviction is a strong belief in something. A person with conviction is one who is not easily influenced by their peers or their environment. A person with conviction is one who does not quit no matter how hard the task. Even in the face of peer pressure or formidable odds, such people are determined to stick to their values and their goals. They have the courage of their convictions.

PURPOSE

In our world of relative abundance, many of the challenges requiring courage which faced our ancestors are no longer a part of our lives. We are sheltered from the elements, and rarely need to face survival situations. The search for physical challenges which test our mettle is all too apparent in the plethora of activities available to us, ranging from endurance contests to thrill-seeking adventures. It seems we are searching for ways to confirm our courage through external experiences, while neglecting the courageous act of looking inward and reflecting on our character. When faced with the pressures of our materialistic culture, we need to summon our courage to discriminate between what we need and what we are influenced to want. Having the courage to understand the inner self is the more difficult task, requiring tenacity and mental toughness above and beyond any physical challenge.

Character Education Year 2 Grades K–6

Courage

Day One:
Discuss the meaning of courage using the definitions on page 107.

Day Two:
Use the discussion questions on page 110 to gain better understandings of courage.

Day Three:
Brainstorm to make a list of people who must use courage every day at work (for example, police, firemen, members of the military, etc.).

Day Four:
Does it take courage to tease a younger student? Why not? What would you say to the student doing the teasing? How would you find the courage to stop the teasing? In small groups, role play the situation.

Day Five:
Create an award to present to a student who exhibited courage this week. Do this at the end of every week this month.

Day Six:
The lion has been called King of the Jungle and has often been used as a symbol of courage. What do you think a lion's courageous roar sounds like? On the count of three—everybody ROAR!

Day Seven:
What types of animals do you think represent bravery? Explain your choices.

Day Eight:
Does having courage mean you should be reckless? Find out the difference in these two terms.

Day Nine:
Choose a bookmark on page 117 that inspires you to have courage. Put it in a place where you will see it often.

Day Ten:
It takes courage to meet new challenges. Have you backed away from any new experiences because you lacked the courage? How can you increase your courage so that you will take on the next new challenge that comes your way?

Day Eleven:
Some people find courage through friends and family. Remember an experience you had where someone else gave you courage. Draw a picture about your experience.

Day Twelve:
Create a large class banner to celebrate courage. Hang it proudly outside your classroom door.

Day Thirteen:
Discuss the kind of courage the first astronauts had to have to be able to blast off into outer space for the first space missions. How do you think their families felt on the day of their launch?

Day Fourteen:
Why does it take courage to try something new or to do something in a way you have never done before? Tell about a time when you really had to convince yourself to use courage to try something new, and how the experience turned out.

Day Fifteen:
Make up a creative story about a character of your own age who was faced with a very difficult decision to make, one that required a great deal of courage. Leave your story unfinished.

Day Sixteen:
Trade your story from yesterday with a partner. Complete your partner's story with a happy ending!

Day Seventeen:
How would our world today be different if Christopher Columbus had not had the courage to continue his voyages in search of a new land? Find out more about his courage and determination and about the people whose courage made it possible for him to continue his exploration.

Day Eighteen:
The first permanent settlers to America had to be very courageous to leave their homes and come to a new world. Pretend you were one of these first settlers, and write or tell about the challenges and the courage it took to leave your home behind.

Day Nineteen:
Make a "badge of courage" for yourself. Think of something you have done this week which entitles you to wear the badge. If you can't think of anything, do something now. Wear your badge with pride!

Day Twenty:
Reflect on what you have learned this month about courage. Do you feel you are ready to accept courage as a lifelong value? If so, how can you begin to practice courage in daily life? If not, what can you do to become more courageous?

COURAGE IN OTHER LANGUAGES

Chinese	*yong*	brave; daring courage
French	*le courage*	strength of character, steadiness or resoluteness in the face of danger, suffering, or difficult situations, zeal for undertaking something or a strong desire to do something
German	*beherzt*	brave, spirited, stouthearted, courageous
Hawaiian	*wiwo'ole*	fearless, brave, bold ('wiwo' means "fearful, bashful, modest, afraid, timid, shy" and 'ole' means "not, without, lacking"—literally, wiwo'ole means "no fear")
Japanese	*yuuki*	gush out spiritual energy
Korean	*yong ki*	brave spirit
Latin	*virtus*	from Latin "cor" (heart); action in accordance with one's heart
Spanish	*coraje*	courage, bravery, valor
Tagalog	*katapangan*	fearless bravery in the face of physical, moral or spiritual danger

DISCUSSION QUESTIONS

- Should you always do what your friends tell you to do?

- What gives you the strength to say "No"?

- If you don't know what to do, who do you ask for help?

- Can you finish your chores or your homework without grumbling or without being reminded?

- If everybody in your group is doing something you think is wrong, do you have the courage not to join them?

- Do you have an inner strength that helps you resist doing something wrong or helps you follow through on what is right?

- Are you able to keep trying when something is difficult?

- Have you been faced with a decision that required courage?

- What resources do you draw from in making difficult decisions?

- What makes a person right—age, wealth, power, fame, or virtue? Why?

- Give an example of something you have a strong opinion about. What could make you change your mind? How do you know when you should?

STORIES AND THOUGHTS FROM SPIRITUAL TRADITIONS

Hinduism

As a man acts, so does he become. A man of good deeds becomes good, a man of evil deeds becomes evil. A man becomes pure through pure deeds, impure through impure deeds.

As a man's desire is, so is his destiny. For as his desire is, so is his will; as his will is, so is his deed; and as his deed is, so is his reward, whether good or bad.

A man acts according to the desires to which he clings. After death he goes to the next world bearing in his mind the subtle impressions of his deeds; and after reaping there the harvest of his deeds; he returns again to this world of action. Thus, he who has desires continues subject to rebirth.

But he in whom desire is stilled suffers no rebirth. After death, having attained to the highest, desiring only Self, he goes to no other world. Realizing Brahman, he becomes Brahman.

– Upanishads

The greatest strength is the ability to forgive.

– Tradition

Christianity

"Be strong, and let your heart take courage."

– Bible, Psalm 31:24

"As you know, we had courage in our God in the face of great opposition."
– Bible, I Thessalonians 2:2

Islam

The bravest is the most in control of himself.

Chinese

"A Good Man will certainly also possess courage; but a brave man is not necessarily GOOD."

– Confucius

ourage —————————————————— UNDERSTANDING

American

Wiley and the Hairy Man

Down by the edge of a swamp, in a small cabin, there lived a boy named Wiley and his mama. Now strange things were known to happen every now and then in those parts. For instance, dogs would start barking wildly for no reason, strange figures would be spotted running through the woods, and laughter could be heard from time to time amongst the trees. People said it might be the Hairy Man up to some mischief.

Each time Wiley would set out from the house his mama would call, "You be careful now, Wiley. You look out for that Hairy Man, y'hear? Never know when he'll be up to no good."

Wiley would reply cheerfully, "Don't you worry, Mama. Got my hound dogs with me all the time, everywhere I go. You know that Hairy Man just can't stand hound dogs!"

Wiley's mama would smile, for indeed she knew that the Hairy Man couldn't abide those hound dogs. In fact, Wiley's mama knew all sorts of things, including a little bit of conjure magic!

One day, Wiley set out to gather a load of wood nearby, so he left his faithful dogs tied up on the porch. Before he knew it he had wandered deep into the swamp in search of wood. He was a lot farther away from home than he had expected to be when he felt a shiver go down his spine. He heard some branches cracking and he spun around quick to see the Hairy Man coming his way.

Oh, was he an ugly fellow! Big and hairy all over with a slobbery yellow grin. It was a crazy grin, and Wiley was not pleased at all to be meeting him. The Hairy Man galloped wildly toward Wiley and stopped suddenly, a couple of inches from his face. "Hello, Wiley," said the Hairy Man in a husky sort of voice.

"Don't you come so close to me, Mister Hairy Man," insisted Wiley. He looked down at the Hairy Man's strange feet only to discover that they weren't feet at all. They were hooves! Now Wiley knew that those weren't feet for climbing, so he scrambled up the nearest tree as fast as he could.

"You come on down, Wiley!" hollered the Hairy Man.

"No sir, Mister Hairy Man. Come on up 'n get me if you want," replied Wiley.

The Hairy Man kept smiling his awful smile. "I'll just be down here waiting for you, Wiley. I'll be waiting until nightfall. Just until you get hungry or tired," the Hairy Man chuckled.

Now Wiley wasn't going to give up to this ugly old Hairy Man. He remembered his dogs back home on the porch and he came up with a plan. "Say, Mister Hairy Man, I hear tell you know some conjure magic," said Wiley.

"Why, I know more conjure magic than anyone in these parts!" boasted the Hairy Man.

"Well," said Wiley, "I'll bet you don't know enough to make something disappear. How 'bout making that tree stump disappear? Can you do that?"

In an instant the tree stump disappeared. "Now, you see that, Wiley? It's gone!"

"Is that all the conjure magic you have, Mister Hairy Man? Let's see you make my shirt disappear," Wiley called down.

"Gone!" cried the Hairy Man as Wiley's shirt vanished.

"You're going to run out of conjure magic soon, Mister Hairy Man. Bet you can't even make this little rope holding up my britches disappear."

"Sure, I can!" yelled the Hairy Man. "Why, I can make every rope in this county disappear now!"

Wiley began to chuckle as he held onto his britches. "Oh yes, you know some mighty wonderful conjure magic. Just the magic I needed, in fact. Here, dogs! Here, dogs!" Wiley called to his dogs that the Hairy Man had just freed from the porch by magic.

Wiley could hear his dogs barking as they ran toward the swamp from the house. The Hairy Man did not wait for the dogs to get any closer, he just turned and ran faster than lightning away into the swamp.

When Wiley and his dogs made it home, Wiley told his mama how he had fooled the Hairy Man. His mama gave him a big hug and said, "Well now, you've fooled the Hairy Man once, son. If you can manage to outwit him two more times he'll stay away for good!"

"I hope I don't have occasion to run into him ever again," said Wiley. "Can't say I like the looks of that hairy face, or that slobbery grin, or those big black hooves."

"Say, Wiley," asked his mama, "did you happen to see if he was carrying a sack?"

"'Matter of fact he was, Mama," nodded Wiley.

"Well, I just thought of another way you can fool that Hairy Man, Wiley," said his mama. "Now listen, you go on into the swamp tomorrow without the dogs and here's what you do." Wiley's mama gave him a plan to trick the Hairy Man once more.

The next morning, Wiley left his faithful dogs shut inside the cabin and walked off toward the swamp. He tried whistling and singing and hopping on one foot to keep his courage up and his mind off the Hairy Man. Then all at once, he felt that same shiver up his spine from the day before.

Suddenly, standing right before him was the Hairy Man.

"Hello again, Wiley," said the Hairy Man, grinning his wicked grin.

"Well, hello there, Mister Hairy Man," said Wiley, trying to smile. "What have you got in that big old sack there?"

"Nothing, Wiley. At least, not yet!" said the Hairy Man, leaning real close to Wiley and laying his sack down right next to him.

"Say, Mister Hairy Man," said Wiley, looking him straight in the eye, "I hear tales of how you can change yourself into any old animal you want. Could they be true?"

"Yes, Wiley," said the Hairy Man, bending right over him, "those tales are true." Now the Hairy Man looked mighty fierce, but Wiley went on.

"You wouldn't be able to change yourself into something big like a bear, would you?" asked Wiley. Before he knew it the Hairy Man had disappeared and there in his place was a huge black bear, grinning and slobbering at Wiley. "I'm impressed," said Wiley, trying to sound brave. "But I bet you can't turn yourself into, say, an alligator."

In an instant the bear vanished and Wiley was looking at the mouth of an alligator, smiling and slobbering at him. "Oh, I see you're mighty fine at turning yourself into something big," said Wiley, "but I bet you can't change into something small, like, for instance, a possum."

Just as Wiley had hoped, the alligator was gone in a flash and in its place was a tiny possum. Wiley scooped up the little animal and shoved it into the sack which lay on the ground. He tied it up real tight and sent it flying into the river. Then he turned and started back home. He was feeling pretty good about outwitting the Hairy Man for the second time when he heard a deep voice bellowing from the river.

"I'm going to get you, Wiley! You just wait and see!" the Hairy Man's voice boomed through the swamp.

With that, Wiley ran as fast as his legs could go. When he arrived back at the cabin huffing and puffing he told his mama what had happened.

"Well now, son," Wiley's mama said as she patted him on the back, "you've managed to trick that Hairy Man twice. I imagine he's good and angry now. We'll just have to come up with a way to fool him again and we'll be rid of him forever and always."

Now Wiley did not like the idea of the Hairy Man coming to his house to get him, but Wiley's mama was calm as she rocked in her rocking chair and came up with a plan. "Wiley," she said, "go to the barn and bring back one of our baby pigs." Wiley did as he was told, but on his way to the barn he thought he saw a strange, wild animal run through the trees. It was as large as a horse, but it had curly hair. His dogs ran barking after it and they disappeared into the trees.

Wiley brought the little pig into the cabin. "Now go and put that baby pig in your bed, Wiley," said his mama, "and pull the covers up over it nice and tight." Just as he was covering up the piglet he got that peculiar shiver up his spine and he could hear thumping and scraping all around the cabin walls. The whole cabin began to shake and Wiley began to tremble a bit, as well.

Suddenly there was a great banging on the door. "Quick, Wiley," his mama whispered, "climb up into the loft and stay out of sight!" Then, quite calmly, Wiley's mama opened the door.

"Where's your boy?" the Hairy Man yelled. "I've come to get him!"

"Well, you can't have him," said Wiley's mama.

"Then I'll have to bite you," said the Hairy Man, stepping closer.

"Well, I suppose I'll have to bite you right back," said Wiley's mama, looking him square in the eye.

"Give him to me, or I'll set your house afire!" threatened the Hairy Man.

"Oh, I've plenty of milk to put out your fire," said Wiley's mama.

"I say give him to me, or I'll make your cow run away, I'll make your well go dry, and I'll make your cotton shrivel and die," yelled the Hairy Man.

"Oh, you wouldn't do all those awful things, would you, Mister Hairy Man? You couldn't be that horrible, could you?" Wiley's mama said in her sweetest voice.

"I can be that horrible and I will!" screamed the Hairy Man.

"Oh, well," said Wiley's mama, "I suppose I should give you my baby then." She turned toward Wiley's bed, then turned back toward the Hairy Man. "If I give him to you, do you swear you'll do me no harm and never come back?"

"I do swear, just give him to me!" the Hairy Man bellowed.

"Go on and take him then," said Wiley's mama, pointing to the bed.

The Hairy Man charged over to the bed and threw off the covers. "There's nothing but a baby pig here!" he yelled.

"Did I say what kind of baby I was giving you? He's mine and I'm giving him to you. Go on, Mister Hairy Man, take him, he belongs to you now." Wiley's mama smiled sweetly at the Hairy Man. "And remember, Mister Hairy Man, you swore you'd leave me be and never come back if I gave you my baby!"

The Hairy Man went wild as he had been fooled for the third time. He stomped about and gnashed his slobbery teeth, then he tore out of the cabin never to be seen in those parts again.

Wiley climbed down from the loft and ran into his mama's arms. Then he called to his dogs who ran in happily from the woods. "We did it, didn't we, Mama? We tricked that awful old Hairy Man three times over!"

"We did, Wiley," smiled Wiley's mama. "Just you and me against that big old Hairy Man."

PROVERBS AND MAXIMS

All progress has resulted from people who took unpopular positions.

— *A. Stevenson*

Courage is the price that life exacts for granting peace.

— *A. Earhart*

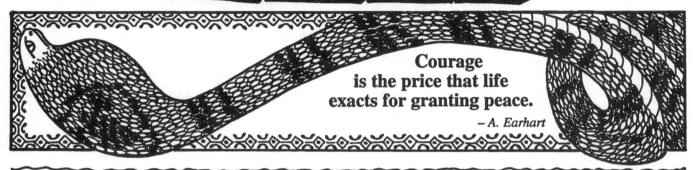

To see what is right and not to do it is lack of courage.

— *Confucius*

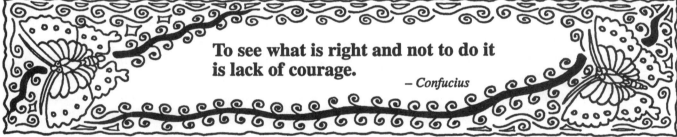

It is not because things are difficult that we do not dare; it is because we do not dare that they are difficult. — *Seneca*

A "no" uttered from the deepest conviction is better and greater than a "yes" merely uttered to please, or what is worse, to avoid trouble.

— *M. Gandhi*

HEROES AND HEROINES

DAW AUNG SAN SUU KYI (1945–)

Born in Rangoon, Burma, she is the daughter of General Aung San Kyi, who was the national leader of Burma until he was assassinated in 1947. She studied politics at Delhi University, while her mother served as ambassador to India and Nepal in 1960. She graduated in 1967 from St. Hugh's College, Oxford University with a degree in philosophy, politics, and economics. In 1988 she returned to Burma to help with her ailing mother, and witnessed the student protests in Rangoon. Drawn into the struggle, she proposed the formation of a People's Consultative Committee during the democratic uprising and on August 26, 1988 addressed a mass rally of 500,000 people, calling for a democratic government. The National League for Democracy was formed and Aung San Suu Kyi was elected secretary general. In the next months she gave hundreds of addresses across Burma, narrowly escaping assassination, and was finally put under house arrest, where she stayed until July 10, 1995. Her non-violent struggle and writing earned her the Nobel Peace Prize in 1991.

ANNE FRANK (1929–1945)

Born in Frankfurt, Germany, she enjoyed a good home with her parents and her sister Margot. After the Nazis took over Germany in 1933, the family moved to Amsterdam, Holland. Anne attended the Montessori School, but when the Nazis occupied Holland in 1940 she was forced to leave the school. When Margot received orders for deportation, Mr. Frank was prepared and moved his family, a second family of three, and an eighth man into two small apartments hidden in the rear of the warehouse where he worked. Friends supplied them with necessities, and they remained quiet during working hours and hidden during the night. They were betrayed, arrested, and sent to Auschwitz, a concentration camp. Later they were sent to Bergen Belsen, where Anne perished. Her personal diary became famous as an example of courage and faith and as an account of life under the Nazi terror.

PROM GOULD (1979–)

Prom was born in Cambodia about the time a Vietnamese invasion ended the genocide of the Khmer Rouge regimes of Pol Pot, responsible for the massacre of 4 million people. He was orphaned by the civil war that followed. When his adoptive parents, Ron and Kim Gould of Honolulu, met Prom, he was twelve years old, weighed 40 pounds and suffered from hemophilia, hepatitis, parasites, malaria, and malnutrition. The Goulds were in Cambodia to complete the adoption procedures for their son Mina and noticed Prom taking care of the younger children. Clearly in a lot of pain, he still had a zest for life, showed an interest in everything around him, and exhibited a courage far beyond his years. When the Goulds learned that adoption procedures between Prom and his projected family had failed, they were given the opportunity of adopting him. They didn't hesitate, and Prom was welcomed into their family. With love, medical care and a lot of food, Prom thrived. His courageous spirit has taken on many challenges: learning English, adapting to a new culture, gaining entrance to school, and learning to paddle outriggers are just a few of his accomplishments. There are more challenges ahead and Prom will meet them with the same optimism, cheerfulness, confidence, and inner strength that delivered him from the horrors of Cambodia.

HELEN KELLER (1880–1968)

Born in Tuscumbia, Alabama, she was deprived of sight and hearing at the age of 19 months due to a severe illness, and soon became mute. She lived in silence and darkness for five years until her parents appealed to Alexander Graham Bell for advice about her education. Ann Sullivan, who was then twenty years old and partially cured of blindness, began to instruct Helen on March 2, 1887. With Ann Sullivan's discipline and dedication, Helen learned the gift of language in one month, learned to read braille, learned to talk, and in 1904 graduated from Radcliffe College. Her education and training represent one of the most extraordinary accomplishments ever achieved in the education of those with similar disabilities. She worked until her death at the age of 88 to help others by writing articles and books, by speaking, and by raising two million dollars for the American Foundation for the Blind. Her greatest gift was the inspiration of her determination and courage.

ROSA LEE MCCAULEY PARKS (1913–)

The early life of this young girl, born in Tuskegee, Alabama, gave no indication that she was destined for greatness. Her mother was a teacher and her father was a carpenter. They moved to Pine Level, Alabama while Rosa was still young, and she was shielded from the harsh realities of racial segregation. She attended high school and college for a short time in Montgomery. She married Raymond Parks in 1932 and they were both active in the voter registration aspect of the civil rights movement. She worked for the NAACP to break down the barriers of segregation in education and public accommodations; little progress was made in the 1940s and early 1950s. In 1955, while working in a Montgomery department store as a tailor's assistant, she made national headlines. Being very tired after work, but not meaning to cause trouble, she simply refused to give up her seat to a white passenger on a racially segregated bus. Her arrest led to a successful boycott of the Montgomery buses by African-American riders. She is still active in civil rights issues.

JACKIE ROBINSON (1919–1972)

Born in Cairo, Georgia as John Roosevelt Robinson, he was the youngest of five children. His sharecropper father abandoned his family five months after Jackie was born, and his mother, determined to create a better life for her family, moved them all to Pasadena, California when Jackie was only sixteen months old. As Jackie grew up, he developed into a sensational athlete and was the first person to earn letters in football, basketball, baseball and track at UCLA. In 1941, after college, he played football with the Los Angeles Bulldogs; however, World War II ended his football career. He began playing baseball in 1945, with the Monarchs of the Negro American Baseball league. Branch Rickey of the Brooklyn Dodgers became aware of his abilities and, with his own act of courage, invited Jackie in 1947 to break the color barrier that existed in major league baseball. In spite of the pressure and prejudice, he played well and was voted Rookie of the Year. It was his spectacular play that led to the Dodgers' first World Series Championship in 1955. His courage was displayed not only on the baseball diamond but also in public, where he spoke out against prejudice and injustice. He retired from baseball in 1956. In later life he suffered quietly and courageously from diabetes, and died from diabetic complications at age 53.

PUT COURAGE INTO ACTION

- Politely say "No" when someone asks you to do something you know is wrong.

- Talk to your parents or teacher about something difficult you face.

- Happily finish all of your chores and homework.

- Practice expressing your real opinion, even when others disagree.

- Read the story of Harriet Tubman, a woman with moral courage.

- Write a description of something about which you have a strong conviction.

- Politely disagree with friends when you think they are wrong.

- Develop strong character by practicing all of the values of the month.

- Choose friends who share these virtues of strong character.

- Make a list of the things about which you have a strong conviction.

COMMUNITY SERVICE IDEAS

- Write a letter to the editor of your local newspaper about a local injustice. This might be a good total class project, with every member of the class signing the letter.

- Volunteer to do what you can for an agency that is working to save endangered species.

- Arrange to play or study with a classmate who has trouble making friends.

- Stand up for a community cause in which you believe by making a poster to display in a prominent place.

BOOKS ON COURAGE

All the Lights in the Night. Arthur A. Levine. New York: Tambourine Books, 1991.

Amazing Grace. Mary Hoffman. New York: Dial Books for Young Readers, 1991.

Call it Courage. Armstrong Sperry. New York: MacMillan Company, 1970.

Follow the Drinking Gourd. Bernadine Connelly. Lincoln: GPN, 1993.

The Girl Who Loved Caterpillars. Jean Merrill. New York: Philomel Books, 1992.

John Henry. Julius Lester. New York: Dial Books, 1994.

Little Engine that Could. Waty Piper. New York: Platt & Monk, 1930.

Loop the Loop. Barbara Dugan. New York: Greenwillow, 1992.

Sir Cedric. Roy Gerard. New York: Farrar, Straus & Giroux, 1984.

Teammates. Peter Galenboch. San Diego: Harcourt Brace, Jovanovich, 1990.

The Book of Virtues. William J. Bennett, ed. New York: Simon and Schuster, 1993.

"The Brave Three Hundred" – p. 472

"Crossing the Rubicon" – p. 477

"I Have A Dream" – p. 572

"If " – p. 476

"The Minotaur" – p. 463

"Our Heroes" – p. 461

"The Road Not Taken" – p. 523

"Rosa Parks" – p. 489

"Ulysses and the Cyclops" – p. 467

Creativity

SUPPORTIVE VALUES

Wonder • Resourcefulness

DEFINITIONS

The ability to bring into existence, to produce through imagination.

Creativity is the ability to bring into existence or to form through imaginative skill. These definitions speak to us of the ability to invent. They describe everything from the visual and performing arts to engineering and the theoretical sciences. It is this ability to be thoughtful and imaginative in our work (which makes us creators in the world) that we want to celebrate this month.

Wonder is an excitedly amazed admiration or astonishment at something awesomely mysterious or new to one's experience.

Resourcefulness is the capability of devising ways and means to handle a situation. The ability to creatively use our resources as individuals, as communities, and as a world are at the crux of this value.

PURPOSE

The ability to create is the distinguishing characteristic of being human. Creativity can be a difficult undertaking because the process is personal. You are sharing a part of yourself with others.

Knowing the vulnerability of creativity, Beethoven wrote: "Advise your critics to exercise more care and good sense with regard to the productions of young authors; for many a one of them may lose their creative spirit, who otherwise might have risen to higher things." We need to nurture the fragile seedling of creativity in our students, urging it to take root, grow strong, blossom, and bear fruit. Many of our students been told exactly what to do so often that they are stumped when given an assignment which they can present as they choose. We need to take more care with our pruning methods and be generous with the fertilizer of encouragement to insure growth. In this way students will discover fulfillment in the creative process and continue to seek and realize their own areas of creativity.

Sustaining a sense of wonder and resourcefulness as educators and nurturing these senses in students are the responsibilities of an educator, for it is wonder which inspires our powers of creativity.

Creativity

Day One:
Discuss the meaning of creativity. Use the definitions on page 123 to get the discussion started.

Day Two:
Use colored chalk, felt tip pens, or crayons to draw while listening to a selection of music. Notice how one creative movement can inspire another.

Day Three:
Each individual person is an original creative work. Make a list of all your personal characteristics. (Brown hair, freckles, blue eyes, a mole on your right elbow, etc.) Be as specific as you can! Mix up all the lists and have each person choose one. Find the person by using the clues on the list.

Day Four:
Nature is constantly recreating itself. Draw a picture of each of nature's four seasons of creativity.

Day Five:
Read the list of words in other languages on page 125. Imagine the creativity it took to create and define these words!

Day Six:
Make a class garden of creativity. Construct flowers using colored tissue paper and pipe cleaners. Stick the flowers in holes punched in a shoe box (which you have painted green). Notice the unique creative styles represented by the flowers.

Day Seven:
Many scientists have sought to solve problems by using their creative thinking skills. Using your science textbook, think about how creative scientists developed the use of the pulley system, proof for the law of gravity, or other scientific wonders.

Day Eight:
Using what you have learned so far about creativity, make a banner or sign to hang up in your classroom, serving as a reminder to use creativity each and every day.

Day Nine:
Use your creative thinking skills to create an original poem, song, story, or drawing.

Day Ten:
Combine all the creative works to form a class book. Make a creative cover for the book and place it on the reading table to be enjoyed by visitors to your classroom.

Day Eleven:
Read a story about creativity from the selection on pages 127–132.

Day Twelve:
Choose a community service project from page 136 to share the gift of creativity.

Day Thirteen:
Put your community service project into action!

Day Fourteen:
Work in small groups to evaluate the amount of creativity used in planning and carrying out the service project. Share the small group opinions in a total group setting and determine the least and the most creative things done.

Day Fifteen:
Choose a proverb bookmark from the list on page 133. Color, cut out, and use it!

Day Sixteen:
Creativity can mean lots of fun. In a group, think of a new game. Be sure to write down all the rules, so that everyone can easily understand how to play. Try to keep it simple and make it a game that everyone can play.

Day Seventeen:
Play the game that you created with your class!

Day Eighteen:
It takes some creative thinking to solve a riddle. Find a riddle in the library and work in small groups to solve the riddle. Create a riddle of your own.

Day Nineteen:
Read about the heroes and heroines who embraced creativity on pages 134–135. Which one do you most admire? Why?

Day Twenty:
Reflect on the lessons of creativity you have learned this month. Think about ways you can begin now to be more creative in your thinking and in your actions.

CREATIVITY IN OTHER LANGUAGES

Chinese   *chuang*   to create, to make, to invent, to begin
              zao   to create, to make, to build, to prepare, to begin from

French   *la créativité*   ability to use one's imagination and inventive powers to create

German   *schöpferisch*   from schöpfer: to scoop, to be generative, productive, creative

Hawaiian *makaku*   creative imagination of an artist (maka means "eye" but also means "beginning, commencement, source" and one of many definitions of forku is "to appear, show, reveal . . . to change into, transform")

Japanese *soozoo*   to create something from wood with a knife (soo—"to cut with a knife, to make something for a first time"; zoo—"to carve with an axe")

Latin   *cogitatio*   from Latin "creare" (to make) (the ability to make things)

Spanish   *facultad creadora*   ability to be creative, original

Tagalog   *pagkamalikhain*   pagka—the essence of something, its nature
              likhain—to make something never made before

DISCUSSION QUESTIONS

• What does it mean to be creative?

• Describe someone who has a good imagination.

• What is something mysterious about life that makes you think a lot? Why is this interesting?

• Is there only one way to solve a problem?

• What are some examples of human creativity? Is everyone creative? Why or why not?

• Why are we inspired by the creativity of others?

• What is something that you are really curious about, something you think about a lot?

• What is a resourceful solution? For instance, to the homeless?

• Who are some creative people you admire? Why are they good models?

• How do you get in touch with your own creativity?

• How would you define a sense of wonder?

• How does being resourceful help solve problems?

STORIES AND THOUGHTS FROM SPIRITUAL TRADITIONS

Buddhism

The greatest creativity is transforming our own mind from ignorance to wisdom, awaking all our inner qualities.

All that we see and hear and feel is a product of the mind. We can create a violent, miserable existence or a loving, happy existence. We are the producer and director of our own movie. We can be miserable or we can be happy. The choice is up to us.

A Zen monk once invited a student to eat brown rice. Thinking she would suffer stomach trouble, the student declined. Later she regretted her decision and recalled his advice, "If there is a task that must be done, no matter how you detest it, do it anyway, thinking, 'I love it, I love it.'" With a creative attitude, even depressing events can be transforming.

In Tibetan Buddhism there is a practice of imagining oneself as an enlightened being, in an enlightened form with enlightened speech and an enlightened mind. As one teacher in America put it, "If you're not enlightened, pretend you're enlightened!" Through creative imaging, we can embody all enlightened qualities.

Another practice is to imagine our enemy as our greatest teacher. When someone insults or irritates us, instead of retaliating in a similar way, we imagine the person as our dear parent, teacher, or friend, surrounded by love in the form of pure light. This practice has the power to dispel the anger and resentment in our mind, and calm the attacker, too!

Respect the changes which inspiration makes in oneself, without analyzing them or calculating (their results). Success will always come when the heart is without disturbance.

Christianity

"A person's gift makes room for them and brings them before great people."
– Bible, Proverbs 18:16

"You are the light of the world. Let your light so shine before others, that they may see your good works."
– Bible, Matthew 5:14,16

The Creation Story

When God began creating the heavens and the earth, the earth was at first a shapeless, chaotic mass, with the Spirit of God brooding over the dark vapors.

The God said, "Let there be light." And light appeared. And God was pleased with it, and divided the light from the darkness. So he let it shine for awhile, and then there was darkness again. He called the light "daytime," and the darkness "nighttime." Together they formed the first day.

And God said, "Let the vapors separate to form the sky above and the oceans below." So God made the sky, dividing the vapor above from the water below. This all happened on the second day.

Then God said, "Let the water beneath the sky be gathered into oceans so that the dry land will emerge." And so it was. Then God named the dry land "earth," and the water "seas." And God was pleased. And he said, "let the earth burst forth with every sort of grass and seed-bearing plant, and fruit trees with seeds inside the fruit, so that these seeds will produce the kinds of plants and fruits they came from." And so it was, and God was pleased. This all occurred on the third day.

Then God said, "Let there be bright lights in the sky to give light to the earth and to identify the day and the night; they shall bring about the seasons on the earth, and mark the days and years." And so it was. For God made two huge lights, the sun and the moon, to shine down upon the earth: the larger one, the sun, to preside over the day and the smaller one, the moon, to preside over the night. He also made the stars. And God set them in the sky to light the earth, and to preside over the day and night, and to divide the light from the darkness. And God was pleased. This all happened on the fourth day.

Then God said, "let the waters fill with fish and other life, and let the skies be filled with birds of every kind. So God created great sea creatures, and every sort of fish and every kind of bird. And God looked at them with pleasure, and blessed them all. "Multiply and stock the oceans," he told them, and to the birds he said, "Let your number increase. Fill the earth!" That ended the fifth day.

And God said, "Let the earth bring forth every kind of animal—cattle and reptiles and wildlife of every kind." And so it was. God made all sorts of wild animals and cattle and reptiles. And God was pleased with what he had done.

The God said, "Let us make a man—someone like ourselves, to be the master of all life upon the earth and in the skies and in the seas."

So God made man like his Maker.

Like God did God make man.

Man and maid did he make them.

And God blessed them and he told them, "Multiply and fill the earth and subdue it; you are masters of the fish and birds and all the animals. And look! I have given you the seed-bearing plants throughout the earth, and all the fruit trees for your food. And I've given all the grass and plants to the animals and birds for their food." Then God looked over all that he had made, and it was excellent in every way. This ended the sixth day.

Now at last the heavens and earth were successfully completed, with all that they contained. So on the seventh day, having finished his task, God ceased from this work he had been doing, and God blessed the seventh day and declared it holy, because it was the day when he ceased this work of creation.

— Bible, Genesis 1:1 - 2:3

Judaism

The Last Miracle

According to the maggid of Mezritch, the creation of Heaven and earth is the revealing of something out of nothing. There are those who do nothing but think about God, they strive to imagine the universe as it was before it was created. They transform the something back into the nothing. This is more miraculous, for as the Talmud says, "Greater than the first miracle is the last."

American

Apellamando's Dreams

Once upon a time, there was a simple little road which led to a drab little village, which was filled with dull little buildings and surrounded by gray little houses. The streets were quiet, folks worked hard, and the children minded their parents.

Now just outside this village, there lived a very special boy named Apellamando. What made him so special was that whenever he dreamed dreams or thought thoughts, his dreams and thoughts would appear in brilliant colors above his head. They would float into the air in bright beautiful pictures. If Apellamando thought about a rainbow, a rainbow would sail up from his forehead. If he thought about a butterfly, a lovely butterfly would hang lightly over his head.

Apellamando managed to keep his gift a secret, except from his four best friends. His friends loved to watch Apellamando's dream float against the sky. "Dream of sailboats, Apellamando!" they would cry. "Think of green and yellow caterpillars, Apellamando!" they would beg. Apellamando was happy to grant his friends' wishes, and they would lie on a patch of grass and watch Apellamando's colorful dreams in all their glorious colors decorate the sky.

One day, as the friends enjoyed watching bright yellow canaries, bunches of balloons, orange and black tigers, and bouquets of flowers drift from Apellamando's head, it began to rain. As the rain fell, it seemed to moisten Apellamando's floating visions and they began to stick to things!

The bright yellow canaries floated over and stuck fast to the door of the bakery. The bunch of balloons stuck to the walls of the Village Square. There were all of Apellamando's colorful dreams stuck to the walls of the gray little houses and the drab little buildings! The children stood stunned in the street when the baker stepped out of his shop and cried, "Who painted these birds on my door?" He spotted the children and yelled, "What do you think you're doing painting all over our clean little village?"

"I'm sorry. I didn't mean for the dreams to stick. But they do add something quite lovely to the gray walls, don't you think?" said an apologetic Apellamando.

"No, I don't think!" yelled the baker in reply. "In fact I think you children should be punished for painting on our property!"

"But you don't understand," the children cried in unison. By this time, many of the townspeople emerged from the buildings. "How dare the children do this to our walls! They must explain themselves!"

When the children tried to explain themselves, the grown-ups became angrier. "No one can make pictures in his head for all to see. No one can share their colorful dreams," the grown-ups said. They decided the children must be lying. The children were sent home to wait for their punishment.

Apellamando hung his head as they left the village streets and headed for the path through the woods to their homes. His friends tried to reassure him, saying it wasn't his fault. Anyway, they liked the buildings so much better with Apellamando's dreams on them. But Apellamando could not be comforted. "I shall never have another dream. Not ever," he sighed.

"But Apellamando, you can't stop dreaming! We love your dreams!" his friends implored.

"No. Never again," Apellamando insisted.

The children walked forlornly through the woods as the sun began to set. They were too unhappy to mind where they were going, and it began to grow dark before they had reached their homes. Finally, they realized that night was about to fall and they were lost.

Hungry, tired, and a bit worried, the children sat down in a clearing.

"This is all my fault," said Apellamando sadly. "I should never have dreamed those dreams."

"But your dreams are lovely," said one friend.

"Yes, and so colorful," said another.

"We loved to look at them. They made us happy," they all agreed.

"But they were good for nothing," Apellamando said dejectedly.

"Wait a minute," said one of the children, "they would be really good for something now, Apellamando."

"No. My mind's made up. I'll not dream another dream ever," Apellamando replied.

"But Apellamando, if you could dream a dream now, it would float up into the air and the grown-ups would see us and find us."

"Yes, please, Apellamando!" the other chimed in.

"I can't!" said Apellamando.

"You must!" cried his friends.

So, reluctantly, Apellamando began thinking of rainbows and sparrows and apple trees, and slowly his dreams floated higher and higher until they hung in the violet sky.

The children's parents had begun to worry, as their children had not arrived home. They had gathered folks from the village to help look for them. All at once, someone yelled "Look!" and pointed to the beautiful images floating over the woods.

In a short while, the village folk found the children and realized they had been wrong about Apellamando. He really could share his colorful dreams. And what a gift it was!

The village is no longer drab and gray. Its walls are splashed with color and its people are happy. There is an old man that the children visit in the Village Square each day. He tells them wonderful stories, and every now and then a beautiful, colorful picture floats up and rests just above his head for everyone to see.

Chinese

"A craftsman, if he means to do good work, must first sharpen his tools."
— *Confucius*

"All men know that beauty and ugliness are correlatives, as are skill and clumsiness; one implies and suggests the other."
— *Lao Tzu*

"Despise thy masterpieces; thus renew the vigor of your creation. Let the straight appear crooked to you, your craft clumsiness; your Music discord."
— *Lao Tzu*

PROVERBS AND MAXIMS

The real voyage of discovery consists not in seeking new lands, but in seeing with new eyes.
— *Proust*

Wonder is the basis of worship.
— *Carlyle*

Happiness lies in the joy of achievement and the thrill of creative effort.
— *F. D. Roosevelt*

He who can no longer pause to wonder and stand rapt in awe is as good as dead; his eyes are closed.
— *Einstein*

Wonder (said Socrates) is very much the affection of a philosopher; for there is no other beginning of philosophy than this.
— *Plato*

HEROES AND HEROINES

LEONARDO DA VINCI (1452–1519)

Born in Vinci, Italy near Florence, he was raised by his father in both towns. He became an apprentice of Andrea del Verrochio, a sculptor, painter, and goldsmith. For about twenty years, age thirty to fifty, he worked in various capacities—as an engineer and architect of cathedrals, a decorator of palaces, an organizer of pageants, and a painter and sculptor—while teaching himself Latin and carrying out anatomical and other scientific research. He served as a painter for a variety of patrons in Milan, Rome, and several French cities. Though there is a scarcity of his paintings, some are well known: *Adoration of the Magi*, *The Last Supper*, and *Mona Lisa*. There is even less of his sculpturing. However, the drawings and sketches of his notebooks show a mixture of social commentary, an interest in ugliness and beauty, a skill in mechanical and anatomical drawing, scientific insight into flying machines, stink bombs, and all kinds of fascinating contraptions, and observations related to geology, geography, botany and astronomy.

CHARLES JOHN HUFFAM DICKENS (1812–1870)

Born in Landport, England (later Portsmouth), he spent his early years on the southern coast, where his father worked for the Navy Pay Office. After losing his job, his father moved the family to London, but things didn't improve. A creditor forced his family into a debtors' prison where they stayed for three months. At age 12, Charles worked in a blacking factory and attended school, where punishment was delivered by blows to his back with a swordlike cane. He worked for a time as a court reporter, while writing short stories under the pen name of Bog. The stories became very popular, and he published a two-volume set at age twenty-four. He was not only an entertaining storyteller, but a social reformer as well. He became the editor of a newspaper, *The Daily News*, and his editorials attacked the social evils of his day. His books, such as *Oliver Twist*, *Nicholas Nickleby*, *David Copperfield*, and *Little Dorritt*, helped form public opinion against the abusive practices of debtors' laws, public almshouses, and child labor.

WALT DISNEY (1901–1966)

Born in Chicago, Illinois and raised partly in Kansas City and partly on a midwestern farm, he acquired some basic art instruction from correspondence courses, but dropped out of high school at age 17. He worked as a commercial illustrator, making primitive, animated, advertising cartoons, and tried to start his own business. When that failed in 1923, he moved to Hollywood where his older brother, Ray, helped him resume cartoon production. The invention of such cartoon characters as Mickey Mouse and Donald Duck, combined with a creative use of music, sound, and folk tales, made his Disney shorts a worldwide success. He expanded his dream, producing his first feature-length cartoon (Snow White) in 1938 and opening his fantasy theme park (Disneyland) in 1957.

THOMAS ALVA EDISON (1847–1931)

Born in Milan, Ohio, he is perhaps the most creative and prolific of all inventors. His mother was a schoolteacher and worked hard to instill in him a love for reading. He began his career as a newsboy in the Grand Trunk Railroad when he was only twelve. In his spare time, he installed a laboratory for experiments in a baggage car and, acquiring a printing press, published the only newspaper ever printed aboard a train. At sixteen he became a telegrapher and bounced from job to job until, at twenty-one, he was considered a failure. However, he was independent, hardworking, and stubborn, and began looking for ways to improve the telegraph. One of his successful early inventions was the quadruplex method (four messages being received at the same time). As he gained backing, he expanded his thinking and soon invented the carbon telephone transmitter and the phonograph. His incandescent lamp was first demonstrated in 1879 when he was only thirty-two. Before his life ended he held at least 1,300 United States patents. His creative inventions improved the lives of people everywhere.

LUDWIG VAN BEETHOVEN (1770–1827)

He was born in Bonn, Germany into a musical family: his grandfather directed the court orchestra and his father sang in the choir. However, the family lived in poverty because of his father's drinking. Beethoven developed a passion for the outdoors and, from an early age, felt that nature was the true source of music. His musical training began at age four. Because he had obvious talent, he was often beaten in efforts to make him practice more. His first compositions were published in 1782 when he was only 12 years old. He studied with many of the world's masters, including Mozart, and, feeling restricted by his teachers' rules, began to create his own style. By the time he wrote his Third Symphony he was known as an original composer. In 1798 he began losing his hearing, and his Ninth Symphony, finished in 1823, was composed after he had become completely deaf.

Creativity————————————————EMBRACING

PUT CREATIVITY INTO ACTION

- Do something creative every week.

- Spend a few minutes every day thinking about the wonders of life. Discuss it with a friend.

- When you can't solve a problem, look for a different way.

- Think about a way in which you are creative. Practice it.

- Talk with an adult about something you wonder about. Ask a lot of questions.

- Find a way you and your parents can make a contribution to a community concern (beach clean-up, graffiti, etc.).

- Practice something creative (drawing, painting, poetry, guitar) regularly for the whole month.

- Read a book that stretches your imagination.

- Look at a difficult situation or assignment you face from a different perspective.

- Join a community service project that offers a resourceful solution to a community concern.

COMMUNITY SERVICE IDEAS

- Make hand-decorated placemats and/or tray favors for people in a retirement home or hospital.

- Make birthday and/or greeting cards for children with life-threatening diseases.

- Tell stories to children in a local hospital.

- Make colorful, cheerful posters to decorate the walls of a senior healthcare center.

- Write a play and present it to children in a daycare center.

- Think of a new and creative way for your class to contribute a unique service to the community.

BOOKS ON CREATIVITY

Butterfly Boy. Laurence Yep. New York: Farrar, Straus & Giroux, 1993.

Camille and the Sunflowers. Laurence Anholt. New York: Barron's, Hauppauge, 1994.

The Day of Ahmed's Secret. Heide and Gilliland. New York: Lothrop, Lee & Shepard Books, 1990.

Fox's Dream. Keizafuro Tejima. New York: Philomel Books, 1987.

Michael the Angel. Laura Fischetto. New York: Doubleday Books for Young Readers, 1993.

Rosie the Cool Cat. Piotr Wilkon. New York: Viking, 1991.

Is Your Bed Still There When You Close the Door? Jane M. Healy. New York: Doubleday, 1992.
  "An Archeologist in Your Bedroom" – p.138
  "Creativity: Balloons" – p. 104
  "Grand Ruler of All Schools" – p. 103
  "If You Had One Wish" – p. 86
  "The Magic Wand" – p. 124
  "Talking to Animals" – p. 101
  "The Time Machine" – p. 130
  "A Tour of Your School" – p. 132

Environmental Awareness

April

SUPPORTIVE VALUES

Beauty • Sacrifice

DEFINITIONS

Understanding that many factors determine the survival of an ecological community.

Becoming conscious of and making an effort to comprehend the complex factors which surround us and ultimately determine our survival is the key to **environmental awareness.** Making an effort to recycle, reduce, and reuse in our daily lives could be one example of an environmentally aware person. Caring for the land, loving the land, and understanding all it has to offer so that we can conserve and replenish it are also necessary aspects of this awareness.

A quality that gives pleasure to the senses or exalts the mind or spirit is **beauty.** Beauty as it pertains to our natural surroundings is our focus for this month's partner value.

Sacrifice is giving up something for an ideal or belief. The willingness to sacrifice self for the greater good of society is a trait which clearly defines a person of character.

PURPOSE

Making an effort to recycle, reduce, and reuse as part of one's daily life is a mark of an environmentally aware person. Understanding our environmental predicament and making our actions of conservation habitual will better equip educators to teach students the importance of these actions.

With our hearts and minds focused on the generations to come and our spirits centered on our obligation to the earth of which we are a part, we cannot help but become more committed to and more aware of the beauty of our environment. In recognizing and preserving the beauty of our earth we are leaving a gift of untold worth for generations to come. We must learn to honor the value of sacrifice, necessary for the survival of our planet, and realize that by giving up some of our conveniences we serve the greater good of all. The environment has taught us to understand that small sacrifices in the present can lead to great benefits in the future.

April

Environmental Awareness

Day One:
Use the definitions on page 139 as a springboard for discussing the meaning of environmental awareness.

Day Two:
There should be world-wide awareness of the need to protect the environment. Look at the list of words in other languages to gain a better understanding of the thoughts around the world that accompany environmental awareness (see page 141).

Day Three:
Work in small groups to consider the impact just one person has on pollution. List the ways in which you contribute to pollution. Do some research to find facts concerning how much waste or trash a person creates each year, how much water a person uses, and how much food is wasted.

Day Four:
Make a list of ways people can reduce the amount of waste they contribute each year. Do you think you could make a serious commitment to living up to your own suggestions?

Day Five:
Why is it important to have clean water and to conserve the water that we have? What can you do to protect the world's water supply?

Day Six:
Make a birdfeeder using recyclable materials (for example, milk cartons). Hang the birdfeeders at home or outside your classroom window.

Day Seven:
Select an endangered animal about which to do a one-page report. Include a picture of the animal in your report. Use completed reports for a classroom or school hallway display.

Day Eight:
Choose a proverb bookmark from page 149. Decorate it, cut it out, and use it!

Day Nine:
Using pictures from magazines or newspapers, create a collage to show wasteful uses of the earth's resources (for example, paper plates, aerosol cans, styrofoam, etc.).

Day Ten:
If your school does not recycle, make a plan for proposing a recycling project to your principal. Discuss ways in which students can be encouraged to recycle.

Day Eleven:
Do you know the difference between renewable resources and nonrenewable resources? If not, find out and make a list of each. Talk about ways to conserve our use of nonrenewable resources.

Day Twelve:
Compose a letter to local officials encouraging them to include environmental concerns in every project they undertake.

Day Thirteen:
If possible, plant a tree in your school yard. If there is not enough money or enough space, make a small window garden and plant hardy wildflower seeds or small plants. Watch them grow.

Day Fourteen:
Do you know that a nocturnal animal is one who sleeps during the day and is awake at night? Turn off all the lights and pull the curtains to make your room dark. Can you imagine what it would be like to be a nocturnal animal? Find out more about the lives of these animals.

Day Fifteen:
Read a story about environmental awareness from the selection on pages 143–148.

Day Sixteen:
Plan and conduct a nature scavenger hunt. The list may include: ants, rocks, pine cones, leaves, feathers, dandelions, etc.

Day Seventeen:
Make a list of environmentally friendly classroom "rules" to hang up around the room (for example,
• "Don't waste water"—hang near the sink;
• "Recycle paper"—hang near the trash bin;
• "Turn the lights off"—hang near the light switch, etc.)

Day Eighteen:
Make a list of recommended environmental household "rules" to take home and share with your family.

Day Nineteen:
Study a micro-environment. With a partner, pick a grassy spot to place a hula hoop or circle made with rope or string. Get on your knees and write down what you see inside the circle (grass, clover, bugs, etc.).

Day Twenty:
Reflect on the lessons you have learned this month about environmental awareness and make a workable plan for embracing environmental awareness as a lifelong value.

ENVIRONMENTAL AWARENESS IN OTHER LANGUAGES

Chinese	*zi* *ran*	self, private, personal, natural; yes, certainly, really, still, nevertheless
French	*la conscience de l'environnement*	to be sensitive to and aware of one's relationship with one's surroundings and the external world
German	*umweltbewußtsein*	consciousness about the environment
Hawaiian	*malama 'aina* *aloha 'aina*	take care of the land love the land (malama means "to take care of, tend, attend, care for, preserve, protect, save, maintain" and 'aina means "land, earth," aloha means "love, affection")
Japanese	*kankyoo*	land without a border, surroundings kan—a round jewel that has even thickness, to go around, a circle kyoo—land border
Latin	*conscientia de rerum natura*	environmental: from Old English en (in) + viron (circle); related to Latin vibrare (to vibrate) awareness: from Gothic "wars" (watchful) (watchfulness of that which is vibrant-alive-around you)
Spanish	*conciencia del medioambiente*	having a conscience about the environment
Tagalog	*kaalamang pangkapaligiran*	kaalamang—being aware and sensitive kapaligiran—the condition of all surrounding things

Environmental Awareness ———————LEARNING ABOUT

DISCUSSION QUESTIONS

- Do you have a responsibility for other living things?

- Are there things you waste or see others waste that could be conserved or recycled?

- How much time do you spend enjoying the beauty of the earth?

- What animal would you miss the most if it became extinct?

- How do your daily decisions affect the future of our planet?

- What changes could you make in your life that would enhance and prolong life on our planet?

- Do you talk with your friends or family about the beauty of the earth? Why or why not?

- What aspect of creation is most endangered?

- Do you think we are facing an environmental crisis?

- Do you think we have over-valued individualism and need to consider the needs of the entire planet?

- How often do you pause for a moment of meditation or prayer in response to the beauty of the earth?

- What concerns or worries you the most about the future?

- How does your family conserve water?

STORIES AND THOUGHTS FROM SPIRITUAL TRADITIONS

Hinduism

He is a true devotee who is firm in the thought, seeing the Lord in all creation, both what is and what is not.

— Ramcaritmanas

For the ignorant, the world is a web, in which to be tangled and strangled. To the wise, the world is God's creation and He is manifested everywhere within it.

— Tradition

Buddhism

The Buddha taught respect not only for human beings, but for all living creatures, near and far, large and small, visible and invisible. Respect for living beings includes respecting their habitats, refraining even from needlessly breaking the branches of trees, for they are the abode of countless beings. Awareness of our environment arises naturally when we reflect on the interrelatedness of all living beings. We depend on living beings for our food, our shelter, and our very life. We are all linked in a vast and complex web of interrelationships, where the welfare of one affects the welfare of the whole.

Let no harm come to living creatures, for each one values its life just as dearly as we do our own. Animals are not always as ordinary as they may seem, either.

The Golden Deer

Once upon a time in India, there was a very special golden deer named Suvarnapar_hva, who was the leader of all the many deer living in the forest. Not only was he as beautiful as silk and gems, he had the gift of human speech and the mind of highest enlightenment. One day while drinking at the bank of a river, he saw a hunter bound with rope and drowning, screaming for help. His friend the raven warned him away, saying, "Beware, this man is evil. He will commit the highest treachery." But Suvarnapar_hva, out of compassion, dived into the river to save him. Having been warned, though, he made the man pledge never to reveal the incident to anyone.

Meanwhile, Queen Moonlight saw this special deer in a dream and wished to see him in reality. The king, determined to fulfill the queen's heartfelt yearning, sent hunters out to capture the deer, but no one was able to sight him. Furious, the king offered a huge reward for the capture of the golden deer. By and by, the hunter who had almost drowned heard about the reward, and being evil and greedy by nature, went to see the king. He broke the promise he had made and betrayed the golden deer.

Soon after, Suvarnapar_hva's friend, the raven, spotted the soldiers of the king approaching with bows and arrows to capture the deer, and warned him from the tree tops. But the golden deer was unafraid. He said, "If they do not capture me, they will capture some other deer. This is my chance to protect others from harm."

Just then the evil hunter raised his bow to kill the golden deer. But as he did so, his hand fell off and dropped to the ground. Suvarnapar_hva went before the king and told him the story of how he had saved the hunter's life. The king was stunned when he heard the tale of the hunter's treachery. He invited the golden deer to stay in the palace, and prepared a jeweled throne for him. There, to the great delight of the people, Suvarnapar_hva taught the path of non-violence and respect for all living creatures.

Zen Buddhism

A Zen master told a child, "I can make a whistle from a pine needle." The child asked, "Can you make a whistle from a pine needle?" When the wind blows, the pine needles sing. The wind can sing, the wind can roar. Each element of nature speaks in its own voice.

Whether you are going or staying or sitting or lying down, the whole world is your own self. You must find out whether the mountains, rivers, grass and forest exist in your own mind or exist outside it.

Christianity

"O Lord our God, you have put people in charge of everything you made."
— *Bible, Psalm 8:6*

"And God saw everything that was made, and behold, it was very good."
— *Bible, Genesis 1:31*

Hawaii

Calabash of the Winds

The weather had been quite unpredictable and the demi-god, Maui, was feeling restless, so he decided to build a kite. He used a strong, lightweight wood for the frame and one of his mother's fine bark cloths, which was beautifully decorated, for the skin of the kite. He then lashed the skin and the frame together with long lengths of a strong bark which he twisted together for added strength. The kite was huge. When it was finished it was forty-five feet across and seventy-five feet long. The neighbors were amazed when they saw it, for none of them had ever seen such an enormous kite before.

There was not enough wind to fly it, so Maui and his friends carried the kite to find the Cave of the Winds, where the Keeper of the Winds lived. Along the way they passed men and women who were busy at work, pounding their bark cloth or planting taro; but when they saw the large kite they left their work and followed the boys to the cave.

Maui called out a greeting at the mouth of the cave and the Keeper of the Winds emerged from the darkness into the daylight to see Maui and his friends holding the kite.

"Dear Keeper of the Winds, could you call some winds so that I can fly my kite?" Maui asked.

The Keeper admired the kite, replying, "It is a fine kite; let's try it." He went inside the cave and returned with a small gourd which was covered by a lid. "This is the small gourd in which I hold the gentle winds."

They carried the kite to a large clearing and Maui chanted softly to the wind to come gently and lift his kite. The Keeper of the Winds slowly lifted the lid off the gourd and tipped it slightly to release a gentle wind. A light breeze lifted the huge kite a little way off the ground. Maui called for more wind and the Keeper uncovered the gourd a little further. The wind was stronger now, and lifted the kite so that it sailed over the trees. Maui let out more cord and called for more wind. His friends and the villagers shouted to the Keeper, "Give him more wind!"

The Keeper was as excited as the crowd, and he turned the gourd upside down as the magnificent kite climbed higher and higher and went out beyond the large, grassy clearing, beyond the tall green trees, and out over the turquoise ocean.

Soon the huge kite began to fall, so Maui and his friends quickly reeled it in and caught it as it came down.

The weather was beautiful the next day, so Maui and his friends carried the kite to the Keeper of the Winds again. "Today you must give me the winds from your large gourd."

"Those winds are not for kites; don't be a fool, Maui," cautioned the Keeper.

"But I am strong and my kite is magnificent," Maui retorted, and he began to chant for the mighty winds to come and fly his kite. The winds in the large gourd inside the cave began to tremble and moan. The Keeper ran inside and struggled to keep the lid on, but it popped off. The winds escaped from the cave and quickly lifted Maui's kite off the ground and shot it straight into the sky. Maui laughed heartily, grabbed tightly onto the cord and planted his feet firmly on the ground. The winds were playing tug-of-war with Maui and his kite, and he was enjoying the battle of strength.

A cloud moved in and Maui could no longer see his great kite, so he called for the winds to return to the large gourd. But they were too far away to hear. Maui tried to reel in his kite. Suddenly he fell down; the cord had broken and he was left holding the stick which had been attached to the end of the kite cord. The winds had won the tug-of-war. They celebrated their victory, and soon a downpour chased everyone home.

The Keeper went into his cave and chanted for over an hour, trying to persuade the winds to return to their home in the large gourd, which they finally did. By the time the winds settled down, all the bark cloth which the women had set out to dry for the day had blown away, and the taro fields were all flooded.

Everyone in the village was very angry with Maui and would have nothing to do with him. The Keeper of the Winds was especially angry with him and would not answer his call when he went to the cave to visit. Maui became more restless with each passing day and finally decided to make another kite, which he flew near his home every day. As he flew the kite more and more he began to notice patterns in the wind, and slowly he came to understand the weather and which winds would bring rain and which would keep it clear.

One day, he saw a neighbor heading out to work in his taro patch and warned him about the approaching rain. The neighbor ignored him, but soon returned, soaking wet from the rain. Soon after, Maui saw another man going fishing, and cautioned him about a storm which Maui knew to be brewing. The fisherman paid no heed and was swept from the rocks where he was fishing and drowned.

After awhile, the villagers became aware of Maui's ability to predict the weather, and they began to rely on his knowledge. Would it be a good day to go fishing, to work in the taro patch, to take a sailing canoe to another island?

The attitude of the people toward Maui began to change, and he was respected for his special skill with his weather kite. They eventually forgave him for the storm brought on by his adventurous spirit, and honored him for his keen awareness of their environment, which enabled them to make safe decisions concerning their everyday work of survival.

Nigeria

Why the Sky is Far Away

Long, long ago the sky was not out of our reach as it is today. On the contrary, it was so close to the earth that people could reach out and touch it. Not only that, it tasted delicious, and if anyone was the least bit hungry all they had to do was reach up and grab hold of a bit of sky and eat it. It was wonderful! Sometimes it tasted like sweet potato, sometimes like roasted meat, or luscious fruit. There was so much of it! Indeed, a never-ending supply of delicious sky.

Because it was so easy to make a meal out of sky, there was very little work to be done. There were no crops to be sown or harvested. There was no cooking and thus no need to fetch water for boiling, or sticks for a fire.

Because there was so little work to do, people spent their time doing wonderful things like weaving beautiful cloth, or carving interesting objects, or telling tales, or making music. There were always exciting festivals to celebrate their happy lives. When festival time came there was a flurry of activity and preparation. The king of this happy land was called the Oba. In the Oba's palace there were servants whose only job it was to carve the sky into beautiful shapes for the festivities.

The sky, however, was growing angrier and angrier with the people. They had grown wasteful. They frequently took more than they could eat and then, without a care, threw the leftovers into the garbage. The heaps of leftover sky got larger and larger. Soon they were everywhere. There were chunks of half-eaten sky here, and barely nibbled bits of sky there.

"I'm tired of seeing myself wasted, strewn in pieces and piled in heaps all over the land," the sky said angrily. So one day, the sky turned very dark. Heavy, threatening clouds hung over the Oba's palace. Thunder rolled and lightning flashed right over the people's heads, and a great voice boomed "Oba! Your people are wasting my great gifts. They take more of me than they can use and toss me carelessly on garbage heaps all over your land. You must warn them, Oba, they must stop being wasteful or the gifts will be taken away!"

The Oba, afraid of losing the delicious sky, quickly dispatched messengers to take the sky's warning to the people. They were told of the sky's anger and warned to take only as much as they could eat and no more. They must not reach for the sky unless they were truly hungry. The people took the warning very seriously, as they did not want to lose their precious sky. For quite awhile they were very careful. Then came the time for the greatest festival of the year, which lasted several days. There was to be music and dancing and feasting. During the first few days of the celebrations, the Oba feared that the people would forget the sky's warning. He took care to make sure that no more sky was carved for the celebration than could be eaten.

Indeed, people continued to heed the sky's warning, but there was a woman in this land who was never satisfied. Whatever she had, it was never enough. She always wanted more jewelry, more children, more food. It was hard for her to obey the Oba's ruling, for she truly loved to eat. On the very last night of the festivities, she and her husband ate and danced into the night.

When she finally returned home, she said to herself, "What a wonderful evening it was. I wish I could relive it all—the music, the dancing, the food!" She gazed up at the sky, and, recalling all the delicious flavors and desiring to taste them all again, she reached up and grabbed a huge chunk. After only a few bites she began to feel quite full and started to toss the remaining piece on the garbage heap. "Oh, no! I mustn't throw this away," she cried and ran to her husband. "Husband dear, you must help me finish this piece of sky!" she begged. Her husband, who was exhausted from all the merriment, could manage only one bite. The woman ran to wake her sleeping children. "Children, you must help me finish this piece of sky!" she implored. But the tired children could only nibble at the chunk. Finally, the woman decided that enough had been eaten away and surely throwing away just a small piece could not be that bad. With that, she tossed the half-eaten piece of sky into the garbage heap.

Suddenly, thunder rolled and lightning flashed and a mighty voice boomed from overhead.

"Oba!" it cried, "Your people have been careless once again. They do not treat me with respect. I will leave you now!" With that, the sky began to rise higher and higher, and it did not stop until it got to be right about where it is today.

From that day on, the people had to work for their food. They had to sow and harvest crops. They had to hunt in the forests. The sky looked down on them as they labored, hopeful that they would learn not to waste the precious gifts of nature.

PROVERBS AND MAXIMS

I am glad I shall never be young without wild country to be young in. Of what avail are forty freedoms without a blank spot on the map?

— *A. Leopold*

Nothing so much enhances a good as to make sacrifices for it.

— *G. Santayana*

There is religion in everything around us, a calm and holy religion in the unbreathing things of nature, which man would do well to imitate.

— *Ruskin*

We need wilderness whether or not we ever set foot in it. We need a refuge even though we may never need to go there . . . We need the possibility of escape as surely as we need hope . . .

— *E. Abbey*

We travel together, passengers of a little spaceship, dependent on its vulnerable reserves of air and soil; all committed for our safety to its security and peace; preserved from annihilation by the care, and the work, and, I will say, the love we give our fragile craft.

— *A. Stevenson*

HEROES AND HEROINES

ANSEL ADAMS (1902–1984)

Born in San Francisco, California, he grew up in the dunes area by the Golden Gate Bridge and developed a love of nature partly by watching the Pacific surf and the low fog moving across the sky. The other reason for his interest came as a result of his being tutored at home and being left by himself a lot; he found himself more responsive to the wild environments than to urban life. His career began as a thirteen-year-old wandering through the 1915 Panama-Pacific Exposition with a Brownie box camera. The following spring he visited Yosemite National Park with his Brownie. "From that day in 1916 my life has been colored and modulated by the great earth gesture of the Sierra." He continued photographing Yosemite every year through the 1970s. Few people have worked as hard or as effectively to preserve the American wilderness. His photographs "articulated" the concept of wilderness values; he touched countless lives with the importance of preserving the remaining wilderness lands.

JOHNNY APPLESEED (1774–1845)

Though born in Massachusetts as John Chapman, there is very little known of his early life. One account mentions that his father served with George Washington and that he grew up with many younger half-brothers and half-sisters. He was a solitary child and would go for long walks in the woods, where he studied the behavior of the animals and birds. When he was 18, he and his brother walked across New York state. The next account has him at 25 in the Ohio River Valley, where he began his life work: traveling through the new land, reading the *Bible* to settlers and planting apple trees wherever he went. He did this for fifty years and earned the respect of Native Americans as a medicine man, because he also planted herbs, made healing poultices, and brewed soothing tea. There are stories of his bravery, such as the time he risked his life to warn settlers of an impending attack by the Native Americans. The orchards he planted may have vanished, but his legend as a caretaker of the environment will last forever.

RACHEL LOUISE CARSON (1907–1964)

Born in Springdale, Pennsylvania, Rachel owed her love of nature to her mother, who taught her as a tiny child the beauty of and a love for nature. Her literary talent became apparent at age ten when she began contributing articles to the *St. Nicholas League,* a children's magazine. She enrolled in the Pennsylvania College for Women with the intention of making writing her career, but a course in biology changed her mind. She rediscovered her interest in science, eventually becoming a member of the zoology staff at the University of Maryland. Combining her scientific skills and her writing ability, she became well known for her books *Under the Sea Wind* (1941) and *The Sea Around Us* (1951). She became a significant figure in the environmental movement and is best known as the author of *Silent Spring*, a controversial study of pesticide misuse, and as a crusader in the struggle for conservation and ecological awareness.

THEODORE ROOSEVELT (1858–1919)

Born in New York City into an old New York Dutch family, he was afforded an excellent education and developed an intellectual curiosity and a love of literature and the arts. To overcome the ill health and physical weakness of his early childhood he became a dedicated proponent of physical culture through sports and outdoor living. He graduated from Harvard and entered law school, but an interest in politics kept him from the legal profession. He was elected governor of New York, then became the twenty-sixth president in 1901 when President McKinley was assassinated. He is listed under Environmental Awareness because of his many successful conservation policies. During his presidency more than 150,000,000 acres were designated as national forests, thus saving not only forests but mineral, coal lands, and waterpower sites. His strong policies and leadership led to the National Conservation Commission and the Reclamation Act of 1902.

BRIAN SCHATZ (1972–)

Born in Ann Harbor, Michigan, he moved with his parents to Honolulu when he was two years old. Brian is the founder of an organization called Youth for Environmental Service (YES). In 1987, Brian went to Sandy Beach at dawn to surf and found it closed due to a sewage spill. This inspired him to get involved in community environmental protection. He found few opportunities for a young person such as himself to make a difference in his community. Through his college years at Pomona College, he began to develop an idea to empower young people to directly address their communities' environmental problems. This idea became YES. Starting with one phone line, limited funding, and some support from the University of Hawaii, he built this organization. It has since grown to include six staff people as well as offices in Honolulu, Maui, Seattle, San Francisco, and Los Angeles. Brian's philosophy is that everyone, young or old, can do something about local problems. All they have to do is take action.

PAUL WATSON (1950–)

Born in Canada, he has become one of the most daring of the environmental activists. He is one of the founders of Greenpeace and the Sea Shepherd Conservation Society. The original Sea Shepherd was a deep water trawler that Watson commissioned as the champion of sea animals that were being hunted into extinction. He scuttled the ship rather than let it be taken over by pirates, and found a cod trawler that he converted into the Sea Shepherd II. Since 1978, he has disrupted government-sanctioned wolf hunts and seal hunts, invented the tactic of tree-spiking to save old-growth forest from lumber companies, rammed Japanese driftnet ships, and confronted Russian whalers on the high seas. He has been arrested, beaten up, pursued by helicopter gunships and nearly killed. He is controversial, complex, and has been denounced as a terrorist by some. However, there is no doubting his passionate defense of whales, seals, seabirds, dolphins, and almost every form of endangered marine species. Future generations will probably consider him a hero.

PUT ENVIRONMENTAL AWARENESS INTO ACTION

- Start recycling paper, glass, plastic, and metal, or get someone else started.
- Avoid disposable plates, cups, and utensils.
- Use the back of discardable paper for scratch paper.
- Turn off lights when not in use.
- Put a water conservation device in your toilet tank.
- Reuse egg cartons and paper bags.
- Give away rather than dispose of unneeded items.
- Turn off the water while you brush your teeth.
- Decrease TV watching and increase reading.
- Sponsor a clothes swap.
- Be responsible and creative with leftover food.
- Take shorter showers.
- Volunteer to pick up litter along your favorite beach or park.
- Use rechargeable batteries.

COMMUNITY SERVICE IDEAS

- Organize a class or Scout Troop project to collect litter around campus with your parents, talking with them about the importance of caring for the land.
- Help with trail maintenance, stream cleaning, or park clean-up with a local environmental group.
- Organize a recycling program in your neighborhood.
- Volunteer at a local nature conservancy.
- Plant a garden or some seeds in a pot. Keep a journal of the growth.
- Organize a class project to secure and plant a tree in your community.

EMBRACING—————*Environmental Awareness*

BOOKS ON ENVIRONMENTAL AWARENESS

Antarctica. Helen Cowcher. New York: Farrar, Straus & Giroux, 1990.

Desert Giant: The World of the Saguaro Cactus. Barbara Bash. Boston: Sierra Club Books, 1990.

Eagle. Judy Allen. Cambridge: Candlewick Press, 1994.

Empty Lot. Dale H. Fife. Boston: Sierra Club Books, 1991.

Farewell to Shady Glade. Bill Peet. Boston: Houghton, 1966.

The Great Kapok Tree: A Tale of the Amazon Rainforest. Lynne Cherry. San Diego: Harcourt Brace, Jovanovich, 1990.

Little House. Virginia L. Burton. Boston: Houghton Mifflin Co., 1942.

Miss Rumphius. Barbara Cooney. New York: Viking Press, 1982.

Our Vanishing Farm Animals: Saving America's Breeds. Catherine Paladino. Boston: Joy Street Books, 1991.

Salamander Room. Anne Mazer. New York: Knopf, 1991.

Tiger. Judy Allen. Cambridge: Candlewick Press, 1992.

Tigress. Helen Cowcher. New York: Farrar, Straus & Giroux, 1991.

Tree of Life: The World of the African Baobab. Barbara Bash. Boston: Sierra Club Books, 1990.

Whistling Thorns. Helen Cowcher. New York: Scholastic, 1993.

Why the Sky is Far Away: A Nigerian Folktale. Mary-Joan Gerson. Boston: Little, Brown, 1992.

Zoo. Anthony Browne. New York: Knopf, 1992.

A Call to Character. Colin Greer and Herbert Kohl, eds. New York: Harper Collins Publisher, 1995.
   "Miss Rumphis" – p. 375
   "Rascal" – p. 366
   "The Story of the Hungry Elephant" – p. 375

Earth Prayers. Elizabeth Roberts and Elias Amidon, eds. San Francisco: Harper, 1991.
   "Bless Thee, O Lord . . . " – p. 225
   "Earth Mother" – p. 14
   "Find the Good Road" – p. 86
   "My Heart Soars" – p. 42
   "Teach Your Children" – p. 10
   "We Live By the Sun" – p. 16

The Moral Compass. William J. Bennett, ed. New York: Simon and Schuster, 1995.
   "The Wonder Tree" – p. 746

Freedom

SUPPORTIVE VALUES

Social Justice • Equality

DEFINITIONS

Being free to make choices and determine actions.

The **freedom** to make our own choices and determine what action we will take in any given situation is the freedom to which we refer this month. This freedom can be our salvation or our nemesis if it is not combined with a full understanding of the values of respect and responsibility.

Treating all people fairly, regardless of race, religion, gender, or sexual preference, is the definition of **social justice**. Akin to this value is **equality**, which asks that we treat all people the same in terms of education, housing, and job opportunities regardless of differences.

PURPOSE

Kenneth Sollitt explains, "Freedom is the opportunity to make decisions. Character is the ability to make right decisions. It can be achieved only in a climate of freedom. For no one learns to make right decisions without being free to make wrong ones." This is the crux of *Character Education*. As paradoxical as it seems, the freedom which allows us to make wrong decisions is the freedom which also enables us to build character. Freedom to make mistakes is an idea that educators embrace, because we know that it is when we strive to understand and correct our mistakes that learning occurs. Giving students the freedom to make mistakes by reassuring them that "there are no mistakes, only lessons" is one of the greatest gifts educators can give.

"We hold these truths to be self-evident: that all [people] are created equal; that they are endowed by their Creator with certain unalienable rights; that among these are life, liberty, and the pursuit of happiness . . . " Thomas Jefferson and the framers of the Constitution made the values of freedom, justice, and equality an integral part of that document. It follows, as Roberta Williams reminds educators, that "When we look for possibilities and potential in every student, then nurture those qualities, all children become successful learners." In this way educators will be encouraging a classroom atmosphere where freedom, equality, and social justice can flourish.

Freedom

Day One:
Use the definitions on page 155 as a springboard to discuss the meaning of freedom.

Day Two:
Can you imagine what it would be like not to have your freedom? As a group, list all of the things you would not be able to do without your freedom.

Day Three:
Using the discussion questions on page 158, discuss your understanding of freedom.

Day Four:
History is full of examples of people fighting for freedom. Name a war where people fought for freedom. Is freedom a value worth fighting for? Why?

Day Five:
Choose a proverb bookmark from page 165 to decorate and cut out. Use it in your social studies book to remind you of those who fought for freedom.

Day Six:
Growing up means increased freedom to make your own choices. What choices do you have the freedom to make every day? Make a list.

Day Seven:
Review the list of choices you made yesterday, and make a list of choices you are not free to make. How many of these are choices you would like to make? Are there some you feel you should be able to make when you are older?

Day Eight:
Democratic nations rest on the basic principle that each individual has certain inalienable rights. Find the historical document that outlines these rights in your country and list them.

Day Nine:
Name some of the benefits of living in a democracy. How do citizens of a democracy sometimes take these benefits for granted and fail to think about how their lives would be different if these freedoms were taken away from them?

Day Ten:
Unfortunately, there are people even today who do not have their freedom. Write a letter to your representative in Congress to remind him or her to keep the value of freedom at the forefront of their policy efforts with foreign nations.

Day Eleven:
Find out the name and address of your congressional representative and mail the letter you wrote. Discuss the importance of all citizens in a democracy learning about the people running for Congress and of going to the polls and voting for the candidate of their choice, once they reach voting age.

Day Twelve:
Read a story about freedom from the selection on pages 159–164.

Day Thirteen:
Remembering the story you read yesterday, illustrate a scene from that story.

Day Fourteen:
Freedom of thought and expression is the root of change in society. List some changes that have occurred throughout history due to this type of freedom (for example, civil rights, women's suffrage, rap music, movies, etc.).

Day Fifteen:
Read about and discuss the lives of the heroes and heroines of freedom on pages 166–167.

Day Sixteen:
Spread the value of freedom by choosing a community service project from page 168 to carry out as a class effort.

Day Seventeen:
Plan your service project and check your plans to make sure you have complete freedom to carry them out.

Day Eighteen:
Put the class community project into action.

Day Nineteen:
Review your choice of service project, your plans for carrying it out, and the results of seeing it through. Was it successful as a group project? What, if anything, would you do differently if you could do it over?

Day Twenty:
Reflect on what you have learned this month about freedom. Celebrate your freedom to live a fulfilled and happy life.

FREEDOM IN OTHER LANGUAGES

Chinese	*zi* *you*	self, private, personal, natural; cause, means, instrument, source, motive; from, by, by way of, through
French	*la liberté*	possibility of acting, thinking and expressing oneself according to one's own choices; state of mind of a person who is not dominated by fear, prejudices, pain, or embarrassment
German	*freiheit*	liberty, freedom, privilege, immunity
Hawaiian	*ku'oko'a*	independence, liberty, freedom (ku means "to stand" and 'oko'a means "different, separate, unrelated, another; whole; entirety")
Japanese	*jiyuu*	be oneself ji —oneself
Latin	*libertas*	from Gothic "freis" (free)
Spanish	*libertad*	liberty, freedom, independence
Tagalog	*kalayaan*	having independence; being free; liberty; having free use

Character Education Year 2 Grades K–6

DISCUSSION QUESTIONS

- How would you define freedom?

- What are you free to do? What shouldn't you do?

- In what ways can children be treated as equal to adults?

- Do you think people should be free to do whatever they want? Why or why not?

- What kind of choices are you free to make every day?

- Should any of these choices be controlled by rules or be given direction by guidelines?

- What are some examples of social justice found on the playground?

- Do you think all people should be seen as equal no matter what kind of job they have or how much money they have? Why?

- What are the freedoms you enjoy the most? Are there any limitations on these freedoms?

- What responsibilities accompany freedom?

- How do you define social justice?

- Have you ever been made to feel unequal to someone? Why do people do that to others? How can the Golden Rule be applied?

UNDERSTANDING ————————————

STORIES AND THOUGHTS FROM SPIRITUAL TRADITIONS

Hinduism

Action rightly renounced brings freedom:
Action rightly performed brings freedom:
Both are better
Than mere shunning of action.　　　　　*– Bhagavad Gita*

External freedom is temporary, it is gone the moment we become attached to things in the world. Internal freedom is permanent, for then our only possession is God.
　　　　　– Tradition

Having requires holding. Holding creates attachment. Attachment causes bondage. To be truly free is to let go of all desires and find peace within.　　*– Tradition*

Buddhism

The greatest freedom is freedom from the delusions of the mind. One who is free from hatred, desire, and ignorance is truly free.

The robe worn by Buddhist monks and nuns symbolizes freedom, freedom from the bondage of ordinary appearances and worldly pursuits. As Zen monastics dress, they repeat this verse:
　　　　"Vast is the robe of liberation
　　　　A formless field of benediction
　　　　As I wear the Buddha's teaching,
　　　　Saving all sentient beings."

Zen Buddhism

The Original Mind is like water, which flows freely without stopping at one spot, whereas the Deluded Mind is like ice, with which one cannot even wash one's hands and face. By melting the ice to water, it will flow anywhere; one can then wash one's hands and feet or anything. In one word, the mind freezes on one spot, it is "stopping." By freezing, there will be no freedom of use. Ice cannot even wash the hands and feet. Melt the mind and let it flow through your whole being and use it at any particular place as needed.

Freedom —————————————————————— UNDERSTANDING

Christianity

"Do not use your freedom as an opportunity for evil."

– Bible, Galatians 5:13

"The Lord sets the prisoners free; the Lord opens the eyes of the blind."

– Bible, Psalm 146:7-8

"And you will know the truth, and the truth will make you free."

– Bible, John 8:32

Islam

If it had been your Lord's Will, they would all have believed—all who are on earth. Will you then compel mankind against their will to believe?

The free will Allah has given us is the free will to worship as we please. It is to Allah alone that we must account for our choice. Men and women of Faith must endeavour to persuade the Faithless to submit to Allah, but we do not have Allah's permission to force anyone against his or her will to believe. Indeed, it is a contradiction in terms. If He had willed it, Allah would have created us without free will, but the merit of Faith is that it is arrived at through the individual's efforts and use of the abilities Allah has given to him to see the Truth. Faith imposed by physical fear, social or financial pressure is not Faith but hypocrisy . . . , for which both the false convert and his converter are guilty.

– Selections from Mishkat-ul-masabi [247] p. 160
The Cow (Baqara) 2:256

Chinese

"One who is free to choose, yet does not prefer to dwell among the Good— how can he be accorded the name of wise?"

– Confucius

"You may rob the Three Armies of their commander-in-chief, but you cannot deprive the humblest peasant of his opinion."

– Confucius

"One may govern a state by restriction; weapons may be used with skill and cunning; but one acquires true command only by freedom, given and taken."

— Lao Tzu

Master Kung said, The gentleman has nine cares. In seeing he is careful to see clearly, in hearing he is careful to hear distinctly, in his looks he is careful to be kindly; in his manner to be respectful, in his words to be loyal, in his work to be diligent. When in doubt he is careful to ask for information; when angry he has a care for the consequences, and when he sees a chance of gain, he thinks carefully whether the pursuit of it would be consonant with the Right.

— The Analects, Book XVI

Hawaii

Hina in the Moon

Hina was unhappy when her husband, Aikanaka, was home. It also saddened her that her son, Maui, would not come and visit as often when Aikanaka was home. Aikanaka, although a brave hunter and warrior, was a lazy man. When he wasn't challenged by daring adventures, he sat at home and expected Hina to do all the work. He was very demanding, and expected everything to be exactly the way he wanted it, although he never lifted a finger to help. Instead, he loved to sit around with his friends and tell stories of his adventures, which he would embellish so that they made him look like a hero.

In the early hours of dawn before the sun was up, Hina was getting the earth oven ready to cook the day's meals. At midday, when the sun was high and hot overhead, she was busy pounding bark to make her bark cloth. In the evening, after the sun had set, she pounded taro to make poi for the evening meal. Late at night, before she went to bed, she hiked to the spring, where she would fill a gourd with water for the next day and return home. Every day, no matter how hard she worked to please her husband, Hina would hear only complaints about everything she did.

One day Aikanaka sent her to get shrimp from the mountain stream. She was exhausted, but obeyed him. As she was sitting beside the stream she saw a rainbow arch nearby. She went over to the beautiful arch and began to climb it, step by step. Everything around her was colorful and peaceful, and she felt content. By noon, however, the sun became too hot. Hina was thirsty and her skin was beginning to blister. She climbed down from the rainbow, and as she was walking home she met her husband on the path. He was angry, and approached her with a frown, demanding to know where she had been and where his shrimp were. He had been to the spring to get water, and that was women's work. Hina said nothing, but took the gourd of water from him and thirstily drained it. Now Aikanaka was extremely angry.

Hina looked beyond her husband and saw a moon rainbow, and knew what she must do. She went into her home and took a gourd and her favorite tapa beater and board for making bark cloth. She quickly went toward the moonbow and began to climb. Aikanaka was astonished, but, when he came to his senses, started after her. The fragile pathway would not support him and in one last effort he lunged after Hina and managed to grab her ankle. She climbed faster and escaped his grip, but twisted her ankle in her effort to break free. She continued upward on the arch toward the moon, surrounded by the stars and the dark, cool night.

She lives there even now. When the sky is covered in clouds, it is Hina laying out her bark cloth to dry in the sun. When the thunder rumbles, she is rolling away the stones which keep the wind from blowing her cloth away. When the lightening flashes, she is shaking her finished cloth. On full moon nights you can see her there in the moon, sitting with her tapa beater and board beside her.

India

Lakshmi's Choice

Surjit Singh of village Kaleswar had a daughter named Lakshmi. She was his only child. Surjit Singh was a wealthy man.

"Surjit! What about marrying your daughter to my son?" the landlord of the area, Vikram Rao, once asked Surjit. That is because Lakshmi was not only beautiful, but also very intelligent and good-natured.

"I wonder if there could be a better match!" commented Surjit. The landlord was happy. But the very next day, the renowned merchant of the area, Kamleshwar, proposed his son's marriage with Lakshmi. Again Surjit could not refuse the proposal, but said that he would leave it to Lakshmi's choice.

When Lakshmi was asked by her parents, she kept quiet. "My child, you must speak out your preference! To us both the young men seem equally good," said her mother.

"Mother, to me both the young men seem equally bad. I have another young man in mind—Vidyadhar," said Lakshmi with a shy smile.

"Vidyadhar? How can he be better than the other two?" asked Surjit Singh with some surprise. Vidyadhar was the headmaster's son. He was a good scholar.

"Father, the other two cannot possess the quality which Vidyadhar has. But Vidyadhar can possess what they have," replied Lakshmi. "You can ask them individually and find out for yourself!"

Lakshmi told her father what exactly he should ask the three young men.

One day Surjit Singh found the landlord's son alone. He went in and briefed a friend of his. The friend came out and asked the young man, "How much interest do you take in your father's estate?"

"Why should I bother? Don't we have our clerks to look after it?" answered the young man.

"Of course, you have enough wealth. But suppose you marry a girl who loves literature and arts. Would you be able to become a scholar?" he was asked.

"That is not my interest!" answered the landlord's son.

Similar questions were put to the merchant's son on another occasion. He too answered in the same way.

It was now Vidyadhar's turn. "Vidyadhar! There is a proposal for Lakshmi's marriage with you. The problem is, you have scholarship, but no wealth. Will you be able to possess wealth if you marry Lakshmi?

"At once!" replied Vidyadhar.

"At once? How?" Surjit Singh's friend asked him.

Vidyadhar laughed and said, "Look here, I do not consider myself eligible for Lakshmi's hand. But that is a different matter. If we are to accept your hypothesis that I marry Lakshmi, don't you see how I grow rich at once?

Lakshmi is her parents' only child. Who will manage their wealth if not their son-in-law?"

The answer was duly reported to Surjit Singh, his wife and Lakshimi.

"Do you see my point, Father? The landlord's son and the merchant's son have wealth, but no scholarship. They cannot develop scholarship either. Vidyadhar has scholarship, but no wealth. But he can automatically become wealthy!" explained Lakshmi. Surjit Singh laughed. Lakshmi married Vidyadhar.

Judaism

The Seder of the Ignorant Man

Once, a rabbi had celebrated the first night of Seder so devoutly that every word, every ritual was perfect, and he felt proud of all that he had performed for the service. When he awoke at dawn he heard a voice say, "More pleasing to me is the Seder of the water-carrier."

The rabbi had to ask many people before he found where this man, the water-carrier, lived. He was a poor man and lived far from town, but the rabbi sent some disciples who went to the house and asked for the man. The wife admitted that her husband was indeed the water-carrier, Hayyim. She explained that he was unavailable since he had had too much to drink the day before and would not be able to speak to the rabbi properly. The disciples insisted that the man come with them, so they woke him and dragged him off to meet the rabbi.

The rabbi questioned Hayyim about the special rituals that he did for Seder, a holy day for the Jews commemorating their release from bondage in Egypt. The water-carrier replied, "I am a poor ignorant man like my father before me and I do not know what the proper rituals are. When my wife asked me to celebrate Seder properly, I said, 'All I know is that our ancestors in Egypt were led to freedom from captivity by God. I also know that we are still in captivity, but I know that God will lead us to freedom, too.' When I said this to her, a table appeared before us, which was covered with a shining cloth and all the dishes for Seder and red wine. I ate and drank and so did my wife, and I said, 'I drink this cup to you, God, because you make us free!' Then we drank and rejoiced and I got tired and fell asleep."

PROVERBS AND MAXIMS

Remember, remember always, that all of us, and you and I especially, are descended from immigrants and revolutionists.

— *F. D. Roosevelt*

Freedom is nothing but a chance to be better.

— *A. Camus*

Freedom is not worth having if it does not connote freedom to err.

— *M. Gandhi*

You can't hold a man down without staying down with him.

— *B. T. Washington*

But what is liberty without wisdom and without virtue? It is the greatest of all possible evils; for it is folly, vice, and madness, without tuition or restraint.

— *Burke*

HEROES AND HEROINES

BADSHAH KHAN (1890–1984)

Born as Abdul Ghaffar Khan, in the village of Utmanzai in the northwest tip of British India, he grew up on his father's farm in the shadow of the Khyber Pass. It was a time of unrest and calls for rebellion against the British rule. When Ghaffar was seven years old, the Frontier War broke out. He never forgot the suffering of his people and the way their strong spirit faded from their eyes. He heard the constant talk of hatred and fear. He grew up admiring the qualities of soldiers and also admiring the views of the headmaster of the mission high school in Peshawar, the Rev. Mr. E.F.E. Wigram. He was torn between going to the university and becoming a professional soldier. Several experiences led him to an Islamic school in Campbellpur and later to a mission school at Aligarh. By 1915 his strong presence and his dedication to India and to Islam earned him a reputation as a brave young reformer, and, at age 25, he was proclaimed Badshah Khan, the King of Khans. But his method was different. From the most violent people in the world he created history's first non-violent army of over 100,000 men. He proved that strong people can be non-violent, and showed how violence has no place in Islam. Along with Gandhi he helped bring freedom to India.

HARRIET TUBMAN (1821–1913)

She was born a slave in the small village of Bucktown in Dorchester County, Maryland. Early in life she witnessed the injustice and terrible inhumanity of slavery. She endured many beatings and many long hours of hard labor, and developed a rebellious nature. She was seriously injured when she tried to help a slave escape; she was near death for months and never completely recovered. In 1849, no longer able to endure slavery, she simply left for the north one night with two of her brothers. Her brothers turned back, but she continued to Pennsylvania, where she quickly became involved in the Underground Railroad, an elaborate network of routes, guides, and hiding places that moved slaves to freedom in the north. She became one of the most active "conductors," and earned the name Moses. In spite of a reward of $40,000 for her capture, she helped at least 300 slaves reach freedom. She worked as a cook and a spy during the Civil War and continued working for human rights well into her eighties, appearing on the same platform as Susan B. Anthony. When she finally received a government pension, she used the money to find homes for the needy; she was still serving others when she died at age 93.

EMBRACING ———————————————————————— *Freedom*

NELSON ROLIHLAHLA MANDELA (1918–)

Born in Transkei, South Africa, he was the son of a chief of the Xhosa. Gifted with a strong will and a quick mind, he decided to fight the oppressive system of apartheid through the practice of law. He studied law at Witwatersrand University and set up his law practice in Johannesburg in 1952. He had joined the African National Congress (ANC) in 1944 and was already committed to a non-violent approach to dismantling apartheid. He was elected president of the ANC in 1951 and this marked the beginning of real turbulence in his life. He spent a total of twenty-seven years in prison, mostly on charges of high treason (apartheid perception of wanting equality, freedom, and dignity for the blacks of South Africa). Even in prison he continued to inspire those still involved in the struggle, and when he was released in February 1990 he received a tumultuous welcome wherever he went. He is the most significant political prisoner of the 20th Century and the most important reformer in South Africa. His life has become a symbol of human rights. He became the first president of a black majority-ruled South Africa and was awarded the Nobel Peace Prize in 1993.

SUN YAT-SEN (1866–1925)

Born into a peasant household in Choyhung in Kwangtung, China, near the Portuguese colony of Macao, he was established by his birthplace as a man of two worlds—China and the West. After a few years in a village school he was sent to Hawaii to join his elder brother. He enrolled in Iolani School, an Episcopal college preparatory school, where he focused on a study of science and religion. He graduated in 1882 and returned to his village in China. He spent his formative years in Hong Kong and, after beginning his medical studies in Canton, returned to Hong Kong, where he graduated from medicine in 1892. He became more interested in politics and was appalled by the Manchu government's corruption, inefficiency, and inability to defend itself against foreign aggressors. He became the preeminent leader of China's republican revolution and was instrumental in the overthrow of the Manchu dynasty in 1911 and the eventual reunification of the country.

MARTIN LUTHER KING, JR. (1929–1968)

Born in Atlanta, Georgia, he attended the Atlanta public schools and graduated from Morehouse College in 1948. He was educated for the ministry at Crozer Theological Seminary and was ordained into the National Baptist Church. He received a doctorate in theology from Boston University in 1955 and it was while he was in Boston that he met and married Coretta Scott. While serving a church in Montgomery, Alabama, he became active in the National Association for the Advancement of Colored People (NAACP) and the Alabama Council on Human Relations. In 1955, when Rosa Parks was arrested for violating a segregated seating ordinance on a public bus, King and Ralph Abernathy, a fellow minister, organized a bus boycott. The boycott ended in triumph for black dignity, and King became a national hero. Organizing "Freedom Riders," voter registrations, lunch counter sit-ins, freedom walks and rallies for civil rights modeled after the non-violent protests of Gandhi, King became one the most important black leaders of his era. He was assassinated on April 4, 1968, while standing on a hotel balcony in Memphis, Tennessee.

Freedom ————————————————— EMBRACING

PUT FREEDOM INTO ACTION

- Make good choices about what you eat.
- Make sure you understand rules and directions; and then follow them.
- Make sure everyone is included in your activities.
- Always treat others fairly and equally.
- Make good choices about language and what you say to others.
- Make sure everyone is invited to play during recess.
- Follow the rules even when no one is looking.
- Stand up and support someone who is treated unequally.
- Make good choices about watching TV and reading.
- Think about the way your language might be affecting others.
- Set an example as a "good sport."
- Always "play fair" in games and in relationships.
- Practice the Golden Rule.

COMMUNITY SERVICE IDEAS

- Write letters for Amnesty International.
- Volunteer with the Humane Society or another animal shelter.
- Create banners extolling the virtue of freedom. Hang them up in your community.
- Plan a class parade to celebrate "freedom."
- Make a scrapbook of poems, stories, and songs with freedom themes. Donate the scrapbook to your school library.

BOOKS ON FREEDOM

All the Lights in the Night. Arthur A. Levine. New York: Tambourine Books, 1991.

To Be a Slave. Julius Lester. New York: Dial Press, 1968.

Follow the Drinking Gourd. Bernadine Connelly. Lincoln: GPN, 1993.

Journey of Meng: A Chinese Legend. Doreen Rappaport. New York: Dial Books for Young Readers, 1991.

Molly's Pilgrim. Barbara Cohen. New York: Lothrop, Lee & Shepard Books, 1983.

Nettie's Trip South. Ann Turner. New York: MacMillan, 1987.

The Red Comb. Fernando Pico. Mahwan: Bridgewater Books, 1994.

Seminole Diary: Remembrances of a Slave. Dolores Johnson. New York: MacMillan, 1994.

Sweet Clara and the Freedom Quilt. Deborah Harris. New York: Knopf, 1993.

Zoo. Anthony Browne. New York: Knopf, 1992.

A Call to Character. Colin Greer and Herbert Kohl, eds. New York: Harper Collins Publishers, 1995.
    "The Candle" – p. 288
    "Harriet Tubman is in My Blood" – p. 64
    "I Have A Dream" – p. 401
    "Just Like Morton" – p. 79
    "Running as a Spiritual Experience" – p. 60
    "Understood Betsy" – p. 58

A 4th Course of Chicken Soup for the Soul. Jack Canfield, "etal." Deerfield Beach: Health Communications, Inc., 1997.
    "Song of the Bird" – p. 150

The Moral Compass. William J. Bennett, ed. New York: Simon and Schuster, 1995.
    "The Bundle" – p. 749
    "The Death of Becket" – p. 357
    "The Pioneer Family" – p. 352
    "The Three Heavy Stones" – p. 748

RESOURCES FOR THE CLASSROOM

The Book of Virtues. William J. Bennett ed. New York: Simon and Schuster, 1993.

A Call to Character. Colin Greer and Herbert Kohl, eds. New York: Harper Collins Publishers, 1995.

Chicken Soup for the Soul. Jack Canfield and Mark Victor Hansen. New York: Guideposts, 1993.

Chicken Soup for the Teenage Soul. Jack Canfield, et al. Deerfield Beach: Health Communications, Inc., 1997.

A 2nd Helping of Chicken Soup for the Soul. Jack Canfield and Mark Victor Hansen. New York: Guideposts, 1995.

A 3rd Serving of Chicken Soup for the Soul. Jack Canfield and Mark Victor Hansen. New York: Guideposts, 1996.

A 4th Course of Chicken Soup for the Soul. Jack Canfield, et al. New York: Guideposts, 1997.

A 5th Portion of Chicken Soup for the Soul. Jack Canfield and Mark Victor Hansen. New York: Guideposts, 1996.

The Moral Compass. William J. Bennett ed. New York: Simon and Schuster, 1995.

Is Your Bed Still There When You Close the Door? Jane M. Healy. New York: Doubleday, 1992.

GENERAL RESOURCES

Books to Build On—A Grade-by-Grade Resource Guide for Parents and Teachers. John Holdren and E.D. Hirsch, Jr., eds. New York: Delta, 1996.

Educating for Character: How our schools can teach respect and responsibility. Thomas Lickona. New York: Bantam, 1991.

The Fifth Discipline. Peter M. Senge. New York: Doubleday, 1990.

Greater Expectations: Overcoming the culture of indulgence in America's homes and schools. William Damon. New York: Free Press, 1995.

How Good People Make Tough Choices. Rushworth M. Kidder. New York: Morrow, 1994.

Positive Discipline. Jane Nelson. New York: Ballantine Books, 1987.

Reclaiming Our Schools: A Handbook on Teaching Character, Academics, and Discipline. 2nd ed. Edward A. Wynne and Kevin Ryan. New Jersey: Prentice-Hall, 1996.

HEROES IN BOOKS

The Great Kapok Tree: A Tale of the Amazon Rainforest. Lynne Cherry. San Diego: Harcourt Brace, Jovanovich, 1990.

Beethoven Lives Upstairs. Barbara Nichol. New York: Orchard Books, 1994.

Lives of the Musicians. Kathleen Krull. San Diego: Harcourt Brace, Jovanovich, 1992.

Galileo. Leonard Everett Fisher. New York: Macmillan Publishing Company, 1992.

Shaka, King of the Zulu. Diane Stanley. New York: Morrow Junior Books, 1988.

The Great Alexander the Great. Joe Lasker. New York: Viking Press, 1983.

Theseus and the Minotaur. C. J. Naden. Mahwah: Troll Associates, 1981.

Perseus and Medusa. C. J. Naden. Mahwah: Troll Associates, 1981.

The Voyage of Osiris: a myth of ancient Egypt. Gerald McDermott. New York: Windmill Books, 1977.

The Sword in the Stone. Hudson Talbott. New York: Books of Wonder, 1991.

Johnny Appleseed: a tall tale. Steven Kellogg. New York: Morrow Junior Books, 1988.

Wolferl: the first six years in the life of Wolfgang Amadeus Mozart. Lisl Weil. New York: Holiday House, 1991.

Paul Bunyan, A Tall Tale. Steven Kellogg. New York: W. Morrow, 1984.

Go Free or Die: a story about Harriet Tubman. Jerry Ferris. Minneapolis: Carolrhoda Books, 1988.

What's the Big Idea Ben Franklin? Jean Fritz. New York: Coward, McCann, Geoghegan, 1976.

Honest Abe. Edith Kunhardt. New York: Greenwillow Books, 1993.

Gilgamesh the King. Ludmila Zeman. Montreal: Tundra Books, 1992.

The Trojan Horse. Warwick Hutton. New York: Margaret K. McElderry Books, 1992.

Mother Teresa, sister to the poor. Patricia Giff. New York: Viking Kestrel, 1986.

Good Queen Bess. Diane Stanley. New York: Four Winds Press, 1990.

Jane Goodall. Eleanor Coerr. New York: Putnam, 1976.

OTHER RESOURCES

Against Borders:
> *Promoting Books for a Multicultural World.* Hazel Rochman. Chicago: American Library Association, 1993.

The Best Years of Their Lives:
> *A Resource Guide for Teenagers in Crisis.* Stephanie Zvirin. Chicago: American Library Association, 1992.
>> A selective, annotative bibliography of fiction and non-fiction self-help works for teenagers, arranged under the following topics:
>>
>> *Family matters*   *School daze*
>> *Me, myself, and I*   *Crack, glue, or a six-pack or two?*
>> *Private property: don't touch*   *Wellness*
>> *Sex stuff*   *One plus one makes three*
>> *Death: romance and reality*

What Would We Do Without You?
> *A Guide to Volunteer Activities for Kids.* Kathy Henderson. White Hall: Betterway Publications, 1990.

Brothers, A Hebrew Legend.
> Florence Freedman. New York: Harper & Row, 1985.
>> This tale of brotherly love exemplifies the values of responsibility, compassion, generosity, commitment, sharing, and family.

Fables.
> Tana Reiff. Syracuse: New Readers Press, 1991.

When I Grew Up Long Ago:
> *family living, going to school, games and parties, cure and death, a comet, falling in love, and other things I remember.* Alvin Shwartz. Philadelphia: Lippincott, 1978.
>> Values from the "good old days."

The Newbery Award Reader:
> *A Collection of Short Fiction by Writers Who Have Won the John Newbery Medal.* Charles G. Waugh and Martin H. Greenberg, eds. San Diego: Harcourt Brace, Jovanovich, 1984.

BIBLIOGRAPHY

Resources for Buddhism

Tokunaga, Keiko, Graduate Student in Zen Buddhism, University of Hawaii, Honolulu, Hawaii.
Tsomo, Karma Lekshe, Philosophy Department, University of Hawaii, Honolulu, Hawaii.

Resources for Chinese Religions

Hsuan, Ko, (Aleister Crowley). *Tao Te Ching*. Maine: Samuel Weiser, Inc., 1995.
Ware, James R. *The Sayings of Confucius*. New York: Mentor Books, 1955.

Resources for Christianity

The Living Bible. Illinois: Tyndale House Publishers, 1971.

Resources for Hawaiian Stories

Alameida, Roy. *Stories of Old Hawaii*. Honolulu: Bess Press, 1997.
Kawaharada, Dennis. *Hawaiian Fishing Legends*. Honolulu: Kalamaka Press, 1992.
Pukui, Mary Kawena. *Folktales of Hawaii*. Honolulu: Bishop Museum Press, 1995.
Pukui, Mary Kawena. *'Olelo No'eau*. Honolulu: Bishop Museum Press, 1983.
Pukui, Mary Kawena. *The Water of Kane*. Honolulu: Kamehameha Schools Press, 1951.
Thompson, Vivian L. *Hawaiian Myths of Earth Sea and Sky*. New York: Holiday, 1996.

Resources for Hinduism

Bhagavad Gita. Trans. Prabhavananda, Swami, and Christopher Isherwood.
　New York: Mentor Books, 1944.
The Upanishads. Trans. Prabhavananda, Swami, and Frederick Manchester.
　New York: Mentor Books, 1948.

Resources for Stories from India

Ayier, V.A.K., *Stories of Vikramaditya*. Bombay: Dharatyia Vidya Bhavan, 1974.
Chandamama, Chandamama Publications: Vadapalani, Madras, India, December 1989,
　March 1994, April 1994.
Lao, Chaman. *Spiritual Stories of India*. Delhi: Publications Division, Ministry of Information &
　Broadcasting, Government of India
Vivekananda, Swami. *Stories for Children*. Calcutta: Advaita Ashrama, 1994.

Resources for Islam

Rumi, Jalal ad-Din. *Discourses of Rumi*. Trans. A.J. Arberry. Great Britain: Curzon Press, 1993.
Brown, Kerry and Martin Palmer. *The Essential Teachings of Islam*. London: Century
　Hutchinson Ltd., ed. 1987.

Darbanid, Afkham and Dick Davis, translators of Farid ud-Din Attar's work, *The Conference of the Birds*. New York: Penguin Books Ltd., 1984.

Fazl, Mirza Abu'l, ed. and translator, Selections from Mishkat-ul-Masabih, *Chowk Minar Anarkali Lahore*. Pakistan: Sind Sagar Academy, 1977.

The Effendi and the Pregnant Pot. Trans. Primerose Gigliesi and Robert C. Friend. Beijing: New World Press, 1982.

Khan, Maulana Wahiduddin. *God-oriented Life: In the Light of Sayings and Deeds of the Prophet Muhammad and his Companions*. New Delhi: Islamic Centre, 1992.

Nizam ad-Din Awliya: Morals for the Heart. Trans. Bruce B. Lawrence. New York: Paulist Press, 1992.

Rumi, Jalal ad-Din. Trans. Reynold A. Nicholson. *Rumi: Poet and Mystic*. London: George Allen and Unwin Ltd.,1968.

Rumi, Jalal ad-Din. Trans. E.H. Whinfield. *Teachings of Rumi: The Masnavi of Maulana Jalalu-'d-Din Muhammad I Rumi*. New York: E.P. Dutton & Co., Inc., 1975.

Yusaf, Ali Abdullah. *The Meaning of the Holy Qur'an*. Brentwood, Maryland: Amana Corporation, 1992.

Resources for Judaism

Buber, Martin. *Tales of the Hasidi*. New York: Schocken Books, 1975.

Fahs, Sophia Lyon and Alice Cobb. *Old Tales for a New Day*. New York: Prometheus Books, 1992.

Schwartz, Howard. *Gabriel's Palace, retold*. Oxford: Oxford University Press, 1993.

Resources for Stories from Other Cultures

Compton, Patricia A. *The Terrible Eek*. New York: Simon and Schuster, 1991.

Demi. *The Empty Pot*. New York: H. Holt, 1990

Freedman, Florence. *Brothers: A Hebrew Legend*. New York: Harper and Row, 1985.

Gerson, Mary-Joan. *Why the Sky is Far Away*. New York: Harcourt Brace, Jovanovich, 1974.

Goble, Paul. *Love Flute*. New York: Maxwell MacMillan International, 1992.

Han, Carolyn. *Tales from Within the Cloud*. Honolulu: University of Hawaii Press, 1997.

Heady, Eleanor B. *Jambo, Sungura*. New York: W.W. Norton and Co., 1965.

Kendall, Carol and Yao-wen Li. *Sweet and Sour Tales from China*. New York: The Seabury Press, 1979.

McDermott, Gerald. *The Stonecutter*. New York: Viking Press, 1975.

Polacco, Patricia. *Appelamando's Dreams*. New York: Philomel Books, 1991.

Rosen, Michael. *Crow and Hawk*. San Diego: Harcourt Brace, 1995.

San Souci, Robert D. *The Faithful Friend*. New York: Simon and Schuster, 1995.

Sierra, Judy. *Wiley and the Hairy Man*. New York: Dutton Children's Books, 1996.

Uchida, Yoshiko. *The Wise Old Woman*. New York: Maxwell MacMillan International, 1994.

Waite, Michael P. *Jojofu*. New York: Lothrop, Lee and Shepard Books, 1996.

STALKER

STALKER

A Novel

FAYE
KELLERMAN

An Imprint of HarperCollins*Publishers*

HarperCollins books may be purchased for educational, business, or sales promotional use. For information please write: Special Markets Department, HarperCollins Publishers Inc., 10 East 53rd Street, New York, NY 10022.

FIRST HARPER LARGE PRINT EDITION 2000

Library of Congress Cataloging-in-Publication Data is available upon request.
ISBN 0-06-019729-3 (Large Print)

00 01 02 03 04 ❖/RRD 10 9 8 7 6 5 4 3 2 1

This Large Print Book carries the
Seal of Approval of N.A.V.H.

This is a work of fiction. Names, characters, places, and incidents either are the product of the author's imagination or are used fictitiously. Any resemblance to actual events, locales, organizations, or persons, living or dead, is entirely coincidental and beyond the intent of either the author or the publisher.

To Jonathan, my #1 guy
To Barney, my #1 agent
To Carrie, editor par excellence,
who is always there for me

STALKER

1

IT SHOULD have happened at night, in a secluded corner of a dimly lit parking lot. Instead, it occurred at one twenty-five in the afternoon. Farin knew the time because she had peeked through the car window, glancing at the clock in her Volvo—purportedly one of the safest cars on the road. Farin was a bug on safety. A fat lot of good that was doing her now.

It wasn't fair because she had done everything right. She had parked in an open area across the street from the playground for God's sakes! There were people in plain view. For instance, there was a man walking a brown pit bull on a leash, the duo strolling down one of the sunlit paths that led up into the mountains. And over to the left, there was a lady in a denim jacket reading the paper. There were kids at the play equipment: a gaggle of toddlers climbing the jungle gym, preschoolers on the slides and wobbly walk-bridge, babies in the infant swings. Mothers were with them, keeping a watchful eye over their charges. Not watching *her*, of course. Scads of people, but none who could help because at the moment, she had a gun in her back.

Farin said, "Just please don't hurt my bab—"

"You shut up! You say one more word, you are dead!" The voice was male. "Look straight ahead!"

Farin obeyed.

The disembodied voice went on. "You turn around, you are dead. You do not look at me. Understand?"

Farin nodded yes, keeping her eyes down. His voice was in the medium to high range. Slightly clipped, perhaps accented.

Immediately, Tara started crying. With shaking hands, Farin clutched her daughter to her chest, and cooed into her seashell ear. Instinctively, she brought her purse over Tara's back, drawing her coat over handbag and child. Farin hoped that if the man did shoot, she and the purse would be the protective bread in the Tara sandwich, the bullet having to penetrate another surface before it could—

The gun's nozzle dug into her backbone. She bit her lip to prevent herself from crying out.

"Drop your purse!" the voice commanded.

Immediately, Farin did as ordered. She heard him rooting through her handbag, doing this single-handedly because the gun was still pressing into her kidneys.

Please let this be a simple purse snatching! She heard a jangle of metal. Her keys? Out of the corner of her eye, she saw the passenger door to her station wagon had been opened. Again, she felt the press of the gun.

"Go in. From passenger's side! You do it or I shoot your baby!"

At the mention of her baby, Farin lost all resolve. Tears poured down from her eyes. Hugging her child, she walked around the front of the car, thoughts of escape cut short by the metal at her tailbone. She paused at the sight of the open door.

"Go on!" he barked. "Do it now!"

With Tara at her bosom, she bent down until she found her footing. Then she slid into her passenger's seat.

"Move across!" he snapped.

Farin tried to figure out how to do this. The car had bucket seats and there was a console between them. With clumsy, halted motions, and still holding Tara, she lifted her butt over the leather-cushioned wall, and into the driver's seat, both now scrunched behind the wheel. Again, Tara started to cry.

"You shut her up!" he barked.

She's a baby! Farin wanted to shout. She's scared! Instead, she began to rock her, singing softly into her ear. He was right beside her, the gun now in her rib cage.

Don't look at him, Farin reminded herself. *Don't look, don't look, don't look!*

Staring straight ahead. But she could tell that the gun had shifted to Tara's head.

Think, Farin! Think!

But nothing came into her hapless brain, not a

thought, not a clue. Fear had penetrated every pore of her being as her heart banged hard against her breastbone. Her chest was tight; her breathing was labored. Within seconds, Farin felt her head go light, along with that ominous darkening of her vision. Sparkles popped through her brain . . . that awful sensation of floating to nothingness.

No, she hadn't been shot. She was going to pass out!

Don't pass out, you fool. You can't afford—

His voice brought her back to reality.

"You give me the girl! Then you drive!"

Tara was still on her lap, little hands grabbing Farin's blouse. Once Tara was out of her grip, Farin knew they both were helpless unless she *did* something.

Farin knew she had to *move*. Without warning, she pivoted around, using the solid weight of her shoulder bone to slam it against his gun-toting hand. Although the sudden move didn't dislodge the gun from his grip, it did push his hand away. Giving Farin about a second to spring into action.

This time, the console was her friend. Because now he had to get over it to do something to *her*. She jerked down on the door handle, then kicked open the metal barrier to the max. Still holding Tara, Farin bolted from her seat, and attempted to run away.

But her shoe caught and she tripped, falling toward the pebbly road.

What a klutz!

Thinking as she plunged downward: *Break the fall with your hip, cover Tara, then kick . . .*

She contorted, managing to land on her hip and shoulder, scraping her right cheek on the unforgiving, rocky asphalt. Immediately, she rolled on top of Tara. Finding her vocal cords, she let out a scream worthy of the best B horror movies.

A deep male voice shouting, *"What's going on over there?"*

Even from her poor vantage point, Farin thought that the shout might belong to the man with the brown pit bull.

Several popping sounds.

Oh God, she thought, *he's shooting at me!*

Farin prepared for the worst—the sting, the pain, the writhing and horror, or whatever was to come . . . because she'd never been shot.

But nothing penetrated her body.

Instead, the popping turned out to be her car's engine. Within moments, the Volvo's tires screeched as they peeled rubber. One of the back radials smashed over her left foot and ankle as the car blasted from its launch pad.

Now came the pain! It burst into her head and made her sob. Loud, but it didn't drown out Tara's piercing cries.

Oh God! My baby is hurt! She called out, "Somebody *help me*!" Her foot and ankle were pulverized, but agony also stabbed her entire lower body—

specifically legs and hips. Her stomach was a
bucking storm, her face felt as if attacked by a rag-
ing hive of bees. She could hardly breathe. She felt
as if she were having a heart attack. At least, she
could wiggle the toes on her right foot so she
knew she wasn't paralyzed.

While moaning back excruciating sobs of an-
guish, she could see the man with the brown pit
bull running toward her. He was yelling for help,
that Farin could tell. The pit bull was barking
wildly . . . menacingly. It was pulling against the
restraints. Suddenly, the dog broke loose from its
owner, galloping toward them at full speed!

Lunging toward them!

A huge leap into the air!

The final touch! She was going to be eaten alive!

The dog was within inches of her face.

She passed out just as the pit bull started to lick
her tearstained cheek.

❑

THE husband was pissed, trying to make Decker go
away by throwing him dirty looks. Not that
Decker blamed the guy. Nor did Decker, or his
twenty-five years of experience, take it personally.
Part of the job with a capital J.

"Look at her!" he exclaimed. "She's in pain—"

"Jason, I'm okay—"

"No, you're not okay!" Jason interrupted.

"You're a wreck. You and Tara have gone through hell!" Anger had made him red faced. Suddenly, his lower lip quivered. "You need your rest, Farin!"

He was about an inch away from breaking down. Decker understood the feeling firsthand, the help-lessness that clouded and infuriated. Men were supposed to protect their families. When they couldn't, the guilt washed over them like a tidal wave.

Truth be told, Farin Henley was a mess. The woman had deep lacerations on her left cheek, probably down her entire body as well. Her left leg was in a thigh-high cast. Not that the leg was bro-ken, the docs had told Decker. But her ankle had sustained multiple fractures. The more the leg was immobilized, the better the ankle would heal.

Even through the scrapes and scratches, Decker could tell that Farin was a "cute" woman. She had a round, pixie face framed with clipped, honey-colored hair. Big, blue eyes, which were red-rimmed at the moment. She appeared to be in her late twenties. Husband Jason was probably around the same age. Light skin surrounding dark brown eyes. He had a head of thick brown hair that had been blow-dried. His black eyebrows were shaped in a perfect arch. His teeth gleamed white al-though he had yet to smile. Medium height, but well built. Jason worked out.

Rather than a direct hit, Decker used the sideswipe approach. He looked down at the crib abutting

Mom's hospital bed, peering at the sleeping form. Tara's porcelain complexion was marred with scratches, but the wounds appeared superficial. The baby was sucking in her slumber.

Decker said, "What is she? About eighteen months?"

Farin wiped her tears. "Exactly."

Jason remained hostile. "What is this? A pathetic attempt to gain rapport?"

"Jason!" Farin scolded.

"Are you going to catch this monster?" Jason rolled his eyes. "Probably not. You have no idea—"

"We have an idea."

The room fell silent.

"And?" Jason asked expectantly.

Decker turned his attention to Farin. "Did you see your assailant's face, Mrs. Henley?"

Farin licked her cracked lips, and shook her head no. "He told me not to look." A hard swallow. "He said he'd shoot me if I did."

Jason said, "You don't look surprised, Lieutenant."

"We've had other reported carjackings," Decker said. "Most of them have been in daylight involving women with small children. The jacker—or jackers because we think it's a ring—tells you not to look or he'll shoot the kid."

"That's right!" Farin exclaimed. "He said he'd shoot . . ." She lowered the volume to a whisper.

"He said he'd shoot . . ." She pointed to Tara's crib. "What happened to the other women? Are they okay?"

"They're okay."

"Well, thank God for that." Farin was quiet. "Did I do the right thing, Lieutenant? By trying to escape?"

"You survived, Mrs. Henley. That means you did the right thing."

"Did the other women escape like I did?"

Decker ran his hands through his graying ginger locks. More silver than red at this point. What the hell! Rina loved him, and people rarely mistook Hannah for his granddaughter. Decker supposed he looked okay. Not *young*, but decent for a rugged, *older* guy. "They're alive," he answered. "They're ongoing cases. I can't tell you the specifics."

The specifics being the home invasions, the robberies, the beatings, and the rapes. The jackings had started two months ago, and had escalated in their violence. If the crimes continued unbridled, murder would be next. He had ten full-time Dees working the area—a joint effort between sex-crimes, CAPS, and GTA. With some luck, the crimes would stay in those three details, and leave Homicide out of the picture.

Jason squirmed. "This asshole has my wife's purse. I already changed the locks and canceled the credit cards."

"That's good thinking."

"Has . . ." Jason closed his eyes for just a second, then opened them. "In the other cases, did any of these . . . these people come back to the house?"

"No," Decker said.

Not yet, he thought.

Relief passed through Jason's eyes. He regarded his wife. "See, I *told* you this guy is a *coward*. Crooks who prey on women are cowards. Just *let* him come to me. He isn't going to come back, Farin. And if he does, I'm *prepared* for the SOB!"

Prepared meaning a gun. A *bad* idea unless Jason knew how to handle a firearm under pressure. Few gun owners did. There was nothing Decker could do to stop this man from buying protection. And he understood the motivation. He just hoped Henley was smart enough to stow the gun away from the kid. He'd have to get Henley alone and mention a few gun safety rules.

Farin said, "I keep thinking there was something I should have done . . . something I should have noticed."

Decker shook his head. "These guys are pros, Mrs. Henley. You did really well."

"So what are you doing to catch them?" Jason demanded to know.

"Talking to people like your wife . . . hoping they can furnish us with some important details."

"You just said the creeps ordered the women not to look."

"Maybe one of them managed to sneak a glance."

"So you have nothing. Basically, you're sitting on your derriere until someone does your work for you."

"Jason!" Farin scolded. "I'm sorry, Lieutenant—"

"You don't have to apologize for my behavior," Jason interrupted. He turned to Decker. "What are you doing about it?"

Five women working undercover, Decker thought. *And it ain't easy, bud, because we can't use babies as decoys. We've got to use dolls or dogs or other undercovers dressed up like elderly. Something to make these motherfuckers think they've got a mark.*

"I wish I could tell you more, Mr. Henley." Decker spoke calmly. "But I can't."

"Probably doing nothing."

Decker didn't answer him. To Farin, he said, "Are you up for walking me through the ordeal?"

"Yes."

"Are you sure?" Jason asked.

"I'm sure."

Decker looked at Jason. "Do you want to hear this?"

"Of course, I want to hear it."

"It'll make you mad."

"I'm already *mad*!" Jason snapped. "I'm furious! I'm . . . I'm . . ." He stopped talking and rubbed his forehead. "Do you have an aspirin on you? I'd ask the nurse, but the hospital charges five bucks per tablet."

Decker took out an ever-present bottle of Advil

from his coat pocket and tossed it to him. "Will this do?"

Jason popped two pills in his mouth and tossed them back. "Thanks."

"No problem." Decker pulled out his notebook and said to Farin, "Take it slowly."

Farin nodded.

Pencil poised, Decker said, "Fire when ready." He grimaced. "Sorry. Bad choice of words."

Farin smiled. "That's okay."

A bad choice of words that Decker had used with the five other carjacking victims. It had gotten a smile out of all of them, and it brought a smile to Farin, as well. Batting one thousand in the smile department. Too bad his solve rate wasn't nearly as impressive.

2

CINDY WASN'T the first cop to show on the scene, but she was the first female officer. By the time she and her partner, Graham Beaudry, were curbside, there was already a sizable gathering in front of the house. The group was confined to the sidewalk area, the lawn having been roped off by yellow crime tape. Items, ejected from the dwelling, lay

"That *isn't* the big picture right now, Officer Decker. There're kids inside. Mamacita starts shooting, we've got real problems."

"How old are they?" Cindy asked.

"Seven and nine." Brown popped a stick of gum into his mouth. "Sarge is figuring out the next move."

"Can't you talk her down?" Beaudry said.

"Not so far," Brown said. "She is *pissed*!" He looked at his watch. "Three-fucking-fifty-two in the afternoon. Couldnah waited for the four o'clock shift."

"Decker!"

Cindy turned and saw Tropper beckoning her with a crooked finger; then he handed her the megaphone. "We're pretty sure she has a gun. If she uses it, it would be bad."

"Very bad," Cindy agreed.

"I want you to talk to her, woman to woman. Keep her distracted. The rest of us are going in to rescue the kids."

Her eyes darted between Sarge and the amplifier. "What if she hears you coming in?"

"You just make sure she *doesn't*. Just keep her engaged in conversation. Keep the tongues wagging. That shouldn't be so hard to do. Here's a chance for you to use some of your fancy college psychology training."

Sarge's lips gave way to a smirk, showing straight but stained teeth. But underneath the sarcasm, Cindy could tell he was tense. At college, she had studied postgraduate criminology, *not* psychology. But now was not the time to correct him.

"What are their names, sir?"

"Ojeda," Sarge answered, overenunciating. "Luis and Estella Ojeda." Then he walked away to confer with the others.

She stood alone, megaphone in hand. Left out of the raid even though she was far slicker on her feet than Beaudry. Then she told herself to be charitable. Perhaps—just perhaps—Tropper really did *feel* she was the only one who could handle this woman. The situation was far too dangerous to be a simple rite of rookie passage. Even so, win or lose, she knew she was going to be judged.

Maybe Tropper wants you to garner some firsthand experience. Hmm. Did he even know what garner meant?

As much as she tried to be one of the gang, deep down, she was an elitist snob. You can take the girl out of the Ivies . . . Sarge was gesticulating . . . giving her the "go" sign. *Confidence*, she told herself. *Show 'em how it's done, college girl.* Depressing the button on the megaphone, she said, "Hey, Estella! You know you have some clothes out here?"

No response. Sarge was making frantic motions that said, *Keep talking, keep talking.*

Cindy said, "Looks like pretty good stuff—"

"Eeez sheet!" Estella yelled out from inside. "All de clozzes is sheet! He give all de nice clozzes to his *puta*!"

Luis said, screaming, "I no have *puta*! She es crazy!"

"He es liar!"

"She es crazy!"

"I *kill* him!"

"Es true," Luis shouted. "She kill me. I no move 'cause she kill me. She es crazy woman!"

Cindy spoke calmly. "Do you have a gun, Estella?"

"She have a big gun!" Luis answered. "She es crazy woman! *Loca en la cabeza!*"

Luis wasn't helping his case. Cindy said, "Come on out, Estella. We'll talk about it."

"I no talk no more times," Estella answered. "*He* talk. All he essays es lies!"

What next, Decker? Say something! Again, Cindy depressed the button. "Hey, where'd you get that little red dress, Estella? Over at Pay-off? I saw one just like it in the store window. I thought it was real cute. You've got good taste."

A moment. Then Estella said, "You buy it?"

"Nah, I didn't buy it."

"Why you no buy it?"

"I'm a redhead," Cindy said. "You gotta have dark hair for that number. You have dark hair, Estella?"

"I have dark hair," Estella answered. A pause. "Some peoples es in my house!"

"No, I'm outside," Cindy said.

"No, I hear peoples in my house!"

"Nah, we're all outside!" Quickly, Cindy said, "You know, Estella, there are lots of people looking at your terrific clothes. You've got great taste. You ever think of doing a yard sale? You could make some real money."

"The clozzes is sheeet!"

"No, they're not shit. I'm telling you, you have good taste." Cindy resisted the temptation to look at her watch. She knew she hadn't been talking for more than a minute though it felt like hours. "I like that slinky little purple dress. You must look dynamite in it."

"Porple no good for redheads," Estella answered.

"Yeah, you're right about that," Cindy said. "I also like the green satin blouse. Green's good for redheads."

"You like it, you take it. I no need no clozzes after I kill him."

Cindy said, "I'm telling you, Estella, you could make some real *money* with these clothes."

A long pause. Then Estella said, "How much you thin'?"

"Hundred bucks—"

"I no care! He gives all de money to de *puta*!"

"*I don' have puta!*" Luis screamed. "She es *crazy*!"

The woman's voice was laced with frenzy. "I no crazy!"

Cindy butted in. "Estella, come out here and we'll talk about it." From the corner of her eye, she saw Sarge leading the kids into one of the cruisers.

Thank goodness for that! But her job was far from finished. "I'll help you pick up the clothes—"

"You *arress* her!" Luis shouted. "You put her crazy ass in jail!"

Cindy said, "Luis, shut the hell up!"

"I shut him up for you—"

"No, no, no, Estella. Come on out. We'll talk—"

"I no move, Missy Redhead. I move, he take de gun. He estrong man. I no move. I no go *no* place. He move, and I shoot hole in his *cojones*."

"I no move, I no move," Luis said. *"Estella, mi amore. Te amo mucho. Tu sabes que tu estas mi corazón!"*

Estella was quiet and that was scary. Sarge suddenly materialized at Cindy's side. "Tell her we'll send a couple of men into the house. Tell her they'll handcuff him. That way, he can't hurt her if she moves. He can't take the gun away. And we'll be there to protect her."

Cindy nodded, and told the woman the plan. Estella was less than convinced of its workability. "I no wan no menses in de house. De menses no listen to de womans never! I hate de menses!"

"How about if I come in?" Cindy blurted out.

"What?" Sarge whispered. "Retract that immediately!"

Cindy took her finger off the button. "Why?"

"Because she's a loose cannon, Decker. Take it back or I'll charge you with insubordination."

Cindy knew he wouldn't do it. Her father wielded far too much power. She said, "I guess I misunderstood you, sir. You said you were sending officers into the house. I'm an officer so I didn't understand the problem. As a matter of fact, I still don't."

It wasn't *exactly* what Tropper had said. Sarge had talked about sending *men* inside. Still, Sarge was stuck. She could claim discrimination. He swore under his breath.

"You come in, Missy Redhead?" Estella was asking.

Cindy looked at Tropper. "What do I say, sir?"

Tropper's jaw was working a mile a minute. "Tell her you'll come in with several other officers—"

"How about with just my partner—"

"Decker, you want more of *us* than *them*. That way, Luis Ojeda doesn't even *think* about an overtake. Now *shut* up and do what I tell you to do!"

His point was a good one. Depressing the button, Cindy said, "Yeah, I'll come in, Estella. But I'm bringing a couple of buddies with me. Just in case Luis tries something funny."

"I no try nothin'," Luis protested. "She kill me."

Cindy said, "Is that okay with you, Estella?"

An elongated moment of silence. Then Estella said, "You come in and put de hancuff on? You arress him?"

"I'll put the handcuffs on him, Estella. You got my word on that."

"Hokay," the woman answered. "You can come in, Missy Redhead."

3

SHE FELT Tropper's breath on down her neck, his presence so palpable it was as if he was giving her little shoves. Flanking him were Graham Beaudry and Rob Brown. Plenty of backup, but she was still point person—the first one out as well as the most vulnerable. They had decided that Estella must see *her* first. It showed that the police could be trusted. In the currently charged atmosphere of police corruption, every point scored by the good guy carried some weight. Cindy's heart smashed against her chest. Yet, the fear invigorated instead of paralyzed.

They had come into the house through the back door—a safer move and less confrontational than front-door entries. The place was stuffy, the air moist and heavy.

Cindy shouted, "We're in the kitchen now, coming into the dining area. *Don't* move, Estella. We don't want any problem."

"Keep talking," Tropper whispered.

She said, "You don't want problems, and neither do we."

"No, I no like problems," Estella said.

"I no like problems, too," Luis agreed.

As Cindy stepped behind the dinette set, she

could see Estella's red-shirted back hunched over, a swath of black hair resting over her shoulders like epaulettes. The woman had a shotgun jammed between her husband's legs.

Cindy stretched her neck far enough to make out Luis's face. Drenched in sweat, his skin looked like steaming milk-laced coffee. A small man with small bones, he possessed a narrow face, which was rather effeminate except for a sparse mustache and a plug of hair between his lower lip and his chin. Traces of acne roughened his cheeks. He resembled a petulant teenager rather than the father of two children.

Leaning backward, she spoke to Tropper. "I see them. He's facing me, but she's got her back to us."

Tropper gave a signal to the others, and the three men drew their weapons. "Okay. You tell her that you're coming out in the open. Tell her we're behind her with our weapons drawn. Tell both of them *not* to move."

"Don't move, Estella," Cindy said. "I'm right in back of your dinette set, but do *not* turn around. I don't want Luis to make a grab for the gun."

"No, I no move," Estella answered.

"Good." Suddenly, Cindy realized that droplets were running down her own forehead. "Now, I'm stepping out into the open so Luis can see me and my buddies. I want him to see that we have guns aimed at his face. So he doesn't try anything dumb. You see me, Luis?"

"I see you—"

"She have red hair?" Estella interrupted.

"*Sí*, she have red hair."

"Real or no real," Estella inquired.

"Es look real," Luis answered.

"It is real." Perspiration rolled down Cindy's nose. "You see our guns, Luis?"

"I see."

"They work, Luis. They work really well and really fast. So don't do anything stupid."

"I no move."

Sarge whispered, "Tell her to remove the shotgun from his balls and lift it into the air. Tell her to move *slowly*. Then you take the gun; we take it from you. After that, you cuff her and the party's over."

"I cuff *her*?"

"Yeah, Decker, you cuff *her*," Tropper barked. "*She's* the one with the barrel in his crotch. What's the problem? Are you gonna do this or not?"

"Yes, sir. Of course, sir." A one-second pause. Then Cindy said, "Estella, I want you to take the gun and slowly, slowly lift it in the air—"

"I move, he take gun."

"He won't move now," Cindy said. "We have three guns pointed at his face."

"I no move, I no move," Luis said, frantically.

But Estella was also agitated. "I no move de gun. Why you no do what you say, Missy Redhead? You say you put hancuffs and arress him. Why you no do that?"

Tropper said, "Keep telling her that he's not going to try anything, that we've got the guns pointed at him!"

Cindy hesitated. "She sounds upset, sir. Why don't I just placate her, and do what I said I was going to do?"

"Because, Decker, if you walk around to cuff Luis, you're in line with her shotgun barrel."

Oh. Good point!

"Go get the gun," Tropper ordered. "Go on! Start talking!"

Cindy wiped her face with her sleeve. "I'd like to do what you want, Estella, but if I handcuff him, I'm right in front of your shotgun. That's not going to work."

"Why? I no shoot you, jus' Luis."

"You could shoot me accidentally. I know you wouldn't mean it, but it's just not going to work."

"You lie to me!" Estella hissed. "You es liar jus' like him!"

"Estella, we have three revolvers aimed at Luis's face. He's not going to move—"

"I no move," Luis concurred.

"Well, I no move, too," Estella said. "Luis es-trong. I move, he take de gun and shoot me."

Cindy blurted out, "How about if I come next to you, and I take the gun?" Immediately, she heard Tropper swear, but didn't dare turn to face him. "If you just stay still, and *don't* move, I can do that. I'll take the gun—"

"Then Luis take gun from you."

"I'm a very big woman, Estella. I could take Luis down in a minute."

Luis said, "She es bery beeeg, Estella! You give her de gun."

Shut up, Luis! Cindy was thinking. *Anything you say, she'll do the opposite.* Time moving in slo-mo, she waited for a response.

Estella said, "Luis is bery estrong—"

"So am I!" Cindy said. "Look, I'll talk so you can hear me, so you know I'm not sneaking up on you. Then I'll tap your shoulder when I'm right behind you—"

"I no sure . . ." Estella said. "I no thin'—"

"I'll talk you through it."

Tropper was growling! "This *isn't* what I ordered!"

"But she's going to go for it, Sarge!" Cindy persisted. "This way I'm not facing the barrel of her gun, and you three will be right behind me."

One second passed, then two . . .

"Please, Sergeant Tropper," Cindy whispered forcefully. "I can disarm her—"

Estella said, "I no *hear* you. Wha' you sayin'? I getting mad."

She looked at Tropper's furious face, knowing he was trapped. If he didn't respond soon, the situation would escalate. His voice snapped like a leather whip. "Do it! But tell her we're right behind you!"

Cindy said, "Okay, Estella, I'm coming in. My buddies are going to be right behind me, so Luis can see them. I'm starting now. I'm taking a couple of steps forward. You hear me, don't you—"

"*Sí*, I hear you! Wha' you thin'? I no have ears?"

"Now I'm taking a couple more steps. Luis is looking right at my buddies . . . at their guns. Is my voice getting closer?"

"*Sí*, I hear you."

"Okay, I'm right behind you now. I'm going to tap your shoulder. Don't move—"

"I no move."

"Luis, you don't move, either—"

"I no move."

"That's good. No one is going to move except me," Cindy said. "Now I'm putting my hand on your shoulder . . ." She touched the woman's bony joint. Estella remained motionless. "That's my hand—"

"Hokay."

"Estella, listen carefully, okay?"

"Hokay."

"I am going to bend down and put my arms around your waist, okay? Don't move—"

"I no move!"

Slowly, Cindy bent over, her chest touching the woman's back, her head peering over Estella's red-clad shoulder. She slipped her arms around a trim middle and wiggled her fingers. "You see my hands?"

"I see."

"You see my fingers?"

"*Sí.*"

"Okay, I'm going to take the gun from you now."

"Hokay."

"*Don't* move!"

"I no move!"

"Luis, if you move and I slip, you no have *cojones*. Do you understand me?"

"I no move, I no move!"

Cindy had had the primary academy training with shotguns. But she hadn't done much private practice with them on the range, choosing to hone an expertise with her service Beretta. But she did know that shotguns weren't warm and fuzzy firearms. They were hard to control, because they were heavy mothers. Estella was keeping hers stabilized by resting the stock in her lap. Her right hand was clenched around the pistol grip, the index finger inside the guard, resting on the trigger. Her left hand was underneath the slide handle—the pump. Both of her hands were shaking noticeably.

Cindy spoke quietly. "Don't move. I'm going to touch your hands." She placed her palms over Estella's fingers. Her skin was hot and damp.

"You feel my hands?"

"*Sí.*"

"Don't move your body, okay?"

"Hokay!"

Cindy began sliding her hands up and down the shotgun, feeling around for a stable, strong area to grip. It was difficult to find a spot because the wood and metal were wet and sticky from Estella's sweat. She hunted until she found a couple of semi-dry places that gave her leverage with the weapon. She grasped the gun, not talking until she was certain she had a strong hold on the weapon.

Finally, she said, "Take your hands away."

"I take my hans off?"

"Yes, take your hands off the gun, but don't move your body."

"You have de gun?"

"Yes, I have the gun. I've got a good grip on it. Take your hands away."

"Hokay . . ." But still she didn't move. "You *está segura* you have de gun?"

"I have the gun." Cindy remained calm. "I have a good hold on it. Take your hands away, but don't move your body."

"Hokay."

As soon as Estella's fingers were off the weapon, Cindy stood up and lifted the shotgun high in the air. Instantly, Beaudry took the gun. Luis jumped up, wiping sweat from his face. He screamed, "You arress that crazy bitch!"

"Cuff her, Decker."

"Wha'?" Estella turned an irate face toward Cindy. She was a pretty woman with big, black eyes, high cheekbones, smooth skin, and deep,

full lips. Why the hell would Luis want someone else?

More than that, what the *hell* did she see in him?
Maybe he had a big—

"Wha' he say?" Estella was screaming. "You
arress him! He have de *puta*!"

Cindy took out the handcuffs from her belt and,
in one fluid motion, turned Estella around and
brought the woman's right arm against her back.
She was seconds away from securing the left arm,
but then Estella suddenly realized what was happening. Wrestling in Cindy's grip, Estella started
spewing out high-pitched Spanish, punctuating
her tirade with curses and spit.

"Don't make this difficult—"

"You es una beetch! You eslying daughter of a put—"

"Let's not get personal." Cindy kneed her in the
back of her legs just hard enough to get Estella to
buckle. Once the woman's legs were bent, it was a
snap to bring her down, and lay her facedown on
the floor. Again, using knees and elbows to restrain
the writhing body, Cindy held Estella's right arm
flat against her back and rooted about for the left
one, which was trying to sock her in the face. Estella was no match for her in strength, but her resistance—the bucking and rolling—made Cindy
sweat from exertion.

Here was the big showdown, and it was *mano a
mano*. Because none of the others were making even
the slightest effort to help her. Instead, they were

standing around, watching with amusement as she struggled. Luis was buoyant, a big smile on his ugly face.

He said, "You go to *cárcel*, you *estúpida, loca*—"

Again, Estella spit in his direction. "He the one with the *puta*! He go to jail! Why *he* no go to jail!"

Luis was doing a victory dance. "Have fun wit de other beeeg ladies—"

"Graham, will you shut him up!" Cindy snapped.

To Luis, Beaudry said, "Shut up!"

Finding the flaying arm, Cindy gripped it and shoved it against Estella's back. She snapped on the loose cuff, then held her manicled arms firmly, and brought Estella to her feet. She said, "We can't send him to jail, Estella, because adultery isn't against the law. Otherwise politicians would have rap sheets a mile long."

Luis made kissy noises at his wife. Struggling against Cindy's hold, Estella tried to break away and kick him.

"Don't do that," Cindy said. "Otherwise, I'll have to tie your feet—"

"I hope de matrona in de *cárcel* is a *beeeg* woman—"

"You es *un diablo* with a *pequeño* pecker—"

"You arress her!" Luis shouted. "Slam her *lardo* ass in jail!"

"I no have *lardo* ass!" Estella screamed. "Your whore have *lardo* ass, beeg, fat ass!"

"Shut up! Both of you!" Cindy broke in. "Luis, you've got to come down to the station, you know."

"Wha'?" Luis's smiled waned. "Me? Wha' I do?"

"We've got to take your statement," Cindy said. "Also, you're going to have to go to court, and speak to a judge if you want to get your kids back. Otherwise, your kids'll end up in foster care."

"*Me?*" Luis's face registered shock. "I go do it?"

"Yeah, *you,* buddy," Cindy said. "Your wife can't do anything if she's in jail."

Tropper was glaring at her. She looked back at him with innocent eyes, and tried to smile. It wasn't easy because she was still restraining Estella. "I was just informing Mr. Ojeda of the procedure for securing his children, Sergeant. That's assuming he wants them."

Estella started foaming at the mouth. "You send de children away, I curse you from *mi cama de muerte*! I speeet on you!"

"No, no, Estella," Luis said gravely. "I no send de children away! I tell de judge. Don' worry."

Ron Brown muttered, "No way a judge is going to give you your kids back. Not with a *shotgun* in the house."

"I no shoot my kids!" Luis was appalled. "You take de gun. I no need it."

Estella was crying. "They take de kids away, Luis! You no let them—"

"They no take de kids!"

"You can petition to get them back, sir," Cindy said. "Or course, if your wife's in jail, you'll be responsible for them. That means you stay home at night baby-sitting while your buddies are out having fun—"

"Decker . . ." growled Tropper.

"Not that I'm trying to influence your decision to press charges, of course."

"They're not going to give them back the kids, anyway," Brown said. "You need to be a *responsible* adult to raise kids."

"Maybe there are other relatives," Beaudry said.

"Her mother." Luis brightened.

"You really think her mother's gonna watch *your* kids after you've slammed her daughter's butt in jail?"

"Decker, you've said enough!"

Cindy slammed her mouth shut. She couldn't understand why Tropper was taking it so personally when she'd seen her colleagues talk other domestic cases out of pressing charges time and time again. Maybe it had something to do with a gun aimed at a pair of nuts.

Estella was sobbing. "They take de kids, Luis! They take de kids!"

Luis's sassy petulance had been replaced by panic. "No, they no take de kids, Estella." He looked at Tropper. "I no charge my wife! She no do nothin'. You let her go! Then, we come down and get de kids."

Tropper was swearing to himself. "I don't believe this!"

Estella said, "He say I no do nothin'. You let me go!"

"It's not that simple," Cindy said. "Even if Luis doesn't press charges, Estella, we've still got to take you down to the station and book you for the illegal possession and negligent use of a firearm."

"Then wha'?" Luis asked.

Cindy said, "She'll wait in jail until her arraignment, which will be in maybe three, four hours. Then a judge will probably let her off on her own recognizance. Which means you won't have to pay any bail—"

"De judge don' put her in jail?"

Cindy shrugged. "I don't know what he'll do. But we'll have to put her in jail until a judge sees her." Tropper was giving her the evil eye. She pretended not to see him. "Usually illegal possession and negligent use of a firearm if it's a first-time offense doesn't warrant jail time. But *I don't know* what a judge will decide. It's not up to me."

"If he says I go home, do we get de kids?" Estella said, anxiously.

"No," Cindy said. "That's up to another judge—"

"But es better if there is a mother, yes?" Luis asked.

"Probably."

"So I no put charges," Luis said. "You let her go."

Brown chuckled with amazement. "She held a gun to his balls, and you're letting her off."

"He es hokay," Estella said.

"I hokay!" Luis confirmed.

Tropper said, "Bring them down. Charge both of them with felony possession."

"Charge me?" Luis said. "I no do *nothin'*."

"Yeah, yeah!" Tropper turned Luis around and cuffed him. "If you're telling me that you were both fooling around with the gun, the charges are possession and negligence against the both of you. That means you and your wife get slammed." Tropper paused. "Unless you change your mind about charging your wife."

"No, I no change my mind!"

"Then you're both under arrest," Tropper stated. "You made your bed, buddy. Now you lie in it."

"That's hokay," Estella said, nodding. "He eslie in de bed, but only with me."

Tropper rolled his eyes and propelled Luis forward. "Let's go!"

As they stepped outside and onto the front porch, cheers and hoots from the neighborhood crowd greeted them. Estella had lowered her head as they walked to the cruisers, but Cindy noticed that Luis was smiling broadly. Probably would have waved if his hands hadn't been cuffed.

His thirty seconds of fame. That's Hollywood for you. Everyone's a friggin' star.

4

Though Bellini's hadn't become Cindy's second living room, at least it was comfortable. More than just a hard-core cop bar, it offered chops and sandwiches as well as salads and soups for the lighter fare. Cozy in size, the place had dim lighting, jazz music, and a big-screen TV, which, at the moment, was airing baseball—Giants–Padres. The floors were pine-planked and worn, and the ceilings held acoustical tiles. A half-dozen tables sat in the center area while red-Naugahyde booths lined the left wall. The right side was dedicated to the bar, its mirrored wall reflecting a black counter, which spanned the length of the restaurant. Technically, the law mandated the eatery to be smoke-free. But the patrons skirted the issue by opening up the back door, claiming the area to be an extension of a nonexistent patio. A moot point because who was going to cite the owner when the law was puffing away?

As Beaudry came in, he waved to a few of his friends. Cindy waved just to feel like one of the gang. Ron Brown was sitting on one of the bar stools, but Tropper wasn't with him. In an eye blink, Cindy caught sight of someone's back as he left the place. It could have been Sarge, but she wasn't sure. There were several others that she knew by name. Andy Lopez was an academy acquaintance. There was also Slick Rick Bederman and his partner, Sean Amory. Bederman was solidly built with dark eyes and thick, curly hair, his face, as always, stamped with arrogance. She had met him once at a party . . . hadn't liked the way he had looked at her. Amory was lighter in his coloring, but also projected 'tude. Beaudry must have caught her ambivalence. He said, "Feel like being social?"

"Maybe later."

They ordered their beers, then took a booth, sipping for a few moments without talking. Beaudry was beating time to the music, fingertips drumming the table. It was soft jazz, the sax singing in a breathy voice which teased like foreplay.

Finally, Beaudry said, "So you did all right today."

"Thanks."

"Chalk one up for the good guys."

Cindy said, "Are we the good guys? You wouldn't know it by reading the papers."

Beaudry waved her off. "This ain't the first scandal and it won't be the last."

"That's too bad."

"Yeah, I suppose." Beaudry picked up his mug. "Still, I'm not losing sleep over it. So you're sure you're okay with today?"

"I'm okay with it." Cindy managed a smile. "I

doubt if Tropper's okay with it. So he's pissed at me. *He's* not the first, he won't be the last."

Beaudry raised his eyebrows, but said nothing.

"What?" Cindy asked. "You're gonna give me some advice?"

"If you're okay with it, I've got nothing to offer."

"So why're you looking at me like that?"

"Like what?"

"Like I've got herpes—"

"You're being touchy, Decker. I'm not looking at you at all. And if I was looking at you, I wouldn't be thinking about herpes. I'd be thinking that you look good in that black pantsuit outfit you're wearing. That it goes good with your hair, which looks pretty when it's loose." He sipped beer. "That wasn't a come-on. I've got a marriage, and I want to make it last. That's just an old-fashioned, blue-collar compliment, so don't go filing any sexual harassment complaints."

"I look good tonight?"

"You look good tonight."

"Thanks." Cindy took another sip of suds, then licked the foam off her lips. "So you think I fucked up?"

"Nah, you didn't fuck up as far as the incident goes. You handled the situation pretty good." He looked around at nothing. "Nah, you didn't fuck up with the situation."

"But I fucked up with Tropper!" Cindy tapped her toe. "Do *you* think I fucked up with Tropper?"

"Not exactly—"

"What does that—"

"Wait, wait, wait!" Beaudry held out his palms in a stop sign. "Give me a sec, okay. You didn't fuck up with him, meaning that he isn't gonna make a federal case out of it. But you might think of doing something nice for him."

"Like what?" She sneered. "Getting him coffee? One lump or two—"

"Don't be a brat. Just . . . think about it."

She laughed. "I haven't been called a brat in a while."

"But you've been called one before."

"Oh yeah."

"It's written all over your face, Decker. 'I am a brat. Not only a brat, but a snotty, educated brat.' "

Cindy maintained the smile, but the eyes dimmed. "That's how you see me?"

"No, that's not how *I* see you." Beaudry sighed. "It's just that you're out there, Decker. Like today. You put yourself . . . *out* there. Right in the firing line. And when you're out there, people notice you. Like Tropper."

"It *worked*."

"That's not the point."

"Silly me, I thought it was."

Beaudry wiped suds off his mouth with his sleeve. "Listen, we don't have to be talking about this. We can talk about other stuff. You tell me your gossip, I'll tell you mine. I'm just trying to . . . you know. Tell you like it is."

She averted her stare. "Look, Graham, no offense, but I'm not in the mood to be dissected."

"That's fair enough."

"On the other hand, no sense being on the outs with Tropper." She stared at her beer. "What should I do for him?"

Beaudry looked around then called her closer. She leaned in, elbows on the table.

He said, "Tropper isn't a stupid man—"

"I didn't say he—"

"Just shut up and listen, okay?" He lowered his voice. "He isn't stupid, Cin. He's got great street smarts. He knows how people operate."

He waited. Cindy said, "I'm listening."

"If you ask him to recount an incident, he's crystal. He can recap from A to Z in perfect detail. The problem comes when he tries to write it down in a report. He's a fish out of water. It takes him centuries to finish his forms. Writing confuses him. He gets things out of order—"

"He can't sequence?"

"Something like that. He's constantly rewriting his reports because the old ones are always messy-looking."

"Why doesn't he just use Word?" she asked. "You know . . . cut and paste?"

"He has trouble with computers. The keyboard

confuses him." Beaudry finished his first brew, held up a finger, signaling the waitress for a second. "Computers probably aren't your problem, right?"

"Not word processing."

"And I don't imagine you have trouble with report writing, either."

"I find it mind-numbing, but it's not difficult. I did lots of papers in college. I usually outlined them before I wrote. You know, occasionally, I'll still outline a report if the incident was complicated—lots of people coming and going. You might suggest he try that."

"I don't suggest anything to Tropper, and you shouldn't either. I think the Sarge got into the academy with a GED. So now you know why he sneers at you."

Beaudry locked eyes with her.

"It's something you should be aware of, Cindy. The guys and gals you're working with are the salt of America. Lots of us are ex-military. We're G-workers who hate the nine-to-five, but still want a good pension. You're from another planet—a college brat who somehow wandered into law enforcement. Not only college, but a *private* college—"

"Let's not forget an Ivy Leaguer."

"See, *that's* what I mean!" Beaudry pounded the table for emphasis.

"I'm sorry." She tried to stop smiling. "It was just too tempting—"

"Forget it."

"Graham, I hear you." She poked her finger into the suds and licked it. "You know, if the guys think I grew up rich, then they're stupid. My father climbed through the ranks the hard way."

"Which brings us to another point, Decker. You gotta stop talking about your father—"

"Ah, c'mon! Now you're getting personal!"

"I'm just telling you for your own good."

"Do I do *anything* right?"

"Not much."

Cindy looked away, biting her lip to control her rising temper.

Beaudry said, "Every time we start shooting the bull, talking about the day, you say things like, 'Yeah, my father once had a case like that.' "

"I'm trying to *relate*."

"It pisses people off. It makes them think that their experiences are nothin' special. Everyone wants to feel special. You already feel special because you've got all this college. You gotta remember that the average Joe on the force is a high school graduate, maybe a couple of years at a junior college like me. If you're real smart, okay, you do a four-year state, then enter the academy with the idea of doing the gold."

"Like my dad—"

"*Stop* mentioning your dad. He isn't a legend, Decker, he's a pencil pusher."

For the first time, Cindy was genuinely offended. "That's crap, Beaudry! He was down in the trenches when the Order blew up."

"Yeah, and a lot of people have said he could have handled that better."

Her face grew red with anger. "What a truckload of bullshit!" She whispered fiercely. "He saved dozens of kids—"

"But lots of adults were pulverized—"

"He wasn't in *charge*, Graham. He wasn't calling the shots!" She winced. "Ah, screw it! I've had enough."

Beaudry caught her arm before she got up. "I'm not criticizing your dad, Cindy. Just repeating what I've heard. You gotta know these things." He let go of her. "Otherwise, you're working blind."

She didn't answer, staring at the bottom of her empty glass. Beaudry said, "Take a refill."

"No, thanks," she said stiffly.

Within moments, a waitress appeared. She wore a low-cut red tank top, a petticoat-red miniskirt topped by a white, ruffled apron, and red heels. Her hair was short, blond, and sprayed stiff. She placed a glass of beer in front of Beaudry.

"How about another for my partner, Jasmine," he said.

"I'm fine, thank you," Cindy said.

Under the table, Beaudry kicked her.

"On the other hand, another would go down real

smooth." Cindy gave the waitress her empty glass and a ten spot.

Jasmine smiled. "Boss says that tonight it's on the house. Just as long as you don't get greedy."

"What did I do to rate?"

"He's been watching you. You came three times this week. He wants to reward your loyalty."

"Tell him thanks." Cindy forced herself to smile. "Really. And keep the bread."

Jasmine's smile turned into a grin. "A cop with class. Be back in a minute."

When she was gone, Beaudry said, "Ten's a big tip."

"Easy come, easy go."

He slid his glass across the table. "Here, take mine."

"No, that's okay." She slid it back.

He took a long swig. "You're pissed, Decker. You look like my wife did when I fucked up with her anniversary gift."

"I'm fine."

Beaudry waved her off. "The gossip about your dad is sour grapes, Cin. The little guys getting back at the one who's made it. Any of us would love to be in Big Decker's shoes. But that's not the point. You keeping talking about Daddy, it looks like you're hanging on to his coattails. It also reminds the rank and file that they haven't gotten as far. Not that your dad doesn't deserve it. His rep is a good one. But you gotta stop being so concerned about him and start being more concerned about yourself. Start thinking about what *you've* done lately."

Again, Cindy averted her glance. She reached across the table and took Beaudry's brew. "So getting back to Tropper . . . what do I do?"

"Tell him you have some free time and it makes you antsy. Ask him if he needs any favors."

"He'll say no."

"Course, he'll say no. Then you say something about the pile of crap lying inside his 'in' box. You say something like, 'Hey, Sarge. Lemme clear some of your paperwork. I'm doing some of my own reports. Lemme type up a couple of your hand-written ones.' "

"He'll see right through it."

"Yeah, he will. He'll know you're trying to kiss ass. But I bet he'll take you up on it. He'll act like it's no big deal. Real casual. But he'll remember it."

"And that'll be that?"

"That'll be that." Beaudry looked around the place. It was filling up by the minute. "I've got to get home to Sherri and the kids. What's today?"

"Today's the twenty-first."

"What day of the week?"

"Thursday."

"Ah . . . that's our chili night. That's a good one. You drink up my beer. I want to save some room for the brewskis with my dinner. Chili and beer. Now there's a perfect marriage for you. If only men and women were chili and beer."

❑

AT that point, she probably should have cut her losses and gone home. Instead, Cindy surveyed the room for civil faces if not friendly ones. Beaudry's comments had left her disconcerted. She didn't want to play the role of the stand-alone, crusading against the world. The maverick made for fine fiction, but was a bitch in reality.

What she wanted was to *blend* in. What the hell was wrong with her?

Ah well, she sighed. She couldn't change the past, so she concentrated on the present. Andy Lopez and his partner, Tim Waters, were still at the bar. Andy seemed like a straight-up guy. Tim didn't impress her much. Conversation with them would be strictly lightweight.

Gotta do better than that.

At one of the tables were Hayley Marx and Rhonda Nordich. About thirty, Hayley was a seven-year vet. She was tall—at least five ten—and had short blond hair and sharp brown eyes. Rhonda was a civilian who worked the front desk at the detectives' squadroom. She was older . . . in her forties, maybe even fifties. She had deep, smoky skin and short kinky hair that was more salt than pepper. Cindy had exchanged pleasantries with Hayley, but had never spoken to Rhonda. But they seemed preferable to Lopez and Waters.

Beer in hand, she stood and ambled over. Hayley looked up, then went back to her white wine. "Get a load off."

"Thanks." Since the two women were across from each other, she was forced to sit beside one. She turned to Rhonda and held out her hand. "Cindy Decker."

"Rhonda Nordich." She shook Cindy's hand. "I worked with your father way back when."

"In Foothills?"

"Yeah, in Foothills. He's at Devonshire now, isn't he?"

She nodded.

"He was a nice guy." Rhonda chuckled and swirled her club soda. "Probably still is. Why do you do that? Talk about a person you knew in the past like they was dead?"

Cindy smiled. "I don't know."

"Well, say hi for me."

"I will."

No one spoke. Everyone drank.

Hayley said, "I see they got you partnered with Beaudry."

"Yeah."

"So what do you think?"

Cindy was taken aback by the frankness of Marx's question. "He's a good guy."

"Yeah?"

"Yeah. Why? Is there something I should know?"

Hayley sipped her Chardonnay. "Well, put it this way. He ain't gonna qualify for the marathon."

"Oh . . . that. Yeah, I already know about that."

"About what?" Rhonda asked.

Cindy said, "He's a little slow with his footwork."

Hayley said, "You know, rumor has it that Slick Rick Bederman requested a transfer because of that. He was wrestling with a perp who had a knife. By the time Beaudry got there, the perp almost sliced an ear off. I'm not saying Beaudry's not a good guy. Just telling you the pitfalls. So don't go thinking I'm talking against him."

"Not at all." Still, Cindy felt uncomfortable. "I appreciate it. But I'm okay with him."

"Suit yourself." Hayley finished her glass of wine. "Are you just drinking tonight or what?"

"I've got nothing special on my roster."

"We're going to have some grub. You're welcome to join us."

Cindy smiled. "Well, there is that two-day-old bowl of pasta in my fridge."

Hayley finally smiled. "That's pathetic."

Rhonda said, "You young ones just don't cook anymore."

Cindy said, "I can cook." A pause. "I just choose *not* to—"

"Uh-huh," Rhonda said.

"It's a volitional thing," Cindy said.

Hayley said, "Now, Rhonda, if you're dying to cook for us—"

"After four kids, I've had enough with feeding mouths. Only mouth I want to feed right now is my own."

Cindy said, "What's good here?"

"How hungry are you?" Hayley asked. "Sandwich hungry? Or steak or chop hungry?"

"More sandwich than chop."

"Try the beef dip," Hayley said.

"Maybe I'll have the beef dip," Rhonda said. "Although I should have the turkey dip. I'm watching the fat."

"Turkey dip's not as good as the beef dip." Hayley turned to Cindy. "It's very dry."

Cindy said, "You know, Rhonda, I'll have the beef dip, and we can split, if you want."

"If you're having the beef dip, then maybe I'll have the tuna," Hayley said. "You don't mind if I steal a little from you . . . although tuna and beef dip don't exactly go together."

"Well, it's not steak and lobster," Cindy said.

"Maybe I'll have the pastrami on rye," Hayley said. "Do you like pastrami, Cindy?"

"I love pastrami."

"Now I'm not touching that!" Rhonda said. "Talk about fat."

"That's no good," Hayley said. "If you want to

split, Ro, I'll take something else. How about ham and cheese?" She turned to Cindy. "You like ham and cheese?"

"Not really. I don't eat ham. I'm Jewish."

"Oh . . ." Hayley thought for a moment. "So you're kosher?"

"No, I'm not kosher, I just don't eat ham. We never had it growing up. Although sometimes we did have bacon."

"That doesn't make any sense."

"I know." She shrugged.

Hayley said, "So if I had a club, you'd split that?"

"Yeah, I'd split that."

"And that's okay with you, Ro?"

"What's in a club?"

"Turkey, bacon, and avocado."

"Skip the avocado. It's not that I don't like avocado." She patted her sizable middle. "It doesn't like me."

Hayley pouted. "But that's the best part."

"All right, so keep the avocado."

Cindy said, "What are we ordering? I'm confused."

"I'll handle it." Hayley motioned Jasmine over. She said, "A beef dip with extra onions and lots of gravy, French fries and slaw, a turkey dip with extra cranberries, mashed potatoes instead of stuffing, and slaw, and a club on toasted rye, half with avocado, half plain."

"You want fries with that, Marx?"

"Yeah, you can give me fries."

"Refill on the wine?"

"Yeah."

"Another Miller Lite for you, hon?"

Cindy thought a moment. "Better make it a Diet Coke."

"Why?" Hayley asked. "How many beers have you had?"

"I just finished number three. I'm okay, but let's not tempt the booze fairy."

"I'm also on number three." Hayley made a face. "Make mine a Diet Coke, too."

"Got it." Jasmine looked over the order, then at Cindy. "Which order is yours?"

"Why?" Hayley asked.

"Because hers is on the house."

Rhonda and Hayley started hooting.

"Why?" Cindy smiled. "What's so funny?"

Hayley said, "Doogle is at it again."

"Who is *Doogle*?"

"The horny leprechaun who owns the place."

Jasmine said, "Don't listen to them, honey. They're just jealous. Now what's your order?"

"What is my order?" Cindy asked the others. "The beef dip?"

"What's the most expensive item we have?" Rhonda asked.

"The club."

"Hers is the club."

Jasmine laughed. "You guys!" She turned and walked away.

Cindy said, "Who is this Doogle?"

"A very little man." Hayley marked about two feet off the ground with her hand. "Hits on all the women."

"On cops?"

"On anything with a moo-moo," Rhonda said.

"A *moo-moo*?"

Hayley said, "He could suck my pussy standing up if I'd let him."

"How tall is he?"

" 'Bout five three. Maybe fifty years old—"

"He sounds perfect," Cindy said. "Actually, he sounds like my last blind date."

"He's got money," Rhonda said.

"Well, that part isn't bad."

"Those types are always stingy," Hayley said. "You know, I make it, I spend it. You lick my balls, and maybe I'll give you meter money."

Cindy laughed. "Been there, done that."

Hayley laughed, too. "Are we sounding drunk yet?"

"No, just plain bitter," Cindy said.

"Uh-oh!" Hayley said. "Look who just walked in. Ole sleaze in a bottle." She gave him a little wave. "Look out, he's coming our way."

Cindy turned around, then felt her skin go hot. She hoped they hadn't noticed, but knew they had.

She was saddled with a near white complexion and that was a dead giveaway. She blushed whenever she became angry, embarrassed, or extremely aroused.

Or so she had been told.

5

HE WAS dressed ninja-style—black T-shirt and black cords under a black leather jacket, a blazer as opposed to a bomber. His dark hair was combed straight back, and silvered at the temples. His eyes gave off that wary cop look that Cindy had seen umpteen times on her father's face. But his body was loose, and at ease. He didn't walk over to them; *he ambled*, as if being a detective afforded him rights to which low-life uniforms weren't privy. He took the empty seat across from Cindy, but he regarded Hayley straight-on. It seemed to unnerve her.

"So what brings you out here?" Hayley managed eye contact while wolfing down the last of her Chardonnay. "Slumming?"

"Some of us actually work after hours, Marx."

"And what are you working on?" Hayley asked. "The new scouts don't come in until September."

He grinned a mouth full of white teeth, while signaling the waitress for a drink. "How you talk to your superiors."

"You aren't my superior," Hayley retorted.

"Not right now, but never say never."

Hayley looked to her left, at Cindy. "Cindy Decker, Scott Oliver."

"We know each other." Oliver's tone was breezy. "I work with her daddy. Or rather I work *for* her daddy now. Big Decker is my loo."

"You work Devonshire?" Rhonda asked.

"Yeah," Oliver answered. "I was there in Homicide a full two years before Deck came on board—the slimy interloper."

"Uh-oh," Cindy said. "Do I want to hear this?"

"Nothing to hear." Oliver flashed her a mouthful of teeth. "I've made my peace with it."

But the look in his eyes said that was debatable. Cindy said, "How is he as a boss?"

"Depends what day you catch him on." Oliver turned his eyes to her. "How is he as a father?"

"Depends what day you—"

"Uh-huh."

Cindy chuckled. "You probably see him more than I do."

"Probably." Oliver returned his attention to Marx. "You're looking well."

"No thanks to the scuzzballs out there."

"Was that a dig at the present company?"

Hayley smiled. "I'm taking the fifth."

Jasmine came over with their food and drink. "Hey, Oliver. I haven't seen you in a long time. Re-visiting old haunts?"

"Wish it were the social thing," Oliver said. "I'm meeting Osmondson."

"So you're doing beeswax. Should I reserve the corner booth?"

"Thank you, that would be nice."

The table fell silent as Jasmine doled out the sandwich plates—the club for Cindy, the turkey dip for Rhonda, and the beef dip for Hayley. She plunked a beer in front of Oliver. "You know what Rolf is drinking these days?"

"Last time I saw him it was straight Stoly," Oliver said.

"I think he's off the booze. I'll bring over a club soda. If he wants something stronger, he can ask for it."

Oliver looked at his beer. "You know what, Jasmine? I've actually got to concentrate tonight. I'll take a club soda."

"I'll switch you," Cindy said. "One Diet Coke for a beer."

Hayley chuckled. "She's going for the buzz."

"Nah, I'm fine—"

"Famous last words."

Oliver gave Cindy his beer. "It's on me. And you can even keep your Diet Coke."

Hayley was looking at the bar stools. Andy Lopez

and Tim Waters were giving them eyes. "You're attracting the gnats."

Oliver laughed. "Nah, Marx, it's your pheromones—"

"No, it's you," Hayley interrupted. "Since you're here, your species thinks it's okay to approach."

"My species?" Oliver said. "Last time I took science, we're the same species."

"Not according to anyone I've ever talked to."

"Now *that* is a very good point." Oliver's eyes went to the door. He stood up. "I see my date."

Cindy turned around. Rolf Osmondson was big, bald, with a sizable belly. He wore a handlebar mustache. He looked as if he'd been exploring the fiords. She said, "He doesn't seem like your type, Scott."

Oliver regarded her with a mock, aghast expression. "Now *you're* getting in the act?"

"Just showing solidarity with my sisters."

Oliver wagged a finger at her. "Don't draw lines in the sand, Decker, unless you're prepared for battle." He ran his index finger across Hayley's shoulders. "See you later, ladies." Then: "Or maybe not."

Cindy watched him go, greeting the Norseman, shaking his hand. They took up the reserved booth in the back. Out of Cindy's range of vision, which, she supposed, was what they wanted: privacy to discuss a case. She sneaked a sidelong look at Hayley, who was clearly upset. The woman was making a stab at her beef dip, tearing off a grizzled corner and chewing it slowly.

No one spoke.

Finally, she said, "He's such an idiot!" Then she whispered, "I'm an intelligent woman. *Why* does he have this effect on me!"

Cindy picked up a French fry. "You know that Sheryl Crow song—'My Favorite Mistake.' We all have them."

"Well, I wish mine wasn't such an asshole!" She got up from her chair. "I gotta go reapply my lipstick."

After Hayley was gone, Rhonda took a bite out of her turkey dip. "Poor thing."

"She covered it well."

"Except her armpits are the size of swimming pools."

"How long were they going together?"

"I don't think they were ever *going* together. It was just a casual thing."

"Not to her," Cindy answered. She glanced at her plate, at the ceiling, at the bar stool. Anywhere but behind her back. Andy Lopez caught her eye. Involuntarily, she nodded, which was a dumb thing to do. Because Andy nudged Tim. Then they both got up.

"Oh dear." Cindy downed some beer for fortification. "Here they come."

Rhonda licked her fingers, which were coated

with turkey gravy. "You be nice. You're way too new to be jaded. How old are you? Twenty-one?"

"Twenty-five."

Rhonda made a surprised face.

"I know. I look young."

"I would think eighteen except you're drinking."

"Hey, Decker." Tim Waters plunked his scotch on the table. He had a medium build with light brown hair, murky green eyes, and bland features. He struck Cindy as Anyman USA. "Heard you were a big hit with Tropper."

"Good news travels fast." Cindy pointed to the chairs. "Take a seat. But bring over another one for Hayley."

Waters said, "After seeing Oliver, we thought she took off."

His smirk was ugly. Cindy stared at him long and hard. It must have been effective, because his cheeks pinked. She said, "No, Hayley's still here . . . just in the john."

Waters grabbed another chair and sat. Andy Lopez took up space next to Rhonda. He was on the small, slight side. But Cindy remembered him in the weight room, bench-pressing 320.

Lopez said, "Actually, Brown said you did okay."

She focused her eyes on him. "That's good to hear." She wrinkled her brow. "So why do I feel that there's an addendum to that statement?"

Lopez stared at her.

She said, "What else did Brown say?"

"Brown's sitting right over there." Waters cocked his head toward the bar stools. "Why don't you go ask him?"

"Because I'm eating my dinner." Cindy gulped down more beer. "What'd he say, Andy?"

"Just that . . ." Lopez stole one of Cindy's French fries. "You know . . ." His voice faded.

"Perhaps he said something about me and frank-furters?" Cindy caught Jasmine's eye, mouthing another beer. "I wasn't hotdoggin' anything!"

"I believe you, Cin—"

"It was a very tense situation. I was doing the best I could."

"Brown said you did good," Waters answered. "What are you bitching about?"

"Because Tropper's pissed."

"Yeah, Tropper's *real* pissed," Lopez said.

Cindy stared at him. "*And?*"

Lopez ate another French fry. "Jesus, Decker, I'm just letting you know. Don't kill the messenger."

Waters said, "Forget it, Decker. Tropper won't do anything."

Almost word for word what Beaudry had said. "How do you know?" Cindy asked. "What? Is he afraid of my father or something?"

Waters sipped his scotch. "Let's just say he has a healthy respect for authority."

Jasmine came with a fresh brew. She regarded Cindy with concern. "You know, maybe you should eat a little. It's good to get something in your stomach so it doesn't go to your head."

Cindy took a bite of her sandwich. It went down like lead. She drank half of her suds. "I'm okay. Honestly."

Waters smiled. "And if you're not okay, I can always drive you home."

"That *won't* be necessary."

Hayley came back, freshly made up. Cindy thought she looked dynamite good. Apparently Waters did, too. His eyes lingered on her chest a bit too long. Marx glared and said, "Who let the riffraff in?"

"I plead guilty." Cindy raised her hand. Mother Jasmine had been right. After four-plus beers, she was getting a definite buzz and needed something in her stomach. She attempted another bite, but it came out a nibble. Andy was glancing at her sandwich with longing in his eyes.

"You want some, Lopez?" Cindy asked. "I'm really not that hungry."

"Well, if you're not going to eat it." Lopez grabbed a half. "Why let it go to waste?"

Suddenly, the smoky air was oppressive, constricting her chest movement. She felt short of breath but didn't dare gasp. The current tension had been magnified by the residual strain from the afternoon. Combined with the liquor, Cindy felt as if she were climbing out of her skin.

She needed out and right away. Quickly, she

stood up. Just as quickly, the room started to spin. She slammed her palms against the table for balance.

"You okay, Decker?" Hayley asked. "Sit down, girl. You look pale."

"No, I'm fine." Attempting a smile. "I'm just tired."

Andy said, "Lemme drive you home, Cin."

She knew he meant it sincerely. And it made sense because she was woozy. But the thought of being alone in a car with him didn't settle well. "Thanks, Andy." Again a smile. "I'm really fine."

"I'll drive you," Rhonda offered. "Hayley can pick me up later—"

"It's not necessary!"

Her voice sounded harsher than she had intended. "Really, Rhonda. Thanks, but I'm fine. I'll see you all later."

She threw her bag over her shoulder. Knowing that they were studying her sobriety, she made sure to walk away on steady feet. But as soon as she got outside, she broke into a sweat. Her heart started pounding, her hands shook, and her vision blurred. She was drowning from the stress of conformity. Standing in the middle of the parking lot, staring at the sea of cars. Where the hell was hers?

"Please, God," she prayed. "Just let me get home in one piece, and I'll never do it again."

She walked down one row, then another. The

misty night air did little for her revitalization. But it did frizz up her hair.

Finally, she spied it—her Saturn. She would have never noticed it except that she had parked under a light. Her car was that sparkly, neon green color that had been in vogue a couple years back. Now the tint was passé, and the coupe looked like an old, painted whore.

She teetered over to her wheels, and fumbled with her keys while perspiration poured off her brow. She managed to unlock the sucker, but then the world started spinning. She shut her eyes, but the reeling wouldn't stop. She leaned against the metal, plopping her head against the thick cool glass, praying she wouldn't upchuck.

"Give me—"

Cindy started, jumping backward, almost plowing into his chest. She turned and glared at him, sweaty face and all. "Do you always sneak up on people like that?"

"Only if they're felons," Oliver answered. "Which is what you're going to be if you drive in that condition. Give me the keys."

She was too sick to argue. She handed him her ring.

"Can you make it around to the other side?"

"I suppose I can *if* I walk slow enough."

Oliver opened the driver's door. "Slide in."

"Thank you."

She managed to trudge her body from the driver's side to the passenger's seat, then threw her head back and closed her eyes. Everything was still spinning. She clutched her legs, hoping the tactile sensation would settle her stomach.

Oliver reached over and fastened her seat belt. "Here. Chew these."

She opened her eyes and stared at the proffered cup. "What is it?"

"Ice chips. It reduces nausea. When you left, you looked a bit unsteady . . . a little green."

She took the cup, biting her lip to hold down her stomach. "Were you spying on me?"

He ignored her. "Where am I going?"

"Philosophically?"

"Cindy—"

"Turn left at the first light—"

"Give me an address."

"To my apartment?"

"Yes, Cindy, to your apartment."

"It's off Bagley. Three blocks north of Venice. You know the area?"

"That's near Culver City, isn't it?"

"Yeah. Exactly." She crunched the frozen water between her teeth and gave him the number. "Sorry about this."

"S'right."

She let out a deep, beer-filled exhalation. She wanted to say more, to explain herself, but she couldn't get the words from her throat. She stared out the windshield, fixing her eyes on the asphalt road ahead.

They rode in silence, the protracted twenty-five minutes feeling like hours. Each turn or lane shift sent acid-coated waves up her esophagus. She sucked ice chips and swallowed often. She wiped sweat from her face with tissues, then wrinkled her nose because the Kleenex stank of beer.

Five pints and she was reeking. She stole a glance at her driver. If the stench was bothering him, he had the decency to remain stoic.

Finally, finally, he parked the car in familiar territory. She somehow got out on her own, dragging her bag along so that the straps scraped the ground. Oliver came over, and Cindy held out her hand for the keys. "I think I can take it from here."

"I need to use your phone."

Cindy opened and closed her mouth, staring at him through squinted, suspicious eyes.

Oliver said, "I've got to call a cab, Cindy. My car is still at Bellini's."

"Oh." Cindy thought for a moment, processing the words. *He has to call a cab.* "I can do it for you."

Oliver kept his eyes on her face, then let out a chuckle. "I suppose you could. But I'd prefer to wait inside rather than freeze my ass off."

"Oh." Cindy thought again. *Yeah, that made sense.* "Sure. Come on in." She nodded but didn't move.

Oliver took her elbow, gently guiding her. "What's the number?"

"Three-oh-two. There's an elevator—"

"We'll take the stairs. The walk'll do you good."

"I'm okay." She blinked. "Really."

He didn't respond. He was pushing her along, his fingers wrapped around her triceps. She felt like an errant child being led to her room. When they got to her unit, Oliver took out the keys and held them aloft. "Which one?"

"The metal one."

"Cindy—"

"Gold . . ." Cindy said. "It's gold. A Schlage. That's as specific as I can get right now."

After several tries, he unlocked the bolt, pushed the door wide open. "After you."

"A real gentleman." Cindy smiled. "Phone's somewhere. Will you excuse me?"

She didn't wait for an answer. She made a beeline for the bedroom and slammed the door shut, peeling off her sweat-soaked, beer-stinking, smoke-reeking pantsuit, cursing herself because the cleaning bill was going to be outrageous. Plopping down on her bed, she lay faceup in her underwear, watching the ceiling fixture go round and round and round and round . . .

Oliver was yelling from the other room.

"What?" she screamed.

"Cab company wants to know the number here," he called back.

"Eight-five—"

"What?"

"Wait a sec." Slowly, she rose from the bed, opened the door a crack, and gave him the number. She heard him repeating it, presumably to the cab company. She was almost at her bed when her stomach lurched. She didn't even try to tame it. A lost cause, she ran to the bathroom, hoping she could retch quietly. But after the first round, she didn't even care about that. When she had finished, she crawled to the sink, and while still on her knees, she washed her mouth and face.

At last, she was able to stand without feeling seasick. She took a gander at her visage in the mirror. She looked how she felt—like warmed-over turd.

She thought about going into her kitchen—fixing herself a cuppa—but *he* was there.

Well, too damn bad! Whose place was it anyway? She donned her pink terry-cloth robe, then gazed one last time in the mirror. Nothing had changed. She still looked horrible—pink nose, sallow complexion, watery eyes, and, thanks to the fog, bright red frizzy hair that made her look as if she were on fire. Still, there was something really nice about talking to a man (even Scott Oliver, who was like her father's age) while looking like shit. It spoke of confidence.

She opened the door to her bedroom and emerged a proud, pink, nappy thing. Oliver's eyes were focused out the window. He pivoted around, hands in his pockets, and stifled a smile when he saw her. "Hard day, Decker?"

"I won't even deign to bother you with my pathetic little story." She went into her kitchenette and filled the coffee carafe with water. "I'm making decaf. You want?"

"Pass." He peeked out the Levelors. "A word of unsolicited advice. Try orange juice. Vitamin C's good for hangovers."

Cindy stared at the coffeepot. "Okay." She spilled the water out in the sink, and took out a pint of orange juice. She poured herself a glass. "Bottoms up."

"What happened, Cindy?"

"It's really not very interesting, Scott."

He shrugged. "Got nothing better to do right now."

"I ruffled some feathers. No big whoop. I'll fix it."

"Learning young." He nodded. "Good for you."

"Thank you," Cindy said. "So why do I detect a note of condescension?"

Oliver went back to the window, busying himself with the slats. "No condescension meant."

She sipped orange juice. It burned as it went down her gullet. "So I'm wrong in assuming that your innocuous off-the-cuff comment bore any sort of indirect ill will toward my dad, right?"

The room fell silent. Stayed that way for a few moments.

"Let's swap favors, all right?" Oliver turned to face her. "I won't say anything to your father about tonight if *you* forget what I said earlier in the evening."

"About my dad being a slimy interloper?"

"That's the one."

"Deal."

Oliver ran his hands through his hair. "He's a good man, Cindy. A good man, and a more than decent boss."

"You don't have to sell him to me." No one spoke for a moment. Then she said, "So what kind of business did you have with Osmondson?"

"We were doing some cross-referencing."

"Does it have anything to do with the carjackings that're plaguing Devonshire?"

Oliver didn't answer right away, wondering just how much he should say. What the hell, she probably talked to her old man anyway. "Maybe."

"Like what?"

"I don't know yet, Cindy. I just picked up the folders."

"Sorry. I don't mean to be nosy." She finished her orange juice and placed it on the counter. "Actually, I do mean to be nosy, but I see I won't get anything out of you, either." She raised a finger. "But that won't stop me from trying. There's always Marge."

"You're feeling better."

"A bit. Although my head's still pounding, and I still smell like a brewery."

"Get some sleep."

A horn cut through the night, the phone ringing shrill and loud. Oliver picked up the receiver. "Yo . . . thanks." He disconnected the line and said, "My cab's here."

"Wait!" Cindy dashed into her bedroom and pulled a twenty out of her wallet. Between the ten she'd given to Jasmine and this twenty, she was down to five bucks and coinage. Which meant, at least, she wouldn't be wasting any more bread on booze. Clutching the bill, she came out and held the money out to him. "For your efforts . . . and the cab fare."

Oliver looked at the crumpled bill, damp from her sweat. Then, he regarded her face. "You've *got* to be kidding." He laughed softly, then tousled her hair and closed the front door behind him.

She remained in place, staring at nothing. She heard his footsteps clacking down the metal staircase, heard a car door slam shut. An engine revved, then roared, but eventually receded until there was silence. The absolute quiet of her apartment.

But within moments, the ambient noises reappeared—the whir of the refrigerator and the humming of the battery-operated wall clock. She glanced around the living room. Her furniture seemed foreign to her eyes—big unfriendly globs of cream cloth. Even the pillows. Instead of decoration, they appeared as evil red eyes, glaring at her with malevolence. Her glass coffee table reflected the eerie green light of her VCR, which flashed an ever-present 12 P.M.

Outside, a loud thumping interrupted her over-wrought imagination and caused her to jump in place.

Calm down.

Just a car stereo with the bass cranked up to the max.

Why was she standing here? What purpose did it serve? None, she decided. She blinked several times. Then she bolted the door and went to bed.

6

HOLLYWOOD HAD six similars over the last two years," Oliver explained. "All of them are opens. Two are out of the loop, but the four I flagged have common details."

They were in Decker's office—not much more than a cubicle except it had a ceiling and a door that closed to afford privacy for those inside. Decker was sitting behind the desk; Oliver and Marge sat on the other side. Decker's phone lights were blinking, but the ringer was off.

Paging through one of the red-marked folders,

Decker took in the basics—the crime, the place, the time, the weapon, the extenuating circumstances. "The woman didn't have a kid. Or did I miss something?" He handed the file back to Oliver.

"No, she didn't have a kid. But she was carrying groceries, which means that her hands were occupied. Perp used the same method of approach. Sneaking up behind her and putting a gun in her back. Asking *her* to drive. Not *all* of our cases involve a kid."

"Only one didn't involve a child," Marge said. "The rest had infants and toddlers."

"So maybe this one was Hollywood's exception," Oliver answered. "Look, I'm just bringing it to your attention. You want to throw it out, be my guest."

"It has been brought and duly registered," Marge said.

Oliver said, "By the way, how's your kid doing?"

Marge tried to hold a smile. "Vega's . . . adapting very well."

"How are *you* adapting to motherhood?" Decker asked.

"I'm doing fine," Marge answered. "Look, the way I figure, even if it does get rocky over the next few years, it's time limited. She's thirteen now. When they're eighteen, they're out of your life, right?"

The men broke into instantaneous laughter.

"What?" Her eyes darted from Oliver to Decker. "Fill me in. I could use some yucks."

Decker shook his head. "Margie, it's just one of those . . . parental things. You've just got to *be* there."

"Why spoil her fantasy?" Oliver asked. "And that's what she's talking about—a *real* fantasy."

Marge said, "I'm going to ignore both of you."

Decker let out a final chuckle, then rummaged through another case file. This one hadn't been flagged. He studied the folder for several minutes. "So you think this one with the lady and the red Ferrari *isn't* a match."

Oliver said, "First off, it's a hard thing to carjack a Ferrari. The car has manual transmission. And even if you can drive a stick, you gotta know how the gears go. And even if you know the gears, you gotta know how to drive a very temperamental car. Also, she was a lone woman and wasn't carrying anything to slow her down. It's not the same MO. Kidnapping for ransom. She was rich."

Marge said, "Sounds like the Armand Crayton case."

Decker said, "Except she didn't die like Crayton. Or maybe she did." He looked at Oliver. "What happened to her?"

"I assumed that the ransom was paid, and she's fine."

"And the kidnappers were never apprehended."

"Obviously not. Otherwise the case wouldn't be open."

"Odd," Decker said. "Kidnapping has the highest solve rate. Did they get the car back?"

"I don't know," Oliver said. "I'll give Osmondson a call and do some follow-up."

Decker said, "This lady drove a red Ferrari, Crayton drove a red Corniche. You don't think there could be a connection?"

"What?" Oliver said. "Like a two-tiered ring?"

"One for high-end, one for low-end."

"A couple of the mother-baby jackings have involved Mercedeses," Marge remarked.

"Two Mercedeses, five Volvos, one Beemer, one Jeep," Decker said. "Not in the same league as Ferraris and Corniches."

"In the Crayton case, the kidnappers didn't ask for ransom," Marge said.

"They never got that far," Decker said. "The car plunged over an embankment and exploded. Crayton was burned to death."

"All I'm saying is that his widow never got a call."

"Armand Crayton had been implicated in criminal activity," Oliver said. "He'd had dealings with scumbags. We never ruled out a hit."

"That's true," Decker said. "When he died, he had several suits against him."

"The Ferrari driver . . . what's her name?"

Decker flipped through the papers. "Elizabeth Tarkum."

"So far as I know, she didn't have a rap sheet. She was just a rich wife in the wrong place at the wrong time."

"A rich, *young* wife," Decker said. "Twenty-six, and she was driving a Ferrari."

Oliver raised his brow. "Crayton was what? Thirty?"

"Thirty-one," Decker said.

Marge said, "What was Crayton involved in? Like a pyramid scheme?"

Oliver said, "He was selling land he didn't own . . . something like that."

"No, he owned the land he was selling," Decker said. "But for some reason, he went bust. Details were always hard to come by. I always had the feeling that someone was fighting me."

"Like who?"

"Don't know," Decker answered. "I sent Webster after the wife, but he never got anywhere."

Marge said, "Maybe this Tarkum lady had some skeletons of her own. You know . . . driving a Ferrari at twenty-six."

"There's nothing to suggest that in the case file," Oliver said.

Decker said, "How old's her husband?"

Oliver shrugged. "Haven't a clue."

Marge picked up her cup and dripped coffee on her lap. Frowning, she wiped the spot off of her pants with her fingers. "That's why I wear black. I can be a slob and no one notices."

Decker handed her the tissue box. "It's why I wear brown. Then you really don't notice."

"You're the only one in the entire department who can get away with baggy brown suits," Oliver said. "They're so out, they're in."

Decker smiled. "That's me. A real trendsetter."

Oliver glanced up from his file. Deck had a deskful of family pictures—Cindy, his little one, Hannah, his stepsons, several of his wife, Rina. They were angled so Oliver could see them. He had never noticed them before. The smell of Marge's coffee had tingled his nose. His stomach growled. He'd left his own cup at his desk. He seized Marge's mug, took a drink, and made a face. "What the hell did you do to this?"

"What?" Marge said. "I put Equal in it—"

"How can you drink that shit?"

"Oliver, it's *my* coffee."

Decker smiled. "You want mine, Scotty? It's black. A little tepid, by now, but it's unadulterated."

"I'll get my own, thanks." He stood and took Decker's mug. "As long as I'm up, I'll pour fresh." His eyes went to Marge. "Do you and your chemicals want a warm-up?"

"At least my chemicals don't give me a hangover."

"You've got a point. Now do you want a fresh cup or not?"

"He gets fresh, I get fresh." She handed him her cup. "Two cream powders, one Equal. *Don't* say a word."

He flashed her the peace sign. "Be back in a sec." Mugs in hand, he walked to his desk to retrieve his own coffee cup when his phone rang. He put down the crockery and picked up the receiver. "Oliver."

"Hi."

He hesitated a moment. "Hi." Then to let her know that he recognized the voice, he added, "How are you feeling?"

"I'll be glad when the day is over."

"What are you doing?" Oliver flipped his wrist, looked at his watch. Ten-thirty. "It's way too early for lunch."

"Code seven—ten-minute break."

"Ah, doughnuts and coffee."

"Just the coffee," Cindy answered. "Everybody's watching the fat." She waited a beat. "Is this a bad time?"

"Sort of." He glanced over his shoulder, eyes on Decker's office. The door was still closed. Then he wondered why he was so concerned. "What's up?"

"I'll make it quick. I just wanted to properly thank you. In my stupor last night, I think I had forgotten."

"Forget it—"

"No, I won't forget it, I'll learn from it. I'm embarrassed, Scott. Not so much that I was tipsy, but that I attempted to drive. That was really stupid. More than that, it was really dangerous."

"Yes, it was."

She laughed over the phone. It was light and airy. "At least you're honest. Anyway, it won't happen again."

"We all mess up," Oliver said softly. "If you learn from it, you're one step ahead."

"Again, thanks for rescuing me. Bye—"

"Look, do you . . . Nothing."

"Would you please complete the sentence?" Cindy requested. "Do I . . . *what*?"

Again Oliver looked over his shoulder. "Maybe we should talk over a cup of coffee. I still know lots of guys in Hollywood. I could fill you in on a couple of things."

"Such as?"

"Give you the lowdown."

"The lowdown on the guys . . ." A pause. "Or the lowdown on me."

"Maybe both."

Cindy sighed. "Don't bother, Oliver. Beaudry has already pointed out my deficiencies. Apparently, they are many and varied."

"Has he told you the good points?"

"He's still searching." A few seconds passed. "*Are* there good points?"

He took another glance behind his back. Marge

had opened the door, holding out her hands like a balance scale—a "what gives" sign. He held up a finger, indicating one minute, and whispered, "This isn't the right time. Look, you get off at three, I get off around five. I'll come to your side of town. How about Musso and Frank at seven?"

"A bit rich for my pocketbook, Oliver."

"It's my treat." He spied Marge motioning to him. "I gotta go. Your father needs my swift insights."

"Don't say hi for me."

"Sweetheart, I have no intention of bringing up your name."

7

TRAFFIC WAS light and should have been moving since the street was zoned for speeds up to thirty-five miles per hour. The trouble was coming from a truck, which was not just crawling, but swerving as well. It was one of those ancient things: a heavy job with lots of primed, curvaceous metal, and a grill big enough to barbecue an ox. The back tail-light had been punched out, the tags were expired, and the exhaust pipe was belching smoke. The bumper was sheared down the middle, and in need of a rechroming. Beaudry typed the license plate number into the MOT—the computer's central hookup into the DMV. A minute later the monitor displayed the basic identification on the truck and its owner.

"Fifty-one Chevrolet," Beaudry said out loud. "Well, that matches. No wants or warrants on the vehicle. Registered to Anatol Petru-ke—" He squinted as he spelled. "P-e-t-r-u-k-i-e-v-i-ch."

"Petrukievich," Cindy said.

"Sounds Russian."

"Probably," Cindy said. "Whoever he is, he's no doubt inebriated." She flipped on the lights and siren. The truck neither slowed down nor sped up. It just kept going at its snail's pace.

Beaudry unhooked the bullhorn. "Pull your vehicle over now!"

"Graham, do you really think he understands what a *vehicle* is?"

"He'll get the message." They rode a few seconds, watching. "Is he slowing?"

"At seven miles an hour, it's hard to tell." She waited. "Yeah, he's skewing his way over to the curb."

"See, he understood what the word *vehicle* meant."

"Maybe it was the flashing lights and siren."

"You're just being a sore loser. Call it, Decker. Heads or tails?"

"Tails."

He tossed the coin, flipped it over to the back of his hand, then showed her the quarter; George Washington was smirking at her.

Beaudry said, "Since it's my call, I say you take the driver."

"I get all the luck." She rolled her eyes. "Who needs luck anyway? A good cop makes her own luck, right?"

"Whatever you say, Decker."

Cindy parked behind the plated dinosaur and got out, leaving the door open for protection. She waited a moment to see if the driver was staying put.

He was—at least for now.

She unsnapped her holster. Cautiously, and with her hands on her hips, she began her approach, moving across the left side of the vehicle. The cabin of the truck was tattooed with a boxed-in ad, reading TOP CHOICE PAINTING in bold black letters. A smiling paintbrush had underlined the words. The phone number was a Hollywood exchange. Mr. Petrukievich was a local. Or at least his business was.

Closing in, Cindy's hand was on her weapon and her eyes were on high alert. As soon as she was at the driver's window, the door started to open.

Forcefully, she said, "Stay inside your truck, sir."

Either he ignored her or didn't understand because the door swung out and a pair of feet planted themselves on the ground. Cindy prepared herself for the worst. Because when he stood, he loomed over her. He was not only tall, but big. Big as in *big* and big-*boned*. As in Dad's size.

"Stay *right* where you are, sir," she ordered.

He froze, his face registering confusion. His complexion was a pale pink, except for the nose, which resembled a gigantic raspberry. Straight amber-colored hair was brushed over his nude chunk of forehead. His beard was thin and blond. He reeked of booze.

Cindy looked for Beaudry's backup, but it appeared as if her partner had his own problems. The truck also held a passenger as big as the driver. Probably equally drunk because Mr. Passenger's gait was wobbly. Graham was trying to keep him upright.

Meanwhile, the driver began rocking on his feet. "I do notink." He nodded vigorously, hair flying over his eyes.

Cindy stood firm, enunciating clearly. "Sir, go *back* inside the truck."

"Back?" It came out *beck*. The man wrinkled his brow, then turned around and showed Cindy his spinal cord.

"No," Cindy said. "Not your back. Back inside the truck. In the *truck*! Turn aroun—turn . . ." She swirled her index finger in a whirlpool motion. The man complied by spinning in circles. "Dees?"

He was drunk as a skunk, but not belligerent. Forget about getting him in the car. She placed a hand on his meaty shoulder to stop his rotating. His body lurched forward while his head continued to loll about. Stumbling, he managed to support his unsteady weight by placing his hands on the hood of the truck. Change the context, and it played as broad comedy. But as the situation stood now, he was a behemoth-size drunk who could turn nasty at any minute.

Warily, Cindy said, "I need to see your license, sir."

The man managed to make eye contact. The orbs were unfocused.

"Your license . . . to drive." Cindy tried to pantomime it. She received a blank stare for her efforts. She called out to Beaudry, "Does your guy speak any English?"

"I don't think so," Beaudry answered. "But he has a good set of teeth. I know because he's smiling a lot."

Cindy looked up at her charge. Burly was a fitting adjective for him. No wonder the former U.S.S.R.'s mascot had been the bear. "Your license to drive." She steered an imaginary car wheel. "Driving."

The man nodded. "Da." He pointed to his truck. He didn't get it.

"License," Cindy repeated louder. As if turning up the volume would increase his comprehension of English. "License."

The man repeated, "Li-cense."

She cried out, "Officer Beaudry, can you get the Breathalyzer?" She figured if he was over the legal limit, she wouldn't even need to see his license. She'd just arrest him on the spot.

"I'm watching someone," Beaudry said. "Just put him through a field sobriety test."

Meaning Beaudry didn't want to leave her alone with *two* drunken big guys. Okay. That was legitimate. So she'd put the driver through a field sobriety test. She could handle that.

She said, "Are you Anatol Petrukievich?"

The man broke into an instant grin. "Da!" He nodded again. "Da!" He launched into a slur of foreign words, ending his oration with a big smile. She smiled back. Then he grinned like a schoolboy.

Great. They were now buddies.

She said, "Lookie here, Anatol."

At the use of his name, his eyes went to her face. Again, the goofy grin.

"Look at my leg. See what I'm doing?" Cindy stood on her right foot and lifted her left about three inches off the ground. She counted to ten aloud. Then she pointed to him. "You! Anatol! Anatol does this, okay? You do it. *Capische?*"

He stared at her.

Which made sense because *capische* was Italian. She put her leg back down and slowly picked it up a second time, once more counting to ten. She pointed at his chest. "You try it."

"*Da!*" He took the challenge and attempted to

stand on his right foot. But he faltered as the last of his toes cleared the sidewalk. Anatol reddened, tried again, and failed again. Clearly, the man's cerebellum was in need of a tune-up. He spoke to her in Russian. From his tone, he appeared to be apologizing.

"No, it's okay," she found herself saying.

"O-key?" He smiled brightly.

"No, not okay." She shook her head. "Not okay, just . . . do this!" She extended her arms out at her shoulder, made fists, then stuck out her right index finger. She brought the tip of the finger to her nose by bending her elbow. She did it without lowering her arms. "Now, Anatol, you do this. You."

The man nodded, but didn't move.

She tried to give him a jump-start by raising his right arm to his shoulder and extending it. But as soon as she let go, the arm fell to his side.

So far, he was getting an F. But there was that thing called a language barrier. Harking back to her life as a grad-school researcher, Cindy decided to gather more objective data before hauling him in. Gently, she turned him around until he faced the Chevy's side. She took his hands and placed them, palms down, on the roof. Then, she brought them behind his back, one at a time, and cuffed him.

Absolutely no resistance.

He was big and drunk, but a damn happy guy.

Carefully, she led him to the cruiser, his feet
dragging against the ground as they approached
the patrol car. His body swayed and staggered with
each step. Cindy found herself propping him up.
The teddy bear was a heavy man with a capital *H*.
She linked her hands around the cuffs and tried to
keep his spine erect. But instead of being his
guide, she found herself being jerked from side to
side as he sidled like a monstrous, stoned crab.

Finally, they reached the cruiser.

"Easy does it, Anatol."

She opened the back door and positioned him
parallel to the seat.

"In." She gave him a gentle prod. "In." She
pushed down on his head so he wouldn't bump
his rather thick skull on the car's ceiling. Partial
success. Anatol's head and body were safely en-
sconced inside, but his shoes still dangled in the
street's gutter.

Holding up an index finger, she declared,
"Wait here."

Anatol grinned. He didn't seem the least bit perturbed. Cindy brought out the Breathalyzer from
the trunk. At the sight of the machine, the Russian's eyes lit up in recognition. Without directions,
he took the protective paper off the blow hose and
exhaled enough sodden breath to knock out a rhino.

"Whew!" Cindy said. "We've got a sizeable BAL.
You are drunk, sir."

Anatol grinned and measured off an inch of space

between his thumb and index finger. "Dis much vodka."

Cindy spread her arms out. "More like this much vodka."

Anatol laughed.

"Do you have one of these?" Cindy reached in her wallet and pulled out her own license.

Anatol shook his head. "No hev."

"You *don't* have your license or you never *had a* license?"

The subtlety of English grammar was lost on him. "No hev."

"I see we're in a rut." Cindy bent down, picked up his paint-splattered gunboat-size shoes, and placed them in the car. She shut the door. "Officer Beaudry," she called out. "I got him trussed and ready to go."

"I'm coming." As Beaudry started toward the cruiser, the other drunk Russian dogged his heels.

Beaudry turned to face him. "No, you stay here." He pointed to the wizened truck. "Sit in there. Call up a lawyer for your friend." Beaudry mimicked a phone call, then pointed to Petrukievich. "Call up help for your friend. He's going to jail."

A perplexed look. "Jail?"

"Yeah, jail."

Cindy watched Beaudry as he tried to act out a prison scene. He wasn't Cagney, but he got the point across.

"Ah!" Drunk Passenger smiled. He got back into

the truck, threw his head back, and closed his eyes. Bunking down for a snooze.

Cindy said, "Do we arrest him as well?"

"For what?" Beaudry answered. "Sleeping? Let's go!"

Since the backseat was divided from the front by a metal grate, *and* since Anatol was still hand-cuffed, they left him sitting solo behind them.

Cindy started the motor, then gripped the automatic transmission shift knob. Something tickled her flesh. A small, yellow Post-it had stuck to her sweaty palm. She peeled the paper off her skin. On it was written the word "Remember," the printing done with a black felt-tipped marker. The dampness on her palm had caused the word to smear. She showed it to Beaudry. "You leave this here?"

He glanced at the paper. "No."

"I didn't, either."

Beaudry shrugged.

Cindy said, "How'd it get here?"

"With traffic being this light, I'm sure it took the freeway—"

"I'm serious—"

"How the hell should I know, Decker? Maybe you put it there and forgot." He smiled. "Maybe that's why it says to remember."

"Very funny."

Beaudry said, "Maybe the guys over at servicing left it there."

"Then I would have noticed it when I drove the

car out of the lot. I *certainly* would have noticed it when I pulled Mr. Petrukievich over. Are you *sure* you didn't put it there?"

"Yes, I'm sure. I'd remember something like that."

Cindy was perturbed, but she didn't say anything. She stared at the paper.

Beaudry said, "Decker, it's late. I'm tired. Let it go. And let's go."

She crumpled the mysterious message. Shifting the car into drive, she released the hand brake and took off. Beaudry called in the arrest, giving the RTO an estimated time of arrival to the stationhouse.

Remember.

Cindy tried to erase it from her mind. "How long do you think it will take to process our friend?"

"What do we have on him?"

"Reckless driving, a DUI with a BAL of over point-two, and operating a moving vehicle without a license."

"Maybe an hour."

"Criminy!"

"Why? You got something planned?"

"Later on."

"I hope you're not tight for time," Beaudry said, "because *if* our drunk tank is filled, then we gotta either take him down to Parker Center or find another substation that can handle him. That means it's gonna take longer."

"Graham, it's three-thirty in the afternoon. How many drunks could there possibly be?"

"Lots of people just hanging, Cin. For them, cocktail hour starts right after the soaps."

❑

WRAPPED in a white terry-cloth towel, Cindy stared into her clothes closet. It was too early in the season to wear the light fabrics. (Besides the fact that it was way too chilly outside.) However, it wasn't heavyweight wool weather, either. That left her with several options.

Option one:

Her midweight, sleeveless black gabardine dress. Always appropriate dinner wear, but way too sexy for a business meeting with a superior, let alone a man who worked with her father. Now, she *could* wear her black blazer over the dress. That would certainly tone it down. But the jacket was a more bluish-black while the dress was more greenish-black. Which never made sense to her; why black came in so many different shades.

Option two:

An olive-drab skirt suit, which looked great with her red hair. But it was militaristic in style, replete with spangles and epaulettes. She had to be in the right mood to wear it. Tonight, she didn't feel like WACing it.

Option three: her last selection.

A single-breasted navy pantsuit—good cut around the hips, not too tight around the ass, no plunging neckline. It said, *I am all business so don't even* think *about it.* Maybe it was even a little unfriendly. She supposed she could gussie it up with a scarf.

Except that she hated scarves.

There were women who were naturals with them, tossing them over their shoulders in a carefree serape manner or winding them like jeweled chokers around the neck. She, on the other hand, never could get the damn things to sit properly. On her, scarves always looked like *weather* wear rather than stylish accessories. Besides, with her red tresses, she had to be careful with multicolored objects.

She unhooked the plain Jane pantsuit from the closet pole and regarded the sedate outfit. It would suffice. To accent it, she'd wear a simple gold chain around her neck and gold stud earrings. Definitely nothing about that ensemble could be deemed inappropriate. Not that she thought that Scott had ideas, but men were men. Even *old* men were men.

She gave herself a final toweling then put on her undergarments. Next came the pants, which fit nicely, even a little loose. Well, that was a nice surprise.

She slipped her arms through the jacket and began to button it. She was shocked to find it pulling across her chest. She took off the blazer and checked herself out in the mirror. Her boobs hadn't gotten any bigger, but her underlying chest musculature sure had. Her shoulders had also widened.

She wondered why she hadn't noticed before. Probably because she wasn't a preener. She checked herself out only when necessary, which meant before dates. And they hadn't happened for a while. Not that this shindig with Scott was a date, but at least it was dinner outside the house with a man who wasn't a relative. She accredited the change in her physique to a regimen of weight lifting and exercise, including a daily workout of a three-mile jog, fifty push-ups, and two hundred crunches.

So the blazer stretched across her chest. No big whoop! She just wouldn't button it. Except now she'd have to wear something *under* the blazer. Her blouses would probably pull, too. So that left her with sweaters. Most of them were too thick and too casual to wear with a suit. Except she did have one black-ribbed turtleneck.

Did black go with navy?

Alas, she thought. Cursed with a pathetic sense of style. If only she had been brought up with a mother who knew about these things. A mother who knew how to knot scarves and how to coordinate separates and just what shade of lipstick would work.

Her mother was just as fashion-blind as she was. Mom's attire consisted mainly of cotton caftans or peasant blouses worn with ruffled skirts. Her jewelry was almost always chunky bead necklaces or Southwestern sterling-and-turquoise numbers. Cindy never understood why her mother dressed in such a shapeless manner since she had a nice trim figure. When Cindy had been heavily into psych, she once had told her mother that wearing loose clothes was akin to denying sexuality. Her mother—also into psych—had said she liked sex just fine (If you want confirmation, go ask your father. *Yeah, right!*), and her choices had more to do with comfort.

Cindy put on the turtleneck. It was tight, but it would suffice. The blazer, of course, softened her protruding bustline. In midsized heels, she stood a svelte five ten, one hundred forty-five. She regarded herself in the mirror. All she needed were sunglasses and a two-way squawk box, and she could have been typecast as a Fed.

She smoothed some blush over her cheekbones, and covered her lips with something gooey and shiny. Rolling her shoulder-length tresses into a knot, she then pinned her hair up with a butterfly clip. She slipped the strap of her bag over her shoulder and went out of the bedroom. Just as she was about to lock up, she tossed a final glance around her living room.

Her eyes landed upon the mantel, staring at it longer than necessary.

Because something struck her as off.

She walked over to the fireplace and studied the

knickknacks perched atop the ledge. There was a bud vase, a small Waterford crystal clock (a birthday gift given by her stepmother, Rina), a dozen miniature porcelain animals (her childhood collection), and several pictures of her parents in silver frames.

That was it!

Hannah's picture was missing. Cindy's eyes scanned the area until they lit on the coffee table. There sat her six-year-old half-sister, a boisterous smile plastered over her little mug. She picked up the silver frame and restored the photo to its rightful place.

How'd it get on the coffee table? Cindy knew she hadn't touched it since she had set it on the mantel.

Or maybe she had moved it when she had last dusted.

God, when was the last time she had dusted?

She checked the clock that read twenty to seven. Even if she were lucky with traffic, she'd barely make it to the restaurant on time.

She'd deal with the picture later. After locking the bolt securely, tugging on the knob to make sure everything was buttoned up, she left her apartment, bolting down the three flights of stairs.

Maybe *Oliver* had moved the picture last night. Maybe he had walked over to her mantel and picked it up, walking around with it as he waited for her. Then, when he went to put it back, he had forgotten where it belonged.

Which really didn't make sense. All he had to do was *look* at the mantel and see the other photographs.

She looked around, checked over her shoulder, then unlocked her car. Sliding into the driver's seat, she immediately locked the car. She took a final glance around before she started the motor.

Maybe Oliver had been walking around with it, then had put it down quickly when she had come into the room. Because he hadn't wanted her to catch him looking at her personal stuff.

Now that made some sense.

You know how it is. You're alone in a strange place; you get curious and start touching things you shouldn't be touching. Then the person comes in and you don't want him or her to see you snooping.

She started the engine, let it idle, then took off. After a block, she checked her rearview mirror. Free and clear—both in front of her and behind her.

No doubt that was it. Oliver probably moved it.

She'd ask him about it . . . *after* he picked up the tab.

8

As she approached the table, Cindy saw Oliver stand up. Like Dad, Scott was from the old school, a guy who probably opened doors and pulled out chairs for the ladies. So unlike her own generation, where every person was on his or her own—good for self-reliance, bad for manners.

Scott looked good. His attire was not only dressier than last night, but also far less slick. He wore a camel-hair jacket over a cream-colored shirt, a red tie, and charcoal slacks. When he held out his hand, Cindy took it. Instead of shaking it, he pulled her forward and gave her a peck on the cheek, leaning over the corner of the table to reach her face. He let go, his eyes giving her a quick once-over.

"You look lovely."

"Thank you. So do you."

"I look lovely?"

"Uh, I mean good. You look good."

"Good is fine. I'll even take lovely. Have a seat."

Cindy slid her body between the tabletop and a red leather banquette, parking herself catercorner to Oliver. The table itself was from another century, surfaced with linoleum designed to look like marble. It was so tiny that their knees touched. She readjusted her position to break the contact. If Scott noticed, he didn't say anything.

The place was a blast from a long-ago past, when Hollywood glamour meant Grauman's Chinese Theatre and the Walk of Fame instead of piercing salons and tattoo parlors. The interior decor could best be described as a hunting lodge, with beamed ceilings, wood-grained moldings, and prints of the chase complete with hart, hare, and hound. Below the coursing images were dark-stained wood panels. Old wood . . . good wood. A mirrored-back bar ran the length of the room, the specialty of the house being a dry martini with an olive or—if you're supersophisticated—a pearl onion. Busboys, identified by green jackets and smiles, poured the water and gave them bread. A waiter, identified by his red jacket and surly expression, handed them menus and asked them if they wanted a drink.

"Wine at dinner?" Oliver asked Cindy.

"Sounds good." She looked up at her server. "Any specials not on the menu?"

The waiter regarded her with suspicion. "The menus are printed *daily*."

"Oh." Cindy perused the carte du jour. "So you have everything on the menu then?"

"Not the linguine and langostino, not the western omelet, not the lobster bisque—"

"So why was the menu printed with linguine and langostino if you don't have it?"

The waiter glared at her. "Do you want to take it up with the owner?"

"Not particularly."

"Are you ready to order, ma'am?"

The menu was extensive and was done in small print. "Can I have a few more minutes?"

The waiter turned and walked away.

Cindy said, "Think we'll ever see him again?"

"If you keep raggin' like that, maybe not."

She shrugged. "Just asked a simple question."

Oliver regarded her face. "You must have been fun to raise."

She smiled. "I don't remember my father complaining."

"Maybe not to you—"

"Why? Has he said anything to you?"

Oliver was taken aback by the force in her voice. "No. Just making conversation. Someone give you a hard time today, Decker?"

"No one . . . unless you're referring to the Russian drunk driver I arrested this afternoon."

He looked up. "How'd it go?"

"He's in the drunk tank sleeping it off, and I'm here. I suppose that's a victory for society as well as for me." She was silent. "Nah, everything at work is fine." She rotated her shoulders. "Just fine."

Oliver put the menu down and studied her face. "You look kind of tense . . . the way you're sitting."

"I'm not tense." She slouched just to prove the

point. "My muscles may be a little stiff. I've been doing some extra typing. You know, hunched over the keyboard with no lumbar support. The department doesn't think ergonomically."

"What are you writing?"

"Case reports. Which are big pains because you have to type them using a certain format. You know, making sure you don't go over the tabs or else the words'll run between the lines instead of on top of them when the form prints out. I thought a hot shower would take care of the aches. Actually, it did, but only for a while."

"Any reason why you're typing so many reports?"

Cindy put down her menu. Immediately, the waiter reappeared. "Have you decided?"

To Cindy, the words sounded like *Have you decided to go* away? *Please?* She said, "Yes, thank you. I'll have the sand dabs. Does that . . . never mind."

"If you have a question, go ahead and ask it. I may sneer, but I don't bite."

Cindy smiled. "How are they prepared?"

"Lightly coated and pan-fried," the waiter answered stoically. "They come with boiled potatoes. If you want French fries, I can get you French fries."

"French fries would be great." She handed him the menu. "Thank you."

"You're welcome." He looked at Oliver. "For you, sir?"

Oliver handed him the menu. "Prawns and your best bottle of Chardonnay."

"Caesar for two to start?"

"Sure."

Without ceremony, the waiter left.

Cindy whispered, "Is he going to spit in our food?"

"I don't think so."

"I was sufficiently polite this time?"

"Better." He smiled. "Why are you typing so many reports?"

"Doing favors." Cindy looked at the ceiling. "Trying to extricate myself from Sergeant Tropper's shit list by completing his reports—his least favorite chore."

"Tropper?" Oliver thought a moment. "He must have been after my time. What'd you do to get on his shit list?"

"You mean *besides* being a college-educated woman? Well, I did have the nerve to handle a tense situation competently. It ruffled his feathers."

Oliver raised his eyebrows. "Department likes team players, Cindy."

"So I should just step aside and let . . ."

She stopped talking, seeing the red-jacketed waiter approach with a bottle of wine and two Caesar salads. He set the plates in front of them, then uncorked and poured the wine, giving Oliver a taste. Scott swirled it, sniffed it, sampled it.

"It's good."

Dutifully, the waiter poured two full glasses, then placed the bottle in an ice bucket. "Ground pepper for the salads?"

"Sure," Cindy answered.

The waiter picked up the pepper mill and plunked it down in front of Cindy. "Help yourself." Then he left.

Cindy gave her salad a healthy dose of pepper. "That man doesn't like me. Maybe it's my red hair."

"Maybe it's the attitude."

"Oh, please!" Cindy speared a chunk of lettuce into her mouth and chewed slowly. "Ordinarily, I would get upset by that. But the food's too good. Tension is bad for digestion."

"Indeed." Oliver raised his wineglass.

They clinked stemware. Cindy said, "To what? To being a good team player?"

"How about to keeping you safe?"

Cindy took a sip. "Safe from the felons or safe from my fellow workers? Aren't you supposed to be giving me some kind of lowdown?"

"Watch your ass."

"Hard to walk when you do that, Scott."

"I'm serious, Cindy. You need to look over your shoulder now and then. You're way too cocky. I don't know if it's the inexperience, the fact that you're educated, the position of your dad, or just your sparkling personality. But you have to be aware of yourself. More important, you've gotta know how your 'tude affects your colleagues. Being out there on the street, your life could depend on any one of them."

"I can take care of myself."

"See, that's a big fallacy. And a dangerous one." He lowered his voice and moved in closer. "You *can't* take care of yourself. Out there, no one can. Everyone has to look out for one another. Policing is a team sport, sweetheart. You want solo activity, become a spy."

"Well, that's an idea. Don't you just love the dark sunglasses."

"You're quick with the repartee. I'll give you that." He sat back. "Unfortunately, your retorts won't do dick against a .357. Or even a .22, for that matter."

"You know, Oliver, even if I *wanted* the help from my *colleagues,* they wouldn't give it to me. So I figure why bother waiting around for it!" She put down her salad fork. "All these crazy hazing rituals they put us women through. They deal with me like I'm one big fraternity prank. Take yesterday. I'm trying to contain this crazy Latina . . . think any of the guys there offered me a finger of help?" She shook her head. "Man, I'd love to have a woman partner, so this whole competition thing wouldn't be an issue."

"It's an issue with your partner?"

She took a healthy swallow of her Chardonnay. "No, Beaudry's not a bad guy."

"So what are you bitching about?"

"I'm not *bitching*! I'm just saying . . . forget it." Cindy retreated into her salad, stabbing at a crouton that kept sliding under the tines. "I'm only talking about work because you *asked* about it. Generally, I keep my mouth shut and do the job. If no one trusts me, what can I do?"

"You're only a rookie, Cin. You couldn't have pissed off everyone that fast."

"It's been eleven months. That's plenty of time." She smiled, but it was a tense one. "So you tell me what's going on."

"First tell me why you think the guys don't trust you."

"A multitude of reasons." She sipped wine. "Starting with the fact that they can't get into my pants."

"Okay. I can buy that. Guys'll try, no big deal. Once they see you're a stand-up gal, they'll get over it."

"I hope you're right."

"What about the women?"

"I haven't been to any of the policewomen meetings yet. Too busy. Maybe I should go."

"Maybe you should."

She sighed. "Even the women I know . . . they have this look in their eyes. I think they view me with suspicion because I'm college educated."

"You're telling me you have no friends? You looked pretty social last night. Tipsy, but social. Did something happen that I don't know about?"

"No, last night was okay. Hayley's nice, actually. Well, I think she's nice." She regarded Scott. "What happened between you two?"

Oliver didn't answer.

Cindy smiled brightly. "I guess we're not going there."

"Good guess."

She poured them both another glass of wine. "I'm still waiting for the lowdown on me."

Oliver said, "We're talking general consensus, not any one opinion."

"Got it."

"You're smart—"

"I could have told you that—"

"Shut up, Decker, and listen. You're smart, quick-thinking, and, more important, quick on your feet. You're good with the masses out there. Calm, assured—not in your face, but you don't back off. You've got good physical energy and good physical strength especially for a broad—"

"Must be the Wheat—"

"You're reliable, you're on time, and don't seem to have any big bad vices. That's the word that gets back to your dad." He looked at her. "I hear that, too. But I also hear other things."

Cindy felt her stomach drop. She was about to blurt out a wiseguy comment, but it stuck in her throat. "Go on."

"You're no problem on the streets, but you've got

this 'I'm superior' 'tude in the stationhouse. You're snotty, Decker. Or like my grandmother used to say, someone who gets above her raising."

"For your information, I'm acting perfectly acceptable for an Ivy Leaguer."

"Well, Decker, to that, I say, you're not in college anymore." Again he leaned over. "You're pissing people off . . . the very people you might need someday. Maybe you should start using some *street* psychology."

"Yeah, yeah—"

"Stop brushing me off and just listen. 'Cause I—like Daddy—have your welfare at heart. Life and death, split-second decisions are *not* analyzed, Cindy. You just jump in there and hope for the best. And the vast majority of us on the force *will* jump in to rescue a colleague at a big risk to our own lives. We're acting on instinct. It's an emotional thing. But we're human, too. I'll jump into the pyre, sure. But I'll do it a lot quicker if I *like* the person. Stop being a snob. Especially because your father isn't like that, and he has much more reason than you to be arrogant—"

"I'm not arrogant!"

Oliver stopped talking and focused in on her face. She was crushed but trying to hide it. He knew he was coming on too strong, although it didn't make his words any less true. Lecturing to her just as he had done with his own sons. He had always been so anxious to get the words out; he had never bothered to think how his brutal remarks had affected them.

Cindy stared into her wineglass. "You want to know the irony of all this?"

Oliver nodded.

"I'm actually shy," she said. "I mask it in superiority. Because in a cop's world, it's better to be egotistical than shy." She looked up and made eye contact with him. "If you give off even an inkling of fear, no one'll ride with you."

"That's true."

"If some of the guys knew how nervous I was, they'd dissolve me in acid."

"Everyone's nervous at first."

"It's different being a woman."

"I'm sure you're right—"

"Better to eat than to be eaten." She stared at her plate. "Who thinks I'm smart, by the way? Or did you make that up to console me?"

"Nah, I didn't make it up. For starters, the detective I was consulting with yesterday—Rolf Osmondson. He says you're smart."

She was skeptical. "I don't know why he'd say that. First time I ever laid eyes on the man was last night."

"Apparently, he's laid eyes on you."

"Suddenly second-grade detectives are noticing uniformed rookies?"

"If the second-grade detective is a heterosexual

male and the uniform rookie is a lovely, young female, you bet your ass he notices. Also, Craig Barrows mentioned you to me."

"Craig Barrows?"

"You don't know him, either?"

"No, I don't think so."

Oliver said, "About my height. Long face. Sandy-colored hair that's thinning. Blue, blood-shot eyes—"

"Yeah, yeah, yeah. Isn't he in Homicide?"

"Yes, he is."

"Sure, now I remember," she said. "About three months after I arrived at Hollywood, one of the vets threw a party and actually invited us rookies. Some of the gold shields were there. I chatted with Detective Barrows for about ten minutes." Cindy pushed away her salad plate. Immediately, the bus-boy removed the dish. She said, "From that one lone conversation, he thinks I'm smart?"

"You must have impressed him."

"I think it was the red hair."

"You attribute an awful lot to your hair, you know that?"

She chuckled and looked up into the dour face of their server. He placed the sand dabs on the table. "For the *lady*."

"Why, thank you." Cindy picked up a French fry and bit it. "Perfect."

The waiter cracked a smile. "You're welcome." He served Oliver his dinner. "More wine?" He looked pointedly at Cindy. "It seems to agree with you."

"Wine agrees with everyone," she stage-whispered to him. "Thank you. Half a glass. I must save room for dessert."

The waiter poured wine for both of them. "Anything else?"

Cindy said, "I believe we're fine." She looked at Oliver. "Are we fine?"

"We're very fine," Oliver answered. "Thank you."

"You're welcome," the waiter said. "Watch out for pin bones."

Again he left.

"Awwww, he cares about us," Cindy said. "He doesn't want us choking on a fish bone. He's definitely thawing."

"Either that or you're buzzed, so your perspective has changed."

"Could be, could be." She ate another French fry. "Why do you say I'm buzzed?"

"You've got color in your formerly pale cheeks."

"Oh, that! It's just the makeup kicking in."

Oliver laughed. "What did you and Craig talk about?"

"Pardon?"

"Craig Barrows. At the party? You chatted for ten minutes?"

"Gosh, it was so long ago." She tried to bring the memory back into focus. "I think we talked about Armand Cray—" She felt her cheeks get hot.

"About the Armand Crayton case. It was me, my partner, Graham Beaudry, and Slick Rick Bederman—"

"When did that take place? About eight months ago?"

"About. The case had been all over the papers. It was such a weird thing with the wife witnessing the whole ordeal." She glanced at Scott, who was staring at her. "Just idle chitchat."

Oliver said, "Cindy, what aren't you telling me?"

"What do you mean?"

"Sweetheart, you're blushing. What's up with Armand Crayton? Did you know the guy?"

"What do you care?"

Oliver audibly plunked down his fork and sat back in his seat. "What do I care? The file is open, darling. What *are* you hiding?"

Cindy waited a moment, then sighed and said, "Okay. Here's the deal. I used to work out at Silver's gym in the Valley before I moved into town. I went there for maybe a year. We struck up a casual acquaintance."

"Did you date him?"

"I said casual—"

"Did you sleep with him?"

"Oliver, do you know the definition of the word *casual*?"

"Sex is casual with lots of people."

"He was married, Scott."

"Meaning?"

"I don't sleep with married guys! Ever!"

"The guy was known as someone who fucked around," Oliver persisted. "Did he ever tell you he was married?"

"No, he didn't. But I, being perceptive and astute, stood clear of his advances."

"So he tried to pick you up?"

"Not in a big way," Cindy said. "You know, sometimes we'd have a drink at the juice bar after our workouts. A couple of times he asked me if I wanted to go someplace else for a cup of coffee. I told him no."

Oliver gulped down a prawn, trying to spit out the tail without looking crass. "What'd you talk about?"

"Nothing that would shed any light on the case."

"Why don't you let me be the judge of that?" Oliver frowned. "What's going on, Cindy? Why are you acting so squirrelly? Knowing you, I think you'd *jump* in head-first to help crack a major homicide. At least, you'd tell your dad—"

He stopped talking.

"Okay. Now, I get it. You *did* tell your dad. You told him, and Big Deck told you not to talk about it. You want to tell me the details? Or should I just ask your father?"

Cindy smiled, wickedly. "Exactly how do you intend to bring it up with him? 'Uh, Deck, I happened to be having dinner with your daughter and—' "

"Oh, fuck you!" Oliver threw a prawn tail at her. "Cindy, fill me in. Pretty please?"

Cindy hesitated, then said, "Our acquaintance was never any big deal, Scott. Our conversations were strictly lightweight—buffing up our bods, how our workouts went. Stuff like that. Once in a while, he mentioned a hot business deal he was doing. I think he was trying to impress me."

"Sounds like it."

"Well, it didn't work. Usually, when he started his business-speak, I zoned out. It wasn't our conversations that alarmed my dad."

"Go on."

"It was one of those extremely bad cases of being in the wrong place at the wrong time. After one of our juice encounters, we were walking back together to our respective cars." Cindy picked up her wine but put the glass down without drinking. "Someone took some potshots at us—"

"Jesus!"

"Yeah, it was frightening." She looked away. "This was several months before he was murdered. I was in the academy by then, so I had my gun. But I didn't use it."

"That was very smart."

"Yeah, that's what Dad said, but I felt like . . ." She blew out air. "I felt that I should have done *something*." Her voice lowered to a whisper. "Oliver, it scared the shit out of me." She felt her eyes moisten. "Not the gunfire, although that was very scary. But the fact that I froze—"

"Why? What'd you do? Just stand there?"

"No, I ducked behind a car."

"That's exactly what you should have done." Oliver sipped wine. "Sure as hell what I would have done."

She was quiet.

Oliver said, "Cindy, what do you think you *should* have done? Turned the parking lot into the O.K. Corral?"

She swiped at her face. "I don't know. I keep thinking what if this had been the streets and—"

Oliver interrupted her. "If, God forbid, something like this happens on the street, you'll know what to do. You'll have your mike, you'll have your gun, and, going back to our *original* discussion, you'll have *backup*. The potshots took you by surprise. Don't worry about it."

"Doesn't shooting always take you by surprise?"

"Sometimes, sure it does," Oliver said. "But when you're working, you're looking out for it."

She looked away. "Maybe."

Oliver said, "So you told your dad about the shooting?"

"Yes." She paused. "But only after Armand Crayton died."

"So you didn't tell him when it first happened?"

"No, I didn't. Because I didn't want to freak him

out. Also, I didn't want to admit that I froze. I was embarrassed."

"Cindy, you didn't *freeze*, you *ducked*! Ducking is different from freezing." He ate another prawn. "Okay, so you told your father about the potshots after Crayton was kidnapped and murdered. And your dad told you not to say anything to anyone."

"Yes."

Oliver analyzed what might have gone on in Pete's head. "Did the shooter get a look at you, Cindy?"

"I . . . don't know. I was really scared when it happened. My initial thought was that the shooter was his wife. That she wrongly assumed that Armand and I were having an affair. But after he was killed, and all the stuff about him came out, I actually *stopped* worrying. Armand had a very long list of detractors. The shots weren't meant for me. They were probably a gift from some disgruntled investor."

"You're not holding back? You never dated him?"

"No, never. We were gym buddies. That's it."

"You told your father all this."

"Yes. And I'm sure that if Dad thought that my involvement was important, he would have told you and Marge and the rest of you guys everything."

"He never said anything to me about it."

"So he didn't think it was important."

"More like he was more concerned with your safety."

"He wouldn't jeopardize the case, Scott. Even for my sake."

Oliver laughed. "Sure, dear!"

"I'm serious. Dad has principles!"

"Dad also loves his family. Between work and your safety, hell, it isn't even close." He waved her off. A busboy thought he was waving at him, because he immediately cleared the plates.

To Cindy, Oliver said, "Do you want dessert?"

"No, I'm pretty full. Thank you, dinner was delicious."

"No prob." Oliver scratched his face. "So you and Craig Barrows were talking about the Crayton case?"

"Just in generalities." Cindy wiped her mouth.

"What kind of generalities?"

"We got on the discussion of follow-home shootings." She perked up. "You know, I think Barrows told me that he and Osmondson were working together on a follow-home that sounded similar to the Crayton case."

Oliver felt like pulling out his notebook, but restrained himself. The conversation was too chockablock. He'd have to grill her in a quiet setting. Take her through the entire thing from start to finish. "Do you remember anything about the case he was referring to?"

Cindy tapped the tabletop. "For some reason, a red Ferrari comes to mind."

Elizabeth Tarkum. Oliver said, "You know what we're working on in Devonshire, don't you?"

"Of course—the carjackings and follow-homes. You think the Crayton case is related to them?"

"Maybe."

Cindy said, "You want to interrogate me, don't you?"

"We call it interviewing."

"Okay," Cindy said. "Suppose I say yes? Do you want to do it behind my dad's back?"

"It might be simpler." Oliver was not at all happy. "How about if I come to your apartment tomorrow evening. You tell me everything you know about Armand Crayton and your conversation with Craig Barrows. If it becomes clear to me that your relationship with Crayton is important to his murder case— or any of our current jacking cases—I'll tell your dad about this dinner . . . which won't be a pretty scene! But if you can shed any light on what's going on with these horrible jackings, I've got no choice."

"You're being very professional." She grinned. "I'm impressed."

"No, I'm not a professional." He rubbed his forehead. "What I am is an idiot for taking you to dinner."

Cindy softened her voice. "You were being nice. Because you felt sorry for me after last night. I appreciate it, Scott."

He smiled, plunking down the credit card to pay the bill. "You're a nice kid."

"Thank you," Cindy said. "Want to go Dutch?"

He laughed. "This one's on me. The next one's on you."

"Is there going to be a next one?"

It was Oliver's turn to blush. Quickly, Cindy changed the conversation. "What time do you want to come to my apartment?"

He stared at her.

"For the interview tomorrow night . . . remember?"

Oliver laughed. "Uh, yeah, I remember. I took my ginkgo biloba. How about seven?"

"Seven it is."

She stared at the tabletop. She had wanted to ask Scott about Hannah's picture; why it was on her coffee table instead of perched atop her mantel. She was feeling quite paranoid especially after their weird conversation. But now it seemed like a suspicious and rude thing to do. So she decided to ask him about it tomorrow. It would make more sense then. He'd interview her; she'd interview him.

"Ready?" he asked.

"Absolutely." She stood. "Walk me to my car?"

"Of course," Oliver answered. "And with any luck, no one will snipe at us."

9

I⊤ HAD been an exhausting morning, but worth the effort. The little number that Stacy had eyed two months ago had been reduced fifty percent. Black, lightweight wool, it was perfect in almost every SoCal season except maybe summer. And even then she could probably wear it at night because so many of the restaurants were overly air-conditioned, the nasty machines breathing arctic ice down on the sexy halter number you wore to look so fine. Trying to look like you're having a good time with frost dripping from your nose, and your breath fogging up the menu. Don't these ultra-hip, ultra-cool, too-too places have any sense of temperature?

Ah well, at least she now owned the perfect black dress for any situation, especially appealing because it was half-off *wholesale*. And since she saved so much money on the dress, she had extra for the shoes, and the scarf, and a couple of pairs of designer stockings that usually cost more than a good meal at a local café. She also had enough for two cashmere sweaters reduced by seventy percent—last year's styles, but the colors were neutral. She loved sweaters. They showed off her tight, perfect body courtesy of genetics and lots of proper physical exercise.

Stacy left the mall through one of the six main entrances, and stepped out into the dirty sunlight, squinting in the glare. Dragging her packages a couple hundred feet, she scanned the acreage of asphalt, trying to spot her red Beemer convertible sold to her by a rich client at a fraction of its worth. It was a sassy, smart bitch, but the problem was that it was so low down to the ground and hard to find among all these sub*urban* vans and souped-up four-wheel-drives. She cursed her stupidity. Why didn't she pay attention to the designated signs—red four, eight purple, whatever. It would have made her life a lot easier, and her arms a lot less tired. Walking through rows and rows of metal, hitting her shoulder on a low-slung rearview mirror.

Was there a landmark she could remember? A tree or a wall or the back of one of the stores or even what side of the boulevard she had parked on? But nothing came to mind. Sweat began to trickle down her brow. It was cloudy but muggy, the moistened air pricking the back of her neck. She touched the crown of her scalp and felt the puff of her tresses, not unlike the aerated fluff of cotton candy.

Great! Her hair was frizzing up. After she spent forty-five goddamn minutes blow-drying it straight, not to mention slopping her hair with all those tonics that promised to keep the dampness and the frizz out of her locks.

Where was the goddamn car?

Another walk through the maze of vehicular steel.

Pretend you're in a funhouse.

Then Stacy remembered that she never liked funhouses.

More walking, and walking, and walking. Feeling so close, yet so far away. Then she hit her head, dummy that she was. She placed her packages on the ground, then rooted in her purse until she found her keys. Holding on to the remote, she pressed down on the *panic button.*

In the not so far distance, she heard her horn's intermittent blare—beep, beep, beep, beep, beep, beep. Ah, such sweet music. She picked up her packages and followed the dulcet tones until her red BMW jumped into her line of vision, looking as welcoming as beefcake. She depressed the panic button once again and the annoying honking ceased.

She hurried over to the car, putting down her packages as she opened the door. Within seconds, she felt the presence of another body breathing on her neck. As she started to turn, she was slammed against the hood of the car, her face pushed against the hot metal, her keys ripped out of her grasp, cutting across her palm. Something hard was pressed against her temple.

A voice said, "Don't move! Don't talk, don't scream, don't do anything. You do anything, you're dead. Am I clear? Nod for yes."

She managed to nod yes, even though she was mashed against the hood.

"You're nice," the voice told her. "You're very nice. But I'm in a hurry, so you're lucky. Now hit the ground, bitch!"

Stacy was confused, her terror only adding to her befuddled state. The voice hissed in her ear. "I said, hit the goddamn ground! Do it now, bitch!"

Hands clenched the nape of her neck and shoved her entire body against the pebbly asphalt. Her forehead smacked against the hard rock ground, her cheek scraped and bleeding. A foot was on her throbbing head, pressing hard against it.

I should yell, she told herself. *I should really yell.* But she couldn't find her vocal cords.

The voice said, "Now, if you're a good little bitch, and you stay where you are and keep your mouth shut for a long, long time, you'll live. If you talk, you'll die. Is that clear?"

Stacy managed to nod.

The foot came off her head and then gave her a sharp kick in the ribs. Her eyes burned as pain shot through her nervous system. Another kick, but this one directed to her back. She moaned as agony squeezed her like a vise. The foot then pushed her aside.

The car door swung open and hit her in the ribs.

Bang went her car door as it slammed shut.

Vroom, vroom went her pretty little convertible engine.

Screech went the tires as the car backed out of its space.

Stacy was left with two overwhelming thoughts. The first was that she was still alive. If this were the worst of it, she'd be okay . . . eventually. Her second notion was that the thief hadn't taken the packages.

At least, she still had her sexy little number.

❑

MARGE was reading from the computer sheet. "We've got another one. A straight carjack. Vic was a lone woman. No kid."

"What kind of car?" Oliver asked.

"BMW convertible. Korman, from GTA, caught the call about twenty minutes ago. I'm sure he's still there. We should go to the scene and find out the details."

Oliver said, "Any reason why *we* weren't called when it came through?"

"We should have been called. Everyone knows that we're working on the carjackings. Someone screwed up."

"See, that's the problem." Oliver stood and put on his jacket. "If our own details don't know each other's business, how can we expect interdepartmental cooperation. You got cases in Hollywood, you got cases here, and who knows where else . . . no one's fitting the pieces together."

"I thought that's what you were doing last night. You met with him long enough. I called you maybe four times in three hours to find out if you learned anything." She closed and locked her file drawer. "Did you?"

Oliver's brain started racing. *What was she talking about?* "Who'd I tell you I was with?"

"Rolf Osmondson from Hollywood." Marge eyed him. "Didn't you take him out to dinner last night?"

Oliver tried to cover. "No, it was the night before."

Marge was insistent. "No, Scott, you told me you were meeting with Osmondson to clarify a few details about the Elizabeth Tarkum case."

That's the trouble with lying when you're over forty. You forget things. Oliver tried to act casual. "Nah, I wasn't with Osmondson. I was on a date. I did phone up a couple of Hollywood Dees. Maybe that's where you're getting mixed up."

"Who?"

Shut up, Marge! "Uh, a guy named Craig Barrows. I didn't mention him to you?"

"No."

"Yeah, well, we talked a little over the phone. Nothing big." He squirmed. "You ready?"

"I'm ready." Marge swung her bag over her shoulder. "I don't think she was hurt too badly. She was talking . . . the woman in the Beemer."

"That's good," Oliver said. "Does she have a name?"

"Stacy Mills. She's a personal trainer."

"Think it's related to Crayton?"

Marge was taken aback. "I don't know. Any reason why it should be related?"

"Car's not typical for our mother-kid jackings."

"It doesn't sound related to Crayton," Marge said. "The jacking took place in the parking lot of the West Hills Outlets."

They walked out of the stationhouse, found Marge's Honda, and then took off. Marge drove the car onto Devonshire, the main artery that linked the north section of the east and west San Fernando Valley. The police station was located in the burbs, which did wonders for the real estate prices in the surrounding area. It gave the illusion that the neighborhood was impenetrable. That wasn't the case, although the response time was quicker. As she drove farther west, the street broadened and the homes thinned. Rolling hillside swept over the acreage: Los Angeles as farmland. Way back when that had been the case—orchards and fields. Go up another forty miles to Oxnard, and it's still the case.

Marge said, "In all this open space around, you'd think a red BMW convertible would be easy to spot."

"It's red?"

"Yeah. Didn't I tell you that?"

"No, you didn't," Oliver said. "Crayton's Corniche was red."

"So are a zillion other cars. But it is interesting." She glanced at her partner. He seemed restless. "Something on your mind, Scott?"

"Nope." He looked at his lap. "Maybe I'm a little tired. Am I acting tired?"

"A little." *Tired and* strange, Marge thought. But she didn't push it. In the distance, she began to see hints of the Spanish tile rooftops. As Marge's Honda chugalugged down the steep curve of the hill, the mall ascended inch by inch over the horizon. It seemed as if the construction had been dropped in the middle of nowhere. But a few miles northeast were wealthy areas—golf course developments and large ranch spreads that appealed to professional athletes and urban mountain men who ascribed to the rugged life as long as their SUVs came with cell phone and computer stations.

The mall was composed of a half-dozen Mediterranean-style buildings that housed, among other things, some high-end discount outlets— Off-Saks, Barneys, Donna Karan, St. John's Sports, Versace, Gucci, and other Italian names real or otherwise. The developer had obviously chosen the spot because the vast amount of land gave the mall room for expansion as well as lots of parking.

Oliver surveyed the blinding sea of chrome. "Where's the crime scene?"

"I think Korman said something about the newly added parking lot."

"How can you tell which building is new? It's all new. Place is one big maze. I hate shopping, and I really hate malls. They represent the worst in human homogenization. They all look the same, they all have the same stores—"

"This is discount—"

"Nothing is individualized anymore," he bemoaned. "Whatever happened to the old-fashioned store? You know, a store . . . fronted by an actual street . . . that has parking in the back—"

"You're showing your age." Marge turned left into miles of asphalt. "You're a well-dressed guy. Where do you get your clothes?"

"I have a few places that know me and my budget. They call right before the sales. I go in after-hours."

"Pretty good service. Sure you aren't fixing someone's ticket?"

"I wish I had the power." He ran his fingers through his black hair. "Would do me wonders with the women."

She smiled. "You're complaining all of a sudden?"

"With women, there's always a complaint, no offense to your gender. I mean, *look* at this place. Look how crowded it is!"

"There're men here. They like to save money, too."

"It's ratio, Marge. Me, I like something, I buy it. With women, it's not just shopping, it's an *adventure*. You'd think they were stalking a snow leopard instead of buying a T-shirt."

Marge rolled her eyes. "Bad night, Oliver?"

He realized he was whining. He stared out the windshield. "These places just depress me."

Marge was disconcerted. It wasn't like Oliver to act this way. Cynical, yes. Obnoxious, yes. But not depressed. She wondered if there was something wrong with his health, but she didn't ask. There was work to be done.

He said, "As a matter of fact, I had a fine night!"

Marge waited for him to explain. When he didn't, she asked, "Does that mean she *had* a brain?"

"For your information, I can attract women that aren't bimbos. When I put my mind to it, I can actually carry on a conversation—"

"Scott, you're acting constipated. What the hell is wrong with you?"

"I told you, I don't like malls . . . there." He pointed. "At three o'clock."

The place was roped off by a yellow crime scene ribbon. Marge eased the Honda over to the spot and pulled in behind one of the four cruisers. Milt Korman had arrived at the scene in a black-and-white. The brass had dictated that unmarkeds were to be used only when the element of surprise was necessary. Otherwise, it was preferred that the Dees use standard cop cars. It gave the appearance of more police out on the road. Marge thought about that as she got out of her Honda. No one said anything to her, so she was a happy camper.

The door to Korman's cruiser was open, and the victim was sitting in the back, her sandal-shod feet dangling outside, brushing the asphalt. She looked to be in her early thirties with a round face and saucer-shaped brown eyes, made bigger by judicious application of eyeliner. Some of the liner had run down her cheeks, giving her an Emmett Kelly sad clown look. She had wedge-cut platinum hair and wore bright copper lipstick.

Korman was leaning against the black-and-white, writing in his pad. He was in his late fifties. A no-nonsense second-grade Dee, he had thick, peppered hair, florid skin, and a misshapen, bulbous nose fashioned from boxing and drink. Upon seeing Oliver and Marge, he waved them over. "This isn't just a standard GTA, it's a jacking. You should have been called right away. Anyway, I'll tell you what I know, and you can question the vic according to your needs. . . . The deal was this. She was shopping, looking for her car . . ." He glanced up, his eyes panning the parking lot. "Big mother place."

"Don't you just hate malls," Oliver said.

"Yeah, I hate shopping," Korman groused. "Anyway, she was lost and was so intent on finding her car, she didn't notice if the perp was following her or not."

"The perp was definitely a he?" Oliver asked.

"She said it was a he."

Marge became animated. "She saw him?"

"No. Hold on a minute." Korman turned cranky. "Let me get this out, okay. She didn't notice anyone following her. She finally found her car by pushing on the panic button."

Oliver said, "Another thing wrong with malls. You always forget where you parked."

"Can I get this out?" Korman asked. "She pushed the panic button, then found her car. Started to open the door, then, at that point, she did sense another being. Never saw the guy. He pushed her down, face-first, on the hood, then shoved her to the ground."

"So she doesn't know it's a he."

"He talked. It was a he."

"Accented?" Oliver asked.

"Don't know." Korman squinted as the chrome bumpers reflected sunlight. "The perp took her keys and her car. I put out an APB right away on the car. No response?"

"Not so far," Oliver answered.

"Weird," Korman said. "How far can you go with a red BMW convertible? It's pretty conspicuous. Unless he had the semi waiting and the perp immediately drove it into the trailer. Maybe we should put out a bulletin to look for a rig big enough to house a car."

"Either that or there's a chop shop nearby."

Korman said, "I haven't heard about it. But there sure as hell been enough carjackings to justify a chop shop in these parts." He shook his head. "You want to interview the vic now?"

"Fine with me," Marge said.

Korman walked them over to his car. "Ms. Mills, I'd like you to meet Detective Dunn and Detective Oliver. They'd like to ask you a few questions."

The woman stole a glance at Marge, then focused her gaze on her nails—long, hard acrylic nails done in the same bright copper tone as her lipstick. Her voice had an air of resignation that comes from being victimized. "I'm tired. I'd like to go home. Can't we do this another time?"

Marge said, "We won't take too long."

Oliver said, "You want us to call somebody for you?"

"I already called my sister."

"And she's coming?"

"Yes." The woman held her head. "I suppose I can talk to you until she gets here. What do you want to know? I didn't see him."

"But you heard him," Marge stated.

"Yeah."

"Male?"

"Definitely."

"What did he sound like?" Oliver asked.

"A *maniac*!" She glared at him, then returned her

eyes to her lap. At this point, Oliver knew that any male was probably at the top of her shit list.

He said, "Did the voice sound accented?"

Stacy pursed her lips. "No, he sounded American. Why?"

"Just trying to gather infor—"

"No, you asked me that for a reason." She became agitated. "Why'd you ask me that? Do you suspect a foreigner?"

Marge said, "I wish I could give you more information, but—"

"You cops are all alike!"

What did she know about cops? Oliver wondered. "Did he have a weapon?"

"I didn't see one. But I think he held a gun to me. I felt something hard against my head." Tears leaked from Stacy's eyes. "He kicked me . . . once in the ribs and once in the back. I'm very strong, but shit . . . he hurt me. I'm in a lot of pain!"

"I'm so sorry." Marge turned to Korman and mouthed the word—*Ambulance?*

Stacy caught it. "I sent the paramedics away." She shrugged. "These ambulances are a scam. All they ever do is rack up hospital bills. They're all in cahoots. . . . I don't want anyone I don't know touching me."

Marge could understand that. "But you will get checked out—"

"My sister will take me to my doctor. She's already called him." She caught her breath. "Think you'll find my car?"

"We're working on it," Korman answered.

"That means no. I'd really like to be left alone until my sister gets here."

Oliver said, "You didn't recognize this guy's voice or anything?"

Stacy regarded him as if he were a moron. "No."

"So you don't think this was some kind of revenge thing?"

"No!" Stacy became jumpy. "Why would I think that? What are you driving at?"

"Ms. Mills," Oliver asked, "did you ever know a man by the name of Armand Crayton?"

Stacy's face lost all expression. "Why are you asking me these *questions*?"

A surprised Oliver regarded Marge. "I'm sorry if I upset—"

"This entire episode *upset* me! You're just another cog on the wheel." She got out of the patrol car. "Can you *leave* now?"

But Oliver pressed on. "It's just that this jacking reminded me of Crayton—"

"Except I'm alive and he's dead!" Stacy shrieked. "Please leave now!"

"I'm trying to help you—"

"I don't need help! *Go away now!*"

"This isn't going to go away, Ms. Mills—"

"Out!" she screamed. Then her face crumpled. "Please, leave . . . *please?*"

"All right." Oliver nodded. "I'll leave." He waited a few moments, then fished through his wallet. "If by any chance you want to talk to me, here's my card." He held out the square piece of paper.

To everyone's surprise, Stacy Mills took the card.

10

FEELING A headache coming on, Decker rubbed his temples. From across his desk, he glanced at Oliver, looking his natty self, and Marge, wearing a utilitarian black pants outfit. He said, "Who brought up Crayton?"

"Yo," Oliver replied.

"Why?" Decker asked.

"Because she drove a red BMW convertible. Crayton's car was a red Corniche, and Tarkum's car was a red Ferrari. Maybe a pattern?"

Marge said, "He hit a nerve. You should have seen the way she reacted. She freaked. Told us to get the hell out. But she took Oliver's business card. Stacy's sitting on something. The question is, what?"

Again, Decker rubbed his temples. What color was Cindy's Saturn? Some weird teal green. It certainly wasn't a luxury car. He sat up straight and tried to appear objective. "What do you think she's hiding?"

Oliver unbuttoned his blue suit jacket, but refrained from loosening his tie. He was hot and wondered why no one else appeared uncomfortable. "Some revenge thing. The same jackers that took down Crayton may be out to get her."

"Did the jacker make any attempt to kidnap her?"

"No." Marge picked a speck of lint off her black pants. "According to Stacy's story, he told her to hit the ground and expressed regrets that he didn't have more time, because she was *nice*."

"Nice, as in he'd like to have raped her?"

"That was the implication," Oliver said. "Agreed, Crayton and Mills aren't mirror images of each other. But I think there's a connection. Especially given Stacy's reaction."

"The crime sounds more like the Elizabeth Tarkum case," Decker said.

"So maybe they're all connected."

Decker said, "And the common thread is . . ."

Oliver shrugged. "Crayton made enemies. There could be lots of reasons for people wanting him dead. Maybe he was associated with these ladies. Because these cases don't fit in with the other jackings. The women weren't carting kids, and the vics weren't forced inside their vehicles."

"So why jack the women now when the Crayton case is old?"

Oliver said, "First off, Elizabeth Tarkum was jacked around six months ago. Second, maybe he figured now was a good time to do Mills because the police might lump her jacking with the ones that have been making the news."

Marge added, "Stacy also said the perp sounded American. Some of our women with kids said the perp sounded foreign."

"But Stacy didn't see him."

"No." Marge regarded Decker—her former partner who was now her superior. Instead of being excited about the information, he looked stressed by it. "Crayton's an open case. I think we should root through the case files again and see if Stacy Mills or Elizabeth Tarkum fit in somewhere."

Decker sat back in his chair. "Let's do this. Compile a list of Crayton's former friends and associates, then go check out if any of them have been threatened or robbed or received any strange phone calls . . . or been shot at."

The room fell silent. Oliver tried to hide his apprehension. But Decker wasn't paying attention to him. He looked up at the ceiling. "This means I've got to talk to my daughter."

Marge widened her eyes. "Cindy? Whatever for?"

"She knew Crayton," he said.

In a heartbeat, Oliver felt enormous relief. But he played along with it and acted confused. "What? *How?*"

"They used to go to the same gym," Decker admitted. "They struck up a casual friendship."

"A *casual* friendship?" Marge repeated.

"That's her version." Decker was pained. "What she told me was this. One day they walked out to the gym's parking lot together. Someone took potshots at them—"

"*Jesus!*" Oliver emoted. "When was this?"

Decker made a face. "Around a year-plus ago. Just before Crayton was murdered."

"And you're just telling us *now*?" Oliver tried to add outrage in his tone of voice.

"That's correct." Decker's face was flat. "I'm just telling you now. She didn't tell me until after Crayton was whacked. When she finally did fess up, I questioned her extensively. She claims she didn't see the shooter, and had no suspicion as to who might have done it. It didn't appear like she was holding back, so I took it for the obvious. That Crayton was the intended target and she was in the wrong place at the wrong time."

"She must have been petrified," Marge said. "Poor thing."

"I'm sure at the time, she was very shaken." Decker took out a cigarette and played with it, rolling it between his fingers. "When she told me, she seemed to be handling it well."

His office fell quiet.

Decker bit the ends of his mustache. "I told her

to keep her mouth shut. I also told her to call me immediately if anything remotely threatening pops up. So far, she hasn't said anything to me, but Cindy keeps her private life . . . well, private."

Oliver shook his leg. "She needs to be told what's going on for her own protection. Also, we've got to talk to her to make sure she's leveled with you."

"I'll talk to her," Decker said.

Oliver said, "Let Marge and me interview her. We can be objective. You can't. Plus, she'll talk more openly to us—"

"I don't know about that."

Marge said, "Pete, she might be embarrassed to tell you if she had a thing with this guy."

Decker winced. "I don't *know* if she was having an affair with him."

"So let Marge and me find out." Oliver attempted to be helpful. "Look, I'll call her, okay? She's in Hollywood, right?" He spoke glibly. "I had wanted to go over the Tarkum case with Rolf Osmondson anyway. Him and this other Dee named Craig Barrows, who had mentioned to some of the guys that Tarkum had some similarities to Crayton—"

"What kind of similarities?" Decker asked.

"Offhand, I don't know. As long as I'm out there, I'll set up an interview with Cindy."

Decker didn't say anything. Oliver took his silence for approval. "I'm not busy tonight. Let's get

this over with for Deck's peace of mind." He
looked at Marge. "How about you?"

"I'll have to make a couple of phone calls . . . rearrange some appointments."

Oliver said, "She should be interviewed pronto.
If you can't do it, I'll do it myself."

Decker's eyes slowly shifted from his desktop to
Oliver's face. Scott was smart enough to catch
the implication. He didn't jump. Instead he
shrugged. "Hey, you can come with us, boss, but
it might inhibit her."

"What makes you think she'll talk to *you*?"

Oliver was frustrated. He really did want to warn
Cindy. And he wanted to talk to her *alone*. But that
had to do with personal reasons. He said, "I think I
could get something out of her. But if you have
doubts, I'll wait for Margie. She's your daughter.
You call the shots."

Decker looked at Marge. "Rearrange your
schedule."

"It shouldn't be a problem," Marge said.

"Great!" Oliver feigned enthusiasm although he
was a tad disappointed that Marge now had to play
tagalong. Deep down, he knew it was best. He
said, "Around eight, Margie?"

"Actually that would work out perfectly," Marge
answered. "Where does she live?"

"Near Culver City," Decker said.

Oliver said, "I was planning to go into Hollywood at around six. I'll meet you at Cindy's around eight." He looked pointedly at Decker. "Is *that* okay with you?"

Reluctantly, Decker agreed. Although he hated losing control, he knew Scott was right. He couldn't be objective. He glanced at his watch. "I'll call her . . . explain the situation and let her know you two are coming by at eight. In the meantime, you two reacquaint yourselves with the Crayton file. Divide up the search and interview as you see fit. Also, you should ask Korman if there's been a proliferation of other luxury red car thefts."

Oliver stood. "Sounds like a plan."

"One more thing." Decker got up and opened his door. "In Stacy Mills's case, the perp ordered her to *hit the ground.* Now, he could have picked out the phrase from the movies or from those real-life cop shows, but you might want to consider that the guy has had some training somewhere."

"Perp's a cop?"

"A cop, a *former* cop, someone rejected from the academy, someone kicked out of the force, HPD, sheriff's department, a security guard, a former security guard, ATF, the military—anyone who wears a uniform and has power needs."

❏

CINDY shifted the receiver over to her other ear. "My father was very vague. How'd this all come out?"

"Your dad brought it up because of a recent case—"

"What?" she screamed. "I can't hear you."

"Your dad brought it up!"

"My dad! Why? What were you guys talking about?"

"Cindy, I can barely hear you." He was at a pay phone about a block away from the stationhouse. Traffic on the boulevard was fierce and loud. Oliver looked around. Not a soul to be seen. And even if someone were, what would he see? "I'll explain when I see you."

"How can you explain things with Marge there?"

Oliver said, "Look . . . your dad said we'd be there around eight, right?"

"Right."

"Marge and I aren't traveling over the hill together. So I'll be there like we planned. Around seven-thirty."

"Make it seven. I've got a lot of questions for you."

Oliver hesitated, then said, "Seven-thirty, Cindy. I'll be there at seven-thirty."

There was silence over the line.

Coolly, Cindy said, "Okay, seven-thirty."

Oliver said, "I have the feeling your dad's going to show up unexpectedly. He doesn't like delegating when it comes to his family. You're his daughter, he's got a personal interest in all this." He waited a beat. "I know he's going to show up at your doorstep with some excuse. I feel it like I feel the wind. Now I can explain being there twenty minutes, even a half hour early . . . traffic was light, I got done with Hollywood early, blah, blah, blah. But I can't explain away showing up an hour early. That would mean that I have *plans*."

"What plans are *those,* Scott?"

"Now you're being a wise guy."

Cindy said, "Okay. Seven-thirty it is. Doesn't matter to me."

"Good. I'll see you later." Oliver smiled as he hung up the phone. Her words said it didn't matter. But her voice said it did.

❏

WEBSTER raked his fingers through caramel-colored hair. He sat slouched over his desktop, a gray tweed jacket hanging over the back of his chair. He had just turned thirty-five, and his wife had mentioned something about a party. As far as Webster was concerned, he didn't want to think about birthdays. Age was a mindset and, since he still looked young, he might as well feel young, too. Although life in the big city sure moved faster than it did in Tupelo. He wondered if L.A.'s frenetic pace aged the body by pumping it full of adrenaline.

He sifted through the Crayton folders: both of

them hefty, containing lots of dog-eared, multicolored pages. There were sections for the autopsy report: graphic photos of a savaged body with exposed bones that had been charred brittle black. There were a dozen black-and-white crash scene photos along with an itemization of what had been found in the burned-out Rolls. Then there was the personal material on Crayton, several sheets depicting a con man with all the rackets, angles, and scams. The files also contained legal documents, stemming from lawsuits of several disgruntled individuals, along with a class action suit that had later been dropped.

Armand had had his fair share of enemies.

Webster looked up from the papers, his baby blues focusing on Marge's face. "Sit. I'm straining my neck."

"Sorry." She pulled up a chair.

Webster said, "Bert and I interviewed the prime suspects. Three or four looked promising . . . the ones most likely to carry a grudge." He handed her a list. "We came up empty."

Marge eased herself back in the chair as she scanned the list. "What did you find?"

"They all had their excuses. Bert and I kept feeling that we were missing something or that someone was holding back. Namely the widow. She kept telling us that it was okay . . . that we were doing our best. Talking like we were schoolkids taking a hard test. Her attitude surprised us. Then I began to reckon that there was this real possibility that she didn't want us to look too hard."

"Why?"

"She was scared of someone coming back to get her."

"Did she mention feeling threatened?"

"Matter of fact, she downplayed it, saying that the kidnapping was a random thing because Armand drove a very noticeable and expensive car. It could have happened to anyone. It was always Bert's and my contention that she wanted the minimum—just to make it look good for Armand's mother. While I feel very bad for this Stacy Mills, I am happy that she breathed some life into the Crayton case."

Marge said, "So you never interviewed either Stacy Mills or Elizabeth Tarkum?"

"No. But I'm sure Armand kept secrets that he took to his grave. With Mills and Tarkum and the wife, you have a distinct advantage over Crayton, Margie. The girls are still alive."

"Who'd you go with first?" Marge asked. "The wife?"

Webster nodded. "Definitely the wife. And if you find out something that I missed, don't rub it in."

11

Armand Crayton had lived in a posh development in the far west portion of the San Fernando Valley. Thirty homes were sprawled over half-acre lots, built around artificial lakes and lagoons, and an emerald-green golf course that rose and dipped like a gentle tide. A resident health club, spa, and two tennis courts were situated in the back, near the foothills, but Oliver and Marge never got that far. Crayton's manse was located in the front section. To get through the gated entrance, Marge rang in through an intercom and announced herself. No response, but a moment later the wrought-iron barrier opened.

It made Marge wonder about how the kidnappers got in or out. She asked Oliver about it.

"Bert had a couple of theories," he answered. "The kidnappers got hold of a magnetic card key, or maybe they rang one of the residences at random, said they had a delivery, and a naïve soul opened the gate. Which would have been a stupid move because all regular delivery people had pass cards. FedEx, UPS, the mail carrier, the local laundry, the gourmet market, mobile pet groomer, et cetera, et cetera."

"Which means there are lots of cards in circulation."

"Yep, they're very easy to come by," Oliver answered. "By the way, the 'ring the house and open the gate' theory wasn't borne out by any of the resident interviews. No one admitted to letting them in."

"An inside job?"

"Probably, but that doesn't mean the wife did it. As far as getting out, the arm lifts automatically. Still, it's not a slam dunk for a kidnapper."

Marge agreed. She parked the car, got out, and stretched, looking at the quiet estate that had once been a crime scene. Mediterranean in style, the house was two-storied—as were all the homes in the neighborhood—and square, accented with cornerstones, windowed balconies, and a roof composed of overlapping red, pseudo-Spanish tiles. It was faced with light, apricot-colored stucco and sat behind a screen of palms, banana plants, and tree ferns. But the place showed signs of neglect. The lawn was a bit overgrown, there were weeds in the planting area, and light gray smudges streaked down the plaster from the window corners giving the impression that the house had been crying. The entrance door was recessed under an arched portico. Marge rang the bell. A young woman in her twenties answered the door.

"Mrs. Crayton?" Marge asked.

"Call me Lark," the woman answered. "Mrs.

Crayton is my former mother-in-law. You're the police?"

"Detective Oliver," Scott said. "This is Detective Dunn. Thank you for agreeing to see us."

"Yeah, sure." Lark opened the door all the way. "Come in."

As Oliver crossed the threshold, he wondered why the hell Tom and Bert hadn't mentioned the widow's comeliness. Tall and slender, with lots of chest filling out a bright, white T-shirt. Legs that didn't quit even if they were hidden under jeans. Her face was all acute angles—a sharp jawline, a strong chin, and pronounced cheekbones. Ash-blond hair had been tied back into a ponytail, gray eyes were outlined in black liner. Naturally lush lips—killer lips.

She brought them through a two-story entry hall and into the living room/family room/den. It was hard to tell what official function the room served because the floor plan was so open. Beige walls surrounded oversized tan and ivory furniture. The floor was covered by plush, ecru carpet. Potted plants added some life to the colorless decor, as did the undraped windows outlining views of the requisite backyard aqua-jeweled pool. She pointed to a sofa, then took a seat on one of the room's enormous chair-and-a-half—the latest in chichi accoutrements.

Lark draped her legs over the chair's arm.

Seductive, Oliver thought. The way she was looking at him gave him goose bumps. That pose had probably served her well in the past. When she spoke, she gazed directly into his eyes. "Did you find out anything new?"

Oliver said, "Nothing earth-shattering, but we're still—"

"Yeah, yeah." Lark broke the stare and lapsed into ennui, picking up a cigarette case from the side table and pushing a button. The lid popped open. She pulled out a smoke and spoke to Marge. "Throw me that lighter, will you?"

Marge hesitated. *Speaking to her in a dismissive voice, as if she were hired help.* She found a silver-etched box on the coffee table and held it aloft. "Is this it?"

"Yeah, yeah," Lark said. "Just throw it over."

Marge resisted the temptation to fastball it. Instead, she tossed it gently. Lark one-handed it, turned the flint wheel, and lit up. She laid the lighter and case back on the coffee table, then blew out a long, languid plume of smoke. Again to Oliver, she said, "So why are you here?"

"There have been a few incidents recently that have piqued our interest."

Lark took another drag. "What kinds of incidents?"

"Carjackings," Marge answered. "We think they might be related to what happened to your husband."

"I don't see how," Lark said. "What I've read about involve women with kids."

"There've been others that maybe you don't know about," Marge answered. "The crimes are escalating. We were just wondering if you've had any threatening calls lately—"

"You think someone's out to get me?" Lark's expression was sour and dubious. "Little late for that, don't you think? My husband's murder happened a year ago."

"So you haven't had any threatening—"

"No. Nothing. I told the cops early on that I thought it was a random thing. Because Armand drove this mother red Corniche, and he dressed very flashy. You know, gold necklaces and a big Oyster Rolex. And he was an out-there kind of guy." Lark tapped her foot. "Someone cased him . . . knew his habits . . . saw him as an easy target because Armand was just . . . out there. No one's coming back for me. Lightning doesn't strike twice, you know."

But it does, Marge thought. She said, "Your husband had made enemies."

"You're successful in business, that's what happens." She took another slow drag on her cigarette. "Never a shortage of resentful people. You know, the papers have made this big thing about Armand being a major player. They never talk about the long hours he put into his business. He had a dream. Some scumbag motherfucker took it away from him." She blew out smoke. "I've done a lot of thinking this past year while waiting for the insurance to come through—"

"Has it?"

"Finally!" Lark announced. "Three weeks ago. Took them long enough, the scumbags. The house is now in escrow. As soon as that's a done deal, I'm gone. Armand and I have a condo in the Marina. It's got everything I need including a doorman. This place is way too big for me . . . not to mention the memories. And I need the house money to pay off Armand's debts. God, he had enough of those. Not to mention the lawsuits." Her voice grew bitter. "Jesus, what a mess. I'm *almost* done with the creditors and bankruptcy court. It's been one hell of a year."

Marge said, "Must have been horrible dealing with monetary issues while still grieving."

"Yeah, well, whatever." Lark crushed out her cigarette in a pottery ashtray. "I've got two more court dates and then the lawyer says I'm a free bird."

"Are you still in contact with any of Armand's former associates?" Marge asked.

"Lady, I'm not even in contact with any of Armand's former *friends*. I'm making a clean break. Not that I didn't have a good ride with Armand. But now I just want *out*."

Not exactly the distraught widow, Oliver thought. But who could blame her? She probably married this guy, expecting to live the good life—

money, drugs, sex, affairs with the delivery boy when the old man was away. Instead, she wound up with a murdered husband, mounting debts, and—the worst possible thing in L.A.—bad press coverage.

Oliver said, "So you haven't received any strange mail or weird phone calls?"

"Unless you mean the breather?"

Oliver stared at her.

"I'm kidding!" Lark said. "No strange calls except from attorneys on the other side. And let me tell you something, Detective Oliver. I'd rather deal with an obscene breather than a lawyer any day of the week."

❑

SHE almost got away with it, but Tropper caught her just as she was leaving the report room. She nodded politely. He returned the greeting with what sounded like an accusation.

"Calling it a day, Officer Decker?"

"And a long day at that, sir," Cindy answered. *How many extra hours did he expect her to put in?*

"Where're you off to?" he asked.

"Dinner with my dad," she lied.

Tropper nodded. "One day I'd like to meet the lieutenant."

Now how do you respond to that? Cindy somehow managed a smile. "Great."

He was silent, seemed to be waiting for more. *Surely he didn't expect an instant invitation?* "Well, I'd better be going." Another forced smile. "Shouldn't keep a superior officer waiting."

"I like that, Decker," the Sarge answered. "That's very good."

"Good day, sir," Cindy answered. Slowly and with great self-control, she turned and walked away. As soon as he was out of sight, she ran to the locker room, angry that sweat had soaked through her clothes. Hayley Marx was there, combing her hair, peering into a mirror with hard-ass eyes. If she noticed Cindy's wet armpits, she didn't comment on them.

"Hey, Decker. We missed you last night at Bellini's."

Cindy opened her locker, then slowly began stripping off her uniform. "What happened?"

"Joey Goudis got drunk and chunked on Andy Lopez—"

"Oh God. Poor Andy!"

"Screw him! He was acting like an asshole, anyway. Spilled his bourbon over my silk blouse."

"Was he drunk?"

"Nah, just being clumsy. He asked about you. Lopez, I mean. He asked who drove you home a couple of nights ago. I told him you drove yourself home. He thought that was dumb because you looked pretty messed. I defended you, but it was dumb, Decker."

"I didn't drive myself home," Cindy said. "I was

going to drive myself home, but I didn't. Scott Oliver took my keys away from me."

Hayley turned around and took in Cindy's face. *"Oliver* took you home?"

Cindy unbuttoned her shirt. "Yep. I suppose it wouldn't have been cool with Dad if they had found me wrapped around a telephone pole with a BAL of one million, and Oliver hadn't interceded."

Hayley waited a few beats, then closed her locker, her eyes still bearing down on Cindy's face. "What did he say to you? Oliver?"

"Before or after I upchucked?"

Hayley suppressed a smile. "Not very good for a first date, Decker."

"It wasn't a date."

Hayley evaluated her sincerity and decided she was telling it legit. "So he took you home, huh?"

"Yeah, Marx. He just took me home. What else do you want to know?"

Hayley rolled her eyes. "I'm acting like a jerk."

"Nah, it's just men. Did your blouse clean out?"

"Don't know yet," Hayley answered. "Haven't gotten it back from the cleaners." She paused. "I haven't even taken it *to* the cleaners. No time. Anyway, Andy seemed disappointed that you didn't choose him as designated driver."

"Tell Andy next time."

"Why don't you come to Bellini's tonight and tell him yourself? Besides, I hear Doogle's running a three-drinks-for-the-price-of-two special."

Cindy smiled internally. Someone in the department *liked* her. Even after she admitted to having
the woman's ex-boyfriend drive her home. Of
course, she wouldn't dare tell Hayley about last
night's dinner . . . or tonight's meeting. What was
the point? Besides, it wasn't her business. It wasn't
anyone's business. "Let's do it tomorrow. I've got to
go marketing. Right now, all I have in my fridge
is a wilted bag of salad, a carton of sour milk, a
six-pack of beer, and a six-pack of Diet Coke."

Hayley smiled. "You can borrow my Miracle
Whip to make salad dressing."

"Sounds like a feast!"

"Shop later on. I'll come with you."

"So shop with me now. I've got an obligation
later on."

"As in a hot date obligation?"

"Only if you're into incest. I think my dad's
coming over."

"You're sick." She hesitated. "He's married, isn't
he . . . your dad."

Cindy laughed. "Yes, he is."

"Does he cheat?"

"My dad is *the* most straitlaced person—"

"Yeah, yeah." Hayley shrugged. "I've heard that
one before!"

"Honest! Anyway, why would you want to mess
around with a married guy?"

"He's a loo. It's good to know people in high
places." She draped an arm around Cindy's bare

shoulder. "Why do you think I'm hanging around you?"

"And here I thought it was my charming personality." Cindy pushed a white turtleneck sweater over her head. "If you want married men, Hayley, you've got a selection out there."

"Ain't that the truth. They're all married or gay." Hayley parked herself on the bench in front of Cindy's locker. "It gets depressing, you know."

"What? Dating married men? I imagine it wouldn't be too fulfilling."

"It's not even that. It's the whole thing. I like the job, but I don't want to be doing this forever."

Cindy nodded but didn't answer. She *loved* the job. Getting somewhere in the department held the number one spot on her to-do list. The *last* thing she wanted was to settle down.

Hayley said, "I'd like the basics one day. You know . . . the picket fence, the pitter-patter, the white van with all those ridiculous cup holders and the bumper sticker that says: Baby on Board. It's lonely being macho. You'll see when you're at it long enough. You've got to be tough. And once you're tough, guys treat you like a guy. Which I guess is their way of accepting you. But it gets to you after a while."

"I'm sure you're right." Cindy zipped up her pants. "How long have you felt the burnout?" Meaning *How long before I feel that way?*

She shrugged. "It creeps up on you, Decker.

Maybe it has something to do with finding the dead baby."

About three months ago, a newborn infant was found in an alley Dumpster. Hayley had been the one to fish her out . . . holding the lifeless naked body in her hands. Cindy restrained from shuddering. She placed a hand on Hayley's shoulder. "You want to go food shopping with me?"

"Nah!" Hayley shook her head. "I'd rather go torture Doogle." She unlatched the top three buttons of her blouse. "Think this'll do?"

"That'll torture 'em all, Hayley."

"Good. That's what I had in mind."

❑

OLIVER checked his watch. It was a quarter to six, leaving him almost no time to make it over the canyon, interview Hollywood, and eat and see Cindy by seven-thirty. Which was going to be a total waste anyway because he knew that Decker was going to show up. Meaning that he wouldn't get a chance to see her alone. And, more likely than not, Decker would stay for the entire interview so he couldn't catch her alone afterward. So maybe what he should do is call Cindy on the cell phone and ask her to meet him for coffee in about an hour. Then they could talk alone for a few minutes, about what was happening with the Crayton case and why Decker brought her up in the first place. And how to handle the questioning. Then they'd leave in separate cars and—

"Hey, Scott, I'm talking to you."

Oliver bolted around. "I didn't hear you, Margie. What's up?"

"How could you not hear me? I'm standing right next to you."

He tapped his temple. "I was concentrating on the Crayton case."

"What in particular?"

Oliver gave her a thoughtful look while his brain tried to think of a response. "How things can change and a dead issue can be jump-started alive. A couple of red cars and . . . boom. Course we're far off from solving anything."

"Well, I was thinking about it, too," Marge said. "Specifically, our conversation with Lark."

"Now there's a queer bird."

"More like a vulture," Marge said. "Scott, do you remember her talking about Armand wearing an Oyster Rolex?"

"Yeah. Sure. What about it?"

Marge said, "It got me thinking. If Crayton was a random thing because he was rich, I was thinking maybe they robbed him before they took him—"

"Didn't have too much time for that, Margie," Oliver said. "Lark saw the whole thing, called the police right away. The chase was pretty close to immediate."

"You're absolutely right. So going over the path

report, I wasn't surprised that he had his wallet on him."

"He was burned up," Oliver said. "The pathologist could tell he had his wallet?"

"The original team found bits of money and patches of leather. Actually, there were bits of high-denomination money."

"So like we said, he wasn't robbed. Although if he was carrying large bills, maybe robbery was the original intent."

"Yeah, that's what I was thinking." Marge cleared her throat. "You know, people wear watches like they're part of their bodies. You put on your clothes, you put on your makeup—well, I put on my makeup. Last and final thing I do is put on my watch. My wrist feels naked without it."

"Don't tell me," Oliver said. "He wasn't wearing a watch. So you think he was robbed?"

"He was wearing a watch, Scott, but it wasn't a Rolex. Enough of it survived for Path to state that it was a Timex."

Oliver decided to play devil's advocate. "So he didn't wear the good stuff that day."

"You picture a guy like Armand going out wearing a Timex?"

"Obviously he did."

"Or somebody switched his timepiece before he was burned to a crisp," Marge answered. "Lark specifically said that she thought the kidnappers were attracted to his flashy stuff—things like the car and his Oyster Rolex. Scott, why mention the watch if it wasn't on him that day?"

"Maybe she's talking in abstracts. Or maybe she didn't know he wasn't wearing it."

"Or maybe she did know."

Oliver said, "What are you saying? That she knew Armand was going to be kidnapped so she took his good watch and gave him a loaner?"

Marge shrugged. "You met the woman. Did she seem grief-stricken?"

"Not at all. You know, Martinez and Webster delved into the woman's past and didn't find anything. They told me that during the interview she said the right things to cover her butt. Also, the insurance company must have looked into her past long and hard before giving her the money. It took them a year to issue the check."

"So maybe we should check out their research. Nothing to lose by calling."

Oliver agreed that a call was in order. Lark was dangerously beautiful and callously aloof. She'd be perfect in the role of the "evil widow." Lark needed to be probed. Although the kind of probing he was thinking about had little to do with the widow's past.

12

THE LINE was long, and service was slow because too many people were waiting for a half-caf, nonfat, soy mocha cap—with a hint of amaretto syrup and go easy on the milk even if it's not real milk—coffee. Cindy was cooling her heels behind five others when Oliver walked in. He looked harried with his black hair mussed and his eyes darting about. It gave him kind of a feral mountain-man look. Yeah, mountain man in a tailored suit and a Gucci tie. She left her place, then hooked her arm through his. "No cup of coffee is worth this long a line. We can grab some McMocha at a McDonald's drive-through and talk in the car."

Oliver smiled. "McMocha?"

"I made that up. Think I should try to sell it to Ray Kroc?"

"He's dead."

"Minor inconvenience."

"Why on earth were you waiting in line?"

"What?"

Oliver broke away, walked up to the counter, and flashed his badge. "I'm in a rush. Two coffees."

Behind the counter was a stunned teen with a pierced nose. She stared at the badge but obligingly filled the order. A moment later the two cops walked outside together, Oliver holding two steaming paper cups of java. He gave them to Cindy and opened the passenger door. "Give the cups back to me."

Cindy got in and took her drink back. After they were inside, she sipped, then said, "Thanks, though it's not my style to flex muscle."

Oliver said, "So, it's okay for you to risk your life every day out on the streets, getting abused by drunks, felons, and various miscreants. But you can't let yourself butt in line to get your cup of coffee—which I *paid* for—"

"I'll pay you back."

"That's not what I meant." Oliver sipped, then gulped. "Not even hot. What's wrong with these people? I'm referring to these asshole corporate places that don't give public servants even a simple break like a free cup of coffee—"

"Ah, the good old days."

"You scoff, but it's true. Nowadays, you can't borrow a tissue to wipe your nose without someone thinking you're on the dole."

"Scott, that's a good thing."

"What is?"

"Not getting things for free. It gives the wrong impression."

"So you're saying that for the average cop, being comped a cup of coffee leads to planting evidence

to obtain murder indictments," he groused.
"You're way too new to be self-righteous."

"But I am anyway. That's the charm of youth. On
a more relevant note, what's happening with the
Crayton case, Scott? How'd my name come up?"

"I told you, your father brought you up."

"In what capacity?"

"As a friend of Armand's—"

"A *casual* friend. I hope he said that."

"He's still reserving judgment."

Cindy made a face. "I knew he didn't believe me.
He gave me that look."

"What look?"

"The parental look that says 'You spent your
milk money on candy, didn't you.' "

"What prompted the whole thing was another
jacking this afternoon," Oliver said. "This one was
a lone woman in a red Beemer. Crayton's car was a
red Corniche, and Elizabeth Tarkum—the woman
that Craig Burrows was talking to you about—
drove a red Ferrari. Tarkum was kidnapped like
Crayton, taken with the car. Later on, she was
dropped off, unharmed but very shaken. We're
looking into a connection between the three cases."

"What kind of a connection? Red cars?"

"That, and maybe these women were associated
with Crayton."

"Associated how?" Cindy asked. "Business or
pleasure?"

"We don't know."

"So you're talking about a long shot."

Oliver said, "We're talking about a year-old un-solved murder that has similarities with current cases. We'd be neglectful if we didn't investigate every angle."

"So what does this have to do with me?" she asked. "I drive a seasick-green Saturn."

Oliver stared at her. "Did you hear what I said, Cindy? Women who may have been associated with Crayton. You're a woman who was *definitely* associated with Crayton. A woman who someone took potshots at. Your dad is worried that kidnap-ping may be next."

"That's utter nonsense."

"Why? Because you want it to be?"

"No, because my association with Armand was minimal. And you don't even know if these jack-ings have anything to do with him. And what are you going to ask me tonight that my father and you haven't already asked?"

"Just to go over your relationship with Armand—"

"I already told you and Dad about that."

"Well, maybe Marge'll have some insights."

"I don't see what."

"We'll also ask you if you've had any unusual phone calls, weird letters—"

"Nothing."

"No threatening messages, no aura of someone following you?"

Cindy hesitated just long enough for Oliver to pick up on it. "What?"

"Nothing," Cindy answered.

"Cindy—"

"Nothing unusual. No weird phone calls, no spooky letters, no one following me. My life is in perfect order, everything buttoned up tight, and nothing out of place . . . unless you mean the picture of my sister that you moved off my mantel."

"What are you talking about?"

"The night you took me home." Cindy tried to remain calm. "While I was in the bathroom trying to hold down my stomach, you were looking at the pictures on my fireplace mantel."

Oliver stared at her.

"Right?" Cindy asked.

"Right. And . . ."

"You were looking at my baby sister's picture. You picked it up—"

"I didn't touch anything." He stopped. "No, I take that back. I used your phone to call my cab and I peeked through your blinds to look for it. So I touched your phone and your blinds. But that was the extent of it."

Cindy stopped talking, trying to figure out her next move.

Oliver said, "I don't touch other people's things, let alone move them around. When I'm casing a house, I walk around with my hands in my pockets. Force of habit from the job. Don't touch what could be evidence. What's this about someone moving your sister's picture?"

Cindy didn't answer, thinking about the night. When she had come out to her living room, his hands had been in his pockets.

Oliver crushed his empty paper cup. "Are you going to answer me or not?"

"Sure." Cindy tried to appear calm. "I thought you moved the picture frame. If you didn't, I probably moved it when I was dusting and forgot to put it back."

A bald lie and they both knew it. Oliver said, "Have your doors been tampered—"

"No—"

"Locks on your windows—"

"Everything's intact—"

"Your drawers haven't been gone through?"

"No—"

"You're sure?"

"Yes—"

"When was the last time you were home?"

"This morning!" She frowned. "Why are you making such a big deal—"

"I'm not making a big deal, I'm asking questions. No weird letters or messages on your machine?"

"I told you no—" She stopped herself.

"Spit it out!" Oliver ordered.

"A Post-it on the wheel of my cruiser," Cindy answered. "It said 'remember'—"

"Oh my God!"

"It was nothing, Scott. Probably a reminder that one of the service guys wrote to himself."

"Do you still have it?"

"No, I threw it away. Stop looking at me like that. How was I to know that it could be significant?"

Oliver checked his watch. It was ten to seven. "I'd like to have a look around your apartment before the others come. See if anything's out of place—"

"You're being ridiculous!"

"You're in denial—"

"No, I'm not. I love myself. If something was off, I'd let you know."

"So humor me. Let me come over early."

Cindy regarded Oliver's intense expression. His voice had also taken on a professional demeanor. All of it gave her a disquieting feeling that she tried to brush off. "Sure, if you think it's that important."

Oliver nodded. "Thank you. Also, you're going to have to tell your dad what you told me . . . about the Post-it and the picture!"

"And freak him out over nothing? Absolutely not! And you're not going to tell him about it, either. Because to admit to the picture, you'd have to admit being in my apartment, and you don't want to do that."

Oliver's tone darkened. "Decker, I have no problem with telling your father that I took you home because you were plastered. I just thought you may have a problem—"

"No problem whatsoever," Cindy said assuredly. "As a matter of fact, I told Hayley Marx about it because I'm the type who has nothing to hide."

Oliver stared at her, a dumbfounded expression stamped across his face. "You didn't *really* do that, did you?"

"Indeed I did." Cindy folded her arms across her chest and waited for his retort.

He said, "Why the *hell* did you tell Hayley Marx that I took you home?"

"What's the big deal, Oliver? I was drunk, you gave me a lift. End of discussion."

Oliver slumped in the seat and slapped his forehead. "I can't believe you did that! It's going to get back to your dad—"

"So what? You were just like . . . doing a public service—"

"*Christ!*" Oliver was pissed. "Of all the people to tell! Hayley Marx and her big mouth! She's a one-woman tabloid! Not to mention the spin she'll put on it to make me look bad."

"She seemed okay with it considering she still likes you."

"Decker, this isn't about Hayley Marx. It's about your dad knowing that I drove you home. I didn't want to deal with it. Especially since I suggested that Marge and I interview you *instead of* him.

Your dad didn't take to the idea right away. Now, he's definitely going to have his suspicions. He's my *boss*, Cindy. Didn't you *think* about that?"

She really hadn't.

He glared at her with a sour face. "I suppose you told Hayley about our dinner as well."

"Now *why* would I do that?"

"Uh, let's see now. Could it be because you speak before you think?"

Cindy glowered at him with hot, fierce eyes. "You're even a bigger asshole than your reputation has it. And, FYI, I'm not going to tell my dad about that night or about the stupid misplaced picture or the Post-it. I'm not going to bring any of this up tonight. So if you want to tell Dad about the picture, you're going to have to tell him about *this* conversation!"

Oliver studied her angry visage. She was impetuous and hot-tempered, and she pissed him off. Still, he tried to modulate his voice. "Did it ever enter your brain that I'm concerned about you? Concerned as a father? Concerned because I *work* with your father? Concerned because despite that fresh, impulsive mouth of yours, I know you're a good kid and would feel terrible if something happened to you."

She stared at her lap, then looked upward and spoke to the car's ceiling. "Funny me. I thought you were concerned because maybe you like me."

"That, too." He waved her off. "I should just

stick to airheads. They're closer to my IQ and have no expectations. Get out of here. Go home. Check your door locks. I'll see you at eight."

"So you're not coming early?"

"No, I'm not coming early." Oliver stared out the windshield.

Cindy drummed the dashboard for a moment, then unlatched the door. "I'll see you at eight then."

"Just watch your ass, okay?"

"Fine. I'll watch my ass."

She got out, closed the door gently, but hesitated before she left.

Waiting for him to stop her.

Screw that! She was just too fucking complicated.

All the good ones came with complications.

Oliver saw her rock on her feet, then tie the arms of her black sweater around her neck. He watched her slowly walk toward her car. The rise and fall of her white turtleneck shirt with each inhalation, her hips swaying against her black slacks. She had a reputation as a fast sprinter. But she also had a graceful walk. He sighed.

Who was watching whose ass?

13

DAD WASN'T waiting for her; Scott had gotten *that* wrong. And her dead bolts and locks were latched and secured. Cindy also studied her doorjamb: no notches or pry marks. Everything appeared undisturbed. Feeling a bit less apprehensive, she unlocked the door and stepped inside her apartment, throwing her black sweater on the couch. A quick glance told her that the place remained just as she had left it. Morning coffee cup still on the side table, the newspaper opened to the editorial page.

Okay. So *that* was taken care of. She was relieved, but she also felt a twinge of disappointment. Her job provided hours of unpredictability and novelty. In contrast, her personal life seemed mundane and listless. Still, she knew she should be careful what she wished for. *Interesting* was an adjective in a Chinese curse.

She picked up the mug and put it in the kitchen sink, then took down a goblet and poured a glass of white wine, knowing it was dumb to drink on an empty stomach. She'd been doing quite a few dumb things of late, most of them having to do with Oliver.

Holding her drink, she came back into her living room, her eyes sweeping over the fireplace mantel.

The family pictures and her porcelain animals were exactly as she had left them: pigs, cats, dogs, and cows aligned together in perfect interspecies unity.

She parked herself in front of the TV and turned on the boob tube with the remote control. The screen filled with images of two people tearing down a supermarket aisle, throwing dozens of cellophane-wrapped hams into their respective shopping carts. Because the sound had been muted, the racing shoppers looked even more comical, as if acting in a Keystone Kops silent movie. She thought about Oliver, wondering if he was scaring her on purpose. Assuming that he was, the next question would be: Why would he want to do that?

Could be he had a Superman complex, the type who stepped in to rescue the damsel in distress. Dad called them HOTS, or Heroes of the Story. No matter how they told the tale, somehow they'd wind up saving the day. The hero—and notice she was thinking about a hero instead of heroine because HOTS were usually male—used phrases like "If I hadn't been there" or "If it wasn't for me" or the pseudo-modest "So they asked me my opinion, and I suggested such-and-such, which just happened to work out perfectly."

So what could turn Oliver into a HOT? An insecurity complex? Or maybe he had been secure until he hit middle age. Maybe his need to be a HOT stemmed from the same fears that propelled him to chase after women half his age. He needed a youth-affirming ego boost. Or perhaps he was trying to make points with the boss by helping his daughter. But that didn't make much sense because he was secretive about their interactions. Then again, just maybe he had legitimate concerns about her safety in this Crayton thing.

Her watch—which she purposely set five minutes fast—read seven thirty-three. She had enough time to make herself some grub. And that probably would be a good idea because she shouldn't do an interview on just a wine-coated stomach. She forced herself up and put a frozen pizza pocket into the toaster.

Ah, the thrill of single life. Even Mom, who was no great whiz in the kitchen, could cook better than this. Cindy did have a standing invitation with her dad and stepmom to come for Friday night dinner, the meal that inaugurated the Jewish Sabbath. Though she hated to impose, maybe this was a good week to take Rina up on it. Her stepmother was very religious; her father had become that way because of her. Their way of life was alien to her. She likened it to a finely crafted Victorian chair—charming and beautiful but impractical for everyday life. But it served her father well, made him happy, and that said a lot.

The pizza pocket popped into the air, landing a half-foot away from the toaster and onto her counter. Gingerly, she picked up the hot pastry and wrapped it in a napkin, munching on it as she headed for her bedroom. What was the dress of choice for being grilled by one's own colleagues . . . or maybe the better choice of word was superiors.

Dad as her superior. After she had spent almost a decade trying to break free from his paternal bonds.

So who told you to go into police enforcement?

She decided to keep on her current outfit—the white turtleneck and black slacks—even though she would have preferred donning jeans and a sweatshirt. Her dress made for a more professional image. Picking up a brush, she smoothed out her red locks, then reapplied her makeup.

Was she nervous about talking to them? Maybe a little. She didn't like her personal life dissected, especially since Crayton had been a poor choice for a friend. She'd look to Marge for support. Marge was cool. She had been her father's partner since Cindy was a teen, had always acted as her advocate when Dad got unreasonable.

She tucked the turtleneck into her pants, then noticed an almost imperceptible stain. She must have dripped coffee, although she didn't recall anything spilling. But that was always a problem with white clothing. Just a speck of brown coffee would show up like a dusted fingerprint. She took off the top and opened her sweater drawer.

Immediately, her heart started hammering—

loud, big thumps. On the surface, everything looked fine. Her tops were folded and neatly stacked. But within an eyeblink, she knew that someone had gone through the drawer. Because her cotton tops were on the right side of the drawer and her woolens were on the left. She always, *always* put her woolens on the right and her cotton sweaters on the left. She quickly opened the three other drawers in the bureau—pants and shorts, sweatshirts and pajamas, underwear, socks, and stockings.

They *seemed* in perfect array. Just the sweater drawer was off.

Or maybe she was wrong.

Or maybe she was going nuts.

As she stared at her clothing, she felt sweat pouring off her brow, her armpits warm and wet, her hands shaking. Her stomach had bunched into a tight, hot knot. Sparkly lights began to dance in her head. She took two steps backward, until her calves knocked against the edge of her bed. She sank down, dropping her head between her knees, red hair cascading down her skull and tickling the carpet. This wasn't from just the sweaters, it was also the booze. She had to stop drinking.

Breathe in, breathe out. Okay, think. When was the last time you straightened your drawers?

A month ago? Maybe even longer? Was it possible that she had reversed the stacks, putting the woolens on the left instead of on the right and the cotton on the right instead of on the left? Because analyzing it with calm eyes, she realized that her sweaters had been folded precisely the way she had always folded her sweaters. And the stacks were neat. She always made nice, neat piles thanks to an obsession with order and detail. Maybe this was nothing more than an overactive imagination due to Oliver's suggestibility.

Damn him!

She threw her head back and plopped her spine down onto her mattress, staring at the ceiling. Still garbed in only pants and a bra, she felt her sweat-coated body evaporating water. The process chilled her skin.

Put some clothes on, Decker.

With great care, she managed to stand up. Trudging over to the evil drawer, she fished out a black ribbed-cotton crew.

Hoping that she was making an unnecessary big deal about this left-right thing. She had probably done it herself although she thought that she might have noticed the reversal. Maybe she only realized it now because she was searching for something awry.

She was about to don the crewneck sweater, but her nose told her she smelled ripe. She needed a shower. Not only would water cleanse her body, it would also clear her mind. She stripped down, stuck her hair in a plastic cap, and turned on the tap until the water steamed. Stepping into the cubicle of hot needles, she bristled, then luxuriated into the combination of pleasure and pain. By the time she emerged from the stall, her skin was lobster pink. Again she felt light-headed, but this time it was from low blood pressure rather than anxiety. Sitting on the seat of her toilet, wrapped in a towel, she dropped her head and tried to stave off an oncoming headache.

Her paranoia was running away with her. After all, how could anyone get in without tampering with the locks? And she had checked the dead bolt on her door and the windows . . . well, at least she had checked the dead bolt.

Maybe she should check the windows before the mod squad descended on her like locusts. Slowly arising, she went into her bedroom and donned all-black attire. She brushed out her hair and put on fresh makeup—just a hint of blush and lipstick—and popped two Advils prophylactically. She picked up the remnants of her pizza pocket and threw it away in the kitchen garbage. While she was there, she checked the side window, which would have been a hard climb because it was flush with the building and two stories up. The lock was latched, the frame devoid of any telltale marks. The paint around the woodwork was without chips and flakes. If the imaginary sweater intruder had somehow gotten inside her house, he hadn't used the doors or the kitchen window.

Or he was a professional.

That didn't sit well with her.

She was about to examine the front windows when the doorbell rang at seven fifty-two—according to her fast watch. Through the peephole, she was relieved to see her father. The last thing she wanted was to be alone with Oliver. She threw open the door and tried to appear normal: giving him a chastising look for showing up even if she was secretly happy to see him.

"Dad . . ."

"I was in the neighborhood."

"Yeah, you're in the neighborhood because you drove yourself to the neighborhood."

Decker smiled. He hoped it was disarming. "Can I come in?"

"I suppose it would be unseemly to let a police lieutenant beg in the halls." She stepped aside. "Come in. I'm not answering anything until the others get here. I've already gone over this before. I'm not repeating myself more than I have to."

"Fair enough." He went over to her mantel and picked up the picture of Hannah. He smiled. "Where was this from? From the zoo, right?"

"Yep. You never saw it before?"

"Actually I think I did. I just forgot how cute it was. You should make me a copy."

Maybe Dad had moved the picture. When was the last time he was here? Months ago. "Admit it. You think number two daughter is cuter than number one."

"I think you're adorable. You just don't look as cute toothless as she does."

"That's a definite point." She picked up her sweater and then put it down again. "Is this interview really necessary?"

Decker shrugged. "We'll find out."

"It's a waste of time. I already told you everything."

"Oliver and Dunn think I might have an objectivity problem." Decker put the picture back on the mantel. "They may be right."

The doorbell rang again. This time it was Marge. She kissed Cindy on the cheek and threw her purse down on the couch. "You fixed this place up since the last time I was here."

"New blinds, a couple of throws, not much else."

Marge looked at Decker. "Why did I know you were going to be here?" Her eyes went to Cindy. "Can you talk if he's around?"

"Yes, of course. This whole thing is unnecessary, Marge. I barely knew the guy."

Marge took out a notepad from her jacket. "You mean Armand Crayton?"

"Yes. We worked out together. End of story."

"Except for the potshots," Marge added.

"I see you filled her in," Cindy said to her father.

"Not the details."

"That's because there are no details." To Marge, Cindy said, "They may have been meant for him, they may have been random. Certainly they weren't meant for me."

Decker said, "Maybe we should wait for Scott before we go any further."

Marge said, "He's running behind. His interviews with Hollywood got off to a late start."

"Is he showing up?" Decker wanted to know.

"Yeah, but it's going to take him a while."

"Does he have something on the jackings?"

"He didn't say."

Cindy said, "Since this might concern me, can someone please tell me what's going on?"

Marge sat on the couch. "Sure bet. Have a seat, Cin. Let me tell you our thoughts." And she did, repeating almost word for word what Oliver had told her an hour earlier. "We're checking out these women to see if they had dealings with Crayton because the jackings are similar. Also, we're talking to women who knew him. That's why we're here."

"First off, I was never a real friend, just a casual acquaintance. We were gym buddies. Nothing beyond that."

"No business dealings?"

"Nope. Even if I had wanted to invest with him, I couldn't have. No money."

Decker said, "Did he talk to you about business?"

"In generalities—"

"Like what?"

"Gosh, it was so long ago . . ." She frowned as she concentrated. "Land deals mostly. If I recall . . . don't hold me to this . . . the idea was to buy the land and turn it around for a quick profit. Catch people while the interest rates were low and real estate was high."

Decker said, "Why do you think he talked to you about it if you had no money?"

"Bragging, Dad," Cindy said. "He was showing off. Probably to make some time with me. It didn't work."

"He put the move on you?" Marge asked.

"Not in a cloddish way," Cindy said. "But if something were to happen, I don't think he would have been unhappy."

"Did he ever suggest meeting you outside the gym?"

"A couple of times for coffee. I said no. That was it." She turned to her father. "I told all of this to you."

"I know. But it sounds different with Marge here."

Marge said, "When you were shot at, Cindy, did someone say anything?"

"No one was shooting at me."

Marge rephrased the statement. "When they shot at Armand and you were there, did someone say anything?"

"No."

Decker said, "Nothing?"

"Nothing. Why would they?"

"Well," Decker began. "If it's a revenge thing against Crayton, someone might say something to identify the reason behind the crime."

"Like in the movies? 'Take that, you bastard.'" She made a face. "*Daaad* . . . Isn't that a little clichéd?"

Criminals were clichés. They were cardboard cutouts— strictly interchangeable parts. Decker said, "So no one spoke?"

"If someone did, I didn't hear it."

"Were you walking or standing when the shooting started?"

"I . . . we . . . standing near his car, I think."

"But you're not sure."

"No, we might have been walking toward his car."

"You were walking him to his car?" Marge asked. "He wasn't walking you to your car?"

"His car was parked closer to the entrance," Cindy said. "And that would make sense, wouldn't it? Someone stationing himself near Crayton's car. Because Crayton was the target, right?"

Nobody answered her, making Cindy even more nervous.

Finally, Marge spoke. "How many shots were fired?"

"I don't know," Cindy said. "I wasn't counting."

"One, two . . . more?"

"Maybe more."

"Any of the bullets come close to you?"

"Sure seemed like it."

"How close?"

"How would I know?" Cindy said. "I ducked behind the car as soon as I heard the pops."

"His car?" Decker asked.

"Yeah, his car. The red Corniche."

"Did his car get hit with bullets?"

"Most likely it did. But it couldn't have been hit that bad. Because he was driving it the next time we met at the gym."

"He *came back* to the gym?" Decker asked.

"Yeah. Guess he figured he was safe. That the shooter wouldn't try the same thing twice."

"That's awfully naïve," Decker said. "And you know for certain he was driving the Corniche when he came back?"

"Yes. Because I asked him how his car was. And he said fine. Then both of us changed the subject. I maybe saw him three, four times after that. I must have been subconsciously avoiding him. Then, of course, when I started working on the force, I didn't have as much time, so I began using the stationhouse gym."

Marge said, "When the shooting started, it seems like you two were almost stationary objects."

"I guess."

"So if the shooter had been pro, he could have probably picked either of you off."

"I suppose." Cindy shrugged. "If you're implying the shooter was after me, then using your same logic, he could have picked me off with one shot as well." The stark reality of the words gave her goose bumps. She rubbed her arms but didn't say anything.

Decker said, "She's saying that maybe the shots were a warning from a jealous wife."

"Oh," Cindy said. "Then again, for all we know, the shots could have been kids getting a kick out of totaling a Rolls."

"That's why I asked if the car was hit," Decker said. "You said the damage wasn't too bad."

"Maybe it was," Cindy said. "I don't remember, Daddy!"

The doorbell rang. Decker stood, but Cindy beat him to it. "Father, it's my place, remember?"

Decker sat back down. "Try to do someone a favor."

Oliver walked in. "Sorry I'm late."

"Did you find out anything?" Decker asked.

"I think you're going to be happy." He took off his jacket and looked at Cindy. "Can I hang this up somewhere?"

"I'll do it for you. Have a seat, Scott." Cindy looked around her living room, anywhere but at him. "Anyone want anything to drink, by the way?"

"Nothing for me, thanks." Oliver sat next to Marge. "Someone bring me up-to-date, please?"

Cindy filled him in. When she was done, she said, "I realize you have this whole revenge thing mapped out. But I had nothing to do with Crayton's business affairs. Why would anyone shoot at me?"

"Crayton was married," Oliver stated. "Could your relationship have been misconstrued as an affair?"

"We were just going over that. I *suppose* if someone wanted to see it that way . . ." She sat back down. "Have you met his wife?"

Oliver looked at Marge. "Interviewed her this morning."

Decker said, "Tell me about her."

Marge said, "Young, gorgeous, chesty, and probably doing fine in the money department now that Crayton's life insurance has come in—"

"Ah!" said Decker. "It came through. When did they pay off?"

"She said three weeks ago," Marge answered.

Decker raised his eyebrows. "It's been over a year. Someone did a thorough investigation."

"We're on it, Loo," Oliver said.

Decker thought a moment. "She was the one who called the cops. Think she could have staged the entire kidnapping?"

"The car crash was real," Marge said. "That's for certain."

"The car fell over the embankment, then exploded." Decker held up a finger. "I wonder how long it took from the point of impact to the point of explosion? Because despite what happens in the movies, when a car tumbles over an embankment, unless it's down a direct drop, the car usually doesn't explode on impact. First the gas line has to break and spill. Then the sparks have to ignite, then the explosion happens only when the gas tank is reached."

Oliver tapped his foot. "Someone detonated the car after the kidnappers escaped?"

"Or the car had been monkeyed with prior to the kidnapping. Let's not lose sight of the fact that Crayton was a con artist. If someone is carjacking women to vent his hatred against Crayton, we should go over his business dealings again."

Cindy said, "Armand talked like a scamster. Always full of ideas, of making a big killing. Like the land thing."

"What exactly was he doing?" Oliver asked.

"Armand told me he was buying land at cheap prices to turn it over for a quick buck."

Decker said, "I've done a little research since we last talked. It seems to me that he was pyramiding, conning from one investor to buy things like land or shares of speculative companies. Then he used those items as collateral for more loans to buy more things. When times are good, no one complains. But when the bottom drops out, he'd be stuck without cash to cover the other investments."

"His wife told us he left her in deep debt," Marge said. "She seemed pissed about it."

"But he had life insurance to cover the debts," Cindy said.

"Who said he took out the policy on himself?" Decker remarked. "Maybe his wife took out the policy on him?"

"We're working on it," Oliver said.

"You seem to be working on lots of stuff," Decker said.

"I know," Oliver answered. "Want to hear what I have on Elizabeth Tarkum?"

"Go," Marge said.

"No investments with Crayton under her name," Oliver said. "But Crayton had a lot of dealings with Tarkum's *husband*, Dexter Bartholomew. Better known in circles as Dex the Tex. Only he's not from Texas. He's from Tulsa, Oklahoma."

"How'd you find *this* out?" Decker asked.

"From the original file—known associates. Bartholomew made money with Armand so he was passed over as a suspect. Besides, no one made a connection between Tarkum and Crayton because of the different last name. Also, the investments were in Dex's name, not Tarkum's. Lastly, the Tarkum jacking took place in Hollywood, not Devonshire. It's only when you go through the two cases at the same time, that it all comes together."

"Tulsa's an oil town," Decker said. "Is he in the business?"

Oliver said, "You better believe it. He manufactures pipes and pipe joints and pressure valves, and all the things you need to get the oil from the wells to the refineries."

"And he invested with Crayton?"

"Yes," Oliver said. "In land sales. Bartholomew made out like a bandit. He's loaded . . . which explains the young wife in the red Ferrari."

"Tell me about the jacking again," Decker said.

"Elizabeth Tarkum went inside her car, turned on the motor. Next thing she knew, she was dumped twenty miles from home. The car was never recovered."

"They knocked her out?"

"She doesn't remember."

"Raped?"

"If she was raped, she didn't file."

Decker said, "Why has it taken us this long to make the connection?"

"Every substation has had carjackings, Loo," Oliver said. "We're just looking into all of them now because we've had a rash of them in our own district. And even if we were looking for similar jackings, Tarkum wouldn't have come up. Because she was a lone woman, not a woman with a kid."

Cindy said, "Uh, can I say something?"

Three pairs of eyes looked in her direction.

She smiled but it was a nervous one. Again she avoided eye contact with Oliver. "One of the detectives down at Hollywood . . . Craig Barrows . . . about ten months ago, at a party, I was talking to him about Armand. Because another jacking had just happened. Now that I think about it, maybe it was the Tarkum case. He mentioned that he thought it sounded similar . . . in a way . . . to the Crayton case."

"How'd it come up?" Marge asked.

"Craig brought it up. I don't know why." Cindy thought for a moment. "Actually, I think Rick Be-derman brought it up. He was the one who caught the original call when the hikers phoned it in."

"Hikers?" Marge asked.

"Yeah, she was found near Griffith Park."

"So, she was left in a remote area just like Crayton," Decker said.

"But miles away from Crayton," Cindy said. "And she wasn't murdered."

"It sure would have been nice to hear about this months ago."

Cindy stiffened. "It was at a party, Dad. I thought Barrows was blowing smoke."

"You could have at least mentioned—"

"Pete . . ." Marge warned.

Decker held up his hands. "Forget it."

Cindy looked down. "I should have—"

"Forget it." Decker stood. "No big deal. I shouldn't even be here."

"As long as you're here, you might as well stay," Cindy said.

Decker smiled at his daughter. "That's very kind of you, Cindy, but it's getting late." He turned to

his detectives. "Let me mull this over. We'll conference in the morning. My office. Ten o'clock."

"I'll walk you to your car," Cindy said.

As soon as they were alone outside, Decker said,
"I'm sorry I embarrassed you."

"I took it as a compliment," Cindy said. "You
treated me like one of your own, not like a daughter." She paused. "Just hearing you guys go over
things I learned a lot. I see street life as an officer,
but I never get a chance to work with the detectives in any meaningful way. This was great!"

Decker hugged her. "You're a sweetie. Take
care . . ." He waited a moment. "Everything's okay
with you, right?"

"What do you mean?"

"No strange letters or phone calls?"

Cindy was prepared for the question. The lie
came out as natural as a yawn. "Nothing."

"No weird people following you home?"

"Daddy, no one has anything against me, I
assure you."

"But you'd tell me if—"

"Absolutely. I'm fine! Go home. Regards to Rina
and the kids. Tell Rina thanks for the invitation for
Friday night. I'll take her up on it."

Decker beamed. "Really?"

"Really." She gave him her warmest smile. "I
need a good meal."

"You got it. Love you, princess."

"I love you, too." She turned and walked away, resisting the urge to unload her problems and confess everything to her dad—the Post-it scrawled with the word *remember* on it, the misplaced picture, the reversed sweater drawer, the general uneasiness she felt. It would have been lovely to have Daddy soothe her worries and allay her fears.

She sighed, thinking: Priests were definitely called fathers for a reason.

14

CINDY WATCHED her father drive off, mindful that he was trying his best. He had been big enough to apologize, no small feat because not only was Cindy a daughter but also an underling. She thought about that as she walked back to her apartment. Opening the door, she wondered what would happen next.

In the three minutes she had been gone, Marge and Scott had usurped her personal space for their workstation, spreading out on her coffee table. She could have been offended. Instead, Cindy thought it was cool: an opportunity to listen and learn. Marge was riffling through sheaves of papers. "Was

Dexter Bartholomew ever interviewed about Crayton's murder?"

"Probably."

"I can't find it."

"I'll help," Cindy offered.

They looked up at her and stared . . . as if they had forgotten she lived there.

"Uh, thanks." Marge handed Cindy a stack. "All you're looking for is an interview sheet with Dexter Bartholomew's name on it. Start with the ones that are tagged blue. Those are from Webster's file." Several silent minutes passed, then Marge was triumphant. "Found it. Bert talked to Bartholomew about a month after Crayton was murdered. I wonder why he waited so long to interview the guy."

"Maybe Bartholomew was out of town," Oliver answered. "Anyway, since Dex made money with Crayton, he wouldn't have been a priority suspect."

Marge said, "From what I can glean from the report, it looks like the majority of Bartholomew's deals with Crayton were closed around two months before Crayton was iced."

Cindy said, "Around the same time that someone took potshots at us."

They stared at her.

"I'm just making an observation," Cindy said. "It probably doesn't mean anything."

Oliver said, "Actually, it's a good point. It's possible that Bartholomew knew something was heating up, that Crayton was going down fast, and that's why he pulled out."

Marge said, "So then we should check up on Crayton's activities just prior to his demise."

"Okay, so we're looking into Bartholomew and his dealings with Crayton. Also Lark and the insurance. What else?" He regarded Cindy. "You weren't going to make coffee, were you?"

She got up. "If you say please."

He gave her a gentle smile. "Please."

Cindy looked down. "Decaf?"

"Please."

"Marge, how about you?"

"I'd love a—" Marge suddenly turned reticent. "We're not keeping you up, are we?"

"Marge, I haven't had a nine o'clock bedtime for twenty years." She walked into the kitchen and started brewing coffee. "Stay as long as you want. So you really think Elizabeth Tarkum is related to Crayton?"

Oliver said, "Possibly."

"How?" Marge asked.

"Any number of ways."

Cindy said, "Maybe someone had a grudge against Dexter Bartholomew regarding his former business dealings with Crayton and took it out on his wife?"

Oliver nodded. "Now that's something to think about."

Cindy felt her face go hot with the compliment. To hide her red face, she busied herself making coffee.

"Sending Dex a message via his wife," Marge said. "So maybe we should also contact those who made money with Crayton. Find out if any of them or their spouses have been threatened." She plunked down the folders. "Tom and Bert must have had some logic behind prioritizing their interviews. It's just not apparent to me."

The room fell quiet as the two detectives sifted through paperwork. In the background, the coffeepot gurgled. Cindy pulled back the drapes on the kitchen window. In a finger snap, she caught a glimpse of something . . . a fleeting shadow. Instantly, a shot of adrenaline coursed through her veins. A split second later she felt the aftermath— a quickened pulse and a coat of sweat. She bit her lip and said nothing, hoping they wouldn't notice her hot cheeks and shaking hands.

And of course they didn't, being too involved in their work. Which was good. As quietly as she could, Cindy tore off a paper towel, wet it down with cold water, and wiped her face. The dousing served a twofold purpose: to wipe the sweat away *and* to take the blush out of her complexion. All this talk about revenge as a motive: It was driving her imagination into a frenzy.

Or was it her imagination?

Of course it was. Forget it, Decker. You're seeing things.

Besides, if she told them what she had seen, Cindy knew they'd stop in an instant. They'd start asking questions. They'd search the area. They'd call out the uniforms. Of course, they wouldn't find anything because whoever or whatever it was would have been long gone. So what would they do next? They'd put a watch on her, follow her, call her up all the time. And tell her father, of course. All this unwanted attention would virtually shut her down as a working cop. Because how could she function with three ace detectives breathing down her neck?

In a moment, she came to the realization. If there were something going on—a big if—she'd have to discover it on her own. The thought scared her, but it also emboldened her. She had to be mistress of her own destiny—without favors. *Not from Tropper, not from Scott, not from Marge, not from Dad—especially not from Dad.*

Without looking up, Oliver asked, "How's the coffee doing?"

Cindy found her voice. "Not too well, Oliver. I think it's singing the blues."

Oliver laughed and caught her eye, then frowned. Immediately, she averted her glance. "It'll be ready in a minute."

Oliver continued to study her, unsure of what he was reading in her face. He raised his eyebrows but went back to his paperwork. Something was off. As he debated the wisdom of asking Cindy what was wrong, Marge spoke. "This case feels like we're starting from scratch. There's something in Crayton's file about land development in Belfleur. Where the hell is Belfleur?"

"Around thirty miles west of Palm Springs," Oliver answered.

"You *know* the place?" Marge said.

"Pass it every time I go down there. It's about two, maybe three freeway exits long. A small little desert town."

"Actually, it has cherry trees." Cindy poured the coffee into three mugs, took out milk and sugar, then brought everything out on a tray. "My folks used to take me cherry picking there."

"They grow cherry trees in the desert?" Marge gave her coffee a dot of milk and sipped. "Ah, this is good."

"Thanks," Cindy said. "Actually Belfleur is not strictly desert. It gets some of its climate from the San Bernardino Mountain area. It's not quite as dry as Palm Springs. And it gets much colder. You need the cold for cherry trees. I know that because when Dad first moved into the ranch house, I wanted him to plant cherry trees. He said we couldn't because it didn't get cold enough." A thoughtful pause. "Funny what you remember from your childhood. Anyway, I'm going back around fifteen years. I don't know what Belfleur is like now."

"Judging from the freeway view, it hasn't

changed much." Oliver picked up the mug and polished off half of it. "If I'm thinking straight, I remember seeing several antiques stores. So Crayton invested there?"

"There was the class action suit about land in Belfleur," Marge said. "But it was either dropped or settled about two months before Crayton died."

"Around the same time that Bartholomew pulled away from Crayton," Oliver said.

"Around the time he was shot at," Cindy said. "So where's the connection?"

"We started off with Elizabeth Tarkum," Marge said. "But instead we got Dexter Bartholomew. You think it's possible that Bartholomew's wife could have been investing with Crayton under her husband's name without the husband knowing about it?"

"Could be," Oliver answered.

Marge nursed her coffee. "You know, I'm thinking we should talk to Bert or Tom again. There's too much going on here—one murder, two carjackings, shady land deals . . . how'd we get into this? Oh yeah, the carjackings in our area. We've digressed a bit."

Oliver said, "Maybe it's all related."

"I don't know, Oliver," Marge said. "This is like that old Chinese finger puzzle—the harder you pull . . . Anyway, if we're going to meet with Decker at ten, let's try to talk to either Bert or Tom beforehand. There's much too much work here for just two people."

"I'll help," Cindy broke in.

Oliver said, "If you have time to help us out, Hollywood ain't working you hard enough."

"I just meant I could read through a couple of files. Take some notes for you two."

"Thanks, Cindy, but we're fine." Marge turned to Scott. "How about we meet with them at around eight? Then afterward, we'll meet with Decker—Big Decker—to hash this out and divide up the tasks . . . which seem to be multiplying by the moment." She checked her watch. "It's getting late."

"It's not even nine-thirty," Cindy protested.

"Yeah, but I don't like to leave Vega alone for more than a couple of hours at a time."

"How's she doing, Marge?" Cindy asked with sincerity.

"Superficially, she's doing just great. Acing ninth grade academically. Emotionally, I wouldn't know because Vega doesn't talk much. I have to depend on nuances to tell if she's happy or not."

"Sounds like a typical teenager to me," Oliver said.

Marge didn't argue because she had no idea what was typical. She knew when she adopted the little thirteen-year-old girl that it wasn't going to be easy. She expected behavioral problems—big ones. Instead what she got was a parent's dream: a bril-

liant student with a strong work ethic and a completely compliant child. The perfect kid . . . which
worried Marge a great deal. Vega had unnaturally
high standards coupled with a fear of showing feelings. Even the psychologist had expressed doubts.
How much could you alter a thirteen-year-old, especially one who had been raised in such a severe—
although not technically abusive—manner? And,
on top of that, Vega was always receiving heaps of
praise and reinforcement and awards at school for
her academic prowess. It was as if the girl had been
doomed to perfection by her superior intellect.

She said, "Let's clean up here and go home."

Oliver said, "You're going to work more once
you get home?"

"Maybe just read a couple more files while I'm
in bed."

He said, "I'll take Bert's, you take Tom's."

"It's a deal." Marge began sorting the files. Tom's
were blue-tagged, Bert's were red. Everything in
bureaucracy was color-coded. It took her about five
minutes to divvy them up. Then she stood. "Cindy,
thanks for everything."

Cindy managed a weak smile. "I just wish I
could help more. I really don't mind reading some
interviews."

Marge patted her back. "I'm sure you wouldn't
mind, but it isn't a good idea. Cindy, you're expecting too much in too short a time. Concentrate
on where you are and stop thinking about where

you want to be. Everyone knows you're book brilliant. You'll get your gold shield soon enough. In the meantime, take all you can out of the streets."

Cindy nodded. "You're right. I should just concentrate on the basics."

"Exactly." Marge kissed her cheek. "Good-bye, honey. Take care of yourself." She turned to Scott. "You ready?"

"You go ahead," Oliver said. "I've got to use the john." To Cindy, he said, "And your bathroom is . . . where?"

Cindy pointed.

"If you don't mind, I'm gonna leave now," Marge said. "I'm anxious to get home." Saying her good-byes, she shut the door behind her.

Cindy started to clean up, knowing what was coming. For lack of anything better, she figured the best defense was a strong offense. Make herself so damn obnoxious that he'd simply give up worrying about her. He came out a minute later, hands in his pockets. She noticed it this time. He had also combed his hair. Picking up on the details. That's what it was all about.

Oliver said, "Are you going to tell me or do I have to pry it out of you?"

She started to rinse out the mugs. "Tell you what?"

"So we're going to play that game. Okay. Fine. I'll ask you. Cindy, what happened in the kitchen about twenty minutes ago?"

"I don't know what you're—"

"Yes, you do know what I'm talking about."

"Everything's fine." She turned off the tap. "Go home."

But he didn't go home. Instead, he walked over to her, put his hands on her shoulders. Speaking to the nape of her neck, he made his voice gentle and alluring. "Tell me what happened."

She turned to face him. Looking right into his eyes. Her own voice was clear and cold. "Nothing happened. But if it's that important to you, I can make something up."

He regarded her but said nothing.

"Go home," she repeated. "I'm tired. I want to go to bed. But I can't if you're around."

"Why are you lying to me?"

Because I don't want to tell you the truth.

"Why don't you trust me?"

Because you're a liar.

"Something's going on," he said. "You've got misplaced pictures and strange notes in your cruisers—"

"It was a note left behind from someone in service—"

"Saying to *remember*?" Oliver grimaced. "Remember *what*?"

"The Alamo, perhaps?"

Oliver said, "Witty, Cin. Now let's move on. Something happened tonight. If you don't tell me, I can't help you."

"Nothing's going on." *And I don't need your help, buster.* She turned her back to him and busied herself with the dishes. "You can let yourself out."

No answer. Still, she knew he was there. She could hear him breathing—low, soft breaths. "Did you hear—"

"Yes, I heard you," Oliver answered. "I can let myself out. All right. I'll let myself out. And let me tell you something, Decker. It'll be a cold day in hell before I let myself back in."

❑

HOLDING a cup of coffee, Martinez came into the interview room. Marge and Oliver were already there. Papers covered nearly two thirds of the table. God only knew how long they'd been at it because he was right on time.

"Hey, Bert," Marge said. "Have a seat."

Martinez laid his mug down on an empty spot. He hung his black jacket over the back of a chair. "Anyone for coffee? I just made a fresh pot."

"There's a pal for you." Oliver glared at Marge. "She refused to make coffee—"

"I didn't refuse," Marge interrupted. "I just said it was your turn."

"I don't make coffee," Oliver said. "It's not that I'm a pig, just that my coffee looks and tastes like mud."

"Because you won't learn how to do it properly—"

"There's no problem here," Martinez said. "The

coffee's made. I said I'd get you both a cup." He sounded disapproving. "Be right back."

Oliver looked at his watch. "We put him in a bad mood in roughly twenty-eight seconds. That's gotta be a record. Especially for an even-tempered guy like Martinez."

"I don't know why you can't make coffee." Now Marge was irked. "You take a scoop—"

"I'm not interested."

"Pour water into the machine—"

"Give it up."

"How'd you stay married for twenty-one years?"

"Twenty-three." Oliver tapped his pencil against his notepad. "I dunno, Marge. I guess even saints have limits."

His tone had become doleful. Marge felt bad. She'd hit a nerve. To cover her embarrassment, she busied herself with paperwork until Martinez came back. He handed each a mug of java, then took a seat. "Tom's gonna be late—if he makes it at all. He took his wife to the ER last night. Her blood pressure skyrocketed again."

"How far along is she?" Marge asked.

"Eight months—"

"They should just induce labor."

"I think they're planning to do that," Martinez said. "Or maybe a C-section. Because she can't go on in her current state. Neither can Tom. Guy hasn't slept through the night in two months. And that's before the baby's born."

"Who's taking care of the other one?" Marge asked. "How old's his little boy?"

"Six." Martinez smoothed his mustache. "Her mother's been living with them—"

"Tom must love that."

"Actually, he's very grateful to her. Also, my wife helps out when Grandma is at her wit's end. James is about the same age as one of my grandsons."

Oliver said, "You work hard to have kids, you work hard to raise them. Then you turn around one day and they're gone along with your youth."

Marge said, "Don't mind him, he's in a foul mood."

Martinez picked up a folder. "Why?"

"Do I need a reason?" Oliver asked.

"What are you doing exactly?" Martinez asked. "Attempting to tie in the recent jackings with Armand Crayton? We tried that. Nothing meshed. So what did I miss?"

"You didn't miss anything. We don't think the Crayton case has anything to do with our current mother-kid jackings." Marge handed him the Tarkum file. "But we think this one may be related: Elizabeth Tarkum, age twenty-six, carjacked about eight months ago. Her husband, Dexter Bartholomew, was a former associate of Armand Crayton."

"Sure, I remember Bartholomew—a man you don't forget." Martinez leafed through the file. "So his wife was carjacked? Where'd the case come from?"

"Hollywood," Oliver answered. "Detective Rolf Osmondson was the primary investigator on it. Both the Crayton and the Tarkum jackings involved expensive red cars. And then we have another one . . . Stacy Mills. Her red BMW was just jacked a couple days ago."

"Expensive red cars," Martinez noted. "Jacker's in a rut. What happened to the Tarkum woman?"

"She was found dazed about twenty miles from where she was jacked."

"So she wasn't murdered like Crayton," Martinez said.

Marge said, "We've been thinking that maybe Crayton wasn't supposed to die."

"Maybe yes, maybe no. At this point, it's all speculation."

"Well, then let's speculate for a minute," Marge said. "Suppose the kidnapping was a revenge thing thought up by someone who lost money investing with Crayton and the kidnappers were people for hire. The plan was to take Crayton and demand a ransom. That way, the duped investor could recover some of his lost money. But something got mucked up. Maybe Lark Crayton wasn't supposed to be home. But she was. She witnessed the kidnapping from the house and phoned it in to the police. Suddenly, the kidnappers had the police on their tail. The Corniche tried to outrun them. Instead, things got wilder and wilder until the car plunged over the embankment. So there went Crayton along with the hopes of getting back the lost money. The avenger investor couldn't get Crayton, so he moved on to one of Crayton's partners."

Martinez said, "Interesting scenario, Margie, except they didn't kidnap Bartholomew, they carjacked the wife. Plus she was found intact, and you never mentioned ransom."

"I don't think there was a ransom demand," Marge said. "Maybe the car was taken in lieu of ransom."

Martinez's look was neutral at best. She sipped coffee, deciding to turn the tables. *Let him suggest a script.* "So what did you and Tom come up with if a revenge motive wasn't on your list?"

"Revenge *was* definitely one of the angles we considered. But we thought about other possibilities, too." Martinez finished his cup. "I'm pouring myself another. Anyone else want a refill?"

Oliver stood. "I'll do it."

Marge stared at him slack-jawed.

Oliver said, "If I get third-degree burns, I'm going to blame you." He took everyone's cups and left.

Martinez said, "He's not a bad guy."

"You don't have to sell him to me," Marge said. "I remember the hospital visits." She smiled at him. "I remember you, too."

"Really?"

"Yeah, I wasn't as zonked out as you thought. I couldn't talk, but I heard everything."

Martinez licked his lips. "I bet you're glad to put all that behind you."

"You bet."

A moment later, Oliver came back. "What's going on? You two look funny."

"We were extolling your virtues," Marge said.

"Virtue*s*?" Oliver distributed the coffee and sat down. "You mean, not only do I have *a* virtue, I have more than one?"

Marge said, "Well, so far the only thing we've come up with is your full head of hair. But we're still working on it."

Oliver smiled, then said, "Bert, what motives did you consider besides a revenge kidnapping?"

"A simple theft that went bad. The guy was driving a Rolls Corniche."

"Crayton had money on him when he died," Oliver told him.

"That's why I said it was a theft gone *bad*."

"So why not just steal the car?" Marge said. "Kidnapping the driver made it a lot more complicated."

"You're assuming it was an organized thing," Martinez said. "Lark Crayton's description made the jackers sound like punk, impulsive kids."

"And you're assuming that Lark was telling you the truth."

"At the time, we interviewed her right away.

There didn't seem to be any reason to doubt her story. She called it in as it was happening. She saw them force Crayton into the trunk at gunpoint. We went over her 911 tape. She sounded like she was in a real panic. There were at least five police cars tailing the Rolls before it went down. The area was heavily wooded. Somehow, the perps got away."

Oliver said, "The perps got away with five cop cars tailing the Rolls?"

"Scott, you know how fast these things happen," Martinez said.

Oliver did know. "Could they have jumped out of the car before it went over?"

"Sure, anything's possible."

"And you haven't ruled out a revenge thing."

"Nah, we never ruled it out, because Crayton was in deep debt."

"He also had a life insurance policy," Marge said.

"Yeah, two mil," Martinez said. "He took it out, and Lark was the beneficiary. Insurance was suspicious, and so were we. But we couldn't trip her up. She kept her story vague and simple . . . almost like she was rehearsed. The more vague and simple, the harder it is to find a chink. We did a background search on her. She wasn't a nun, but she didn't have a sheet. Did insurance ever pay off the policy?"

"Three weeks ago," Oliver said.

"So insurance didn't find anything on her, either."

"Yeah, we want to talk to them about that. The offices open at nine. We'll call and see what they turned up." Marge warmed her hands on the coffee mug. "You really think the kidnapping was done by punk kids?"

"At first, no. Tom and I were sure it was some disgruntled investor. But after countless hours of interviewing . . . well, you've seen all the reports. We couldn't find anything. We were hoping that insurance came up with dirt on Lark Crayton. But if they paid off . . ."

Marge said, "What about Dex Bartholomew?"

"What about him?"

"Did he seem off to you?"

"Completely. Guy's an eccentric from the get-go. But we couldn't find anything to link him to Crayton's death." Martinez looked down at the Tarkum file. "That was before you found this. We must have gone through a hundred people. It seemed like such a simple thing. Guy owes money, somewhere there has to be a grudge. But we just didn't get anywhere with that angle. Okay, so the grudge doesn't pan out. The wife is beneficiary of a two-mil insurance policy. You go with that angle. And that doesn't work out, either. After a while, you think, hey maybe it was just plain old bad luck. Crayton being in the wrong place at the wrong time." He hefted the Tarkum folder. "Maybe it'll open a door. I assume someone interviewed Bartholomew with regards to his wife's carjacking?"

"Osmondson," Oliver said.

"Did he bring up Crayton?" Martinez asked.

Oliver shook his head. "I don't know if he was aware of the link to Crayton until I told him about it. Bartholomew needs to be interviewed again. You were primary first time around. Do you want to do it?"

Martinez said, "Since the Tarkum thing is your baby, you two go ahead with the husband/wife interviews."

Marge spoke to her partner. "You take Elizabeth Tarkum, the wife, I'll do Dex." She smiled. "Doing Dex sounds like doing a designer drug, eh?"

"Wishful thinking." Oliver tapped his pencil again. "Any reason why you want it boy/girl, boy/girl? If Tarkum was having an affair with Crayton, she'd admit it easier to you."

Marge was taken aback. "Why do you think she was having an affair with Crayton?"

"She's a young woman married to an old man. Then Crayton comes along, throwing away cash like bubblegum wrappers. He partied big time and had a rep for being a playboy." Oliver shrugged. "But if your gut says you can do this . . ."

"Okay," Marge said. "I'll take Dexter Bartholomew. Also if he's this oil millionaire macho man, he's less likely to posture with me—a woman."

Oliver said, "That's true enough. It's hard to play wienie wag with a wienieless opponent."

"Wienieless in the physical dimension only," Marge said. "Because I can swagger along with the best of them."

15

Marge had a picture in her mind of the Texas technically Oklahoma—oilman. Dexter Bartholomew would be a bruiser of a guy; around six eight with a giant ten-gallon hat perched atop the head and wisps of sandy-colored hair—touched with gray—peeking out from the brim. He'd have a florid face and a bulbous nose from too much drinking. Piggy deep-set eyes would stare from a wide forehead. He'd dress in khakis with a string tie, and a saggy, baggy beer gut would hang over a genuine croc belt. A deep voice, for sure, with an exaggerated drawl.

When his secretary brought her into Bartholomew's office, she shook hands with a man no taller than five three. She towered over him, a slim man with long, tapered fingers and manicured nails. Dex didn't wear a hat. But he had donned a designer navy pin-striped suit. His shirt was white, his tie bright gold and held in place by a diamond tack. A bit of flash, yes, but it was tasteful. He had a brown croc belt, so she'd gotten that right, and matching croc loafers housed his feet. He had a small head to go with his small body. Bald on top with sandy hair fringing the base of his skull. (She'd gotten the hair color right, too.) Brown eyes—though not piggish—rested behind glasses. An aquiline nose bisected his face with perfect symmetry. He flashed her large, white teeth. Marge figured it had been meant to be a smile. Instead, he came across like a wolverine baring his fangs.

She managed to smile back.

The office was as comfy as a hotel lobby—furnished like one as well, but the room had class. The walls had been wainscoted with walnut paneling on the bottom, ruby red walls on top. Lots of seating arrangements; there were several wing chairs upholstered in blue oiled leather, a half-dozen carved wooden chairs with floral patterns on the seats, and three sofas—one covered with a deep pink silk, another in white jacquard silk, and the third done up in needlepoint tapestry. Several Persian rugs covered the dark-stained running-board floors. Lots of side tables dressed with floral arrangements. It was stylized but elegant, the two things at odds with the Old World look being a straight-grained sleek, rosewood desk and the abstract artwork gracing the walls. The place was situated in a high-rise on Sunset, so it presumedly had a view. But all Marge could make out were bits of rooftops through the haze of L.A.'s smoke-colored marine layer.

"Well, come on in," Dex told her, pumping her hand. "You got business, I got business. It behooves me to let you do your business. Because the sooner you do your business, the sooner I can go back to doing my business. Which I'm not doing now because I'm talking to you."

Marge extricated her hand and nodded. He had the drawl—a big one—but the voice was high and tinny. He spoke at a machine-gun clip. She looked around for a place to park herself. He caught her indecision immediately.

"Sit anywhere you like, young lady. You can sit on the chair, you can sit on the sofa, you can even sit on the floor. Once I had a client who loved to sit on the floor. He came from somewhere in the Mideast where they do a lot of floor sitting because they don't have a surplus of chairs over there. I thought about that as a business for a while . . . importing chairs to the Mideast. Not these kinds of chairs. These are English—nineteenth-century Victorian. Nice to look at, but not top quality when it comes to collectibles. See, I keep the good ones at home where I don't have all these philistines putting their derrieres on five-hundred-dollar-a-yard fabric. Or worse, parking their *be*-hinds on the original fabric, which is as frail as a woman with consumption. Back home, I got Queen Anne chairs, I got Georgian chairs, I got Regency chairs. I also got an original Chippendale chesterfield desk and a serpentine sideboard. Big pieces meant for another time. I had to break apart the doorframe to get them inside the house. The dealer told me she'd requisitioned them from a castle in northern England, but that's a long story and probably apocryphal as well. The main thing to take out of this is that the pieces are in perfect condition with the original finish and hardware. The Regency pieces are pretty wild—the Egyptoid stuff. My wife likes that kind of thing. Are you interested in English furniture at all or am I boring you to tears? Go on. Speak up!"

"No, sir, I don't know much about it," Marge said. "Except that the office looks lovely."

"Now, I am *so* glad you like it," Dex said. "See, I can tell right away that you are a lady with taste. I can tell that. I can tell that and lots of things because I am a perceptive man. But no sense going into that right now. Because you have business, and I have business. So I suggest we forget about the aesthetics and get down to business. Because that's what we're all here for. So have a seat. Because we're not going to do business until you sit down and until I sit down. So sit down."

Marge took a wing chair. Dex sprawled out on the tapestry couch. His eyes stared from behind his glasses. "I assume that, being a detective, you intend to do some detecting. Now if you just want to tell me what this is all about, I may even be able to help you. Go on. I'm listening . . . all ears . . . all eyes and ears. That's your clue to speak, Detective."

His gaze was laser intense. She offered him a smile, but he wasn't buying. She said, "Just a couple of questions regarding your wife's ordeal—"

Dex butted in. "You want to talk about my wife's ordeal? You want to *talk* about my wife's ordeal? *You want to talk about my wife's ordeal?* Well, ma'am, if you want to talk about my wife's ordeal, you should be talking to my wife and not to me. 'Cause, y'see, what do I know about my wife's ordeal? Was I there? I'm asking you, was I there? *Was I there?*"

"I don't believe you were—"

"Damn right, I wasn't there. No, ma'am, I was nowhere *near there.* Because if I had been there, those idiots would have been signed, sealed, and delivered, you know what I'm talking about? I tell you what I'm talking about. I'm talking about the real thing. Done with! Finito! No one gets away with that kind of stuff with me. But I wasn't there. That's the problem. While Elizabeth was cruising around Hollywood Boulevard, I was here doing my thing."

"You manufacture oil equipment, Mr. Bartholomew?" Marge asked.

"That is only part of the picture. If you want to be satisfied with part of the picture, then fine. I manufacture oil equipment. But if you want the whole picture, that is not the whole picture. Yes, I do manufacture oil equipment. But first of all, I don't do it in this office . . . or even in this state. This office here is dedicated to my businesses and my finances and my investments, as well as the companies' businesses and finances. Now, that's not my offices in Tulsa and Oklahoma City."

"No?"

"No, ma'am, my offices there are whole 'nother animals, which're bluer than blue collar." He sat up and leaned over to her, speaking earnestly. "You see, Detective, to understand this world—which is slowly closing in . . . you know, imploding because of technology and the Internet . . . you're laughing, but I'm not joking."

His face had become flushed. Marge said, "No, sir, I'm not laughing. I see your point—"

"You don't see my point because I haven't told you my point," Dex broke in. "Technology is a good thing. Yes, it is. It's a good thing. But it is a very dangerous thing. But that doesn't have anything to do with what we're talking about." He paused. "What were we talking about?"

"How to understand the world."

"Precisely. You got to relate to all sorts of people—rich, poor, black, white, women, men, children, criminals—everyone. You really got to talk to anyone and everyone. Gotta have that patter down, you know what I'm talking about. The patter, the speech, the spiel, the pitch. You don't have that, you can kiss your business ass good-bye. Now! Why are you here?"

"To talk about your wife's carjacking—"

"And whether I was there or not. And I wasn't. I told you that. I assure you, I wasn't there. So why are you talking to me about it?"

Marge knew she had to talk fast and in short sentences. "Any idea who might have done it?"

"Now, if I *had* an idea of who might have done it, don't you think I would have talked to the police about it? Now, you are the police. You *are* the police. And I'm telling you right here and now, I don't know who did it. I don't have the faintest idea who did it, and furthermore, I'd just as soon forget about who did it for Elizabeth's sake. Because every time someone has the bad taste to bring it up, she gets all tense. And let me tell you something, I don't need a tense wife. No, that's not what a man wants—a tense wife. So no, I don't know who did it. Furthermore, I don't even have any idea who did it. Any other questions?"

Marge honed in on his face. "Have you ever considered that the jacking had something to do with Armand Crayton?"

Again Dex showed his teeth. The wolverine was going in for the kill. "Armand Crayton. Uh-huh. You want me to tell you something about Armand Crayton? I'll tell you something about Armand

Crayton. He didn't deserve to die like that. No, ma'am, he didn't deserve that at all."

"You had business dealings with him," Marge pointed out.

"Yes, I did have some minor business dealings with him."

"You made money—"

"Well, of course, I *made* money! That's the idea, Detective, to make money in business."

"Some people lost money—"

"If some damn fool invested with Crayton and lost money, then . . . well, then I'd say, don't go into business. 'Cause you don't know what you're doing. Because what you shouldn't be doing is losing money. Now that's not to say I've never lost money. Course I lost money. But not money I couldn't afford to lose. See, that's the difference between whether it works and it don't work. It's what you can afford to lose. The fuck-you money, pardon my French. The catbird seat. You always want to be in the catbird seat."

"Maybe Crayton wasn't telling his clients all the risks involv—"

"*Caveat Emporium* or whatever the saying is! Let the buyer watch his ass. You can't watch your ass, you shouldn't be in business. I watched my ass, I made money with Crayton. You don't watch your ass, you lose money. And that's not what I do . . . lose money. I make money. That's what I do. Any other questions. Because frankly, Miss Detective, I don't see much rhyme or reason to your questions."

"Whether or not you made money with Crayton is irrelevant to our investigation, Mr. Bartholomew. The point is—"

"Making money is irrelevant to your investigation, but it's relevant to me. That's the whole point of business . . . to make money. So if your investigation isn't relevant to me, why should I answer your questions? Can you answer me that?"

Marge tried to hold on to her patience. "Mr. Bartholomew—"

"What I'm asking you, Detective, is what are you driving at? What *are* you driving at!"

Marge blurted out, "Someone may have kidnapped your wife for revenge on Crayton—"

"Bah and humbug!" Bartholomew brushed her off. "Elizabeth had nothing to do with Crayton. She didn't even like the man. She thought he was a piss bucket, excuse my French. Every time we went over there, she moaned and groaned and carried on like she was Marie Antoinette being carted off to the guillotine."

Marge broke in. "You were social friends with Crayton?"

"I'm social friends with everyone—"

"By that I mean you went to his house and he came to yours?"

"You're interrupting me," Dex said. "Now, if you go on interrupting me, you're not going to know what I mean. But if you don't interrupt me, then I'll tell you what I mean and you won't have to wonder what I mean. 'Cause I'll tell you what I mean."

"Okay, sir," Marge said. "What do you mean?"

"What were we talking about again?"

"You being social friends with Mr. Crayton."

"I'm social with all my business associates. Because that's how you do good business. You do good business by being a person first and a businessman later. Course, if you aren't much of a businessman being a person isn't gonna help much. Gotta have both—the person and the business horse sense. Am I making myself clear?"

"Had you ever been to Mr. Crayton's house?"

"Didn't I tell you that, Detective? Didn't I say to you that dragging Elizabeth to Crayton's house was akin to sending Antoinette to the rack—"

"Guillotine—"

"Rack, guillotine . . . some instrument of torture."

"You must have hundreds of business associates."

"Maybe even thousands—"

"Do you and your wife go to everyone's house?"

"Now, you interrupted me again. But I see your point. And I'll explain it to you. No, I don't go to every business associate's house. Not if the associate lives in Singapore, not if he lives in Japan or China or Europe or Australia unless I'm visiting Singapore or Japan or China or Australia. You see what I'm getting at?"

"You do a lot of foreign business."

"Damn if you aren't a smart girl." He grinned with sharp teeth. "Yes, I do lots of foreign business. Crayton is a local boy, so if he invites me over to dinner, well, being a gentleman, I go. You get invited, you go. Unless you detest the man. I didn't detest the man. I found him to have a certain amount of charm. And then there was his wife; she was lovely. Which I think is the main reason that Elizabeth didn't want us going over there. She disliked Crayton, but she detested Lark. Because Lark is young and beautiful. You know how wives are."

"Jealous?"

"I like the word *protective*. Elizabeth is protective of me, y'see, because I'm the only thing in her life that's worth protecting. But I liked going to Armand's, because he was a funny guy. Yes, he was very funny. Truly entertaining. And Lark, being a young and lovely thing, kept Elizabeth on her toes. Yes, it did. And when you're sixty-one with a twenty-six-year-old wife, it's nice when she's kept on her toes."

"So she was jealous of Lark?"

"I told you I don't like the word *jealous*. Elizabeth was protective of me when it came to Lark. Because Lark knew winners and losers. And where she wasn't so sure about her husband, she was damn sure that I was a winner. Unfortunately for her, I'm taken. But we all know how fast that can change."

"Do you like Elizabeth being protective?"

"I do like it. I like being protected by a young woman very much. You got that right. So why don't you quit your questions now while you're on a high note?"

"Did you ever have Lark and Armand over to your house?"

He broke into staccato laughter. "Now, it's one thing to let yourself be dragged over to the house of a person you detest. It's another to entertain people you abhor. Even I couldn't ask Elizabeth to do that. So, in answer to your question, no, we never had them over to my place. Which was a shame. Because Armand Crayton had no taste in design. No, I take that back. Armand had taste. He just had terrible taste. And I might have been able to teach him a thing or two about designing elements if he would have stuck around longer."

Bartholomew stood up.

"In summary, Detective, I don't know who kidnapped my wife, I don't know why he or she did it, and it had nothing to do with the Armand Crayton murder because Elizabeth had nothing to do with Crayton. So I have nothing more to tell you. Furthermore, I have an appointment and that appointment's not with you. So if you'll excuse my bluntness, you have to go. And even if you won't excuse it, you still have to go. I hope you got what you wanted. Good-bye!"

He stuck out a waiting hand. Marge paused, then stood and shook hands. "Thank you for your time, Mr. Bartholomew."

"You should thank me for my time, Detective. Because I make roughly twenty thousand dollars an hour. So I figure that this little interview cost me around ten grand—the price of a little diamond pin that my wife was looking at. And now, because of this interview costing me ten grand, I'm not going to buy it for her." Again the feral smile. "So I guess you served a purpose. Because if she asks me why I didn't buy her the pin, I'll tell her to blame it on the police."

16

CRUISING DOWN the Hollywood Freeway, Cindy tried to empty her mind of today's garbage. Being grumpy and sleep-deprived was bad enough. But then Beaudry had the audacity to be in a bad mood as well, making it a shift from hell. He had basically bowed out of every arrest, giving her all the dirty work, which he could do because he was the vet and she was the rookie. No matter that she was six weeks away from permanent status, he was the boss. So she took orders and tried to maintain. Two angry cops with loaded weapons and a shotgun, holed up together for eight, tension-filled hours. It was a miracle that police officers didn't routinely shoot one another.

Then, there was Tropper, who was suddenly her buddy, giving her the nod and his paperwork. She was usually pretty good at reading people, but she couldn't tell if he was interested in her as a workhorse or as a lay. She found herself avoiding him, sidestepping around his cubicle, then wondering if she was being obvious about it.

Her car started shaking. She had worked herself up to a righteous indignation and in the process had pressed the pedal to the metal. She was now going around eighty, so instinctively she looked around for an evil ticket-giving cop. Then she smiled. She *was* the enemy. If she were pulled over by LAPD, she probably wouldn't get a ticket. But highway patrol was another thing. They'd cite her because times were tough, revenue was scarce, and there was no interagency cooperation anymore. Born too late to fix tickets: What a pisser!

Again she gave a quick glance in her rearview mirror as she lessened the force on the gas pedal. No cop cars, but a red Toyota Camry with a dented fender and no front license plate—a thirty-six-dollar ticket—was keeping pace with her even though she was still going seventy-five. The car appeared to be around five years old and in need of a good wash. She turned on her right-hand signal and moved over to the next lane. Then she slowed, waiting for the Camry to pass her so that she could get the back plate. But it didn't. It slowed as well.

Actually, it did more than just slow. It changed lanes, then dropped two car-lengths behind her. She thought a moment, wondering why it was important to her to get the Camry's license plate. She was off-duty, going to her father's house for what hopefully would be a relaxing dinner, so what the hell did she care about some misdemeanor license plate infraction?

Her mind wasn't on her driving. Now she was going too slowly. Cars were passing her on the left *and* on the right. She increased her speed, then glanced in her driver's mirror. The red Camry had narrowed the distance between them, one lane over and a half car-length behind.

Forget about it, Decker.

Though Cindy didn't know why Beaudry had been in a bad mood, she damn well knew why she was crabby. It had something to do with cryptic messages, misplaced pictures, rearranged sweaters, and Scott Oliver. Her resentment toward him surprised her, so she knew it was more than just his obnoxious behavior. She was lonely; Scott had been a brief reprieve.

Again, her eyes danced to the rearview mirror. The Camry was still with her. Involuntarily, her chest tightened and her stomach knotted. She entertained a thought that the car was following her, but that was ridiculous. Why would someone be following her? The Crayton case rearing its ugly head? But the Tarkum woman—or her husband Dex—had been involved with Crayton financially. She had nothing to do with the Craytons or his shenanigans. Yet the damn Camry was still with her.

C'mon, Decker. You're getting paranoid.

Suddenly, she hit the interchange to the Valley— where the 101 meets the 170—and the steady stream of cars slackened to a sluggish crawl, the freeway arteries clogged as far as the eye could see. A quick turn behind her back and she realized that the Camry had dropped out of sight. Involuntarily, she let out a gush of air.

Not that she was really worried, she told herself. Only now she was irritated. She was east and south of where she wanted to be. In general, the 101 was notoriously bad at this time of the evening. Adding that it was Friday, she was in for one thick traffic jam. As she battled the stop and go, she thought about her bad luck with men. All of her relationships had involved unattainable guys. Not married men per se, but rather guys with baggage or commitment insecurities and/or career aspira-tions who put personal relationships in a distant second place. Then there were *her* hangups and goals, including her career aspirations in law en-forcement that basically got in the way of every-thing else.

She thought about all this as she idled on the freeway, screening her eyes from a sun-reflecting wall of chrome bumpers now at a standstill. Surface streets *had* to be better than this. She inched to the right, and using a pinch of space, she nudged her car into the abutting lane. She rolled down her window and tried eye contact with the black SUV Jeep next to her. The bastard was pretending not to see her.

You're not going anywhere, bub. Why're you being so stubborn?

Again she thought of Oliver, cutting in line at the coffee shop yesterday, using badge muscle when he should have behaved like a civilian. Cindy thought his behavior rude and snobbish. *Ah well, how the mighty succumb when stuck in traffic jams!* She let go with a horn honk, attracting Mr. SUV Jeep's attention. He glared at her, and she responded by showing him her badge.

He paled.

She shouted, "Move over! I gotta get somewhere!"

He did.

So she was turning into a jackass. But she was able to laugh about it. Inching her way over to the right-hand side, she finally exited at Laurel and merged with the oncoming traffic from the canyon. The streets were dense with cars, except now she had traffic lights to deal with.

Maybe getting off the freeway wasn't such a

charmed idea. But now she was stuck. For forty minutes, she maneuvered the Saturn through the dense metal fog of Valley commuter traffic, then picked up the 405 at Burbank and Sepulveda. The freeway wasn't empty, but at least the cars were moving. Since she had a while to go before her father's exit, she figured she might as well let speed work for her and began the arduous process of moving over to the left. A gap between an Explorer and a Volvo provided her with the opportunity for advancement. Just a quick glance over her shoulder to be safe . . .

Instantly, her heart took off. The dented red Camry had suddenly materialized.

Bastard! Bastard, bastard, bastard!

Think, Decker!

Okay, the car's following you. So get a license plate number, run it in, get the down and dirty on this dude. A good strategy except that when she slowed, so did the Camry—always *behind* her.

She could play it safe and call it in. Have a local cruiser come from behind and read off the plates. She could do that easily. She had a cell phone in her purse. Except how would that look to the big boys: her being tailed by a broken-down car (one that needed a wash to boot) and not being able to handle it. At the very least, she should be able to get the Camry's plates. *That* was a basic.

Since Camry man's goal was to avoid a head-to-head, she'd have to catch him by surprise. She could do that if she pulled a U-turn, gunned the accelerator, and whizzed past him before he could react. But that couldn't be done on the freeway. She had to get off. She assumed the car would get off, too. But *where* to get off? She was still twenty minutes from her father's new house. She knew that area pretty well, but not as well as the northeast Valley, where Dad had kept a ranch house for over a decade. Located around the foothills, the northeast area was less populated and eventually merged into Angeles Crest National Forest. Lots of dirt roadways and hilly terrain. Deeper into the hills, the streets cut through a heavy cover of brush and foliage.

Quiet . . . isolated . . .

She wondered if the Camry would be stupid enough to follow her. Because once she started into the mountains, he'd have to know that she had made his tail. She merged back into the 118, then joined up with the 210 North. She sped up, then slowed down. The Camry kept pace.

Okay, she had no choice then. She'd lead him to his own demise. Find the spot, then suddenly swing around before he knew what hit him. If he rabbited at that point, she could still get the plate.

As the freeway thinned, the cars sped faster, her Saturn cruising around seventy. Because visibility was better, the Camry had dropped farther back. Heart slamming against her chest, she rooted through her purse with her free hand until she found her gun. It felt good in her grip, and though she would have liked to leave it out on the seat, she kept it in her bag. Next, she lifted her foot off the gas pedal and slowed. It was amazing. Her self-pitying thoughts had disappeared as she designed a mental game plan.

Reaching Foothill Boulevard, she got off the freeway and waited at the traffic light. From behind, she spied the Camry now only one car-length behind. The light changed and she plowed forward on the four-lane street. The first ten minutes of driving took her through the commercial area, passing a couple of strip malls, a newly remodeled Kmart, a couple of brickyards, U-Hauls for rent, lumber companies, and a nursery.

One mile, two miles, three . . .

The Camry was there, but in the background. And with each turn and twist, it had dropped back. She could pull the U-turn now and hope for the best. But there were still lots of cars. Best to make the move when she was farther along. She figured maybe another mile.

Gradually, the commercial buildings gave way to untamed, open lands of thick grass sprinkled with wildflowers and patches of brush as she headed into the mountains. The road began to climb. She could hear the car engine whine under the ascent. As she moved up the hillside, the lane narrowed, cutting through dense overgrowth.

Her eyes swept over the rearview mirror: The

Camry was gone. Well, that was and wasn't good. She did feel an immediate sense of relief, but she was also sorely disappointed in herself. She should have gotten the plates!

Had it dropped out completely or was it still following her at a very safe distance behind? And if it was still following her, perhaps she should turn around and try to catch it. No sense driving deep in the foothills by yourself, trying to lure a phantom car. The road continued its tortuous pathway, winding and curling, plowing through untamed woodlands. She felt very isolated.

Turn around, Cindy! This isn't cool!

Except now she couldn't because the asphalt had turned into a skinny two-lane rut that was sided by hundred-foot drops. Daylight became muted as the foliage laced over much of the sun-giving skies.

Cindy made a face. At the time, it seemed like a good idea to lead Camry man here. God, she was *impulsive*!

Don't panic!

She knew there had to be a turnabout somewhere.

Get a grip, Decker. Paranoia is a dangerous thing.

She traveled another half a minute and there was still no turnabout. But the small ribbon of asphalt widened just enough to constitute a lane *and* a shoulder. And her car was small enough to take advantage of the several feet of off-road space.

She pulled over to the right and waited for a bit. No Camry came chugging up behind her.

Damn! Another opportunity bites the big one!

She turned around, heading back toward Dad's house, wondering if she should mention Camry man to him. Of course, if she did, he'd either go ballistic with worry or think she was an incompetent jerk . . . which she was.

Down the road. Down, down, down, her tires screeching as she rounded the curves. Yes, she was driving too fast. Yes, she was shaken more than she'd care to admit even though the Camry was old, dented, and needed a wash.

Down, down, down until once again she was on level terrain, back on Foothill, back to the freeway. She switched on the radio, then turned it off. The music was giving her a massive headache. Or maybe it was just adding to the one already there. She was about fifteen minutes from her dad's. It would be good to get there even if it wouldn't be wholly relaxing. Hannah would snag her as soon as she walked through the door, asking her to play dolls or do video games or watch her Rollerblade—the six-year-old was quite good . . .

Mr. Camry was back.

How the hell had she missed him!

Two car-lengths back. She'd have to pull a quick U-turn. All she needed was a little clearance. One, two three . . . there it was.

Now or never, Deck. Put some feeling into it.

She turned the wheel full-rotation, her tires shrieking protest. But her tactics backfired; her sudden movement a clear giveaway to the Camry that she was on to it. The car bolted forward and sped off. Immediately, she flip-flopped, pulling another U-turn in the midst of traffic, causing an Explorer and a Taurus to slam on the brakes, both of them inches from plowing into her broadside and from crashing into each other. They blared out their rage in a symphony of horn honks accompanied by curses.

Fuck you, she thought, *I'm being chased, you morons!*

She had nearly wiped out, but the gravity of her rashness barely registered. She was charged with anger, internal voices admonishing her foolishness while her actual voice was yelling strings of obscenities. The Camry was several hundred feet up, but pulling away by the moment. She floored her gas pedal, weaving in and out of rush-hour commuter traffic at unsafe speeds as she tried to close distance between them. Camry must have been some kind of pro driver because the car moved seamlessly while she dived and ducked to keep pace with it. Finally, she saw the car whoosh onto the 210 on-ramp. She honked at the autos in front of her, changed lanes, then entered the freeway proper about four cars behind her quarry.

Traffic was steady but there was room for maneuvering. Squinting while speeding, Cindy could make out part of the license plate: 4-A-C—then either an O or a D . . .

Keep on the tail, baby! Keep it in sight if nothing else.

She was gaining some ground but the Saturn had severe speed limitations. It wasn't meant for movie-stunt chases.

And neither are you!

As the license plate became clearer, she read the letters and numbers out loud until she had it committed to short-term memory. A few more repetitions and long-term memory would kick in. The interchange was coming up and the Camry had decided to merge back onto the 405. The driver must have gunned its motor because the car jerked back, then sped off at warp speed. When Cindy tried to push the car, the engine shook and rattled in protest. Still, she was able to keep the red car in her line of vision.

One mile, one and a half, two miles . . .

She could call in the license plate but operating the phone would require her to slow down, and that would cause her to fall behind even farther. Knowing the license gave her an edge and made her feel cocky. Now she wanted to pull the SOB over and find out who the hell he was and why he was following her. At least she assumed it was a he.

Two and a half miles, three miles . . .

The car got off at Devonshire. Perfect! The route he was taking was on the way to her dad's. Perhaps she could catch a criminal *and* make it to dinner on time. She finagled her way over to the far right lane and exited at a madman's speed. But just as she reached the bottom of the off-ramp, she was caught by a red light. Forced to stop, she hit the wheel and cursed loudly as she spied a flash of Camry red tear down Devonshire east.

Stuck, stuck, stuck! Even though she was the first car in the left-hand lane! She was tempted to try the turn, but that would be too much fate-tempting. She already had used up her allotment of lucky breaks. Pecking around in her purse for the cell phone, she bemoaned the fact that she needed to make a left turn and was living in the U.S. and not Britain or Japan or Australia. When the operator came on, she asked for the nearest DMV. But by the time she had the number, the light had changed to green. Feeling immortal, she did a classic no-no, immediately turning left, relying on that half-second brain-to-pedal reaction time to jump out in front of oncoming traffic. She bore down on the gas. To her surprise, she caught sight of the Camry.

Which pleased her at first, but then, when rational thought kicked in, it startled her. Logic dictated that he should have turned off onto a side street and been long gone.

So what was he doing here within catchable range?

If he had disappeared, she would have called in the plates and let it go at that. But now he was getting personal. Taunting her like some modern-day gingerbread man. Well, she'd be damned if she was going to be bettered by some cookie-aping asshole.

She juiced the engine and shot forward, trying to close the distance. But the Camry must have had some added muscle to its ordinary engine because it leapt ahead, racing down Devonshire, swinging in and out of traffic lanes with the deftness of a pickpocket. Going faster whenever she kicked out of the jams. Mocking her, deriding her.

Can't catch me, I'm the gingerbread man.

And here she was playing the fool. Retracing her steps as he pushed her farther east, past the commercial buildings, past the markets and strip malls, past the residences sprinkled with large citrus and apricot trees laden with green fruit; arboreal leftovers that spoke of agricultural Los Angeles. She raced with the Camry, the car having the good luck to make every light. Finally, it encountered a red and cross-traffic, so it was forced to swerve on two wheels and hang a hairpin turn to the right, almost colliding with an oncoming station wagon filled with kids. Cindy screamed as the Camry missed the wagon by the width of a fingernail.

Okay! That was it! She was calling it in.

Just as soon as she had a free hand.

Because now she felt it incumbent to follow the bastard, not to lose him. She leaned on the horn, holding up her badge to the blocking cars and squeezing into the spaces they gave her. Within moments, she was free and clear. The Camry had turned into a distant speck. She floored the pedal and her car jackrabbited as if spring-loaded. Still pressing the horn, she tore forward until the Camry went from being a dot to a definite form. From a form it became a car.

Her car started shaking, the doors rattling in complaint, the windows humming in indignation. She had images of the vehicle coming apart, of tires spinning from under the chassis and metal parts flying outward with centrifugal force.

Why was she hotdogging this? She had the license number, she had a description of the car. Why didn't she leave it at that? She should be playing by the rules. Instead, she was winging it cowboy style. But she couldn't stop herself.

Pushing the car harder until it trembled like a cowering puppy.

This is crazy!

She saw the Camry make a sharp right, spin out, find its wheels, and zoom off. She saw it grazing the foothills, hugging the pathways back into Angeles Crest National Forest. Another sharp right, then a left, then a right, it burrowed deeper into the wilderness, toward the nature preserve, winding up the twisting roads and lanes. As Cindy continued to push her Saturn, she heard a telltale cough of the motor, informing her that the engine was about to go belly-up. Since she couldn't go any faster, she lost the Camry, leaving behind the wind of its exhaust.

With nothing left to do, she slowed to a reasonable pace, her heart going a mile a minute. She picked up her phone to call in the license plate, but a road sign distracted her. On it was printed: LANE ENDS 200 FEET.

Lane ends.

Sure enough, the road reached a cul-de-sac fronted by a nature park replete with picnic benches and barbecue grills. Behind the flat mesa of lawn and tables was hillside with trails slicing through overly tall grasses thanks to the recent rains, towering eucalyptus, canopied sycamores, California oak, and brush and chaparral.

There was an empty rutted lot for parking. She pulled in and killed the motor, noticing that the hood was belching smoke—which was why she kept a two-gallon container of water in the trunk. She decided to have a peek around while the engine was cooling. Gripping her bag, she got out and shut the door. She took her gun out although she couldn't see why she'd use it. The place seemed devoid of human life except for hers.

She looked into the distance, shielding her eyes with a tent of fingers. Squinting as she took in the area. Nothing appeared to be out of place. A few lazy birds hovered in the milky sky. No signs or sounds of the invasion from *Homo sapiens*, only the chittering of birds, the buzzing of insects basking in the last bits of sunlight. Dusk was at hand.

She ambled about the picnic area, hoping to find some tire tracks skittering off the dirt path, but no indentations popped up. A quick examination of the surrounding brush showed the foliage intact. Nothing had been pushed down, knocked over, or displaced. She had to have missed a turnoff somewhere between the time she lost sight of the Camry and when she'd got up here. It was a very likely scenario since she hadn't been paying attention to anything but finding the Camry.

Again she scouted around the grounds, but saw only vast expanses of tree, grass, and copse, a funnel of gnats spinning in the sunlight. The near silence was shortly broken by the plaintive wail of a coyote. A moment later its call was answered by others as loud and piercing as a convoy of sirens. It lasted almost a minute and made her heart jump. Her eyes darted from side to side as she slapped away pesky gnats.

Then, in the distance, she heard the rumbling noise of an approaching car, its motor sounds magnified by the Doppler effect. An acrid smell pierced her nose. Had the Camry doubled around and was it now going to *trap* her? She found herself running back to her car, diving into the driver's seat, and crouching down low, gun in hand, her eyes just above the visibility line of her window, staring at the road.

An old white Mustang appeared, its motor rumbling as gravel churned under the tires. It pulled about ten feet away, then the motor's growling died.

Silence.

Cindy felt the gun slip from her sweaty grip. She wiped her right palm on her pants and held the butt tightly, feeling her chest thump. Then the Mustang's door opened and she heard the sound of shoes scraping gravel, as if the rocks were being shushed. Her stomach was raw acid and pain jabbed her skull.

Come on, baby! Cindy thought. *Come into my friggin' view.*

Scrape, scrape, scrape. Whoever it might be was moving slowly. Finally, Cindy caught sight of a pair of flat black loafers covered by cuffs from black slack pants—women's pants. She raised her head an inch to get a better view.

To her utter astonishment, she was looking at Hayley Marx. Her colleague was wearing a loose-fitting silk blazer over a white shirt. A yellow and black scarf was casually tied around her neck. Bizarre did not even approximate Cindy's stunned emotions.

"Hey," Hayley called out.

Cindy popped into view and Hayley jumped back. Cindy saw the woman's hand dive into her purse, so she rolled down the window and shouted, "It's Decker."

"Decker?" Hayley's shock sounded genuine. "What the hell are you doing up here?"

Cindy placed her gun in her purse, opened the car door, and got out slowly. She took a couple of steps forward, noticing that her so-called friend had her hand in her purse, presumedly hunting for her own gun. "I could ask you the same thing, Marx."

Hayley stared at her, then broke into a smile. "We're kinda staring each other down here."

"Gunfight at the O.K. Corral," Cindy said.

Neither spoke. Cindy forced herself to breathe slowly, cock her hip, and wait for an explanation, as if Marx were a child who had broken something. Hayley took the bait. "Your car's smoking like a bong head. Being a public servant, I figured maybe somebody needs some help."

Cindy's temptation was to look at the car, but she didn't. "Yeah, I understand that. But why are you *here?*" Thoughts were bouncing in her brain. "Me, I was just hanging out, killing time before I go to my dad's. He lives about twenty minutes away and I didn't want to be too early." Nervous laughter. "You know how that is."

"Remarkable." Hayley's giggle was anxious as well. "I was killing time, too. I'm meeting Scott Oliver and didn't want to show up too early." Another grin. "You know how *that* is."

It took a half-second for Cindy to recover from her shock. Oliver had just told her how he couldn't stand Marx. *"Oliver?"* She feigned disinterest. "What are you? A masochist?"

Hayley laughed. "That could be." She took her hand out of her purse and held them both up in a helpless gesture. "I left him a message on his machine yesterday. He called me back." Again a shrug. "I don't know what came over me."

Cindy smiled, but inside she was pained. She walked toward Hayley. "We're talking to each other like from ten feet away."

Hayley met her, then went over to Cindy's Saturn. "What the eff happened to your wheels? Wanna pop the hood?"

"Yeah, I was just letting it cool off first—"

"This is cooled off?"

Cindy sighed. "Perfect topper to a shitty day." She got back into her car and opened the hood. Smoke billowed into the darkening sky. She popped the trunk. "I got some water in there."

"I'll get it." Hayley fetched the water and an old dirty towel. She moved over to the front of the car and started fanning away exhaust. "Amazing . . . both of us meeting up here like this."

"Do you believe in coincidences?" Cindy questioned.

"Not much," Hayley answered. "But this is certainly one."

Maybe yes, maybe no. At this point, Cindy's skepticism was off the charts. "How'd you even know about this place?"

"Didn't," Hayley said. "I left the city early to avoid traffic, so I've just been driving around . . . can I use this to open the radiator cap?"

"Yeah." Cindy got out of the car and joined her. "When are you due to meet Oliver?"

Hayley checked her watch. "About an hour—"

"Whoa, you really did leave early."

"I'm nervous," Hayley admitted. "Driving calms me down. Wanna go out for a drink or something before our respective engagements?"

Cindy looked at her watch. "I should be going to my father's. You want to do something tomorrow or are you working?"

"No, I'm off. Wanna do lunch or dinner?"

"Dinner. Saturday night is too depressing alone."

"Really," Hayley said. "But I reserve the right to cancel if Oliver happens to be any less of a dickhead than I remember."

"Deal." Cindy felt very low. "Good luck."

"I'll need it. I really do think I'm a first-class idiot. Want me to use up all the water?"

"Yeah, go ahead. I'll get more when I get to Dad's."

Hayley regarded Cindy. "You look a little pale."

Cindy smiled. "Like I said, it's been a shitty day—"

"Why were you crouching down in your car?"

Now they were eyeing each other again. Cindy said, "Isolated up here. Just wanted to see who was coming my way."

Hayley broke the staring contest. "You're even more paranoid than me. Is something bothering you, Decker?"

Cindy ran her tongue in her cheek. Then she said, "The world, Hayley. The world is bothering me."

17

WITH HAYLEY on her tail, Cindy gently guided the Saturn down the hillside. The hood was still hot, but the engine had ceased smoking. Dad's place wasn't that far, and Cindy was pretty sure the car would make it. A mile down, they parted ways, Hayley sending her off with a smile and a wave. Perhaps a little too enthusiastic a wave, Cindy thought. She wondered just how much Hayley had believed her. She also wondered just how much she had believed Hayley. Still, they were meeting tomorrow and maybe they'd iron out their mutual wariness. At the moment, Hayley was not high on the worry list. A red Camry was on her mind, not a white Mustang.

Theories tumbled in her brain, starting with Crayton. Was she next in a long list of victims? But why would she inspire *revenge*? She was a plain Jane, not much in the scheme of things. So maybe it had nothing to do with Armand. Cindy knew that the area had been plagued with recent carjackings. But if this had been an attempted theft he had to have been the most timid jacker on earth. Besides, the area's jackers had been preying upon unsuspecting women with children, ladies who had parked in isolated spots. She had been on a very public road in open view. Perfect for a tail, bad for a kidnapping.

But someone had been following her.

A chill went down her spine.

Deep breathe, Decker. You can handle it!

By the time she found herself in front of her father's new house, she had gained the upper hand on her emotions. She wasn't relaxed but she wasn't as tense.

The place was not nearly as large as her father's old ranch, but the area was less remote, ergo deemed better for the kids. Except that Rina's sons were almost gone. Sammy, the older one, was graduating from high school and leaving for Israel in less than six months. Jake was going into the eleventh grade, but was planning to leave in a year. Dad's new family would be down to one kid, her half-sister, Hannah. Cindy wondered why they had bothered to uproot themselves—not to mention a year's worth of fiddling with the house—for one little girl who had seemed perfectly happy on the old ranch. Then again, Hannah would be happy anywhere. The child was pure sunshine in contrast to Dad's older daughter, who, at the moment, was sullen and suspicious.

She parked in the newly tarred driveway, the oil gleaming in the bright sunlight. As soon as she got out, the radiator started spraying out plumes of steam. Rina had stepped out to meet her. Her step-mother wore a loose-fitting dress and her black hair was pinned under a red tam. Together they stared at the car and frowned.

"It doesn't look happy," Rina said.

"It isn't." Cindy shook her head.

"Want me to follow you down to the nearest service station? It's about six blocks from here."

"It's just overheated. I'll douse it with coolant before I leave."

"Who were you racing?"

My imagination, perhaps.

"I'll have your dad look at it before Shabbos," Rina continued. "I wouldn't want you to get stuck anywhere."

Cindy resisted the urge to shudder. "Now that's *not* necessary. Don't even tell him. He'll just worry." She managed a smile. "I have to make a phone call. Can I make it from the house rather than on the cell?"

"Of course." The two of them strolled to the front door. Rina put her arm around her step-daughter and said, "You look tired, Cindy."

"It's been a long day."

"By the looks of it, not a particularly good day, either."

Cindy let out a stiff laugh. "True, true."

Rina gave her shoulder a slight squeeze. "Maybe I can drown your troubles in copious amounts of food."

"If anyone is up to the task, you're it." As soon as Cindy crossed the front threshold, her nose did a happy dance. The cooking smells were savory and aromatic. Her mouth began to water. *Nothing but a Pavlovian dog.* She said, "Smells heavenly."

"Thank you. I hope you're hungry."

"Starved almost beyond redemption."

"Oh, dear."

"Only your turkey can save me."

"That's too bad because I made chicken and rack of lamb."

"That'll do in a pinch." Cindy looked around the remodeled living room. They had opened up the low, flat ceiling, replacing it with a fifteen-foot cathedral number secured with pecan wood beams. Tall picture windows let in lots of natural light. The walls were paneled in the same wood as the ceiling, and hosted an enormous entertainment unit—TV, stereo, CD, bookshelves, video shelves, and dozens upon dozens of framed pictures. Gone were Dad's leather and buckskin furniture. Instead there were upholstered couches and chairs in all sorts of blue-and-white prints—gingham checks, solids, Delft patterns. Lots of denim throw pillows edged with white lace or eyelet. A solo rocker sat on one side of the stone fireplace; on the other was an oxblood leather chair and ottoman looking like a lost ship in a blue sea—an homage to her father's taste, no doubt. The floors were done in wide wood planks; the area rug was oatmeal-colored and woven with various textures to emulate waves.

"This is cool," Cindy said. "Really homey."

"Grab a chair and sit a spell."

"Did you do the throw pillows?"

Rina nodded. "And I refinished the rocker. Your dad did the wall unit."

"Super. It came out fab."

"That it did. He somehow squeezed it in between the extra bathroom and bedroom. Our next project is the kitchen, Lord deliver us. We're waiting until Sammy leaves. One less eating child."

Cindy smiled. "As opposed to children who don't eat?"

"That would be your sister."

"Where is she?"

"Watching a video."

"Should I say hi?"

Rina regarded her stepdaughter. "Why don't you let it ride? That way you can relax a little before dinner."

"I won't argue."

Jingling car keys with one hand and carrying leaflets with the other, Sammy walked into the living room. He wore a white shirt, black slacks, and black shoes. His hair was wet and looked much darker than its natural sandy color. Much of the locks were hidden by a black velvet yarmulke. He picked up a pillow and threw it at Cindy. "Hey, Red."

Cindy one-handed it. "Hey." Sammy had recently cleared six feet. Nearly eighteen, he was almost a man. And a good-looking one at that. She realized her voice sounded listless, so she tried a pleasant smile. It didn't quite work.

Sammy eyed his stepsister. "Hard day?"

"Something like that."

"You can give me the details over dinner. I gotta go put these in shul before Shabbos." He held up the leaflets. "I had to write a lecture on this week's Torah section, which has to do with the various sacrifices. Not exactly easy biblical reading, but I did a fantastic job. Wanna read it?"

"Will I understand any of it?"

"Of course. I not only write brilliantly but I'm also terse and lucid."

Cindy laughed. "I meant is it in English or Hebrew?"

Sammy handed her his lecture. "It's mostly in English and the little bit of Hebrew is translated." He turned to his mother. "Did you read this, Eema?"

"No."

Sammy handed her one. "Concrete proof that

your thousands of dollars of Jewish day-school education was not for naught."

"When are you coming back?" Rina asked. "It's a quarter to six."

"When are you lighting candles?"

"Six-fifteen."

"The way I drive, it's plenty of time," Sammy crowed. "Besides, Dad's not even home yet."

Rina stared at him. "What does that have to do with you?"

"Absolutely nothing. See you." Sammy slammed the door behind him. Rina jumped at the noise. "Things I *won't* miss when he leaves." She felt her eyes get misty and looked down. "Use the phone in our bedroom, Cin. It'll be quieter."

"Thanks. Where is your bedroom?"

"End of the hallway. The one with the view of the backyard weeds. Landscaping hasn't been a top priority."

"The front looks okay."

"That's because the front has all those wonderful oaks and sycamores." A kitchen timer dinged. "My cookies are calling. Find your way into the kitchen when you're done. It won't take away your troubles, but at least it smells good."

Cindy nodded, feeling cared for if not actually better. She went down a short hallway, its walls decorated by a mishmash of photographs and Hannah's preschool artwork. The left side held a closed door vibrating with each thump of an overactive bass line—the boys' room. On the right side was another closed door leaking the maniacal yelps of a toon being squashed by a falling safe or a frying pan—Hannah's room.

She went to the end and entered the master bedroom. The majority of space was taken up by a twin and a double bed pushed together to make a larger-than-king-size mattress. Though her father was very tall, she knew that wasn't the reason behind the weird bed arrangement. It had something to do with Jewish religious purity. Rina had tried to explain it to her once, but Cindy listened with only half an ear: her fields of interest didn't extend to fertility rites.

When around her father's family, she felt at a loss religiously, like somehow she was spiritually inferior. It wasn't due to Rina's attitude; it had more to do with the fact that her six-year-old sister read Hebrew better than she did. Cindy knew it was simply because her sister was educated—and smart—but it still made her feel small. Oftentimes, she sensed that her father, raised Christian and only Jewish for the last eight years, had similar feelings. Still, he masked it well. When he made Kiddush—the ritual blessing over the wine for the Sabbath dinner—he seemed to speak the Hebrew words flawlessly.

The phone was on Rina's side, so she sat on her bed and sank into a fluffy comforter. Cindy would have loved to curl up and go to sleep. Instead she picked up the phone and called in the license plate number of the errant Camry. Of course, the woman put her on hold. Cindy's eyes swept around the space. Rina had chosen pale yellows, sky blues, and whites for the decor, pulling off the cheer without the cheese. The picture window did indeed show a magnificent view of a weed-choked lot. Still, interspersed with the flotsam were some bright yellow dandelions, the purple florets of statice flowers, and orange California poppies, their papery leaves swaying in the breeze. There were also a half-dozen mature, leafy trees. The property went back quite a ways, plenty of room for Hannah to run around and play queen of the forest. (Did kids still do that?)

A few moments later the woman was back on the line.

The plates were stolen: no big surprise. They had been taken off an unrecovered vehicle. On the surface, that wasn't too big a thing. Stolen cars were often dissected, their parts parceled out to various fences and sold to the highest bidder. But the fact that *this* plate came from a stolen car made her think about all the recent carjackings, along with the Tarkum case and the newest one.

Pressing further, Cindy was able to get the name and make of the vehicle from which the plates had been stolen—an early nineties Volvo diesel wagon. The woman was looking up the information on its former owner when her father walked into the room. He looked hot and sweaty and beat. She hung up immediately. "Hey there."

Decker kissed her forehead. "You didn't have to cut the conversation short for my sake."

"You look rushed."

"Not at all. I've got a whole twenty minutes to shower and shave."

"A whole twenty," Cindy repeated. "That isn't even enough time for me to do my eyebrows."

"What do you need to do them for?" He threw his jacket on the bed and began to loosen his tie. "All you ever do is furrow them in disgust!"

"Yadda, yadda, yadda." She stood up. "I think I'll go help Rina. I can toss a salad with the best of them." She kissed her father's cheek. "Thanks for having me over. I can really use a good meal."

"Anytime." Her father went into the bathroom, turned on the shower, then came back out. "I have a special assignment for you. Marge and her daughter, Vega, are coming for dinner—"

"Cool."

"Vega is still very baffled by the outside world. Our customs are probably going to throw her for a loop. I'd like you to act as liaison."

"More like an interpreter."

Decker sat down on the bed and took off his shoes. "That, too. How's it going, sweetheart? You look tired."

"I am tired."

"Everything okay?"

"Dandy."

Decker said, "You don't sound like you mean it."

"I think it's just starvation. I'm looking forward to dinner. It'll be nice not to eat something out of a can. Get ready for Shabbos. We'll talk later."

Decker smiled at her. But her troubled expression made his heart sink. If only he didn't care so much.

❑

RINA told her to use the kitchen phone. She also told her to watch the broccoli so that it didn't get overcooked while she got dressed for Shabbos. The area was small, the counters were old, the refrigerator was cramped and crammed, and the oven and cooktop could have come out of a 1950s appliance advertisement. Claustrophobic, the kitchen did need a complete overhaul. But it didn't stop Rina from cooking up a storm; the food looked fabulous and smelled even better. Cindy's salivary glands were working overtime. Her own mother's kitchen had been redone as a caterer's kitchen—spacious and modern. But Mom never cooked and Mom never catered. Now that it was just her and Alan, they spent most of their time traveling or eating out. So the fancy kitchen remained as dark as most theaters on Monday night.

She took out her notebook, then got DMV back on the line and, of course, was put on hold again.

Comforted by the aroma of rosemary, she held the receiver in the crook of her neck while she stirred the florets with the garlic cloves, taking the pot off the fire when the broccoli turned bright green. She had tossed the salad by the time the woman returned with the information.

The original plates belonged to a couple named Sam and Roseanne Barkley. Looking up the address in the *Thomas Guide,* Cindy saw that they lived four miles away from Dad, on a side street. Probably a neighborhood of houses as opposed to apartments or condos, although she was just guessing on that one. A few more calls and she had Roseanne's driver's license number. From that Cindy got the woman's height, weight, and age: brown hair, hazel eyes, twenty-nine years old— prime breeding years. Roseanne could easily have a baby. Cindy wondered if the woman had been a recent carjacking victim. To get those kinds of specifics she'd have to find the original case report, and that would be hard to do over the phone. Anyway, as it was Friday and after 6 P.M., most of the detectives were gone.

She could ask Dad about Roseanne Barkley. Dad knew all the cases under his auspices. But then he'd start asking the questions. Which meant she'd eventually have to get into the Camry. It was unfair to drag him into her affairs on his Sabbath. Let the man have one day of rest.

She could ask Oli— But he was out with Hayley.

There was Marge. True, it was her weekend and she was off same as Cindy's dad. But Friday wasn't any holy day for her, and Cindy knew she could talk without Marge going postal. Sometimes during the course of the evening she'd pull Marge aside. If this Roseanne woman had been a carjacking victim, Cindy owed it to her colleagues to let them know about the Camry. She stashed the notebook in her purse and looked up from the kitchen table. Rina was observing her with a look on her face.

Cindy said, "I'm fine and so is your broccoli."

Rina checked the vegetable and gave it a quick stir. "Perfect. Your father's worried about you."

"Dad's always worried about something."

"Yes, but this seems different. Is everything okay?"

Before Cindy could answer, the doorbell rang. Rina said, "That must be Marge and Vega."

"I'll do the honors." Cindy got up. But by the time she got to the door, Jacob already had his fingers wrapped around the knob. He had grown, too, not quite as tall as his brother, but on his way there. His dress shirt was untucked from his pants, the tassels of his prayer shawl peeking out from under. Black slacks and black loafers. His fingers raked through wet black hair then secured his yarmulke to his head with a bobby pin. "Hi," he said to her.

"Hi," Cindy answered.

Jacob opened the door. He looked at Marge, then down at Vega. Though she was thirteen, Vega was small as well as small-boned. Her mocha-colored skin was smooth and stretched over wide cheek-bones. Her blue eyes were always observing and evaluating.

"Hi, Jacob," Marge said. "This is my daughter, Vega."

The teenager cracked a smile. It opened up his face, gave him some life. "Hi. Come on in."

Vega regarded him with a grave expression. "Thank you."

"You're welcome."

No one moved. Finally Marge said, "You can go in."

Vega took a tentative step forward. As soon as Marge was in hugging distance, she reached out and embraced Cindy. "How're you doing?"

"Good."

"No one taking potshots at you?"

"Not today." Cindy blushed.

Jacob said, "What's this?"

"Nothing," Cindy said. "Happened a long time ago."

"That makes sense. No one ever tells me any-thing." Jacob moped. "Can I get anyone some water or something?"

"We're fine, thanks." Marge took Vega's hand. "You can sit down."

Vega was still taking in her surroundings.

"Have a seat on the couch, Vega," Marge said.

But the girl was reluctant. Jacob spoke to her. "Marge told me you play chess. I've got to go to shul . . . to temple. But after dinner I'll play you a game if you want."

Vega was wide-eyed. "You go to a *temple*?"

Jacob said, "Uh, it's not like *your* temple was. It's a temple for Jewish people. I'm Jewish. Do you know what that is?"

"It is a religion."

"Yes. It's my religion."

Vega looked at Marge, then at Jacob. Marge said, "You can ask questions, Vega. It's fine."

"I have a request," the petite teen stated. "I'd like to go with Jacob to the temple."

Marge felt a wave of guilt. In her enthusiasm to introduce Vega to modern America, she hadn't given religion a single thought. Almost an atheist, Marge rarely thought about God. But in this moment of epiphany it was clear how much Vega had missed her spirituality.

"Is that okay, Jacob?" When the boy hesitated, Vega picked up on his reluctance. "It is okay if you do not prefer it."

Rina walked in. "Hello, hello, hello!" She hugged Marge and smiled at Vega. "How are you, Vega?"

"I am fine, Rina, thank you very much. You have a lovely house."

"Thank you." Rina had spent time with Vega

many times before, but this was the first time the child had been in the new house. "I hope you're hungry because I made a lot of food."

Vega smiled, but her eyes were sad.

Jacob said, "She wants to go to shul, Eema."

"Who?" Rina asked.

"Vega," Jacob answered.

"I see it is a problem for me to go," Vega said. "I will stay here."

"No, it's no problem," Rina said. "It's just that men and women sit separately and I usually don't go to services Friday night."

"If that's the only problem, I shall sit by myself," Vega said. "I do not mind."

"Services are in a different language," Rina said. "If you go, I'd like someone to be there to explain everything." She turned to Marge. "If you don't mind watching Hannah and the rack of lamb, I'd be delighted to go."

Marge said, "I don't mind at all."

Vega's face lit up. "Do you pray there?"

"Yes, we do lots of praying." She turned to her stepdaughter. "You'll keep an eye on your sister and the food, too?"

"Marge and I'll be just fine."

Sammy came rushing through the door. "Made it with four minutes to spare. You ready, Yonkel? Where's Dad? We're late."

"I'm here, I'm here." Decker came out of the bedroom.

Vega looked at the three males. "Is it your religion to have your hair wet when you pray?"

The three broke into laughter. Vega looked terrified from what she assumed was a horrible faux pas. But then Rina put her arm around her. "No, you don't need wet hair to pray. But it sure looks like it. We can't shower tomorrow, so people often take a shower right before the Sabbath. Sometimes they don't have time to dry their hair properly." To Decker, she said, "I'm going to shul."

"You are?" Decker asked.

"Yes. Vega wants to come. Marge and Cindy will watch Hannah. Yaakov, tell your sister to turn off the TV. It's time to light candles. You want to light a candle for the Sabbath, Vega? I have extra."

"If that would be all right," Vega said.

Marge felt more pangs of guilt. In one minute, Rina had developed more rapport with Vega than she had in six months.

"I'll light, too," Cindy blurted out.

Decker stared at his daughter.

Cindy stared back. "I am Jewish, you know."

Rina sensed tension. "You want to come to shul, Cindy?"

Cindy knew Rina was trying to be inclusive. But their Orthodox synagogue always made her feel so ignorant. She had trouble following the text and had to take her cues about standing from everyone else. Still, she knew more about Judaism than Vega. If the teenager was brave enough to forge into foreign territory, what the hell was her problem?

Then again, if she stayed home, she could talk to Marge about Roseanne Barkley and the stolen plates.

But wasn't it good to take a break from work once in a while? And maybe she did owe a higher source a couple of thank-yous. She'd been pretty remiss in her gratitude of late.

Rina was talking, ". . . tell you what. Why don't we *all* go?"

"Me?" Marge said, pointing to her chest. "Are you kidding?"

"We're wearing pants," Cindy remarked.

Rina answered, "No one will care. I think it would be nice . . . if you don't mind the food being a little overdone—"

Sammy said. "Eema, it's *late*."

"So go. We'll catch up."

"No, we'll wait for everyone," Decker announced. "I want to go as a family . . . for once."

Sammy groaned. "Hannah's not even dressed."

"Get her dressed."

"I'll get her dressed," Cindy said.

Rina said, "Let the boys get her dressed, Cindy. We've got to light candles."

"I don't want to hang anyone up," Cindy said.

"Not at all. Go light candles. We'll wait for you." Decker gave Vega a friendly smile. "It'll give us a chance to dry our hair."

18

Dinner wasn't burned. In fact, Decker found it gourmet and fabulous—vegetable soup with beef bones, tabbouleh salad with mint leaves, rack of lamb, barbecued chicken, broccoli, roasted rosemary potatoes. Yes, the food was superb, practically the only thing about the meal that *was* commendable. Cindy was upset about something but trying to hide it, Marge was low and trying to hide it, Sammy was cracking wise, Jacob was sullen, and Hannah was grumpy from the long walk home. A cranky crew except for Vega, who was floating as they walked back from shul. Never had Decker heard a kid ask so many questions. Coming from Vega—who rarely spoke, let alone initiated conversation—the queries were especially surprising. They were all about religion and directed to Rina, no doubt why Marge was feeling low.

For the first twenty minutes everyone ate and complimented Rina's cooking. Then once again Vega started barraging Rina with questions. One after another until Marge broke in. "Vega, honey, give Rina a chance to catch her breath."

To everyone's surprise, Vega giggled. Marge was visibly flabbergasted. It was the first time she had ever heard the teen laugh.

Rina said, "I know you're curious, Vega. Maybe some other time we can sit down and talk about this in more detail."

Vega played with her tabbouleh salad, piling grain after grain into a precarious mountain awaiting the avalanche. "I am very curious about the animal sacrifices of your holy book . . . the ones that Sammy wrote about."

Curious was quite the understatement. During the services, Marge was constantly shushing an overly enthusiastic Vega, who, with profound discovery, kept pointing out sentences in the Jewish prayer book. She still recalled the teachings from the cult in which she'd been brought up.

Our father Jupiter had quoted us this very passage, Mother Marge. So this religion is related to ours.

I don't know about that.

But it must be!

Shhh . . .

How else would father Jupiter come across these exact words?

Perhaps he read the prayers—

Or was truly God's chosen. Perhaps God told him the words as well as the Jews.

Marge had wanted to scream, *He cribbed them, Vega, what do you think?* But as she was in a house of worship—as a guest no less—she restrained herself. During the services, she had been as restless as a tomcat. To combat the uneasiness, she devised mental ways to stay calm, studying the room as if it were a crime scene filled with suspects.

Rina alternated between praying and baby-sitting. She kept doling out her gold jewelry to Hannah to keep her quiet. The little girl used them as toys, trying them on, then preening to an imaginary audience. It kept her occupied, and that was good. Except that she kept dropping Rina's bracelet. It drove Marge crazy, but Rina took it with equanimity. Cindy, to Marge's surprise, prayed with great intensity. There was definitely something going on with her.

As for the men? Well, she had no idea about the men. The entire time, they had been hidden from view behind a series of makeshift screens that separated the men from the women. The walk home was refreshing, except for Vega's questions, which were becoming increasingly annoying. Once seated at the table Marge thought that Vega would calm down. But, in fact, it was just the opposite. The girl was on a roll and that was that.

Vega said, "I find all the Jewish prayer books truly fascinating."

"Well, that makes one of us," Jacob said.

Decker glanced at his stepson. Up until six months ago, Jacob had been a behavioral dream. Easygoing and outwardly smiling, he had been a model child—except that he had been dabbling in drugs and had underperformed in school—getting

C's when he should have been pulling A's. Then certain things had come out, which had led him into once-a-week therapy. Within a couple of months he had sworn off drugs and his grades had skyrocketed, but so had his moods. He still wasn't as contentious as Sammy, but he had developed an expertise at eye rolling, scowling, and slamming doors. He had turned from a nice but self-destructive kid into a saturnine teen slowly making his way in the world. Decker knew the latter was better than the former, but sometimes the attitude was hard to swallow.

Vega said, "Rina, why would a God so strong and so powerful need animal sacrifices?"

Marge put down her fork. "Vega, enough!"

All eyes went to Marge. The teen blushed and turned her head.

Sammy stuttered out, "Actually, it's a very good question."

Vega glanced at him, then looked at her lap. Hannah was sulky. "I'm bored. Can somebody read me a book?"

"I'll read you a book," Jacob said. "I'm bored, too."

Again Decker's eyes shot to his son, wondering if he should reprimand his rudeness. Luckily, Rina jumped in with a glare.

Jacob remained calm. "Just trying to put myself in Hannah's place, Eema. She must find this conversation completely stulti—"

"Thank you for being helpful, Yonkel," Rina interrupted. "We can do without the editorializing. You can finish your dinner first."

Jacob shrugged, then began to nibble lamb off the bone.

"You know, if I eat another bite, I'll explode," Cindy said. "If it's okay with your Eema, I'll read you a book, Hannah Banana. I haven't spent any time with you and that's not good."

Hannah looked at her mother with expectant eyes. Rina nodded.

The little girl clapped her hands. "Will you read me two books, Cindy Mindy Bindy?"

"Sure."

"Six books?"

"Now you're pushing it—"

"Four?"

"Maybe—"

Decker said, "Hannah, pick out the books first. So Cindy can see how *long* they are before she commits—"

"How long could a child's book be?"

Decker said, "To her, *Charlotte's Web* is one book."

"Oh." Cindy frowned. "Let's pick out the books together."

Rina got up from the table and began to clear. Decker stood, holding a platter of lamb. He'd be brown-bagging it in style for the next couple of days. Marge stood, too.

Decker said, "Margie, you are a guest."

Abruptly, Vega blurted out, "Why is that a good question?"

Marge looked at her. "What is?"

"Sammy said that my question about animal sacrifices was a good one. May I ask why it was a good one?"

Marge was about to sigh heavily, but Decker took her arm. "Actually, you're much more like family than a guest." He handed her a tureen of potatoes. "Take this into the kitchen. Let Vega and Sammy hash out the sacrifices."

"Do you mind?" she asked Sammy.

"Not at all." He grinned. "Gets me out of clearing the dirty dishes."

Decker pulled Marge with him. When they got to the kitchen, Rina smiled at Marge. "She's just curious—"

"Never talks to *me* like that."

Rina said, "Kids are very different with their parents."

"Completely different." Decker spoke softly. "People say such nice things about how well the boys behave. I swear they must be talking about aliens because they couldn't be talking about my sons."

"They're not *that* bad!"

"Not to you, Rina, which is good," Decker said. "There really is something about this father-son conflict. Furthermore, it's complicated by the fact that I'm not their biological father—"

"I don't think that's a big issue," Rina broke in.

"Of course it's an issue. Sammy planned his whole year in Israel around it."

"Gush is a good yeshiva—"

"Gush is the yeshiva his father went to. Discussion closed. No matter that I think it's dangerous. What the hell! I only pay the bills around here."

"Where should I put this, Rina?" Marge was still holding the tureen.

Rina took it and placed it on the counter that had been specified for meat dishes. To Decker, she said, "I'm sorry if he's giving you a hard time. He gives me a hard time, too."

"I know he does. And I'm not complaining. I love Sammy. He's a terrific kid. He's wonderful. He's just . . ."

"He has a mouth," Rina said.

"He's getting better," Decker said. "I had a mouth, too. If you don't mouth off to your parents when you're a teenager, there's something wrong." He turned to Marge. "Which brings us to another issue. As Vega feels more and more comfortable with you, she'll get more and more opinionated."

"That would be wonderful!" Marge said. "The problem is, she doesn't talk to me. I'd love to have debates with her—"

"Be careful what you wish for, Marge," Rina stated.

Decker nodded. "Kids like heroes who are not their parents. You could say one thing, Rina could say the exact same thing. Vega will process your words differently than Rina's. Did you ever get hold of Dexter Bartholomew, by the way?"

"God, what a piece of work he is!" Automatically, Marge felt her muscles relax. Work was known territory. "There's so many things that are off with that guy, I don't know where to begin."

"Off as in weird? Or as in suspicious?" Decker asked.

"Very weird and somewhat suspicious. He kept monopolizing the conversation."

"How so?"

Rina broke in. "People, can the moratorium on business at least extend until after dessert?"

"Sorry," Marge said.

"My fault," Decker said. "I'm incorrigible."

"Yes, you are," Rina agreed.

"Eema?" Sammy cried out.

"Oh God!" Marge exclaimed. "I left her too long with Sammy. He's going to kill her."

"You're projecting," Decker said under his breath.

They all went back into the dining room. Sammy said, "Maybe you can help. I've been explaining to Vega the reasons behind the biblical sacrifices. In Hebrew, the word *korban*—sacrifice—doesn't literally mean sacrifice. The root word comes from the word *to become close*. An offering to God is not for His sake, it is for our sake. God doesn't need offerings. But by sacrificing to God, it draws us closer to Him."

"Killing an animal draws you closer to God?" Marge was dubious.

"Closer to your insignificance," Rina explained.

"I don't need a sacrifice for that," Decker said.

"Poor Dad," Sammy said. "Are you feeling beleaguered?"

"Not at the moment, but I'm sure you can change all that."

Rina went on. "We don't butcher our own meat. It's done for us, and by the time we buy it, everything has been sanitized. That's not how it should be. You should think about what went into the meat. That something living died so that you could eat it. I think if we had to slaughter our own cows, we'd all be vegetarians."

Vega said, "So why does your religion advocate eating meat?"

"It doesn't advocate it, Vega, it just allows it," Sammy said. "It's not the ideal."

"Although it's very tasty," Decker added.

"Mankind was vegetarian before the great flood," Sammy said. "You know about Noah and the flood?"

Vega shook her head.

Sammy said, "We were supposed to be vegetarians. The fact that we're not is a flaw. But God recognizes man as a flawed creature and allows us to eat meat. But only if we think about it. That's why there are so many Jewish rituals involved in the slaughtering of meat."

Rina said, "When Jews sacrificed to God, there was a covert message that they were thanking God for letting us live. The animal's life was in their hands just like their lives were in God's hands. Killing animals for food—even if it's permissible—is supposed to remind us of our vulnerability. Knowing your own limitations and mortality brings you closer to God."

Cindy came back into the dining room. She must have been listening in, because she picked up on the conversation. "It's true. Being vulnerable does make you reevaluate your significance in this world."

Decker gave her a questioning look. Cindy shrugged and said, "She wants to play Fish, Rina. I told her I'd ask you."

Rina looked around the table. "Is Jacob with you?"

Cindy nodded.

"What *is it* with that boy?" Rina muttered to herself. To Cindy, she said, "Tell her that Eema says only a few games. No more than that, Cindy, no matter how much she begs."

"When she acts up, I'll give her back to you. That's the beauty of being a big sister."

Vega was squinting, looking very grave. "Sacrifices are very interesting! Perhaps I should take notes."

"I find sacrifices disconcerting," Marge said. "If killing is wrong, why not outlaw it?"

Rina said, "The Jewish way incorporates human weakness by ritualizing it."

"Not *all* human weakness," Decker said.

"Well, not adultery, if that's what you meant," Rina said.

Decker smiled.

"But there are lots of sexual things that are ritualized," Sammy said.

"Like the mikvah?" Decker said.

"Well, that. But I was thinking about *eshet yafat toar*—"

"What's that?" Decker asked.

"I'll explain it to you later," Rina said. "We're going way off field. Sammy, go get your brother and finish clearing the dishes."

"I will help you clear," Vega said to Sammy. "I am in the same age range as you. We can discuss this further while I wash the dishes and you dry them. That way Jacob can rest with his sister."

"I agree, Eema," Sammy said. "I'll pick up the slack. Leave Yonkie alone. He's wiped."

"Why?" Rina asked.

"He's studying for the first time in his life." Sammy handed Vega a bowl of salad. "Take this into the kitchen."

As soon as the table was free of kids, Marge slumped in her seat. She said to Rina and Decker, "She exhausts me! I'm not cut out for heavy conversation. It's too spooky."

"No argument there," Decker said.

Marge sighed. "I'd better supervise in the kitchen. I wouldn't want her to tire Sammy."

Rina said, "Marge, I have to fix dessert anyway." She started stacking dirty dishes. "You stay and talk to Peter. I insist."

Marge knew she should get up and assert her role as mother, but she couldn't bear the idea of talking about God again. "Actually, it would be nice."

Rina locked eyes with her husband. "Besides, Peter is dying to talk about work—"

"No, no, no!" Decker took Rina's pile of dishes and stood. "Don't blame this on me." He carried the china to the kitchen, then returned to the dining room. "All's peaceful for the moment."

Rina had an armful of serving plates. "I can take it from here."

Decker watched her disappear into the kitchen, then said, "Tell me about Bartholomew."

Marge recapped her afternoon interview. Talking about suspects, she was on firm ground. It amazed her how she could be so professionally competent and so parentally incompetent.

"He wouldn't let you speak?"

"Not a word."

"His manner, or was he hiding something?" Decker asked.

"I think both," Marge said. "I don't know if he had anything to do with Crayton's death, but I'd betcha what he did with Crayton businesswise was shady."

"What was the business? Land flipping?"

"Maybe . . . in an obscure place called Belfleur— off the 10 near Palm Springs. I wanted to ask Bartholomew about it, but I never got that far."

"Didn't Bartholomew break business ties before Crayton died?"

"Only a few months before," Marge answered. "I'm thinking that if someone was seeking revenge against Crayton—and Dex had been involved— then maybe that someone would also seek revenge against Bartholomew. But he couldn't get to Bartholomew because he was too well protected. So he took his revenge via the wife by jacking her car."

"If he was only out for monetary revenge, there are easier ways than carjacking."

"So he was out for more than monetary revenge," Marge replied. "Steal the car *and* freak out the wife. You know, nothing gets to a man like freaking out his wife. Although I have a feeling that Dex doesn't give a shit about his wife. But that doesn't mean a guy like Dex would put up with someone else messing with his wife."

"Weren't we supposed to interview Elizabeth Tarkum?"

"Scott's been trying to set one up, but she hasn't been available. He's not home, but I left a message on his machine to call me when he gets in. But knowing Scott, that may be a while."

Cindy walked into the room. "A while for what?"

"For Scott to get home tonight," Marge said. "I want to find out if he interviewed Elizabeth Tarkum."

"The jacked red Ferrari," Cindy said.

"The very one," Decker said.

Cindy felt her nerves jump. "Why? Did another jacking go down?"

"Lord, I hope not," Decker said.

Cindy tried to be casual. "So this is just follow-up?"

Decker regarded his daughter's face, going from being concerned to suspicious. "You seem tense, Cindy. Is there something you're not telling us?"

"No," she lied.

Silence.

Decker said, "Because if something was amiss, you would tell me."

"Dad, it's been a hard week. You should know."

Decker *did* know. He also knew that this was more than the usual "hard week." He hoped it was only personal problems.

Cindy said, "Hannah's asking for you. She wants you to tuck her in."

Without a word, Decker got up and left.

"Talk about being tense," Cindy stated. "I think Dad's the one who looks drained."

"The jackings are taking their toll on him."

Cindy lowered her voice. "Marge, does the name Roseanne Barkley ring any bells?"

Marge narrowed her eyes. "Why are you asking?"

"Don't get overly excited." Cindy had been planning her cover all night. "On the way over here there was a red Camry driving erratically. I called in the plates and they were stolen. When I tried to pull the car over, the Camry rabbited. Rather than chase it in a civilian car, I called it in to the RTO. Very professional of me, don't you think?"

"I'm reserving judgment," Marge answered. "Have you called back to find out if anyone's spotted the car?"

Cindy nodded. "No luck." She swirled her finger in the pile of bread crumbs. "I'll call again when I get home. I don't want to do it here. They don't use the phone on their Sabbath. I don't want to be disrespectful. So you've never heard of Roseanne Barkley?"

"Never said that," Marge answered. "Barkley was one of our first jacking victims—six months ago roughly. She was assaulted in an underground parking lot. Pushed down and kicked, but otherwise okay. She had been with her kid. They were returning from the pediatrician." She examined Cindy's face. "Okay, kiddo. Your dad isn't here. So what aren't you telling me?"

"You think I'm holding back?" Cindy acted indignant. "I have to defend my actions to my superiors, not to my friends." She regarded Marge. "At least, I thought we were friends—"

"Don't divert the issue with platitudes about friendship," Marge said. "If something serious is going on, I should know about it. Your father, too."

"And if something serious is going on, I'll tell the both of you."

"Were you planning on telling your dad about the Camry?"

"Eventually. I decided to ask you first because you react without anxiety or rancor. With Dad, nothing is ever simple."

"So what can you tell me about the Camry?"

"At least five years old. Dent on the right-hand side. Faded red paint job."

Decker came back into the dining room. Marge stood up. "I'm going to go into the kitchen and make sure Vega hasn't bored your wife and son to tears."

"While you're there, tell Rina to go say good night to Hannah. She's waiting for her mommy."

"Will do. I also have to make a phone call. Is that okay?"

"Of course," Decker said. "What's wrong?"

"Ask your daughter."

After Marge left, Decker looked at Cindy. Using a nondescript voice, she related her Camry story. It took her around thirty seconds. By the time she was done, her father's eyes had darkened. Rina chose that moment to pass by. She took one look at her husband, another at her stepdaughter, then shook her head. "I'm not even going to ask."

Decker forced out a smile. "Everything's fine."

Rina said nothing, happy to flee to the safety of Hannah's room. As soon as she left, Decker said, "A bravura performance, Cynthia. Now try the truth."

"Nothing to add. Sorry. I could embellish—"

"Cut the crap," Decker whispered fiercely. "Rina told me your car was smoking badly. That, in conjunction with what you just told me, you know what that says to me?"

Cindy felt her stomach churn, but she didn't answer.

Decker said, "One of two things: Either you were chasing the Camry or the Camry was chasing you. I hope it was the first scenario, that you overestimated your ability as a cop and decided to apprehend the car single-handedly. But then you lost the car. Being as you're a rookie, you were too embarrassed to admit it. See, that's what I'm hoping it was. But if it was the second option, that someone was chasing you, you damn well better tell me right now. Not only because you're my daughter but because it's your duty as a cop. Because this may have relevance to the jackings that are going on."

He was glaring at her . . . downright smoldering. Cindy tried to maintain her composure. He had touched upon the truth, but hadn't quite nailed it down shut. The Camry wasn't technically chasing her . . . just tailing her.

"This is why I don't talk to you," Cindy remarked.

"Because I know a bullshit artist when I see one?" Decker ground his teeth together. "Okay. You're pissed at me, I'm pissed at you. That's not going to change. But you are going to tell me what really went down before I lose it, right?"

Cindy averted her eyes, hoping they weren't watering. She said, "The car was driving erratically. I was following it at a safe distance, doing all the things I was taught."

"So you didn't call the plates in—"

"Will you let me finish?"

"Go on."

"I was about to call in the plates, but the car bolted. Obviously, my tail stank, and I gave myself away. Once I was going at high speeds, I couldn't call it in. I didn't have a radio transmitter mike, only my cell phone, and who the hell punches numbers on a handheld cell doing eighty-five?"

"You lost sight of the Camry."

"I did."

"Where'd you lose him?"

"North Valley, near your old house."

"On the surface streets?"

"No. In the mountains near Angeles Crest. I was too spooked to go it alone up there."

"So you pulled back. That was smart. So why didn't you call it in as soon as you pulled back?"

"Because I was embarrassed by my incompetence, if you must know. Besides, I was very unnerved by the incident, my car was overheating, and I was alone. My main goal was making it to your house without breaking down. As soon as I got here, I called it in. That's when I found out about the stolen plates and this Roseanne Barkley woman. Now you're up-to-date. I have nothing to add, and glaring at me won't help."

Decker let out a deep sigh. "Are you okay?"

"Fine." Cindy's voice was flat. "Just hound dog from my ineptitude. I'll tell you what I know about the car. But I don't want to discuss me."

"Fair enough." Decker attempted a conciliatory look. "Friends?"

"Always, Dad."

Decker said, "We should find out if someone's spotted the Camry."

"Marge is calling the stationhouse." Cindy licked her lips. "I'm sorry I lied to you. But even if I hadn't lied to you, that isn't a promise to tell you everything that goes on in my life."

"Your personal business is none of my business—"

"Can I quote you on that?"

"I just want to know you're safe," Decker said.

"Like when you were sixteen and first started driving . . . you'd come home late at night. I wanted you to call me—"

"I'm not sixteen anymore, Dad."

"Okay. So it was a bad example—"

"It was a *telling* example. You love me, I know you want me to be okay all the time—"

"Not okay. Just safe."

"That's impossible. Especially considering the field I chose for myself."

Marge walked in from the kitchen. Her expression was flat. She said, "Think Rina will mind watching Vega?"

Decker stood. "What is it?"

"They found the Camry," Marge answered. "More like they found the license plate. The car is now toast."

19

She'd expected their common professions to bring them closer. Instead it appeared to be driving a wedge between them. Cindy stared out the window from the backseat of Rina's white Volvo V70 station wagon. Marge was driving, Dad sat shotgun. The car had been a recent purchase and not a cheap one. Cindy supposed that between Dad's new house and all the remodeling, his bank account wasn't being fully funded. Adding the jackings to empty wallet syndrome, Dad had to be completely stressed out. He certainly was acting like an obsessively driven man, underscored by the fact that he was with them, working on his Sabbath, when nothing really *demanded* his presence.

She continued to sit with her nose pressed against the glass.

If Rina had objected to Dad's decision to work on the holy day, she did so in private. Probably an unwritten law between them: Dad's work lay entirely within his domain, and his decisions regarding his job were immutable. When Rina had kissed him good-bye, she didn't seem angry. But then again Dad was trying hard to work within the letter of the law if not the spirit. According to their beliefs, turning electricity on or off desecrated the Sabbath. So Marge had opened the car door to prevent Dad from turning on the interior auto lights. It was probably the reason she was driving now.

They were now at the base of the mountains, heading into Angeles Crest National Park.

Decker turned his head to face her. His eyes were focused and intense. "You followed the Camry up this particular road?"

"Yes." But Cindy was less than positive. There were many pathways into the mountains and at night the roads looked different, more isolated and forbidding. Darkness in the woods was more than just lack of light; it was something tangible. It enveloped and smothered. "I lost him farther up."

"How much farther up?"

"I'd say about a mile, mile and a half. After the road turned steeper." She tried to sort out her thoughts. "It was so strange, Dad. I know I lost visual contact with the car. But I was behind it the entire time. I wasn't going much slower than he was. Then the road dead-ended, and the car wasn't anywhere in sight. A Camry's not an off-road vehicle. Where could it have gone?"

"Over the ledge of the mountain," Marge said wryly.

"Not while I was there," Cindy said. "I think I would have heard two thousand tons of steel colliding into solid bedrock."

Decker said, "After you lost sight of the vehicle, it probably hooked a turn somewhere and ditched you in the process."

"I looked for turnoffs from the main road. I really, really looked. I couldn't find one."

"The forest is dense," Marge said. "He could have taken the car off-road for a tiny bit and hidden in the brush, waiting until you came back down."

"I would have noticed a smoking car—"

"It was smoking?" Decker asked.

She sighed. "Maybe not. I guess I said that because my car was smoking. All I know is when I came back down, I didn't *see* any turnoff. I certainly didn't see or hear any crash." She shook her head, glad that the car was dark so they couldn't see her embarrassment. "I should have called it in as soon as I suspected something. Maybe if I had, someone with more experience would have stopped the Camry before it took a five-hundred-foot nosedive. I feel indirectly responsible for the death of the driver."

"Who says the driver's dead?" Decker said. "You told me you didn't hear a crash. Maybe the car was pushed off the ledge after you left the scene."

Cindy sat up. "You think so?"

"Did the investigators mention a body?" Decker asked Marge.

"I didn't talk to anyone on-site," Marge said. "The deputy I spoke to said they were in the process of sorting through the wreckage."

Marge rolled the windows partway down. A musty fragrance wafted through the car—thick and moist. The rumble of the engine was artificial and pronounced when contrasted with the sounds of nature's nighttime. Shifting into low gear, she started crawling up the hill. Her headlights, even with the brights on, did little to illuminate the utter blackness. She turned on an interior car light and handed Decker a sheaf of paper. "Can you read me the directions?"

"Against the law to drive with interior lights." Cindy quoted the penal code number. "I should have gone to law school."

Decker turned around and tried out a sympathetic smile. "As your father, I'd like you to forget about what happened and move on. But as a cop, I'd tell you to think about what went wrong. God knows that self-examination interferes with personal happiness. And God knows, above all, I want you to be happy. But what I want isn't as important as what you want. You want to be a good cop. That sometimes means being upset with yourself."

Well, she had the upset part down pat. "Thanks for being straight with me."

"Thanks for taking it so well." Decker unfolded the directions and read out loud. "Go up for exactly four tenths of a mile. You'll have to slow down and look around very carefully. In between two sycamores, there is a rut in the ground. That's the turnoff . . ." He turned around and looked at Cindy. "There's your missing turnoff."

"Yep." She was trying to take it with a professional attitude. But in reality she felt doubly stupid. She had blown the tail *and* missed the turnoff.

"Go on the rutted lane for another mile," Decker continued. "You'll have to go very, very slow because the lane is very narrow, and there are steep drops—"

"How steep?" Marge broke in.

"It doesn't say," Decker muttered. "I should have stayed home. We can barely see in the dark, let alone learn much."

"I told you I would have handled it alone."

"*No one* should be driving this alone."

"I would have paged Scott. He wasn't talking like he had a hot date. I'm sure he wouldn't have minded subbing so you could have your Sabbath in peace."

He wasn't talking like he had a hot date. Cindy contained a smile, then chastised herself. *Why are you dwelling on him?* And of course she knew why. Thinking about Scott was preferable to feeling inept.

Marge had slowed the Volvo. "I'm four-tenths—"

"There are the sycamores," Decker pointed out.

"There's *a road* between those two mothers?" Marge brought the car to a baby crawl and inched the wheel to the left. "If you say so."

"Are you going to scratch up the car?" Decker asked.

"It's a possibility."

"Be careful—"

"Would you like to drive?"

"This doesn't make sense," Cindy interrupted.

"What doesn't?" Decker asked.

"How could a speeding car negotiate such a sharp, unmarked turn?"

"Obviously he knew the area better than you did," Decker said.

"Even so, Daddy, he was racing and this is nearly a ninety-degree turn. In my humble and often wrong opinion, if the car had attempted the turn going that fast, it would have slammed into the trees."

"Possibly," Decker said.

Conceding her a point. Hallelujah!

The car was bouncing wildly as they coursed the pockmarked passageway. Marge switched her headlights on to high-beam intensity. The pie-wedge ray illuminated thick foliage and lines and shadows.

"It's Jurassic up here," Cindy remarked. "Who reported the accident? Trapper John?"

"Maybe it was noticed by a traffic helicopter," Decker remarked.

"Yeah, after all this is a main artery of commuter traffic. I bet the area's chock-full of sig-alerts."

"Cindy, you've got a sharp wit. But right now it isn't doing you any good."

"That doesn't negate my point. Who reported this?"

Abruptly, the car vaulted upward, causing Decker to hit his head on the ceiling. In deference to the holy day, he swore silently.

"Are you all right?" Cindy asked.

Decker rubbed his head. "I'm *fine,* thank you."

"Your head took a real knocking," Cindy said. "I heard that."

"God is punishing me for violating Shabbat."

Marge chuckled. "If life were only that simple."

Decker asked Marge, "Do you know who reported the crash?"

"No, I don't, although it had to be someone with eagle eyesight. I can't see a goddamn thing. I'm getting spooked, like any second I'm going over the cliff—"

"I'll drive if you want," Cindy offered. "I've got excellent eyesight."

"No, I'll manage." Marge's nostrils suddenly flared. "I just got a sharp whiff of gasoline."

"Ditto," Decker replied.

"Acrid," Cindy said.

An appropriate adjective, Decker thought. That sickening smell of petroleum burning everything and everyone in its line of fire. He'd lived with it daily during his tour in Nam.

Marge squinted. "I see light ahead." The car bounded into the air and landed with a thud on its tires. "Ho boy. I hope Rina has plenty of padding on her butt because she ain't gonna have any shocks left."

The faint wattage of illumination was rapidly growing in width and intensity. The stench of seared foliage and petrol soaked through the air. Cindy put her palm over her nose. Within moments, she saw the outlines of parked vehicles up ahead.

"Man, it stinks," Decker commented. "We can park anywhere you'd like."

Cindy chuckled, but it lacked levity.

"What is it?" Decker asked.

"Just the situation. We're heading toward the light like moths to a flame. Sure hope the heat doesn't fry us to death."

Marge made a face and chided her. "You're too young to be that jaded and cynical."

"Chronological age is irrelevant," Cindy retorted. "It's time on the street. I'm only twenty-five, but in cop years I'm ready for Social Security."

❑

THEY parked at the top of the ledge, behind a tow truck. There were sheriff's cars, there were highway patrol cars, there was an ambulance, and there were several red county fire department standard utility vehicles used when the area was inaccessible to the traditional, oversize fire trucks. Single-file, the three of them slowly sidled down the mountain, using a six-inch-wide dirt pathway that had been recently cleared, and a series of temporary handrails that had been set up by the firemen—the Sherpas of the expedition, Cindy joked. But even with the handrails, the descent was steep and difficult with torn root clumps undermining Cindy's footing. To make matters worse, she couldn't go at her own pace. She was sandwiched between her father, who took the lead, and Marge, who kept sliding forward while she groused about the slippery soles of her shoes. It took them time to make it down without a calamity.

Standing at the edge of the ravaged ravine, Cindy wiped sweat from her brow as hot white lights spilled out from several spots, illuminating a blackened pit of foliage and a charred car frame. Bits and pieces of strewn metal could be seen, winking in the beams as far as two hundred feet away from the crash site. The main area was roped off with yellow tape. Inside the restricted circle stood a couple dozen men from the various agencies including four firemen wearing jackets emblazoned with ARSON on the back. There were also a couple of green-scrubbed medicos from the county coroner's office. The sight made Cindy's stomach tank. And as if that wasn't bad enough, she had to cope with the fetid stench of gasoline. Normally, her father carried face masks. But because they had gone out in Rina's car, they were all out of luck.

A man in sheriff's khakis came out of the inner circle to greet them. Decker stepped forward and held out his badge. "Detective Lieutenant Peter Decker. This is Detective Dunn, and Officer Decker. We're from LAPD."

"Detective Deputy Bryant Bowler."

The man's forehead was raining dirty droplets of sweat, drawing streaks over his brow. His entire body—clothes, hands, and face—was blanketed with soot. Even when he took off his face mask, his physical characteristics were hard to make out because of the ash. He seemed somewhere between twenty-five and forty with blue eyes. Judging by a glint of orange peeking through ember-coated tresses, the hair was probably flaming red when washed.

Bowler said, "You're far from your stomping ground. What brings LAPD here?"

"Actually, that's my doing," Cindy said. "I was here earlier in the evening."

Bowler jerked his head back. "You were *here*? In this *area*?"

"Well, not in this exact spot, but yes, in the area," Cindy explained. "I was in pursuit of the Camry—"

"What? Which Camry? You mean the vehicle we're working on?"

Decker said, "Perhaps if Officer Decker explained the entire incident, things would become clearer."

Giving her the opening to tell her tale, because by this time, it was a tale. She decided to be spare with the details because she didn't remember exactly what she had told her father. She spoke slowly, deciding that her words sounded consistent enough to her ears. Wrapping it up, she mentally prepared herself for the onslaught of questions. "As we were ascending the hill, the Camry continued to travel at dangerously high speeds. So I made a conscious decision to slow down even if it meant discontinuing the pursuit and losing the visual contact of the vehicle."

"Is that what happened?" Bowler asked.

"Pardon?" Cindy asked.

"Did you lose visual contact?"

"Yes. Still, I kept going until the road dead-ended."

"At Prenner's Park."

"I didn't catch the name of the grounds. It's a picnic area."

Bowler nodded. "That's Prenner's Park."

Cindy said, "The Camry must have used this road to escape. I failed to notice this turnoff both going up and coming down."

"That would make sense," Bowler said. "Even in daylight, it's nearly impossible to find this road. You just gotta know it's there."

"I stayed at the site for another ten minutes to check things. I'll tell you one thing, Deputy. I never heard any crash."

"What time was this?"

"Around five."

Decker said, "When she called in the plates, she found out that the Camry's license plate was pulled from one of our carjacked vehicles."

"So that's where you all fit in," Bowler said.

Marge nodded.

"The Camry was a stolen vehicle," Bowler said.

"The plates on the Camry were stolen from a vehicle that was carjacked six months ago," Decker answered. "I don't know about the Camry itself. I haven't called up my Dees from GTA. At this point, our priorities are the jackings rather than auto theft. That's why we're curious about the identity of the driver."

"No driver so far," Bowler said. "We think the car was pushed."

Cindy felt a rush of enormous relief. "So there's no body?"

"We're still looking, but we won't be surprised if we don't find nothing."

Decker said, "Who determined that the vehicle was pushed?"

"Mutual consensus," Bowler said. "Because of the tire tracks."

"No skid marks?"

"Nope."

Decker knew that tire tracks laid down differently at different speeds. A speeding car will kick up lots of dirt, and have short, squashed impressions. Also, there will usually be skid marks from the driver frantically trying to stop the car. A vehicle that has been manually pushed will kick up far less splatter and have longer, clearer tread impressions. No skid marks, either.

Bowler said, "We were lucky. The ground condition was a good *amigo*—just moist enough to get some good impressions and firm enough to hold them tight."

"What about footprints?"

"They're a little harder to find. We do have some smudges. Might be partials."

Marge said, "Place stinks of gasoline. Was an accelerant used to help the exploding gas tank along?"

Bowler said, "Arson's here. You want to talk to them?"

"Eventually," Decker said. "How did the pusher or push*ers* leave the crash site?"

"Well, see, we're working on that. It's hard to tell if there was more than one vehicle because, unfortunately, there's been lots of in and out confounding traffic. So even if there were other car impressions, they could be obliterated by now. We can't see them in the dark, either. Could be they drove the Camry up here, pushed it over, then left on a bike or motorbike or even on foot. It isn't a hard walk down the mountain, especially in daylight. We haven't checked all the impressions yet and won't do so until morning." He craned his neck and looked upward. "You got any theories that can help, we're all ears."

"Who reported the burning vehicle?" Cindy wanted to know.

"Local traffic helicopter saw some distant plumes of smoke. The pilot went in and pinpointed the crash site for us. Weather was kind also. No wind, not particularly dry, and very clear. And it rained a couple nights ago, so we had some ground saturation. We got the fire equipment in before the flames had a chance to skyrocket. Even with that you can see the damage." Bowler heard his name being called. " 'Scuse me."

After he left, Cindy said, "*Mea culpa*, Father. I scoffed at your suggestion that the crash was spotted by a traffic helicopter. Although technically he didn't spot the crash, he spotted the fire."

"I still win points," Decker said.

"That you do," Cindy admitted. "Well, what now?"

"They're going to want you to make a statement," Decker said. "Then I suggest we go home. For starters, I'm out of my jurisdiction. And they've got plenty of techs here. Besides, I can't really work the way I want being as it's the Sabbath."

"What kind of statement?" Cindy asked.

"Just tell them what you told us."

"I'll have to sign it?" she said.

"Of course." Decker stared at her. "Why? Do you have a problem with that?"

"No," she responded quickly. "I just want to make sure that I don't make some kind of costly mistake by not remembering something correctly."

"Just take your time." Decker's expression was intense and penetrating. "There's no hurry. We'll all wait until you're done."

Cindy nodded, feeling sick but hiding it. She was going to have to fudge, saying that she was following the car instead of the other way around. Playing loose with the facts: She hoped it wouldn't come back to haunt her. Dad's eyes were still boring into hers. She averted her glance and said, "I wonder who originally owned the Camry?"

Marge said, "Hard to get that information without the correct license plates, but not impossible. If the crash investigators determine the year of the car's make, we could work backward. Find out how many red Camrys were sold in California in that year."

"Like a zillion," Cindy said.

"A little less than that," Marge said.

Cindy said, "If someone felt the car had to be destroyed, why do it this way? Why not just . . . hide it somewhere? Or chop it up and sell it for parts?"

Decker said, "My thoughts exactly. Maybe the car was involved in some other crime and the owner wanted it massacred beyond recognition. Could be there was crime evidence in it."

"Like what?" Cindy asked. "Like blood? Oooo, this is getting Gothic."

Decker regarded his daughter. "Are you sure you've leveled with me?"

"Yes," Cindy said. "Why do you keep asking?"

"Protection works two ways," Decker said. "I want to protect you. But I think sometimes that you want to protect me."

"I've leveled with you, Dad. Can we put it to rest?"

Decker slowly nodded his head. "Okay. I won't ask again."

Cindy blew out air. "What kind of crime evidence?"

"Just like you said, Officer Decker. Blood, hair, fibers, body parts—"

"Now you're getting gross."

Decker smiled. "Something definitive that might point to a specific crime. Something where the owner would feel there was no choice but to trash the car."

"Crashing and burning a car attracts a lot more attention than chopping it for parts," Marge said.

"I agree," Cindy said. "And if you want to destroy evidence, why leave on the stolen license plates?"

Decker chuckled. "Because someone slipped up. Or someone just never thought about the license plates. We Americans seem to be obsessed with the brilliance of the devious criminal mind. In reality, most felons are just plain dumb."

20

Hot, sweaty, tired, dirty, disgusted, self-loathing, inept, and more than a little bit frightened. And this was just a *partial* list of adjectives she'd use to describe her raw emotions. What Cindy desperately needed was a shoulder to cry on, but with no one available she'd have to settle for a hot bath and bed.

It was well after the witching hour when they finally returned from their forest foray, but the only one who was sleeping was Hannah. An exhausted Marge had grabbed Vega, who was still filled with questions, and left muttering apologies to Rina for taking her husband away on the Sabbath. When it had been Cindy's turn to say good-bye, both Rina and Decker had begged her to stay until the morning, her father being particularly worried about her driving home. True, Cindy's weariness bordered on debilitating, and equally true, her car had been spewing smoke signals earlier in the evening. Still, she had stubbornly refused to spend the night. She needed her own shower, her own mattress, her own space.

Call when you get in, Dad had pleaded. *Please?*

You worry too much. Besides, you won't answer the phone because of the Sabbath.

I'll wait up to hear your voice.

Dad, please don't.

Okay, I won't wait up. But leave a message anyway.

Reluctantly, she agreed. He was concerned because he knew deep in his heart that something was amiss. If only he weren't so damn perceptive.

She drove home in a state of paranoia. Hypervigilant, she made each look over her shoulder count, eyes constantly meandering from the front to the back, from her rearview mirror to her side mirrors. She changed lanes often; she made abrupt moves. She'd suddenly speed up, she'd slow down. If she'd seen herself driving, she'd have pulled herself over on a DUI. But she did have rhyme and reason for her blunt actions. Her erratic driving was meant to bring out a tail.

But there was no tail. At least, no one *appeared* to be following her. Getting off the 10 freeway at National, she twisted and turned her way toward home. There was still some early Saturday morning traffic buzzing along, a car radio thumping out rap at an ear-splitting level. Cindy cited the violation in her head, then turned east, just slightly north of Culver City. The route home took her past her favorite Indian vegetarian restaurant and sweet shop, an army surplus store, a designer clothing outlet, a law corporation that advertised on daytime TV during the soaps, a health-food store chain that was always jammed with alternative health foodies, and a series of old one-story buildings that had somehow made it through L.A.'s numerous earthquakes.

A quick left, then a right, and she found herself tooling down suburban streets lined with apartment buildings. It was an integrated area: African Americans, Hispanics, Indians (from India), Asians, Jews, and some working-class whites thrown in for contrast. She loved the pulse of this sleepy town, a throwback to a gentler L.A., housing so many different people with their different languages, their regional dress, and their varied cuisines. She had only lived in the area for seven months, yet, for her, it was as right as rain.

She pulled into her parking space in front of the building and turned off the motor, her eyes scouting her surroundings. The area appeared quiet . . .

deserted. With great caution, she opened the car door and got out—keys in left hand, the fingers of her right wrapped around the butt of her gun. No one jumped from the shadows, no one popped out of anywhere. Boringly serene and that was the way she liked it. Still, she felt her breathing quicken. It had been such a long night . . .

Walking to the front of her building, up the steps.

Constantly glancing behind.

Jingling the keys while holding fast to her gun.

By now she was panting, sweating . . .

Get ahold of yourself, Decker.

A look to the left . . . to the right . . . over her shoulder.

Slipping the key into the lock . . .

Something was terribly, terribly wrong. As she inserted the key, the door opened to an inch's worth of space with no dead bolt latched to hold it in place. For a moment, she felt her head going light, her chest banging like a bass drum. Then she quickly regained her senses. Standing stock-still, trying to evaluate the situation without panicking.

She left the key halfway in the lock, then liberated her gun from her purse.

Door unlocked. Was someone there? Was someone still there? Dark inside. Is there any noise? Do you hear anything?

But she was only able to discern the frantic sounds of her own raspy gulps of oxygen.

Keep thinking. Go inside or go away? Call someone? But who? Police?

She *was* the police.

Don't press your luck! Get away, get away! Get away! *Or maybe . . . maybe just a quick peek inside. If you're going to do that, don't touch anything. Don't touch . . . get away makes more sense. Who to call? Who to call? Just a quick peek.*

With the barrel of the gun, she further nudged the door ajar. A fetid whiff assaulted her nostrils. After tonight she thought she was beyond smelling, but she was proven wrong. Another prod with her gun. By now there was an eight-inch gap of space connecting the outside of her apartment to the inside. She stopped, she listened, she looked, but she couldn't see a thing. Her place was dark.

No sounds except for her breathing. Sweat pouring off her brow onto her nose and mouth. She licked up the dirty, salty water with the tip of her tongue. Her armpits were soaked; there was dampness between her legs.

Did she piss in her pants? No, just sweat . . . lots and lots of sweat.

Again she pushed the door with her gun. Now she could make out things even in the darkness. Things in disarray . . .

Get away!

But that would show weakness. She refused to show *weakness*, even to herself. Taking a baby step forward, but a foot outside the door just in case.

Using the barrel of her gun, she flipped on the living room lights. A fraction of a second for her eyes to adjust. When they did, she wished they hadn't. It was more than disarray. Her home, her *refuge*—someone had turned into *refuse*—a literal garbage dump of wreckage and breakage, of shit and trash. A sickening altar to some demon god, constructed by some maniac, some horrible, terrible, sadistic . . .

Tears welled in her eyes. Her brain shut down. She couldn't even think, she was so stunned. Instead, all she could do was stare in helplessness. Her very being had been violated, ravaged by some two-legged wild animal. She slumped, then leaned against the doorjamb for support, her gun still in her shaking hand.

Don't fritz out on me now, she mentally yelled. *Someone may still be there.*

She swallowed, forced herself into action, holding her service piece with a two-grip stance. Her eyes surveyed the terrain, specifically the floor and how to step around the piles of tossed books mixed with littered pictures and broken glass—a massive, reeking mountain of a mess!

Think!

How to move so she wouldn't trip. How to get cover if needed. The couch was still upright . . . more like the frame was upright. The back was intact but several cushions had been ripped.

Get a plan! Check the place out!

First, she looked through the living room, then the kitchen, then the bedroom and bathroom. The advantage of a small apartment: fewer rooms to check out when someone guts them. Methodically, she crept forward, her eyes panning across the open interior doors, her footwork planned and careful as she sidestepped mounds of trash and filth. Turning on the kitchen light, what she saw knocked the wind from her roiling gut. Pots, pans, food, rubbish, shards of broken dishes, scattered cutlery, puddles of milk, juices, and maybe urine for as much as she could tell. Certainly stank like someone had pissed.

But her kitchen wall clock remained intact. According to the cat with the swinging tail, it was one twenty-two.

Opening the refrigerator with the back of her hand, she saw a catastrophe of sticky food, broken eggs, and spilled drinks. She closed it immediately and opened the cupboards: The maniac had had the courtesy to save some of her dishes—around half intact, half dumped on the floor scattering ceramic dust.

She moved back into the living room, debris crunching under her feet as hot tears ran down her cheeks. Slowly making her way into the bedroom, each step forward agonizing because she knew what she'd find. Turning on the light, she saw it was worse than she imagined. Her clothing, her pictures, her perfume bottles, her combs and brushes, her jewelry, her makeup, her shoes and underwear and socks and hose—all of it scattered and tossed and disregarded. Her bedding had been ripped off her mattress, her comforter vomiting up pieces of hypoallergenic foam. On top of her mattress cover was a steaming pile of what looked to be dog shit.

She sniffed back tears and bit her lip to keep it from shaking.

Her drawers half open with her garments spilling out. Her closet door . . . it was half closed.

Someone hiding?

With great trepidation, Cindy approached. Her footwork was steady but far from silent. Each step gave her presence away. Imagining herself in a raid.

Take a deep breath, she told herself. *A deep breath now. One . . . two . . . three. Go!*

She kicked the door open and pointed her gun at her hanging pink robe.

"Freeze!" she screamed.

But there was no response, only the grating noises made by her choppy breathing. Using her foot, she kicked through her apparel, filtered through the garments just to make sure no one was hiding. Clearly no one was there. When she was satisfied, she came out from her clothing niche, desperately trying to staunch the flow of tears. Suffused with resignation and despair, she inched her way over to the bathroom. She knew what to expect because some of the contents of her medicine cabinet were lying on the floor between the two rooms. As she neared her bathroom, she felt a chill down her back. She bolted around, but no one was there.

Going crazy, are we?

Shut up! She said it out loud.

Now she was talking to herself.

She turned back to the bathroom. Felt the chill again and was about to look over her shoulder. Before she could pivot, a voice from behind shouted, *"Freeze! Don't move, don't move, don't move!"*

She froze, paralyzed by fear. Fear that seemed somewhat out of place. Because she knew rationally that maniacs don't say freeze. Cops say freeze.

"It's me, Cindy," the voice said. "Scott Oliver. *Don't* move!"

She remained motionless.

"I am crouched by the side of your bed, staring at a pile of shit with my gun drawn over the mattress. I can see you. You're holding your revolver in your right hand. I'm telling you all this because I don't want to stand up and have you shoot me. I'd really like to avoid any stupid tragedy, okay?"

She didn't answer. He spoke softly but forcefully at the same time. How did he do that?

Oliver said, "Okay. How about you turn around first so you can see me . . . or the gun? Then I stand up."

She remained silent.

Oliver said, "Or I can stand up first, but then you can't see what's going on."

"I'll turn around," Cindy said. Her voice sounded tremulous, as if she were talking underwater.

Oliver said, "Fine. Just don't shoot—"

"I won't shoot." She turned around. "I see your gun."

"Good. I'm getting up now." As he stood, he heard his knees crack. Clearly getting too old for this. When he was on his feet, he almost gasped when he saw her. Her face was sodden and covered with dirt. Staring at him with wild eyes, she looked feral. For a full minute, they locked eyes. Neither spoke and neither moved. Finally he said, "Are you alone?"

She didn't answer.

"I mean . . ." He swallowed hard. "Is someone here? I mean, can I put my gun down? Or maybe someone's still in the place . . . I mean have you checked everything out?"

She still didn't answer.

He held up his revolver, then slowly put it down on the bed. "I'm going to walk toward you—"

"Don't!"

"Sure. Okay! Fine. I'll stay here. Won't move a muscle. You tell me what . . ." Again he swallowed. "Are you all right?"

She didn't answer. She couldn't answer.

"I mean . . . I know you're not all right . . ." He sighed heavily and looked at the ceiling. "Do you need to go to the hospital?"

She shook her head.

"Were you assaulted?"

She shook her head again. "I . . . It was like this when I came home." Then she said, "Why are you here?"

"I left a message on your machine . . ." He smiled, but the side of his mouth twitched. He was sweating buckets. "I suppose you haven't gotten around to checking your messages. Jesus fucking Christ, what the hell happened?"

She stared at him.

Oliver said, "Marge called me about fifteen, twenty minutes ago . . . she told me about the Camry and the . . . you following it and it going over the mountain and the crash. And . . ." He exhaled deeply and blew it out. He folded his arms across his chest to prevent his hands from shaking. "And she wanted me . . . or her and me . . . or she and I . . . to go over there tomorrow . . . to the crash site . . . and check it out and . . . and I was in the area and knew you were coming back, so I figured you'd be up. So I thought I'd ask you a couple of questions . . . about the crash. And about the car . . . you know, to get background. And maybe I thought it would be nice to see you."

She remained motionless.

Oliver licked his lips. "I saw the light on in your place, but the door was open so . . . I saw this fucking mess . . . I wanted to make sure . . ." He stopped talking. "I . . . I . . . I think you get the picture."

"Where were you?" Cindy asked softly.

"Pardon?"

Her cheeks were wet and felt as if they were on fire. "You said you were in the area." She cleared her throat. "Where were you?"

"I was out in the area . . . just out. What difference does it make? I was ou—" Again he smiled. Again his mouth twitched. "You don't think that I . . ." He stopped talking.

Slowly, she neared him, emphasizing each step— one, two, three, four, five, six. Until she was right in front of his face. Until she could see every pore oozing brine from his face. Until she could almost taste the salt of his sweat. Until she smelled the anxiety in his sour bad breath. She whispered, "I know where you were. You were at Hayley Marx's apartment. You were fucking her, weren't you? So why didn't you just come out and say, 'I was at Hayley Marx's apartment, *fucking* her!' Huh? Why didn't you just say that?"

Oliver felt his face go hot. He chuckled and shrugged, his eyes darting about the room. "Okay. I was out fucking Hayley Marx."

She threw back her hand and smacked him across the face. "You *bastard! You fucking asshole bastard!*" She slapped him again, catching his nose against the palm of her hand. Immediately blood began to pour from his nostrils. Instead of deterring her actions, it heightened them. She slammed her fist into his shoulder. Then she started pummeling him. Punching him until it made her hands hurt; he made no effort to block her jabs. *"You filthy, rotten, son of a bitch—"*

The phone rang, shocking her into passivity. Sobbing, she jumped back and hugged herself. "Oh God, I'm sorry, Scott. I'm so sorry, I'm so very sor—"

"It's okay," he croaked out, holding his hand over his nose. "Your phone's ring—"

"I am so, so sorry—"

"Cindy, your phone—"

"Oh God, oh God, oh God—"

"Shhhh . . ."

"So sorr—"

"Quiet!" Oliver barked. "I'm trying to hear your machine . . ." He swabbed his bloody nose with his shirt. "It's your dad. I'll get—"

"No!" She grabbed his arm. *"No, no, no!"*

"He wants to know where you are—"

"No!" Cindy dug her nails into his arm. "If you tell him about this, then he'll know I lied about the car."

He yanked his arm away and rubbed his forearm. "What car? What are you talking—"

"I'll have to tell him that the Camry was following me instead of me following it. And then he'll know I lied. And he'll never, ever trust . . . and I signed that statement—"

"The Camry was tailing you?" Oliver asked. *"You didn't tell your father that there was a car tailing you?"*

"You don't understand!" she wailed. "I couldn't, Scott! I just couldn't. If I did, he'd take over and—"

"Cindy, you've got to—"

"No!"

"Then let me—"

"No, no, no! You can't tell him, Scott. You've got to promise me that you . . . just promise me—"

"Cindy, at this point, we have no choice—"

"Then he'll know you're here—"

"Cindy, I don't fucking care if he knows I'm here. You *need* him, baby. As a matter of fact, *I* need him. I could do with a little professional input."

"You can't tell him!"

"I've got to tell him!"

Again she hauled back and attempted to slug him. But this time he grabbed her wrists. "Stop hitting me!"

"Let me go!" she screamed. "Let me go, let me . . ." Suddenly, she wilted against his chest and started sobbing—big, deep, uncontrollable wails. Oliver released his grip on her arms, then hugged her tightly.

"It's okay!"

"It's *not* okay!"

She was right. It wasn't okay. He felt his skin prick with anger. *Who the fucking hell did this?* "I am so fucking *sorry* . . ." Again the phone rang. Oliver started, jumped back, breaking the contact. Sweating with a spasm in his right eyelid. Not to mention his nose, which was still leaking blood.

Yet he could keep his voice controlled and even. "That has to be your dad again. He's worried that you didn't make it home. If you don't tell him you're okay, he's going to call out the National Guard. Or, at the very least, come over here."

"I'll talk to him," Cindy said.

"You're in no state—"

"I'm *fine*! Just let me calm—" Three rings. "I can do it!" A fourth ring. Now or never. She picked up the bedroom receiver. "I'm fine. Stop worrying, Daddy."

A long pause over the line. Then Decker said, "You don't sound fine."

"I'm tired."

"It took you long enough to get home—"

Her voice cracked. "I drove slowly. Carefully. Just like you like."

"Cindy, I know something's wrong. If you don't tell me—"

"Nothing's wrong," she shouted. "Nothing is wrong except you bugging me."

"Cindy—"

"Just leave me alone!" She hung up with a loud thump. Her body was trembling as if grabbed by seizures. Then her head went light and her knees became weak. Short of breath, she succumbed to her panic and stress, buckling under her own weight. Oliver caught her, then wondered where to put her. Certainly not on the bed next to the shit:

The entire fucking room was a stinking trash heap. He looped his arm under her shoulder, then picked her up, carrying her across-the-threshold style into her living room. He found a soil-free spot on her torn sofa and laid her down.

Predictably, the phone rang. Scott tiptoed over the trash and picked up the receiver. "It's Oliver. She's fine physically, but her place has been tossed and trashed. It's bad. You'd better get over here."

Decker was not one who was easily shocked. Still, it took him a couple of seconds to find his voice. "But she's okay?"

"She's okay. She wasn't assaulted. She just came home and found her place wrecked."

"Did she call the cops?"

"I don't think so. I haven't, either."

"Don't. Wait till I get there. You need evidence bags?"

"Lots."

"I'm out the door."

Oliver heard the line break. He hung up the receiver. That was Deck to a tee. Whatever he was thinking, he was way too much the pro to start asking questions.

21

WHEN DECKER knocked on the door, it opened by itself, revealing a slice of jaundiced light. Using his handkerchief, he pushed the wooden barrier and exposed the mess, eyes attempting to process the disgust and violation. But his rage interfered—deep, primal *rage*!

"Careful where you step," Oliver said to him. "I haven't gone over any of this."

"Where is she?" Decker's voice came out a growl.

"Taking a bath." Oliver sneaked a sidelong glance at his boss; Deck looked glazed, eyes frozen and without light. "I told her to soak for a while. She had a Polaroid camera, so I took pictures and drew sketches before I wiped down the tub. The bathroom snapshots and sketches are on the mantel. Next to the figurines—which someone arranged in obscene positions."

Decker stepped inside and shut the door. He didn't go over to the mantel. Instead, he honed in on Oliver. Scott wore gloves and a face mask. When he saw Decker staring at him, he removed the mask. "What?"

"You tell me," Decker said.

"I got here around one-thirty. Apparently, she

came home ten minutes earlier and found it like this."

"Does she have any ideas about this?"

"I think she does, but we didn't get that far."

Choose your words carefully, Decker told himself. "You've been here before, haven't you . . . in this apartment."

Oliver tried to appear casual. But sweat dotted his upper lip. "I was here with you and Marge a couple of nights ago asking her questions—"

"Oliver—"

"Once before that," Oliver broke in. "I took her home from Bellini's. You familiar with the place?"

"Should I be?"

"It's a cops' bar in Hollywood. When I went out to meet with Osmondson—to get Hollywood's carjacking files—I saw her there. She was piling on the beers pretty heavily. When she got up to leave, she looked unsteady. I didn't want her driving, so I drove her home. You can guess why I didn't tell about it."

Cindy had asked him not to. Decker kept calm. "She was drunk?"

"Actually, she was more sick than anything else."

"That's not like her." Although Decker realized that he knew little about his daughter's personal life. "Was she upset about something?"

Oliver shrugged. "She's the new kid on the block and Hollywood's a tough division . . . very established in the old school. Hard place to break in. I'm sure she was upset about lots of things."

"Was she getting flak from someone?"

"She's young, she's female, she's smart, and she has a big mouth. I'm sure she's getting lots of flak. Did she give me any specifics? No. I was simply the taxicab that night."

Decker said, "Did she call you to come by tonight?"

"No, I just . . . happened to be in the area. I'd thought I'd stop by."

No one spoke. The seconds dragged on, the silence more accusing than words. Oliver bumbled on.

"Marge called me around twelve-thirty. She told me about you three going out and investigating a Camry that went over a mountain cliff in Angeles Crest. Apparently, Cindy was tailing it and lost it somewhere up there." He looked at Decker for confirmation.

"And?" Decker asked.

"Marge wanted us . . . meaning her and me . . . to go out there tomorrow. Which is technically today. Since I dropped my date off around ten minutes from here, I thought I'd ask your daughter a couple of questions—"

"At one-thirty in the morning," Decker said flatly.

"I saw the light on in her place. I figured she was up." Oliver stuck his gloved hands in his pockets.

"What are you asking me? Did I come here with designs? No, I didn't. But even if I did, that isn't any of your business."

"On the contrary, my daughter's welfare is very much my goddamn business—"

"I didn't say goddamn—"

"It was implied." Decker felt his fingers tighten into fists; an involuntary action because Scott was right. Cindy's personal life was hers to mess up as she saw fit. As for Oliver, he wasn't exactly a stand-up guy, but he'd always been out front. And he was here, in Cindy's apartment, helping her out, sorting through the muck when he could have jumped ship using any one of a variety of excuses. Still, Decker couldn't let go, his voice ripe with anger. "You know anything about this?"

"Not a clue," Scott shot back. "Why the hell would I know anything?"

Decker could barely refrain from punching him. "Stop being defensive. I just thought maybe she told you something she hasn't told me."

Beneath his solid fury, Decker sounded hurt. Oliver said, "Actually, she did babble out that the Camry was following her and not the other way aroun—"

"Good grief!" Decker slumped against the wall, feeling a mixture of hot indignation and failure. "God Almighty, I *wish* she would have told me that. It certainly puts a different perspective on the situation."

Oliver said, "Look, can we leave aside the personal garbage for a moment and concentrate on the crime scene—"

"I never did like you."

"I don't like you, either," Oliver said. "I think you're arrogant and smug and egotistical and full of yourself because you had the dumb luck to marry a beautiful young woman who you blindsided into thinking you're someone you're not. And you probably think I'm a superficial, callous, badly behaved, pathetic, aging baby boomer with an unhealthy obsession with youth and young girls in particular. But I'm a good cop and so are you. Can we move on now?"

"Go on."

"You can't tell at first glance . . . well, at least, I couldn't tell at first glance." Oliver looked around the room. "There's a lot of mess, but not much actual damage. Her expensive things made it through without a hitch."

"Not the couch."

"Even the couch isn't totally demolished. It's ripped, but nothing that couldn't be handled with a strong needle and thread. Her TV's whole. Even the remote works. I know 'cause I tried it. Her stereo's intact. Her jewelry's all there—"

"It wasn't a robbery," Decker stated. "So what was it?" For the first time, he took in the room like a cop. "Looks like someone was looking for something. She hint at that?"

"Not to me." Oliver's head did a one-eighty turn about the room. "It's something personal, Deck. Take a look at the figurines on the mantel."

Decker did a two-step around the fallen picture frames and broken shards of glass, Hannah's little face peering out as if trapped in a fish tank. Without thinking, he picked it up and pocketed it. Then, with hesitancy, he went over to the fireplace.

Cindy had always collected animal figurines. What sat on the ledge of her mantel constituted only a portion of her menagerie. Some pervert had turned it into a bestial orgy. Pigs atop pigs, missionary style. Horses humping one another from the back, two cows nosing the butt of another. Typical animal behavior actually, except the way it had been set up, it was anything but innocent.

"Creative sort." Decker was fuming, but he managed to keep his voice even. "More original than writing threatening words in lipstick on the bathroom mirror."

Oliver stopped what he was doing. "Did you ever come across anything like that?"

"No."

"Me, either. He did leave a calling card; shit on Cindy's mattress."

Decker stared at him. "Shit metaphorically or literal shit?"

"Literal."

"Good Lord!" Decker grimaced. "Human?"

"I'm no shit expert, but I'm thinking canine

variety. I bagged it and took it outside because it was stinking up the place."

"That's damage." Decker rubbed his forehead. "Disgusting damage but not expensive damage. Someone wanting to frighten her. My poor little baby." He suddenly felt old, as if his life had been an erosion of years, wearing him down like tides against the mountains. Studying Oliver, Decker realized he was just as weary. He wondered if Cindy's vibrant youth only emphasized to Scott his own steady, inescapable march toward death.

Oliver stroked his chin as if he needed a shave. "Anyway, I didn't powder anything for prints. You have a print kit?"

"In the trunk. I'll do what I can, but eventually we should call in some techs. We should give Cindy the courtesy of letting her know our plans."

"Good idea. I left a checklist for the bedroom on the dresser," Oliver said. "You want me to call Marge?"

"Let her be with her daughter." Suddenly, Decker squinted and frowned. "What the hell happened to your nose?"

Gingerly, Oliver touched his face. "Your daught—Cindy got mad at me. Actually, it was more like she was angry with this and took it out on me. That's okay. I knew where she was coming from."

Decker winced. "Does it hurt?"

"Hell, yeah, it hurts. Cindy's strong. She punches like she means it."

❏

WEARING her fuzzy pink bathrobe, Cindy trudged out of the bathroom, her feet housed in slippers with soles that scuffled against the floor. She stopped when she saw her dad, unsure of how to engage him. She tried out a smile, but it quickly faded, settling for a dispirited "Hi."

Decker felt his heart tighten; she looked so young and vulnerable. Her hair was hidden under a mound of piled towel, her face colorless and devoid of expression. Decker put down an evidence bag, noting his daughter's gaze fixed on the mess in her room, part of the walls dusted with black ink. "What can I do for you?"

"Find any latents?"

"Nothing so far. Oliver and I are thinking about calling in some techs—"

"Sure, let the whole world know I'm a total boob."

Decker tried to figure out his next move. "So what would you like to do?"

"Is burying my head in an oven an option?"

Decker approached her as one nears a wounded animal. He stopped in front of her. "Can I give you a hug?"

"Sure, if it'll make you feel better."

"Will it make you feel better?"

"Dad, I think I'm beyond kissing the boo-boo."

Decker hugged her anyway. "I love you, princess."

She lay against his chest, her posture stiff and unyielding. "I love you, too."

"We'll get through this—"

"Wrong." She pushed out of the embrace. "*I'll* get through this. I'm going through it. Not you."

He knew she was distraught, but how could he comfort her if she refused his overtures? Ironically, it seemed that the more sensitive he was, the more she pounced, interpreting his tenderness as a weakness. If being gentle wasn't going to work, he might as well be himself. "I'll need to ask you some questions."

"Sure. Go ahead."

"This time you'll have to be honest."

"Not a problem."

But Decker wasn't sure about that.

Cindy said, "Thanks for taking the shit off my bed."

"Oliver did it."

"Let's hear it for Scott's hidden altruism. Rah, rah—"

"Why don't we go in the living room—"

"More like my former living room." She took off the towel. Waves of rust-tinged hair tumbled to her shoulders. "Is St. Scott still here?"

Decker nodded.

"Maybe I should get dressed then," Cindy said. "Ah, forget it. No need to stand on formalities. He's seen me faint, he's seen me drunk, he's seen me barf . . . more like heard me barf. I supposed he filled you in."

"He didn't get into specifics. You don't have to, either."

"Just trying to be honest. I'm a real pain in the butt for you, aren't I?"

Decker put his arm around his daughter. "I love you. Stop diluting that fact with self-pity."

"Viewing the current circumstances, I think my self-pity is excusable."

"Indeed." Decker guided her into the living room. Cindy's eyes jumped about, surveying the mess. "It's not as bad as I remember. I think St. Scott cleaned up." She shouted, "Hey, Oliver. Is janitorial work part of the job description?"

From the kitchen Oliver shouted back, "I don't do windows, but I do do coffee. You want some?"

"Do I have a coffeepot left?" Cindy asked.

"You do."

"Do I have coffee?"

Oliver opened the fridge, then wrinkled his nose. It wasn't a pretty sight. "I'd say the ripper left about half a bag of Peet's for you."

"I'd love some coffee," Decker said.

"It's regular not decaf," Cindy answered.

"That's all right," Decker said.

"It's more than all right. At this hour in the morning, it's a necessity." Oliver poured tap water into her still-standing coffeemaker. "Besides, I've been known to exist days without sleep. Although, I suppose being in a drunken stupor could be considered a subcategory of sleep."

Cindy smiled and leaned against her father. Decker hugged her shoulders. "Sit down, sweetheart."

"Where? My couch is a mess." Cindy looked around and settled atop an intact, upholstered arm of her couch, her limp hands settling into her lap. "The floors are cleaner. What'd you do with all the garbage?"

"Bagged it." Oliver came back into the living room. "Your dad and I will sift through it later on. Marge'll probably help out as well."

"Does she *have* to know about this?" Cindy moaned.

"Cin, this isn't your fault. You didn't bring this on," Decker said. "The more heads we have working for us, the better off we all are."

"As long as you don't call in Culver City police. This is still my place and I have the right *not* to report it—"

"What if it's some serial burglar or rapist?" Decker said. "It's your obligation—"

"If you really think that's what *this* is, then call them up. And if you do that, then don't ask me any more questions about Armand Crayton. Besides,

Crayton's been dead for over a year. I don't see how this could have *anything* to do with him."

"Then why'd you bring him up?" Decker said.

"I don't know!" She shook her head. "You said I didn't bring this on. But I keep thinking that maybe I *did* bring this on . . . that maybe I offended someone."

Oliver said, "Like who?"

"That's a problem," Cindy said. "I offend lots of people."

Decker took out his notebook. "I know you have suspicions. You've been troubled for a while."

"That was just self-centered angst. Up until now I never felt troubled about being in *physical* danger."

"So start with the basics, Ms. Decker," Oliver said. "Any guys acting weird around you lately?"

"No."

"Anyone seem hostile toward you?" Decker said.

"No."

"You blow off anyone in the last few weeks?"

"I don't blow people off," Cindy said. "I just kind of . . . work my way around them. If I want my distance from certain miscreants, I avoid them."

"Are you in that kind of situation now?" Decker asked.

"I was speaking metaphorically. No one's interested in me."

"The contrary, Cindy, someone is very interested in you. You're being stalked. Scott told me that the

Camry was following you. Why didn't you say something to me?"

Cindy didn't answer. There was no need to state the obvious. Decker didn't press it. But he couldn't quite keep his irritation from surfacing. "When did you notice that the car was tailing you?"

"I was over the hill . . . in the Valley. Somewhere on the Hollywood Freeway going into the 134. That's when I first noticed it. But it could have been tailing me from the start, from the moment I left the police station."

"So what really happened?" Decker asked. "This time the truth, please."

Cindy took in her father's skeptical eyes. "No need for the reprimand. It wasn't my intention to chase down the Camry. I just wanted to get the plates. But I was too obvious. Or the driver was very astute. As soon as I made a couple of maneuvers on him, he fled. I got caught up in the situation. I started chasing him."

"The Camry fled from you?" Decker asked.

"Yes."

"And you lost it in Angeles Crest?"

"Yes."

Decker said, "And up until now nothing strange has been going on?"

Oliver jumped in. "Why don't you start with the picture frame—"

"What picture frame?" Decker asked.

"The one that had been moved off her mantel. It

had a picture of Hannah in it." Oliver's eyes skipped across the room. "I can't find it as a matter of fact."

"I have it." Decker removed Hannah's picture from his pocket. "I picked it up from the floor."

"Tampering with evidence, Dad?" Cindy said.

"At least you haven't lost your sense of humor. Tell me about this picture frame."

"It was so insignificant, it's hardly worth mentioning," Cindy said.

"Not so insignificant that you didn't ask me about it." Oliver turned to Decker. "The day after I took her home, she called me and asked if I had moved Hannah's picture from the mantel to the table, was it?"

"Yeah, the table," Cindy answered. "I found it on the table. I don't remember putting it there. I always keep the family photos on the mantel." She shrugged. "As long as we're getting silly, I suppose I should mention the Post-it."

Oliver said, "Someone left a Post-it in her cruiser with the word *remember* on it."

"Jesus!" Decker said. "Remember *what?*"

"I don't know, Dad!" Cindy snapped. "I don't think it was even meant for me. And no, I don't have it. I threw it away. How was I to know it could be important?"

Decker held his tongue. "Anything else we should know about?"

"Okay. I'm telling you everything now. I keep

my cotton sweaters on the left side, the wool on the right. I found them reversed. Maybe I did it. Maybe the home wrecker did it."

"Someone went through your things before tonight?" Decker said.

"Maybe." Cindy crossed, then recrossed her legs, trying to find a comfortable position. The arm of the sofa simply wasn't made for sitting. "That is all of it. I swear, even if you put me on the rack, I have nothing more to add."

Decker asked, "When did all this start to happen?"

"The night Scott brought me home. That's when I first noticed that the picture was out of place."

Decker said, "Give me the date."

"I have it. That's when I met Osmondson . . ." Oliver thumbed through his pocket calendar and gave him the date.

Decker said, "Around a week ago." He turned to Oliver. "Any jackings on that date?"

"No," Oliver said. "Anything else happen to you on that day, Cindy?"

"Nothing."

"What about work?" Decker said. "Did you arrest anyone that swore a vendetta against you?"

Cindy shook her head. "Perps talk, perps make threats all the time. But I can't recall anything particularly nerve-racking."

"What did you do that day?" Decker asked.

"I don't remember offhand," Cindy said.

Oliver said, "Did you piss off anyone at work?"

"I don't *know*!"

"Cindy, you remember the night in Bellini's. You were sitting at a table with Hayley and some other woman—a black gal . . . she didn't look like a cop. More like a civilian."

"Rhonda," Cindy said. "She's a secretary for Detectives."

"I know Rhonda," Decker said.

"Yeah, she mentioned you. She says hi—"

"Can I get a thought out?" Oliver barked. "Okay, it was you and Hayley and Rhonda. What were you talking about?"

"Men. How all the good ones are married or gay. I wasn't in a good mood and I was shooting down beers."

"Why weren't you in a good mood?" Decker asked.

"Dad, I'm never in a good mood."

Decker smoothed his mustache. "Okay. Let's try this. The women . . . did you come in with them? Did you meet them there?"

She exhaled. "Actually, I came in with Graham . . . Graham Beaudry . . . my partner."

"When you were first assigned to him, you said he was okay," Decker said. "Do you still feel that way?"

"Yes, basically. Graham's a bit lazy, but not a bad sort."

"Has he ever put the make on you?" Decker asked.

"No."

"Any subtle signs?" Oliver wondered.

"No. Beaudry treats me like a human being."

Oliver said, "Who doesn't treat you like a human being?"

"Everyone treats me okay to my face," Cindy said. "Behind my back, they whisper."

"About what?" Decker asked.

"Being snotty . . . too smart for my own good . . . arrogant because I have a lieutenant father."

"Any of it true?" Decker asked.

"All of it is true." Cindy bit her bottom lip. "I think that was the day we confronted the lady with the gun at her husband's balls. I was talking to Beaudry about the arrest."

"What about it?" Decker asked.

"The lady . . . her name was . . ." Cindy screwed up her face. "Estella . . . lovely Estella Ojeda. She was thoroughly pissed off at her husband. She found out about his *puta* and was pointing a sawed-off shotgun at her husband's *cojones*. I talked her down almost single-handedly. I handled it masterfully."

"Did Beaudry have a problem with that?" Decker asked.

"Beaudry didn't. But I sure as hell pissed off my sergeant."

Decker and Oliver exchanged glances. Decker said, "How so?"

"By showing him up. He'd been making wisecracks about my being educated—like I was the snooty ivory-tower intellect while he had all the street smarts. He'd sent me in thinking I'd blow it. I proved him wrong. At the bar, Beaudry was telling me that I was off-base and I didn't do myself a favor by embarrassing him."

Decker said, "That's certainly true. Who's the sergeant?"

"Tropper."

"Does he have a first name?"

"Clark," Cindy replied. "Anyway, he's nothing to worry about. For the last week I've been typing his reports on my own time to get on his good side." She smiled, but it was forced. "He hasn't hassled me since." What she didn't tell them was that Tropper had gone from ice to fire. She didn't have to tell them. The info was stamped on her face, which both of them read quite well.

Decker said, "Does he come on to you, Cindy?"

"No—"

Decker said, "If you have any inkling that he may be responsible for this—"

"I have no inklings, Dad." Cindy shrugged. "Of course, I'm not sure of anything right now. Is Tropper capable of doing this? Of course he is. He's a macho cop with a Wild West attitude. But why would he want to hassle me? I've cut his paperwork in half."

Decker spoke to Oliver. "You worked Hollywood. What do you know about Tropper?"

"Nothing. He came on after I left. I can find out—"

"Do that," Decker said. "It'll look better coming from you than from me." He focused in on Cindy. "Any other guys take an interest in you?"

She shrugged. "No one really. Well, there's Andy Lopez. I went to the academy with him. He offered to drive me home the night I got drunk. I declined."

"Do you think it made him angry?" Decker asked.

"No, he didn't seem angry. But then later on Hayley Marx . . . the cop I was with when I got tipsy . . . she told me he was hurt. That she thought he had a crush on me."

"Does he?"

"We're casual acquaintances," Cindy said. "I don't know what he thinks about me."

"Okay," Decker said. "Anyone else we should know about?"

"Speaking of Hayley Marx . . ." Cindy licked her lips and turned to Oliver. "Did she mention that we ran into each other last night?"

"She mentioned seeing you," Oliver said. "She didn't go into details. Why?"

"Do you know where I met up with her?"

"No."

"At Prenner's Park," Cindy said. "The park where the road dead-ends. I pulled over because my car was smoking. All of a sudden, Hayley Marx shows up out of nowhere."

Decker was too stunned to speak. He raised his brows. "You didn't think this was *odd* enough to mention?"

"I thought it was awfully odd. But I knew she couldn't have been following me. She was driving a Mustang, not a Camry."

"Cars can be switched," Decker said.

"Not that fast—"

"Yes, that fast."

"Dad, she couldn't have possibly done *this*." Her arm glided through air, showcasing the room. "Scott was with her the entire evening."

"She could have hired out," Decker said.

"Why would she? She doesn't have anything against me. She even acts like she likes me. I just thought it was—well . . . strange."

"Too strange to be a coincidence," Decker answered. "She seems to have a vested interest in your personal life . . . telling you about Andy Lopez—"

"It sounds worse than it is, Dad. We were just spouting harmless girl talk—"

"Maybe she was riling up this Lopez fellow against you—"

"Now you're getting paranoid—"

"Cindy, I am working within a framework!" Decker raised his voice. "Look at this mess!"

"I agree it's a mess," Cindy answered calmly. "I just have doubts that Hayley is involved."

"Even though she just happens to run into you in the middle of the wilderness?" Decker said. "What did she say she was doing up there?"

"Killing time before she met with Oliver."

"What time was it?"

"Around five. She said she was going to meet Scott later."

"That's all true," Oliver said.

Decker said, "I don't buy it for one second. Why would she be roaming around Angeles Crest?"

"She probably took the same route out that I did, Dad. And if she thought like me, she probably got off the freeway when it jammed up. Maybe she decided to go to Angeles Crest to mellow out."

"No, she didn't," Decker said. "She went there because she was following you—"

"She wasn't driving a Camry!"

"I didn't say she was the Camry person. I'm not even saying she was behind the Camry person. But it's just too weird to pass off as one of those strange things."

Oliver said, "It does sound weird. Still, she told me she saw Cindy. And Cindy's right. Hayley couldn't have trashed the place because I was with her the entire evening."

"Hayley is one of the few women who talk to me," Cindy said. "Why would she do this?"

"I'm not considering motive right now, Cindy,"

Decker said. "Only candidates. And from what you've told me, you've built up quite a good slate of those in the running."

22

BY FOUR in the morning, most of the mess had been sorted, cataloged, and carted away. The floors had been swept and vacuumed—the dust bags saved for evidence, of course—the counters had been cleaned, and her fridge had been restored albeit barren in the food department. Her sleeping quarters had been freshened, the air thick with the scent of lilac room deodorant. Her comforter was gone, but she did have a spare blanket and her sheets were clean, crisp, and free of debris. Tidied up, her place was tolerable, even livable, but it went down like a bad aftertaste. As dictated by good manners, Oliver had left her place first.

Her father insisted on stalling, begging her to come home with him. But she declined his invitation with a weary smile, telling him to go home to his family. She'd be fine. And even if she wouldn't be fine, she'd have to learn on her own how to be fine again. Literally pushing him out the door. As soon as he left, she swung the dead bolt into the jamb, then leaned against the door, exhaling aloud. Her place was sterile, as welcoming as a budget hotel. All her personal touches had been bagged and taken away by her father and Oliver. They would keep it quiet for now, but who knew how long that would last. She surveyed the space with dry eyes and detachment.

Wired by raw nerves dipped in stress hormones, she trembled more from her body's natural chemicals than from fear, feeling much too unsettled to sleep. If she was going to spend the remainder of the night awake and sane, she needed a game plan. She could take two approaches: She could bemoan her fate and eventually freak out, or she could remain aloof and treat her situation as if she were the primary cop who caught the call.

That would mean securing pencil and paper and writing stuff down. She wondered if she even had pencil and paper. She kept her supplies in one of the kitchen drawers, and most of their contents had been dumped during the raid. Did she have any supplies left? She felt restless and mean, stalked by an unknown hunter with unclear intentions. Was this just a warning? If he really meant harm, why attack her house?

Write it down!

Which meant she was back to square one: Get pencil and paper. Sleep deprived and unsteady, she trudged over to the kitchen area and opened her supply drawer. It now contained her cutlery. She took out the cutlery tray and opened the cutlery drawer, now empty except for a can opener and a measuring spoon for coffee. The wood was still damp from where Oliver had washed it down. She really should have lined her drawers with coated paper. It would have made the cleanup so much easier. She removed the can opener and the measuring spoon and put the items in the cutlery tray, placing the entire ensemble back in the silverware drawer. Her supply drawer was now empty. She was without provisions.

How could she get anything done without provisions?

There was a twenty-four-hour drugstore about five minutes by car from where she lived. It was time to check out who actually shopped at five o-clock in the morning. She put on her coat, picked up her purse, rooting through it to make sure her gun was accessible. Lastly, she took out her keys. She spied out the window, discerning only odd, lifeless forms and shapes in charcoal and steel. With great caution, she opened the door, then locked it, venturing out to her car.

Though her poor Saturn had run the gauntlet, it started up valiantly after a few preliminary sputters, reminding her of an invalid trying to hide the illness. Again she checked her purse for her revolver. She put the car into gear and puttered her way over to Buy Rite Drugs, her eyes jockeying back between the windshield and the rearview mirror. She pulled into a near-empty parking lot. The inside was a ghost town: empty, long, brightly lit aisles reflecting polished linoleum floors. The fluorescent tubes hummed as she walked. As she passed shelves of analgesics, she spotted a frantic mother buying a hefty supply of Infant's Tylenol. A moment later she noted a hype with greased hair and stringy arms, clumsily holding a box of tissues and a half-dozen assorted candy bars. She made her way into the stationery supplies and picked up a ream of lined paper, a bag of pencils, a bag of felt-tipped pens, a box of paperclips, two pads of Post-its, two pencil sharpeners, a yellow highlight marker, and a three-ring binder. She threw it all in a shopping cart.

While she was there, she picked up milk, eggs, margarine, orange juice, two boxes of Neapolitan ice cream, a box of corn flakes, a bag of sugar, and a bottle of pancake syrup that she'd probably never use. But the bogeyman had spilled out her old syrup and psychologically she needed to replace it. So as long as she bought the syrup, she might as well try making pancakes via a mix. And while she was on a pancake kick, she bought a can of blueberries because, hell, what could be more cheerful than blueberry pancakes, orange juice, and fresh coffee? Which reminded her that she needed coffee, having used up the last remaining bag four hours ago.

She checked her watch. Starbucks would open in twenty minutes. Might as well get the good stuff. She dawdled away twenty minutes by buying a birthday card for her mother (her birthday was next month), sorting through discontinued makeup items from a table marked ALL SALES FINAL, and browsing through a magazine rack.

She checked out around five-fifty and walked to the parking lot. Night was still nursing its beer, but dawn was up and coming, the horizon a wash of purples and pinks. Everything was so still and fresh. Things had to get better!

After buying coffee and a newly baked croissant, she was on her way home, noticing that her heart-beat quickened the closer she got to her apartment. By the time she was slogging up the stairs, she felt an all-out adrenaline rush—heart thumping, head throbbing, hands clammy and quivering. Her system was on hyper-alert and she couldn't stop the shakes.

Though she took out her gun, she knew it was for show only. She was trembling so hard, she couldn't have shot a whale from ten feet away. Somehow she managed to insert the key in the lock. Somehow she managed to open the door. Still holding her gun, she kicked her bags inside with her right foot, stepping into the living room at the same time. One more shove and she and the groceries were inside. She locked the dead bolt, put

down her gun, and sank to the floor, holding her
head between her hands, squeezing her eyes shut to
prevent them from overflowing with water.

Deep-breathe!

*Better yet. Do something normal! Something so utterly
mundane that it could be done by a decorticate monkey!*

She stowed her gun back in her purse, then stood
up and picked up the bags, and began to put the
groceries away. As her fridge filled, it gave her
heart. So much heart that she thought she might
forget about the croissant and attempt the pancakes. Her search for her mixing bowl was interrupted by a modulated knock. Instantly her heart
took flight. Rationally she knew it was a friend because intruders didn't give warning. Still, out came
the gun. A check through the peephole; it was
Scott carrying a grocery bag. She let him inside but
made a point of looking at her watch. "The early-
bird special is down the block. All the cholesterol
and ptomaine you can eat for two ninety-nine."

"As tempting as it sounds, I decided to bag it."
He held up the paper sack. "I have fresh rolls, butter, strawberry jam, grapefruit juice, and whole
bean coffee with a grinder." He grinned. "Yuppi-
fied to the max." A second glance and he noticed
the revolver in her shaking hand. "You can put the
gun away. I promise I'll behave."

Her smile was laced with tears. "Thanks."

He put his bag on the counter, then noticed her

empty grocery bags. "Looks like we had the same idea. Where'd you go?"

"Buy Rite Drugs. I bought some pancake mix. I was going to make blueberry pancakes." She held up the can and offered it by way of proof. "Here are the blueberries."

"I see that."

"I've never made pancakes before," Cindy said. "Do you think it's difficult?"

"No, it's not difficult with a mix. I used to make them all the time when my boys were young. Back when I had a purpose to life."

"Such a devoted father. My dad never made me pancakes, let alone blueberry pancakes."

"Guess that makes me the superior parent." Oliver smiled. "For some reason, you look very wiped out. Why don't you let me whip up a batch?"

"He buys me food, then cooks for me. How lucky can a woman get?"

Slowly, Oliver walked over to her and put his hand around hers. He slipped the gun from her grip and laid it on the kitchen counter. "I've got a great idea. Go lie down, and I'll not only make you pancakes, I'll scramble up some eggs. Then I'll set the table and call you when everything's ready. Full-service butler and cook and I don't require a tip."

"Can't beat that."

"No, you can't. Go to bed, Cin. The chef needs some elbow room."

But she didn't move. "You live forty-five minutes away. Obviously, you didn't go home."

"Obviously."

"Where'd you go?"

Oliver chuckled. "Drank some strong coffee, then went grocery shopping. Go to bed."

"Sure it's not too—"

"I have to tank up anyway," Oliver said. "Gotta meet with Marge and find out about a Camry that took a nosedive."

"Oh yeah. I forgot about that."

"Go to bed."

Go to bed . . . *her* bed that was now free of shit. She wanted to ask Oliver what he had done with the pile, but she figured it might dampen his enthusiasm for cooking. Rule number one: If a guy wants to cook for you, let him.

"I'll walk you in," Scott said.

"I think I can find my bed without your help."

"Think so?"

Cindy nodded, then kissed his cheek. "Thanks, Oliver. This means a lot to me."

He turned, then brushed her lips. "You're welcome. Go lie down."

She paused, knowing that she could make it more. With a single touch of her fingers on his, she could make it a lot more. So tired, yet aroused. So weary, yet energized by the smell of his cologne and body oils from his all-night vigil. Her own body was a sorry concoction of out-of-whack hormones.

"I'll be in the bedroom," she said.

"I know." With that, he started to open her supply drawer, now jammed with office accoutrements. He opened the cutlery drawer and pulled out the can opener. "You switched drawers on me."

Cindy stared at him. "I would never switch a man's drawers."

Oliver burst into laughter. "Get out of here!"

He sounded like he meant it. Slowly, Cindy made her way to her bedroom, almost molding with the mattress as she slipped inside the covers. Within minutes, the fragrance of homemade cooking tweaked her olfactory system. She had only meant to close her eyes for a moment . . . just for a moment. But her bed was so comforting and the smell was so wonderful and she couldn't seem to reopen her eyes. Besides, she wasn't alone. Oliver was here . . .

❑

SHE awoke in a hot, wet sweat, her chest drumming an arrhythmic cadence. Too scared to move but not too scared to open her eyes. For a moment, she spun with vertigo, but after a fashion the room decided to stop pirouetting. She managed to take in the face of her nightstand clock. It was a little after two. No doubt still the afternoon because the sun was up and this wasn't the North Pole in the summer. The wonderful cooking smells had dissipated, leaving in their wake the stale odor of congealed grease. Getting up on two feet was no easy trick, but eventually she did find her balance *and* her pink robe to boot. She trudged out into her living room.

Scott was gone, and his pancakes had been wrapped in Saran and stowed in the fridge. The dishes had been washed. The counters had been cleaned, just as she had left them, except now she had a coffee grinder. She opened the refrigerator once again and took out a bag of whole beans, placing a scoop in the grinder.

The sucker worked, turning the beans into aromatic mocha sand. At this point, she didn't even care about the coffee. The fragrance was enough to lift her spirits. She put on a pot, then headed for the shower. Did a backtrack and checked the door. Of course it was locked, but since Oliver didn't have a key, it wasn't bolted. She remedied the situation with a twist of her wrist.

Once out of the shower, she dressed in loose sweats, her damp hair tickling the back of her neck. She reheated the pancakes in the microwave, poured herself a glass of orange juice, and doused her coffee with half-and-half. She was in breakfast heaven, scarfing down butter and sugar and fat and all the bad stuff, but relishing each bite. She made it through half a stack when the phone rang, sending her heart into paroxysms. Taking a deep breath, she lifted the portable out of the cradle. "Hi."

"Are we still on for dinner?"

Mom.

"Uh . . . sure," Cindy replied. "That'd be great."

A pause. Mom said, "You forgot about it."

"Not at all—"

"Yes, you did. But I won't hold it against you."

She was already holding it against her. Cindy said, "What time, Mom?"

"How about five?"

That was only three hours away. "Mom, that's a little early. I ate a late lunch—"

"See. I told you, you forgot about it. Why else would you eat a late lunch?"

Sherlock had caught her in her fib. Cindy was annoyed. "You never eat so early. What's going on?"

"I just thought maybe we'd *chat* before dinner." Another guilt-inducing pause. "But if it's too hard for you to get here—"

"How about six-thirty?" Cindy interrupted.

"I suppose—"

"Great," Cindy chirped. "I'll see you then."

She hung up, placing the phone on her kitchen table, dreading the upcoming date. As of late, she had much more in common with her father than with her mother. And it seemed that every time Mom had found out about a dinner at Dad's, she had followed it up with an invitation of her own. She loved her mother but wondered why she was still competing for her daughter's love nearly twelve years after the divorce when both parties seemed happily remarried. Real relationships were tricky jobs. It was no wonder there were so many lonely hearts surfing the chat rooms. Electronic boyfriends were perfect. In the privacy of the mind, they were always perfect. They never farted or burped, they never hogged the conversation (probably because their fingers got tired of typing), and they were forced to listen to what you had to say because they were more or less forced to read your response. If only the tactile part could be worked out—the hugging, the kissing, the holding, the stroking, the sex . . .

By now, her pancakes had lost their luster, leaving a buttery film on her teeth. She put the half-eaten stack back in the refrigerator, spilled out the orange juice, but helped herself to a second cup of coffee. Time to get down to business.

Out came the paper and pencil.

First she wrote down *Crayton?* Why would the mess in her apartment have anything to do with Armand Crayton? Even if Scott and Marge and her father were on the verge of digging up something about the case, why would the perp take it out on her?

But what if the perp had known about her prior acquaintance with Crayton, and thought she knew something about his murder.

But then why would he satisfy himself with just

messing up the apartment? Why not just . . .
gulp . . . kill her? Was this a warning of some sort?

Warning about what?

Remember.

If it wasn't Crayton, who could it be? Her dad
had suggested three possibilities—Lopez, Marx,
and Tropper. Take them and the motives one
by one.

Suppose Lopez trashed her place because she
didn't let him drive her home. Rather unstable
gent if that indeed was the case. She'd watch him
over the next couple of days, talk to him . . .
maybe even mention the incident and judge his reaction. But she'd have to do it subtly so as not to
arouse suspicion.

She put a check by Andy Lopez's name.

Tropper. Everyone at the scene had witnessed her
triumph with Estella and how she got the gun
away from her, deflecting what could have been a
tragedy of domestic violence. Despite Tropper's
best efforts to make her look like a fool, Cindy had
come through like a hero. Tropper was pissed, not
only because she emerged victorious but also because her victory was done in public. He had tried
to put her in her place, and instead she put him
down. He had to have felt some embarrassment.
Could he still be holding a grudge?

If he was, he was nursing it slowly, allowing
Cindy to type up his reports, fetch his coffee, and
do his filing. Clark Tropper seemed more amiable

than he had ten days ago. Downright friendly at
times . . . asking her to introduce him to her father. Maybe *presumptuous* was the correct word. Was
he luring her into believing all was fine, while re-
arranging her animals into Kama Sutra positions?

The phone rang again. She picked it up from the
table and punched in the talk button. "Yo."

"Weren't we supposed to hook up?"

It was Hayley Marx. Cindy said, "We left it that
you were supposed to call me."

"Yeah, you're right. I overslept."

"So, it must have gone well last night," Cindy
announced. She hoped her voice was appropriately
casual as well as bored.

"It was all right." She sounded less than enthusiastic. "He was preoccupied."

Cindy bit her lip. "About what?"

"He mentioned all the carjackings that are going
on in his area. I think the heat's on. You'd probably
know more about it than I would since your dad's
in Devonshire."

"You think my dad talks to me about work?"

"I dunno. You two seem close."

"We are close. But Dad keeps his work to
himself."

Hayley said, "That's cops in general—tight-
lipped. Anyway, lunch has come and gone. How
about dinner?"

"Where were you ten minutes ago? My mom just
called. I'm going over to her place at six-thirty."

"Dinner with Dad, then with Mom?" Hayley commented. "Cindy, you've got to get a life."

Mocking her. Cindy said nothing.

Hayley's voice sounded casual. "I suppose we could go out to Bellini's afterward. How about if I meet you there at, say . . . nine?"

How long did she have to stay at her mom's to be polite? "Make it nine-thirty. If I leave too early, I'll hear about it from Mom for the next month."

"I think you're too enmeshed with your parents."

"And I think you should give up the closet psychology."

Hayley's laugh was full. "Okay. Bellini's at nine-thirty. It ain't all that great, but at least they know my name."

Then she disconnected the line. Picking up the pencil, Cindy tapped it against the sheet several times. Under the title of candidates, she wrote down *Hayley Marx* at the top of her list.

23

DECKER WOKE up with a blistering headache. He wasn't used to sleeping in the daytime, and this particular sleep had been cruel, replete with distorted images that he was now desperately trying to erase. His sheets were sweat-soaked and his face felt swollen and itchy. Despite the pounding in his head, he realized the house was quiet. It was close to five. His family had probably gone back to shul, the boys for Mincha services and Rina had most likely taken Hannah to the afternoon youth program. Decker labored as he got out of bed, the soles of his feet tingling when they touched the ground. Trudging to the bathroom, he wiped his face and neck with a wet towel, brushed his teeth, then ingested a couple of Advil, knowing that while the tabs might not conquer the pain, they might hold back the army of throbbing nerve endings.

He put on his bathrobe and ventured out, finding Rina stretched out on the couch, her head and feet propped up on pillows of lace and satin. She looked up from her book, then closed it. "How are you feeling?"

"Do you really want me to answer that?"

Rina took her feet off the couch. "Come, sit down."

"You don't want me near you."

"S'right. I'm used to musky, wild beasts." She tapped the seat cushion. "Sit."

Decker did so, albeit reluctantly. "Where are our progeny?"

"The boys took Hannah back to shul."

"Did they offer or did you make a request?"

"Actually, they offered."

Decker raised his eyebrow. "They actually displayed some altruism. That's nice. She didn't call, did she."

"No."

"You're sure?"

"I didn't hear anything, and there're no new messages on the machine." Rina shrugged. "You knew she wasn't going to."

"No. It would have been a nice courtesy, but I guess that's asking too much."

"It has more to do with assertion than courtesy, Peter."

"You're right about that," Decker answered. "Anything I do will be interpreted as interference. You know, as pissed as I am at Oliver, there's this side that says, hey, he's a good cop. If she's willing to accept his help, that's not so bad. So wait till this resolves. And then when it's all over, I'll go ahead and beat the crap out of him—"

"Peter—"

"I'm kidding."

"No, you're not."

He rubbed his forehead. "Do you *believe* his story? He just *happened* to be there when she got drunk."

Rina said, "Actually, I do."

Peter gave her an incredulous look. "You can't be serious."

"Peter, you knew he was in Hollywood, talking to that detective about the carjackings. It seems reasonable that he might run into Cindy."

Decker grumped. "I don't believe in coincidences. I bet he *planned* to meet her there and this drunk story is just a cover. They're doing this to spite me."

"With all due respect, I don't see Scott as a predator. He'd never seek Cindy out, but if she was around and needy . . . I could see him saying, 'Well, why not?' Cindy, on the other hand, is very anxious to prove that she's your equal. By coopting Oliver, she's become one of your detectives, *de facto*—"

"Oh, please!"

"Which makes you not just her father but her peer. Which is why she's so stubborn about accepting your help. She doesn't want to break this facade about you two being equals." She took his hand. "We know she's terrified. I'm just wondering if there's a way we can help her without getting in her face."

"There's a way," Decker said. "I can find out who this bastard is and mow him down. It would be preferable to do it with her help, but not essential. If she's keeping secrets from me, then I can keep secrets from her."

"That's all very well and fine except you haven't any ideas about his identity."

"She gave me some ideas," Decker said. "I'm not exactly starting from square one."

Rina said, "What kind of ideas?"

"A couple of co-workers. And I'm still not ruling

out that this has something to do with the Crayton case."

"That was over a year ago."

"But it's not over. We all feel that some of these recent jackings are connected to it."

"What about the other jackings?"

Decker looked pained. "We're still working out the details. Why does she *do* this to me? She knows how much I worry." He bounced up and took the cell phone from its recharger. "Drives me crazy! I guess I have to realize that I'm the adult in this relationship."

"Maybe that's part of the problem. That you feel you're the only adult."

He stared at her. "Since when have you become so shrinky?" He made a face. "It's those community college courses you're taking. I hope it's a passing phase. Whenever the wife starts getting too interested in psychology, watch out for the marriage."

Rina laughed. "Don't worry. You're stuck with me."

"I certainly hope so." Cindy's machine kicked in. Decker dutifully waited for the beep. "Hi, sweetheart, I just called to find out how you're doing. Please call me back and let me know you're okay. I love you." He punched the end button. "Done."

"Except now you're worried about her not being home."

"Exactly." Decker tried her cell phone. When he

didn't get any response other than that terrifically maddening recorded message—*the mobile customer you are trying to reach is unavailable*—he paged her. Either she was slow to respond or she was purposely ignoring him. After ten minutes of flattening the floor, he gave up and sank into the couch. He held his head. "I'm at a loss here. Help me. What should I do?"

Rina took his hand. He was suffering. She was suffering, too. Yet she had to be the rational one, her concerns and feelings secondary because Cindy was his daughter. "You want to go over there, don't you?"

"I don't know!"

Rina said, "I think that when kids are born, they should be implanted with subdermal locators. The nurse could put it in right when he or she does the silver nitrate drops."

"Wouldn't that be nice."

"Instead of schlepping out there, why don't you page Oliver?" Rina suggested. "Maybe he's with her."

"I don't want to think about that." He wrinkled his nose. "But it's a good idea." He punched in Oliver's pager and waited, pacing until he heard the phone come to life. Decker picked up the receiver with shaking hands. "Yo."

"What's up?" Oliver answered. "Is Cindy okay?"

Decker's heart sank. If Oliver was asking, it

meant she wasn't with him. "I certainly hope so. I thought that maybe she was with you."

Oliver hesitated. Now there was a real change of heart. But at this point Deck was probably so nervous, he'd accept any kind of protection. Oliver figured he fell somewhere between a territorial ape and a pit bull in Decker's mind. "She's not with me," he said. "I've been at the Camry's crash site with Marge for the last three hours. Is there a specific problem with her?"

"No. She's just not home. Maybe I'll swing by just to make sure."

"Marge and I have about fifteen, twenty more minutes here. I know it's your Sabbath. If you want, we'll go by. Save you the bother . . . if you want."

Trying to be diplomatic by asking him, Decker thought. "Did you see her this morning, Scott?"

Oliver inhaled sharply. Was Decker about to grill him? But before Scott could answer, Decker said, "I was wondering if she told you anything new. Anything she didn't feel comfortable telling me?"

Okay. So that was it. Decker was scared shitless, taking help from anyone because Cindy was his daughter, a cop, *and* a reckless kid. "Actually, I did stop by around six. I made her breakfast, but she fell asleep before I was done cooking. No, she didn't tell me anything new."

"That's unfortunate." Decker shifted the phone

into his other hand. "Find out anything at the crash site?"

"Amazingly, the techs pulled a couple of prints off the driver's wheel."

"When was this?"

"No more than a half hour ago. With this new computerized national fingerprint network, if the prints are there, we'd know something in a couple of hours *if* this was a weekday. As it is, we'll have to wait until Monday."

"Anything else?"

"Nothing you probably don't know. Yes, it appears that the car was pushed and doused with an accelerant. An amateur job, though, because too many things were left to chance. Someone was depending on the explosion to ignite the accelerant. A pro would have had some kind of remote device just in case it didn't burst into flames. If we trace the driver through the fingerprints, maybe we can open some doors to the jackings. Provided we can find the driver. I'm sure Cindy got a better look at him than she remembers."

"Probably. I'd ask her about it if I could *find* her. I've tried her pager, her cell phone, her personal phone. I'd try her at work, but first off, she's not on duty, and second, if it got out that I was calling to check up on her, she'd explode. You don't carry the baggage I do. Maybe you could call up Hollywood for me."

"Sure, if that's what you want."

Trouble was, Decker didn't know what he wanted. He said, "Did you ever get hold of Elizabeth Tarkum?"

"She's away for the weekend." Oliver made a snorting noise. "Now there's a novel idea. People taking off work on weekends. I'll try Tarkum on Monday morning."

"Marge tell you about her conversation with Dexter Bartholomew?"

"That he got off on flirting with Crayton's wife. And he didn't want anything to do with his wife's jacking, or, for obvious reasons, with Crayton's death. We started kicking around some possibilities. First, a thing between Dexter Bartholomew and Lark Crayton. Then we thought about an affair between Crayton and Elizabeth Tarkum, which makes more sense because they were both victims."

"Dex popping Crayton as revenge, then having his wife carjacked to teach her a lesson. Kind of a stupid plan. Carjacking is a weird way to perpetrate a revenge crime. And two similar carjackings of two socially acquainted people would automatically throw suspicions on the spouses. Which is exactly what's happening."

"Except that we didn't connect them for over a year because the crimes happened in two different divisions. We might not have ever put the two together. It's only because we've got a bunch of recent unsolved jackings that forced us to look elsewhere. An arrogant guy like Dex probably thought he got away with it."

"And now that we're digging this up again?" Decker asked.

"People who might have known something about the original Crayton jacking would watch their ass. That could include Cindy. I'm sure she doesn't know jackshit about Crayton. But if Dex thinks she does, that might . . . you know what I'm saying."

Indeed Decker did. But hearing it so concisely gave his already wired nervous system a start. "What about Stacy Mills? You said you felt she was hiding something. Why don't you and Marge go track her down? Impress upon her the need to be forthright. Maybe she was a friend of Lark or Armand, and one of them confided in her."

"I have no problem with that, but what about Cindy?"

Decker held back a sigh. "I'll swing by her place simply because I'm too nervous sitting here and doing nothing. It's probably a total waste of time. She's not home. I don't know what I expect to accomplish."

"Peace of mind maybe."

"Oliver, I gave up on that romantic notion a long time ago."

24

OLIVER AND Dunn reached the condo development right as the sun was setting, bleaching white
a dozen low-profile pink stucco buildings that
were topped with Spanish tile roofs. The apartments were scattered over golf-course-type acreage
with lots of rises and dips made green by liberal
use of lawn sprinklers. Not a lot of flowers or
bushes, but there were several lily ponds, a couple
of swimming pools, a quad of tennis courts, and
many bubbling Jacuzzis. The structures were identical and it took the duo a few passes before they
found Stacy Mills's specific abode which had been
christened The Windsome.

The aerobics instructor lived on the second floor:
a two-bedroom, two-bath unit with a niche that
passed for a state-of-the-art kitchen. She answered
the knock, her expression sour and suspicious. She
was a wiry thing in black latex, her arms well defined if not big. She seemed very nervous, her eyes
skipping between the two cops. Her eggplant-
painted lips were pressed against each other as if
glued shut. "Since you're not going away, you
might as well come in."

She led them into her carton-size living room,
which held two mullioned French doors leading

out to a patio. The walls held several prints of saccharine-sweet sunsets, the floor was covered in cream-colored pile carpet. The furniture was chunky and square, the couches and chairs upholstered in what passed as chic. But to Marge's eyes, the cloth looked more like Granny's white slipcovers. There were no throw pillows atop the couches, only two white, long-haired, ennui-stricken cats, which blended in with the fabric.

Oliver chose one of the chairs; Marge abutted one of the bored cats. It lifted its head, then decided to roll over. Marge stroked its belly and it purred contentedly. Stacy's eyes narrowed, regarding the cat like an errant lover.

"How long is this going to take?" Stacy snapped. "I have clients."

Marge settled into the couch. She wore a plain white blouse tucked into gray slacks; her jacket was midnight blue and unstructured. She pulled out her notebook from a floppy straw bag. "What kind of work do you do?"

"I'm a personal trainer. I work with many important people—industry people."

Industry meaning Hollywood. Oliver said, "How long have you worked as a PT?"

"What is this? A job interview?" Stacy exhaled, clamping her arms across her chest. "Why am I talking to you? You haven't recovered the car, right?"

"Right," Marge answered.

"So what good are you? I've got a dinner date in a few hours. Can you leave?"

Oliver said, "How long have you worked as a personal trainer?"

Stacy regarded him with steely eyes. "Didn't you just ask me that?"

"Yes, but you haven't answered the question." He reached for his notebook tucked into the inside pocket of his lightweight, gray jacket—a previously owned Valentino that he picked up at a fraction of its retail cost, probably a discard from someone in the *Industry*. He completed the designer blazer with a sky-blue shirt, patterned tie, charcoal pants, and black tie shoes. "It's a simple question, Ms. Mills."

"About ten years."

"Really?" Oliver smiled. "You started your field while still in your teens?"

"Ha, ha, ha . . ." But the compliment wasn't lost on Stacy. "I work hard at looking good. It's my stock-in-trade."

"I'll bet," Marge said. "No one wants to get advice from someone who doesn't look the part. Like your obese doctor telling you to lose weight."

Stacy said, "Can we dispense with the chitchat and get down to business? Exactly why are you here?"

Marge said, "I'd like to ask you a few questions about Armand Crayton—"

"I knew it!" Stacy began to pace, arms swinging

like rotor blades, her feet squashing the white nap of her carpet. "I didn't *know* him. But if it'll get you out of here quicker, I'll say I did."

Marge said, "You didn't know him?"

"That's right!"

"Did you ever meet him?" Oliver asked.

Stacy glared at him. "Yes."

"And you still insist you didn't know him?"

"I exchanged hellos with him. 'Hello, how are you. Hi, how you doing? Hey, what's up?' That's not *knowing* a person."

"Sounds to me like you saw him on a regular basis," Marge said. "Would you care to explain?"

"Not really."

Abruptly, Oliver sat up. "I interviewed Lark Crayton. She takes good care of herself. She's one of your clients, right?"

"Was," Stacy corrected. "I stopped working with her after he died. First off, she was in no state to train. Secondly, money became tight."

"Did you like her?" Oliver said.

"She paid her bills. For me, that constitutes liking a person."

"Did you have a personal relationship with her?"

"No." Stacy stopped walking about. "Anything else?"

"People tell their trainers all sorts of personal stuff, don't they?" Marge said.

"Yes, they do."

"You must feel like a shrink half of the time."

"Yes, I do," Stacy said. "But a good trainer, like a good shrink, keeps confidentiality."

"But unlike a shrink," Marge said, "you're not bound by rules of confidentiality."

"It gets out I talk about things, I lose my clients, Detective."

"It doesn't have to get out," Oliver said.

"Why don't I believe you?"

"Because you're perceptive," Oliver answered. "I'm a rotten guy for a boyfriend, but an honest cop." He turned to Marge for confirmation.

"I can vouch for the honest cop part," Marge answered. "Look, we all know that the carjacking scared you—"

"Of course, it *scared* me! It *terrified* me! You want to get me to trust you, solve the damn crime. And don't tell me you need my help to do that. You should be able to do that without my help. That's why I pay taxes!"

Oliver said, "Ms. Mills, your clients pay you to help them stay in shape or get into shape. But no matter what you do, if they don't exercise and watch their diet, you're not going to work miracles. That's all we're asking. If you give us a little background, it could go a long way."

Marge said, "We know Lark was dissatisfied with Crayton. Fill us in on the details."

Stacy checked her watch. Then she marched over to the fridge and took out a water bottle. She gulped greedily as if Crayton had sucked out her life force. "What do you want to know? She was unhappy with her marriage. So what else is new in this city?"

"What were her specific complaints?" Marge asked.

"He worked too hard, he worked too long. He wasn't around, he had women on the side. He didn't make enough, though she seemed to have lots of money to my eye. But I've worked long enough to know that lots of SoCals live on the edge, especially those in the Industry. Even the ones who make it can't seem to hold onto it. It's amazing how fast they go through the millions. If it's not cars, it's clothes. If it's not clothes, it's jewelry. Actually, if they'd stick to clothes and jewelry and fancy cars, they'd be okay. It's the lavish parties, the chartered jets, the hundred-foot yacht, the three vacation homes along with the residence in Holmby Hills and the apartment in New York. You think they live in any of the zillions of houses? I have this one client . . . he's got a four-thousand-square-foot Upper East Side apartment in New York with a view of the park that was decorated by some *Architectural Digest* biggie. I think the place was featured in *Architectural Digest*. Do you think he stays in the apartment when he's in New York? No, of course not. That would make too much sense. He rents out a suite at the Carlyle because he likes the room service. If he stays at his apartment, he's gotta get a cook and a maid and a valet and a

haircut guy and a gym guy: It's easier to use the
hotel's services. So I ask him, 'Why do you keep
the apartment? It must cost a fortune in upkeep.'
You know what he says?"

"What?" Marge duly responded.

"He's says he uses it for entertaining—for his parties. Can't have a dinner party at a hotel. But when
the party's over, his hired help cleans up, and he goes
back to a clean hotel room. Can you beat that?"

Marge smiled. "Maybe you can borrow it from
him at a reduced rate?"

"He's offered to take me more than once. Supposedly to keep him in shape when he's in New York.
Yeah, to keep his pecker muscles in shape." She
bent down and picked up a cat. The feline was passive and drooped in her arms like a muffler. "Let
me tell you something. I earn my money honestly.
I'm nobody's whore."

Oliver said, "You have a lot in common with us.
We're pushed around all the time—"

"Who says I'm pushed around!" Stacy sounded
resentful.

"Maybe you aren't, but we are," Marge answered.
"We can't move without worrying about the
ACLU or the IAD or some other citizens' group
bringing charges against us. And it's hard to be
methodical when arresting someone who's drunk
or stoned or irrationally angry."

"Sorry, but I don't bleed for cops," Stacy said,
stroking her pet.

"And you shouldn't," Marge said. "I'm not bitching. I knew the job when I got into it. I imagine that you did, too. You tell people you work for all these rich movie stars who offer you perks and free trips and whatnots. They think you got it made. But everything has a price, right?"

Stacy said, "Excuse me, but what does all this have to do with Crayton?"

"You tell us," Oliver said. "You're the one who reacted so strongly when we mentioned his name."

Stacy turned away, placing the cat back onto the sofa. "Okay. This is it. Armand was a typical case in point. With a little charm and a lot of ambition, he pyramided his way up. He had the house, the beautiful wife, the clothes, the Rolls, the parties, and the clients who invested with him. But beneath the surface it was built on quicksand, just waiting to cave in." A breath, then an exhale. "Lark told me she was worried. He was up to his neck in shenanigans."

"What kind of shenanigans?" Oliver asked.

"Lark didn't get into specifics, only that Armand was behind in payments and needed some quick cash. His lifestyle was eating him up. But he couldn't sell off his stuff because that would alert people that he was in trouble. Meanwhile, she's spending a hundred bucks an hour to have me watch her sweat. Lark kept obsessing on the car. The Corniche was leased, of course, and the payments were taking a hefty bite out of his wallet."

"Why didn't he walk away from it?"

"He couldn't get out of the contract without stiff penalties, let alone ruin the image. When people see you desperate, they chuck you out like vomit. Look, I'm not totally innocent of that kind of thing. I have to keep a certain face for show. I drive a Beemer . . . well, I used to drive a Beemer. You need a good car for show, but I got mine at a very good price—all cash. Now it's gone, but insurance'll take care of me. I could easily be in hock like the rest. But I'm not because I'm the bargain-shopping queen." She turned to Oliver. "Like your jacket. It looks like Valentino. I could get that today for seventy-five percent off retail because it's last year's style."

Oliver said, "I didn't do badly. I got it last year for sixty off."

"No, that's not bad at all. Where'd you get it?"

"Retails for Less."

"I've been there. Off-seasons and seconds."

"And previously owned."

"Good for you. If Hollywood had your money sense, movies wouldn't cost twelve bucks a pop."

Marge said, "Getting back to the Rolls. Armand wanted to get out of the lease?"

"According to Lark, yes. All my information about Armand was according to Lark. So if it turns out to be bullshit, don't blame me."

Oliver said, "Did Armand have any ideas on how to break the contract?"

Stacy sighed. "She mentioned something to me about him faking an accident . . . you know, ramming it into a wall and totaling it. She asked me if I thought that would look suspicious."

"What did you say?"

"I told her I thought it was a real dumb idea. It not only would look phony but he could hurt himself. Crashing into walls to total cars isn't something that should be done by amateurs."

"What'd she say?"

"She dropped the subject."

"And that was that?" Oliver said.

"No," Stacy admitted. "A couple weeks later she asked me if I knew anyone who'd be willing to not only steal a car but to get rid of it. Like because I train lots of people, I know a big criminal element." She stopped talking, again folding her arms across her breast. "I was really insulted."

"What did you tell her?"

"I told her I don't know anyone. I tried to be calm, but it really pissed me off. Then when the carjacking happened . . . only it turned out to be more than just a jacking. Man, I was nervous. If she had planned this, and I kinda knew what was going on . . . what did that mean for me? I must have spent six months looking over my shoulder, waiting for something to happen."

"How many days passed between the time she asked you about stealing the car and the actual jacking?"

"About a month."

"So, for a month, she didn't mention anything about the Corniche?"

"No . . . well, no more schemes. She still complained about Armand, though. How he couldn't manage money. When the jacking happened, I called her to offer my condolences. She wasn't home at the time, but she did call me back a week later, telling me she was in no state to see anyone. And even if she was in a state to see someone, she couldn't afford me anymore. I returned that phone call, but again she wasn't home. That was the last of it. Until last week—when I was carjacked."

She tapped her foot, then again took a big swig from her water bottle.

"I let my guard down because it's hard to live in a state of paranoia. Big mistake."

"Why do you think you were carjacked?" Oliver asked.

"Who knows? The car's flashy, I look vulnerable, a random thing, or . . . a reminder to keep my mouth shut." Stacy's eyes moistened. "I don't know. If someone wanted to warn me, why wait a year?" She stared at the detectives. "Right?"

Marge and Oliver nodded simultaneously. But it didn't seem to console her.

"This has been a real nightmare," Stacy went on. "I can't eat, I can't sleep. I take on more clients than I should because work seems to drive away the fear. That's the only positive. I'm making more money than usual." She stood and picked up the other cat. This one sensed the tension and squirmed in her arms. But Stacy held on tight. Maybe a little too tight. "The way I'm working . . . it can't go on forever. I'm wrecked!"

"Couple more questions, Stacy, and then we'll leave you in peace," Marge said. "Lark ever talk about her social life?"

"What do you mean?"

"Did she talk about her friends?"

"Yeah, sure. She talked about everything."

"Do you remember names?"

"Oh boy." She pondered the question. "Most of her chatter was background noise. I just said uh-huh a lot and told her to keep breathing."

"Did she ever mention the name Dexter Bartholomew?" Oliver asked.

"Dexter Bartholomew?" Stacy shook her head. "Not that I can recall."

"Doesn't ring any sort of a bell?"

"No. Should it?"

"Not necessarily," Marge answered. "How about Elizabeth Tarkum?"

She thought a moment, then shook her head again. "No."

"You don't recall any specific names?" Marge asked.

Stacy looked pained. "This is a year-old memory so I could be totally off-base. A couple of times Lark talked to me about a guy who was her ace in the hole. She didn't have to worry about anything because he had mucho clout."

Mucho clout! "A cop?" Marge suggested.

Stacy thought about that. "Could be. Way she was talking, I figured it was some Mafia guy. But a cop would be more reasonable, right?"

"Right," Marge answered. "Do you recall a name?"

"Something Germanic comes to mind, but that's as much as I remember." She shook her head, then got up and opened the door. "I really do have a dinner date."

"Thanks for your time," Marge said.

Stacy practically slammed the door on their heels. They walked in silence for a few moments, noticing the chill in the air. Marge tightened her jacket. "It's a cop and that's why she's holding back the name. She's scared witless. Bad cops are dangerous."

"Hey, even good cops are dangerous."

"All the more reason she's quaking," Marge said. "So do we press Lark for the name of the ace in the hole or go back and press Stacy?"

"If we go back and press Stacy, she's going to bolt."

"Yeah, I think you're right. Lark may do the same now that the insurance came through. Maybe we should just sit tight until we reach the company on Monday?"

Oliver raised his eyebrows. "If we ever get to

Monday. Man, this has been one hell of a weekend. And it's not even over."

Marge stopped walking. "You're expecting *more*?"

He faced her, making eye-to-eye contact. "I'm worried about Cindy. Deck hasn't heard from her and she's not answering her pages. That's not good. I'm going over there."

Marge lowered her voice. "You're involved with her, aren't you?"

Oliver looked away. "I plead the fifth."

❑

CINDY'S foot was on the gas pedal by nine-thirty, meaning she'd be late to Bellini's and would have to endure Hayley's inevitable ribbing. She had given three hours of her undivided attention to her mother, yet Mom seemed insulted when Cindy had to go, as if love was measured in minutes of idle conversation. Still, her mother's house was familiar, unlike Bellini's, which was noisy, crowded, and filled with tipsy cops whose macho posturing and dares often turned ugly in a finger snap.

Shielding her eyes from the incandescent glare, Cindy scouted the room and found Hayley at a table, along with Andy Lopez and his partner, five-year vet Tim Waters, in almost a replay of a week ago. The table held others as well, including slick Rick Bederman, staring at Hayley with intense brooding eyes. As he spoke, he twisted his wedding ring as if the jewelry was uncomfortable. On Bederman's left was his partner, Sean Amory, also married, but that didn't stop his baby blue eyes from scoping out the ladies. Lastly, there was Carolyn Evert—a six-year vet who was a five-ten and leggy blonde. They were chugging down shooters and laughing themselves red-faced. Absent were Tropper, Ron Brown, and Beaudry. Cindy couldn't help but wonder . . .

Seeing all these people, Cindy's first impulse was to turn and walk out. The combined events over the last several days were giving her high anxiety—rapid heartbeat, sweaty palms, jumpy eyes. But she was determined to conquer her fears. With calculation, she ambled over to the table, pulled out a chair, and sat with her stomach against the back of it, squishing herself between Bederman and Evert. Hayley handed her a shooter. "How was Mama?"

Cindy emptied the contents of the shot glass in a single swallow. "Neurotic." She turned to Carolyn Evert. "I'm Cindy Decker. I hate your legs. Not that they're bad. Just that I wish they were mine."

"Genetics, girlfriend," Carolyn answered. "Just like your red hair."

"I'll swap you," Cindy said.

"Be careful what you wish for." Carolyn picked up a lock of Cindy's tresses. "I might take you up on it one day."

"Take another shooter, Cin," Hayley said. "Drown out your problems with Mr. Cuervo."

Taking the glass, raising it to her lips, but not really drinking. The first chugalug satisfied her social obligations. Now she concentrated on keeping her wits. "So what happened in the wonderful world of Hollywood in my absence?"

Lopez said, "The usual." He had his hands clasped around a tumbler of something cold and clear. "Sleazeballs and assholes."

Carolyn said, "We were just wondering where Doogle was. I don't have a lot of cash, and I was kind of hoping my sleek legs would extend my credit past the hundred mark."

"I'm sure they would if they were open," Waters said.

"In your dreams," Carolyn answered. "You wanna loan me a twenty spot, aqua boy?"

"What'll it get me?"

"Goodwill," Carolyn answered. "Maybe the next time I see you, you can kiss my feet. And think of this, Waters. My feet are attached to my legs."

Waters nodded in contemplation, then gave her two tens.

Lopez smirked. "Wasn't that movie money for you and the little woman?"

"I'll take her to the Rialto. Every seat two seventy-five all the time."

Carolyn held up the bills. "Thank you, Waters."

"The least you can do is sit with me while I tell you my troubles." He looked pointedly at Cindy. "It's getting crowded here. I think I see a spare booth in the corner."

Carolyn sighed. "You ain't gettin' any. Let's keep that clear. But if you have the need to talk, I suppose twenty bucks can buy you a couple of ears for a bit."

Waters stood up. "I just need a shoulder to cry on. And being as yours is so lovely—"

"Yadda, yadda, yadda." Carolyn arose from her seat. "See you all later. Timmy needs to express his feminine side."

Hayley watched them for a moment, then surveyed the room like it was uncharted territory. At first, she appeared to be looking for someone, then abruptly she turned to Cindy. "Don't take it personal . . . them leaving. They've been at it all night."

"As long as it's not my breath."

"Your breath is fine," Bederman said.

Cindy gave him a smile but said nothing.

Bederman said, "How's your partner doing?"

"Beaudry?" Cindy shrugged. "He's fine . . . oh, that's right. You used to partner with him."

"Yep."

Cindy nodded, leaving the unasked question of *Why'd you request a transfer?* floating in the miasma.

Bederman said, "Beaudry tells me you're smart."

"You two still talk?" Cindy said.

"All the time. He's a great guy. We just aren't partners anymore."

Cindy expected him to elaborate. But he didn't. "Well, that's nice to hear. I know Beaudry thinks I'm a wiseass."

"Everyone thinks you're a wiseass, Decker," Lopez broke in. "You're real wise with a real good ass."

"That's a real knee-slapper, Lopez," Hayley commented dryly. "You must be a riot with the twelve-year-old boys."

Lopez's face darkened. Cindy felt her heart in her chest. Lopez was still on her list of would-be stalkers and the last thing she needed was for him to be pissed. She tried to deflect his embarrassment with a smile. But all it did was encourage him to keep putting his foot in his mouth. He said, "Marx, on the other hand, has a rep for being very hard . . . that is, when she's not being too easy."

The table ooohed, but Hayley just laughed it off. "Oh, my, my, Andy, you are one swift animal with clever quips. You should challenge the results of your recent IQ test. Surely they made a mistake when they listed you at the imbecile level."

The nastiness was making everyone queasy. Sean Amory said, "Why don't you give him a break, Marx? He's a rookie."

"Being a rookie is no excuse for being unfunny."

"Being a vet is no excuse for being a bitch."

Lopez stood, knocking over his chair. "See you guys later."

Hayley shoved a handful of peanuts into her mouth. "Well, that told me off." She looked at Bederman and Amory. "You think I'm a bitch?"

"All women are bitches sometimes," Bederman said. "Just like all guys are bastards sometimes. But you really should pick on someone your own size."

"He's taller than me!"

"He was imitating Waters," Amory piped in. "He's got a prick for a partner. He thinks you have to be a prick. Cut him some slack."

"Why should I? He's a jerk."

No one spoke. Then Hayley got up. "It's not enough being a fucking woman in a male-dominated, paramilitaristic organization, I also gotta play Florence what's-her-face to the weaker members of your sex to keep their thingies from shriveling up like sausage casing. I'll be right back."

The table had suddenly become roomy. Cindy had emptied it from seven people down to three in less than five minutes. She felt exposed. It appeared to her that the remaining two men were studying her but pretending not to. Bederman broke the interlude. "You're a quiet one."

Cindy smiled. "It's safer that way."

Bederman was about to pour himself another drink. Then he stopped. "I should be getting home. I told my wife by ten." He checked his watch and turned to Amory. "What about you?"

"You go," Amory said. "I'll sit with the youngun till Marx gets back."

"It's fine really," Cindy said. "I don't need a baby-sitter. And I don't mind solitude."

Amory smiled. "Then you've come to the wrong place."

"Why are you here?" Bederman said.

"At Bellini's?" Cindy asked. "Hayley. We agreed to meet here. In lieu of dinner."

"You like Hayley?" Bederman asked.

"As a matter of fact, I do."

"She made a lot of wrong turns," Bederman said. "Fucked a lot of married men. Now she's bitter. Don't go that route."

"Don't worry. It's not me."

Bederman stared at her for a moment. "What is you?"

She wasn't sure whether he was sizing her up. Whether he was about to make a move on her. That was just dandy: some other male to be concerned about. "Bederman, that's a good question with many answers. Right now, me is slightly tired with a bit of a headache."

"Need an Advil?"

"I've taken several, thank you."

"Can I give you a lift somewhere?" he asked innocently.

"No, I have my car. But thanks."

Bederman suddenly seemed to lose interest. He turned his attention to Amory. "You coming over to watch the game tomorrow?"

"Yeah. I'm bringing the family."

"You bring the family and the beer. I'll provide the eats."

"Deal."

Bederman left. Cindy glanced over her shoulder. Hayley was sitting next to Lopez, her body leaning toward him, nodding as Andy talked. Apparently, they had reached some kind of truce. To Amory, she said, "I'm really okay."

"I'm sure you are. You know, I don't like Marx, but Lopez was a jerk for talking about your ass like that. You shouldn't let him get away with it."

"I'll deal with him, but not in public. I don't like embarrassing people."

"You didn't mind stepping over Tropper."

Cindy felt a squirt of adrenaline course through her body. "You *couldn't* mean that domestic about a week ago. That was no big deal."

"Maybe not to you, but the sergeant wasn't pleased. If your last name wasn't what it was, you'd have a big black mark on your quarterly assessment report. But being as your dad carries some weight, Tropper backed off."

"Amory, I was just trying my best."

"The best thing isn't always the proper thing."

"I've been making it up to him." She blushed at the way it came out. "By helping him out with his paperwork, I mean."

"Yeah, everyone knows you've been typing his reports; they're coherent."

"Oh no." Cindy made a face. "Are people gibing him about that?"

"They think you're sleeping with him. And Tropper isn't correcting them."

Without thinking, Cindy yanked her head back, as if punched in the chin. "That's not only false, it's totally ludicrous!" But she felt more fear than outrage.

Amory spread out his arms. "Don't kill the messenger. You could maybe help yourself out and stop typing his reports."

"It was Beaudry who suggested I do it."

"Maybe he didn't give you such good advice."

Cindy stared at him, uncertain if he were friend or foe. "Maybe I should just do my job and stop listening to people. Who thinks I'm sleeping with Tropper?"

"Camps seem to be split," Amory said. "The macho types are saying, 'Yeah, well, typical of a broad trying to get ahead.' Then there are other apes who know your name is Decker and you're not stupid . . . or at least not *that* stupid. Especially to do something like that with Tropper."

"I am not sleeping with Clark Tropper. Actually, I'm not sleeping with anyone at the moment, cops or no cops. I am at a complete standstill in the love-life department."

"That could be changed."

"Not with *any* of you guys," Cindy said. "Thank you, but I'll maintain my nunlike status. You could do me a favor and spread the word."

"That you're a nun."

"That I'm *off-limits*."

Amory stood up. "I think that's my exit line."

"Nice talking to you, Amory." In a few short minutes, Cindy had completely cleared the table. Man, wasn't she the life of the party. In what seemed like an eternity, she waited by herself until Hayley had the grace to return. She gave Cindy a quizzical look. "You look wiped."

"Amory just told me that people think I'm sleeping with Tropper. Is that true?"

"I think Amory was hoping you were sleeping with Tropper," she said. "If you were stupid enough to do that, you'd be stupid enough to fall for one of his lines."

"You didn't answer the question. Have you heard any comments like that?"

"Nothing serious. Amory's a pussy hound. He was trying a line out. It didn't work. Let it pass."

Cindy didn't bother asking how she knew about Sean. "What about Bederman?"

"Don't even ask." Marx rubbed her forehead. "God, I'm sick of this fucking place. Why are we here?"

Because you suggested it! Cindy wanted to say. Instead she said, "Let's go somewhere quiet for coffee."

"That sounds good. How about your place?"

Why the hell would Hayley want to go to her apartment? To finish off a job she started last night? But, by her tone of voice, the invitation almost sounded romantic . . . like she wanted something cozy. With the way that Cindy felt about guys at the moment, it almost sounded tempting. *Almost.* "Did you work things out with Lopez?"

"Yeah, sure."

"Where is he?" Cindy looked around. "I don't see him. Where'd he go?"

"I dunno." Hayley searched the room. "I left him at the bar. Who cares? Let's just get out of here."

Cindy swung her purse over her shoulder. "You know where I live?"

"Haven't a clue."

"Then follow me home. I could use a good cop watching over my tail."

Hayley frowned. "Why's that?"

"It means I've had some incidents lately. Let's go."

Hayley didn't move. "What kind of incidents?"

She sounded concerned more than surprised. Cindy should have been suspicious, cautious. Instead she found herself wanting to confide in this woman. What was it about her that inspired Cindy's trust?

"I'll tell you all about it later," Cindy said. "Just not here. Especially not here."

25

EIGHT MESSAGES according to the phone machine. But it would have been unwise to listen to them with Hayley in the room. Cindy was amazed at how fresh the apartment looked—scrubbed and straightened with her kitchen counters clear of debris, as if the place had undergone spring cleaning. Hayley's eyes canvassed the space, landing on the couch and its stitched-up upholstery.

"What happened to your furniture?" she asked. "Looks like someone went crazy with a knife." She regarded Cindy's face. "Is this an example of the incidents you were referring to or did you just get this secondhand?"

"No, it was whole when I left for work on Friday."

"Jeez, Louise!" Hayley wrinkled her brow. "What happened?"

"If I knew, I'd tell you."

"Someone broke in." Hayley shook her head. "Wow! No wonder you look so drained. Why didn't you tell me right away?"

Cindy shrugged.

Hayley said, "So when did it happen?"

"Last night. Probably when I was at my dad's. Sit down. I'll make coffee."

"Have anything stronger?"

"Yes, but I'm not going to serve it. I don't need it and neither do you."

"That's probably true." Hayley tossed her purse on the floor and sat down next to the jigsaw stitching. She fingered it gently, then spoke out. "Did you call the cops?"

"My dad came over and poked around." Cindy poured water into her coffeemaker, then came back into her living room. She suddenly felt heavy, as if her feet were shod in iron. "This wasn't random. My place was trashed, and some of my things were ruined, but my valuables weren't missing."

Hayley nodded.

"The suggestion box is open," Cindy said, "Who'd you piss off?"

"I don't know." The phone rang. Wordlessly, Cindy picked up the receiver. "Hi, Dad. I just got in."

"You don't believe in returning your pages? I called your house, I called your pager, I called your cell—"

"I didn't get any of it, Dad . . . well, I don't know about the house. I just got home. I was at Mom's and then I went out with a friend." Here she was, at twenty-five, still explaining herself to her father. "I turned my cellular off, but my pager's on. How many times did you page me?"

"About a half-dozen times."

She pulled her pager from her belt. "Nothing's registering, hold on and let . . . it's not turning on. The battery must be dead." She slid open the small plastic cover. "Actually, the battery is gone."

The line was quiet. Then Decker said, "I'm coming over—"

"Dad, it's not necessary. I've got company right now. I'm all right."

"Who's there? Oliver?"

"Hayley Marx."

"I don't know which one is worse."

Despite herself, Cindy smiled. "I'll call you back later. I'm sorry you were worried."

"When was the last time you took your pager off your body, Cindy?"

"I don't know, Dad. I'll have to think about it."

"You don't have any idea?"

"I usually wear it when I'm out. Sometimes I leave it in my desk at work because I don't want to get distracted on the job. I'll have to think about it," she said again.

"Was your pager working Friday?"

"Dad, I'll have to *think* about it. As soon as I have some answers, I'll call you."

Her voice sounded unsteady. Decker desperately wanted to take away her pain. This unrelenting concern for his children's welfare was eroding him like sand, grain by grain. "Okay. Just call me before you go to bed. Check your locks, check your windows!"

"I will call you and I will check my locks and windows. Bye now." Cindy hung up and glared at her pager, then at Hayley. "I need to go to the drugstore and get a battery."

"Somebody removed it from your pager?"

"Appears that way."

"This is serious." Hayley pulled her pager from her purse and took out the battery. "Here. Put this in. Just to see if you have any messages."

"Thanks." Cindy inserted the battery into the fittings. Instantly, the compact black box vibrated back to life. She riffled through the numbers, counting five from Dad, two from Mom, along with a couple of numbers whose combinations seemed vaguely familiar—maybe Marge's or even Oliver's. She'd check them out later. She gave the battery back to Hayley. "Here you go."

"Cindy, was this the first time someone broke into your place?"

"Yes. Why?" She inspected her with hard eyes. "You seem to have some . . . familiarity with the situation, Hayley. You want to tell me about it?"

"Stop glaring at me," Hayley said. "I'm on your side. Can I have some coffee now?"

Cindy broke her stare. "Yeah. Sure." She poured two hot mugs of thick, strong coffee. She gave a mug to Hayley, then made herself comfortable on one of her armchairs. "If you can shed some light on this mess, I'm all ears."

Hayley took a protracted sip of coffee. "It's just a hunch, okay. But maybe . . . just *maybe,* this was some kind of hazing ritual."

Cindy was incredulous. "You're saying this was done by *cops?* Cops that I *work* with!?"

"Possi—"

"You're actually telling me that . . . that *cops* broke into my apartment and left dog shit on my bed—"

"Someone left dog shit on your bed?" Hayley appeared appalled. "That's horrible!"

"Not to mention disgusting." Cindy was breathing hard. "Do you *know* anything about this?"

Hayley kept looking around for somewhere to put her mug.

"Just put it on the floor." Cindy stood up, her fury barely under control. She made her voice soft and strong and spoke very slowly. "You can't have it both ways! Either you did know or you didn't know!"

"I said it was just a hunch—"

"And just *what* are you basing your hunch on—"

"Stop looking at me like that!" Hayley laid her coffee cup down. "I just know what some of these guys are capable of doing, especially to rookie women. Cin, we're not exactly dealing with PC guys, here. We're talking high school graduate, working stiffs who like a little excitement and want a good pension. Why do you think I've been keeping watch over you—"

"Well, if you've been keeping watch over me, you fucked up somewhere." No one spoke, giving Cindy a moment to absorb what had been said. She took in a breath and let it out. "You didn't fuck up. I'm not your responsibility. Sorry for the outburst."

Hayley waved her off. "If someone broke into my apartment, trashed it, and left dog shit on my bed, I'd be frozen. It's amazing you're talking in full sentences."

"You should have seen me twelve hours ago." Cindy collected her thoughts. "Things have happened to you." A statement as opposed to a question. "What?"

Hayley's jaw began to work overtime. "At least it didn't involve excrement."

"What happened?" Cindy asked.

"In the beginning, my car broke down a lot. One time it was the hose, one time it was the battery, one time it was the distributor cap, one time it was out of gas . . . that time I had just left Bellini's. It was three o'clock in the morning and no one was around. My gas gauge read half full, but I was as dry as dust—"

"Why didn't you *tell* me?"

"Tell you what? That the guys we work with are assholes? You already know that!"

"Hayley, at least it would have put me on alert. This way, I was totally blindsided!"

"I'm sorry."

"How long did it last?"

"Most of my rookie year. Then they found others to pick on. I should have said something. I didn't and that was a conscious decision. I didn't want to poison the well, Cindy. I thought that maybe it wouldn't happen to you because of your dad. And you've also been here for a while. We walk a very thin line, between being one of them and being one of us. The more we women can blend in and not cause trouble, the more they'll like us."

"What is this?" Cindy barked. "Junior high?"

"Decker, it's not just a matter of being popular. It's life and death. They've got to feel that we're one of them. Otherwise, they aren't going to put their asses on the line when we need it. So I say, let them have their fun. Then what you hope is that they had enough of a good time to save you when it really matters."

"If destroying a house and putting dog shit on somebody's bed is the old boys' idea of fun, then something is terribly rotten in the state of Hollywood."

Hayley nodded. "Excrement seems extreme."

"*Seems?*" Cindy was still pacing. "You're saying someone at the stationhouse did this as a . . . rite of passage?"

"Possibly. Maybe it was Tropper. You pissed him off a while back, right? Maybe he did it to get even."

"It was over a week ago. And I've been helping him out ever since."

"He could still be carrying a grudge."

"Is he the type?"

"Yes. Definitely."

Hayley seemed anxious to pin the blame on Tropper. He *was* a logical choice, but Cindy wasn't quite ready to proclaim Hayley innocent. What did she mean by "keeping watch" over her? Cindy asked her that very question.

"Just keeping my eyes and ears open," Hayley responded.

"And?"

She looked at her lap. "You hear things. 'Decker's smart, she's a pain in the ass, she's not up to her father, she's got a nice ass.' Does it mean anything?" She shrugged. "Most of the dirt had to do with that hot domestic where you showed up Tropper. Your partner kept telling the story, over and over—"

"Graham?"

Hayley nodded.

"What was his spin on it?"

"That you did real good. And that you burned Tropper's butt. And that's why you're typing up his reports. To get back on his good side, and not to sleep with him. I think he got a kick out of it. You know Beaudry. He's so straight that he can't picture anyone bucking authority—"

"When did you hear this *sleeping with Tropper* rumor?"

"After you started helping the Sarge out. Beaudry was talking to Bederman, who was off on one of his famous antiwomen, anti-affirmative-action tirades, trying to hide his pig attitudes with some kind of perverse reasoning. Bederman has a hard-on for you, you know. And I don't mean the sexual kind. Although maybe that's part of it, too."

"I know he doesn't like me. I don't know why. I've maybe talked to the guy a few times, including tonight."

"What does logic have to do with it? Maybe it's because he's seen us together. Bederman hates my guts. Did he try to pick you up tonight?"

"No. But he did warn me not to follow in your ways, saying you've fucked a lot of married men."

Hayley winced. "He's right about that."

Cindy said, "Did it end badly?"

"They all end badly."

"And because it ended badly for you, Bederman doesn't like me?"

"Could be. Also, maybe it's because you're partners with his old partner—"

"But Beaudry didn't ask for the transfer from Bederman. It was the other way around. So why would he care about my being Graham's partner?"

"Maybe he feels Graham likes you better—"

"For God's sake, Hayley, we're supposed to be grown-ups!"

"It's stupid, but unfortunately, it's reality!" She looked up at her. "Will you sit down? You're making me even more nervous than I am."

Cindy gave her a quick once-over. "Why should you be nervous?"

"Because it's very unpleasant to talk about this. Brings back bad memories of how I fucked up my chances. Maybe that's why I've taken it upon myself to be your rabbi. You still have a clean slate. And you've got the brains for it. If I can't do it for myself, maybe I can help you to do it."

"Do what?"

"Go for the gold of course. You've got the brains, but you also have to learn to play the game."

Cindy studied Hayley's face: it registered nothing. She started to pace again but thought better of it and plopped into her armchair. "How about starting by being honest with me. First of all, what were you doing up in Angeles Crest?"

"Making sure you were okay."

"Meaning you *followed* me out from the stationhouse up into the mountains?" Cindy was flabbergasted. "Why on *earth* would you do that?"

"Hold on," Hayley cautioned. "It wasn't like that at all. We left the stationhouse at around the same time, right? We walked out to the parking lot together. We were going in the same direction, right?"

Cindy was quiet.

"Right?"

"Right, right. But—"

"Wait a sec," Hayley interrupted. "You asked me a question, let me answer it. I wasn't following you, Decker. I was following the Camry that I thought might be following *you*. My first thought was that one of the guys was maybe planning on taking away your distributor cap."

"You saw the license plate, then."

"Yes. I did, and I called it in—stolen plates. So I figure it was one of the Dees in GTA playing tricks using some of his old evidence—"

"Do you seriously expect me to *buy* that?"

"I'm not selling so I don't care if you're buying. But that *is* what I thought."

"Some detective is purposely lifting hot license plates from the evidence room in order to stalk me." Cindy nodded her head. "Well, that makes perfect sense."

Hayley reacted without emotion. "You're green, so you don't know. But these kinds of things happen. The big stuff makes headlines only when *pounds* of cocaine are missing. But no one cares about an ounce . . . or a necklace here and a ring there . . . or that old TV, or a ten-year-old stereo. Evidence has *boxes* of pilfered license plates from stolen vehicles."

Cindy's head was reeling. "You actually thought . . . that the Camry was a joke?"

"Not a joke, a *prank*!" Hayley said. "That's why I kept an eye on it. I had time to kill. I figured if it could save you some . . . inconvenience, why not? When you started switching lanes, I knew that you picked up on the tail. Which impressed me, being that you're a rookie. When the Camry doubled back and tried to shake you, I thought for sure I was right. It was one of the guys trying to stick it to you. You should have just called it in, Decker, then let it go."

"I couldn't call it in, because I was going too fast."

"That's what I'm *saying*," Hayley remarked. "You should have dropped it. Instead, you played hot dog and tried to solo it out. The guy could have been a real bad ass with a Magnum .44. He could have popped you before you knew what was flying. As it was, you almost caused a couple of bad sig-alerts."

Cindy digested the story. Parts of the tale had to be fabrication, yet some aspects struck her as truthful. She and Marx had left the stationhouse at the same time. And they had been going in the same direction. And Marx couldn't have trashed her apartment because she had been with Oliver. So what was really going on?

"Anyway"—Hayley regarded her nails, then dropped her hands in her lap—"you started up the mountain, I pulled back, knowing you'd eventually come back down. But when you didn't, I began to get a little concerned so I went up to look for you. When I saw you and your smoking car, I thought I was right. Someone had messed with your car. That's why I accompanied you back down the mountain. Once I saw your car was working okay, I left." Again she studied her hands. "That's all of it, Decker. I've run out of explanations."

"Why didn't you immediately tell me your suspicions?"

"I should have. It's tricky, Cin. Knowing who to trust and who to look out for. I'm sure you're having those same thoughts right now. Am I legit or what?"

"Are you?"

"How should I answer that?" Hayley said. "Yes, I am legit. But you don't really know that. It's one of those cases where only time will tell."

26

As SOON as Decker hung up, he resisted the urge to call her again. He would have been happy sleeping with the line open, the receiver tucked under his pillow all night, using the phone like a modified infant intercom system. But though Cindy was still his daughter, she wasn't a baby. He turned off the nightstand lamp and wrapped himself in his covers, pretending that slumber would eventually come and drown out his woes. Moments passed, then he felt Rina stroking his back.

He purred. "That feels good."

"Everything okay?"

"For the time being."

"Do you think she'll be able to sleep?"

"I hope so. She's young . . . resilient . . . determined. Traits that'll serve her well, but make it hard to be her father."

More silence. More rubbing.

Decker said, "Keep going, you're on a roll."

"Any spot in particular?" Rina asked.

"It all feels good." Then Decker analyzed his response. "Well, *if* you were asking for a custom order, I'd tell you that my favorite spot wasn't on my back."

"Are you up for it?" Rina giggled. "I didn't mean it like that."

Decker turned around and faced her. "I don't know. We could try, but I won't promise anything."

"Trying is good. Maybe it'll . . . loosen you up."

"Sex as a muscle relaxant." He sighed. "How in the world do you stay married to me?"

"First let's make love. Then we'll talk."

"I might be too tired to talk afterward," Decker said.

"Then we'll go to sleep. That's okay, too."

Decker thought about it. Sex then sleep. It sounded like a plan.

❑

IN that twilight stage of nocturnal slumber, Cindy heard the knocking, but it took a few seconds before she registered what it actually was. That it meant that someone was at the door. Seconds ticked by before her chest tightened, her heart slamming against her sternum. Maybe it was Dad. (And if it was Dad, did she really want to answer it?) More likely, it was Oliver.

The knocking had stopped.

She thought, *If you're Oliver, don't go away. Hang on a sec.*

Slowly, she swung her legs over her bed and donned her fuzzy pink robe. One eye was open; the other had crusted shut. (Had she been crying in her sleep?) As she walked to the front door, she rubbed the sealed lid with the sleeve of her robe until it sprang open. "Who is it?"

"Oliver."

First she peeked into the peephole. Then she undid the chain that she had just installed an hour ago. She'd been in the hardware section, looking for the batteries, and she saw the flimsy links that were supposed to keep out the bogeyman. She figured why not. Not much in the way of real protection, but a layer is a layer. Finally, she opened the door.

"Hi. Come in."

"You were sleeping."

"Were is the correct tense, yes."

"I'll go home."

"Don't be silly," Cindy admonished him. "Come in means come in."

Her eyes were on him as he walked in and sat down on her mangled couch. She liked his jacket and told him so.

"Yeah?" He brushed off a piece of dirt. "It's Valentino."

"It's real sharp."

"Yeah? Thanks." He smiled at her. "Nice of you to notice. How are you? How long did you sleep?"

"About four or five hours."

"Then you're still in sleep deprivation. You need like a good twelve hours."

"Yes, I do." She looked at his eroded face. "What about you?"

"I'll be fine."

"You're far from home. What are you doing here? Checking up on me? They have phones for that, Oliver."

"Phones aren't good unless someone answers them. I didn't see your dad here, so I figured I . . ." He threw up his hands and stood up. "Don't worry about me. It's Sunday tomorrow. I'm going to stay in bed, eat nachos, and watch the game."

"You forgot the beer."

"Yeah, I did. Good night."

"You want to crash out on the sofa, Oliver? You couldn't ruin it any worse than it is."

"How long is your couch?"

"It's a seven-footer."

He thought for a moment. "You have clean sheets?"

"Very clean. You and my dad washed them all."

"That's right." Oliver started shaking his leg. "I'll be honest. I'm beat. I spent the better part of the day at the crash site—"

"Oh God. How was that?"

"Nothing big, nothing unexpected. But it was dirty work. I did shower off, so don't worry about me dirtying up your furniture."

"Your sweat hasn't preyed upon my thoughts."

Oliver managed a tired smile. "Sleeping here would be nice. If it's all right with you."

"It's fine with me." Cindy felt something gripping her throat, making it swell. "As a matter of fact, I'd probably sleep better."

Oliver's smile broadened. "That'd be great."

Cindy approached him, until they were face-to-face, her hands on his chest. Slowly, she slid them up to his shoulders. "I'd sleep even better if I wasn't alone."

"You're not alone—"

"I meant alone in my bed." She stepped away from him and hit his chest. "You can't be that dense!"

He took her into his arms, pressing her body into his own, as the inseam of his pants became restrictive. He embraced her tightly, his legs so weak he could barely remain upright. The stress of the day combined with the wind of lust. She was such a kid, the same age as one of his sons. She was somebody's daughter, somebody's little girl. But the main thing was, she wasn't *his* little girl. To him, Cindy was a young fireball of red hair with a perfect tight ass. That's the way he had to think about it. Because if he thought about her—the person— he'd wither to dried fruit. "I just want to make sure that you know what you're doing."

"Do you know what you're doing?"

"No."

She said, "Well, it's comforting to know you're not an expert on everything."

❑

CONSIDERING how nervous he had been, he thought he did real good. She seemed to like it. At least, it knocked her out cold. She was breathing with deep, luscious breaths. He envied her, sleeping the sleep of youth. After his sons were born, he was cursed with an overactive "wake" center that never entirely shut down, even during the dead of night.

This wasn't one of his better decisions . . . being with her. But he made so many bad decisions in his life, this certainly wasn't one of the worst. It did complicate things. What made it bad was that he liked her. He was going to want to do it again. And she seemed to like him. She'd probably want to do it again, too. Then . . . if they did it enough times . . . that would mean they were in a relationship. And that would be very complicated. Decker wouldn't like it, but Decker didn't like him anyway. So that wouldn't change things much.

No, that wasn't true. It would change lots of . . .

"You awake, Oliver?"

The sound of her voice startled him. "Yeah. Sorry, am I moving too much?"

"You're not moving at all."

"Oh . . ." He took in a breath and let it out. Maybe she hadn't been sleeping. Maybe he didn't knock her out. Maybe he wasn't as good as he thought he'd been. "What's up?"

She said, "Hayley Marx was over here earlier."

The sound of that name tweaked his stomach. He hoped she wasn't going to go all emotional on him. "Yeah?"

"We talked quite a bit."

Uh-oh, Oliver thought. *This can't be good news for my ego.*

"Actually, she *suggested* that maybe . . . maybe this thing was like an in-house joke."

"What?"

"Breaking into my apartment," Cindy said. "That maybe some of the guys at the station did it as a prank."

Oliver sat up in the bed and drew the sheets over his knees. Okay, so maybe she and Hayley didn't talk about him. So maybe he wasn't on her mind at all. She was still back on the break-in. He should have felt relieved that he just wasn't all that important. Instead he was crushed. Well, if he couldn't dazzle her with his sexual prowess, maybe he could bowl her over with his finely honed skills as a detective. *"What* is Marx suggesting?"

"How did she put it?" Cindy turned over and sat up alongside him, resting her head on his shoulder. "That this was maybe like a hazing thing—"

"Come again?"

"Like the guys at work were testing my mettle."

"By putting shit on your bed?"

Cindy was quiet. Though dark, she could make out his profile—the straight line of his nose, the crisp angle of his chin. "What do you think?"

"What do you mean?" *Not a swift comeback. Not at all dazzling.* "Are you asking my opinion?"

"Yeah, I'm asking your opinion. Do you think the break-in could have been a prank done by some of the guys at the stationhouse?"

This time she had phrased it very clearly. Oliver finally understood that she wanted help, and that this wasn't a theoretical discussion. "Some of the guys on the force are assholes. And some of them are real assholes to women, especially women rookies. But anyone who'd leave shit on your bed has problems."

"So you don't agree with Marx."

"Cindy, the guy who did this wasn't fooling around. He didn't teepee your house or . . . or short-sheet your bed. He trashed your place with malice and forethought. The jerk who did this was angry and violent and holds either some kind of personal vendetta against you or harbors some psycho sick sexual fantasy with you as his costar. For Marx to suggest this was a male cop fraternity prank is making light out of something very serious. Frankly, it makes me wonder about her judgment. It makes me . . . a little suspicious of her actually."

"Why? Do you think she's behind this?"

"I don't know. Could she be?"

"I don't see why she would be." Cindy sat up straight. "Unless she thinks that I . . . I took you from her or . . . I don't know how'd she find out about you and me . . ." Her voice got hard. "Unless you said something—"

"C'mon." Oliver frowned. "Even I'm not that big of a putz."

"Well, you're the only thing she could hold against me."

"Hate to admit it, but I don't think I'm that important to her." Oliver felt his entire body stiffen *except* for his dick, which was as limp as wilted celery. "The night wasn't charged with passion."

She snuggled against his chest. "I'm sorry."

"Like hell you are." He pushed her away. "In answer to your original question, no, I don't think this was a cop prank. I know what cops are capable of doing. I've done a few nasty things in my day. But I've never attacked anyone's furniture, and I've never even considered leaving dog shit on anyone's bed *including* my ex-wife's!"

Cindy felt deflated. For some reason, she had hoped it had been a fellow officer. It struck her as less menacing than some anonymous pervert. Yet she knew how deadly cops could be. For one thing, they always carried guns. "Then, I'm out of ideas. How about you?"

"The old brain has shut down for the evening."

"That's too bad."

"Cynthia, maybe we should try to . . . I don't know . . . enjoy the moment."

The room fell quiet. "Then again, maybe not." Oliver glanced at her bedside clock: three-twenty. "Maybe we should just try to get some sleep."

"You go ahead." She grabbed a paperback off her nightstand. "I need to wind down—"

"All right, all right." Oliver took hold of her fleeing arm and brought her close to his body. "Like father like daughter—all business. Tell me Marx's words of wisdom, as close to the real thing as you remember."

Cindy rubbed her eyes. "She said it might be a kind of hazing ritual. For me to prove myself."

"What'd she base it on?"

"Pranks that were played on her." She went over Marx's car stories. "Those kinds of things happen, right?"

"Yes, those kinds of things happen."

"Credible, correct?"

"Completely credible."

"It's disgusting."

"And stupid, and very dangerous." He looked down. "Like I said, I plead guilty to my fair share of moronic practical jokes. But never dumping shit on someone's personal effects. If for no other reason than who the hell wants to handle it? What else did you two talk about?"

"Just who might have done it. Coming up with a list of candidates."

"Who's tops on the list?"

"Tropper."

"The sergeant you outsmarted."

"That's the one."

"What about the other guy? Lopez?"

"Yeah, we talked a little about him. Man, she really dissed him last night. He was acting moronic to me, and Hayley gave it to him. It was nasty. She went over later and had a heart-to-heart. I think she actually apologized."

"Why was Lopez giving it to you?"

"He was trying to be funny. He's also imitating

his partner—a guy named Tim Waters, who's a real jerk."

"Don't know him."

"Hayley tells me that Waters is a pussy hound."

"Most cops are. What other things did Marx lay on you?"

Hayley had said a lot of things now that Cindy thought about it. "She told me that Bederman didn't like me. Specifically, she said the guy had a hard-on for me and not the sexual kind. Though for the life of me, I wouldn't know why. I've maybe had ten minutes' worth of conversation with him."

"Bederman, Bederman . . ." Oliver mulled the name over in his brain. "He sounds vaguely familiar. What's his first name? Rich or something like that?"

"Rick."

"Yeah, he was coming in just as I was leaving. Came in as a first- or second-year vet. This must have been about ten years ago. What is he? Around thirty-five?"

"About."

"A real swaggerer. I remember not liking him. Could be I was jealous and viewed him as competition, though."

"Honest of you to admit that."

"What the fuck do I got to hide? I'm beyond it now. Why does she think he doesn't like you?"

"I don't know."

"What kind of contact have you had with him?"

"I told you. Ten minutes' worth of conversation, including last night."

"You talked to him last night?"

"Yeah, he and his partner were sitting with Marx when I walked into Bellini's."

"What'd you and this guy talk about?"

"We didn't talk until Marx left the table to make nice to Lopez, who had stalked away in anger. Bederman told me that I shouldn't sleep around with married men like Marx did. It screwed her up."

"He's absolutely right. But it's weird for him to be telling you that. You say something like that when you want a piece of tail. You know, you're Mr. Sincere with the friendly word of advice. Meanwhile he wants to dive in your pants. You put him down or anything?"

"No, not at all. I listened, but I thought he was out of order considering I was with Hayley. Then after he left, his partner, Sean Amory, started making veiled passes. By now, I was getting fed up. So I told him I was out of commission as far as dating cops was concerned, and I also told him to spread the word. We left it at that."

In the dark, she felt her face go hot. Lucky that Oliver couldn't see it. "I guess that was a premature statement being as I'm here in bed with you."

Oliver let out a small chuckle. But clearly his thoughts were elsewhere. "You have any professional contact with either of these subspecies?"

"We've—we being Graham and I—we've

assisted Bederman and Amory on a couple of calls.
I think they assisted us a few times. Bederman
used to be Graham's partner. They're still friendly,
according to Bederman—"

"*Really?*"

A pause. "Obviously, you find that significant."

"I find it interesting. What's Graham's last
name?"

"Beaudry."

"Yeah, what does Beaudry think about Bederman?"

"Graham doesn't talk about Bederman. But Bederman told me that Graham thought I was
smart . . . this is so provincial! He likes me, but
she doesn't like him and they like her . . . blah,
blah, blah."

"Why aren't they partners if they still like each
other?"

"It just didn't work out."

"Who asked for the transfer?"

"Bederman."

"Ask your partner why he's still friendly with
him if Bederman wanted out."

"What should I expect to hear?"

"Probably not the truth," Oliver commented.
"You ask for a transfer from a guy, it's supposed to
mean you don't get along."

Cindy was quiet. "The rumor is that Bederman
asked for the transfer because Graham is slow."

"Slow?"

"A slow runner, slow physically. In foot pursuits, Bederman was doing all the heavy work while Graham made a big show of slapping on the handcuffs."

"Have you found that to be true?"

"Beaudry wouldn't set any Olympic records, but I don't think he's malingering." She thought back to her encounter with the drunk Russian just a couple of days ago. She was the one who had been doing all the sweating.

"But the rumor has merit?" Oliver asked.

"It really isn't that bad—"

"You spread a rumor like that about your ex-partner, it isn't going to sit well with him."

"Graham's an easygoing kind of guy—"

"No, Cindy, that doesn't explain squat. He's not gonna put up with that kind of crap without a rumor of his own. And if he isn't doing it, that says something. I know the way the uniforms work. Something's not right."

Cindy was quiet.

Oliver said, "You stay friendly with a guy after the transfer, it says to me, you two have to split up from each other because it's dangerous to stay together."

"I haven't any idea what you're talking about."

"They did something dirty together, Cindy. They got away with it and wanted to split up before people started sniffing around them as a unit."

"No, I don't think you're right."

"Why not?"

"Because I know Graham. He's not dirty."

"How do you know?"

Cindy stalled but couldn't come up with a response.

"How long have you been with him?" Oliver asked. "Six months? Eight months? That's nothing, Decker. Nothing at all. I was once with a guy for two years before I realized he was on the take."

"What'd you do?"

"Requested a transfer. But I'll tell you something. We didn't remain friends."

"When was this?"

"In my early days at Hollywood. Back when I still believed in truth, justice, and all that crap."

"Did you fink on him?"

"Nope! He was stealing from drug busts. Not a good thing, but it wasn't murder. You see cash on the table and wind up pocketing a twenty. Then it's a fifty or a hundred. No one knows. No one gets hurt. It's tempting. I was tempted. But I didn't do it. That's the difference."

"What happened to your ex-partner?"

"He took retirement after putting in his twenty. Last I heard he was working as a security guard."

Cindy winced. It seemed like a rather pedestrian ending to what should have been a morality tale. "So he didn't get caught?"

"No, he didn't. Most don't *if* they're not too greedy. But if you stay around long enough, you begin to nose them out. They're the ones who never get anywhere. They just can't seem to climb up the ranks no matter how many merit badges are on their Scout uniforms, because they're too busy looking over their shoulders. It wasn't morality that kept me straight. It was fear of getting caught and pushing my dreams down the toilet. My family's full of cops, but none of them have earned gold. Man, I was a determined sucker in my youth."

"You succeeded."

"Damn right, I did. Then, as soon as I got it, I screwed up."

"Not professionally—"

"Untrue. Professionally and personally. You can't mess up one without messing up the other. There's a reason why your dad is where he is and why I'm where I am. I got too sidetracked, believing my own PR. Then I got too old. Anyway, *I'm* not important right now. I'm just telling you all this because I know when two and two make five. Something's off. And you're telling me that this one bar conversation and seeing him a couple other times has been your only contact with Bederman?"

She brought her knees up to her chest. "I told you about the party when I was first assigned to Hollywood."

"Yeah, the introduction rookie party. It was right around the time that Crayton was axed. You were talking to Craig Barrows, too."

"What a memory. I don't remember Bederman saying much of anything."

"So what was he doing?"

"Just listening to me talking about Crayton."

Suddenly, Oliver was very interested. "What specifically were you saying about Crayton?"

"Just that I knew him from the gym."

"You mention anything about being shot at?"

"No, Oliver, I have some common sense."

"Did he ask you any questions or offer any comments?"

"None that I can recall."

Crayton, Bederman, and Barrows: How did they fit together? Bederman worked in Hollywood. The Tarkum kidnapping was in Hollywood. Crayton's murder happened in Devonshire. If Stacy Mills was to be believed, Lark Crayton was probably behind Crayton's carjacking, maybe even behind the murder. Was she also behind Stacy Mills's carjacking? Oliver said, "Does the name Stacy Mills ring any bells?"

Cindy sat up straight, feeling her heart take off. "You *know* her?"

Now Oliver shot up into an upright, sitting position. "*You* know her?"

"From the gym where Armand and I used to work out—"

"Man oh man," Oliver recited. "She was recently carjacked—"

"What?" Cindy felt her lungs tighten. "When did this happen? Is she okay?"

"She's fine, but she's got a truth problem. She admitted knowing Lark Crayton. What about Armand Crayton. Was she a friend of his?"

"I don't know if they were friends. I did see them talking several times."

Oliver's voice was infused with enthusiasm. "Anything intimate appear to pass between them?"

"Not that I can tell." Cindy took a deep breath. "Poor girl! This is *awful*!"

But now Oliver was less than sympathetic. The bitch had lied to Marge and him. She did know Armand. Maybe she knew him too intimately, and that's why she was afraid of Lark. "Did Stacy Mills know that you and Crayton were friends—"

"Acquaintances—"

"Don't nitpick. Was she aware that you knew Crayton?"

"Sure. We all talked a couple of times, had juice together." Cindy licked her lips. "She knew I was going into the academy. She said if I got fed up with being a cop, I should try out being a personal trainer. That's what she was . . . a personal trainer."

"She still is. At least she wasn't lying about that."

"What did she lie about?" Cindy asked.

"She told us that she worked with Lark Crayton and barely knew Armand."

"Maybe it was true. They never appeared like best friends."

"Stacy said that Armand's wife thought he had a woman on the side. Maybe that was you. Maybe that's why you were shot at. Were you friendlier with Armand than she was?"

"I wasn't all that friendly—"

"Who talked to Armand more?" Oliver butted in. "Stacy or you?"

"I can see where this is leading. That Stacy was jealous of Armand and me. Or Lark was jealous. From my observation, Stacy didn't seem very interested in him."

"Maybe she wasn't. She kept saying that she knew Lark better than Armand. Maybe she was getting paid to spy for Lark, and reported back that Armand was fooling around with you."

"There's no way that Stacy could have thought that," Cindy cried out. "Armand and I were never close, Oliver."

"But suppose Stacy was getting paid to tell Lark *something*. If she had nothing to report, Lark wouldn't keep paying her money, right?" Oliver tried to assemble his ideas. "Stacy impresses me as a woman concerned about money."

"So Lark Crayton shot at us because Stacy reported to her that Armand and I were having an affair."

"More likely, Lark hired someone to shoot at you. According to Stacy, at that time, Lark was doing lots of things, most of them centered around trying to get rid of Armand. Not that I believe Stacy, but I'm betting that like all liars, she mixes truth with fiction."

"God, you're sure she's okay?"

"A lot better than you," Oliver said. "Her apartment is whole."

"I can't believe . . ." She bit her lip to keep it steady. "What is going on!"

An idea tumbled around Oliver's brain. *A possible cop who was Lark's ace in the hole. Bederman.* He said, "Rick Bederman . . . does that sound German to you?"

"What?"

"Does the name Bederman sound German?"

"To me, it sounds American—"

"But if you had to tag a European nationality on to it, what would it be?"

"English . . . Dutch . . . maybe German. Is there a point?"

"Stacy Mills told Marge and me that Lark had an ace in the hole—"

"Up her sleeve."

"What?"

"Isn't *an ace up her sleeve* the usual expression?"

"You're distracting me."

"Go on."

"Lark had some guy with clout and a German name in her pocket. I'm thinking cop and I'm thinking Bederman."

"Why would it be Bederman? Lark lives in Foothills, Bederman works in Hollywood. Where's the link?"

"Dexter Bartholomew," Oliver said. "His own wife was carjacked. Marge and I are thinking that Dex hired out to give the old lady a warning because she was fooling around with Crayton."

"Dex carjacked his own wife?"

"Possibly."

"Do you have any evidence to back this up?"

"No." Oliver rubbed his eyes. "I think I need a pencil and paper to figure this one out. I have to start making diagrams. I know it's all related but I'm too tired to figure it out."

"Lark hired Bederman to warn me off . . . or maybe scare Armand. Then Dexter Bartholomew hired Bederman to carjack his own wife as punishment for a supposed affair."

"Something like that."

"So who was hired to carjack poor Stacy Mills? And why *now*? Why not a year ago? Or even six months ago?"

"Because we've just started churning up all this mess by reinterviewing them." He turned to Cindy. "And all this crap with your apartment . . . maybe this is *your* warning."

"Warning about what?"

"I don't know," Oliver admitted.

"Why not carjack me like the other women?"

"Hard to carjack a cop . . . she has a gun."

Cindy sighed. "I'm way too tired to assimilate all this stuff."

"So am I." Oliver yawned to prove his point. "Let's talk about it in the morning when your father gets here. Maybe he can add something fresh."

"My father's coming over in the morning?"

"Yeah."

"He told you that?"

"No, but I know fathers and I know Deck, and putting the two of them together means your father's gonna be here tomorrow morning . . . say around ten." Oliver stood up. "That's why I'm gonna sleep on the couch tonight. That way, when he wakes both of us up, it'll look presentable. He'll have suspicions, but he won't know for sure."

Cindy became pensive. "You'd prefer to keep this hidden."

"Hell, yeah, I prefer to keep it hidden. I work with the man, Cindy. If confronted, I'd tell the truth. But Deck isn't going to confront me, and I'm not going to admit anything. If that seems cowardly, so be it."

"Actually, I think it makes perfect sense."

Oliver breathed a sigh of relief. At this point, she was almost too good, acting like a guy instead of a girl. But maybe that's the way it was with this new generation.

Cindy said, "I just have one more request."

"Talk to me, darling."

"Since it's not likely that Dad's gonna show up

within the next . . . say thirty minutes . . . perhaps we should take advantage of the situation."

Oliver grinned. "That's a great idea in the abstract. But you're young and I'm old. So if I do fall asleep, don't take it personally."

"You know you're awfully self-deprecating."

"I do that on purpose. At my age, it's the only thing that seems to work with the girls."

Cindy pulled him down. "I hope this doesn't ruin the mood, but I do like you, Oliver. You've been nice to me and I find that very attractive in a man."

Oliver brushed his lips against hers. "I like you, too. And it doesn't hurt that I find you incredibly sexy." He looked deeply into her eyes, mostly to avoid looking at her breasts. "Baby, you are so beautiful, nothing you could say would ruin the mood."

27

THE KNOCKING was soft, but being as Oliver was such a light sleeper, he was up with his hand on the knob by the third muted thud. He swung open the door, put his finger to his lips, then he cocked a thumb toward Cindy's bedroom. Decker's face was flat; from experience, Oliver knew that meant the loo was pissed. Perhaps it was Oliver's dress—shorts and nothing else. Good thing he was spent. Even at this age, he still woke up with occasional boners. He stepped aside, watching Decker's eyes as they skittered about the room, landing on the rumpled sheets on the couch. With nothing left to do, Oliver decided to slip on his pants.

Decker kept his eyes glued to the sheets. It wasn't cold inside so why the hell were they trying to snow him? Maybe Cindy was trying to be considerate of his feelings. Or it had been Oliver's idea. Why rub it in if they had to work together. "Is everything all right?"

"Yeah, she's fine. But we did some talking last night." Oliver strapped on his watch. It was eleven. At least, Deck had the decency to come at a civil hour. "I'll tell you all about it. Let's grab some coffee somewhere."

"I don't mind talking here," Decker said.

"I do. I don't want Cindy to hear what we talk about. You know how it is when you go over cases. You discuss the extremes. It's enough to make you paranoid."

Decker's face finally showed emotion. That ravaged look that revealed a hundred years of pain. "What's wrong, Oliver?"

"Loo, I'm not sure if anything's wrong beyond the usual shit that women go through when they're rookies."

"What kind of shit?"

"That's what I want to talk about." Oliver buttoned up his shirt, tucked the tail into his pants, then slid on the jacket. He smelled as ripe as rotten vegetables. He should have taken a shower after she'd fallen asleep. Ah, well, let Decker suffer the olfactory insult. "I guess I should leave a note."

Saying what? Thanks for the fuck, the dirty bastard. Decker pushed the thought out of his mind, reiterating what he had told himself before. It said something that Oliver was here. Maybe for his own sexual purposes, but the fact remained that he was looking after his daughter.

". . . where she keeps paper and pencils?"

Decker tuned into Oliver's voice. "Uh, she used to keep them in the kitchen drawer."

Oliver went into the kitchen. Thick slabs of sunlight coursed through the sheer window coverings, sending his overstrained eyes into pupil shock. Blinded, he slid open the drawer and wrote a cursory note. *Went out for coffee with your dad. Be back in an hour or so.* He placed it on the coffeemaker, then went back into the living room. He picked up his briefcase and put on his sunglasses. It helped to readjust his eyes.

He said, "You got a key to lock up?"

Decker resisted the urge to retort, *You mean she hasn't given you one yet, you stinking SOB.* Then he stopped himself. Would he be this angry if Scott

were closer to her age? Or would he be angry if
Oliver was screwing a young girl who wasn't his
daughter? Maybe he should try . . . just . . . *try* to
look at this more objectively. Who was the vulnerable one here? Oliver was getting on in years, and
Cindy was fresh and full of choices. Plus, Cindy
didn't suffer fools, often speaking her mind without considering human frailties and egos. If anyone
would take a fall, it would be him. In which case,
he should pity Oliver. It's hard to take falls when
you're old.

Oliver said, "Lieutenant, are you with me here?"

"Yeah, yeah." Decker held up his key ring. "I've
got a key. Let's go."

❑

ALL the designer coffee places were packed with a
Sunday brunch crowd. They settled on an ancient
coffee shop with worn gray-tiled floors, worn
oxblood booths, and worn waitresses in tired, faded
brown uniforms and white clodhopper shoes with
thick rubber soles. Asking for a booth in the back,
they trailed Sally as she and her larger-than-life
blond beehive led them past the counter area
where two male down-and-outers were nursing
coffee and nibbling on toast. A far cry from the designer espresso and butter croissants being sold
across the street at Star$s. They were seated in an

empty area, and it took only moments for Sally to return with two steaming mugs of java. She took out her pad and waited.

Decker pulled a ten out of his wallet. "I'm fine with coffee." He handed her the bill. "This is for the privacy."

She took the bills. "Cops or criminals?"

Decker smiled, showed her his badge.

"Ah, a big-shot detective. Should I feel honored?"

"Depends on who the cop is," Decker answered.

"Ain't that the truth. Between the cops and criminals, it's hard to tell the difference. You read about that detective who just had his ass hauled in for bank robbery? And what about that entire unit who invented stories and put all those kids behind bars."

"Not a good endorsement of L.A.'s finest."

Sally smiled. It crinkled her face, but made her look younger at the same time. "Well, you paid for privacy, I might as well give you some. Would you like me to leave a pot? That is a pot of coffee."

Oliver smiled at her. "That would be great."

"Just wave if you change your mind about food."

"I'll do that."

After she left, Oliver spoke, keeping his voice low. "I know I'm talking like an old fart, but Sally the waitress is absolutely right. Some of the young studs in blue are truly sick. Which fits into the topic of Cindy. You know how it is with rookies,

especially rookie women. They're tested. Sometimes things go overboard."

Decker sipped his coffee, then made a face.
Strong brew. Or maybe it was just the sour taste in
his mouth. "Breaking into an apartment is a hell of
a prank."

"But it's something to think about. Apparently,
Hayley Marx had some things done to her when
the guys broke her cherry at Hollywood. She was
the one who suggested that maybe these were
hazing rituals."

"What kinds of things?"

"Her vehicle was constantly dying on her for one
reason or another. She could be lying, but the complaints sounded legit. Plus, we know that Cindy's
got a couple of guys on her ass." Oliver began to
tick them off. "There's Tropper, the Sarge who she
showed up. Guy could be a grudge holder. And
then there's the punk rookie Andy Lopez, who was
making lewd comments to her last night—"

"What *kinds* of comments?"

"Talking crudely about her ass or something—"

"*Bastard!* I'll kill him!"

"I don't doubt it, Pete. But for time's sake, can I
go on?" Oliver leaned in. "There's Lopez's partner,
Tim Waters, who's a big pussy hound. But I'm
keeping them on the back burner, because according to Hayley Marx, there's this blue named Rick
Bederman who has it out for her."

Decker's eyes darkened. "You know him?"

"I recall him slightly. Macho asshole from what I remember. But it was a long time ago."

"Why does he have it in for her?"

"Cindy doesn't know. But let me take a wild stab and say it's a sexual thing. In case you haven't noticed, Cin isn't shy about being a woman."

Decker hid his emotions behind a coffee cup. He was angry, he was embarrassed. Most of all, he was a father. "Did this Bederman come on to her?"

"He gave her advice not to fuck married men—"

"Bastard—"

"Yeah, he doesn't sound like a sweetheart. But what makes it interesting is that he was partnered with Cindy's current partner, Graham Beaudry. And . . ." He wagged his finger for emphasis. "What makes that *even more interesting* is that even though Bederman requested a transfer, he and Beaudry are still friends."

Oliver went through last night's conversation, item by item. His memory wasn't quite as sharp as he had wished it, and he should have taken notes. But that would have been difficult considering he was in bed and naked while his clothes and notebook were in the living room. Decker didn't interrupt, not even once, but early on, he took out a notebook. Oliver wondered what he was scribbling down. He knew there would be questions later, and there were.

Decker tried to settle comfortably into the booth, but the stuffing was sparse and his butt kept feeling springs. He said, "Beaudry and Bederman . . . you think they did something dirty."

"It crossed my mind."

Decker nodded. "If that's the case, I'd say that Bederman wasn't giving Cindy a friendly tip. Nor was he trying to get into her pants. By telling her not to fuck around with married men, the implicit message was don't fuck *with me*. Then the next question would be, why would he say that to her? The logical answer? He must think that Cindy knows something about him. He thinks Cindy has dirt on him."

"What kind of dirt?"

"I don't know, Oliver, you're the one she talks to." Decker looked at the ceiling. "Let's say for a moment that I could be objective on this. If she was a stranger to me, the first question I'd ask her is do you have dirt on him, and judge her reaction."

"She told me she's barely talked to the guy . . ."

"Okay." Decker bit his lip. "Do you think she was telling the truth?"

Oliver stared at him. "Decker, we're talking about your daughter—"

"I know that!" Decker snapped back. "Answer the damn question! The one thing you are is a perceptive cop."

The one thing! "Yes, I think she was telling the truth. I don't think she has a notion as to why this asshole was talking to her like that." Oliver was appalled. "I can't believe what you just asked me! You're one lucky motherfucker that I'm trustworthy."

"Why do you think I asked you?" Decker shifted his position again. "It still doesn't mean I like you, only that I trust your integrity as a cop."

Oliver didn't respond. In his screwy way, he knew Decker was complimenting him. "Unless she's one great liar, I think she's clueless."

"So you know what that says to me? It says to me that Bederman *thinks* she knows the dirt on him. What kind of dirt and where would she find it out?"

"Possibly from Beaudry," Oliver answered. "Just because Bederman says they're still friends doesn't make it so. It's tied into the Crayton case, Deck. Bederman was listening in when Cindy spoke about Armand being her workout buddy. Maybe Bederman had his paws in that case and thinks Cindy knows something. Someone did take potshots at her."

"That was a while ago."

"Yeah, Decker, but we just started messing with the case again. First we interview Lark Crayton, then Stacy Mills gets jacked. Then Marge talks to Bartholomew, and Cindy's apartment gets trashed. Not to mention someone following her in a Camry that was conveniently pushed off a mountain sort of like the way that Crayton died. You see a pattern here?"

"How does Bederman fit in?"

"Lark mentioned that she had someone with clout as an ace in the hole. How about a cop and how about Bederman? Didn't you say we should think cop in Stacy Mills's carjacking?"

"I suggested it," Decker said.

"Lark wanted Armand to have an accident. She needed a pro to arrange things and Bederman was the man."

"So get me something to tie Lark to Bederman."

"Elizabeth Tarkum's jacking took place in Hollywood. Bederman works in Hollywood. Maybe Dex approached Bederman to do his wife's jacking and Lark happened to overhear—"

"You just don't *happen* to overhear something like that, Scott. Besides, Tarkum happened *after* Crayton."

"So maybe Dex arranged both of them," Oliver said. "It brings us back to the theory that Dex's wife and Armand were having an affair. Bartholomew wanted to teach them a lesson."

"You think Dex contracted Crayton's murder," Decker whispered. "Just a little while ago, you thought that Lark contracted her own husband's murder."

"She and Dex were in it together."

Decker said, "I could understand Dex contracting Crayton's murder. I don't think he'd be stupid enough to draw attention to himself by contracting his own wife's carjacking. Someone would put two and two together just like we're trying to do."

Oliver said, "Stupid yes, but Dex is one arrogant alpha dog. Marge said the guy is off the scale when it comes to self-importance." He swallowed the dregs of the coffee, then made a face. "Where is Margie, by the way? She should be here with us, thrashing this case around."

"She and Vega are at the park with Rina and Hannah."

"What the fuck is wrong with her?" Oliver griped. "She used to be a workaholic."

Decker smiled. "She found a life—"

"Loo," Oliver said, "a life is being in love with some stud muffin. A life is flying down to Vegas to catch a show and throw some dice. A life is partying till dawn. What kind of life is that? Taking a kid to the park, getting dust in your lungs and dog crap on your shoes 'cause some jerk doesn't believe in curbing his animal!"

"Getting feisty, Oliver?" Decker smiled. "Maybe it's lack of sleep."

"Maybe it's because I've been busy *baby-sitting*." Oliver tapped the table. "Okay. Suppose Stacy Mills was telling the truth . . . which is a stretch. Suppose Lark was stupid enough to try to murder her husband. First time out, she gets someone to fire a few potshots at him and his chippy, but that doesn't work."

"Cindy wasn't having an affair with him."

"But what if Lark thought they were having an affair. Maybe Stacy Mills—who knew that Cindy was Armand's workout partner—was feeding Lark incorrect info to keep herself in Lark's good graces. Anyway, the upshot is that now Lark knows who Cindy is. She keeps that info on the back burner. Now flash forward. Armand is becoming even more of a liability. She knows she needs help from a professional. She talks to Stacy again. After all, Stacy has been spying for her. So maybe she can get her a hit man. That doesn't pan out. Stacy may know how to gossip, but she doesn't know diddly about hiring a professional popper. So Lark talks to Dex, who decides to give her a couple of names because he doesn't like Armand. You like it so far?"

"It's interesting." Decker consulted his notes. "So Lark is talking to Dex, who's giving her some names of hit men. Then what?"

Oliver regarded him with awe. "You wrote all that down?"

"It's all in the key words. You want to finish up?"

"Okay. Lark asked Dex for a little help and Dex gave her Bederman."

"Why would Dex help her out?"

" 'Cause he was pissed at Armand for screwing his wife," Oliver answered. "Then, on her own, Lark decides to get Tarkum and uses her same contact—Bederman. Great, now things are going along fine for a couple months, half a year, more. Then we get a rash of carjackings and start looking in other areas. And I happen to come across Tarkum in Hollywood and start asking questions.

To see if I can't tie it into these recent jackings. And, of course, I can't because Tarkum is probably unrelated to Devonshire's jackings. You said that yourself."

"I said it might be unrelated," Decker said.

Oliver said, "So now I come across Tarkum, and you think of Crayton because the two jackings both involve rich people with fancy cars instead of hapless mothers and children in beaten-up cars. Then I tell Osmondson that Tarkum reminds me of Crayton. And Osmondson starts talking about it, and Bederman finds out. He gets a little nervous. First thing he does is contact Lark. She admits to him that she had a bad case of little loose lips with Stacy Mills, and tells Bederman to scare her into silence. Which of course makes us even more curious because now instead of just two similars we have three similars. But Lark doesn't bother to think about that. She just wants Stacy out of the picture."

Decker said, "Why would Bederman agree to do it?"

"To save his skin."

"He's a cop, Scott. He'd have to know that it would pique our curiosity."

"So maybe Bederman is stupid."

"Or maybe . . ." Decker thought a moment. "Maybe Bederman thought he could stuff the Mills jacking in with the others in Devonshire. Then *I* get into the act, and start reinvestigating Crayton.

Bederman gets nervous because Cindy is not only my daughter but also *knew* Crayton."

"And then Bederman starts thinking that maybe he didn't plug as many holes as he thought," Oliver said. "So he gets a little *more* nervous. He has to know how much Cindy knows. How does he find that out?"

"Through Beaudry," Decker said. "Bederman can't pump Cindy, because he's afraid that she might talk to me, and then he'd be in real trouble. So what does he do? He asks his ex-partner to do him a favor and pump her for him. So why would Beaudry agree to something like that?"

"I think I might know," Oliver asked. "Cindy told me that Beaudry has a rep of being slow physically. Maybe Bederman's pulled him out of a couple of tight squeezes, and he figured it was time for Beaudry to pay the piper. The problem is that it hasn't been Beaudry who's doing the pumping, it's been more like Hayley. I still can't figure out whose side she's on."

Decker paused, then said, *"Has* Beaudry pumped Cindy for information about Crayton?"

Oliver said, "I'll ask her. Or you can ask her. Somebody should ask her."

"It's a nice theory," Decker said. "Of course, I'd like it a lot better if we found something that ties Bederman into the case."

Oliver said, "I'll start looking." He paused. "Be nice if I had my *partner—*"

"Leave Marge alone. She's waited a long time for this."

"I know. I wish her well. Hope she knows what she'd doing. I sure didn't."

"No one does. That's the marvelous thing about parenthood. There are no formal rules."

28

IT WAS a suspension bridge fashioned from slats of gray oak and held together by bolts of some kind of superstrength steel. The construction had to be superstrength to weather the abuse given to it: hour after hour, day after day, and year after year of jackhammer jumping.

Rina's voice could barely be heard above the school-age squeals. "Hannah, stop running! That little girl is trying to get across."

Miraculously, Hannah halted in her tracks, put her hand to her missing-a-front-tooth mouth, and giggled. "Sorry." She went over to the tot of around two and held out her hand. She spoke in an exaggeratedly maternal tone, making the pitch of her child-soprano range even higher. It was a wonder the dogs didn't start howling. "You want some help, sweetie?"

The girl of two stuck her thumb in her mouth. Hannah took the other hand and walked her across the wobbly bridge. Once the tot was safe on the other side, Hannah resumed her wild play. Marge was watching her in awe.

Rina said, "I know. She's hyperactive in the sense that she never stops."

"You must be exhausted."

"I would be *if* I didn't say to myself it's the last time and it goes so quickly . . . which it does." Rina looked around. The park was relatively quiet, the usual crowd sleeping in because it was Sunday. It was a nice park, meaning it was small enough for Rina to keep her eye on Hannah. There was a fenced-off region that contained lots of play equipment—climbing apparatus, monkey bars, swings, and slides, some of them with loads of twists and turns and tubes that could rival theme parks. The majority of the recreational zone was devoted to a block-long grassy section big enough for football and baseball—there was a backstop and one set of splintered, paint-peeling bleachers—with room left over for picnic benches and built-in barbecues. The curb abutting the park had filled up with cars, but there were plenty of spaces across the street.

"Where's Vega?" Rina asked.

Marge pointed to a far bench near the diamond's backstop. Vega was curled up, her eyes buried in a book. "I brought her here to teach her how to ride a bike. Nobody can say I'm not trying."

Rina was puzzled. "Trying to do what?"

Marge frowned. "What do you think?"

"I don't know. That's why I'm asking you."

"I'm trying to make her . . . no, that's not the right word." Marge gave an exasperated sigh. "I'm trying to *help* her catch up on the childhood she missed. You know, do things like . . . like ride a bike or skate or listen to music I can't stand or jeez, even watch TV."

Rina held back a smile. "You want her to watch TV?"

"Not be glued to the TV!" Marge gave up. "I know I must sound like an idiot. My kid reads all the time! Such problems. But it's to the exclusion of everything else. It isn't healthy."

"Probably not healthy for her eyes. But it's great for the brain—"

"You don't understand."

Rina shrugged philosophically. "Maybe not."

Now Marge felt doubly stupid. She had just told a mother of three, who had been raising kids for nearly twenty years, that she didn't understand child rearing. And here was Marge, the expert, having had custody of one teenaged girl for eight months. She tapped her foot. "You don't think it's a problem? That she reads all day?"

"Correct me if I'm wrong. But I don't think you're concerned about her reading, you're concerned about her ability to integrate socially."

Marge was quiet. "So what do I do?"

Rina put her arm around Marge's waist. She would have looped it around her shoulder, except that Marge was too tall. "Personally, I think you're doing great. She seems very happy—"

"She's so *quiet*. Except with you! Man, she talks to you. Maybe I'm just not the right—"

"Stop it."

"Okay, okay." Marge made a face. "Look, I know she went through an ordeal! I know she grew up in an isolated, weird environment. But she's not in that environment anymore. There's an entire world out there."

Rina smiled. There were things she could tell her friend, but she refrained from giving lots of advice because it usually backfired. "I wouldn't worry too much."

"Really?"

Rina nodded, then yelled, "Hannah, stop screaming!" Softly, she said, "I swear that child is going to give herself throat polyps."

"See, you worry, too!" Marge pointed out.

"Pardon?"

"You worry about Hannah getting throat polyps!"

Rina laughed. "Yes, I worry. I worry whether Sammy will be safe in Israel. I worry about Jacob, and wonder if he'll ever survive adolescence. I worry about Hannah. She's so little and vulnerable. I worry about Peter every single day he straps on his gun and goes to work. But no matter how

much I worry, how much I fret, how much I wring
my hands and pound my forehead, I know that my
getting an ulcer is *not* going to help. More likely,
it'll probably hurt because I won't be in good shape
when my family *really* needs me. So my credo is
to bury my head in the sand and don't think about
the bad until it smacks me in the face. Crises
happen to everyone sooner or later. Why antici-
pate them?"

Immediately, Marge felt her stomach turn over.
Rina spoke from experience—widowed at twenty-
four, raising two small boys by herself, a victim of
crime at twenty-six, hysterectomy at thirty. And
here was Marge, complaining because her adopted
daughter read too much.

Rina went on. "Vega's a lovely girl, Marge.
You're giving her lots of emotional sunshine. You
watch. She'll bloom beautifully."

"What wouldn't I give for your attitude!"

"It's because of your profession. All you ever see
is the bad people and people in distress. You wonder how I'm so calm as a mother, I wonder how you
and Peter and Scott and the lot of you go out there
every day."

Marge chuckled. "You're trying to shut me up
with flattery."

"Maybe."

They both laughed. At that moment, Hannah lost
her footing on one of the ladders and fell to the
ground, landing on her rear. "Oh dear!" Rina ran to

her, picking up the tearful little girl. "What happened, sweetie?"

"I fell down and hurt myself!" A wail. "Oh, look! I'm *bleeding*!"

Sure enough, a trickle of blood was leaking from her left kneecap. The right one fared better, but was still scraped raw. "Oh my!" Rina brushed off the seat of Hannah's dress. "Maybe we should go to the bathroom and wash that off—"

"I want to go *home*!" she screeched.

Rina looked at her watch. It was a little after twelve. They had been there almost two hours. On top of being mortally wounded, the child was probably tired and hungry. She picked up Hannah, who threw her bony arms around her mother's neck. "Are you tired?"

"I'm not tired!" Hannah said, between sobs. "See!" She scrambled down from her mother's grip and did ten jumping jacks, her standard act that served to contradict her parents whenever they claimed she was tired. "I just hurt myself!"

More sobbing.

"Okay." Rina picked her up again. "How about we go home and get some lunch?"

Hannah nodded and sniffed. Marge was at their side. "What's the verdict?"

"I think she's had enough."

"Good going, Hannah," Marge said. "I've had enough, too. Next time I take Vega out, I'll take her to the library. At least I'll be off my feet!"

"Marge—"

"I'm kidding." She stared at Vega. "If I shout from here, do you think she'll hear me?"

Rina picked up a bag filled with sand toys and snacks. "Let's just walk over there. My vocal cords have had it."

"Here!" Marge took the bag. "I'll get it."

They had made it about halfway across the lawn when Marge's nose started twitching. A telltale raw odor that came from an animal's excrement. "You smell something?"

"I do." Rina put Hannah down and checked her shoes. "I hate to add to your already jolly mood, but it isn't coming from me."

Marge checked the bottoms of her sneakers. "Oh God!"

"Eeeeeuuuuu!" Her bloody knee temporarily forgotten, Hannah was holding her nose. "Peeeeeyeuuuuuw! It *stinks!*"

"That's enough, Hannah!" Rina took back her tote bag and pulled out a packet of wipes.

Marge snatched the wet towels and muttered, "This is fu—perfect! Just perfect!"

"Can I help?"

"Not unless you want to clean my shoes!"

"I'll pass—"

"What kind of friend are you?"

"Eeeeeuuuuu! Gross!"

"Cool it with the commentary, kid," Marge snapped.

Rina smiled. "How about if you clean yourself off and I take Hannah to the car. We'll wait for you there."

"You know what I hate about athletic shoes?"

"All the grooves—"

"Exactly! Ick! What a fu—what a mess!"

"Vega's coming over. Maybe you can get her to clean your shoes?"

"Yeah, right!"

"Eeeeuuu—"

Rina clamped her hand over Hannah's mouth. The little girl giggled. She was clearly delighted at being disgusted and grossed-out. With the stench growing stronger, Rina figured it was a good time to make an exit. She picked up her oversize tote. "See you in a moment."

As she trudged her way to her Volvo, she realized how heavy Hannah was. A ring of sweat was sitting behind the collar of her shirt and her back felt a twinge. Hannah was still the youngest, but she wasn't a baby.

"Sweetie, I have to put you down."

"Please?" Hannah begged. She tightened her legs around her mother. "My knee hurts."

With the dog stuff gone as a distraction, Hannah had gone back to her earlier wounds. "My back hurts," Rina explained.

Reluctantly, the girl slid down. "I'm sorry, Eema."

"Thank you, sweetheart."

Hannah used to call her Mommy. Since starting first grade, she'd switched to Eema, to be big like her older brothers. The first-grader said, "I'll help you carry the bag—"

"It's okay. I have the bag."

"No, I'll help you." She began yanking the straps. Since Rina didn't want to play tug of war, she ceded the sack to the victor. She watched Hannah struggle, her red curls bouncing as she walked unsteadily. Her eyes caught the sun, reflecting back a deep olive color. She looked like she should have been a Colleen or a Megan.

Rina said, "Can I give you some help?"

"No, I can do it." Grunt, grunt. Moaning and sighing, she was in top-notch form, doing her best imitation of Sarah Heartburn. "I . . . ugh . . . got it."

All of her kids were so different. Her sons, born from the same mother and father, were diametric opposites. Shmuel was serious, Yonkie was lighthearted . . . at least he was until he reached the magic sixteen mark with his hormones kicking into high gear.

They reached the curb to cross the street. Rina bent down and picked up one of Hannah's soft little hands. She took the bag with the other. "C'mon," she said.

Together, mother and daughter, they crossed the street. Rina reached inside the bottomless pit of the bag and fished out her keys. She opened the hatch door to her station wagon and immediately Hannah climbed in the back.

"Hannah," Rina scolded. "Come around the right way. Stop climbing over the upholstery."

"Please, please, please?"

Rina sighed. "Get out of the way so I don't slam this on you." She shut the hatch with force, kicking up dust from the dirty carpet. She sneezed loudly as Hannah disappeared into the bowels of the Volvo. Walking to the driver's door, she started excavating the bottom of her purse for a tissue.

Simultaneously, as foreign fingers grasped her right arm, something cold and hard dug into her backbone. Instinctively, she knew what was pressing against her spine. She realized what was happening, even before he spoke.

"You scream or you move, then I kill you."

The voice was raspy . . . accented. Rina stood in place as the gun pushed deeper into her back. Unlike the other carjack victims, she knew the drill. She knew what he was going to do. But that was neither here nor there because she was immobilized by fear.

The voice said, "You listen or you're dead. You walk to other side of the car, and open the door. Do it!"

Rina translated, *He's telling me to walk over to the passenger's side. You know what's going to happen. Use it to your advantage.*

She looked out at the park, at the distant people

and a distant Marge, who was still messing with her shoes.

For God's sake, look up at me! she shrieked inside her head.

But Marge was completely absorbed in her task.

Rina was on her own. She thought of the memorial service of Yizkor, a prayer she still said for her late husband.

Man is like a breath, his days are like a passing shadow . . .

Don't think about that now!

If she screamed, she would probably get shot. But it might be worth it because Hannah was in the car.

"You go now!" he whispered vehemently. "You go or I shoot you dead!"

Hannah was in that car!

Dead or not dead, she wouldn't let him have the car when Hannah was inside!

Slowly, Rina started to move toward the passenger door, again turning her head toward Marge. Out of the corner of her eye, she saw Vega looking in her direction, the two of them locking eyes for just a millisecond. But it was enough because the teen began tapping Marge's shoulder. The gun burrowed itself into her muscles until she winced in pain.

He growled. "You look straight. Go!"

Do something!

Okay, Marge. I'll make a deal. I'll do something, if

you do something. And, God, it wouldn't hurt if you helped things along.

Rina let her keys fall from her hand until they dropped to the ground; the kerplunk was audible.

"What you do—"

"I dropped my keys—"

"What!"

With all her weight, Rina fell to the ground, breaking contact with the muzzle of the firearm for just a moment. Perhaps a moment would be enough. She curled up in a compact ball, holding her body tightly packed with her knees against her chest, her forearms covering her ears. She couldn't hear Marge's voice saying, "Police! Freeze!" But she could hear the deafening pop of gunfire, and feel the wind of whizzing bullets. She drew herself inward and started to sob as something big and smelly slammed onto her back, oozing hot, wet liquid down her neck. She screamed, shaking off the intruder with jerky, uncontrolled movements. She was still screaming even as Vega put her arms around her. Still screaming even as Marge brought her up to her feet and hugged her tightly.

"You're okay, you're okay, you're okay!" Marge was telling her.

Shaking uncontrollably, Rina couldn't speak. She could barely support her own weight.

"You're fine," Marge assured her as she rocked her back and forth. "You're fine, you're fine, you're fine!"

A sudden energy bolt of maternal instinct shot through Rina's veins. She pushed Marge away and breathed out, *"Hannah!"* Rushing over to the back door, she threw it open. The little girl was jumping on the bench seat. She saw her mother's face, saw her sickly pale complexion and the tears running down her cheeks. The little girl retreated inwardly. "Eema, sorry I jumped on the seat. I'll put on my seat belt now. Don't be mad. Please don't be mad!"

She burst into tears.

Completely oblivious as to what had just happened.

People began rushing over. Marge displayed her badge, telling everyone to step back. Such authority and calm in her voice. Just a minute ago, Rina had been conversing with just another insecure mother. The two versions of Marge didn't seem to match, but wasn't that the way it was with people. Using Marge's professional confidence as a springboard, Rina managed to find her own voice. "Hannah, come out of the car this instant!"

"I'm soorrrrry, Eema!"

"Get out!" Rina yelled, pulling her daughter forward by the arm. The little girl slid across the seat on her belly and was weeping hysterically by the time she was liberated from the car. Rina longed to hug and kiss her, because, as a mother, that was what *she* needed to do. What Hannah required was swift removal from the scene before any of its grisly nature sank in. She turned her daughter from the gruesome sight and barked orders to Vega. "Take Hannah across the street, back to the park, and play with her until you hear from me!"

"I want to stay with you!" Hannah wailed.

"Go!" Rina commanded Vega.

The young teen, having been raised in a cult, was good at following orders. She picked up the squalling child and ran with her across the street. When they were out of sight, Rina buried her head into the welcoming folds of her palms, weeping so hard her shoulders were moving. People were talking to her, but all she heard was white noise. After a few moments, she admonished herself for lack of control, told herself to get a grip on it. She was alive and safe: Hannah was alive and safe. What more did she want? She should be thanking Marge, thanking Vega for spotting her, thanking Hashem for making it come out all right!

Silently, she said the prayer of *Gomel*, thanking God for delivering her from harm's way. After she was done, she felt a bit calmer. It felt good to be doing something. She peeked through her hands and saw Marge gesticulating as she held her cell phone.

You have a cell phone! Rina told herself. *Page Peter!*

Marge was somehow managing to maintain order while speaking at a machine gun pace into her phone. Rina wiped her eyes, and picked up her tote, spilling out most of its contents, including her cell phone. But it had been built well, humming beautifully after she pressed the power button. With trembling hands, she punched in the correct numbers and managed to page her husband.

Waiting for the return call . . .

Marge was still directing piles of people traffic. "Back away! Back off!" She glanced at Rina, yelling out, "Where are the kids?"

"I sent Hannah with Vega back into the park. I don't want them to be a part of this."

They're already a part of it, Marge said to herself. *At least, Vega was.* Thinking about Rina's words: Crises happen to everyone sooner or later.

In retrospect, dog shit seemed pretty damn benign.

"Are you okay?" she asked Rina.

"Yes, I'm okay." Rina managed a scared smile. "I know that because you told me I'm okay!"

Marge reached out her arms to Rina. Putting aside her duties as cop, because she was, first and foremost, a person. They embraced, hugging each other with the knowledge and appreciation that each body was whole.

"Thank you," Rina whispered.

"Thank Vega. She was the one who saw you."

"Well, thank you for not shooting me."

"Thank you for dropping down and giving me a clear shot." Marge was breathing heavily. "Look, do Vega a favor and take her to synagogue again."

"Absolutely." She held back tears. "I could use a little God myself."

Marge continued to hold her tightly, as much for her own sake as for Rina's. Then, she realized things were getting out of control. Reluctantly, she stepped back from Rina, and started shooing the lookie-loos away from the crime scene.

A crime scene that she created! Well, she didn't create the crime scene. More like she redirected it. More like, Rina directed it. Her improvisational pratfall gave Marge a clear view of the perp . . . a clear angle.

Marge looked over to Rina and gave her the thumbs-up sign. "You did good, kid! You did real good!"

Despite her best efforts, Rina started to cry, an unbridled wellspring of emotions pouring forth—joy, anger, fear, relief, an appreciation for every breath she took.

Thank you, *Hashem,* she said to herself. Thank you for saving me.

And maybe, just maybe, it was her *emmunah*—her faith—that had allowed her to think clearly, that gave her some kind of plan.

In the background, she heard the undulating wails of approaching sirens. It almost drowned out the ringing of her cellular.

Peter calling back from her page. Answer the phone.

But she hesitated, unwilling to let go of this overwhelming wind of gratitude. How lucky she had been. Thank you, God—the creator and director of life—for saving her. And thank you, dear Margie, for playing one heck of a starring role.

She pressed the *On* button. Peter's deep, sweet voice came through the receiver. For a moment, Rina couldn't speak.

And then she did.

29

SOMEONE HAD brought her water; another had offered a Tylenol. Since Peter was prone to headaches, Rina always carried Advil in her purse. She declined the Tylenol, but used the water to swallow the Advil. Not that the analgesic would help much. She couldn't stop shaking. A squadron of police black-and-whites had encircled the area like wagons around a camp, the beacon lights atop their cruisers flashing intermittently. Officers had cordoned off a wide band of curbside with yellow crime scene tape. Rina was in the thick of it, leaning against the backside of her Volvo, just yards away from the dead body. A pair of paramedics waited for the coroner's wagon, while a duo of uniforms held vigil over the corpse. A white-and-red ambulance stood several yards away reminding her of the tenuous nature of life.

Oddly, she felt protected. Few dared to approach her for fear of messing up evidence. Also, she had a clear view of Hannah on the swings. Her little daughter had a serious expression on her face as she pumped her legs. It said, Eema had given her the assignment of playing and she was going to play. Vega stood nearby, her eyes fixed on the child. Not once had she approached Marge for help; it would never have occurred to Vega to ask.

Rina stared at her bloodstained dress. She should have asked Peter to bring her a change. First off, forensics might want her clothes, though she wouldn't know what they'd do with them. More important, it made her sick to be wearing someone's life forces. But she couldn't dwell on that now. She needed to ready herself for the eventual onslaught of questions.

Uniformed officials flitted like mosquitoes. Some seemed to be gathering witnesses, others appeared to be taking statements. And there were several groups still waiting for orders. The randomness suggested that no one had taken charge. That would change when someone from Homicide came onto the scene.

The irony was that Marge was from Homicide, but obviously she couldn't lead the investigation because of her involvement. Rina felt for her. An officer-involved shooting meant a probe by the Officer Involved Shooting team. Not that this should be a problem as her actions were justifiable. And she had lots of witnesses to back her up. Still, taking someone's life, even in a rightful situation, was an onerous burden.

Rina continued to shiver even though some kind soul had given her a denim jacket. She hugged herself as she rocked on her feet. She looked around, making eye contact with a uniformed officer. He hesitated, then sidestepped the yellow tape, and swaggered over to her, pad in hand. He had a dense build to match his dense mop of black hair. Brown eyes stared at her with ferocious intensity.

He started his spiel. "If you don't mind, ma'am, I'd like to ask you a few questions."

In a toe tap, Marge was at her side. She flashed her badge. "She does mind. She's waiting for her husband, Lieutenant Decker. Please give her the courtesy of a little privacy."

Red-faced, the uniform backed away, muttering some apologies.

Marge put her hands on her hips. "How are you holding up?"

Rina rubbed her arms. "I could ask you the same question."

"I'm all right." Marge chewed gum, and surveyed the area, trying to appear casual. "This kind of thing is familiar territory."

"Familiar territory with a twist," Rina said.

"A big twist . . . thank God, that's Webster's Audi. You stay here." Marge jogged over to the car. Tom got out and smoothed down his jacket. He had returned to his usual self—from frazzled expectant parent to super dude in super duds, sporting a white shirt, khaki pants, and a black linen blazer—slightly wrinkled to give it that perfect look. "Your timing could have been a mite better," he drawled out. "My wife just gave birth to a perfect little girl about six hours ago."

"Congrats! Still, there's nothing more you can do for her. I'd say my timing was exquisite."

Webster put his arm around Marge. "Are you okay?"

"Been better." She bit her lip and clasped her hands to keep them from shaking. "Not looking forward to all the bureaucracy. Do you know who's coming from the OIS team?"

"So far, we got Hodges and Arness. Being as it's Sunday, it takes a while to find everyone."

Marge nodded. "Hodges and Arness are good guys."

"Yeah, it's going to be fine, Margie. You want to tell me what all happened?"

Marge gave him a quick rundown. Then she said, "I've been trying to give the Blues some direction, but I'm hog-tied because of . . . of what happened. No one knows what's flying."

"Bert's due out here any moment. We'll all handle the investigation of the body, let the shooting team handle you. Where's the corpse?"

"It's sprawled against Rina's Volvo." Marge began walking him over to the spot. "I did everything by the book, Tom. But ask me anyway."

"Did you warn the perp?"

"Yes."

"People heard you?"

"I hope so."

"Was there imminent danger?"

"Yes. He had a weapon, and he pointed it at me."

"Did he fire?"

"I think so, but I couldn't swear to it because it happened so fast. It would firm up my case if he fired."

"It would help. You didn't touch anything, right?"

"Nothing. The gun's right where he dropped it. Looks to be a .38 Colt revolver." She coughed. "I posted a couple of uniforms to guard it and the body."

"How many rounds did you fire?"

"Three."

"You checked your gun then?"

She nodded. "Yeah. I checked."

"Well, you didn't empty the gun," Webster said. "Shows you were in control. That's good. Did you check the perp for vital signs?"

"Checked the jugular *and* the brachial artery. I couldn't detect any pulse . . . not unless you count his aorta gushing like a fountain. It was a straight-on chest shot. I mean . . . look at me!"

Webster did. Her clothing was a mass of red inkblots.

"I kept trying to plug him up while I talked to 911." She was talking as much to herself as to Tom. "I don't remember the conversation, but it's recorded on tape."

"Did you move the body?"

"From where he landed, I moved it enough to check the wounds and check for vitals. That's when I got blasted. I kept my face out of the way, and my hands don't have any open cuts. Hopefully, I'm okay . . . just pray that the bastard didn't have AIDS." Her heavy sigh held back the tears. "God, it was awful! I kept stuffing the hole in his chest with his shirt . . . to try to stop the bleeding. I knew it was a waste of time. He was a goner on impact."

"But you can say you tried."

"Yeah, that's certainly true. The ambulance must have come about a minute later . . . they saw me working on him."

"Piece of cake. You're gonna be just fine. Just sit back and compose yourself."

"That's a tall order." She shook her head. "Every time I close my eyes, I see this red river charge toward me. Fresh blood is really warm . . . hot. I'm still sticky from him! It's horrible!"

"Can I do anything for you?"

"Just find out about the stiff. Maybe his identity will break the jackings. The way he did it was identical to the Farin Henley case . . . right down to the Volvo station wagon."

"That would be a hoot. You breaking your own case. Course, it would have helped a mite if you hadn't *killed* the guy."

"I'm going to ignore that." Then Marge burst into laughter—at odds with her wet eyes.

❑

DECKER vaulted over the crime tape. Before Rina could protest, he grabbed her shoulders and squeezed her tightly. She was determined not to cry, but she did leak a few tears.

"Do you need a doctor?" Decker asked.

"A shrink would help."

"That can be arranged." Decker held her at arm's length then drew her back into his chest. "Where's Hannah?"

"Across . . ." Rina cleared her throat. "She's with Vega in the park. See her? She's sliding down that twisty thing?"

Decker looked. Little orange curls bounced as Hannah's body whooshed down the turns of the metal apparatus. How close she came to being a statistic . . .

"Poor thing must be starved," Rina said.

"Lieutenant—"

"Not now!" Decker barked.

The officer retreated. Decker took a deep breath and let it out. "I called your parents—"

"Peter, why on earth did you—"

"Because it was better to hear it from me than from the TV news." Decker mopped up a sweaty brow with a handkerchief. "We're both going to be occupied for a while. I figured they could watch Hannah—"

"I don't want her involved! She didn't see anything, she doesn't even know what went on."

"I know. That's why I need your folks. We'll get her out of here as fast as we can. Ordinarily, I'd ask Cindy but she's in no shape to do anything right now."

"Poor Peter," Rina said. "You must be a nervous wreck!"

"Poor *me*? Poor *you*! It's amazing you're still standing on two feet." Decker ran his hand over his face. "This sure puts things in perspective. Makes you just want to . . . kiss the day!"

"I've been thanking God nonstop." Rina's lower lip began to tremble. "Peter, what do I tell Hannah? She thinks I'm mad at her for jumping on the backseat. I know I should go over there and say something, but I'm so nervous, I don't know what to do!"

Decker lessened his grip on his wife. "Give me a few minutes to get things squared away and I'll take care of her. Has anyone taken your statement?"

"Some officer tried to ask me questions, but Marge shooed him away."

Decker nodded, pulling away from his wife to analyze the scene. There were around a dozen uniformed officers doing traffic and crowd control. The coroner's wagon had arrived, the attendants waiting for the police photographer to finish up so they could take the body away. But before they did, the OIS team would examine the body for entrance and exit wounds, giving Marge the physical evidence she needed to exonerate her actions. Also, Martinez was there, waiting to go through the pockets of the victim for ID.

Marge was with Oliver, speaking with her hands as well as her mouth. Decker called out his name. Scott turned around, gave Marge's shoulder a final pat, then jogged up to the tape, stepping over the barrier with careful, deliberate movements. His limbs felt numb from a poor night's sleep.

"I'm so sorry, Mrs. Decker," Oliver said. "Do you need a doctor or anything?"

"No, I'm okay."

Decker said, "Take a statement from her. When you're done, I'll drive her home—"

"I can drive, Peter."

"First off, the Volvo stays here for a while. Secondly, I wouldn't dream of letting you drive after what happened."

"So after I'm done, I can take Hannah and Vega with me and go home?"

Decker nodded.

"So why did you call my parents?"

"Just in case you need to rest. Wouldn't hurt for you to have a little help."

"Then you'll tell Marge that I have Vega?"

"Yes. Vega might have to make a statement herself. I'll see what I can do about that." He wagged a finger at Oliver. "You take good care of her."

"Of course."

Decker evaluated his detective. Oliver looked worn to the bone. "Have someone with you to verify her statement. Report back to me, then go home and get some real sleep. Sleep . . . as in your *own* bed."

Oliver ignored the sarcasm and pulled out a notepad. "I'll do that. Someone should look after Detective Dunn until the shooting team gets here. She's a bit nervous."

Decker regarded Marge, who was pacing in tiny circles. "I'll go over there." He kissed Rina's cheek, then brushed his lips against hers. "I love you."

"I love you, too."

But Decker was reluctant to leave. He forced out a weak smile, then backed away. He realized he looked ludicrous, so he turned and walked over to his former partner. He put his hand on her shoulder. "I think I owe you some thanks."

"Hell, I'm just so grateful it worked out. Hopefully, the shooting team will see it that way." Marge bit her thumbnail. "When's Hodges getting here?"

"He's on his way."

"Is he going to interview me?"

"I don't know how they've worked out the division of labor. They'll take you back to the stationhouse for the statement." Decker put his arm around her. "You're not going to have any problems with this, Margie. No one's going to try to trip you up. Just take it slow and you'll be fine."

She nodded.

Decker said, "You want to show me where you were standing?"

She took him to the exact spot. There were still bits of dog excrement clinging to the blades of grass. "I was kneeling here, cleaning my shoes . . ." Marge crouched down to reenact the scene. "Vega tapped me on the shoulder. I looked up . . . saw Rina."

Decker knelt beside her. From this position, he had a good view of the driver's side of the Volvo. "Then what?"

"I stood up . . . got my gun out. I started running over . . ." She squinted. "I remember a few people were in the line of fire, I told them to get back, get back—"

"Are they still here?"

"Yeah, Webster's talking to one of them right now. That older fat guy with the gray ponytail in the blue workout suit."

Decker gave the man a once-over. "Go on."

Walking several yards, she suddenly stopped behind the thick trunk of a eucalyptus tree spewing the scent of menthol. "I took cover right . . . here. See? There's my footprint and my knee print."

"You were kneeling."

"Absolutely. Better control. From the position, I had a clean view. Rina had dropped down to the ground—"

"Why?"

"I don't know. You'll have to ask her. But it was a brilliant move. It gave me a clear shot at the perp. I identified myself. The perp turned toward me, his weapon pointed in my direction. I opened fire."

"Three rounds."

"Yeah. Tom told you?"

"Tom told me. Did you call for backup before you opened fire?"

"Afterward. I couldn't handle the phone and my gun at the same time. And based on the present situation coupled with the past history of the on-going jackings, I assessed that immediate action was necessary. There wasn't enough time to wait for help."

Decker looked around, across the expanse of park area. "If he shot at you, the bullets could be anywhere."

"I've thought about that."

"I'm sure you have." Decker looked at his feet, then squatted down to examine the ground about him. He put up markers next to Marge's footprints. Then he examined the tree trunk. Starting at the bottom, Decker's eyes started walking up the dips and folds of the shaggy bark. Around twenty inches off the ground, he stopped and stared.

"Look here. Something nicked off the bark. See we have a nice radial, half-moon pattern. This looks like a bullet graze. Martinez will bag the hands just as soon as the photographer's gone. We're going to find residue. I'm sure he shot at you."

"So that's good. Be better if we had the bullet."

"We'll search the park. But even so, you're all right. The nick should help the shooting team with their angles and trajectories." He marked the spot with a piece of tape. "Guy was a good aim. You're lucky."

"Hodges is here," Marge announced.

Decker stood up. "Rina's making a statement now. After she's done, she'll take Hannah and Vega to our house. Depending on what Hodges and the others want, we may have to talk to Vega."

"I know."

"But maybe not." Decker waved the detective over. Hodges, like all members of the OIS team, was from Robbery/Homicide. He was a good detective—analytical—and a decent fellow. He was still muscular in his build, but had grown soft around the middle. A man with a face filled with character—graying hair, gray eyes, and lots of facial crags and creases. In his early fifties, he was two and a half years off his twenty-five-year pension.

"Lieutenant," Hodges said.

"Are you doing the interviewing or the analyzing?"

"Arness and Renquist are on their way down." Hodges turned to Marge. "Renquist will take you down to the stationhouse. He'll take a statement from you. How're you feeling?"

Marge nodded nervously. "I'm all right."

"Good." Hodges shifted on his feet. "I'll wait for Arness. You looked like you were looking for something, Loo. Kneeling down and all. Find anything?"

"Just what I marked off with tape. Here on the tree and Detective Dunn's prints on the grass. How long do you think the analysis is going to take?"

"Usual."

"Three . . . four hours?"

"About."

"Scott's getting a statement from my wife. Then I'd like to take her home. So I'll be gone about a half hour . . . maybe forty-five minutes."

"I'm real sorry about your wife. What a bitch of a thing to happen."

"She's all right. That's all that matters."

"Thank God."

"Loo?" Martinez ran across the street and stopped in front of the trio. "Hey, Ross, how's the curve ball coming?"

"We're a shoo-in against Van Nuys, Bertie. Parks twisted his ankle on a skiing trip. The Department won't let him pitch. Threatened him with suspension if he did. He isn't going to risk it being three years from pension." Hodges turned to Decker. "When are you gonna join the team, Loo? Bet you've belted your fair share out of the park."

"See the size of my strike zone?" Decker remarked. "Besides, I was slow when I was young, I'm even slower now."

"That's the whole point of the over-forty league, sir," Hodges stated.

"As tempting as it sounds, I'll still pass."

"There's Renquist." Hodges waved him over, then turned to Marge. "You'll be fine. Just take it slow. Good luck."

"I'm all right," Marge said. And for the first time, she almost meant it. She had saved Rina's life: that made her a hero. And the guys were acting so nice and normal. Maybe things would actually be all right.

Decker said, "Did you have something, Bert?"

"Yeah. Right!" Martinez suddenly remembered why he was there. "I went through the pockets of the perp."

Hodges said, "Did you move the bod—"

"No, I didn't move the body—"

"Screw up the angles—"

"I didn't move the body!"

"I moved the body," Marge said.

"Don't say anything yet," Hodges said. "Wait for Renquist."

"What'd you find, Bert?"

"Okay. His driver's license says he's Luk-Duc Penn, twenty-five, five six, one-thirty. No green card, so maybe he's legal. He lives . . . lived in Oxnard." Martinez gave Decker the exact address. "We're spending all this time on looking at similars in L.A. and the guy lives out of town. From this area, all he has to do is take the 101 North and within thirty, forty minutes, he's in another jurisdiction. Wide-open spaces between here and Oxnard. You can get to the backfields without using conventional routes."

"Oxnard's mainly Hispanic," Marge said.

"It's mainly *migrant*," Martinez said. "Because of all the agriculture, it's a magnet for anyone poor and illiterate. Look at the recent influx of Southeast Asians in SoCal. They compete with the Central American migrants for jobs and probably compete in the crime market as well. If we start hunting up north, I'm sure we'll find chop shops."

"Sounds reasonable," Decker said. "Let's contact the Oxnard PD and a judge up there, and grab ourselves a couple of warrants."

30

Having been a recent crime statistic herself, Cindy felt genuine empathy about what had happened to Rina and Hannah. Her immediate reaction wasn't just emotional, but physical, being overcome with that terrible sensation of momentary light-headedness. But her father had assured her that they were *fine*, whatever that meant because how could *anyone* be fine after such an ordeal. Dad had also been quick to tell her that Hannah hadn't seen anything. And that the carjacker had been shot dead by Marge. Cindy's immediate reaction was relief. Rina wouldn't have to go through a trial, and they could honestly tell Hannah that the bad man was gone for good.

Then, after she had hung up the phone and thought about what had occurred, she sank under the enormous burden of being forced to take a life. The incident roiled up questions in Cindy's mind. Could she shoot to kill? At this point, she felt that she could. Yet, when someone had shot at her and Crayton, she had ducked behind a car, frozen with fear.

Heart beating wildly, she had an immediate impulse to fly over the freeway, and see that her sister and Rina were indeed *fine*. But things were a mess right now.

Why don't you check up on us in about an hour? her father had said. Then he had added, *I'm still thinking about you. Are you okay?*

I'm fine, Daddy. Really. Everything here is almost back to normal. She hesitated. *Actually, I can't help but wonder why all this garbage is happening to us.*

Her dad had laughed, but it was without mirth. *I know that no one is without problems. So, I guess it's our turn. I just hope that if I'm taking some kind of big life test, I've passed the damn thing already.*

I'm really sorry, Dad. Are you okay?

My family's fine, I'm fine. He paused. *I love you, princess. Please be careful. Ease your old man's psychic pain and, at the very least, keep in touch.*

I will, Dad. Don't worry. I'll take care of myself.

She felt horrible for him. But there *was* this tiny, tiny upside. She finally had time to herself. With Dad occupied with the latest developments, he couldn't dwell on her. That went for Marge and Oliver, too. The freedom gave her space to think . . . to analyze.

She picked up the morning coffeepot and began to wash it. Her thoughts drifted back to last night with Scott. It had all happened so fast and furiously that she wondered if it had happened at all. The whole thing was made even more surreal because she had woken up and found him gone. (Although the couch was covered with rumpled bedding, so she knew he had slept there. And there was the minimal note—*Call you later.*) And when he *had* phoned her, it had only been to tell her that he had been with her father, but now they both had to leave because of what had happened at the park.

She dried the carafe and put it back into the machine.

A really weird night, but infinitely better than the night before. She didn't remember the sex too well—her mind had truly been elsewhere—but she did recall the discussion about Bederman, about how Scott had said that partners don't usually break up and still remain best friends. It made her curious about Graham and about Rick Bederman since his behavior last night had been odd, talking against Hayley like that. It made Cindy wonder if there hadn't been another reason for Bederman wanting out of the partnership.

To get the transfer, Rick would have had to put down his request in writing. Ergo, the department would have a written record of the request in Bederman's file. If she could just get hold of the file, she'd find out the ostensible reason behind the transfer. Wouldn't that be nice?

But there were problems. Files not only were confidential, but were kept downtown in Parker Center. Access to the folders was just about impossible without the proper paperwork, and the personnel department was shut down on weekends, the room probably locked up tight. Maybe there was a civilian skeleton crew kept on to man other necessary offices, but that was about it. Going downtown was out.

She started wiping the counter with the dish-towel, but it was sodden by now, leaving streaks across the Formica. She draped the cloth over the faucet, and released a couple of sheets of paper towels from the dowel. Thinking as she wiped, she concluded most stationhouses were quiet over the weekends. Detectives tried to work a schedule of weekdays, nine to five. Not that they weren't avail-able, but it was an on-call system, and if the case could wait until Monday, it did.

Cindy threw away the wet paper towels, and went to the fridge. Pulling out a cluster of grapes, she popped one into her mouth, the sweet, fleshy explo-sion drowning out a sour taste that had previously languished. She sank into her couch, put up her feet, and thought as she ate.

Hollywood had to have some rudimentary file system on its cops. After all, there were attendance records, requests for vacation days, accounting of sick days, and leaves of absence. Roll call was usu-ally done by hand by the watch commander, but Cindy figured that the handwritten information probably got logged into a computer by a civilian, someone who was now home watching the game or planting flowers or out for the day. Perhaps she'd have some luck gaining access to the stationhouse's local computer software. Certainly she'd have an easier time getting in the building.

But if the stationhouse were less populated, would her presence there attract more or less attention?

Finishing the grapes, she held the empty branches and turned them over in her hands. The fruit was a meshwork, a system. Just like everything in life, one had to know how to work the system. If someone asked, she could always say she was catching up on report writing, or helping out Tropper because he had been swamped with paperwork. People knew she'd been doing that, so no one would doubt her in that regard.

The downside was that it would take time to break any kind of software code. And there was the possibility that she couldn't break it at all. And if she did break it, what was she looking for? Still, she got off the couch and picked up her bag. It was better to *be* doing something than to wonder if you *should be* doing something.

She unlocked the door, stepped outside her apartment, and then bolted the door shut. She looked around, her eyes scanning the walkways, the stairs, the street, the rooftops . . . all that was about her.

By now, vigilance had become habit.

❑

FIRST, she changed into her uniform because she thought she'd fit in better. Then, she went to the report room and pretended to be tidying up the loose ends of her paperwork. She was lucky. The stationhouse was quiet, and those that were there didn't seem interested in a rookie typing up forms. Beyond a few passing glances, she moved about either unnoticed or disregarded.

When the timing seemed right, she got up and moved down the hallway to where the stationhouse's records were likely to be kept. Getting into the cubicle turned out to be a snap. The lock was minimal, and she penetrated it with a simple credit card. Why bother with a dead bolt because who would steal stuff from a police station? Except that stuff did have a way of disappearing: pencils, pens, paper, pads, envelopes, folders, Post-its. Cindy figured it was like people in a hotel room, taking stationery not because they needed it, but because it was there.

Breaking into the computer was as complicated as turning on the switch. Within seconds, she faced around two dozen window options. She checked them out, one by one, until she came to a sheet program that listed the daily assignments—rotations, car assignments, street assignments, court dates, days off, days on, who patrolled with whom, which detectives were assigned to what details. The schedules were filed by date; the cops were filed alphabetically. It wasn't hard to find out Bederman's daily assignments over the past few years, but it would be time consuming.

She did have the time, but what was the point?

Finding out Rick's attendance record told her nothing about the man. But it was better than pacing the floors of her tiny apartment, jumping up at nonexistent sounds, peeking through the curtains every five minutes, and checking the locks, door-jambs, and windowsills for pry marks, pick marks, or other scratches.

Her favorite computer key turned out to be the Backward one. Going back, date by date, month by month. It was boring, it was stupid, and it accomplished nothing. Rick was there at roll call by six-thirty, he logged out by three-thirty. Six days on, three days off. Sometimes he took longer shifts to get more days off in a row.

Two months into the past, then three months, then six months. The flesh beneath her eyes began to twitch as she scaled through the massive piles of small print. There was nothing subjective on these charts, no comments good or bad about any individual. Just record keeping.

Eight months, nine months, eleven months . . . right around the time Cindy became a part of Hollywood. Prior to her arrival, Graham Beaudry's assignments had him riding solo. A few flips back in time, then, to Cindy's amazement, she found out that Graham had been partnered with another woman named Nicole Martin. As she looked backward in the files, she discovered that Graham had worked with her for over *a year*.

That was odd. Everyone talked about Graham and

Rick being former partners, but no one had mentioned Nicole Martin to Cindy. Not even Graham had spoken about her. Cindy followed Martin's path for a while. Further hunting showed that Nicole had been transferred to Pacific—specifically into Detectives, Juvenile Detail. To verify, she called up Pacific and asked for Detective Martin's voice mail. When the machine kicked in, she hung up.

Okay. Graham's last partner got the gold. Maybe that's why Graham never mentioned her, too embarrassed because Martin had gone on to bigger things. Still, even Hayley never mentioned her. Maybe Hayley was embarrassed as well, because Martin went gold and she was still pounding the streets.

It was all very odd. Or, rather, it could be that Cindy didn't understand the organization. There were so many unwritten rules and laws and the only way to learn about them was by breaking them unwittingly.

It made for very nervous rookies.

Before Nicole, Graham had been with Bederman.

So what was Bederman's history after he and Graham had split? Going into this thing, Cindy had assumed that Bederman had immediately hooked up with his current partner, Sean Amory. But looking over the roll call sheets, she was reminded once again why she never went to Vegas. Her assumptions were always wrong.

Not only had Bederman *not* been partnered with Sean, but *also* he had not been partnered with anyone. Plus, Bederman had transferred to the Evening Watch. No, not the *Evening* Watch—the *Night* Watch. Wee hours in the morning. The least favorite shift of most officers because the calls were usually serious ones. Shunned by those who would prefer normal working hours *unless* you just happened to be hooked on vices.

Which of course wasn't fair at all. Plenty of decent officers worked the watch. Some of them just liked being free during the daylight hours, some were single mothers and fathers who liked the hours because it allowed them time with the kids—breakfast before they went to school, then dinner before they went off to work, and the kids went to bed.

But being on the night shift also meant getting away with the hanky-panky and not having to explain anything to the wife. Being on the night shift meant easier access to the dark side—literally and figuratively. Because there was that element, those cops who thrived on thrill, who got their kicks out of skirting the boundaries, hanging around the sleaze—the hookers, the pimps, the pushers, the punks—thinking that they'd never be affected, that they'd never succumb. But they always did. Many past news items were testaments to cops who had fallen from grace.

But Cindy had no indication that Rick had been

one of those. He could have had a very legitimate reason for wanting the night shift. She knew he had young children. Maybe his wife had to work days, so Bederman worked nights to be with the kids. He didn't impress her as being domestic. But then again, didn't he say something about leaving early to be home with his wife? So maybe she had him all wrong. Maybe he was a straight shooter.

Her logic was objective, but her gut feeling was skeptical.

Rick had spent about two years on the dark side. And those same two years just happened to be the same two years of Armand Crayton's greatest financial success. It was during those specific two years that Crayton was throwing parties, buying Rolls-Royces, making plans, *and* dealing with Dexter Bartholomew.

Coincidence?

Again, Cindy scrolled through the assignment charts—backward, then forward, then backward again, charting the Beaudry/Bederman progression. A half hour later, she felt she had it down, surprised by the results.

Beaudry and Bederman had been partners for nearly *ten* years. They had started right around the time Oliver had remembered Bederman coming into Hollywood. Right around the time that Oliver had left and gone to Devonshire.

Partners for *ten* years.

If Bederman had been leery of Beaudry's physical

ability to catch criminals, he certainly took his time doing something about it.

Scott was right on. Something wasn't making sense.

Okay, Cindy told herself. They had been partners for ten years. Then what? Then, they split up, Beaudry riding with Nicole Martin, and Bederman working nights by himself.

Then Martin was promoted to Detective, and Beaudry rode solo for six months. Back at the ranch, around the same time, Bederman switched to the day shift once again where he rode solo for three months. Finally, his assignment sheet showed him with current partner Sean Amory.

Amazing what you can find out by perusing simple assignment records!

Doing the math, Cindy noted the three-month period where both Bederman and Beaudry were on the day shift together, but riding solo. Which meant that if they had wanted to partner together, they could have.

Obviously, they purposely chose *not* to do it.

Why?

Who didn't want whom? Or was it mutual?

Or was she just doing mental pyrotechnics to make sense out of her own disorganized life?

And what, if anything, did it have to do with Crayton?

She logged off the computer, took her hand-written material, and stuffed it into her bag. She looked around, then sneaked out of the office, down to her locker to change, then out to the parking lot. As soon as she hit the outside air, she exhaled deeply. She hadn't noticed how tense she had been. It felt good to get out of there.

Looking around, she opened her car door and slipped behind the wheel, locking her Saturn before she started the motor. Her mind had turned to errant cops, thinking about the most recent scandals that had been plaguing the LAPD. How could she not think about them? It was an old story: cops being corrupted by money. She couldn't help but wonder whether or not Bederman had been living the fast life for those two years he had worked the night shift during the peak period of Armand's glory. She tried to recall hers and Armand's conversations, all his dreams and his schemes. Mostly, she'd listened with half an ear because she'd thought Armand a big scamster. That he was trying to get money from her . . . trying to get into her pants.

Since he wasn't successful at any of those endeavors, Cindy wondered what he got out of their casual relationship. Maybe it was just an ear. Still, he seemed to listen intently when she talked about the academy and her dreams of being a cop.

Could Armand have possibly viewed her as an "in" on the force? Did he think that she was corruptible? Was he throwing out lures to see what would bite? And wasn't that how it worked for

Lark Crayton as well? Throwing out ideas to Stacy Mills to see what would catch?

If Armand were going to catch a big fish, he'd have to use bigger bait than just promises. Cindy thought about how everyone had been concentrating on Crayton's carjacking. Maybe they should have been concentrating on what led up to the jacking, namely what Armand did for a living.

What did Cindy's father say Crayton had been involved with? Something about land swapping down near Palm Springs. What town was it? Something with flowers in it . . . a foreign name that didn't describe the place at all. Something like Las Flores only it was in French. Les Fleurs? Belle Fleur?

That was it. Belfleur. One word. They couldn't even get the French right.

She started the car's motor, but didn't head home.

To her shock, she found herself going southeast until she hit Arlington. Then, as if hit by forces beyond her control, she was going east on the 10 freeway.

But the forces weren't beyond her control. She knew what she was doing. She was taking a ride out to Belfleur in the hopes that maybe some local could give her a hint as to what went wrong with Armand Crayton's schemes.

It was a long shot, but hell, maybe just this *once*, her bet would pay off.

31

IT WAS Sunday, with temperatures hovering in the seventies, so it should have been a beautiful afternoon. But the morning coastal fog had refused to burn off, turning the heavens an insipid milky blue, as if the ethers were suffering from anoxia. The travel was ugly as exhaust from the cars, trucks, and buses enveloped the buildings, making everything appear washed out. But traffic was light, and that was a joy. Even Cindy's worn Saturn seemed to be chugging along at a decent speed, enjoying a rare moment devoid of snarled lanes and sig-alerts.

The drive east took her past downtown L.A., past towering commercial buildings, business hotels, the spanking new sports arena, and convention centers. Beyond them stood the older mercantile buildings of East L.A. and the City of Commerce—miles upon miles of tired structures. A few were being renovated, but too many had been left to rot. As she continued east, she eventually hit the refineries, the factories belching out crud through smokestacks, reminiscent of the old-fashioned locomotives except that the illusion carried none of the romance. There were also dozens of car dealerships, each announcing a sale of the century, using

bloated balloon cartoon figures—obese Tweety
birds and Sylvesters wafting in the light breeze,
frozen smiles on their faces. This was the SoCal
that everyone would just as soon forget.

She cranked up Sheryl Crow on her CD player,
the singer's low-key but bruised voice chanting the
vagaries of life. She advanced the disc to selection
number eight, never tiring of the line about being
a stranger in one's own life—the ultimate statement of alienation. Precisely why it was good for
her to be *doing* things, be they as mundane as looking up attendance records, or driving one hundred
miles with no concrete goal in mind. Action was
always better than rumination.

As she moved out of the big city and its woes,
she drove by dozens of bedroom communities that
lined the freeway. The developments looked identical—two-story town houses with peaked, tarpa-
per roofs and white siding. In an inspirational
quirk, a few developments dared to have blue siding. Older cars were parked in driveways, lawns
were studded with bikes and balls. An occasional
tree swayed in the breeze produced by a steady
stream of high-speed cars. One home right after
the other. Servicing the local residents were monstrous malls—marooned islands in asphalt seas.

Not the scenic route, but Cindy didn't mind. It
was wonderful to be out of the city, away from the
malevolent forces that had been plaguing her. Not
that she was carefree. Constant checks in her side

and rearview mirrors reminded her that those naïve days were gone. To draw out possible tails, she sped up, she slowed down. She changed lanes frequently. She felt around in her purse for her gun, she made sure her cell phone was on. She switched radio stations constantly to prevent her mind from going into freeway hypnosis. She opened the window, she closed the window. She turned up the volume of her stereo. Anything to keep her active and alert. Still, there was residual fear, that nagging sensation that she was missing something.

As she approached hour number two on the road, she once again looked into her rearview mirror. Out of all the cars she had started with, there remained a blue Lexus driven by a lone white male, a white Ford Explorer occupied by two twenty-something women, an army green Range Rover occupied by two forty-something women, and a silver Volvo that housed a family. The vehicles were traveling at a steady rate, but they had kept at a sizable distance behind her. Plus, they didn't switch lanes when the Saturn did. Cindy figured she was safe for the moment.

Her stomach rumbling, she reached into her purse and brought out an apple. Thirty minutes later, she ate some grapes.

The terrain had turned from cityscape to landscape. A panorama of virginal scrubland as she headed east into the inland valley, into the edges of the Mojave Desert. Plains of sand-washed acreage pushed against granite, snow-tipped mountains. There was no lead-up to this change in geography; the ground was flat and arid until it abruptly hit the foothills of piled rock. But the air had turned crystalline. No industry around to pollute it, no shoreline fog to obscure it.

Cindy was surprised to see actual exit signs for such a small community like Belfleur, one of them boasting the town to be the antiques capital of the Inland Empire. From the edge of the freeway, Cindy actually spotted several antiques stores. As soon as she could get over to the right-hand lane and exit, she did. She was relieved that none of the four cars behind her had followed her lead. A moment later, she was riding down Main Street—a four-lane band of dust-coated asphalt that paralleled the freeway. Since there didn't seem to be any centralization of business, she parked when the mood hit. She pulled up curbside, got out, and peered over the monotonous topography—level and tan.

The area was a pinch shy of ghost town status. There were no other pedestrians, and few signs of life. Belfleur was small, and while it made a pretense at being quaint, it couldn't pull it off. The compact stores were erected slapdash from grainy stucco, streaked gray from either rain or plumbing problems. On one side of the street, Cindy passed a deli, a coffee shop, and a market—all closed. The other side held a secondhand-clothing store—

which was also closed—but lining the sidewalk were a hardware store and a liquor store, both of them open. A hundred feet later, there was only open space with a clear view of the mountains. Five more minutes of walking led her to another coffee shop, also open and with people inside. Cindy had a talk with her stomach, and decided that at the moment, she was more curious than hungry. She'd grab some grub on the way back.

About a quarter-mile down the main drag, she came upon a mall of antiques shops. Entering one of them, she found herself looking at items better suited to a thrift shop. Lots of old books and clothing . . . odd lots of dishes that could have been pieces from great-grandma's cheap china set. There was a shelf filled with rusted tins that were once used to hold dry goods. Another shelf was stocked with chipped porcelain figurines stamped MADE IN JAPAN. Cindy did notice a few pieces of good-quality iridescent carnival glass, but the prices weren't any bargain. Still, since Mom collected it and she didn't want to leave empty-handed, she picked up a cup-and-saucer set and examined it for flaws. Finding the pieces to be in pristine condition, she brought them over to the counter.

A forty-plus woman was behind the register. A very short haircut emphasized a very long jawline. Blue eyes sat in nests of tiny crinkles, wrinkles, and crow's feet. Her face was without adornment—no makeup or jewelry. Her clothing was simple—a short-sleeve, blue surfer Hawaiian shirt and a pair of baggy jeans. Cindy handed her the cup and saucer.

"This is nice," the woman said. She studied the price. "I should have asked more for it. Too bad. My loss, your gain."

Cindy nodded and smiled. "Nice shirt."

"Thanks," the woman answered. "We've got a stack of them over on the left. Did you see them?"

"Uh, no."

"Want me to show you them?"

"Sure."

The woman came out from behind the counter and began leading Cindy through the maze of crowded aisles. "They're the real thing from the fifties and sixties. One hundred percent rayon. Not cotton. The cotton ones don't drape well. We also have some bowling shirts if you're interested."

"I don't bowl."

"That's okay. Most of our customers don't bowl either. It's just the latest thing in Gen-Y dress. You know, too hip, gotta go. What do you do?"

Cindy was momentarily floored by the question. She gave her stock answer. "Student."

"U of Redlands?"

"Uh, no. UCSD."

"Nice place to go to school." The woman quickly rooted through the piles of cloth, then pulled out a pink shirt decorated with Hawaiian hula dancers. "This should be your size."

"It's nice." She actually thought that it was kind of neat. "How much?"

"Forty."

"Wow! That much?"

"Like I said, it's the real thing."

"What do you think it cost new?"

"Five, six bucks. I'll give it to you for thirty. That's what I charge Ron Harrison in West Hollywood. He marks them up a hundred percent." She smiled. "Just slip it on over your blouse. See what you think."

Cindy slipped on the shirt. "It's a little big."

"They're supposed to be big."

"I look like a Mafia moll trying to hide a gun."

"We get them, too." The woman smiled. "Okay, I'll go to twenty-five. I paid twenty for it. Surely you wouldn't begrudge me five bucks."

"You're talking me into it," Cindy stated. "I don't need it."

"Need is completely different from want. Do you want it?"

"I wouldn't mind."

"Buy it. You won't be sorry."

Cindy threw up her hands, then handed her back the shirt. "Just call me sucker. I'll take it."

"It looks good on you. And if you do change your mind, just bring it into Ron Harrison. Tell him Elaine sent you."

"I'll keep that in mind."

"You want some cappuccino or an espresso? I've got a machine in the back."

"I'm fine—"

"I'm fixing one for myself."

"Okay, I'll take a cappuccino."

"Come in the back then."

Cindy followed Elaine into the back of the store. The machine was squeezed between old appliances, specifically iceboxes. "People still use these things?"

"Nah, strictly for decoration—even though most of them do work. We get a lot of L.A. designers in here looking for odds and ends."

"Really?"

"Yeah, really. You sound surprised. Why would they pay fifty percent more to shop in a fancified store when they can get the same thing here if they sniff around a bit? We really have some treasures in here."

"Who's we?"

"Pardon?"

"You said we," Cindy replied. "Do you own the place?"

"Me and my friend."

"Oh."

"What's with the 'oh'?" Elaine challenged. "You have something against lesbians?"

"Not at all." Cindy groped for the right words. "It's just that I didn't expect to see any gays in a town this small."

"We've got a lot of gays here in Belfleur."

"Yeah?"

"Yeah. Mostly lesbians. We've also got a few older queers. You have antiques, you have gays. Stereotypes aren't based on fiction, you know." She took a carton of milk out of one of the old iceboxes and began to steam it. "What's your name?"

"Cindy."

"So, Cindy. What brings you specifically to Belfleur?"

"Actually, I'm sort of hunting around for information."

Elaine stopped steaming and faced her. "You're no student."

"I'm a student of life."

"That's as corny as Fritos. What kind of information are you seeking?"

"That's the big question."

"It's the big one for me," Elaine said. "It shouldn't be for you. You should know what you want."

Cindy decided on honesty. "About a year ago, there was a big carjacking murder in Los Angeles—"

"Armand Crayton."

"You knew him."

"Of course. Everyone knew Armand. Now, he must have bought a dozen Hawaiian shirts from me." Elaine paused. "I wonder if the widow still has them?"

"What did you think of him?"

Elaine handed her the cappuccino. "What are you? Like a private eye or something?"

"A cop," Cindy said. "But I'll still take the shirt and the cup and saucer. Tell me about Armand Crayton."

"A real operator in every sense of the word. First, he tried the sexual allure. When I didn't bite for obvious reasons, he tried the business angle, but that didn't work either. But he must have charmed his way into the hearts of more than a few suckers. I know for a fact that dozens of people had bought into his schemes. Most of them were not from around here, I'll tell you that much."

"Bought into what? A land development of some sort?"

"It was supposed to be a resort with private condos as well as rentals. Desert Bloom Estates. They had a whole mock-up of the place sitting in Armand's office—"

"Armand had an office here?"

"For a while, yeah, he had an office. Just for the locals, to show us that he had *plans* so we wouldn't think he was a total con man. Of course it was horse manure, but the model was nice. It was complete with buildings and little pieces of blue cellophane for the pools. And there were these tiny little trees and cacti landscaping. Some of the units even showed furniture. You know the dated pink and green Southwest stuff. But I guess the investors weren't exactly the sophisticated type. They marketed Belfleur as an upscale Palm Springs with the desert warmth but without the extreme heat. We have the change of seasons as you go deeper into San Berdoo, near where all the orchards are. It's real woody up there. Course it gets cold up there, too. That's why we can grow cherries and apples. We get a real chill during the winter. You pass any of the cherry trees?"

"No."

"Keep going northeast into the mountains. It's going to be a good fruit crop. Come back in June. We've got U-pick, U-haul farms. Cherries for a fraction of what you pay in the market."

"You own a cherry orchard, too?"

Elaine smiled. "Now that would be very enterprising of me. But no, I don't have any cherry trees."

"How about Armand? Was he interested in cherries?"

"Only the human, virgin kind." Elaine laughed at her own joke.

"That sounds like Armand."

"You knew him?"

"Not well. But you didn't have to know Armand well to realize what he was after."

"True, true, and too true."

"So Armand wanted to turn the area into a desert resort."

"See, *that's* what the problem was," Elaine explained. "Belfleur isn't hot enough year round to be a desert spa. And it isn't cold enough to be a ski resort. Plus, I'm betting when word got around and people realized they hadn't invested in any Garden of Eden, they backpedaled. Most of his investors were out-of-towners looking to make a fast buck. It never works that way."

"You're right about that," Cindy agreed. "Do you know how much the plots originally cost?"

Elaine sipped her cappuccino, receiving a milk mustache in the process. She licked it off with the tip of her tongue. "You know, you should be talking to Ray. He's not only a genuine old-timer, but he was more involved with Armand than I certainly was. He's the town Realtor." Elaine faced the front of the store. "Go east on Main, past the trailer park, past the big Wal-Mart shopping center with the Taco Bell and the Starbucks, almost to the end of Belfleur. The town merges into Haciendaville. If you reached Haciendaville, you went too far. His place is on the left side."

"His office is open today?"

"His office?" Elaine smiled. "That's funny . . . his office. Anyway, he's always there except Sunday morning when he's at church. Ray's straight, a rabid Republican, and a Baptist to boot. But don't be put off. Despite all that, he's a good guy."

❑

IT WAS a tiny storefront with filmy windows that usually accompanied places boarded up for good. The gold lettering on the glass said RAYMOND HARP. Underneath the name was the word REALTOR. Cindy opened the glass door and went inside. A man was slouched in an oversized chair with his feet propped up on a bridge table, its plastic top made up to look like simulated wood. He was smoking a cigar. He wore a white suit and a Panama hat, and sported a white beard. He had a round face, pale skin, and very dark eyes. He was typecast for the elderly plantation gentleman, or the old corrupt Southern judge. And Cindy wasn't far off. When he asked—without moving—if she needed help, she detected a slight drawl. But it was more Texas than Deep South.

"My name is Cindy Decker. Are you Mr. Harp?"

"Pleased to meet you, Cindy Decker." The man tipped his hat. "And no, I'm not Mr. Harp. I'm Mr. Harp*er,* if you must know. The E and R got scratched off the window ages ago. Never bothered to put 'em back up since everyone in town knows who I am."

Cindy nodded and attempted to give him a friendly smile as she looked around. The file cabinet was ancient with papers sticking out even though the drawers were closed. The soda machine was vintage quality and probably worth more than anything Elaine had in her antiques shop. "So you are Raymond Harper, then."

"Achully I'm *Elgin* Harper. Ray was my brother, and he moved out twenty-five years ago. Never bothered to correct that, either. Lots of people call me Ray. But if you're asking my true Christian name, it's Elgin Harper." He smiled, showing brown teeth, then blew a smoke ring. "Now what can I do for you, Cindy Decker?"

"I'm thinking about buying a weekend escape. I heard that prices are cheaper here than in Palm Springs."

There was a pause. Then Harper said, "You're talking about a second home *here*?" He swung his feet off the desk. "And just *what* do you intend to do with a house here?"

"Just relax." Cindy kept at it. "Maybe drive into the mountains and do some hiking. Also, since it's close to Palm Springs, I can drive into the city when I want a little more action."

Harper eyed her. "Are you a hooker?"

Cindy burst into laughter. "No, sir, I am not a hooker."

Harper didn't answer.

"I'm *not* a hooker," Cindy reiterated. "Honest."

"Then what do you do?"

"Why are you so curious?" Cindy asked.

"Because a pretty lady comes in here asking for a retreat. A lady who wears slacks instead of jeans and a fancy sweater that shows off a healthy chest, excuse

my impertinence. Listen, you want to ply your trade,
I won't object. I could give you a slew of referrals.
Heck, being a red-blooded Republican male, I may
even come to you myself. But I still go to church.
That means I'm not gonna sell to you and get in
trouble with the locals. Not that we're too overly
Christian. You see all the antiques stores we got?"

"I met Elaine."

"She's one of many. Hell, we got more queens in
this here city than in Europe. But we don't want
any of your type bringing in imported trash. We
got enough with our own local trash. You want
customers, try the reservations for that kind of
shenanigans."

"I am not a hooker."

"Well, maybe not. But you're not being truthful.
What *do* you want?"

Cindy glanced around. "You've been here a long
time, haven't you, Ray? Or is it Elgin?"

"It's whatever you want to call me, honey." He
started laughing. It turned into a hacking cough.
"And yes, I've been here a while. Hey, I bet you're
a bondsman. Who skipped bail this time?"

"I'm not a bondsman. I'm not even a
bondswoman."

"Well, you're some kind of person looking for information. You're packing." He pointed to her
bag. "I can see the piece dragging down at the bottom of your bag. If you're going to rob me, go
away. Only money here is in the soda machine."

Harper stood up. His protruding belly fell over his belt and hung down, nearly hiding his genitals. He put his hands on his hips and took a step forward. "So what do you want, young lady?"

"Okay," Cindy said. "This is the deal, Mr. Harper. I'll tell you what I know about Armand Crayton and you fill in the rest."

"What's in it for me, Cindy Decker?"

"Who knows? Maybe by talking, we can figure out who murdered Crayton."

"And why would I care about that?"

"You didn't like Armand?"

"As a matter of fact, I found him an agreeable young lad. But if you're asking who killed him, I'll tell you there's a long list of candidates. Armand disappointed quite a few people."

"Tell me about them," Cindy persisted.

Harper blew another smoke ring. "I think I'm gonna sit down again. This may take a while. You might want to pull up a chair yourself." He held up his cigar. "This bothering you?"

"No, not at all. I love the smell of a cheap cigar. It reminds me of back alley gambling and barroom brawls."

"Now there's a thought." Harper sank into his chair and put his feet back up. "You wanna make up some coffee?"

"I suppose I can do that." She searched around the room. "Where's the coffeepot?"

"In the john, right next to the toilet paper."

"Lovely."

"No, it ain't the Ritz, thank you very much."

Cindy went inside the bathroom. It was small, but surprisingly spotless. Even the grout that held together the white tile floor was clean. The machine rested on a shelf, along with the coffee, its accoutrements, and three mugs. She poured the water into the apparatus and waited for it to gurgle. As the coffee brewed, she tried to formulate her questions. But there were so many of them, she gave up.

A few minutes later she walked back into the office—so to speak—and handed him a fresh cup. "What do you take?"

"Three packets of powder, three lumps of sugar."

She took the cup from him and prepared it to his liking.

Harper said, "I could get into this. A beautiful woman fixing coffee for me." A fraction of a wait, then he said, "*Any* woman fixing coffee for me."

"I bet you do okay in the woman department." She pulled up a chair. "That ah-shucks demeanor. Gets 'em every time. Now . . ." She sipped her coffee. "What can you tell me about Armand and Desert Bloom Estates?"

"The gentleman almost pulled it off. Quite a feat, Cindy, because this land doesn't have a whole bunch of natural resources to sell it. Yet, Armand approached the land like it had been kissed by King Midas of Crete. Man, that boy could talk a good case. And he was nice to the locals, though everyone knew it was with self-serving interest. Still, he was polite. I'll give him that much."

"Who were his investors?"

"I'd say fools, but that would be harsh. You've got to remember, Cindy, that the stock market was booming with everything e-this or e-that. People were throwing capital into companies that had never turned a profit. Guess Armand figured he might as well ride *that* wave. Housing was booming, and empty land was at a premium—if you lived in Silicon Valley or Seattle that is. What's the first thing they teach you in real estate buying school—location, location, location. Well, here in Belfleur, hi-tech means a calculator. Doesn't take a genius to figure that one out. What can I tell you? Belfleur didn't really participate in the boom."

Harper stubbed out his cigar and took a swig of his coffee.

"Sure we had a few Hollywood types with their ponytails and second wives that got it in their heads to be gentlemen farmers and bought some fruit orchards, but that was about it. All that was true until Crayton came along. But, you see, Armand wasn't in the real estate business. He was in the dream business. He sold dreams to anyone willing to believe them."

He arched his hand across the air, making an imaginary banner.

"Desert Bloom Estates. All you ever wanted in a dream getaway. Pools and sauna and gyms and massages and mud baths and salt rubs. The place to come when you want to be pampered. And who doesn't want to be pampered. Heck, I get excited when a pretty young lady makes me coffee." He winked at her. "Real excited."

"You're getting red in the face, Mr. Harper. Just what is your blood pressure?"

"I don't know 'cause it's rising by the minute."

"Just watch yourself," Cindy admonished. "My CPR skills are rusty."

"It may be worth it."

"Who actually owned the Desert Bloom land?"

"That would be Armand."

"So he actually was selling land that he owned."

"Well, I suppose technically the bank owned it. But Armand had the deeds. Mr. Crayton owned the plots, and more important, the rights to develop them."

"Who were Armand's clientele?"

"Lots of working-class stiffs from Los Angeles. And for a while it looked like Armand was going to pull it off. The locals were ecstatic."

"Did any of the locals buy in?"

"Most didn't. Don't think they fully trusted Armand and they turned out to be right. But that was neither here nor there. A development like Desert Bloom could completely revitalize the town. City planning commission couldn't wait to approve the plans. This was what everyone was waiting for. They, like the rest of us, could almost taste that influx of fresh greenery. And it was promising for a while. Armand had down-payment money and everything. How do I know? Because Crayton had his business accounts banked locally. And there was money in the account. Real money. We all thought that the project looked like a go."

"So what happened?"

"Guess you don't follow the market much."

"I would if I had money."

"Touché," Harper said. "I know that situation. Well, Cindy, what happened is that the market dipped . . . a big dip."

"Armand pulled out," Cindy said.

"No, he didn't pull out. But his partner did, the actual man with the money to develop. When the plug was pulled by Dex, everything fell through."

"Dex being Dexter Bartholomew," Cindy said.

Harper regarded her. "Yep, you've done your homework. The good old boy from Oklahoma had us all going for a while. But then . . ." He snapped his fingers. "Gone. He suddenly refused to develop Desert Bloom, claiming that Armand didn't have enough initial buyers to develop a project of such magnitude. Hell, he needed way more money just to get started. You know, to run the utility lines— the water, the sewage, the electricity, the phone lines, though God knows there were plenty of phone lines already set up. But everyone here knew what the real story was. Dex took a beating in the market and didn't have the play money anymore."

"But Armand had banked the down-payment money."

"Yes, ma'am, he did."

"So he refunded his investors."

"No, ma'am, he didn't. I said he banked the money. I never did say the money stayed in the bank permanently."

"He spent it."

"Yes, he did. Not on wine, women, and song—although I'm sure that was part of it. Mostly, he spent it to acquire more land to make the development even bigger. When the bust hit, and Dex pulled out, Armand was left with a slew of angry investors."

"Any particular irate citizen come to mind?"

"Nope." Harper sighed. "It was very pi-tee-ful. Dex left Crayton with worthless land and a lot of explaining to do. In the end, he was forced to declare bankruptcy. The bank took back the land that Armand owned, and the dream vanished. Now the people who had already bought plots, course they still owned the land. But now it was worthless. There was a class action suit, but nothing ever came of it because Crayton didn't have anything. Of course, that didn't stop him from living in a fancy house or driving a fancy car. Which really tweaked a few noses."

"Never let them see you sweat, Mr. Harper."

"Mebbe, though it wouldn't have hurt to be a little more sensitive to the situation."

Cindy drank her coffee, remembering Crayton. He was a man of flash and dreams, as insubstantial as a Hollywood pitch line. She said, "You know, the rumor was that Bartholomew actually made money off Armand. But it sure doesn't sound like that was the case."

Harper chuckled. "Don't cry for Dex. Once Armand went broke, Dex—as a gentleman's courtesy to those unfortunate souls who went bust—offered to buy back the land. His largesse was tempered by the fact that he offered deep discount prices. Still, twenty percent on the dollar is better than zero. Dex did just fine."

"How's that if the land's worthless?"

"Worthless as a housing development, but not worthless as land. Lots of stone underneath here, Cindy Decker. Good, solid stone. But you need capital to quarry it up. Lucky for Dex that he had capital from his oil pipe business. If you keep going northeast, you'll run into the pits. Now we Belfleurians are a forgiving type, so we don't hold it against him. Also, he's created more than a few local jobs. Dex is doing just fine, thank you very much."

"And everybody sold out to him?"

"Almost." Harper broke into a big smile. "See, I

don't believe in selling land at a deep discount if it's my money. I'd rather sit on it."

"You were an initial buyer in Desert Bloom Estates, Mr. Harper?"

Harper hung his head in mock shame. "I regretfully admit that I got caught up in the frenzy. Sometimes I think that I'm just a crazy old fool."

Crazy like a fox, Cindy thought. "You don't seem so upset by it."

"I'm not. And it turned out to be a good thing. Because my little plot actually bisects key parts of Dex's quarry. Makes it very hard for him to get from point A to point B without trespassing on it."

"He's offered you a premium price for it, then."

"Many times, Cindy, many times. But I don't believe in gouging the man. Instead, I just charge him a *tiny* bit of money every time he crosses my land."

"Just a tiny bit."

"A tiny, tiny bit," Harper said.

"How many times does he cross your land a day?"

" 'Bout two hundred." Harper burped. "Those tiny bits do add up."

"Aren't the others resentful?"

"Mebbe a few. More are impressed with my real estate savvy." He took his feet off the table. "Are you impressed?"

"Yes, I am." Cindy looked at the ceiling, then

said, "You wouldn't, by any chance, have a list of Crayton's investors . . . would you?"

"If I had a list, that would be a confidential thing, young lady."

Cindy looked at Harper, but said nothing.

Harper said, "Course we could negotiate a price." His smile widened. "And it doesn't have to be money."

Cindy said, "What do you have in mind?"

"I could relax my impeccable standards for . . . say, a quick blow-job."

Cindy pulled out her badge. "You've just solicited a police officer."

Harper's grin remained in place, but it lost its wolfish leer. "Ah, you can do better than that, Cindy Decker. We both know you have no authority here."

"I could still make trouble for you, Elgin."

"Nah, you don't understand the system." Harper got up. "I got *friends* in the department."

Cindy supposed that was true enough. She moved in close, then gave him a peck on the cheek. She whispered, "Please?"

"Give me tongue and we might have a deal."

"Elgin, I wouldn't want to be responsible for your infarct." She beamed. "Be a love and help me."

Harper sneered. "I suppose it won't create much of a problem if you take a quick peek at it here in the office."

"Thank you, sir."

"We're back to 'sir,' are we? I liked it better when you called me Elgin. You know why I'm doing this for you? You didn't wrinkle your nose at my cigar. City folks can stuff pounds of cocaine up their noses, but a little tobacco smoke riles them into hysteria. You're okay, Cindy Decker. You know how to work people."

"Why thank you, Elgin. It was very kind of you to say that."

Harper yanked out a drawer from his ancient file cabinet. It squeaked when it opened. "I'll have to get organized one day."

"What for?" Cindy asked. "You seem to know your way around your paperwork."

"More or less." Harper rooted through sheaves of multicolored papers—yellow, pink, white, blue-lined paper, graph paper, *newspaper*. It was a total mess. But a minute later, victory was his. "Here we go." He handed her the list, and looked at his wall clock. "I'll give you thirty seconds, young lady. Fair enough?"

"Fair enough, Elgin." Cindy gave the list a quick once-over. She didn't even need the thirty seconds. Since the names were in alphabetical order, Richard Bederman was placed almost at the top.

32

HAVING THE information but not knowing what to do with it. Yes, Rick Bederman had been one of the investors from the ill-fated Desert Bloom Estates, but Cindy had nothing to connect him to any crime. And why would Bederman, more than anyone else on the list, enact revenge on Crayton and Bartholomew? Lastly, what, if anything, did that have to do with her recent problems?

It was after seven, dark by the time she got home. She pulled into her outdoor parking space and checked her rearview mirror before she unlocked the door. All was quiet. She quickly got out of the car and climbed up the two flights of stairs to her unit. But before she went inside, she checked the bottom of her door. She had strung a tress of her hair from the edge of the door to the frame. It was still there and that was encouraging. Unlocking the door, she stepped into the living room, then bolted the lock. To her delight, the place was undisturbed. Even the magazine she had left on the coffee table was still open to the same page—a Lexus advertisement. Things were looking up.

She put on a pot of decaf and checked her phone messages. The longest one was from Mom telling her how much she'd enjoyed dinner and would like to do it again when Cindy *had more time* to stay and chat awhile. That was okay. Mom's complaints were normal, and normal was good. There were other communications including two from Scott (*Hi, how are you? Are you okay? Things are going well. Call.*), two from Dad (*Just tell me you're okay!*), and one from Hayley Marx (*Call when you a get a minute.*). There had also been several hang-ups. Under ordinary circumstances, she wouldn't have given them a second thought, but the events of the past week had magnified every seemingly potential threat.

What she should have done was return the calls to assure everyone that she was okay. But she was entirely spent, most of the fatigue coming from a lack of nutrition. The doughnut from the Belfleur coffee shop had done little to tide her over. Perhaps after dinner she'd have more energy to make chitchat.

She made a sliced smoked turkey sandwich with tomato and lettuce, smearing on generous amounts of mustard and mayo. Putting down the place mat, she set up a table for one, tucking the napkin under the flatware. She swiped the countertop while the espresso bean blend was brewing away, leaking its heavenly aroma. When the coffee was ready, she sat down for a solo dinner. She was becoming a regular domestic animal, and this made her happy. Just last week, she was feeling sorry for

herself. Now she was thrilled with the privacy and
the ordinariness of the situation: eating dinner
unmolested.

She was ravenous, each bite awakening her taste
buds. She forced herself to eat slowly, to savor the
moment. After she was done, she wiped her
mouth, cleared the dishes, and then treated herself
to a glass of white wine for dessert—an imported
Vouvray given to her by an old high school friend
after she graduated from the academy. It was
lemony and light. As she sipped her drink, she
washed her dish, her cup, her fork and knife. When
she had finished with supper, she took out a piece
of paper and a pencil, then sat down at the table,
and began making diagrams—the who, what,
and where.

No matter how she mutated the possibilities, she
kept coming back to the same obvious conclusion:
After Bederman got burned, he kidnapped and
killed Crayton for revenge, and carjacked Dex's
wife to pawn her Ferrari and recover some of his
lost money from the Desert Bloom project. What
would make a person go to such extremes?

Theory A: Bederman invested all his money with
Crayton and was now broke. He needed cash to
survive.

Rebuttal: If Bederman was going to resort to
crime to solve his financial problems, there were
ways for a cop to get instant money—lean on a
dealer or a pimp or, like Scott said, just skim a cou-

ple of ounces from the supply room. Far easier methods than kidnapping a prominent citizen's wife for ransom. But maybe because of the scandals, lots of cops were looking over their shoulders. Maybe the supply room wasn't an option anymore.

Theory B: He not only wanted the money, he wanted to teach Crayton and Dexter Bartholomew a lesson.

Rebuttal: Murder is one hell of a lesson, not to mention tricky business. Especially knocking off someone like Crayton. Armand's life and finances were bound to be scrutinized, meaning the Desert Bloom fiasco would come out. But, then again, just *how much* would really come out? Because here she was—a novice—finding out things that the original teams hadn't. True, it could be that at the time of Crayton's murder, the people in Belfleur hadn't been so forthcoming. Perhaps they had been so overwhelmed or scared by the killing that they had hidden, forgotten, or repressed crucial information. Certainly, Cindy couldn't picture Elgin Harper just handing over the list of investors. She had gone in a year after the murder. By then, people felt safer talking.

But since there was no statute of limitations on murder, the killer could always be brought to justice. The killer would always be fair game. Bederman would know that. Would he be willing to take that big a risk, seeking revenge while knowing he could be hauled in at any moment?

Theory C: Bederman wanted the money, wanted to teach Crayton and Dex a lesson, *and* he didn't care about the risk. Again, her thoughts kept coming back to all the recent scandals. The phony setups with cops thinking they're above the law because they put their asses on the line every night. So what if they pick up a little drug money, or grab a little hooker pussy, or pocket a little graft to look the other way *just this one time.*

Bederman could have been one of those. And maybe he had thought he beat the system, because the crime was still unsolved an entire year later. But there was a kicker. None of the big-time spender schtick seemed to apply to Bederman. So far as *she* knew, he hadn't been taking any expensive vacations, or bought any designer duds, or leased any fancy cars. His idea of recreation was drinking at cop bars after work or Sunday barbecues, watching the game with the guys. As for mistresses, Bederman didn't need money to get a woman on the side. There was a subspecies of the feminine sex who gravitated toward anything in power and/or in a uniform.

She doodled on her paper, making swirls and whirls, doing her name in bubble letters. She felt like a kid struggling to write an in-class essay.

Did Bederman have a woman on the side? Was that why he changed to the night shift? Lark had mentioned an ace in the hole. Scott felt that Bederman was as good a candidate as any.

She needed help in sorting out the information. She needed Scott or Marge or Dad. They'd know what to do with the data. But that would mean explaining to them how she *got* all this information. Not that she did anything illegal, but she was still uncomfortable about it. She was supposed to be working as a uniform cop, not as a detective.

The flip side was that Crayton was *Dad's* unsolved case. She'd be doing him a big favor, giving him the information, not to mention the possibility of reeling in a dirty cop.

The door knocker interrupted her thoughts, the loud thumping making her jump. She sprang up, and peered through the peephole, shocked to be looking at Rick Bederman's face. Panic swelled in her body as she gave him a curt "Just a minute."

Had he followed her home?

No, she was *sure* he hadn't. She'd checked. She'd *checked*!

Quickly, she picked up her notes and stuffed them into the kitchen drawer. Then she took out her gun, gripping it tightly in her hand. She forced herself to inhale, then exhale slowly. She did unlatch the bolt, but kept the chain on when she opened the door.

"What do you want?"

Bederman seemed annoyed. "Uh, can I come in, please?"

Instantly, Cindy sized up her options, deciding that fear not only lowered her Q as a cop, but also immediately stamped her with a big V for victim. She couldn't allow him to see her as a victim. She took off the chain and swung open the door, trying to appear peeved but casual at the same time. "What are you doing here?"

Bederman's eyes fell to her gun. "Planning on shooting someone?"

"Hope not." She stepped away from the threshold. "Come in."

Bederman walked into her living room, his eyes still on her revolver. Finally, he glanced around, his gaze settling on a lone spring poking out of her sofa cushion. "I think you need new furniture."

"My furniture was fine until someone vandalized my apartment this weekend."

Bederman's eyes widened. "You're kidding!"

"No, I'm not. Have a seat."

"Is that why you're holding your piece?"

"Probably. At the moment, I'm not a trusting person."

"You opened the door for me."

"Any reason why I shouldn't?"

Bederman smiled. He wore a tweed jacket over a white shirt and jeans. Cowboy boots on his feet. "Take it easy. You sound very uptight."

"I call it businesslike. What can I do for you, Officer Bederman? You're still welcome to sit down, you know."

Bederman stalled, then finally sat down on one of her chairs. More like sank into it. He placed his hands underneath his neck, and spread his legs wide open. Like he expected a blow-job. But his face was tense. "I didn't come here to make time with you."

Silence. Cindy waited for the explanation.

"Actually, I came here because I wanted to . . . you know, dispose you of that idea."

Dispel, Cindy thought. Or maybe he did want to dispose her. She remained silent.

Bederman leaned forward, elbows on his knees. "I'm a confident person. I come on strong. Too strong, some say." He unbuttoned his jacket, showing her his filled holster. "I was talking to Graham this afternoon—"

"At your barbecue?"

"Yeah, how'd you . . . oh, you heard me and Tim talking last night."

Cindy nodded.

"Yeah, it was at the barbecue. Graham was there. I somehow got to telling him about what I told you . . . about Hayley Marx making mistakes . . . and that you shouldn't make those mistakes." He scratched his nose. "Graham told me that what I said . . . it could leave you with the wrong impression."

"Meaning?"

Bederman gnashed his teeth, causing his cheeks to bulge. "Meaning that I got a solid marriage and I want to keep it that way. I don't want any rumors that could be of the nasty kind."

"Most rumors are nasty."

"Yeah. Right. Anyway, I'd like it if you'd just forget about what I said. I'm the first to admit that it wasn't very smart of me to talk like that."

"Far as I'm concerned, it's forgotten."

Bederman fidgeted. "All right. Good. Forgotten. Not that I think I did anything wrong . . . just that I don't want you to get the wrong impression."

No one spoke for a moment. Then Cindy stood up. "I know what you mean. You can go now. Mission accomplished."

Slowly, Bederman got to his feet. "You don't like me, do you?"

"Bederman, I don't know you well enough to dislike you. And right now, I'm distrustful. Do you blame me?"

"Nope." Bederman buttoned his jacket. "You don't think *I* did anything, do you?"

Cindy's lie was smooth. "Why in the world would I think *you'd* be responsible for trashing my apartment?"

"Just that you're still holding the gun."

She looked at her piece. "Figured I might as well clean it. Nothing better to do."

"Well, I'd better be getting back." But he didn't move. "Any ideas about the perp?"

"Some."

"You want to talk about it? I might be able to

help. I've been at this kind of thing much longer than you have."

Establishing his superiority. If she rejected him, he'd take it personally. *Change the subject, idiot!* "Who won, by the way?"

Bederman made a face. "What are you talking about?"

"The game. Weren't you guys watching the Sunday Dodgers' game?"

"Yeah, we were. The Dodgers won. Why are you asking? You got money riding on it?"

"Wish I did because the spread would have been great. I can't believe they actually won. They must have had an enormous lead because they always blow their lead."

"They were ahead six-nothing until McGwire hammered a bases loaded into right field at the bottom of the seventh. Then they put in this new kid from the bullpen. Maybe they brought him up . . . I don't know, a month ago from Albuquerque. Somehow, he managed to stall the opposition for the last two innings. Not that they didn't get hits off of him. Just no runs."

"Amazing."

Bederman smiled. "You like baseball, Decker?"

"I take an interest in all the sports. It helps me keep up with the guys."

"That's important to you?" Bederman's eyes held her straight on. "To keep up with the guys?"

Cindy kept her gaze steady. "I like to get along, Rick. Just ask Graham. You two are still real tight even after your breakup. That's not the usual. Know what it tells me? That you like to get along, too."

"Sure I like to get along. But believe me, I can hold my ground. You don't want to mess with me, ever."

A veiled threat or was it just posturing? "I'll keep that in mind."

"Do that."

"Okay. See you later, then."

But Bederman made no attempt to move. "See, with Graham, it was nothing personal. That's why we still get along. It was nothing personal."

"Good to hear—"

"It was no big deal, Cindy. My wife was working a demanding job with early hours, and I decided that I should be there in the morning for the kids. So I transferred to Night Watch. That way I could help while my wife was at work. You know, make 'em breakfast, take 'em to school. Kids have to have a father, too, you know."

"I know. I adore my dad."

Bederman stiffened. "That's right. Your dad is a detective—lieutenant, right?"

Cindy nodded. *As if he hadn't known.*

"Must be nice."

"It doesn't affect me, Bederman. I still get my fair share of shit. When did you sleep?"

"What?"

"Doing the watch, helping the kids in the day," Cindy said. "You must have been working pretty hard. Did you ever sleep?"

"Yeah, sure. During the day when the kids were in school, I slept then. It was tough, though. Eventually, my wife quit the job for something less . . . demanding. I went back to days as soon as I could."

"That must have been a relief."

"It was. But that's off the original point. I just wanted to tell you that the breakup was nothing personal. He's a good guy and a good partner."

She smiled and stood. "You're right."

Bederman smiled back—a big, toothy smile. Cindy could tell that he liked being right. Slowly, he stood up, then ambled his way out. She was thrilled to lock the door behind him.

❑

"He hasn't gotten back from Oxnard yet," Rina said. "I'll tell him you called. He'll be very grateful. You know how he worries."

"I know." Cindy shifted the phone to her other ear. "So you don't have any idea when he's coming home?"

"No, but it's probably going to be late. It's going very well. And when it goes well, it means long hours." Rina paused. "Cindy, you sound like you need something. Are you in trouble?"

"Not at all—"

"But you're bothered by something specific," Rina said. "Why don't you just call him on his cell. I know he wouldn't mind."

"Nah, it's not important enough to interrupt his business. I know they've all been waiting a long time for a break in the jackings. I just wanted to go over some ideas, but it'll keep."

"Honey, you're welcome to come over and wait. After what we have both gone through, we could use a little company."

Cindy felt her face go hot. She had been so wrapped up in her affairs, she had completely forgotten about Rina's woes. Quickly, she asked, "How are you doing? How is Hannah doing? Do you want me to come over there and help out with her?"

"Hannah's asleep, *boruch Hashem*. Whether or not she stays asleep is a different story."

Cindy sighed. "How about if I swing by in an hour—around ten. Would that be too late?"

"Not at all. I'll see you then."

"Bye."

"Cindy?"

"Yeah?"

"Be careful, please. And bring your gun."

❏

CINDY stopped before she closed her apartment door. From the passageway, she could see the street. She looked over each car, and decided she recognized them all. The VW Bug belonged to the girl with the long dark hair who played salsa music. The Taurus belonged to the couple who argued over money and lived in an apartment across the street. The Mitsubishi four-wheel drive was owned by Greig, a set designer for the Ahmanson.

She shut the door and bolted it. Gun in hand, she descended the stairway, speed-walked to her car, got in, then locked up with the simple click of a button. She started the motor, checked her gas gauge—full—and backed out of her space, checking the rearview and side mirrors. She threw the gear into drive and zoomed away.

The streets were quiet, which made it easy for her to spot any tail. Nothing jumped out. She got on the freeway, and pressed the pedal to the metal until she was going at a good, fast clip. Twenty minutes into her drive, the engine started to whine. Moments later it began to sputter and her car started decelerating even though her gas gauge still read full. Heart beating wildly, she depressed the gas pedal, but that didn't do anything. The car was definitely slowing. *If* she didn't get over to the right soon, she'd be stuck in the middle lane of the freeway with cars, trucks, semis, and other heavy vehicles whizzing by her in every direction, not to mention the possibility of a fatal rear-end collision. It was dark, and travelers didn't expect lanes being blocked by stalled cars.

Think!

Trying to keep a grip on her runaway panic, she managed to maneuver her Saturn on to the right shoulder. A moment later, it coughed and died. All she could hear was her own shallow breathing. She blew on her hands while she looked in her rearview mirror, keeping that position for a few minutes. No one appeared to be stopping, which was a sad commentary on Los Angeles, but very good because it appeared that nobody had been following her.

She knew she had to do something. And she would. But first, she just wanted to rid herself of the tension, the awful feeling of being set up. Rooting through her purse, she found the number for Triple A in her address computer, then dialed out on her cellular.

It told her the system was busy.

Her breathing quickened.

Again she dialed out.

Again the system was busy.

She went into the back of her phone, played with the battery, and tried again.

The steady beep, beep, beep told her that either her number had been cloned or somebody had tampered with the phone itself. Either was very disconcerting.

Instantaneously, her chest tightened. Yelling at herself because the panic had to stop. She was a damn officer of the law. She had to do better than this. She felt around her purse for her gun. At least, she knew *that* was working.

A pair of bright lights grew in her rearview mirror, filling up the reflective space. She turned around, saw the car slowing behind her . . . slow, slow, slow until it parked around twenty feet away. But it wasn't just any car. It was . . . *highway patrol*!

Yes!

Never had that CHP emblem looked so cool.

Cindy looked down at her right hand gripped around the butt of her service revolver. It wouldn't be cool for him to see her holding a gun. It might give him the wrong impression. She put the gun back, but took out her ID and badge. She slid over the console and got out on the passenger's side, walking a few feet until his face came into view.

At first, she thought she was imagining things, but she knew she wasn't. The agitation she felt was both horrific and overwhelming. It made her head go light and her knees shake. She willed herself to stand erect, because her other thoughts were either to run or to faint—untenable options because he had a shotgun. He was carrying it so that the length was nestled against his arm, and the barrel was pointing down. But that position could change in an eye blink.

Play dumb!

Which wasn't hard. She *was* dumb!

Did he follow her or had he been waiting outside her apartment all this time?

But she would have noticed a highway patrol car—

"Having car problems, Decker?" he said. "Maybe I can help."

His voice broke into her terrified thoughts.

"Have you always moonlighted for the highway patrol?" she asked. "The uniform looks swell on you."

He slowly raised his outstretched arm, like a Nazi about to give a Heil Hitler, but stopped short with the barrel of the gun aimed at her stomach. "If you want to live a little longer, you should shut up. And don't do anything silly. Things like running or screaming or trying to hotdog it in a one-on-one. Because my trigger finger's twitching, and I'll cut you down as easily as I'll cut a fart. You get it?"

"Got it."

"Who knows, Decker? Maybe with those fancy words of yours, you can talk me down." He smiled. Cindy could make out the teeth in the moonlight. He said, "You're a clever gal. What do you think?"

"I'm going to give it a try."

"C'mon." He waved the gun from left to right, then lowered it. But the barrel was still near her groin. She had heard that stomach wounds were very painful—excruciatingly painful. But death was worse.

He was talking. ". . . going to take a little ride.

Just the two of us. We'll take my car. Gentleman always does the driving. Besides, maybe you've always wanted to see the inside of a highway patrol vehicle."

"Golly gee! Will you turn on the siren and flash the lights, too?"

"Always the wiseass." He was now glaring at her. "Let's see how funny you are when you're begging for mercy."

She thought about faking him out, telling him that she had phoned her dad and he was on the way. But maybe that would set him into a panic of rash reaction. Never panic someone holding a shotgun. She could feel his eyes boring in, her mind emptying of ideas and blanking out conscious thought. But Freud did have something with that little gizmo called the *unconscious*. Because seconds later, she found that she had leapt over the side railing, and was rolling like a ball down the embankment of the freeway. Hugging herself and praying . . . *where did that come from?*

One second, two seconds, three and four.

Fire exploded past her head. She screamed, pain stinging her scalp as buckshot grazed her cranium. She dove into brush and dropped onto her belly, creeping to a spot that afforded the best camouflage, trying to hide and escape at the same time. Blood was seeping from the side of her head. She touched the wound and winced, then inhaled deeply, trying to get air into her lungs. As she slithered along the solid ground, stones and rocks scraped her stomach.

She could hear him coming down, making his descent, the sounds of thick soles dragging loose earth. She needed to get away.

What do animals do when they're being hunted?

They run. *(That would make her visible.)*

They crawl and creep and hide. *(Crawling or creeping made noise.)*

They fight. *(He had a gun and outweighed her by seventy pounds of muscles and years of experience!)*

They play dead.

Go for it, kid!

She stopped in her tracks, trying to paralyze every muscle in her body. It was hard because her bladder and bowels weren't in great shape. Though she managed to hold still, she could still hear her own terrified breathing. Even with the cars racing by, it was audible. If she could hear it, maybe he could hear it, too. She opened her mouth, hoping not only to get in more oxygen but also to decrease the gasping breaths.

But his footsteps kept getting closer. Silently, she turned her head until his form, silhouetted by moonlight, became visible. He was scouting out the brush for her body, pulling back the limbs of the foliage, parting the bushy leaves and peering inside for her.

He was the hunter, she was prey. How long could it last? How long could *she* last?

If he found her, crouched like a wounded animal, she was as good as dead meat. She'd have to have a plan if he came upon her. Because she did have the element of surprise.

Her confused and addled thoughts pointed to two choices. Because it was unlikely that she could outrun him without being shot—he was noted as a terrific marksman—she figured she'd have to attack him directly or try to dislodge the gun from his grip. If she could disable him, it would be easier to dislodge the gun. But if she fell short of the mark, she'd be dead.

Gun or him? Gun or him?

Then she thought: *You don't have to make that decision now. Seize whatever meager opportunity he'll give you.*

He came closer and closer, his eyes running over the terrain, moving in on her. Parting the leaves with the barrel of the gun, which would mean that the barrel would be pointing at her face if he found her. Feet were always more deadly than arms.

Imagine yourself to be a kangaroo.

What's my motivation?

He's going to blow off your head if you don't succeed.

A foot away . . . then it came down to inches. Eleven, ten, nine . . .

She held her breath and silently positioned herself.

Eight inches, seven inches.

The leaves began to separate, letting in the moonlight.

She caught him hard between the legs. As he doubled over, she thrust her feet upward and pushed them into the cartilage of his nose. Instantly, it shot out blood. She bolted up, grabbed his arm as she had been taught at the academy, and gave it a solid twist, wrenching it with all her force. But he'd also gone to the academy. He'd been taught the same maneuvers. Despite his handicaps—a throbbing groin and a bleeding nose—he pulled from a bottomless reservoir of strength.

She should have made the break to freedom when she'd had the opportunity. Except that she didn't want that. She wanted to win! Under her force, she saw the gun slip from his grip. She was almost there. Then it was hand to hand. She was smaller, more agile. Without the gun, she had a chance.

But then he fooled her. His left hand had the audacity to reach around her neck, pulling her back tightly against his chest. She was forced to let go of his left hand, then tried to do the old flip she had learned from the academy.

He had also gone to the academy. He was prepared. And he was strong . . . so strong.

The light was fading.

So were the sounds.

I love you, Mom.

33

Decker gripped his cellular phone. *"How long ago did she call?"*

Rina stemmed her own anxiety to keep him calm. "She said she'd be here at around ten—"

"That was *an hour* ago! Did you call her?"

"Yes, of course. She's not answering her phones or her pager. Maybe she's going over the mountains. Sometimes the reception isn't so good."

But Decker wasn't hearing it. The fear was immediate and raw. "How *many* times have you tried to call her?"

"Around a half-dozen," Rina admitted.

"Good God!" He paced as he spoke. "I'm coming home. But first I'm going to call up Hollywood and ask them to send a cruiser by her house. Hopefully, it won't be driven by one of those assholes that have been giving her a hard time. Okay . . ." He was talking as much to himself as he was to Rina. "First we'll see if she's home. Next we'll see if her car's gone. If her car's gone, I'll put out a bulletin on it. Which means I'd better call CHP. To get to the house, she'd take the freeway."

"Do you want me to go out looking for her?"

"Absolutely not! You stay by the phone. God, what a nightmare!"

Rina closed her eyes. She didn't know what to say other than to agree with his assessment. Obviously, that certainly wouldn't be productive. "I'll call you immediately if something comes up—"

"She didn't say anything about what she wanted to talk to me about?"

"No, nothing."

"Not a hint?"

Rina hesitated, to weigh her words carefully. "Nothing specific. She did seem rather . . . enthusiastic over the phone. Like she found out something—"

"Oh, great! That's even more ominous! Her poking around stuff, pissing people off—"

"Peter, maybe I'm wrong—"

"You're never wrong! What made you use the word *enthusiastic*?"

"Maybe the correct word is preoccupied. She forgot to ask about Hannah's welfare until I mentioned the incident in passing. Then she got all concerned about how Hannah was doing. That's not her at all . . . to forget about her sister. You know how she feels about Hannah."

"Cindy hasn't been home all day! She's been nosing around something, and it caught up with her. God, how can someone so smart be so damn *stupid*!"

"Maybe she just got a flat tire."

"Right. And chickens have lips!" Decker cursed

under his breath. "Maybe Scott knows something. I've got to go."

"Peter, don't worry. It'll work out."

Decker wanted to believe her. He really wanted to believe her. He also wanted to believe that good was rewarded and evil was punished. But even the great prophet Moses wasn't privileged to know God's system of justice. Why should he, a mere mortal, be privy to the crazy way the world worked?

❑

THE car wasn't in her parking space, so it was logical that Cindy was still out. Ridiculous to try the apartment, but Hayley figured what the hell. Nothing better to do. Maybe Cindy had taken her car into the shop, and was driving a loaner. The Saturn was sure smoking pretty bad on Friday. It would make sense for Cindy to check it out. Hayley climbed up the two flights of steps, and knocked hard for several moments. Of course, no one answered.

So what? No big deal that she wasn't home.

But something prevented Hayley from turning around and going home. This itch . . . this pang in her stomach . . . like something from another sphere was talking to her. Telling her that something was wrong. So she took out a hairpin and tried to pick the lock. As soon as she realized it was a dead bolt, she stopped and gave up.

Now she definitely should have turned around and gone home. But the itch was growing stronger, propelling her to start in on the windows. They were locked: no big whoop about that. Someone had broken into her apartment, so Cindy was probably extra-diligent about locking her windows.

At that point, she would have surely turned around and gone home *if* she hadn't seen fresh scratches near the sills that made her feel downright jumpy. She pounded on the window, but that didn't accomplish anything except rattle the glass. No more options save two—go home or break the glass.

She exhaled out loud. Then she wrapped her jacket around her fist and gave it all she had, punching a jagged hole in the pane. She snaked her hand in, avoided a particularly lethal shard of glass, and somehow managed to unclick the lock with her padded fingertips. Up came the window and a moment later, Hayley was inside.

She called out Cindy's name, but no one responded. Scoping out the rooms, she found nothing lurking behind the shower curtain. Norman Bates had decided not to camp here today.

Now she felt doubly stupid: A. She was worried about a grown woman, a cop nonetheless, and B. she'd broken the window, which she'd probably have to pay for. And how would she explain it to Cindy, who was already looking at her like she was a little weird. Who could blame her? Cindy couldn't possibly understand what drove Hayley to break the window or tail that Camry. How could Hayley explain her unfailing intuition, stemming from that dreadful day when she had been stuck for three hours in the middle of Joshua Tree National Park in blistering desert heat because some asshole in the department thought it funny to drain her radiator fluid and run down her phone battery. Luckily, some Good Samaritan motorist did eventually stop. And miracle of miracles, he wasn't a psycho or a pervert. He was just a nice guy who let her use his cell phone, and waited with her until Triple A showed up. Later, after she was safe, she had sent him money—fifty bucks, which had been a lot, back then. The envelope came back stamped: Return to Sender . . . addressee unknown. At that point, Hayley swore up and down that he had been her guardian angel. And who couldn't use a guardian angel— someone looking after your ass? Cindy was a nice kid with potential *if* the jerks didn't get in her way.

For the sake of completion, Hayley gave the place a quick once-over. Everything seemed okay (except for the broken window, which she should board up before she left). Without thinking, Hayley pressed the button on Cindy's phone message machine: one from Mom, a couple from Daddy, and a couple from Oliver. Not that Scott said his name but Hayley recognized the voice. She smiled, having known something was up from the moment he had followed Cindy out of Bellini's. It seemed so predictable. Cindy was trying to prove something to her father, and Oliver was trying to prove something to his boss. The two of them were a chemical reaction waiting for the catalyst.

Out of habit and boredom, she started opening drawers, first in the bedroom, then the desk in the living room, and finally in the kitchen. That's when she came across notes with Bederman's name scribbled all over the pages. The papers had been stuffed behind a cow-shaped pot holder. Hayley smoothed out the sheaves then sorted them one by one. Lots of charts and diagrams, and lots of doodling . . . Bederman's name, Cindy's name in bubble letters, and the name Armand Crayton with arrows pointing every which way. The last page she looked at gave directions to a place called Belfleur.

Where the hell was Belfleur?

More important, where the hell was Cindy?

Someone, in a beaten-up red Camry, had tailed Cindy into the hills last Friday. Then someone had trashed the kid's apartment. Now she wasn't home, and it was past eleven, and she was up to something that had to do with Armand Crayton.

Crayton was dead.

This wasn't looking good, and the itch was

growing by the second. Rooting through her pocketbook, Hayley found her electronic notebook and looked up Oliver's cellular number. As the phone rang, she wondered how she would explain herself to him, whether he'd think she was a partial or an absolute idiot.

He picked up on the third ring. "Detective Oliver."

His voice sounded tense. She said, "It's Hayley Marx."

"What's up?"

"Do you have Cindy Decker's father's phone number?" she stammered out. "I need to talk to him."

"Why?" Scott shot out. "What's this about?"

His agitation was palpable. She said, "Maybe you can help me, Scott. Do you know where Cindy Decker is?"

"No!" he barked out. "Why do you want to know?"

"Probably for the same reason you're snapping at me. I'm worried. I'm at her apartment now, her car isn't here. She hasn't been home all day. I know her place was broken into—"

"*Where* are you exactly?"

"Inside her apartment," Hayley repeated. "I broke the window and let myself in. Because I have this . . . this feeling—"

"What feeling?" Oliver cried out. "What's wrong? Anything out of place?"

"No, except for the window, which I'll board up.

But I found some notes in her handwriting. They had Rick Bederman's name on them. Even creepier, some also had Armand Crayton—"

"Oh God!" Oliver moaned. *Did the bastard get to her?* "Her stepmom just called her dad about five minutes ago. Cindy is supposedly on her way to her father's house, but she hasn't shown up."

"Well, maybe I can help with that. In her notes, she wrote down directions to a place called Belfleur. Do you know what that's about?"

"Yeah, I have an idea," Oliver muttered. "This isn't good. Her dad was here a few seconds ago, but left after his wife called. We were all in Oxnard, raiding a chop shop. Hold on. Let me see if I can catch him."

Hayley waited, noticing that her breathing was shallow. It seemed as if she had been put on hold for a very long time. Then an anxious, deep voice broke through the line.

"Tell me everything that you know."

Hayley cleared her throat. "I know that a Camry had tailed her on Friday. I know that the Camry fell down the mountainside. I know that her house was broken into. I found some scratches on her windowsills. Other than that, nothing seems out of order, sir."

"So why are you calling me?"

Hayley's throat became dry. "I don't know how to say this—"

"Then just spit it out."

She cleared her throat. "There's some odd men in my division, Lieutenant."

"Tell me."

"Well, she had Rick Bederman's name scrawled on some of her notes."

"Okay. What about Bederman's partner, Tim Waters?"

"He's also odd. But there were no notes with his name on them."

"She also mentioned some kid that she went to the academy with—Andy Lopez. What do you know about him?"

"He's a jerk, but he doesn't strike me as dangerous. She also didn't write his name down."

"She had a run-in with a sergeant there—"

"Clark Tropper. She's been typing up some papers for him. I thought they ironed things out."

"Maybe not. Do you have phone numbers for any of these yahoos?"

"I can get them in a snap. I'll call them for you, if you want."

"No, I'll call. Just get me the numbers."

"Sir, it might be less obvious if I call Bederman. But I'll do whatever you want."

She was right. Decker said, "Do you think Bederman would hurt her?"

"Yeah, if she made him angry enough. All of these men have tempers."

Decker told her to hold a moment. To Oliver, he said, "This Marx girl. Can she be trusted?"

Oliver thought long and hard. "She's a pain in the butt. Sarcastic, bitchy, intrusive. But I never recall her being dishonest. What does she want?"

"She wants to call up Bederman and sound him out. If she's sincere, it's a good idea because it'll look less suspicious. But if she's setting us up, then it's a bad idea."

"If she's setting us up at Bederman's behest, then he knows about this phone call, Deck." Oliver ran his hand through his thick, greasy hair. "Marx isn't the sharpest knife in the block, but I'd take the chance. Because right now, she's a lot closer to the situation than either of us."

Decker hoped that Oliver was right. To Marx, he said, "All right. You take Bederman and Waters and Lopez. They're your peers. Tropper's a sergeant. You call him up, you're in a one-down position. Being a loo, I'm in a one-up position. I'll take Tropper."

"That makes sense." Hayley cleared her throat. "Sir, again, I don't know how to tell you this, so . . . I put a tracer on Cindy's car—"

"You *what*!?"

"I put a tracer on Cindy's Saturn. After that guy in the Camry tailed her into the mountains, I got concerned. When I first started on the force, some wise guy in the department made sure my car broke down in the middle of the desert. It was so traumatic that I swore to myself it wouldn't happen to any other woman rookie if I could help it. I know I must sound idiotic. But as God is my witness, I like your daughter." Hayley's eyes started watering. "I'd feel horrible if anything should happen to her." She sniffed back an onslaught of tears. "Do you want me to activate it?"

"Hell, yeah, activate it!"

She winced at the aggression in his voice. "Okay, sir. I'll do that. The mechanism is back at my house. I'm fifteen minutes away from it. I'll call you as soon as I get a signal. Then I'll take care of Bederman. I'm sorry about this, sir."

"So am I." Decker gave her six phone numbers. "Call any of those lines if you hear anything, no matter how trivial it seems to you."

"I will."

Decker hung up. To Oliver, he said, "Hayley said she was worried about Cindy, so she put a tracer on her car. Goddamn it, *I* should have done that! What the *fuck* is wrong with me?"

What the fuck is wrong with both of us? Oliver said, "Marx is smarter than I gave her credit for. Always been my downfall . . . underestimating the gray matter of women. That's why my ex has a new Mercedes and I'm driving a ten-year-old Plymouth."

34

FIRST SHE felt a deep throbbing in her head; sharp, stabbing thrusts underneath her eyeballs and a dull, aching soreness in her ribs. The pain was so intense that it almost shut out all other sensations. But Cindy wouldn't allow that to happen, because she wanted to live. She concentrated on her other senses, which were rendered almost nil by the agony, forcing herself to bring them to consciousness. The rhythmic rumble of the engine bounced her incapacitated body up and down. It was only a few millimeters, but in her compromised position they were enough to send electric shockwaves down her spine and through her teeth. She hurt in a new way, as if an alien had descended upon her and was eating her up, tendon by tendon, bone by bone.

Concentrate!

Slowly, other stimuli crept into her cognizance; the back of her hands crunched against each other, her ankles were tightly affixed together. The taut ropes were chafing her skin or, worse, cutting into her flesh. There was also something thick and nappy stuffed into her mouth, tasting vaguely medicinal. Her ears discerned background sounds: cars whooshing past, an occasional horn or ambulance. There were the kinetics of the car speeding along, not stopping or doing any sharp turns. They were probably on a freeway. Her eyes could see, except that there was nothing really to see, just shadows and darkness. A part of her did not want to remember what had brought her to this doom. But she did remember.

Cindy knew exactly how she had gotten there. Except for the blackout—that period of time after her useless efforts to save herself. She didn't recall being bound or gagged, but that was certainly how she had ended up. Being vanquished was a horrible feeling. Doing everything she could have done, and still it had not been enough.

Her solace was that she was still alive. If he had wanted to murder her from the top, he could have done so. Obviously, he had other things in store. Unpleasant things . . . torturous things.

The chemical smell permeated her nostrils, making her woozy enough to be passive but not too woozy to think. And *if* she was going to get out of this, she'd have to think.

Country music was playing on the radio. Her dad liked country music; Cindy did not. But whenever they were in a car together, she deferred to him. She knew a couple of the singers—artists as they called themselves. She knew this one: Cheli Wright being a single white female looking for love. The lyrics and the upbeat tempo seemed to be mocking her pathetic state. Just a week ago she

had thought her lack of a love life was an insur-
mountable problem. Then, just days ago, after
being stalked, her personal effects were violated.
She had been sure that things couldn't get worse.

Well, they had.

What wouldn't she give to be just aggravated
about silly issues like her love life or stupid co-
workers or unpaid bills or driving an ugly car. If
only God would grant her one more day to be irritated at Mom for her intrusiveness or to be annoyed at Dad for being so controlling. One more
day to use her cell phone or eat a sandwich or put
on her uniform or go to the bathroom.

Without realizing it, she was crying, tears running silently down her face until her cloth gag absorbed them. By now, she could feel it as a gag,
bisecting her mouth and slicing across her face, finally being knotted at the back of her neck. She
had something to be thankful for. He hadn't taped
her face, so she could breathe easily. And another
thing to be grateful about: Her hands were bound
by ropes and not cuffs. That surprised her. She
would have figured him for a cuff man.

Which said to her that maybe . . . just *maybe
baby*, he didn't want to hurt her *too much*. Now that
could be wishful thinking. But he hadn't killed her
when he had the chance. And he must have had
lots of chances because she hadn't remembered his
tying her up—

"You awake, Decker?"

His voice snapped her into superconsciousness . . . hyperalertness. She should have been using the quiet time for planning and scheming. Instead she had been free-associating—great if she had been in therapy, but very bad since she was being kidnapped and probably about to be tortured.

"I know you're up. I can hear the difference in your breathing. Come on, Officer Decker. It's okay to give me a sign of life. Grunt or something."

She could have grunted. She could have given him some kind of signal that she had heard him. Perhaps that's what she should have done. Encouraged him and kept him talking. Instead she said nothing, did nothing.

He kept waiting. She stayed frozen: out of fear, out of defiance.

"I know damn well you can hear me, Decker. Let me tell you something, *Officer*. You aren't in any position to jive me, so cut the crap and answer me."

If she didn't give him a sign, he'd probably hurt her. He was used to giving orders and having them obeyed. She was now paying the price for having questioned his absolute authority. Sure enough, when she didn't respond, he turned around and whacked her across the cheek. It wasn't even a hard whack. But because she was so sore from what had probably been a previous beating, it stung her face like a splash of boiling water. Damn well made her want to pass out again. Instead she moaned.

"That wasn't hard at all, Decker. Just a little love

pat! Buck up!" Then he said, "You know, Decker? With your brains and connections, if you just had played it straight, you would've made it in the shade. Know what I'm saying? But you got this problem, Decker. You push things. It was bad enough, having this little bitch mouth off to me, showing me up. But then, when you started eating shit, I was going to . . . cut you some slack."

How gracious, Cindy thought. Even in her thoughts, she couldn't stop the sarcasm.

He continued to talk. "Because if you made gold—more like *when* you made gold—you wouldn't think I was a total son of a bitch. Do you get what I'm saying?"

Cindy did get what he was saying. She got it perfectly. She ate shit for him, and he was going to forgive her. So how the hell did she foul up? Last she remembered, she was still capitulating to the asshole. What merited true forgiveness from this prick? A blow job in the supply room?

"Yep, you sure had me fooled. I thought you were really trying to kiss my ass. But stupid, uneducated me. I couldn't see that you were setting me up, sucking up to me while trying to stick it up me. That was really rotten, Cindy. It really pissed me off. You're gonna pay for that. Pay big time. I'm telling you this so you'll understand."

But Cindy didn't understand a damn thing. What had she done to give him the false impression that she was trying to screw him?

He was tisk-tisking at her now. "You could have left well enough alone, just played the game. You had to go and stick your nose where it didn't belong!"

What the hell was he talking about? She hadn't been scheming against him . . . she hadn't been doing anything that remotely could be misconstrued—

"What were you trying to prove by going down there, huh?"

Going down where?

"Trying to upsmart Daddy like you upsmarted me?"

Outsmart, Cindy thought.

"Bragging that you can solve things that Daddy can't. Is that your style with authority? You know what, Decker? Daddy should have given you a sharp kick in the pants a long time ago. Then you wouldn't have been in this mess, because you would have known your place instead of being so damn nosy! I tried to warn you off. I sent you notes. I chased you around. I gave you signs—little and big signs. Nothing worked. Now you've found out things, and look where it got you!"

She grunted.

He said, "I can't understand a word you're saying."

Maybe if you took the gag off, you would! Seconds later, she got her wish. In a swift, rough motion, he yanked the gag down until it rested around her neck like a bandanna. The tug was so violent against her jaw, she felt as if he had taken out a couple of bottom teeth as well. "Sir, I don't know what you're talking about."

She wasn't surprised that she was slurring her words. Her mouth and lips were bloated with edema. What astonished her was that he understood her. At least, she thought he understood her because he laughed. It was a hard laugh, a low-pitched cackle of a warlock, if there were such things as warlocks. And maybe there were because she felt this was pretty damn close to Wells's vision of hell.

He said, "With your fancy degree and fancy words, I would have thought you could do better than that!"

"I can't because I don't know what . . ." She stopped talking. If the conversation continued this way, it would soon bog down to a predictable rut. She'd say this, he'd say that.

Use your fancy degree!

Her mind flashed back to her psych courses, specifically to Milton Erickson, and the art of the unexpected. "Thanks for taking off the gag. I really appreciate it."

Silence.

"What am I smelling?" Cindy continued on, desperately fighting the effects of the soporific gag. "Something like chloroform? Where in the world did you get it? They don't use it in hospitals anymore. You must have searched long and hard. But then again, I see you as a pretty resourceful guy."

"How would you know?"

"I'm a smarty pants, remember?"

Again, no one spoke.

She tried again. "Can I say something without you getting offended?"

"Probably not."

"Can I try?"

"Can I stop you?"

"You could put the gag on again. By now, we both know I'm pretty much under your control."

He didn't answer. Cindy took his silence as a signal to continue. "Sir, you think I was trying to screw you. Tell me how."

"Don't give that bullshit!" He hit the dash so hard, it made her aching body jump. He was panting now . . . louder than she was. "Don't fucking *lie* to me. You're in no position to fucking *lie* to me, Decker! We both know damn well why you went out to Belfleur!"

She opened her mouth, then closed it, her jaws pounding with pain. Her brain began to spin. Belfleur, Belfleur . . . what did he have to do with Belfleur?

And then it hit her like his hand across her face.

She had been so *intent* on Bederman, so *sure* of his guilt, she hadn't even bothered to check the rest of the list! If she had, she would have no doubt found his name—and maybe others as well. Who knew how many cops were on the list? She was not a big believer in conspiracy theories, but at the moment, she could only think of that. All of them! They were out to get her because they thought she knew something. She did know something. She knew that they had something to do with Crayton's death . . . and Bartholomew's kidnapping . . . and Mills's carjacking. She knew something, but she didn't know everything. Certainly she didn't know enough information to die for. But he didn't know that. He thought she had it all figured out. He had overestimated her abilities, while she had under-estimated his.

❑

DECKER didn't wait for Oliver to cut the motor. As soon as Scott pulled up behind Cindy's car, Decker was out.

God bless Hayley Marx and her tracer. Or rather, God bless her for the moment because Decker still wasn't sure about her. He vaulted over to the Saturn's driver's door, but found it locked. The passenger's door, however, was shut but unlocked. Heart pounding, he threw it open and peered inside.

She wasn't there.

He popped the trunk.

She wasn't there, either.

Simultaneously, he felt both happy and panic-stricken. He hadn't found a body—thank you, thank you, God—but she was gone. The uncertainty drove him to frenetic action. He rooted through her bag, finding her wallet and her gun. Money inside the wallet. She had a tube of lipstick, pens . . . loose credit-card receipts. He pocketed them. Where was her billfold containing her badge and ID? Marge touched his shoulder and he jumped.

"Sorry," she said. "I didn't mean—"

"Her gun's here." Decker turned to her, breathing hard. "She didn't even have a chance to go for her gun!"

"We'll find her, Pete—"

"You tell me how!" Decker wiped away moisture from his cheeks. "Tell me *how*!"

Oliver had walked over. "You know, there's lots of brush down the embankment. Maybe she ran out of the car, and didn't have time to take her gun—"

"She would have taken her gun!" Decker got out of the car and began to pace. "Why wouldn't she grab her gun? The bastard just snatched her out from behind the wheel—"

"Except the driver's door was locked," Oliver said.

"What?"

"You snatch someone from behind the wheel,

assumedly you grab them around the neck and drag them over to your car. You don't take time out to close and lock the door—"

"You kick it with your fucking foot!" Decker said.

Marge whispered a silent "Shut up" to Oliver, then rubbed her forehead. "Peter, we have to call it in as a crime scene—"

"So call it in!"

She did. Then she took out a flashlight. "I'll be down in the embankment area. See if I can find anything."

An ominous statement because everyone knew what she meant. Oliver knew he should go with Marge and help. But the thought of Cindy down there, dead, shot dread through his veins. The image would haunt him forever. He cursed his self-ishness and his weakness, but couldn't overcome it. He regarded Decker. The big man was leaning against the Saturn for support, his meaty hand covering his face.

To Marge, Oliver said, "Maybe I should stay up here." He cocked his head toward Decker.

"Yeah, maybe you should." Marge took a few steps, then tripped. She forced herself not to cry until she was out of eyeshot and earshot. When she was halfway down the embankment, she wept softly, wiping away tears as she searched for what she hoped she wouldn't find.

Oliver placed his hand on Decker's shoulder. The

big man turned around and stared with glazed eyes. "Why didn't she take her gun?"

"I don't know."

"It doesn't make *sense*!" Decker swallowed back tears. "She took her badge, but she didn't take her gun—"

"She took *her badge*?"

"Yeah," Decker said. "She took her badge. At least her badge isn't in her purse. It doesn't make any sense."

"Nothing makes sense because we don't know what's going on."

"Well, thank you for that pithy explanation." Decker stomped away from Oliver and began to walk back and forth. The uselessness of his actions made them pitiable. Paralyzed, Oliver watched him for a moment, trying to shake stupor from his shoulders. Slowly, he put one foot in front of another, bending down to search Cindy's car. It smelled of her and that drove him crazy. Using his nose, he realized that it *only* smelled of her. Whoever had done this . . . he hadn't dragged her out. She had come to him.

Oliver forced concentration upon his brain, taking out a flashlight though it provided dim illumination. He went through her purse. The first thing he noticed was that Decker was right. Her gun was sitting at the bottom of her bag. So was her pocketbook with the money still in the billfold. So where was her standard-issue police wallet, which contained her officer's badge and ID? Maybe it had fallen out. Cindy's bag was more of a sack. It wasn't zipped up, meaning things could easily tumble out. He began to search the car . . . under the mats and seat cushions, in between the seats and the console, in the glove compartments and door recesses.

Nothing.

He heard sirens in the distance. Soon the place would be crawling with cops. If she were near, they'd find her.

Without thinking, his hand went to the ignition to turn on the motor, just to see if the car was working. But there weren't any keys in the slot.

Come to think of it, Oliver didn't recall seeing keys in her purse. He searched again.

No badge *and* no keys.

He waited a moment, then got out of the car and walked around it, shining the light on the ground. Maybe she dropped her keys. But he didn't find anything. No keys, no billfold, not even any footprints to speak of, at least not in this light. Nothing to suggest anything sinister. He walked several yards behind the car and illuminated the pavement. Tire tracks that didn't extend to Cindy's Saturn. Different tire tracks, but that wasn't exactly a big deal. One would expect to find tire tracks on the shoulder of the freeway. That's where cars pull over when they have road problems. But these seemed fresh, like the car—

"You find anything?"

Oliver was startled. "You crept up on me."

"Sorry. What're you thinking?"

He regarded his boss. The ravages of hell had trod over Decker's face. With the flashlight, Oliver traced the beam of light over the ground. "Look at these."

"Tire tracks."

"Look new to you?"

"The bastard pulled up behind her," Decker said. "He saw that her car had stalled, pulled up, then dragged her out of the car."

Oliver hesitated, then said, "Cindy wears sneakers most of the time, doesn't she?"

Decker didn't answer because he knew where Oliver was going. No drag marks had been left from the shoes.

Oliver said, "You know what else I didn't find in her purse? Keys."

Decker looked at him.

"For what it's worth," Oliver said, "I think she got out voluntarily, took her badge and keys, and met someone. Maybe we got it all wrong. Maybe someone was stalled on the shoulder, and she went to help him and it turned out he was a psycho—"

"Someone was stalking her. If she had bothered to take her billfold and keys, she would have taken her gun, Scott. She *would* have taken her gun."

No one spoke.

"But she did take her keys." Decker was thinking

out loud. "She got out and took her keys so she didn't accidentally lock herself out . . . she took her badge but not her gun—"

Think! *Think!*

But nothing came.

Decker said, "Heard from Marx?"

"She still hasn't tracked down Bederman or Tropper."

"Bastards! Call her again!" Decker barked. "Maybe she's lying!"

Oliver took out his phone and started dialing. In an instant, an idea invaded Decker's thoughts. What did Bederman and Tropper and Marx and all the others have in common? They were all *cops*.

"Hang up for a second!" Decker shouted.

Oliver pressed the end button. "What?"

"How about this? She was stalled, Scott. She was stalled because some fucking psycho in her department was playing games with her car. So here she was, stalled on the freeway, then suddenly someone pulls over to help her. If it were just Joe Blow, she would have taken out her gun to meet him. But it wasn't Joe Blow. It was someone she wasn't afraid to meet."

"Someone she knew."

"No, that would make her even more suspicious . . . if someone she knew just happened to find her stalled on the freeway."

Decker was right, of course. Oliver said, "Go on."

"How about a cruiser?" Decker suggested.

Oliver hit his forehead. "Of course. She sees a cop pulling behind her. She'd know better than to approach a cop with her gun in her hand."

"And that's why she took her ID. To identify herself—"

"Pete!" Marge called out.

"Oh God!" Decker's knees buckled. Oliver caught him before he caved in. Marge came running over and spoke rapidly. "I didn't find anything . . . I mean I didn't find her." She broke into tears. "I mean I didn't find her body!"

"What did you find?" Oliver asked.

The sirens got louder.

Marge said, "There are lots of crushed bushes. I think there was a struggle down there."

"Blood?" Decker asked.

"Not that I can see."

But Decker sensed that she was telling partial truths. He felt his head going light. "I've got to sit down."

Marge eased him into Cindy's car. He felt hot tears well up in his eyes. He blinked them back and looked away.

Oliver said, "Marge, get me my cell phone. Or better yet, can you call up Hollywood, and find out if Tropper or Bederman is on duty. If they're not, find out if either had checked out a patrol car, or if a cruiser's missing."

"Why?"

Oliver explained Decker's theory.

"I'll do it right away." Marge turned to use her cell phone.

"Also . . ." Decker cleared his throat. "Also, call up CHP."

"Why?"

"Just . . ." Again, Decker cleared his throat, along with a sharp intake of air. He felt as if he were suffocating even though the night air was clear and crisp. "Ask if all their cruisers are accounted for."

Marge looked at him.

Decker said, "If I were Cindy . . . not knowing who was with me or who was against me . . . I'd be suspicious of a patrol car. It might be Bederman . . . it might be Tropper." Another big breath. "But a CHP cruiser . . . if I were stalled and I saw a CHP cruiser . . . I'd be very happy. I'd get out of the car without my gun . . . but with my badge . . . and say . . . and say, 'Hey, can you help me?' "

35

FROM THE safety of her car, Hayley spoke into her cell phone. "Lopez is accounted for. He's been at his parents' for the last four hours. Tropper's still a question mark. I did get hold of Bederman's wife. She expects him back any moment—"

"Back from where?" Oliver interrupted.

"From a drive. He goes out for a drive by himself sometimes—"

"That sounds like total bullshit to me."

Hayley felt the same way. "He's got a pager. I'm trying to track him down."

"If he hasn't answered, Marx, he doesn't want to answer!"

"You want to put out an APB on the car?"

"I'd love to except we don't have anything concrete on him. Plus, he's a cop." Oliver was very conflicted. "Give me the license plate."

"He's got two civilian cars—a Ford Aerostar minivan and a Camaro convertible. His wife said he took the Camaro . . . which is his car." Hayley gave him both license plate numbers. "But I'm also thinking, Scott, that if he's doing something nasty maybe he has the van and the wife isn't coming clean."

"Why don't you go to the house and see what's missing?"

"Yeah, sure . . . good idea. I'm also five minutes away from Graham Beaudry's house. He's Cindy's current partner—"

"Isn't he also Bederman's *ex*-partner?"

"Yeah. But they're still friends. They still hang together."

"Right. Cindy told me that. I think it's weird."

"You gotta know Graham. He's just that kind of guy. I'm thinking that maybe Graham knows where Bederman is. Or at least, maybe he knows where Bederman hangs out. Because they are still friends."

"You checked Bellini's?"

"Yeah, I called. He's not there. Graham's a nice guy. Let me ask—"

"You're looking at Graham as a nice guy. You ever consider him as a possible perp?"

"I don't see it, but if he is involved, then I definitely should go see him. So what should I do first? See Graham or check out Bederman's vehicle?"

No one spoke for a moment.

Hayley changed the subject to give him time to think. "How's it going over there?"

"We've located some torn bits of clothing."

"Hers?"

"I don't know, Hayley."

His voice sounded flat. She said, "But . . . you know . . . you haven't found her."

"We wouldn't be having this conversation, if we had."

"It was a stupid question."

"No, it wasn't." Oliver softened his voice. "It was a very normal question. I'm real testy."

"Understandable. How's the lieutenant?"

"Stuck in hell."

The conversation was playing hard on Hayley's

already overwrought anxiety level. She felt her throat swell. "So what should I do?"

"You're close to Beaudry's house?"

"Five minutes."

"Go check him out. Call if you find out anything."

"Likewise." She disconnected the line, and started the motor of her car—a ten-year-old Mustang that had been giving her problems of late. Something about a nervous transmission. But she couldn't afford to repair it. She had renamed the wheels "bucking bronco." Sure enough, when she put it in drive, it hesitated before lunging forward. Seconds later, she was on her way to Beaudry's.

Graham lived in a simple one-story house in a residential area of one-story houses. The neighborhood was hilly, and the streets moved up and down like a baby roller coaster. Since the suburb was near the ocean, the homes at the top had a nice view. But Beaudry lived at the base of the knoll in a white, wood-sided home with flower beds lining the walkway. No skyline or ocean view, but the area was not at all unpleasant. She parked across the street and was about to get out when a car in his driveway came alive with red, backup lights. There was just enough light for her to make out the license plate.

Bederman.

She let him go for a half block, and followed him

without headlights until they were on Venice Boulevard. Then she popped the illumination switch and dropped back a couple of car lengths, following him east for several miles. When he turned into the residential area of Culver City, she again tailed him without headlights. His particular block was a flat street with a gated condo development on one side, and faceless one-story homes on the other. Bederman pulled into the condo driveway, inserted a card into the magnetic slot, and the mechanical arm lifted upward, allowing him entrance.

Hayley continued on for another half block and then parked the car, thinking about what to do next. If Bederman had been at Graham's for the past two hours, he couldn't have been with Cindy unless Bederman and Beaudry were in on it together. Nothing surprised Hayley anymore. She had seen the best of fathers brought down for diddling their daughters, she had seen pastors who were wife beaters. She had arrested rich kids for shoplifting candy bars, she had seen poverty-stricken illiterates do the most amazing heroics. Appearance meant nothing and lots of times first impressions were wrong. Still, there was something off-kilter when she tried to picture Bederman and Beaudry hanging at a Sunday barbecue planning Cindy's demise. She called up Scott and told him what had happened.

She said, "He was driving the Camaro. I found

that somewhat encouraging. Mainly because it's harder to hide a body in a car that small. Even the trunk is small."

"Yeah." Except that Oliver was discouraged. He would have been far happier had Hayley found Bederman with Cindy—alive and gagged and whatnot. Instead, the verdict was still out, the terror of the uncertain rotting away his ability to think.

"Are you there, Scott?"

"Yeah, I'm here." In body, he was there. But his mind wasn't processing.

Hayley said, "I don't think Bederman's going anywhere for a while. Maybe I should concentrate on Graham."

Oliver thought about that. "Maybe Bederman's switching cars and is going to go out again."

"Do you want me to wait here?"

"As opposed to . . ."

"Going to Beaudry's place. I'm just thinking that if Bederman did something nasty, maybe he went to Graham's to confess or something."

"Maybe he went there to ask Graham to give him an alibi," Oliver said. "What do you hope to accomplish by talking to Beaudry?"

"I have a better relationship with Graham than I do with Bederman. And he is Cindy's current partner. On the surface, they seem to get along. I'm just thinking that I'd get more out of Beaudry than I would out of Bederman."

"What do you expect to get out of Beaudry?"

"If there's something off about Bederman." She sighed. "I don't know. I'm not a detective. How about a little guidance?"

That was always Hayley's style—straight out with it. Oliver said, "Nothing much is happening here . . . which I suppose is better than finding something. Look, Hayley, I'll do Bederman, you do Beaudry. I should be there in . . . twenty minutes."

"Want me to wait for you?"

"Yeah . . . wait for me." Silence for several seconds. "Any word from Tropper?"

"No. I called about three minutes ago. Maybe we should put out the APB on him?"

"It's the same problem, Hayley. We don't have anything on him. Not answering your pager isn't a crime. Also, if he's in a cop car, putting an APB on his civilian car won't do any good. It might even hurt because Tropper has tactical lines on the car's radio. If he has Cindy and hears that we're looking for him, it could panic him."

Hayley agreed. "So maybe we should crash his apartment or something?"

"Yeah, who needs due process— Hold on. What?"

Hayley heard muffled speech in the background. From what she could tell, there was excitement in the voices. She rubbed her hands together as she waited. It was getting cold in the car and the coffee she had purchased an hour ago was a mass of cold mocha and congealing cream. A moment later, Oliver came back on the line.

"Hayley, do you know if Tropper or any of them has anything to do with CHP?"

"I'm not sure what you're asking me."

"We think whoever took Cindy was using an official cruiser—maybe a CHP vehicle. Do you know anyone in Hollywood who has a CHP officer as a friend?"

"No. But I'm sure there's someone out there who fits the category."

"What do you know about Tropper?" Oliver asked.

"Not much. He's been with Hollywood for at least ten years. Hard-nosed kind of guy. He's got a good record."

"How many times has he gotten bagged with an excess force complaint?"

"Nothing to tag him as a problem."

"You're sure?"

"No, I'm not *sure*."

"Married?"

"Divorced."

"Kids?"

"I'm not sure. We're not buddies."

Oliver said, "I'll go to Tropper's. You might as well talk to Graham."

"You know, all these dudes live within twenty minutes of each other. Do you have Tropper's civilian license plate? Just in case?"

"Yeah. But if you happen to come across it, don't even think about going after him by yourself!"

"I wouldn't do that," Hayley lied. "But who knows? Maybe I'll get extremely lucky and bump into the car. If I have the license, I can call you up."

"I think that's unlikely."

"Stranger things have happened."

❑

BUT Hayley did not get extremely lucky: not that she didn't try. She drove around for a half-hour trying to second-guess where Tropper might be, but she came away empty-handed. She was stippled with anxiety—fearful for Cindy's safety, for her own safety as well. Hayley couldn't help wondering if she was the next victim on some psycho's list.

It was close to one when she finally arrived at Beaudry's house. The windows were dark, but the porch light over the door was on. Approaching the place, she felt trepidation. On the one hand, she wanted Graham to be a good guy. On the other, she had to view him as a potential psycho.

She rang the bell. Several minutes elapsed before a light went on from the inside, someone peering out the peephole. Beaudry opened the door, his hair a carpet of cowlicks, his squinting eyes made into slashes by the harsh light from the porch. He was clad in robe and slippers. With his fingers, he tented his brow so he could see her better. "What the hell are you doing here?"

"Cindy's missing—"

"What!" His mouth dropped open. "What do you mean, 'missing'?"

"Can I come in?"

He retreated and she came into his house. His mouth was still agape. "What's going on?"

Hayley regarded his expression—projecting the proper image of being shocked and appalled. "Did you know she was having trouble, Graham?"

"What kind of trouble?"

"Male Chauvinist Pig trouble."

Beaudry blinked several times. "From who?"

"From lots of people. From your friend, Bederman, for starts. Then there was Clark Tropper—"

"Tropper gives everyone a hard time." He stared at her. "Do you think Tropper hurt her?"

"I don't know." Hayley was amazed at how cool and casual she sounded. "She's missing, and he's not answering his pages. Any idea where he might be?"

But Beaudry sidestepped the question. "How long has she been missing?"

"About three hours—"

"That's not too bad."

"Lots can happen in three hours, Graham."

"I know that." He started pacing. "What happened?"

"She was en route to her father's. She never

showed up. Her car was left abandoned on the shoulder of the freeway—"

"Oh my God!"

From the way he responded, Hayley couldn't keep accusation out of her voice. "Do you know anything about it?"

Beaudry stiffened. "I don't like your tone, Marx."

"That's because I'm fucking scared, Beaudry!"

A female voice called out. "Graham? What is it?"

The wife. Hayley had woken her up. She cocked her head in the voice's direction. "Take care of her."

"Oh my God! What a horrible mess!" Graham rubbed his face. "Hayley, I'm on your side—"

Hayley interrupted him, her fury barely under control. "If you fucking A are on my side, then tell me what you *know*!?"

"Graham?" The voice was very plaintive this time.

"Hold on! I'll be right there!" he shouted. To Hayley, he said, "Lemme get rid of her, then I'll tell you everything. I'll make it quick."

After he disappeared down a dark hallway, Hayley looked around the living room. Matching muslin slipcovers, white sofa and love seat. A glass coffee table rimmed with brass matched the side tables. Wall-to-wall carpet in a low pile weave. There were landscapes and seascapes on the walls. Everything matched, but looked plastic. Or maybe she was just jealous because the house seemed so perfect and her life was so messy. Ten minutes later, he returned, dressed in proper street clothes, a gun in his hand. "Shouldn't we be doing something to help? Like look for her, maybe?"

"Look *where*, Graham? Look in Rick Bederman's Aerostar?"

"Rick's been with me for the last couple of hours."

"Doing *what*? Establishing an alibi?"

"Maybe."

The admission shocked Hayley. "What's going on?"

"I'll tell you what I know, but it isn't much." Graham's voice was tense. "Bederman has a problem with Cindy. I told him he should lay off her, but he's got this problem with her."

"He wants to fuck her?"

"Rick wants to fuck everyone, but that's not the problem. It had to do with the Armand Crayton case. You remember that—"

"Go on."

"Rick was fucking Crayton's wife. They had like a two-year affair. She's got pictures."

"Who does?"

"The wife. Lark."

"Lark has pictures of Rick and her fucking?"

"Actually, they're videos. You wanna know the stupid thing? Rick took the videos, not her. That guy is such a fucking moron—"

"But you're still friends with him?"

"Because he's got a wife who is my wife's best

friend. Because he's got children. You partner with a guy for a long time, he does you favors, you do him favors!"

"It's nice that you're a loyal friend, but what does this have to do with Cindy?"

"The Crayton case is still an open file. Right after the murder, Bederman broke off the diddling with Lark, but the two of them were still tangled up. First off, Rick had invested in Crayton's business and lost money. Money that he didn't want his wife to find out about. Second, there were the videos. So he struck some kind of deal with Lark. She'd keep her mouth shut about the two of them and he'd do her favors—"

"What *kind* of favors?"

"How to handle the cops when they questioned her."

"You mean how to lie to the cops."

"Yeah, that's what I mean."

"Lark had her husband killed, didn't she?"

"I don't know that. Rick doesn't know, either." Beaudry was adamant. "But he was worried enough to help her out when she asked for help. You gotta understand the position he was in. He was scared about his wife finding out about the affair. He was terrified about being implicated in Crayton's murder—"

"Did he do it?"

"He swears up and down he didn't do it. Mostly, I believe him. But not entirely. There was a reason

I didn't partner with him after he came back to day shift."

"But you stayed his friend."

"Yeah. I stayed his friend."

"You're an idiot!"

"Tell me about it! I don't know what's wrong with me. Eighteen years on the force and I still feel . . . sorry for people."

"How about feeling sorry for Cindy?"

"I feel horrible for her, Marx! If Rick hurt her, I'll nail that motherfucker." Beaudry stared at the ceiling. "Rick thinks that Cindy somehow found out about the affair. He thinks she's gonna tell her dad and blow the case open. Then the cops are gonna come looking for him, and plant the murder charge on him. He's especially worried because he knows that Cindy doesn't like him."

"When did he tell you all this?"

"Today. I was at his house for a barbecue. He made some stupid comments to Cindy. I told him time and time again to lay off Cindy. He shouldn't be talking to her *especially* if he's worried about her and her daddy. So what does the idiot do? He goes over to her place! He said he made it right! He said it was all worked out, but he was nervous, Hayley. All I can tell you is that he's been with me for the last two, three hours."

"But the timing is perfect, Graham! She was going to see her dad. Maybe she did have something on him. So he doctors her car, follows her on the freeway, and waits for her to stall out. Then he pulls over in his cruiser—"

"Rick wasn't working today. Why would he be driving a cruiser?"

"The Dees on the case seem to think that the perp was driving a cruiser. Because Cindy left her gun behind when she went out to meet him."

"You're telling me that Rick signed out a cruiser just to kidnap Cindy?"

"You're the one who's telling me he's a moron!"

"Let's go see Rick." Beaudry took a coat out of the hall closet. "You want to drive?"

"Yeah, I'll drive."

Beaudry opened the door and locked it behind them. "You say her car was found on the shoulder of the freeway?"

"Yeah. The 405 going into the Valley."

"And when was the last time they heard from her?"

"Around nine. Why?"

"I'm just trying to figure out the timing."

Hayley unlocked her car and they both got in. Beaudry said, "If he did do it, he'd be working on a real tight schedule. He left my house after the barbecue around eight. Then he'd have to drive down to Hollywood to get a cruiser, then drive to Cindy's house and doctor her car. That means he has to know that she has plans to go out. Then he has to follow her, take her off the 405, and do something nasty to her. Then to make it back to my house by nine-ish—"

"You said nine, *nine-thirty*."

"It's still a very tight schedule."

He was right. It was a squeeze. Hayley started the motor. "Maybe he had already checked out the cruiser."

"And what did he do with it? Park it in his garage? You know you just don't go in and check out a cruiser. They keep records, Hayley. If he was gonna do something nasty using a cruiser that he checked out, it would kinda mark him."

"So someone down there did him a favor and let him borrow one without checking it out."

"The mileage wouldn't match."

"So maybe he stole a cruiser."

"Then someone would have reported it missing."

"Graham, I don't even know that Cindy was pulled over by a cruiser. Matter of fact, Scott Oliver . . . he's the detective on the case . . . he thinks it might have been CHP—"

"*CHP?*" Beaudry hit his head. "Why didn't you tell me that in the first place? You know how the government auctions off old stuff to raise money? You know, you can buy old buses or fire engines or cop cars. Course the vehicles are labeled not in service and all that jazz, but if you know what you're doing, you can restore it in a snap. It's against the law to do that—"

"And the *point* is?"

"Tropper bought a deacquisitioned CHP cruiser around a year ago."

36

DECKER HUNG up the radio mike. "He only has plates for his civilian car. No CHP-type vehicle registered under his name."

Oliver said, "He's gotta have something if he's driving the vehicle."

"I'm sure he has a couple of bogus ones. Plates aren't hard to make."

"Bastard!" Oliver glared out the windshield. "The Camry that Cindy was following . . . it had a plate from one of our early jacking victims. Maybe he stole some plates from the evidence room."

Decker said, "CHP uses official plates. He had them made up. Anyway, we don't even *need* the license number. How many CHP cruisers can there possibly be?" He threw his head back and closed his eyes. "The car wouldn't be hard to spot *if* he's just driving around. But we know the bastard's going to light. We need to figure out *where*."

Since Oliver didn't have an answer, he didn't speak, driving through tense silence. He pretended not to notice the moisture in Decker's eyes, executing a series of turns down narrow, darkened streets until he reached Bederman's block, where Hayley's car was parked curbside. Since Marge had left minutes before they had, she had already arrived, her Honda nosing the rear bumper of Marx's vehicle. Oliver saw the silhouettes of four figures assembled around the streetlight—Marge and Hayley and two men whom he didn't recognize. As the car slowed, Decker opened his eyes, sat upright, and started punching his right hand into the flesh of his left. As soon as Oliver pulled over, Decker got out and leapt toward them.

"I'm ready to kill someone. At this point, anyone will do." He spoke with such assurance no one doubted his words. "I want some answers now!"

Sets of eyes went to Bederman. Though he was a man of sizable stature, he shrank under Decker's scrutiny. "I'm not swearing to any of this—"

Decker grabbed him by the jacket collar and jerked him forward, towering over the man by a good three inches. "Do you *know* where they are?"

"No!" Bederman offered no resistance. "No, sir, I swear I don't! I swear I'm just as worried—"

"*No, you're not just as worried!*" Decker screamed. "*You couldn't possibly be just as worried, you fucking idiot! DO YOU KNOW WHERE THEY ARE?*"

Bederman broke into a cold sweat. "No! I'd tell you if I knew. I don't know!"

Decker said nothing, still restraining Bederman by his clothing.

Hayley cut in, her voice soft and trembling. "It has something to do with the Crayton case, sir. Bederman had invested with Crayton. So had Tropper. Both had lost money, but Tropper lost more."

Decker let go of Bederman, pushing him back several inches. He turned down the vocal volume, but he was still yelling. "What does that have to do with *Cindy*?"

Bederman managed to get the words out of his throat. "Tropper was pissed big time. He talked to me about getting even with the bastards. He said I owed it to him."

"Because you talked him into investing with Crayton?" Oliver asked.

"No," Bederman said. "It was the other way around. He talked *me* into investing with Crayton. He was buddy-buddy with Dexter Bartholomew."

"Where'd he know Bartholomew from?" Marge asked.

"Tropper pulled him over for a routine traffic violation," Bederman said. "Dex paid him off. It was the start of a very beautiful relationship."

"And Tropper just . . . *told* you this?" Decker asked.

"I found out from Lark."

"Rick was fucking her," Beaudry explained.

Oliver said, "So why did *you* owe *Tropper* if he talked you into investing?"

Bederman started to speak but couldn't. Beaudry filled in. "Tropper covered for him during the affair."

Bederman looked at him. "This never would have happened if you had covered for me."

Beaudry said, "Shut the fuck up, Rick!"

"Good idea!" Marge added.

Decker screamed, *"What does this have to do with Cindy?"*

"I'm not positive, sir," Bederman admitted. "I think Cindy found out things—"

"What things?" Decker asked. "Like who killed Crayton? Did Tropper murder Crayton?"

"Maybe." Bederman paused. "I couldn't swear to it, though."

Decker said, "Why would Tropper think Cindy would have information about that?"

"Because you guys were poking the Crayton case again." Bederman zeroed in on Oliver. "Tropper heard that you were at Bellini's, asking Osmondson questions about carjackings. He figured it had to be Crayton. What else could it have been?"

"That had nothing to do with Crayton," Marge said. "It had to do with jackings we were having in Devonshire."

"Well, Tropper thought it was Crayton!" Bederman retorted. "At least that's what he told me. He thought that you were onto something, using Cindy as a spy because she was the lieutenant's daughter—"

"*What?*" Decker screamed.

"Sir, I don't know what he was thinking! The man's violent as well as crazy!"

"Was Tropper having Cindy followed?" Marge asked.

Bederman looked away. "Maybe—"

Again, Decker grabbed him. He was sweating, shaking, and out of control. This time, he kneed Bederman in the balls, then pushed him to the ground. "I'm going to fucking *kill* you!"

Instantly, Bederman doubled over in pain. "I swear I never hurt—"

Decker kicked him in the ribs. "I'm going to *stomp you* to death!"

Marge placed a hand on his shoulder. "Take it easy, Pete!"

Oliver got between Decker and the writhing Bederman. "Could you hold off for a few more seconds, Deck? I got more questions for him."

Decker walked away, then abruptly turned around and came back. He plucked Bederman off the ground as easily as one retrieves a dropped coin. He propped Rick onto his feet, and spoke to him nose to nose. "*Why . . .*" Decker cleared his throat. "*Why* did that fucking bastard decide to kidnap her *today?*"

"I don't know!" Bederman whispered. "He didn't confide in me." There were tears in his eyes. "He just asked me to go see her—"

"Today?"

"Yeah, today!"

"*Why?*"

"To pump her. Try to find out if she knew anything. I didn't find out anything. I didn't even pump her because I didn't want to know if she did know anything. Believe it or not, I wound up going over there to apologize—"

Hayley broke in. "You know, while he was inside talking to her, I'm sure Tropper was outside, rigging her car—"

Again, Decker shoved his face against Bederman's. *"DID YOU FUCKING KNOW THAT?"*

"No, I swear I didn't!" The officer swallowed hard. "The only thing I ever did for the bastard was to . . . to scare the crap outta Stacy Mills. That's the only thing I ever did—"

Once more, Decker kneed him and pushed him down.

Marge said, "You gotta stop doing that, Peter! You're gonna kill him!"

"That's the fucking idea!" Decker yelled out. "Why did you scare Stacy Mills?"

"Because Lark said that she was shooting off her mouth!"

"Did Lark have Crayton killed?"

"I don't know!"

Oliver said, "Did Tropper threaten to tell your wife about the affair?"

"Yes. That's why I went over to Cindy's house . . . to pump her. Tropper told me to. He wanted to find out how much she knew about Crayton."

"Why would your wife believe Tropper if he told her about the affair?"

Beaudry said, "Tropper had pictures . . . videos actually—"

"Oh, for chrissakes!" Decker resisted the temptation to break Bederman's face. "He took videos of you fucking this bimbo?"

"Actually, Rick took them . . . kept them with Lark." Beaudry shrugged. "She must have given them to Tropper."

"So you fucked up *my daughter* to hide your dirty movies! I need to kill you, Bederman! I'll start with your nose—"

"Sir?" Hayley broke in.

Decker turned around to look at her.

"Cindy was out all afternoon, sir," Hayley continued. "Do you know where she was?"

Decker shook his head. "No. Do *you* know where she was?"

"I saw some notes in her apartment," Hayley said. "Directions to a place called Belfleur—"

"Oh my God! Wait a minute, wait a minute." Decker pulled out several folded credit card receipts that he had taken from Cindy's purse. He read the first one, then stopped cold on reaching the second slip. "The receipt is dated yesterday afternoon from Elaine's Antiques in Belfleur!"

"Where Bartholomew and Crayton had land investments," Oliver said. "If Tropper followed her down there, he might think she was on to something."

"She probably *was* on to something!" Decker said. "That's why she wanted to see me! How could she be so damn *stupid*!"

"She wasn't stupid," Hayley said. "She was careless because she's young!"

Decker lifted Bederman off the ground. "Give us your best shot, Bederman! Where do you think Tropper would have taken her?"

"Don't you think I'd tell you if I knew?" Bederman moaned.

Decker spat as he spoke. "I think you're a fuckup and a liar, so no, I don't think you'd tell me—"

Oliver broke in. "Pete, we've got to think. We've got to reason this out. We know Crayton was kidnapped and murdered. That was probably Tropper's doing—"

Marge said, "We don't know if Crayton was murdered on purpose."

Oliver said, "We don't know that he wasn't. All we know is that the Rolls fell over the embankment. It could have been an accident, it could have been on purpose."

Decker released his stronghold on Bederman, but still held the man's jacket. "The Camry that Cindy followed on Friday. We know it was pushed over the cliff *on purpose*. Where did Crayton's Rolls jump the railing? Somewhere in Angeles Crest, right?"

"Yes, I believe so," Oliver said.

Marge said, "I remember Tom saying something about double investigation teams because it was in two divisions. I think it was in Angeles Crest."

"So we have two cars jumping the railing around the same spot," Oliver said.

"Did Tropper have Cindy *followed*?" Decker yelled at Bederman.

"I don't know—"

"God, you're *useless*!" Decker shoved him away.

"That Friday, sir, Cindy and I left the stationhouse around the same time," Hayley remarked. "The Camry left around the same time, too. It was parked outside the stationhouse, not in the police lot, but something made me suspicious. That's why I tailed her. I knew she was going out to see you, sir. It was a long distance. I was afraid that her car might break down—"

"Was it *Tropper*?" Decker interrupted.

Hayley said, "Sir, I don't know."

"So assume it was Tropper or one of his stooges," Oliver said. "Two cars over two embankments in the same proximity . . ." Oliver's eyes widened. "Maybe Tropper thought that's where Cindy was going on Friday . . . to Crayton's original crash site. Maybe Tropper was trying to head her off because he left something behind or was afraid that she'd discover something. Then you have Cindy going down to Belfleur yesterday. This just confirms in his mind that she's on to his dirty secrets."

"What's *the point,* Oliver!" Decker growled.

Oliver said, "Let's hunt around the crash site, Pete. We don't know where the bastard is! But that's as good a guess as any!"

❑

FROM her limited perspective, Cindy could swear that the night was getting progressively darker. Tropper had placed her facedown—actually she was staring somewhere between the floor mat and the back of his seat—but if she craned her neck to the max, she could see out the top third of the passenger's rear window. What she saw were branches and leaves. What it told her was that she was deep in some kind of rural area. She guessed it had to be Angeles Crest. She could ascertain this not only by the foliage but also by the length of time it had taken to get here. There were also the sinewy, mountainous curves that felt different from other turns. The gag still rested around her neck like a bandanna, still spewing out chemical smells. But because it wasn't directly about her nose, she could breathe easier and think more clearly.

She said, "Sergeant, this area seems familiar. By any chance, did you tail me here on Friday?"

"Not me *personally,* no."

He expected her to ask who did tail her. But Cindy kept quiet, wanting to keep him off-guard.

Several seconds went by. Then Tropper said, "You do know why we're here?"

"I have a few suspicions. They're probably wrong—"

"Don't patronize me, Officer! I am still your superior."

"Yes, sir, that's definitely true."

"Is that scorn in your voice, Officer Decker?"

"Sir, that is fear and nothing else. Well, that's not entirely true. Maybe I am a little curious."

He waited for more. But she held out until he spoke. "Go on," Tropper said. "Curious about what?"

"I know you're angry with me—"

"Damn right, I'm angry. You were bullshitting me, Officer. I don't like that."

"Sir, I sincerely regret my snotty attitude toward you last week." So much had happened in a week. So, so much . . . "All I ever wanted to do was make it right—"

"Make it right by spying on me." Tropper let out a derisive laugh. "That's a good one, Decker."

She sensed that he would warp anything she would say. So she didn't answer. But that didn't stop her from thinking. *Spying* on him? How in the world would she have ever associated him with the Crayton case?

"C'mon, girl!" Tropper interrupted her thoughts. "I don't have the fancy education like you do, but I'm not a retard. I've seen you hanging around that greasy old detective guy, feeding him stuff about me. I know he was pumping Osmondson for information. I know he works for your father, and the Crayton case is a big fat bunion on Daddy's toe. I'm not stupid like you think I am."

"I don't think you're stupid at all—"

"*Now* you don't think I'm stupid."

Again, Cindy was quiet. She should have been trying to figure out a mode of escape. What to do if he pulls the car over, takes her for a walk in the woods, and plans to shoot her dead. Maybe she should think about how to fake a death or how to escape. Or maybe he'd push the car over the side railing and off the cliff with her in it. Maybe he'd make the engine explode and burn her to a crisp. Thinking about those kinds of things filled her with panic and dread. Those kinds of things would make her lose control of her mind as well as her bladder and bowels. Right now, with a swollen face, a bullet graze wound at her temple, *and* aching sides and bound arms *and* feet, a split lip *and* being slightly high as well as nauseated, she didn't want poop in her pants.

So instead, she thought about Tropper, trying to bring some logic to his demented thinking. Tropper had seen her talking to Scott. Scott and Dad were working the Crayton case. So Tropper must have thought that she was kissing up to him, trying to get information about him only to fink to her dad or Scott. But how in the world was she supposed to associate Tropper with Crayton in the first place?

Obviously, he thought she was on to him when she went to Belfleur. But his crazy thinking had started before the trek. He had admitted to being behind the Camry incident. No doubt, he vandalized her apartment.

But why would he think that she knew about him? Just because she was talking to Scott? Maybe that was enough for a guy as paranoid as Tropper.

Unless . . . *unless* Tropper had been the sniper a year ago. He had seen her with Crayton as they walked out of the gym.

"We're almost there," he said.

Almost where? "Okay."

"You know where we're going, right?"

"Should I know?"

"Yeah, you should know, Decker. It's his final resting place. I'm sure you've come here before to throw off some flowers or something."

So she figured it out; good going, girl. Unfortunately being clever wasn't going to help much right now. "He was never my boyfriend, sir. I know you thought that when you shot at us, but I swear to you he was just a friend. Not even a friend, Sergeant. He was more like an acquaintance. He was friendly to me like he was to everyone because he wanted money out of me, like he did out of everyone he met. I thought he was—"

She stopped herself. She wasn't about to tell

Tropper, who had invested his hard-earned cash with Crayton, that she knew better than to fall for Armand's pitch. That she thought Armand a con man from the start.

"I didn't have any money to invest with him. Eventually, he stopped being so friendly."

Tropper's laughter was hard and mean. "You expect me to believe you? He probably gave you a cut."

"Sir, I wish he had. Unfortunately, all he gave me were half-truths and downright lies. I don't care what Lark told you. I wasn't his lover, thank God!"

"It wasn't Lark."

Cindy was quiet. "Lark didn't hire you to shoot at us?"

"No."

"Ah . . ." Cindy nodded. "Okay."

"Okay, *what*?" Tropper exclaimed.

"If it wasn't Lark, it had to be Dexter Bartholomew. What did he have against Crayton? Was Crayton messing with Bartholomew's wife?"

"Yeah, but that wasn't a sore point because Bart was messing with Lark. Bart was pissed because Crayton had stolen the deposit money from escrow. Money that Bart was going to use for building and financing. But I think you know that."

"Actually, I didn't," Cindy said. "Maybe I don't want to know so much."

"What difference does it make, Decker? You're dead either way."

The coldness in his voice shot ice water through

her body. She shivered, but willed herself to keep going. *Above all, show no weakness.* To a guy like Tropper, weakness was probably an aphrodisiac. "I heard that Bartholomew actually made money on Belfleur because Crayton went bust. I heard that Bartholomew bought back the parcels at deep discount. It was Crayton who lost out."

"You got it the wrong way, lady. Crayton bought back the parcels at deep discount."

"Sergeant, Bartholomew owns the land down there," Cindy said. "I know that for a fact."

"Sure he owns the land," Tropper said. "Now that Crayton's dead, he owns the land. Crayton's dying solved everybody's problems. Lark would eventually get the insurance money, Bartholomew got his land, and I got my money back and then some."

"By doing Bartholomew a couple of favors—"

"By doing everyone some favors. Crayton was a piece of shit. He deserved what he got."

"Lark was in on his death?"

"We gave her a couple of choices. She could help out or she could die with him. She was more than happy to cooperate especially when Bart threatened to expose the affairs. It would make the cops very curious."

"Affairs? As in more than one?"

"You surely can't think that Bart was the only one."

"Who else?"

"You tell me, Miss College Graduate!"

"Bederman?"

"Very good."

"How about his partner?"

"Beaudry's a straight arrow—"

"Not Beaudry. Sean Amory."

Tropper smiled. "Yeah, that's right. Bederman's with Amory now. Yeah, he was screwing her—"

"How about yourself, sir? As a matter of fact . . ." Cindy tried to sit up, but of course, couldn't move. "Didn't you get a divorce about that time?"

Tropper didn't answer.

Cindy smiled for the first time. "What happened, sir? Did she make some fancy promise to you that she couldn't keep?"

Tropper turned around and punched her in the jaw. Cindy's face exploded into thousands of tiny stars as pain shot through her head. Her and her big mouth . . . always getting her into trouble. But what the hell! Like Tropper said, she was dead anyway.

37

BEING STUBBORN did have its good points. Like when every pore of the body was in excruciating pain and the most sensible thing to do was to pass out cold. But Cindy refused to slip into the nether-world for much the same reason that she couldn't keep her mouth shut—sheer force of mulish will. Tropper was screaming at her, but it was all one big aural blur since her head was ringing bells. Finally, he stopped talking. A few moments later, the tinnitus abated, and all that was left was her wracked body. Her bowels cramped and her bladder leaked, but she somehow kept rudi-mentary control over her basic functions.

His tantrum being over, he was now quiet. Cindy was silent because she couldn't talk. Re-markably, she still could hear, and hear well. Slith-ering through the wilds of the mountainous roads for the last umpteen minutes, she analyzed the sounds of nature's spooky orchestra—hooting, flut-tering, whistling, and the occasional piercing howl that sent a shiver down her spine. There was also the car's purring engine, which served as back-ground noise. She had gotten used to the rhyme and rhythm, so she was shocked when she heard what she thought *might* be some distant mechani-cal rumblings. Something that *might* indicate an-other car in the mountains.

Her fantasies soared. Maybe, just maybe, Hayley Marx had followed her again! She became elated at the idea although her rational side argued it was too much to hope for.

What would she have given to see that Mustang again?

Perhaps she was dreaming about the engines, her grip on reality rather tenuous at best. But then suddenly Tropper was squirming. Cindy could tell this because the back of the driver's seat—which she had been staring at for the entire ride—was suddenly full of activity, moving as if the leather covering encased a living being.

And then the noises became . . . not loud, but *louder*.

"Shit!" Tropper announced.

So, he had heard something, too! Okay, Cindy thought. Someone was out there. But so what? Why should Tropper be worried? What harm could another car do to him, and what help could it give to her? She couldn't scream, she couldn't move. Cars in the area were irrelevant.

The thought was utterly depressing!

But then she began to reason a bit.

The fact that Tropper had said, "Shit," meant that he was concerned. So maybe he was seeing things he didn't like. Like another . . . cop car?

Again her hopes flew upward.

After all, hadn't she called Rina at around nine and told her that she'd be at her dad's in around an hour? And when Cindy didn't show up, wouldn't Rina do something?

Of course, she'd do something!

Rina was all action! She would have called her dad! She would have called the police! She might have even gone out looking for her in her own car!

Oh my God! Cindy finally figured it out. Maybe someone was actually out there looking for her!

Through swollen lips, she mumbled, "Sir, do you have the time?"

"Shut up!" Tropper barked.

Be that way! She'd figure it out for herself. She had stalled on the freeway around ten-thirty. Then Tropper showed up, they made scary chitchat, he ordered her in his car . . . she jumped the rail and ran from him. That had to have taken at least fifteen, twenty minutes. Then they had struggled. Maybe another twenty minutes. Eventually, he had knocked her out, tied her up, and dragged her into his car. Figure a half hour for that. So maybe he hit the road again around eleven, eleven-thirty. They'd been driving for at least an hour, maybe longer. So it was probably around one-ish.

Yes, Rina would have done something by now. And definitely people would be out looking for her.

But why in this area? If they found her car on the 405 coming out to the Valley, why would they look for her here?

Then she thought some more, imparting reason to circuitous logic to keep her spirits up. Weren't they near the area where the Camry went over the railing? Didn't it make sense to look around here again?

She sure hoped it did!

She *prayed* it did!

The sounds became more distinct. They were car engines, and more than one of them. Cindy felt a lopsided smile spread across her face. *Knowing Dad, he had sent out the National Guard.*

"Shit!" Tropper exclaimed once again. "We're going to have to speed things up!"

Oh God, she thought. *I hope the bastard doesn't shoot me on the spot.*

"This changes things." Tropper paused. "But not too much."

He took a sudden series of turns and soon Cindy could feel the vehicle bumping and bouncing. He had taken his car off-road, or at the very least onto an unpaved road.

Tropper said, "You ever go camping?"

She knew he was waiting for her to answer. She managed to slur the words out. "Yeah, I've been . . . camping."

"I used to go camping all the time," Tropper said. "That was when I still had a family. That was before Crayton and his cunt wife and all those dick people infected my life."

Several silent seconds ticked by.

"Yeah, I went camping a lot," Tropper said. "I know this place like the back of my hand."

Goody gumdrops for you, she told herself. It wasn't common sense that prevented her from saying those words out loud. It was physical discomfort.

"We're not too far away from it now," Tropper said. "You know what I'm talking about, don't you?"

Cindy didn't answer.

"The spot!" Tropper said. "Where the Corniche made its fateful plunge . . . how'd you like to join your boyfriend?"

"He wasn't my boyfriend," Cindy muttered.

He turned around and peered down at her. Even in the dark, she could make out his big ugly face.

"What's that you say?" Tropper said. "You're not talking too good. Did I knock out your teeth?"

She ran her bloodied tongue over the tips of her incisors. They were not only ragged but also a bit shorter of length. Still, they were in her mouth and that counted for something.

"It would save me some work if I did knock them out," Tropper said. "I'm gonna have to smash your face in. Otherwise, forensics will have something to work with. Don't worry. I promise that you'll be out after the first swing."

The engine sounds had grown louder. That gave her courage.

She murmured, "Hard to smash me up when they're out there looking for me."

"You think so?"

"Yeah . . ." She tried to steady her breathing. "Yeah, I think so."

"Maybe you're right." Tropper spoke calmly. "See, that's why I took this baby off-road. Hell, they can look all they want. They'll never find us."

Oh yeah? she thought. *They'll find us.*

Please let them find us!

But how? Being a lone car hidden in thousands of acres of woods, how in the *world* would anyone find them? Tropper's car wasn't very loud and they were deep in the bowels of the forest. She could tell by looking out the window. The foliage was as thick as fog.

Wait a minute!

Wait a friggin' minute!

She could actually *see* the foliage! Which meant that Tropper was still driving with his lights on! A faint glimmer of hope, but one that she clung to. As he continued to drive, the car bounded as they traversed uneven road, its sides scratching against the thick brush as if someone were raking his nails against the blackboard. It gave her chills and that astounded her . . . that she still had any nerve endings left that weren't causing her pain.

Tropper announced, "We're just about there!"

Cindy's heart slammed against her chest, her breathing quickened until she was almost choking. All this time, no matter how much she hurt, no matter how bleak the situation, she had never given dying an actual thought.

Now, as the car began to slow, mortality slapped her in the face!

This was it! She was going to die!

At last, her bladder gave way. The stream of warm liquid comforted her . . . that her body at least was still alive.

The car slowed—slowed, slowed, and then

stopped! He turned off the motor and sat a moment. With his car engine shut down, all she heard were ambient forest voices and faraway rumblings.

So much dashed hope.

She heard the squeak of an opening car door. By the movement of the seat, she knew he was getting out. A moment later the back door opened. She had been pushed against it for so long she almost fell out of the newly expanded space.

He bent down until his face was atop hers, his dark eyes burning hellish holes in her own orbs, his smelly breath smothering her own. "Man, do you look fucked-up!"

Her bladder may have exploded, but she had enough rebelliousness left to keep her eyes dry.

"I'd like to say I'm sorry, Officer Decker," Tropper commented, "but you're a wiseass, and it's just as well for it to end this way. You just hang on tight for a sec. I'll be right back."

She heard his footsteps crunch dry leaves as he walked. A moment later, she heard the trunk pop. He took something out that lightened the load of the car. Then he walked back to her and held the object aloft.

It was a sledgehammer!

If there were an appropriate time to panic . . . to cry and beg and plead and make false promises, this would have been the perfect moment.

But stubbornness and a strange, ill-placed sense

of dignity kept her quiet. Instead, she offered no resistance, feeling a strange calm come over her.

He waited, expecting her to do something, say something. When she didn't, he said, "Because you're a fellow officer . . . I won't make you suffer."

She muttered a serene thank-you, then closed her eyes and waited . . . and waited . . . and waited.

She opened her eyes. He was staring at her. What did he want?

What *did* he want?

Slowly, he raised the hammer, then after an interminably long second, he lowered the implement.

"I can't get any leverage," he grumbled. "If I do it in this small space, I might ruin the car. Not to mention make you suffer. I wanted to take you out in the first blow." He tapped his foot. "Tell you what. If you promise not to run away, I'll take you out of the car. And walk you over to a real pretty spot near the edge of the mountains. That way, you can leave this world while looking at this beautiful, starry sky."

Cindy felt her lip tremble. She bit it back. "That sounds great."

"I swear, Decker," Tropper continued, "if you do run away, I'll catch you. And then I will make it hurt."

"I hear you, Sergeant."

Again he waited a moment. "You sure are calm for someone who's gonna die."

"I'm pretty nervous inside, sir."

"Well, you're hiding it very well." He reached over and untied her legs. In one swift movement, he dragged her out and lifted her up, his hand grasping the ties that secured her hands behind her back. She felt her knees buckle under, but he held her erect by her bound hands. "I just gave you a compliment, Decker. You're not going to go pussy on me now, are you?"

"Not on purpose, sir."

"Stand up!"

She stood as erect as possible. "I'm ready, sir."

"I like your style, Decker."

"Thank you. Are you sure we can't work out another solution?"

"I'm sure." Tropper grasped her idle hands, still bound behind her back, and edged her forward. "Let's go for a walk until we find a good spot."

His grip wasn't all that strong. For a moment, she thought about running. But how fast could her injured body take her? How far could she possibly get? He'd catch up, and be very mad. She really didn't want to be maimed and tortured.

She must have been walking slowly, because he pushed her forward. This time, he was rough. Dried brush and twigs snapped beneath their feet. The sounds had been so distracting that it took a few seconds before they both heard it—the distinct thwack, thwack, thwack of faraway helicopter rotors. And she didn't need a working knowledge of physics and the Doppler effect to know that the sound was growing rather than receding in loudness.

They looked up simultaneously. Three or four of them homing in on them.

How did they know?

The headlights! Cindy remembered. Not only had Tropper been *driving* with the headlights, he had parked with them *still* on, never bothering to shut them off. Cindy could see them in the distance, shining like Moses' rays.

"Shit!" Tropper screamed.

Opportunity had knocked, and Cindy took advantage. Instantly, she sprinted forward. Tropper darted after her, his long stride overtaking her in a matter of seconds. He leapt forward, grabbing her by her hands, but his unsteady balance made him slam into her body, causing them to stumble and fall. Quickly, he got to his feet, raised the sledgehammer, and slammed it down. She rolled to her side, missing the impact by a fraction of an inch. The swing of the heavy maul had caused him to pitch forward, giving her just enough time to get back on her feet and tear off. Again he caught her, yanking her back by the collar of her clothes, nearly choking her. But by this time, the helicopters had closed in on them, shining their search beams on the ground, lighting up the darkened area like a night shoot on a set.

Cindy allowed herself a half smile as Tropper

looked up and let out a string of obscenities. If the sergeant had been a smart man, he would have dropped her and saved his own skin by making a dash to the car. Instead, he tightened his grip on her and tried to run *with her* back to the car. Since she didn't have much strength to resist him—and fearing that if she did, he'd pound her unconscious—she let her body go slack, knowing that her dead weight would slow him down even further, hoping he would figure out to drop her!

But he didn't. Instead he cursed her and kicked her limp legs. "Get up! *Get up!* GET UP!" Seeing that his screams had no effect on her behavior, Tropper looped his arms around her waist, squeezed, and towed her back, dragging her legs against the hard, rough ground. Cindy felt her clothing rip, the skin of her calves being scraped raw and red. But his movements were slow and ungainly, giving the air units time to zero in on them, hoping they would stand out like a pimple on a porcelain complexion.

Cindy saw the copters close ranks, hovering above until she felt the breeze of the rotors as well as the heat of searchlights. If she squinted to avoid the glare, she could actually make out the faces of the sharpshooters in position. The sound was deafening, almost blasting out the roar of the upcoming sirens. Almost . . . but not quite.

Seconds later, she could hear words coming through the megaphone! They were surrounded, he should let go of her and give himself up or they'd shoot—something like that. Perhaps that's what she thought they should say from all the movies she had watched. She really couldn't understand anything too well because not only was she stunned by the fear that prevented her brain from processing too much, but also the orders were coming fast and furious.

Tropper paid them no heed. Successfully reaching the car, he yanked opened the driver's door, shoving her inside first, then slid behind the wheel. Within moments, he gunned the engine and sped deep into the forest.

The helicopters' searchlights continued to follow them through the overgrown maze of flora, streaking like comets through the sky. Ironically, the illumination made it easier for Tropper to see in the dark. He depressed the accelerator, causing the car to fly forward. Cindy screamed as the car skidded, barely keeping contact with the soft dirt road that was more like a hiking trail. In the rearview mirror, she could make out the blue and red strobic blinks from the cruisers' bar lights, the beacons inside going around and around and around. They remained several car lengths behind.

Tropper increased the speed, trees whizzing by them. One wrong move and they'd be smashed beyond recognition.

"Oh my God!" Cindy panicked as her heart beat out of control. "Oh my God, oh my God—"

"Shut up!" Tropper snapped back.

Her eyes darted to the control panel of his CHP car. The speedometer needle kept climbing—forty, fifty, sixty. Tropper was wearing his seat belt (funny how some habits are permanently affixed in the brain) but not tethered by the restraint, she was bouncing around the interior. To make matters worse, her hands were tied. If he crashed, he'd have the air bag and the seat belt; she would be hurled through the windshield, her face sliced up like bologna, and she wouldn't even be able to use her palms for protection. The car continued to rocket forward, scraping against brush, skidding when the tires hit rocks, stones, and oversized roots. One part of her wanted to close her eyes; the other part refused to let her tune out.

"You're going to get us both killed!" she screamed. *"GIVE IT UP!"*

A second later she screamed again as the car's front tire hit a felled log and went flying forward. The car landed with a thump and continued on.

"Oh my God!" she cried out. "Oh my God, oh my God—"

"Shut up—"

"You shut up!"

"You shut up!" Tropper swerved to the right then to the left and seconds later he was back on the main mountain road—a narrow, two-lane highway, but at least it was paved. By this time, a caravan of police cars was behind them. The air units followed from above.

Again, Cindy's eyes landed on the speedometer's gauge. He was going over sixty, taking the turns at race car speeds. The cruisers had fallen back even farther, forced to reduce their speeds even as Tropper accelerated. But the air units kept them in the spotlight.

Twisting and turning, Cindy felt her stomach lurch at each turn. Bile spewed out of her stomach and up through her throat. Sweat poured onto her clammy brow. If she was scared before—facing Tropper and a sledgehammer—she was terrified now. If he kept this up, she was definitely going to die.

Her stomach weakened further and she vomited.

Tropper sniffed the puke in disgust. To show his displeasure, he depressed the gas pedal until it was flat with the floor of the car.

Going into a hairpin turn.

Missing it by just a fraction of an inch.

Cindy screamed as the car plunged through the railing.

Being hurled forward through millions of needles of pain.

Soaring through the star-studded heavens.

If she hadn't been in so much pain, it would have been beautiful.

The last thing she heard was a deafening explosion.

The last thing she saw was the eruption of intense, bright light.

The last thing she felt was warmth from a sudden wave of heat.

And then, it was all gone!

Dark . . . cold . . . silent.

38

Mom was venting again; this time the scapegoat was Dr. Heinz, one of the primary ER physicians who had treated Cindy when she had initially been brought in. Not that Cindy remembered Heinz, or a damn thing about that night, even though people had told her that she was talking when the paramedics had wheeled her through the Emergency Room doors.

"If one more person calls her *lucky,* I'm going to *strangle* someone!" Mom had reached the breaking point, and then some. "Winning the lottery is *lucky*! Breaking the slots in Vegas is *lucky*! Being stalked, kidnapped, beaten, and falling down a drop of God knows how many feet is *not lucky*! I daresay that isn't a definition of lucky in any culture of the world, including tribes that mutilate themselves in the name of beauty!"

The doctor's eyes shifted from Mom to Alan, who had taken on the role of Mom's long-suffering husband, and then again to Mom. He returned the outburst with a patient smile. Cindy understood her mother's frustration—and even agreed with it—but still, she could show more restraint. On top of being embarrassing, Mom's speaker-busting volume made Cindy's head throb. She could hear it through the bandages that encased her skull and wrapped around her ears. At the moment, most of her upper body was packaged in bandages, constricting her chest, making it painful for her to breathe. Of course, the broken ribs sure weren't helping.

Her eyes closed. If she didn't move, she looked as if she were sleeping—the image she wanted to foster. When she slept, nobody bugged her, and the pain wasn't as pronounced. But it was hard to sleep when Mom was yelling. So Cindy rested, monitoring the standoff between parent and doctor through hooded eyes.

It was hard for Mom to look at her. It was equally hard for Cindy to look at her mother, whose eyes held constant tears, always on the *brink* of breaking down. Cindy longed to tell her to get over it, but she wouldn't do it, no matter how much the pain bit her wracked body. Over the years, moms had earned themselves some cheesy rights including the right to look pitiful and scared when their only daughters (in this case, only child) fell down hundred-foot drops. It would have been an even bigger descent if Cindy hadn't had the good fortune to land in a tree. Leaves were softer than packed dirt, and the arbors saved her from another hundred feet of accelerating G-forces.

"You'll have to excuse me," the doctor was saying. "We physicians fall prey to thinking from a medical point of view. I say she's lucky because broken ribs mend very quickly. The collarbones have incomplete fractures. And the single break in her right arm radius is clean. The rest of her long bones are miraculously intact."

Mom regarded him with steely eyes. "Dr. Heinz!" She enunciated very clearly. "My daughter is not a specimen! She is a person! Just . . . look at her!"

"I understand, ma'am—"

"No, you *don't* understand!" Mom protested. Again she regarded her daughter with those awful wet eyes. This times, the water overflowed. "You don't understand at all!" Sob. "I'm grateful that she's here . . . but the situation isn't at all *lucky*!"

Leave it to Dad to choose this Kodak moment to walk into the hospital room. Mom gave him a granite-hard glance, quickly swiping at her eyes, then composing just enough to give her exit line with drama. Arising from her vigil by Cindy's bedside, she marched toward the door, saying something about being downstairs in the cafeteria, drinking the awful coffee *if* anybody needed her.

Alan quickly followed. Before he left, he said, "She's a bit overwrought."

"It's completely understandable," Dr. Heinz answered.

"Yes, it is." He looked at Cindy, then at Decker and repeated, "Yes, it is."

After they had gone, Decker said, "Am I interrupting anything medical?"

"I was just going over her chart," Dr. Heinz answered. "The most recent tests. Everything looks good, Lieutenant. Her vitals are still very strong."

Cindy raised her arm an inch off the bed and twirled her index finger in the air.

The doctor stifled a chuckle. "I have duly registered your opinion, Officer Decker." He smiled. "Feistiness is a good sign. It indicates recovery. It will get better, I promise you."

With her eyes still closed, Cindy mouthed, "Thank you." Through some miracle, she managed to vocalize the same words.

"Why, you're very welcome! I'll be back later."

Decker forced a smile on his face as he stood up and shook the doctor's hand. "Thanks for everything."

"Glad to be of service." Heinz pumped Decker's hand. He placed Cindy's chart in the slot mounted on the hospital door, then left. Suddenly, Decker was alone with his daughter. Panic shot through him. This was the first time he had come in when she was already awake . . . not only awake but

conscious enough to make a feisty gesture . . . and
Decker didn't know what to say to her. He envied
his ex-wife's anger and her capacity to express it.
He looked around the hospital room, trying to
find a clue as to how to behave. All he saw were
robotic, beeping machines along with dozens of
floral and/or balloon arrangements anchored down
with teddy bears and other absurdly cute stuffed
animals.

Cindy saw him staring at them. "Give them to
Hannah."

Decker turned and focused on his daughter.
"What, sweetheart?"

Cindy sighed. Her mind was clear, but her
speech wasn't. "The teddy bears . . . ted-dy bears."

Decker's eyes squinted in confusion.

Cindy pointed to the arrangements.

"You want to smell the flowers, sweetheart?"
Decker asked.

Cindy shook her head, closed her eyes, and went
quiet.

Decker felt his body tense up with frustration.
He couldn't even understand his own daughter. He
felt like screaming! He felt like smashing something! Like taking a hammer to the place and raz-
ing it to the ground. Instead, he sat like a lifeless
stump, trying desperately to figure out his next
move.

Cindy reached out for his hand.

Thank God! Decker thought. Something he

could do. He took it, he stroked it, he kissed it. It was crisscrossed with dozens of splintery scratches. Her face was covered with them as well. Some were scabbing over, some were still red and raw. There were creams and ointments over cuts, but the doctors had elected to keep her face exposed to the air. She looked awful in the main, but pretty well intact considering what she had gone through.

Besides the baby cuts, she had come away with several deep slashes and jagged wounds. One traversed the back of her hand—a stitched-up, Z-shaped laceration that was still pink and puffy, but had finally stopped oozing.

Despite Jan's protests, Cindy had been lucky. Being ejected through the windshield meant she hadn't been inside the car when it had exploded on impact. She had also had the good fortune to be dropped into a large, leafy sycamore that slowed her fall with its thousands of auxiliary newly leafing branches, but cradled her in the crook of its boughs. They had a hard time finding her, a hell of a time getting her down. She had been pricked by hundreds of microscopic pieces of glass, sliced up by large, lethal shards, and had been bleeding from every conceivable surface area of skin. She had been on the verge of shock. But by the grace of God, she was alive and conscious. Not only that, even as they drove her in, as she shivered and trembled and moaned and groaned and cried out in agony, she could move every finger on her hands, wiggle every toe on her feet. It had only taken three days for her to go from the ICU to a regular hospital bed.

The wonderful, recuperative powers of youth!

Again, Decker attempted light conversation. "Beautiful flowers, princess. Lots of them. You must have lots of fans out there."

Many more detractors, Cindy thought. Instead, she gave her father's fingers a gentle squeeze.

"I like those yellow roses especially."

Cindy managed a nod. They were from Scott. Some of the cops at Hollywood had come to visit out of obligation, but Oliver had come out of genuine concern. She appreciated his thoughtfulness, his caring, and his kind, encouraging words. And she knew he had been instrumental in rescuing her. But when he left the room, it was as if he had never been. She rarely thought about him, knowing that the deep feelings just weren't there yet—if they came at all. (Did he sense it as well?) Whatever the relationship was, it was definitely *not* the romance of the century. A bit sad, now that she thought about it.

Sad, but not at all tragic.

Tragic was Armand Crayton's calculated ruin and death, all of it planned by Bartholomew, and executed by Tropper, all because of Crayton's sexual indiscretions with Dexter's wife. Tragic were the injustices she had suffered via Tropper's hand. Tragic did not define the end of a brief, albeit enjoyable, romp with a good-looking guy whose self-esteem was defined by how many young girls he got into the sack.

She closed her eyes. She knew she was short-changing Oliver—that there was sincerity lurking in his being—but right now, she was far too stressed out to be fair. Cindy realized that anger was not a beneficial emotion. Prolonged, it festered into boils of raw, naked venom, poisoning each and every social encounter. But right now it beat the hell out of depression!

A white-capped nurse appeared, breaking into a smile when she saw Decker holding his daughter's hand. "That's so sweet!" she cooed. "She is one lucky girl!"

It was good that Cindy couldn't talk. She didn't trust her mouth if her thoughts were any indication of what she would say.

The nurse, whose name tag defined her as M. Villa, told her it was time for her pain medication.

Decker kissed his daughter's hand. "Well, that should help you, right, sweetheart?"

Even Dad was sounding dorky. But she squeezed his hand back to show she loved him.

The nurse started injecting something into Cindy's IV. It took very little time for Cindy to feel warm and fuzzy. Moments later, Rina burst into the room, her hands carrying a stack of magazines. She unceremoniously placed them at Cindy's bedside. "I brought lots of gardening magazines because they have pictures. I figured you might be tired of TV and too wiped out to read." She stared right at Cindy's face. "Look at you. You're scabbing over already."

Cindy muttered, "Does it look bad?"

"What?" Decker asked.

"She asked if it looked bad," Rina interpreted. "Well, the facial scratches don't look deep at all. I'd say give it a few weeks. By then you can hide whatever is left with foundation. I know you use foundation. You do it well, too. Sometimes, I hardly see your freckles."

Cindy nodded.

Rina said, "Your face will be fine. Just don't look in the mirror. It's like weighing yourself after you've had a baby. Hannah drew you several pictures. Do you want me to tape them up on the wall?"

Cindy nodded yes. "Give her the teddy bears."

"What teddy bears?" Rina looked around the room. "Oh, from the flower arrangements. Later. Right now, you keep them. When Hannah comes to visit you, she can play with them. Where's your mother?"

Decker said, "Jan's in the cafeteria, drinking bad coffee. Why?"

"No offense meant to her, but I'm probably the last person she'll want to see. My main concern is that Cindy has some peace. It's hard enough with people walking in and out, sticking and poking you." Again she stared at Cindy. "I can't get over how fast you're healing. It seems almost hourly. The boys want to visit tonight. I told them to hold off for a few days."

Cindy nodded. The pain medication was making her woozy and very happy—the joys of Demerol.

"Hannah's a different story," Rina went on. "Kids aren't squeamish." She turned to Decker. "Remember when my mother had shingles in her eye three years ago. The entire left side of her face was swollen, bumpy, and red. It was very strange in contrast to her perfectly normal right side. Hannah just went over to her, kissed her good side, and said, 'Omah, read me a book!' She wasn't even polite about it, just demanded to be read to. Didn't give a second thought to her grandmother's feelings or her face." Rina laughed. "If you want to see her, I'll bring her for a few minutes. More than that, she'll exhaust you."

Cindy said, "Bring her."

"Okay." Rina stood up. "I'm going to go now." She kissed Cindy's forehead. "I'll see you later. Get some sleep."

Cindy nodded. "I am tired."

Decker arose. "I'll walk you to the elevator." He waited until they were at least fifty feet from the room. Then he whispered to his wife. "How in the world can you understand her?"

"It comes from raising kids," Rina answered matter-of-factly. "Not the little ones. They're easy to understand. They shout and scream whatever's on their mind. It's the teenagers! Either they mumble a lot, or I'm truly going deaf because I can't understand a word they say." She smiled. "I meant what I said. It's miraculous how good she looks. Her lip is whole, and her nose will look better than it ever did."

"She always wanted a nose job."

"Well, she got one. I just hope the doctor didn't make it too small. Cindy had a patrician nose . . . very stately in contrast to all these California button noses. It gave her . . . class."

Decker sighed. "I don't know how you do it."

"Do what?"

"Be so . . . so upbeat without being phony. You're so sure of yourself. When you tell Cindy that she's going to be fine, I can tell that Cindy believes every word you say. When I'm around her, I feel like such an oaf. I don't know what to say or what to do! I'm her father, for goodness' sakes."

They reached the elevators. Rina pushed the down button.

Decker said, "I can't talk to my own daughter! What the hell is wrong with me?"

"That's precisely it, Peter. You're the father, but I'm only a stepmother. I love Cindy dearly, but because I never nurtured her, I still can drum up some objectivity. If this were Hannah, *chasvachalelah*, I'd be a basket case."

The elevator dinged. She faced her husband and reached out her arms to him. They went from a simple hug to a deep embrace as Decker drew Rina to his breast. She felt his fingers go under her beret and weave themselves into the strands of her hair. She heard him take deep, short breaths, felt his chest heaving. They stood there for a while, letting elevators come and go. When she finally looked up, his eyes were wet and red, but his cheeks were dry.

He choked out, "I guess it just wasn't her time."

"No, it wasn't," Rina answered. "God has too many plans for her. That much I know. I'm just not sure . . . exactly what they are. But isn't that life, Peter? For better or worse, it's the ultimate mystery!"

39

SHE DIDN'T want to come, she didn't want to be here. But Marx had declared that a three-month hiatus had been long enough. And now that Cindy had passed the rookie stage, she needed to confront the devil head on, and get back on the horse, blah, blah, blah. Since Marx seemed to be enjoying the role of mentor, Cindy didn't want to argue. She knew she owed Hayley, so she subjected herself to this awful ritual. And now, here she was in Bellini's, trying to ignore the stony silences and

hostile stares from her fellow officers as she and
Hayley walked through the bar to find an empty
table.

At work, it was bad enough—the snarls, snickers,
and smirks. But Cindy could turn her back and ignore them, concentrating on the Job—which she did
and did well. Since Graham had acted decent from
the get-go . . . even if he hadn't been overly sensitive—not that she expected him to be her therapist,
but some understanding *might* have been nice.

She could get through the day, hiding behind the
trials of daily street life. But at Bellini's there were
no shields, no protective barriers, no barbwire
fences. She couldn't bury herself behind paperwork
or phone calls or weight machines. Here, everything was open. She wanted to keep her eyes on her
beer, but she was paranoid about her safety, constantly looking over her shoulder or into the mirrors to see who was coming in or going out.

Had she been in any other profession, she would
have been long gone, leaving behind her a legacy of
pithy statements and phone calls from her lawyers.
Instead, out of deference to her father, and Marge
Dunn, and Scott Oliver, and Hayley and Graham,
and all the others who had *tried,* she hacked it out,
day to day, wondering how long she could last.

Hayley was talking. "So the guy starts waving
something, we don't know what it is, but we know
it's not a gun or something hard 'cause it's like
flapping around. So Ray and Raul were there with

us . . . Raul makes his approach— Decker, are you listening?"

Cindy sipped beer. "Raul is making an approach—"

"You're not interested—"

"Of course, I'm interested. What's he waving?"

Hayley let out a small laugh. "Wait, wait, there's a buildup."

Cindy glanced into the surrounding mirrors. People were staring at her, but no one was coming up to her. That was good. "Go on."

"Okay, okay." Again Hayley chuckled. "So Raul approaches with the gun on his hip, tells the perp to drop whatever he's waving. So the perp, being an asshole like most perps are, throws it at him, hits him smack in the face—"

"God, that's scary—"

Hayley broke up. "Turns out it was his condom—"

"Oh God—"

"A *used* condom!"

"That's repulsive!"

"Asshole's lucky that Raul didn't shoot him on the spot!"

"It would have been justifiable," Cindy said.

"Absolute— Decker, what are you looking at? Stop twitching and turning. No one cares about you."

"You care." Cindy produced a tarnished smile. "You're about the only one."

"Oh, fuck you and your self-pity!"

Cindy raised her glass. "Thanks, as always, for bringing me back to earth!"

"Graham's coming over," Hayley said. She looked up and smiled. "How's it going?"

"Not so bad, Marx." Beaudry pulled up a chair and sat down.

"Buy you a beer?" Cindy offered.

"Nah, gotta get going. Monday night football."

"Can't miss the game," Cindy said.

"Rick's coming over," Beaudry announced.

"Send him my regards," Cindy answered.

"I don't think so," Beaudry said.

Cindy paused, ran her tongue inside her cheeks. "When did he make bail?"

"He's been out for around a month."

Cindy raised her brow. "That long?"

"Yeah, that long."

"Dare I ask how he's doing?"

"For a former cop about to be indicted for car-jacking and assault who's in the process of a nasty divorce, I'd say he's doing pretty shitty." Beaudry shook his head. "I don't feel sorry for him. It's his own damn fault. But what can I tell you? The man's got nothing! I figure he might as well have a nice place to watch the game."

"Does he know we're still together?" Cindy said.

"Yeah, he knows. Sometimes he asks about you. I don't say anything. It's none of his business. I knew what I was doing when I left him. I also know what I'm doing by staying with you. This time I'm gonna back a winner."

Cindy let out a surprised chuckle. "You think so?"

"I know so. Sure you're in the toilet now. But check you out in a year after all this has died down because some other shit has grabbed the headlines. You'll be in like Flynn for taking the gold, and you'll think about this discussion, and you won't forget your old pal Graham Beaudry."

"No, indeed, I won't forget my old pal Graham."

Beaudry stood up. "See you tomorrow, then?"

"As always."

Beaudry turned and left.

Neither Hayley nor Cindy spoke right away. Then Marx said, "You trust him?"

"Yes, I do. It may be a mistake, but you have to trust someone."

"True. I think if he was going to fuck you up, he would have done it by now."

Cindy glanced over her shoulder. "The guy has integrity . . . to stay with me—"

"Why the hell shouldn't he stay with you?" Hayley said. "You do most of the shitty fieldwork and almost all his work."

"I must cause him some heat."

"I don't think so," Hayley replied. "Graham's a duck. Things just roll off his back. Look at him. He's still friends with Rick . . . are you listening?"

"Someone just walked through the door. She

looks like she's coming over," Cindy replied. "Medium height, short dark hair, beanpole thin . . . kind of pretty . . . I don't know her."

Hayley turned around, raised her eyebrow. "Petra Conner. Homicide."

"The Cart Ramsey case?"

"That's the one. Talk about getting heat. Man, her ass was on the burner for a long, long time."

Cindy said, "So what the hell does she want with me?"

Hayley shook her head, but a smile was lurking on her lips.

"What?" Cindy whispered.

"Shhhh," Hayley said.

Petra took up Graham's empty chair, sitting down without being asked to do so. She looked much younger from afar, but up close Cindy could see the lines and furrows. At first, Cindy thought she was dressed entirely in black. But upon further inspection, the blouse was dark, dark navy. She signaled the waitress, held up a single, slender index finger, and nodded. Then she turned to Hayley. "Did you tell her?"

"No, I didn't—"

Petra dismissed her with a wave. "I'm Petra Conner."

"Hayley just told me." Cindy held out her hand, and Petra took it. "Nice shirt. What is it? Kind of a jaquard print?"

"Yeah, it's got some texture to it."

"It's nice," Cindy repeated.

"Thanks."

Jasmine, the waitress, came over with a single glass of white wine. Petra said, "Refills, anyone?"

"I'm fine," Cindy said. "Last time I drank too much, it got me into trouble."

"Isn't that the way it always is?" Petra answered.

Cindy laughed. "I suppose you're right." The table fell into an awkward silence. Awkward for Cindy, but maybe not for Conner. She watched Petra sip her wine, somehow pulling off being delicate and earthy. The woman had it together—one of the lucky ones.

Petra said, "I'm here as one of the good guys."

Cindy gave her a barely perceptible nod. She didn't trust anyone, especially someone who said she was one of the good guys.

She leaned in closely. "Tropper was no big deal. He was a jerk from day one. No one misses him except maybe his kids. But Bederman was on the force for over ten years. He made a lot of friends, did a lot of favors. You know cops and loyalty: the blue code of silence and all that stuff. It's really out. I'm sure this isn't news to you. But it's always a good idea to state things out in the open. This is something you need to be aware of."

"That I've made enemies."

"Quite a lot of them," Petra said casually. "The *other* thing you need to know is that while you have some nutty guys wanting you out, there are a selective, important few who are watching you, Officer. You crack up mentally, you're out. You weather the mess, you'll go somewhere."

Cindy stared at her, then looked at her beer. "Okay. Thanks."

Petra waited a few moments, then said, "It's not easy. Guys can be jerks, cops can be jerks. To-gether—cops and guys—you get premium-quality jerks. But that's just the way it is."

Cindy nodded.

"Decker, we have an infinite capacity for guilt," Petra said. "I still feel like it was my fault that my ex left me, making excuses for his rotten behavior. But, in reality, he screwed up. And that's the way it is for you. *Rick Bederman* screwed up. *You* didn't. Get it straight, okay?"

"Okay," Cindy answered.

"That's what I've been telling her," Hayley re-marked.

"Yeah, but it means more coming from me." Petra laughed. "Okay, that's that! Secondly, the ac-tual *reason* that I'm here is our bowling league—"

"What?" Cindy asked, laughing.

"The Women's Law Enforcement Bowling League. Hollywood took third last year. The cap-tain has recruited me and demands that this year we do better." Petra was straight-faced. "Bowling is a very tactical sport, not to mention all the hand/eye coordination. Bowling's great for the gross motor skills in the same way that painting is good for the fine motor. Hayley was supposed to tell you all this but she didn't want to *impose* because she thought you were still *fragile*—"

"That's so sweet," Cindy said.

"It's stupid!" Petra announced. "You have strong forearms, Decker. And I've seen you at the range. I know you're a good shot. Do you bowl?"

"Only like a recreational thing," Cindy said. "I've never been in a league."

"Well, you're in one now!" Petra told her. "Practice is Tuesdays/ Saturdays at Mar Vista. Seven o-clock." She stood. "See you then."

Cindy said, "I broke my arm three months ago."

"It was your left arm," Petra said. "You're right-handed." She turned to Hayley. "You make sure she gets there."

"All of a sudden she's my responsibility?" Hayley said.

"Yes," Petra answered. "That's it exactly."

Petra left as bluntly as she came. Cindy figured it was a good time to take her leave as well. She got up from the table. "I'm tired, Hayley. I need my beauty sleep."

"I'll walk you out."

"I can make it to the car by myself." But Cindy's voice lacked conviction.

Hayley saved face. "I'm tired, too. Let's go."

Again, they endured the rough sea of angry stares and comments. Cindy walked with her head held high. Her head never felt so heavy. Once in the

parking lot, she unlocked her Saturn and slid inside. She turned on the motor. "It starts. Go
home!"

Hayley slammed the door shut, but Cindy didn't
take off right away. Instead, she waited, watching
Hayley walk to her car, listening for the motor to
kick in and her headlights to go on. When it was
clear that Marx's car was in working order, Cindy
took off.

Heading straight for home. It took her about
twenty minutes to reach Robertson and Venice.
Home was five minutes away. She should have
turned on National. Instead, she went west on
Venice. If she kept going west, she'd eventually hit
the ocean. She stopped when she reached the gaudy
orange sign announcing Mar Vista Bowl. She
pulled into the parking lot and killed the engine.
What the hell! Worse comes to worst, she'd bleed
off some anger and frustration in a constructive
manner.

She sat at the wheel for a moment. She felt like
crying, but she didn't. She couldn't. It had been so
long since she had shown real emotion that she had
somehow forgotten how.

She had always wondered what had made her
father tick.

Now she knew.